THE WORKS OF SRI CHINMOY

POETRY

VOLUME II

THE WORKS OF SRI CHINMOY

POETRY

VOLUME II

TOME 2

★ ★

TEN THOUSAND FLOWER-FLAMES
PART 51 TO 100

207 FLOWER-FLAMES

LYON · OXFORD

GANAPATI PRESS

LXXXVI

© 2016 THE SRI CHINMOY CENTRE

ISBN 978-1-9113190-6-1

See appendix for notice regarding this edition.

FIRST EDITION WENT TO PRESS ON 13 AUGUST 2016

POETRY

VOLUME II

TEN THOUSAND FLOWER-FLAMES

PART 51 TO 100

5001.

My Lord,
I have one request:
May my heart sing the song
Of universal oneness.
My Lord,
I have one more request:
May my life sing the song
Of transcendental newness.

5002.

Before I call,
God's Compassion-Eye answers.
Before I start,
God's Compassion-Heart
Finishes the race for me.

5003.

I am not sure of my identity.
To me, this is not
An indispensable necessity.
My only necessity
Is to love my Inner Pilot
And to please Him in His own Way
Throughout Eternity.

5004.

You are not happy
Because your mind is not happy
In spite of having mustered
World-domineering power.

5005.

Serve the crying earth.
You will be happy.
Love the smiling Heaven.
You will be happy.

5006.

A faithless heart
Marks the very beginning
Of a soulless dream.

5007.

True, you are fighting a losing battle
Against impurity,
But continue.
Someday, somehow,
You are bound to win.

5008.

Unless you dare to be
Your real and transcendental Self,
No matter what you do,
No matter what you say,
No matter what you become,
You will still remain
A reality completely out of date.

5009.

Allow him to enjoy
His superficial superiority.
You try to enjoy
The purity of your heart's
Satisfaction-unity.

5010.

There is always tomorrow
For those who do not try at all,
And also for those
Who do not want to give up.

5011.

As your good voice
Is pleasing you,
Even so, your right choice
Will please God.

5012.

Your heart's soulful cry
Is your only protection
Against the reign
Of merciless misunderstanding.

5013.

You will never be able to enjoy
The beauty of your own
    self-perfection
Precisely because of
Your self-satisfied grandeur.

5014.

Amazing is the power
Of burning sighs.
They can stretch themselves
To Heaven's loftiest heights.

5015.

If your heart's inner purity
Is active and illumining,
Then your life's outer beauty
Has to be active and fulfilling.

5016.

There are two things you can do.
You have been doing one thing
All the time:
You have been feeding your
    senses.
But when will you do the other
    thing?
When will you stop denying
The hunger of your soul?

5017.

There is no difference between
Your voice of ignorance
And your choice of autocracy.

5018.

The heart gives spontaneously.
The eyes see immediately.
The hands accept gratefully.
God dances smilingly.

5019.

Unless you are a challenger
Of stark oblivion,
How can you once more be the
   enjoyer
Of your perfect union with God?

5020.

Do not hide yourself.
Do not cry to be heard.
Do not try to convince others
To manifest you.

5021.

His is the vision-eye
That increases the beauty of
   Heavenly hours
And the purity of earthly days.

5022.

How can he sleep
When his dreams do not allow
   him
To sleep?
How can he smile
When his God is all
In tears?

5023.

Because your mind is
A world-forsaker,
Your poor heart is compelled to
   become
A world-loser.

5024.

My Lord, I am happy
Because You are the Lord of my
   life.
Can You not make me perfect
By becoming the Lord of my
   thoughts?

5025.

Doubt cramps your mind,
Fear cramps your heart,
Failure cramps your life,
Only because unconsciously
You want to perish
In your own narrow vision-cave.

5026.

It seems that everybody
Is familiar with descent.
In his case, he deliberately chose
The memorable game of
   deplorable descent.

5027.

My heart does double duty.
It surrenders to God
To know God's Illumination-Will.
It binds mankind
To fulfil its own temptation-will.

5028.

His love of praise
Is so great
That he does not mind
Even if it is all founded upon
Himalayan falsehood.

5029.

Your defeats in life's battlefield
Will soon be ending,
Because your mind is no longer
   indifferent
To your heart's spontaneous
   enthusiasm.

5030.

What is my confidence,
If not my faith in God?
What is my faith in God,
If not my oneness-satisfaction?

5031.

Everybody knows
That I am not a great man.
But only my God and I know
That I have a good heart.

5032.

My mind's humility
Is my deep wisdom.
My heart's gratitude
Is my deeper wisdom.
My life's surrender
Is my deepest wisdom.

5033.

If you do not
Accept defeat,
God Himself
Will befriend you.

5034.

You are a burdened heart.
You are a confused mind.
But you can and you will be
  liberated.

5035.

God does not mind
If and when I cover His Body
With my bitter failures.
But He does mind
If and when I do not cover my
  heart
With His transcendental
  Satisfaction-Victory.

5036.

If you believe in God,
You get God's Power.
If you believe in God's Power,
You get God's Peace.
If you believe in God's Peace,
You get God's Joy.
If you believe in God's Joy,
Then you will before long become
Another God.

5037.

If you pray to God
For forgiveness,
God will grant you forgiveness.
If you meditate on God
For another chance in life,
God will grant you another
  chance.
But the paramount questions are:
Will your haughty mind allow you
To pray to God for forgiveness?
Will your impure heart allow you
To meditate on God for another
  chance?

5038.

A possessive mind wants much
But gets very little —
Next to nothing.
A submissive heart needs nothing
But gets the utmost —
Also the best.

5039.

Self-insight
And
Ignorance-night
Are two eternal strangers.

5040.

You think of God.
That is what you know and do.
God loves you.
That is what He knows and does.

5041.

Because you are a starless walker,
Your abrupt descent
Is made of ruthless and tireless
   despair.

5042.

Stop your self-indulgence.
You will have a longer life.
Stop your world criticism.
You will have an immortal life.

5043.

God does not mind
If each man is the manifestation
Of his own inadequacy.
But He does mind
If an individual enjoys his
   unwillingness
To transcend his life's
   incapacity-weakness.

5044.

Between war-weapons and
   peace-weapons
There should always be
   love-weapons.
Then only shall we be able
To bask in the sunshine of
   oneness-bliss.

5045.

Do not worry!
He who worries buries himself
With the unsolicited help
Of today's powerful hands
And tomorrow's indifferent eyes.

5046.

To say that God has created
Confusion for your mind
Is as absurd as telling the world
That you can teach God
The art of perfection.

5047.

Your Master does not hide from
   you.
It is your visionless eyes
And your restless mind
That do not allow you to recognise
   him
Even while he is standing
Right in front of you
With his Eternity's
   Compassion-Eye.

5048.

If you are a stranger to me,
You will be satisfied
Only with my greatness.
If you are dear to me,
You will be satisfied
Only with my goodness.
But my Lord Supreme
Will not care for
My Himalayan greatness
Or my sun-vast goodness.
He will care only for my oneness
With His Eternity's Vision-Light
And
His Infinity's Reality-Delight.

5049.

Now that you have shattered
The yoke of your self-imposed
   burden,
God will grant you
His own secret and sacred
Satisfaction-Delight.

5050.

God has not tempted you.
He knows everything
Except the art of temptation.
It is you who have tempted
   yourself.

5051.

You thought you would be able
To discover yourself
By fulfilling your temptation-life,
But look what you have done!
Instead of finding yourself,
You have bound yourself.

5052.

Not only do desires pass away,
The man of desires also passes
   away.
But the man of aspiration lives
   forever
Inside the complete
   Satisfaction-Heart
Of his Beloved Supreme.

5053.

Because of your generous heart,
God has given you
His prosperous Life.
Because of your pure eye,
God has given you
His Vision-Light.
Because you long for perfection
In everything you do and say,
God has given you
His own Satisfaction unparalleled.

5054.

Since you indulge
Your perplexed mind,
How can you have
A relaxed heart?
Since you indulge
Your restless vital,
How can you have
A guileless body?

5055.

God loves you
No matter what you have done
And no matter what you are doing now.
But do you think you will be able
To love God
If He loves your doubtful
   poison-mind
More than He loves your soulful
   nectar-heart?

5056.

Only your suspicious mind
Can ruin the beauty
Of your soulful eyes.
Only your ferocious vital
Can destroy the purity
Of your bountiful heart.

5057.

Who says that it is an easy task
To graduate from the university
Of the mind's ignorance-night?
I do not, I cannot and I shall not
Agree with them.

5058.

Faith in God
Awakens soulful tears.
Love of God
Fulfils divine promises.

5059.

God gave him
One hundred and one
   incarnations
To realise Him.
But in each incarnation
He was punctual and perfect
In being late to invoke God,
Pray to God
And meditate on God.

5060.

If you invade the privacy-world
Of human thoughts,
You will be sadly disappointed.
But if you enter the purity-heart
Of human life,
You will be richly rewarded.

5061.

A sympathetic ear
Is amazingly great.
A sympathetic heart
Is perpetually perfect.

5062.

Heaven will be Heaven to me
Only if I can carry there
My heart's climbing cry.

5063.

Each sad tear
Gives birth
To a glad breath.

5064.

To love
Is to become
A silver dream-boat.

5065.

A soulful smile from Above
Can easily lighten a heavy heart.
My own heart is a radiant
   example.

5066.

In just a twinkling of its
   vision-eye,
The world-soul has made
The world-body beautiful.

5067.

Cheerfulness
Is the sunlit path
To Heaven's fruitfulness.

5068.

I am happy
Only when I admire
My heart's sacred dreams.

5069.

A soulful heart is always available
To accept the blame
When the doubtful mind
Does everything wrong.

5070.

Things change.
Years bring new values.
Yet the aspiration-heart always
  remains
The safest and by far the best
  haven.

5071.

The inner beauty
Is a "must" for every seeker
Of the transcendental Height.

5072.

To his extreme sorrow
His rest has deteriorated
Into an incurable idleness.

5073.

Only one teacher is needed
And that teacher
Is your heart's experience-delight.

5074.

Slavery means
Possession-hunger.
Mastery means
Renunciation-feast.

5075.

Not your doubting mind
But your aspiring heart
Is the direct representative
Of your illumining soul.

5076.

Self-knowledge means
A complete freedom
From ignorance-demand.

5077.

Yesterday I went to
  ignorance-king
Uninvited.
Today God has come to me
Uninvited.
Tomorrow I shall, without fail, go
  to God
Whether He invites me or not.

5078.

To see beyond myself
Is to find and feel
My inseparable oneness
With my Beloved Supreme.

5079.

Only a genuine seeker
Knows that his inner hunger
Is infinitely more powerful
Than his outer hunger.

5080.

If you sincerely and soulfully
    repent,
God will not allow the
    temptation-serpent
To torment you —
Not even mildly,
Not to speak of powerfully.

5081.

Some think I close my eyes
To ignore them,
But it is not true.
I close my eyes to pray
Most soulfully for them.

5082.

Not once but twice will you know
The real man in a genuine seeker:
Once when you mercilessly
    criticise
His doubtful poison-mind —
Needless to say,
He will love you far beyond
Your imagination's flight;
Once when you unreservedly love
His fruitful nectar-heart —
Needless to say,
He will immediately admire you
    unreservedly
For helping him find
His long-lost vision eye.

5083.

Your heart was born to sing
A soulful song of a new creation.
Why then do you compel it to sing
A doleful and funereal song?

5084.

In the inner world,
When the flood of intelligence
And a drop of wisdom challenge
    each other
The drop always wins.

5085.

A weak man is understood
Only by God's Compassion.
A stupid man is understood
Only by God's Forgiveness.

5086.

Your creation of truth
Will no longer remain unheralded
For your cry for perfection
Is swiftly reaching its
    zenith-height.

5087.

Selflessness within,
Fruitfulness without.
Service-cry within,
Perfection-smile without.

5088.

Do not say
That you alone can do it.
Say that God does it in and
    through you.
Then lo, it is all done.

5089.

God is not
Going to look for you
In your life's shallow
    amusements.
How can your heart
Find satisfaction
In your life's pointless activities?

5090.

How can there be peace
When the main speaker
At the world's conference table
Is not given the chance to speak
With His Silence-Eye?

5091.

God is just.
This is what
An intelligent mind thinks.
God is love.
This is what
A pure heart feels.
God is all.
This is what
A wise soul knows.
God is another man.
This is what
The compassionate Lord
Tells the world.

5092.

It is too early for me to say
That God is for me,
But it is not too early for me to say
That I am all for God.

5093.

I am not going back to Heaven
Without earth's aspiration-cry
In infinite measure.
I am not coming back to earth
Without Heaven's
　satisfaction-treasure
In measureless measure.

5094.

A judge quite often
Suffers from his loneliness.
Let us sympathise
With his loneliness
And forgive his beastly crimes.

5095.

Look!
Your self-gratification
Is being denounced
By your own self-destruction.

5096.

Just as other sincere seekers
Have realised God,
So can you realise God,
If you value the purity
Of your heart's sincerity-cry.

5097.

I am always ready to die
With my heart-realities
To fulfil the Himalayan heights
Of my soul-dreams.

5098.

Two supreme commitments
I have made:
I shall carry my heart to Heaven
To spread humanity's cry of
　helplessness.
I shall bring down my soul to
　earth
To spread divinity's light of
　fulness.

5099.

To say and to do the right thing
In this world
And to represent the world
Is to take a risk.
But I must say
It is a risk worth taking
For its goal is life-fulfilling.

5100.

My mind's sincerity gives me
The silver opportunity
To do something great for this
    world.
My heart's purity gives me
The golden opportunity
To be somebody good for God.

5101.

Choose something entirely
    different
And soulfully new today.
Look, your glorious victory-hour
Is fast approaching.

5102.

Do not expect anything
From this unsatisfied
And dissatisfied world.
Do not expect anything
From the satisfied
And fulfilled Heaven either.
Then you will always remain
Far from the reach of sorrow.

5103.

Yesterday
Your mind was nebulous.
Today
Your mind is puzzled.
Tomorrow
Your mind will be confused.
Why, why, why?
Because yesterday
You did not love your heart,
Today
You are not crying with your heart
And tomorrow
You will be unwilling
To smile with your heart.

5104.

My morning's inner teacher
Is my surrender-life.
My evening's inner teacher
Is my gratitude-heart.

5105.

Two sermons of ignorance-night:
I do not care
Whether God thinks of me;
I am quite sure
I could have created a better
    world.

5106.

Your burning temper
Has consumed all at once
Your heart's purity-cry
And
Your eyes' beauty-smile.

5107.

My heart,
I shall always faithfully follow
    you.
No matter where you go,
No matter when you go,
No matter how you go,
I shall follow you.
You are eternally mine.
Do tell me
That I am also eternally yours.

5108.

The fate of mere mortals
Need not and must not remain
A ceaselessly helpless cry.
It will eventually and inevitably
Be transformed into
A sleeplessly self-giving smile.

5109.

Hate never wins.
A powerful love
At times wins,
At times does not.
But a soulful oneness
Always and always wins.

5110.

If you cannot treasure
Beauty's faith and purity's
    gratitude
Inside your mind,
Then yours will be
The mind-sky with no stars.
No, not even one!

5111.

Each humility-life
Unmistakably owns
Teeming noble, life-inspiring,
Supremely divine qualities.

5112.

His illumination-mind
Soothes the four corners
Of the world
With the beauty
Of Eternity's moon.
His perfection-heart
Illumines the four corners
Of the world
With the power
Of Immortality's sun.

5113.

My fame is not lasting.
Even the experience of fame
Is not lasting.
But the Compassion
Of my Beloved Supreme
In and through my fame
Is everlasting.

5114.

My Lord,
My heart's gratitude-world
Is Yours
And it will forever remain Yours
Whether or not You grant me
An iota of Your own
   Compassion-World.

5115.

I shall follow Your Footsteps,
My Lord, I shall,
With my heart's morning cry
And my life's evening smile.

5116.

Do not let any chance pass by,
Especially when God knocks
At your heart's door
To open your heart's
Gratitude-fragrance-flower.

5117.

O my heart,
I am always buffeted
By the surging ocean
Of my mind's doubts.
Yet I know that
My conscious and constant
   oneness
With your aspiration-world
Is my only God-realisation-hope
And
My only
   God-manifestation-promise.

5118.

You want to know
What God will accept from you
And what God
Will not accept from you?
I tell you,
God will accept everything from you
Except one thing:
Your malicious disobedience-indulgence.

5119.

God will transform my mind
Only after I have informed Him
That I shall live always inside
My heart's soulful beauty
And
My life's powerful purity.

5120.

In the morning
My heart's surrender-drops
Are my Lord's
Most powerful possessions.
In the evening
My life's gratitude-flames
Are my Lord's
Most powerful possessions.

5121.

O current of desires,
You think that you are
Extremely powerful,
But you are not!
My Lord's Compassion-Grace
Will make you flow
Into the river of aspiration-light.

5122.

Miracles were perhaps necessary
At the very start
Of your aspiration-life.
But once you have successfully
Started your inner journey,
Not only are miracles unnecessary,
But they may hinder your speedy progress
Far beyond your imagination.

5123.

God has openly fed you
With His Compassion-Sea.
Will you not even secretly
Feed Him
With your heart's gratitude-drops?

5124.

Ignorance and stupidity fooled
   you.
They donned the cloak of
   innocence.
Alas, you could not see
Through their tricks!

5125.

Unless you desert mercilessly
Your stupid self,
The steps of your soulful heart
Will never be able to lead you
To your destined goal.

5126.

Before I accepted
The life of aspiration,
My tears were the tears
Of real sorrow.
Now that I have accepted
The life of aspiration,
My tears are not tears of sorrow
But tears of real joy.

5127.

Two souls I have:
In my outer life
I wear smartly
God's Protection-soul.
In my inner life
I wear soulfully
God's Compassion-soul.

5128.

There are two essential truths:
The mind does not know the
   Truth
And at the same time
Does not want to know the Truth.
The heart knows the Truth
And yet wants to know
More of the Truth.

5129.

Wait for God's choice Hour.
Your mind's indomitable strength
And your heart's immeasurable
   splendour
Will, without fail,
Reach their final goal:
God-Satisfaction in God's own
   Way.

5130.

In his dying hours
He prayed to God most soulfully
To grant him a fragrant and
    grateful
Surrender-life.

5131.

The manifestation of my soul's
Blue-gold vision
Is my life's white-green mission
Unparalleled.

5132.

"Become supremely good."
This was the first message
That I received from Heaven.
"Become enormously great."
This was the first and last message
That I received from earth.

5133.

First we have to prove to ourselves
That we belong to the Unknown.
Then a day will come
When we will have to realise
That we belong to the
    Unknowable.

5134.

Unless and until
We create a conscious
Love for the Unknown,
We will never be able to create
Any love for the Unknowable.
Unless and until
We can love the Unknowable,
We will not be ready
For the infinite Light and Delight
Of our Beloved Supreme.

5135.

By taking your life
You don't accomplish anything.
If you have failed,
Then wait for another hour,
God's choice Hour,
To do something great for God.

5136.

Some people
Have the inborn tendency
To stick to their promise.
But to surrender to God's Will
Is the infinitely higher way.

5137.

We shall try to do
Something extraordinary
Only if it is the Will of God.
Otherwise, while accomplishing
Something great,
We may go away,
Far, farther, farthest,
From the Will of God.

5138.

You can easily remember your
   Master
In everything that you do
If you can make yourself
Sincerely feel
That the very thing you are doing
Is for nobody else but him.

5139.

Each time you feel insecure,
Think of yourself
As tinier than the tiniest
And think of your Master
As the vast ocean,
Which is your own highest
   Reality.
Don't think of anybody else
Around you, behind you
Or in front of you.
Only throw yourself into the
   ocean,
Your Master,
And then become the ocean.

5140.

If you want to make progress,
Only think of your heart's
   happiness
And how you can keep
Your entire being happy.
Wherever you go,
Carry happiness with you.

5141.

If you want to make the fastest
   progress,
At least seven times a day,
Perhaps for only five seconds,
But with a very strong inner
   intensity,
Be consciously aware of your
   spirituality.
You are on a very, very special
   path.
You are not an ordinary,
   unaspiring person.
You are a chosen instrument of
   the Supreme.

5142.

If you want to feel newness
In the new year,
You have to get that very newness
From the new year itself.
The new year has all newness:
New promise,
New success,
New progress.

5143.

Secretly,
Thousands of years ago,
We got everything from the
  Source.
Only now
Are we giving back to the Source
What we long ago received.

5144.

Today your vessel is tiny.
Every day
Make your vessel larger,
And every day
God will fill it.

5145.

Tell yourself
That although you may not be
Doing the right thing,
You are more than ready to do it,
And you *will* do it,
Unconditionally.

5146.

A desire-life is nothing but
A subtraction-sadness.
An aspiration-life is another name
For an addition-gladness.

5147.

If you wage war
Against your unbelief,
God will immediately grant you
His own Confidence-Light.

5148.

Words about God
Are on your lips,
But your hands are full
Of Satan's deeds.

5149.

Your life's prayer
Must unveil the truth.
Your heart's meditation
Must prevail over falsehood.

5150.

Faith cares
Neither for your past misdeeds
Nor for your future misdeeds,
But only for your present good
   deeds.

5151.

When nobody dares to challenge
Your faith in God,
That is the time
For God's Hour to approach you
Lovingly, speedily and
   satisfactorily.

5152.

Hope is a future reality,
A hidden reality,
Waiting for its revelation
In the heart of the Eternal Now.

5153.

There are two kinds of faith:
Faith in one's own
Insecure capacity
And faith in God's
All-illumining
   Compassion-Light.

5154.

Hope says:
"I shall one day please God."
Faith says:
"My Lord is already pleased
With me."

5155.

The outer man
Is decaying.
The inner man
Is preparing.
The God-man
Is revealing.

5156.

I do not have to remind God
Of all His Promises,
For God sleeplessly
And unconditionally
Wants to reveal Himself
In and through
My tiny little heart.

5157.

God's sacred Possession
And man's sacred possession
Are one and the same:
Humanity's self-transcending cry.

5158.

You do not have to
Stand up for yourself.
God's Compassion-Eye
Has already compelled God
To stand up for you,
For you alone.

5159.

I may not know
Whether it is God's fault
Or my fault
That I am useless,
But I do know
That God has tried
Infinitely more than I have tried
To perfect my nature,
Illumine my heart
And
Liberate my life.

5160.

No defeat can make
My whole life miserable.
But the lingering effects
Of defeats
Have turned me practically insane.

5161.

Do not lose,
Do not sacrifice
Your life's integrity-flower.
If you lose or sacrifice it,
Your poor life will be compelled to dance
With a totally useless futility.

5162.

Be indifferent to your subtle,
Clever and tempting tiredness.
God will take it away immediately
So you can be a close member of
His inner Family
And walk sleeplessly along
His Eternity's Victory-Road.

5163.

Failure is only
A matter of feeling.
Success is only
A matter of striving.
Progress is only
A matter of self-giving.

5164.

Unless the seeker asks,
Do not tell him where God is.
Unless the seeker needs,
Do not supply him
With God's Compassion-Flood.

5165.

You are a real problem to yourself
If and when you are unwilling
To change your frustration-mind,
Insecurity-heart and failure-life.

5166.

God will teach you Himself
   tomorrow,
If you unlearn what your
Suspicious mind and inauspicious
   life
Have taught you today.

5167.

Simplicity and universality
Are two complementary
Vision-realities
And two inseparable
Perfection-satisfactions.

5168.

Neither resist
God-Beauty's descent from Above
Nor resent
Man-duty's ascent from below.

5169.

If your life lives
In the doubting mind,
Not too long, rest assured,
Will you be able to avoid
The serpentine quagmire
Of life-devastating contradictions.

5170.

If you have
The burning desire to serve,
Then first become
The glowing desire to be cheerful
Before serving,
While serving
And after serving.

5171.

Freedom from self-mortification
Will glorify your Heaven-bound
   heart.
Freedom from self-glorification
Will beautify your earth-bound
   mind.

5172.

Do not ask a barren intellectual
   giant
Anything about God.
He will cleverly and quickly,
If not shamelessly,
Supply you with a maze of
   uninspiring
Plus discouraging
   misinformation.

5173.

Buffeted by cruel
   unreality-strokes,
His vision is denied
Tomorrow's heart-illumining
And life-fulfilling dawn.

5174.

My poor mind is incapable of
   gratitude.
My rich heart is not only capable
   of gratitude
But also capable of constant,
Cheerful and self-giving
   servitude.

5175.

An impossible hope:
To have a faultless friend.
Not only possible but also
   available
Here, there and everywhere:
A faithless friend.

5176.

O my light-searching mind,
If you fail,
It is better to be embarrassed
Than ashamed.
O my God-manifesting heart,
If you fail,
It is better to be ashamed
Than embarrassed.

5177.

A constantly blundering doubt:
This is what our human mind
Primarily is.
A sleeplessly self-giving life:
This is what our divine heart
Precisely is.

5178.

Fear no wrong.
Your heart should know this.
Love no wrong.
Your mind should know this.

5179.

If you struggle to control yourself,
God will smilingly help you enrol
In His
   Life-Transformation-School.

5180.

Do you need protection
Against your wandering
   thoughts?
Then climb up quickly
The magical ladder of will-power.

5181.

Cry within powerfully.
Smile without soulfully.
You will be able to operate
Easily and successfully
On the malignant
   ignorance-tumour.

5182.

Do not allow anybody
To subject your mind to ridicule.
Do not allow anybody
To subject your heart to
   deception.

5183.

A suspicious mind
Is a most frightening challenger.
Alas, my precious heart and my
   auspicious life
Have no capacity to smash its
   pride.

5184.

Each base thought
Defiles everything that is sacred
Immediately.
Each pure thought
Immortalises everything that is
   willing to change
Unmistakably and unreservedly.

5185.

You are afraid to befriend
A sound-life.
That means you do not have
An all-loving heart.
You are afraid to befriend
A silence-life.
That means you do not have
An all-knowing mind.

5186.

His universe collapsed
When his mind deceived his heart
And when his heart disobeyed his soul.

5187.

Breaking asunder the strong grip
Of wild emotions,
His heart sat at the
    Protection-Feet
Of his supreme Satisfaction-Lord.

5188.

Every unforeseen uncomely
    occurrence
Has the incalculable capacity
For a devastating recurrence.

5189.

At the time of my soul-journey's
    start
I thought I did not need
The smiling Eye of Heaven
Or the serving hand of earth.
Alas, where am I now?
I am crying at the feet
Of an unavoidable and inevitable
Failure-end.

5190.

Your mind is shattered.
Do you know why?
Because God wants you to enjoy
Freely and unconditionally
His Heart's Ecstasy-Sea.

5191.

You are indifferent to the
    pleasure-life.
Therefore, God has freed you
Once and for all
From the imponderable
    pressure-world.

5192.

Earth-bound hopes
Flicker and die.
Heaven-free attempts
Succeed and proceed.

5193.

No frustration,
O my vital,
If you want to be happy.
No sophistication,
O my mind,
If you want to be happy.
No hesitation,
O my heart,
If you want to be happy.

5194.

All eyes will be on you
When your own eyes look within
And drink deep the delight
Of your universal oneness-heart.

5195.

An obedience-thought
Has enlarged the freedom
Of my mind.
A gratitude-smile
Has increased the ecstasy
Of my heart.

5196.

If you want to look at your
     yesterday
As totally unimportant,
Then invoke the blessingful
     presence
Of tomorrow's sky, tomorrow's
     sun
And tomorrow's moon
Inside your today's
     receptivity-heart.

5197.

O silence of Eternity,
Do make my heart beautiful.
O sound of a fleeting second,
I shall make your contribution
Everlastingly and timelessly
     fruitful.

5198.

His eyes are pale with guilty fears.
Do you know why?
Because his life has not become
     one
With his heart's climbing tears.

5199.

I do not live
On the praises of this world.
I do not live
On the indifference of the higher
  worlds.
I live inside the Compassion-Eye
Of my Lord Supreme.

5200.

May my mind's sincerity
Spread like a silver dawn.
May my heart's purity
Radiate like a golden morn.

5201.

Just outside your heart's door
God in His supreme Beauty
Is standing.
Just inside your heart's door
God in His supreme Duty
Is working.

5202.

Man's conscious oneness
With God's Will,
And man's conscious offering of
  gratitude
To God's Compassion
Will make man's future slavery to
  ignorance
Impossible.

5203.

My first decision:
I shall not criticise the world
Any more.
My last decision:
I shall love the world
Exactly the same way
My Lord Supreme loves the world.

5204.

Weakness must quickly aspire
For strength.
Strength must unmistakably
  aspire
For oneness,
The only satisfaction.

5205.

To make your life real
You must be more affectionate
To your heart
And more indifferent
To your mind;
You must be more strict
With your vital
And more patient
With your body.

5206.

Live in naturalness
If you want to grow
Into the fulness
Of God's Vision-Reality.

5207.

What you really need
Is Eternity's emptiness
Within
And Infinity's fulness
Without.

5208.

The power of inspiration
Tells me to realise God.
The power of aspiration tells me
How close my heart is to God,
How far my mind is from God
And why my little ego-"I"
Can never realise God.

5209.

A tempted mind thinks
That everything is beautiful.
A liberated life knows
That everything is meaningful.

5210.

A non-existent sincerity
His mind has.
A non-existent purity
His heart is.
But an all-existent divinity
His life will before long become.

5211.

Your mind cherishes
A cluster of memorised ideas.
How do you then expect
The nectar-delight of Himalayan
    ideals?

5212.

O noisy ambitions,
Your tortures are infinitely worse
Than the tortures of the doubtful
And suspicious mind.

5213.

Not only do my soul and my heart
    enjoy,
But also my stupid mind enjoys,
The Fragrance of God's Breathing
While I silently and
    unconditionally meditate.

5214.

He who does not suffer
From ingratitude's cruel blows
Is divinely great,
Supremely good
And
Transcendentally perfect.

5215.

Intuition travels alone
In supreme secrecy
To prove to the world
That God the Creator
Keeps all His Promises
To God the creation.

5216.

Two perfectly useless concepts:
I can do whatever I want.
My life can do without
Any higher guidance.

5217.

My mind needs the Bible
Because it is so soulful.
My heart needs the Christ
Because He is so fruitful.

5218.

When the mind does not pray,
The heart sighs
And the soul sheds sleepless tears.

5219.

The inner beauty does not die;
It grows and glows.
It grows to feed the outer world.
It glows to dance with the inner
    world.

5220.

The entire world can see
The most powerful competition
Between the mind's deliberate
    unwillingness
To realise God
And the heart's sleepless
    willingness
Not only to realise
But also to manifest God.

5221.

He no longer accuses
His doubting mind.
He no longer accuses
His insecure heart.
He accuses only
His weak soul.

5222.

The troubled mind
Can and will find rest
Only when it learns
The magic art of complete
    surrender
To God's Will.

5223.

Yes, I can and shall
Realise God.
Yes, my life can and will
Manifest God.

5224.

He is beautiful, supremely
    beautiful,
Not because he has inside his body
An inconceivable array of stars,
But because every day he sees
The Face of his Beloved Supreme
And every day he plays with
The Heart of his Beloved
    Supreme.

5225.

O my heart,
Do not die unsung.
O my mind,
Do not die unsettled.
O my vital,
Do not die unchallenged.
O my body,
Do not die untransformed.

5226.

If you want to climb
The sky's long stairs,
You have to love the Unknown
And bow to the Unknowable.

5227.

If you live inside your heart,
With your soul
And for your Beloved Supreme,
Then you can never be homeless.

5228.

An impure vital
Is the first danger sign
In a seeker's aspiration-life.

5229.

What you need
Is an imperial thunderbolt
To frighten your unaspiring heart
And your ungrateful life.

5230.

Humility, humility:
The crown of success-light
Which alone can destroy
The wild arrogance of decades
In man's unaspiring nature.

5231.

The first surprise:
God has gladly become man.
The last surprise:
Man shall infallibly become God.

5232.

His strength has failed.
His surrender has succeeded.
His gratitude has received the prize.

5233.

True freedom is not
To build and break in one's own way,
But to grow and glow
Only in God's Way.

5234.

Unless you live sleeplessly
For God the Vision-Eye,
How can you eventually grow
Into God the Reality-Delight?

5235.

Love is something to give.
Devotion is something to give.
Surrender is something to give.
Gratitude is something to become.

5236.

Gratitude is not only
The absence of imperfection
But also the conscious presence
Of the bountiful God.

5237.

An evil thought
May or may not break bones.
But an evil thought
Can and does break hearts.

5238.

The Infinite has cheerfully
   embraced
The finite
So that mortals can successfully
   grow into
The Immortal.

5239.

Always it is God's Compassion-Sea
That saves and illumines the
   seeker,
And not the seeker's merit-drops.

5240.

We really live
When we give to God what we
   have:
Ignorance.
We really live
When we do not give to the world
Our shallow wisdom.

5241.

A prayerless heart
Is a powerless life.
A prayerful heart
Is a fruitful life.

5242.

O my eyes,
I feel sorry for you
Because you cannot love the world
Without hoping to be loved in
   return.
O my heart,
I am so proud of you
Because you do not expect the
   world
To love you,
Although your life
Is a sleepless love for the world.

5243.

An anxiety-mind
And an insecurity-heart
Are the seeds
Of a most tragic end.

5244.

Like an arrow that wings
Through darkness,
His aspiration wings
Into the beauty of Light.

5245.

The illusion of possibility
Can never solve any problem
Either in the desire-life
Or in the aspiration-life.

5246.

History either obeys the will
Of some chosen men
Or accepts the despair-hearts
Of ordinary mortals.

5247.

Muster your determination
If you want to succeed
In the battlefield of life.
Surrender yourself
Constantly and cheerfully to
  God's Will
If you want to proceed
With the spiritual leaders of
  humanity.

5248.

The agony of wild impatience
Tortures humanity's mind
And ruins the poise
Of humanity's heart.

5249.

A confusion-mind
And a contradiction-vital
Live together
In the same absolutely dark room.

5250.

The last flicker of life
Awakened him to see
Once and for all
The countless Himalayan
  blunders
In his life.

5251.

If you choose yourself,
You have nothing to gain
And nothing to lose.
If you choose God,
You not only gain everything,
But also reign over everybody.

5252.

Every day you will meet
With a fresh disappointment
If you want to conquer your
  loving heart
With your doubting mind.

5253.

An uncritical friendship:
Did it ever exist?
Does it exist now?
Will it ever exist in the future?
The answers are all unmistakable:
No, no, no!

5254.

Whenever there is a collision
Between my heart's dream
And my mind's reality,
I always take the side of my heart,
For each dream of my heart
Is newness and sweetness
   incarnate.

5255.

How can you be happy,
How can you be satisfied,
When to discover beauty's truth
You search all the ugly faces
And not all the beautiful hearts?

5256.

My mind's suspicion-night
Is a binding chain around
   nothing.
My heart's wisdom-light
Is a loving chain around
   everything
That I unmistakably have and
   eternally am.

5257.

I need no nest
Until I see that others
Are properly rested.
I need no rest
Until I see that others
Are completely satisfied.

5258.

Is it your impurity-mind
That is killing you?
Is it your insecurity-heart
That is killing you?
Is it your fear of impossibility
That is killing you?
Dive deep within
And get the correct answer.

5259.

As you are looking for
Constant recognition
In the outer world,
Even so, sleepless perdition
Is looking for you
In the inner world.

5260.

A loser's heart of sorrow
Is apt to sadden my heart
But also to illumine my life.

5261.

Selflessness means
That the breath of happiness
Is here
And the life of happiness
Is now.

5262.

To fulfil an unhappy promise
I look at my own eyes.
To fulfil a happy promise
I look at God's Heart.

5263.

A sweet whisper
From an unknown goal
Has perfected my heart
And liberated my life.

5264.

If your mind still has
Chains of expectation,
You will definitely be doomed
To dire disappointments.

5265.

Unless you can muster all your
    life-activities
Into a soulful sacrifice,
Do not expect to become
A choice instrument
Of your Lord Supreme.

5266.

I am very busy,
And I intend to remain so.
No matter how desperately
Death wants to meet with me,
I simply cannot afford to grant
An interview to death today.

5267.

God the creation
Yields only to a soulful server.
God the Creator
Yields only to a dream-flooded
　lover.

5268.

You can make a bold attempt
To be your true self
Only when you treasure
An atmosphere of silence-delight
　within
And an atmosphere of
　silence-light without.

5269.

God commands the strength I
　have
To richly increase.
Death commands the strength I
　have
To quickly decrease.

5270.

The loneliness
Of your yesterday's mind
Must not puncture
The newness-beauty
Of your today's heart.

5271.

Success without self-admiration
Is divinely great.
Success after God-adoration
Is supremely and eternally good.

5272.

The robust conviction of your
　mind
And the tall superiority of your
　vital
Must pale into the insignificance
Of nothingness
Before you can have an iota
Of God's Satisfaction-Bliss.

5273.

Self-praise is ready
To strangle you.
God's Forgiveness-Heart is more
　than ready
To forgive you
In season and out of season.

5274.

Before you hurt others,
Hurt yourself first.
It will make you wise.
Before you love yourself,
Try to love others first.
It will make you perfect.

5275.

If you purchase knowledge,
You will be able to go as far as
The door of your mind.
If you acquire wisdom,
You will be able to fly to the
   highest Beyond,
Sit at God's Protection-Feet
And look at God's
   Satisfaction-Eye.

5276.

What your mind needs
Is a lightning-swift insight.
What your heart needs
Is a soft and sweet touch
From your Eternity's Beloved
   Supreme.

5277.

My mind thinks
It is an impossible task
For me to pray to God.
My heart feels
It is an extremely easy task
For me to claim God.

5278.

I had thoroughly read
God's Heart
Long before I studied
God's Face.

5279.

What is it that I need
And God does not need?
Determination-fire.
What is it that God
Constantly cares for
And I never care for?
My own self-transcendence.

5280.

Success you want?
Then become a self-styled
Man of duty.
Progress you want?
Then become a God-created
Flower of purity.

5281.

First I must appreciate
The sweetness of my silence-heart.
Then only shall I appreciate
The fruitfulness of my
   fulness-soul.

5282.

My soul has invited me
To share its supernal beauty.
I am now inviting my soul
To share my infernal insecurity.

5283.

I shall fear God
So that I can learn from Him
How to create fear
Inside my own suspicious mind.

5284.

Each faithful heart
Embodies the sacred beauty
Of Heaven's silver dreams.

5285.

His reverent regard
For the Compassion-Eye of
   Heaven
Has given him an unprecedented
And permanent joy.

5286.

My heart pines
For the music of my soul
Inside my confusion-cleared
   mind.

5287.

Earth, O earth,
Do tell me something new today.
Tell me, have you not yet seen
God's Vision-Eye?
Heaven, O Heaven,
Do tell me something new today.
Tell me, have you not yet felt
The quenchless thirst of helpless
   humanity?

5288.

Earth loves him
Because inside his heart
Earth has found a moon of hope.
Heaven loves him
Because inside his eyes
Heaven has found a sun of
   promise.

5289.

I just tell my heart what to do —
That is all —
And my heart does it.
It loves God.
I tell my mind what to do,
How to do it and why to do it.
Even then, my mind is totally
   reluctant
To do it.
It does not love God.

5290.

Even God does not want me to do
Two things in one single day.
Why then do I have to blame
   myself?
Today I have emptied my
   stupidity-sea.
Tomorrow I shall completely fill
My divinity-ocean.

5291.

God does not love me:
This is not what I want
To tell the world.
I need God, only God:
This is what I want
To tell the world.

5292.

I may not know who God is,
But I do know where God lives.
He lives beyond the grasp
Of my desire-life,
Within my aspiration-breath.

5293.

I am grateful to God
For having faith in my wishful
   dreams.
I am grateful to God
For having faith
Even in my fearful realities.

5294.

What God actually needs
Is not my life's soulfulness.
What God desperately needs
Is my mind's immediate
   willingness.

5295.

His outwardly restless life
Puzzles me.
His inwardly ascetic life
Puzzles me.
His unconditionally surrendered
   soul
Puzzles me.
To me, he is three insoluble
   puzzles.

5296.

Do not laugh at him.
Today he is absolutely loyal
To himself.
Tomorrow he may be loyal to you.
And who knows,
The day after tomorrow
He may be loyal to God, and to
   God alone.
Therefore, his absolute perfection
Need not remain a far cry.

5297.

God had to build a special prison
To imprison your impurity-mind.
Now God is building a new prison
To imprison your
   insecurity-heart.

5298.

He regards himself as an
   exception,
The only exception,
When Heaven is indifferent
To all human beings.
He regards himself as an
   exception,
The only exception,
When earth does not cry to reach
The highest heights of Heaven.

5299.

In a twinkling
He saw into my heart
And knew that my soulful
   happiness
Would remain young forever and
   forever.

5300.

O my soul,
Let us renew our old dream.
Let us sing the song
Of God's full manifestation on
   earth.

5301.

My joy shall know no bounds
If God shows me His
   Compassion-Eye
At this very moment.
But if He wants to show me
His Compassion-Eye
In the very distant future,
With equal cheerfulness
I can and I shall wait.

5302.

If you want to own
Time's telescope
To see the head of the past
And the heart of the future,
Then become inseparably one
With the waves of your heart's
Oneness-sea.

5303.

Life is tension,
Life is apprehension.
Yet this same life
In the distant future
Will embody God's
　　Manifestation-Light
And God's Satisfaction-Delight.

5304.

What you want
Is an attention-drum.
What you actually need
Is a transformation-flute.

5305.

If you do not know the truth,
Then wait; wait for the right time.
God will come to you
And smile at your
　　preparation-hour.
If you know the truth,
Then also wait; wait for God
To descend upon you
With His Satisfaction-Shower.

5306.

The heart is beautiful
Because it breathes in
Purity-breath.
The soul is fruitful
Because it breathes in
Divinity-breath.

5307.

My Lord, since spirituality
Is a very difficult subject,
May I start studying it
With a minute-life of surrender
And
A second-life of gratitude?

5308.

There are two realities:
One is a God-embracing reality,
The other is a
　　satisfaction-destroying
Reality.
At every moment we have to make
Our faultless choice.

5309.

The heart of an unconditional
　　seeker
Lives in God's Promise-World.
The life of an unconditional
　　seeker
Lives in God's Delight-World.

5310.

Your heart will enter into
Alarming danger
If it ever sees eye-to-eye
With the mind's poison-doubt.

5311.

Surrender is peace-expansion.
Gratitude is delight-expansion.
Oneness is birthless and deathless
Satisfaction-expansion.

5312.

When we listen to
The whispering dictates
Of our conscience-light,
We can easily escape
The jaws of death.

5313.

God is so pleased
With his heart's compassion-sky
And his life's dedication-sun,
That God has asked him to stay
All the time
Inside His Heart of Pride.

5314.

Before you pray and meditate,
You must invoke the deer-speed.
While you are praying and
    meditating,
You must invoke the
    elephant-confidence.
After you have prayed and
    meditated,
You must invoke the lion-victory.

5315.

To live in the desire-world
Is to forget how to smile.
To love in the aspiration-world
Is to become an expert
In the art of smiling.

5316.

Can you dare to believe
That God wants your heart
To be His Eternity's partner
And wants your soul
To be His Immortality's
    collaborator?

5317.

In my desire-life
Nothingness-hunger
Is my frustration-friend.
In my aspiration-life
Fulness-feast
Is my illumination-friend.

5318.

As long as you are willing
To muster your inner courage
To achieve a perfect life,
God's Compassion-Flood
Will, without fail,
Wait for you.

5319.

My eyes have a special love
For the aspiration-shrine.
My life has a special love
For the dedication-shrine.
My soul has a special love
For the surrender-shrine.

5320.

Man's service-hands
And God's Benediction-Eye
And Satisfaction-Heart
Always live together.

5321.

A life of daring promise
Is specially blessed
With an ever-transcending
  horizon.

5322.

Remain not
In your beggar-life of desire.
Choose to live like an emperor
In your life of aspiration.

5323.

If I lose faith in my Lord Supreme,
He can and He will forgive me.
But if I lose faith in myself,
Who knows,
I may not want to
Or may not be able to
Forgive myself.

5324.

If each moment of your life
Can be made into a sacrifice,
God's Perfection-Life and
  Satisfaction-Heart
Will claim you as their very own.

5325.

If you want to serve God,
As you must,
Then detach yourself
From your unreal self:
Ego-bondage.

5326.

Before your mind dares
To suspect others,
Can you not dare
To look into your mind's eye
With greater suspicion?

5327.

The perfection-love
That the divinity of purity attracts
Is bound to last
For Eternity.

5328.

This world is full
Of God-fearing men.
We do not need any more.
What we need now
Is just a few
God-loving and God-serving
　　seekers.

5329.

The animal hunger
Tells us that self-indulgence
Is necessary.
The divine hunger
Tells us that God-effulgence
Is indispensable.

5330.

God invites us all.
Only the self-made men
And self-satisfied men
Proudly and foolishly
Decline His Invitation.

5331.

Poverty is dying for
Self-indulgence.
Plenty is enjoying
Self-indulgence.
An awakened soul
Is longing for
Self-effulgence.

5332.

The distance between
God's Grace and God's Face
Is so negligible
That God does not want us
To measure it.

5333.

I take the Heaven-bound train
To see the Face of God,
And then I take the earth-bound train
To sit at the Feet of God.

5334.

My sincerity is the hyphen,
The golden connecting link,
Between my life's perfection
And my Lord's Satisfaction.

5335.

Long have I been
On the mountain peak of hope.
Now I want to stand
On the solid ground of powerful practicality.

5336.

Let there be
Countless delays and detours.
I shall not mind as long as I know
That in the process of evolution
I shall one day be able to sit
Consciously, soulfully and unconditionally
At the Feet of my Lord, my Beloved Supreme.

5337.

My heart's cry is infinitely stronger
Than what I have already done wrong
And what I am going to do wrong
In the near or distant future.
Such being the case,
I can never be doomed
To utter disappointment.

5338.

I have tried to please the world
By smiling at the world.
Now I see that this
Is not the right way.
Therefore, I shall try another way:
From now on,
I shall try to please the world
By crying for the world.
I do hope that this way
Will be successful.

5339.

Three old friends of mine
Are still with me:
My mind's sincerity,
My heart's purity
And
My life's gratitude.

5340.

Your brave determination
May or may not enable you to conquer
Your powerful nervousness,
But your soulful oneness
With God the creation
Will definitely enable you to conquer
Your unthinkably torturing nervousness.

5341.

The outer world
Doubts his sincerity-mind.
The inner world
Doubts his purity-heart.
But he is not lost at all.
Do you know why?
Because he does not doubt himself.
As long as he has implicit faith in himself,
He need not worry
What the outer world thinks of him
Or what the inner world thinks of him.

5342.

On earth
My heart soulfully celebrates
The victory of
God's Compassion-Height.
In Heaven
My soul powerfully celebrates
The victory of
God's Justice-Light.

5343.

There was a time
When I liked my mind's
Lamb-white days.
But now
I like my heart's
Blue-gold hours
Infinitely better.

5344.

My mind's constant complaint:
This world is extremely imperfect.
My heart's sleepless complaint:
Its own perfection
Is still a far cry.

5345.

His mind is a cry
Of unsatisfied desire.
His heart is a cry
Of soulful and grateful aspiration.

5346.

God does not mind
If my mind does not think of Him.
But my soul becomes extremely
  sad.
God does not mind
If my heart does not pray to Him.
But my soul becomes extremely
  and extremely
Furious.

5347.

When his ignorance-burden
  increases,
Man thinks that he is lost,
Totally lost.
But he does not know that God,
Out of His infinite Bounty,
Will give him another chance
To be good and to be perfect.

5348.

Humanity's victory depends on
Humanity's gratitude and
  surrender.
Divinity's Victory depends on
Divinity's Compassion and
  Forgiveness.

5349.

I enjoyed the first moment of
  freedom
In my life
The day I was able to tell my mind,
"Mind, shut up and sit down!"
And to tell my heart,
"Heart, wake up and climb up!"

5350.

When my mind loves
The quality of freshness,
When my heart loves
The quality of soulfulness
And when my life loves
The quality of newness,
God immediately comes down
With His Quality of Fulness,
And this Fulness is all for me.

5351.

When danger threatens you
  mercilessly,
Immediately use a completely
  new vision.
Feel that God, the Supreme
  Saviour,
Is fast approaching to rescue you.

5352.

Your pride's ceaseless errors
Will compel you to enter
Into life's abysmal abyss,
And there you will see
That you are nothing
But a useless creature,
Empty of hope.

5353.

If you soulfully and unreservedly become
A pilgrim of inner beauty,
Then you will without fail
Have an easy road to Heaven.

5354.

You are doomed to constant failure.
Do you know why?
Because your mind is controlled
By ceaseless and fruitless greed.

5355.

My Beloved Supreme
Lovingly and unreservedly loves
My reality-cries during the day
And my dream-smiles during the night.

5356.

If your heart has the strength
To transcend and transcend and transcend,
Then the Lord Supreme
Will without fail grant you
His Eternity's Length,
Infinity's Length
And Immortality's Length
To enjoy.

5357.

When he realised God for himself,
God said to him,
"My son, I may use you
In the distant future."
When he realised God for others,
God said to him,
"My son, I shall use you
In the near future."
When he realised God for God,
God said to him,
"My son, I am using you
And I shall use you
Sleeplessly and eternally."

5358.

I cannot perfectly say
Whether I love God or not.
But I can unmistakably
And spontaneously say
That God loves my life.
Something more,
He has made my heart
A fit instrument of His,
So He can choose me.

5359.

With my purity-heart
I love the Beauty-Face
Of my Beloved Supreme.
With my purity-body
I serve the Vision-Eye
Of my Beloved Supreme.

5360.

If your heart is always soulful,
Then you are ready to go
To the unaspiring souls
And inspire them
To follow your way,
For your way is God's Way,
And God's Way is the only way.

5361.

My Lord,
Early in the morning every day
Do grant me a heart of poverty
So that I can be humble.
My Lord,
In the evening every day
Do grant me a heart of plenty
So that I can be grateful
And perfect.

5362.

Happiness will follow you
If you follow the footsteps
Of the purity-sages
Who sing sleeplessly
For your heart's illumination
And your life's perfection.
Where do they sing?
They sing inside the
    silence-haunted heart
Of your unconscious universality.

5363.

Only my purity-heart
Can and will silence
The market-noise of my mind.

5364.

Man's unparalleled gift
To God
Is his daily gratitude-heart.

5365.

A purity-heart is always hungry
Not for worldly possessions
But for Heavenly blessings.
And these blessings
Are God's constant Compassion.

5366.

A seeker's heart is blessed
With the capacity
To smell the Fragrance
Of God's Heart of Beauty
Any time it wants to.

5367.

Everybody has a life of obedience.
This obedience-life you have to
   offer
Either to your ignorant, unlit
And limited mind
Or to your beautiful, soulful
And fruitful heart.

5368.

A man of purity
Does not have to know
How to approach the world,
For his Lord Supreme
Approaches the world
In and through him.

5369.

The Peace of my Beloved Supreme
Will eventually break the pride
Of my mind's self-imposed
   turmoil.

5370.

In the morning
I need the freedom to adore
The Beauty of God the creation.
In the evening
I need the freedom to adore
The Responsibility of God the
   Creator.

5371.

My humility-life
Is my conscious oneness
With the illumining and fulfilling
   Universality
Of my Beloved Supreme.

5372.

I shall surrender to my Beloved
　Supreme
What I have:
An uncertain mind.
I shall surrender to my Beloved
　Supreme
What I am:
An insecure heart.
When I surrender
Both my uncertain mind and my
　insecure heart,
Then only shall I become
His choice instrument.

5373.

The beauty of self-giving
Will eventually be transformed
Into the divinity of
　God-becoming.

5374.

A gratitude-heart
Has the message
Of God's Manifestation here on
　earth
And is the fulfilment
Of God's transcendental Promise
　to mankind.

5375.

My life's only task
Is to become inseparably one
With my soul's task,
And this task is to consciously
And unconditionally
Manifest my Lord Supreme
At every moment here on earth.

5376.

My heart has to become
Spontaneous joy
Before my mind can see joy
In God's entire creation.

5377.

Only a humility-life
Can breathe in the endless breath
From Above
Which not only energises
The seeker's limited world
But also radiates
Throughout God's entire world.

5378.

To swim every day in the ocean
Of my Lord's Heart of Delight,
I need only two things:
An experience and a realisation.
The experience is:
"I am for my Beloved Supreme,"
And the realisation is:
"I am of my Beloved Supreme."

5379.

I need only one courage,
And that is the courage to tell the
   whole world
That I am for God, God alone,
Even if God wants to be for
   somebody else.
This is the only courage
That accelerates my own progress
And also humanity's progress
In and through me.

5380.

It is easy
To feel security inside the heart
When the mind enjoys clarity.
It is easier than the easiest
To feel security inside the heart
When the heart unconditionally
   follows
The soul's dictates.

5381.

My Lord Supreme,
You have given me now
What You have brought for me:
Your Vision-Satisfaction-Smile.
And I am giving You
What at this moment I am:
My heart of gratitude-cry.

5382.

When I establish my conscious
   oneness
With my Beloved Supreme,
I see that my life has become all
   newness,
And I feel that my Lord's Fulness
Is delightfully claiming me
As its very own.

5383.

My oneness-heart is my
   fulness-life
And my Lord's complete
   Satisfaction
In His own flowering Vision.

5384.

The four great challenges of a
  seeker-heart
Are to see beauty's eyes,
Purity's heart,
Humility's life
And
Divinity's head.

5385.

The Japanese are helpful
Because they are surrounded by
  beauty.
Beauty is truth,
And truth is always self-giving.

5386.

When we look at a flower,
We get the fragrance of the flower.
Lo, for a few seconds
Our consciousness ascends
And we become self-giving.

5387.

As long as my heart
Knows the complete truth,
I do not care whether my mind
Knows the truth
Or even cares
For the truth.

5388.

I have failed,
Not because I have not attempted.
I have attempted time and again
Soulfully, even sleeplessly.
I have failed
Because I have not made even one
  attempt
At my Lord Supreme's choice
  Hour.
What was I trying to accomplish?
I was trying to reach
The summit-height of Heaven.

5389.

Faith in myself
Awakens my heart.
Faith in God
Immortalises my life.

5390.

God smiles at everything and
  everyone.
But His Smile is most beautiful
And most powerful
When He smiles at a purity-heart.

5391.

In God's inner Family
There are three particular
   members
Who are very special to God:
One-pointedness,
Soulfulness
And
Selflessness.

5392.

With my purity-soul
At every moment
I shall manifest God inside my
   heart.
With my purity-heart
At every moment
I shall live inside my mind.
With my purity-mind
At every moment
I shall energise my vital.
With my purity-vital
At every moment
I shall keep my body awake.

5393.

I shall every day soulfully pray
To my Lord Supreme
To grant me the purity-key
Of my body, my vital and my mind
So that at any moment I can open
   up
My heart's security-door.

5394.

When my Lord asked me
To enter into the world,
I asked Him only one thing:
"My Lord, what shall I do
And what can I do for You
To please You?"
My Lord said to me:
"My child, try to feed Me
At least once every day
With your heart's adamantine
Determination-speed.
If you can do that,
I shall be pleased with you
Far beyond your imagination's
   flight."

5395.

God's Vision in Reality is
   beautiful.
God's Reality in Vision is
   powerful.
God's Vision-Reality is fruitful.
God's Reality-Vision is always
   truthful
To the Creator in Him
And to the creation in Him.

5396.

A security-heart
Is a beautiful flower,
And that beautiful flower
I now am.
A responsibility-life
Is a most energising fruit,
And that energising fruit
I shall before long become.

5397.

Only a life of discipline
Has the capacity to run
Faster than the fastest
To the Infinite.
A life of discipline
Simplifies all the seeker's human problems
And expedites his Godward journey
Far beyond the seeker's own imagination.

5398.

My Lord, since You have given me
A beauty-mind,
Can You not give me at every moment
Purity-thoughts?
My Lord, since You have given me
Purity-thoughts,
Can You not show me at every moment
Your Satisfaction-Eye?
My Lord, since You have given me
Your Satisfaction-Eye,
Can you not make my life
A perfection-gratitude
Worthy of Your Satisfaction-Eye?

5399.

When I came into the world
And breathed in for the first time,
My Lord Supreme granted me the boon
Of breathing in the Fragrance of His Faith-flower
Inside my heart.
Today He is smelling
The fragrance of my gratitude-flower.
I am happy
Not because He has given me something,
Not because I have given Him something,
But because I see that His Eyes
Are all Light
And feel that His Heart
Is all Delight.

5400.

The whole world is looking for miracles.
Every day it is dying to see miracles.
But can there be any miracle
More challenging, more illumining
And more fulfilling
Than to see and feel the infinite Beauty
Of my Beloved Supreme
Inside this tinier than the tiniest
Gratitude-heart of mine?

5401.

My heart-breaking misfortunes
Today shall breathe their last,
For today God's life-transforming Hour
Has blessingfully touched the breath
Of my heart's aspiration-cry.

5402.

O my heart,
Reside not inside the dungeon of despair.
You can easily live inside
The Freedom-Palace of God's Dream-Beauty.
Try, you shall succeed!

5403.

The human life is but
A labyrinth of contradictions.
It does not know how to pray,
Yet it thinks it can easily realise God.
It is always full of problems,
Yet it thinks it is enjoying
Perfect perfection.

5404.

God's first Hymn:
"Secretly I shall grow."
Man's first hymn:
"Sacredly I shall become."

5405.

Something refuses, out of fear,
To reveal itself
Before the all-transforming
   Heavenly Light.
What is it?
The deathless frown of
   ignorance-night.

5406.

Your devotion to anger
You have already shown to the
   world
For a very long time.
Now can you not show
Your devotion to self-perfection?
Try, you easily can.
Lo, you have marvellously
   succeeded!

5407.

His self-giving heart
Is a soaring citadel.
In it no fear, no doubt breathe.
It is perfect perfection
In God's stupendous Satisfaction.

5408.

The oneness of love and duty
Is the perfect fulness
Of a seeker's own inmost divinity.

5409.

Heaven said hello to him
Before he saw
The Face of God
And long before he sat
At the Feet of God.

5410.

If confidence is misplaced,
Man sees not his inner face
And fails to run in God's
Most precious Divinity-Race.

5411.

Uncouple the soul-divinity
From the body-ignorance.
You are bound to be free.
You are bound to be happy.
You are bound to be perfect.

5412.

Bravely my mind
Shall contest with doubt.
Sleeplessly my heart
Shall contest with impurity.
Uncompromisingly my soul
Shall contest with ignorance.

5413.

In the middle of Eternity
He felt his heart's sincerity-cry.
In the middle of Infinity
He saw his soul's divinity-smile.

5414.

If you want to live
In the paradise of
   self-compliments,
You can.
But do not expect others
To live with you.
Why?
Your paradise is too small,
Plus full of dangers.

5415.

His heart's beauty is starving
For God's full Manifestation.
His soul's vision is starving
For God's absolute Satisfaction.

5416.

Two old questions:
How can a weakling ever realise
   God?
How can God care for me
When I am so bad?

5417.

The dreamlessness of dust
Awakens my heart,
Purifies my mind
And illumines my poor little life.

5418.

O knowledge-flames,
Can you not eclipse
   ignorance-night?
Try, I am sure you can.
O wisdom-sun,
Do feed my knowledge-flames
And make them exactly like you.
Since you can do it easily,
Will you not do it for me?

5419.

My sound-life loves
God the creation.
My silence-life becomes
God the Creator.

5420.

His life's scattering smiles
And his heart's streaming tears
Have together made him
A choice and perfect instrument
 of God.

5421.

I saw time's first sunrise.
I could not believe my eyes!
It was the soul-beauty
 unparalleled.

5422.

Where has God gone?
He has gone to Heaven
To receive your heart's
Climbing gratitude-flames.

5423.

A strange new disease:
The heart is suspecting
Its own sterling faith in God.

5424.

If you think that
In the outer world
Your mind does not need
God's Forgiveness
And your heart does not need
God's Compassion,
Then you must realise that
In the inner world
You are unmistakably
And completely lost.

5425.

Mine is a sinking mind.
Mine is a rising heart.
Mine is a flying soul.
Mine is a smiling God.

5426.

With His Blessing-Eye God
 examines
Every sick human thought
And then cures it
With His nursing Heart.

5427.

I can't stand my mind.
It thinks that it knows
Everything and everyone.
Yet it does not even know
How to discard its useless
    treasures
Even in an infinitesimal measure.

5428.

O physical world, stop sleeping.
O vital world, stop pushing.
O mental world, stop doubting.
O psychic world, stop hesitating.

5429.

My companions
From the beginningless
    Beginning:
Eternity's beautiful cry,
Infinity's soulful smile,
Immortality's fruitful silence.

5430.

When my mind completely
    surrenders
To my heart,
And when my heart offers its
    victory-light
To my soul,
I shall triumphantly enjoy
A never-ending celebration.

5431.

Heaven's smiles of farewell
Gave him the joy
Of fulfilling promise.
Earth's tears of farewell
Gave him the satisfaction
Of fulfilled promise.

5432.

The art of pure perfection
Is not an impossible dream
But an inevitable reality.

5433.

Generously erase yourself
If you want to see
The palace of Light and Delight
Inside the depths of your own
Exquisite trance-bound heart.

5434.

Every mind is a new question.
Every heart is a perfect answer.
Every soul is a transcendental
    Vision
And a universal Reality.

5435.

When love starts ruling my mind,
Compassion shall shelter my body
And perfection shall touch my
   heart.

5436.

A soulful cry and a powerful smile
Together have made
A secret and sacred passage
From my heart's depth
To my soul's height.

5437.

An all-consuming ego-night
Has enveloped his mind.
Therefore, he sees not
His soul-beauty's gratitude-heart.

5438.

Heaven and I wept together
When my mind deliberately
Refused to change
And my heart unconsciously
Forgot to climb.

5439.

Nothing can threaten
My soul's silence-heart.
Nothing can weaken
My life's gratitude-breath.

5440.

Your desire for the permanence
Of your body
Is rejected by Heaven
And ridiculed by earth.

5441.

In secrecy's silence-breath
Heaven slowly descends.
In ecstasy's sound-life
Earth quickly ascends.

5442.

Simplicity has deserted him.
Therefore, his eye's beauty
Sings no more.
Sincerity has deserted him.
Therefore, his heart's purity
Dances no more.

5443.

God does not need me,
Not because I do not love Him
But because I feel no need for
   Him.

5444.

A true God-seeker knows
That victory never comes too late.
It always comes unmistakably
At God's choice Hour.

5445.

What can I expect from myself
When I am a bundle of desires?
What can I not expect from myself
When my life becomes
A climbing aspiration-flame?

5446.

Because your mind has become
A spreading wave of anxiety,
Your heart is finding it extremely
   difficult
To maintain its pristine purity.

5447.

Reduce your life's attachments.
The growing and glowing
   enlightenment-bird
Will come and sit on your heart's
Soulful and fruitful
   detachment-tree.

5448.

Each divine thought
Is a never-slumbering plant
In God's Cosmic Vision-Garden.

5449.

You have no right to announce
What you have.
You have no right to announce
What you renounce.
You have only the right to
   announce
That God is sleeplessly for you,
Only for you.

5450.

God cannot be found,
God will not be found,
In your dark, unlit
And impure mind-cave.
He can be found
And will always be found
In your sunlit, spacious
And precious heart-palace.

5451.

When I enjoy labour,
I stand close to God.
Between us there is nothing
And nobody.
When I enjoy leisure,
No matter how close I want
To remain to God,
I always see the Satanic smile
Of an undivine force
In between God and me.

5452.

What am I doing inside my mind?
I am desperately trying
To save my dying friend:
Sincerity.
What am I doing inside my heart?
I am soulfully trying
To save my dying friend:
Purity.
What am I doing inside my life?
I am sleeplessly trying
To save my dying friend:
Integrity.

5453.

How can your mind be truly
   happy
When it proudly and shamelessly
   enjoys
The chill winds of ingratitude?

5454.

Is sincerity enough?
No, you need determination, too.
With determination are you
   complete?
No, you need God's Grace,
Without a shadow of a doubt,
To be amazingly perfect.

5455.

God always chooses
A self-giving heart
To play His Role on earth
And a death-denying soul
To play His Role in Heaven.

5456.

Each auspicious splendour
In the inner world
Reveals ultimately a precious
   wonder
In the outer world.

5457.

From life's dawn I have received
Two invaluable gifts:
A soulful love for perfection
And
A fruitful gratitude for
   satisfaction.

5458.

Today his heart's joy
Knows no bounds
Because the rapture of inspiration
Is marching through his
   silence-mind.

5459.

His heart is flooded
With immortal memories of
   Heaven.
Therefore, God is now granting
   him
The rarest opportunity
To walk closer alongside Him.

5460.

His mind's three triumphant
   conclusions:
He saw God before God saw him.
He taught God how to show
His Compassion-Eye to mankind.
He will never fail God,
Although God has failed him
Time and again.

5461.

Today your heart
Has passed a momentous test.
Today you sincerely and
   unmistakably feel
That delight is another name for
   self-giving.

5462.

Teeming doubts on tip-toe
Entered into his mind
Only to destroy his mind's
   silence-light
And forcefully employ him
To serve in the great army of
   ignorance-night.

5463.

The countless deceptions
Of a thoughtless evil-doer
Cannot compel God to lose faith
   in him.
But his unwillingness to change
   can,
Unmistakably can.

5464.

Why do friendships fail?
Because of a subtle serpentine
Ego-interference.
How can friendship ever last?
By becoming only one thing:
A birthless and deathless
　oneness-love.

5465.

My conscience-drops made me
　stop.
My faith-flames made me run.
My surrender-gratitude made me
　win.

5466.

My faith looks forward
In the morning
To see God's Face.
My faith looks inward
In the evening
To sit at God's Feet.

5467.

His heart's devotion-stream
Flows sleeplessly and powerfully.
Therefore, he is a choice member
Of his Lord's inner Family.

5468.

Self-doubt refuses to rest.
Self-faith refuses to fear.
Self-giving refuses to deceive.

5469.

Ego-protection blocks perfection.
Perfection missing,
Satisfaction-boat not sailing,
But sinking.

5470.

To solve every problem,
Solve your own problems first.
To love each and every human
　being,
Love God first.

5471.

Two are the requests
That reach God:
Lord, do give me the capacity
To love You only.
Lord, do give me the necessity
To love You only.

5472.

Sail beyond the secret sorrow-river
To reach the sea
Of Eternity's infinite Delight.

5473.

Awareness is a spiritual power,
And this spiritual power
Loves only one thing:
The Hour of God's Satisfaction
Inside man's silver dream-boat.

5474.

Life's worst disaster
Is when life does not awaken
Or cannot awaken
When God's God-Hour strikes.

5475.

God says to me
That He will give me three things
If I give Him only one thing.
If I can give Him
Only one gratitude-flame,
Then in return He will give me
His Compassion-Sea,
His Perfection-Sky
And His Satisfaction-Sun.

5476.

He is chained to an unhappy past,
Yet he thinks that someday,
   somehow
He will grant the world
A sky-vast delight.

5477.

When we do not avail ourselves
Of opportunity,
Opportunity goes away.
Then the time comes when we feel
A desperate need for opportunity,
But opportunity does not appear.
Our deplorable fate
And our earthly existence
Are forced by the higher forces
To remain together and helplessly
   wait
For death's hour to arrive.

5478.

In the inner world
The most often-asked questions
   are:
Do you want to see God?
Where is your universal passport?

5479.

A soulful smile
Can kindle the universe.
A breathless cry
Can feed the universe.

5480.

What has experience taught me?
Nobody has to remain unrealised.
What has realisation taught me?
Everybody is an unmanifested
    God.

5481.

Your vital is puzzling you.
Your mind is baffling you.
Therefore, you are sad.
But this sadness will not last
    forever.
Wait soulfully for God's choice
    Hour.

5482.

If you want to have
A continuous and precious
    evolution,
Then give up what you do not
    need,
A helpless cry,
And accept what you do need,
A powerful smile.

5483.

What you have now
Is a flaming temper.
What you need
Is a flaming love.
Inside your flaming love
One day, to your surprise,
You will see a growing and
    glowing God.

5484.

In perfect silence-hush
My heart remains loyal
To my soul's perfection-vision.

5485.

Since your mind has penetrating
Intuitive vision-light,
Since your heart is a constant
Self-transcendence-delight,
You are perfect,
More than perfect.

5486.

Love the battlefield of life,
For joy is always breathing
Secretly and openly
In both your victory and your
    defeat.

5487.

When death invades you,
Do you not see
New sparks of wonder,
Extremely illumining,
In that experience?

5488.

He is weeping like a helpless child.
Do you know why?
Precisely because of the flood
Of his remembrance.

5489.

If you can consecrate
Your voyage on Beauty's mystic
   boat,
Then complete satisfaction
Will be yours.

5490.

I am weary of myself.
My life is but a hopeless journey
With not an iota of ecstasy.

5491.

If you cannot make the correct
   choice,
Try at least to suspect your choice.
You will be able to keep yourself
Free from the heavy burden
Of fruitless accomplishments.

5492.

My purity-heart has discovered
The supreme Truth:
My Lord's Compassion-Eye
And my Lord's Forgiveness-Heart
Are by far its nearest and dearest
Neighbours.

5493.

My hesitation is a serious
Imperfection of my mind.
My hesitation is a dangerous
Frustration of my heart.
My hesitation is an utter
Dissatisfaction of my soul.

5494.

My mind's impurity,
My heart's insecurity
And my life's futility
Stay together
And will die together.

5495.

O my mind,
Be not afraid
Of never-ending changes,
For they will eventually lead you
To
    Perfection-Satisfaction-Delight.

5496.

Let me detach myself completely
From the world of earthly
   knowing
So that I can grow into
The world of Heavenly becoming.

5497.

Time and again
Opportunity knocks
At our heart's door.
Time and again
We do not avail ourselves
Of these opportunities.
Then we blame God
And curse ourselves.

5498.

If your heart can love
The lives of the unlovable,
Then you become a revealed jewel
In Heaven's treasure-safe.

5499.

My Inner Pilot
Can grant me abiding happiness
Only after I have taught myself
How to become an
    obedience-smile.

5500.

Switch your loyalty to God.
You have given enough,
More than enough,
To this ungrateful world.
Give God one second of your
   selfless heart,
And He will grant you
His Eternity's Nectar-Smile.

5501.

No more tomorrows.
No more todays.
It is now, at this very moment,
That I shall become a divinely
   good
And supremely chosen
   instrument
Of my Lord Supreme.

5502.

Only your purity-flooded
Silence-mind
Can tame
Your restless and goalless vital.

5503.

Just because the busy thoughts
Outnumber the quiet thoughts,
Today's mental world
Is unlit and confused.

5504.

You can never enjoy
Ignorance-sleep
If you have a sincere and dear love
For the unfathomable deeps.

5505.

An ordinary and unaspiring man
Is the product of feeble dreams.
A great seeker and God-lover
Is the product of powerful
And fruitful visions.

5506.

In the battlefield of life
Only the goalless fighters
Are godless failures.

5507.

Each time I am inspired,
I become a song of God's Beauty.
Each time I aspire,
I become the music of God's Duty.

5508.

Victory and defeat are interwoven.
Do not try to separate them,
But try to go beyond them
If your heart longs for abiding
    peace.

5509.

You do not have to hide your
    promise;
Just hide your pride
And transform your promise.
God Himself will be proud of you,
Far more than you could ever
Be proud of yourself.

5510.

Today's
Proud ambition
Tomorrow becomes
A helpless victim to itself.

5511.

Unless God's Compassion-Flood
    descends
Into your entire being,
Your life will remain
An unblossomed, tiny little bud.

5512.

It is only your heart's
   aspiration-cry
That can liberate your mind
From the intense apprehension
Of an absolutely futile
   nothingness.

5513.

Fight and fight against
The despondency of your vital,
If you want to bring to the fore
Your loving and aspiring heart's
Oneness-supremacy.

5514.

O heart, my heart,
Try to outweep the false tears
Of the mind.
Try! You will make the
   aspiration-world
Immensely happy.

5515.

His heart's inner sun
Was stunned
When his life
Carelessly and stupidly descended
Fast, very fast.

5516.

He has two ancient playmates:
His heart's selfless cry
And
His life's shadowless smile.

5517.

The beauty of Heaven
Silently sank inside his heart
When his life refused to accept
The soundless sound of his soul,
The great and good
   God-representative.

5518.

My mind and my heart
Do not dare to mix with you
Not because you are too great,
Not because you are too good,
But because your uninspiring
And unaspiring words
Always cast darkness
On my blossoming and glowing
   soul.

5519.

Everything may bend
If necessity demands.
But God's Justice-Light,
When decreed by God Himself,
Will never bend.

5520.

God has infinitely more important
Things to do
Than to please
My constantly curious whims.

5521.

You do not have to go to hell
To see what hell looks like.
If you allow yourself
To mix with your insane
   thoughts,
Then hell itself will come and visit
   you.

5522.

When God chose you
To be a truth-seeker and a
   God-lover,
He gave you a secret haven
Of sacred silence
Inside your heart.

5523.

Two absurd absurdities:
The pure heart
Will deceive the confused mind;
The sure soul
Will deceive the crying heart.

5524.

When his treacherous mind
Communes with him,
His heart suffers
From frustration-blows.
When his precious heart
Communes with him,
His mind suffers
From self-imposed
   suspicion-tortures.

5525.

An insincere mind
And an impure heart
Are unconsciously willing victims
Of powerful sorrows.

5526.

Each moment will seem to be
A fruitful Eternity
If we love the beauty
Of our heart's cry
And the duty
Of our life's smile.

5527.

God's unconditional Love
Has awakened my heart.
Now it is my heart's bounden duty
To awaken the younger members
 of its family
With its God-given unconditional
 love.

5528.

As God's Justice-Light
Does not sanction
Anything uninspiring,
Even so,
God's Compassion-Height
Does not sanction
Anything unaspiring.

5529.

My heart is happy
When it remembers
Its past soulful tears.
My mind is happy
When it remembers
Its past powerful smiles.

5530.

If you are thinking of collecting
The harvest of happiness,
Then look forward
With the beauty of the morning
 dawn
And with the purity of the
 evening stars.

5531.

Through tremendous suffering
He learnt the meaning of the
 inner life.
Now he is teaching others
The meaning of the inner life
Through the joy of his song.

5532.

May oblivion hide
My mind's teeming doubts
And my heart's crying fears.

5533.

How can you expect to see
The beauty of your oneness-love
For God's creation
If you have already allowed
Your breath to be stained
With dark hatred?

5534.

Since the kingdom of your mind
Is flooded with ruthless scorn,
Your heart cannot be anything
Other than a palace
Of throbbing despair.

5535.

Let not the hostile forces
Capture my mind any more,
For now I have become absolutely
   one
With the inner faith
That creates a new and illumining
   creation
For me and through me.

5536.

Outwardly, in public,
You are more than ready
To hate your doubting mind.
Inwardly, in private,
You cherish your doubting mind.
What else is it,
If not the height
Of your hypocrisy?

5537.

His heart's celestial beauty
Was slowly killed
By his mind's dragon-frowns.

5538.

If you deliberately refuse to accept
The beauty and power
Of consciousness-light,
Then your entire being
Will be compelled to face
A sudden and fierce
   confusion-night.

5539.

Hope begins
Inside the searching mind.
Promise begins
Inside the loving heart.
Satisfaction begins
Inside the illumining soul.

5540.

The voice of beauty asks my mind
To go forward
Farther than the farthest
In order to become happy.
The voice of purity tells my heart
To dive inward
Deeper than the deepest
In order to become perfect.

5541.

Love ceaselessly struggles
To increase itself.
Peace sleeplessly struggles
To fulfil itself.

5542.

My life's beauty has given me
The capacity to appreciate
God the creation.
My heart's purity has given me
The capacity to love
God the Creator.

5543.

For a selfless seeker
Eternity's progress-road
Is paved with God's own Light
And Delight.

5544.

Do not think that if you drink
The water of self-contempt
For your past misdeeds,
God will be pleased with you.
No, He will not!
However,
Out of His infinite Bounty,
He may grant you another chance.

5545.

There are two prophetic songs:
Today God will walk with me;
Tomorrow I shall work for God.

5546.

A powerful person
May not get even one faithful
    friend,
But a soulful person
Will have the entire world
As his loving and intimate friend.

5547.

Your mind may at times know
The beauty of hope,
But your heart always knows
The power of hope.

5548.

O power of oblivion,
Will you kindly hide
My depression-torture
Today?
O power of oblivion,
Will you kindly hide
The pride of destruction-night
Tomorrow?
This is the only way
My mind can move forward
And my heart can dive inward.

5549.

Slowly and steadily
Kill the doubt-snake
That has encircled your searching
　mind
And enveloped your crying heart.

5550.

You do not have to guard your
　soul.
Only do not resist your soul
When it tries to guard you,
Guide you and illumine you
In God's own Way.

5551.

If you obey God's Will
Consciously, soulfully and
　unreservedly,
Then you will never inherit
　disgrace
From any corner of the world.

5552.

It is not God's Justice-Light
But God's Compassion-Height
That silences and illumines
Not only the uncontrolled
But also the uncontrollable vital
　in us.

5553.

Master your resentments
Towards the world and towards
　yourself.
You will before long
Make the fastest ascent.

5554.

Peace may not follow him
Whose life is the proof of
　goodness,
But God's blessingful
　Satisfaction-Light
Without fail follows him.

5555.

The outer hunger rules
The human in me mercilessly.
The inner hunger rules
The divine in me gloriously.

5556.

If you have a detached mind
And if you have a devoted heart,
Then your life of total
　transformation
Cannot and will not remain a far
　cry.

5557.

In the morning
Use your purity-breath
To illumine the world within you.
In the evening
Use the selfsame breath
To liberate the world around you.

5558.

Who can measure
The beauty of the heart?
A breathless God-dreamer
And
A selfless God-lover.

5559.

Since you are wanting
In self-control,
How can you expect God
To perform His Satisfaction-Role
In and through you?

5560.

Be careful in choosing!
If you make a mistake,
You will never be able to hear
God's life-transforming Voice.

5561.

Only my cheerfully and
    unconditionally
Self-giving heart
Has the velocity and capacity
To capture the wings
Of fleeting time.

5562.

Breathlessly I love You, my Lord,
In my heart's dreams.
Sleeplessly I need You, my Lord,
In my life's realities.

5563.

Reduce the earth-bound mind
To nothingness
If you want to be happy.
Multiply the beauty of
The Heaven-free heart
Until it reaches Infinity
If you want to be perfect.

5564.

A rash of the world's deficiencies
You are bound to incur
If you do not offer
Your self-giving and
    earth-fulfilling life
Efficiently.

5565.

His silence-tree
And its own life-tears
Are sheltering not only those
Who are longing for light
But also those
Who are longing for
   service-delight.

5566.

The streaming tears
Of the soul's sorrowful eyes
Can easily be felt
By the seeker's heart.
They alone can purify, illumine
And immortalise the seeker.

5567.

Two paramount questions:
Do I have to love God
   unconditionally
In His own Way?
Does God have to love me
In all my weaknesses
In my own way?

5568.

In the morning if I forget
To offer my gratitude-heart
To my Lord Supreme,
Then in the evening I offer Him
My universe of tears.

5569.

If you become a victim
To earthly fame,
How can you expect to discover
The satisfaction-waves of
   Heavenly gains?

5570.

His mind is as secret
As a dream-bud.
His heart is as sacred
As a reality-flower.

5571.

A dry intellectual mind
Is undoubtedly an ineffectual
Life-transforming hope.
Therefore, live not in the arid
   desert
Of intellectual pride.

5572.

The whispers of the prophets:
You will see God face to face.
You will consciously become
A participant in God's Eternity's
   Race.
You are another God.
What you need is your Atlantic
   manifestation
Through your Himalayan
   revelation.

5573.

Two precious dreams:
I shall realise God without fail
In this life;
God shall be proud of me
Permanently.

5574.

Inside the circle of anger
Fear and doubt unconsciously
   abide.
Outside the circle of anger
Beauty's God-rapture openly
   abides.

5575.

Yours is the opportunity
To enjoy the power of choice.
God's is the Divinity
To grant you the choice of power.

5576.

No end to sadness for him
Who mechanically thinks and
   thinks.
No end to joy for him
Who prayerfully meditates and
   meditates.

5577.

Self-discovery is not an accident.
Neither is life-mastery.
God-realisation is not a mystery.
Neither is earth-transformation.

5578.

His sadness sadly crawled
And finally collapsed.
Then he surrendered himself
To Heaven
And became the cheerful
   hero-pride
Of earth.

5579.

Unless you take
The life of aspiration seriously
Right from the beginning,
Your mind's curiosity
Will fade away
And your uncertain heart
Will miserably fail.

5580.

If your heart does not create
A solid citadel
Against your mind's wild
   tempests,
Then your life will meet with
Nothing else but downright
   failure.

5581.

If you live in the desire-world,
The separation-wall between you
   and God
Will swell and expand.
Therefore, accept the world
That is within you:
The union-world,
Where you and God are eternally
   united
In God's infinite Vision-Delight.

5582.

What does my aspiration-cry do?
It carefully and triumphantly
   renovates
My old world.
What does my dedication-smile
   do?
It invites God the Supreme Guest
To come once again
And live in my newly revealed
   world.

5583.

Until his ignorance-night
Completely vanishes,
His will be the role to cry,
And his Lord's will be the role to
   sigh.

5584.

He does not pray,
He does not meditate.
Yet he expects the fruits
Of prayer and meditation.
Since this is not possible,
He is forced to enlarge
The confines of his despair.

5585.

A Dream of God
Easily made infinite human
   beings.
The reality of a single man
Can amazingly satisfy the
   Absolute Supreme.

5586.

If earth gets tired
Of loving Heaven,
Heaven does not mind.
Perhaps God also does not mind.
But if ever Heaven gets tired
Of loving earth,
Earth will helplessly weep,
And God will use nothing
But His Volcano-Ire.

5587.

The human life is
A molehill-height of hopes.
The divine life is
A mountain peak of fulfilment.

5588.

On the summit of ages
This imperishable message was written:
Each promise of God and each hope of man
Together shall strive,
Together shall succeed,
Together shall transcend.

5589.

Only the arrows
Of your silence-life
Can pierce the veil
Of your mind's ruthless
Suspicion-nights.

5590.

O my ego,
I have all along either pleased you
Or tried to please you.
Can you not please me only once
In this lifetime?
"O God-seeker,
What do you want from me?"
I want your death, immediate death.
"O seeker, granted.
From today on you will be able
To walk along the sunlit road of aspiration,
Dedication and
God-manifestation."

5591.

There is only one highway to Heaven,
And that highway
Is our constant and unconditional
Self-giving way.

5592.

The footsteps of envy
Must not trespass
On the hallowed ground
Of my heart's oneness-life.

5593.

Society's cheap joy
You openly enjoy.
How can you then
Hope to secretly enjoy
Divinity's invaluable
Heart-embracing
And life-illumining joy?

5594.

Since you resigned
From your life's inner career
Long before your mind-power
    faded,
Your heart-power will fade
Long before its career is meant to
    end.

5595.

God's supremely chosen
    instruments
Are extremely embarrassed
To go back to Heaven
Without having radically changed
The uncomely face of this world.

5596.

Death's journey begins and ends
When your heart remains
Untouched and unperturbed by
    earth's noise
And offers its grateful
    existence-life
To the Lord Supreme.

5597.

Life's journey begins and ends
Inside God's Eternity's Eye,
Infinity's Heart
And Immortality's Body.

5598.

You want to escape.
Do you not know
That you cannot escape?
You can escape
From your friends and dear ones.
You can escape
From your society.
You can escape
From your country.
You can escape
From each and every one.
But you cannot escape
From your mind.
No matter where you go,
Your mind will follow you
And torture you.

5599.

If you really want to escape
From your mind,
Then you have to go
Beyond the mind.
How do you do that?
You have to make friends
With the blue bird
That is deep inside your heart.
This blue bird will help you fly
In the firmament of Light and
   Delight.

5600.

When you pray,
Think of a lost child within you
Crying helplessly.
When you meditate,
Think of a morning flower
Smiling and smiling,
Radiating its beauty
And offering its fragrance.
This is how you can make friends
With your soul
And fly with it infinitely higher
Than the confines of the mind.

5601.

This entire year, 1983,
Has a very special significance.
This is the year of meditation.
I most sincerely urge you
To meditate, meditate, meditate!
Alone or with others,
At home or anywhere,
Whenever you are free
Meditate, meditate, meditate!

5602.

As God's choice Hour does not
   arrive
Every hour, every day, every week,
Every month or even every year,
Who knows, a year of this kind
May not appear again for a long
   time.
If you want to become God's
   choice instrument,
Then avail yourself of the golden
   opportunity
That this year of meditation
   offers.

5603.

Meditate, meditate, meditate!
Pay more attention to your
   meditation.
Spend more time in meditation.
Meditate soulfully, prayerfully
   and devotedly.

5604.

If you do not meditate,
Then your heart will remain
  insecure
And your mind will remain
  impure.
With an impure mind
And an insecure heart
You will not be able to please
Your Beloved Supreme.

5605.

Security, which is confidence,
You badly need.
Purity, which is inner assurance,
You badly need.
Both purity and security can and
  will come
Only from your meditation.

5606.

Whether you are meditating
In your Master's physical presence
Or somewhere else is
  unimportant.
No matter where you are,
If you think of your Master
And meditate soulfully,
You are bound to get his inner
  guidance.
And this inner guidance,
Which is his inner oneness with
  you,
Will last forever and forever.

5607.

In your early morning meditation
Be regular, be punctual and be
  sincere.
If you do not meditate regularly
  and punctually,
The Supreme will forgive you,
Your Master will forgive you,
But you will never be able
To forgive yourself, never!
If you deceive yourself in your
  meditation,
There will eventually come a time
When you will spontaneously
  become
Absolutely sincere.
Then it is you who will not be able
To forgive yourself.

5608.

My aspiration's self-transcending
  horizon
Tells me what I can do for God.
My dedication's all-loving
  service-hands
Tell me and show me
What God has already done for
  me.

5609.

If you resist God's
   Compassion-Light,
Then nothingness-night
Will haunt you at every moment
And destroy your hope-paradise.

5610.

When you choose,
You choose a better life
For yourself.
When God chooses,
He chooses a supremely perfect
   life
For you.

5611.

Two common sense experiences:
I need God's Heart of Compassion,
God loves my heart of aspiration.

5612.

Enthusiasm has determination
   inside it
In disguise.
Determination has peace inside it
In disguise.
Peace has perfection inside it
In disguise.

5613.

The difference between
Your mind's impurity
And your heart's insecurity
Is absolutely negligible.
The difference between
Your heart's purity
And your life's luminosity
Is absolutely negligible.

5614.

Suffering is an inner thief.
We must by all means try to catch
   it.
If we cannot,
Our life will remain a victim
To untold miseries.

5615.

Beauty likes to touch
The feet of Divinity.
Divinity likes to feel
The heart of Immortality.
Immortality likes to grow
With God's ever-transcending
   Vision-Eye.

5616.

If man offers
His service-hands
And his love-heart,
Then God grants him
His Compassion-Eye
And His Satisfaction-Crown.

5617.

A completely new vision:
My aspiration-flame,
No matter how weak and feeble,
Can never be doomed to a
   failure-life.
A life of success
Lovingly, cheerfully and proudly
Awaits my aspiration-life.

5618.

As the human mind
Quite often enjoys
Turbulent self-contradictions,
Even so, the divine heart
Always enjoys
Divinely inspired
   God-affirmations.

5619.

Your mind is eclipsed
By worldly thoughts.
Alas!
Therefore, your soul is forced to
   suffer
An indefinite delay.
Alas, alas!

5620.

O my mind,
Instead of dying for
An ever-new curiosity,
Can you not long for
An ever-fresh luminosity?
Thus you will be able to please
The Real in you:
Your own Eternity's blue bird,
Your soul.

5621.

Alas, your innocent heart
Has to perish
Because of your mind's
Unthinkable stupidity:
Your mind has feasted
On poison-doubt.

5622.

When the hour of death
   approaches,
With your heart's aspiration-cry
You can secretly climb up
God's hidden Tower of
   Immortality.

5623.

The bounden duty of a seeker's
   heart
Is not to allow
Teeming doubt-clouds
To eclipse his inner sun.

5624.

A perfection-life
We can never acquire
On our own.
But God the Compassion-Heart
Is more than ready
To acquire it for us.

5625.

A self-giving heart
Marks the glorious beginning
Of a God-becoming soul.

5626.

What I need
Is not the extinction
Of ambition
But the fire-pure transformation
Of ambition
Into an astounding dedication.

5627.

God-realisation is not beyond
The range of aspiration.
God-manifestation is not beyond
The range of dedication.

5628.

A self-giving heart
Is a beautiful nest of security.
A self-doubting mind
Is a desolate cave of insecurity.

5629.

My obedience means
My higher life is successfully
   operating
In and through my lower life.
My disobedience means
My higher life and my lower life
Are both in trouble.

5630.

What is belief?
A flight into the realm of fulness.
What is disbelief?
A plunge into the abysmal abyss
Of useless nothingness.

5631.

How can you hope to succeed in
   life
When you are allowing
Your disappointed mind
To accompany you on your
   journey?

5632.

A searching mind is one step
   forward
Towards the aspiration-goal.
An aspiring heart is one step
   forward
Towards the realisation-goal.

5633.

From Above
What my body needs
Is a compassion-gift.
What my vital needs
Is a salvation-gift.
What my mind needs
Is an illumination-gift.
What my heart needs
Is a liberation-gift.
What my life needs
Is a perfection-gift.

5634.

Surrender is a
   miracle-achievement.
This my mind knows.
Gratitude is a
   miracle-achievement.
This my heart knows.

5635.

Faith helps my heart-flower
   blossom
Petal by petal in perfect perfection
So that it can respond
To my soul's delight-call.

5636.

The soul-birds come down
Into the world-arena
To awaken the higher realities
That are fast asleep
Inside the earth's ignorance-body.

5637.

Yesterday Eternity came to me
With its oneness-soul.
Today Infinity has come to me
With its oneness-role.
Tomorrow immortality will come
   to me
With its oneness-goal.

5638.

I desired,
Yet not quite desired,
An earthly sound-mind.
I loved,
Yet not quite loved,
A Heavenly silence-heart.

5639.

To take shelter inside
The fragrance-purity of your heart
Is to discover a stepping-stone
To God-realisation.

5640.

Even a great mind
Can be invaded
By chaotic confusion.
But a good heart
Is always embraced
By kaleidoscopic beauty.

5641.

Do not wait!
If you really want God
To be always on your side,
Then immediately choose to serve.

5642.

Not your solitude-companion
But your gratitude-companion
Can definitely and will
   immediately
Please God.

5643.

Round and round my silver
   dreams
Revolve my Lord's Vision-Eye
And my Lord's
   Compassion-Heart.

5644.

If you can have a free access
To patience-light,
Then you can run very fast
On the high road to Heaven.

5645.

A universally
Heart-winning man
Is a breathlessly
Self-giving soul.

5646.

Outwardly and openly
He shows a face of joy,
But inwardly and secretly
He is weighed down
By his heart's excruciating pangs.

5647.

This time I have brought down to earth
Two souvenirs from my trip to Heaven:
A heart-awakening conch
And
A life-transforming flute.

5648.

If you are preoccupied with
 yourself,
How can you watch
The life-transforming free play
Of God's Heart?

5649.

Your mind's miscellaneous
 thoughts
Will never allow you to build
A monument that will withstand
Time's giant frowns.

5650.

God overheard
My foolish prayers.
As a result,
His Heart is extremely sad.

5651.

To unfold the heart-flower
Of my life,
Every day my soul sings
A sun-song to my Beloved
 Supreme.

5652.

You are already the Lord
Of my illumination-dreams.
Do also be the Lord
Of my oblivion-sleep.

5653.

To be a most faithful
Companion of God,
What I need is a tiny
   gratitude-plant
Inside my heart.

5654.

God loves me,
And He tells me that
He will love me infinitely more
If I attempt for Him
Any so-called impossible task.

5655.

Do not ask for too little.
When you do that,
God's Heart of Magnanimity
Is embarrassed.

5656.

A lingering thought
In a poverty-stricken mind:
This is what your light-forsaken,
Deplorable and doomed life is.

5657.

I dearly love
The abode of the ancient sages,
For there they are always exulting
In Ecstasy supreme.

5658.

Is it possible for you to be loved
By God powerfully,
When you are so heartlessly
   indifferent
To His creation-child?

5659.

If you meditate on
God's Forgiveness-Depth,
Then you are repaying
God's Compassion-Height.

5660.

You will remain unnoticed
Both by Heaven and by earth
If you do not show your heart's
Flaming and glowing
   compassion-touch.

5661.

The more my outer world
Consciously needs perfection,
The sooner my inner world
Shall grant its prayer.

5662.

You have not forgotten me
Even at the end
Of your life's long dream.
Therefore, you are my heart's
Peerless friend.

5663.

His mind is now a confessed
   failure
Because it allowed itself
To be possessed by an irresistible
   desire
To command others.

5664.

If necessity demands,
You can speak well of yourself.
But there is no necessity
For you to speak ill of others.

5665.

"My Lord,
Do show me the way."
This is a good prayer.
"My Lord,
Do be my Guide."
This is a better prayer.
"My Lord,
Do manifest Yourself in Your own
   Way
Through any heart You choose."
This is by far the best prayer.

5666.

My mind's new discovery:
God loves my mind.
My heart's new discovery:
God is for my heart.
My life's new discovery:
I shall unmistakably please God
From this very moment.

5667.

My mind's outer resolution
Shall make my body
A fit instrument of God.
My heart's inner revolution
Shall make my life
A perfect instrument of God.

5668.

From now on I shall keep
The suspicion-snake behind me,
The faithfulness-dog beside me,
The promise-deer before me.

5669.

Humanity's dream
Is perfect perfection.
Divinity's dream
Is supreme satisfaction.
The Dream of the Supreme
Is to make each human being
A conscious and living God.

5670.

Disobedient people God created.
So what can the Master do?
But this much the Master knows:
Disobedient people will always fail.

5671.

If disciples cannot meet
With their Master's simplest request,
Is the Master such a fool
To believe that these unfortunate disciples
Will ever please him?

5672.

You may feel that something
Is the easiest thing,
But the easiest can be the most difficult.
For when you consider something to be easy,
That is the time
The hostile forces attack you
And make you feel how weak you are.
You say that you can do it,
But the world will see and God will see
That you cannot!

5673.

Four words your Master
Does not want to hear
When he has asked you to do
   something:
"I did not know!"
If you always say you did not
   know,
Then you will remain ignorant
Throughout Eternity.

5674.

If you are a good disciple,
You will always try to please your
   Master.
If you are satisfied
With being a bad disciple,
Then just stay in his boat,
Sleeping all the time,
Snoring all the time.
But remember,
A good disciple will behave
In a totally different way.

5675.

I have only three goals in life:
I shall continuously fight
Against ignorance-night.
I shall cheerfully unlearn the
   lessons
That my earth-bound mind has
   taught me.
I shall, without fail,
Manifest my Lord Supreme
When the supreme Hour strikes.

5676.

We can fulfil
Our journey's course
Only if we can regulate
Our thought-life
And emancipate
Our action-life.

5677.

If your mind is charged
With an adamantine
   determination,
Then your heart is bound to enjoy
A satisfaction-feast.

5678.

If your mind can be
Brutally sincere
To your heart,
And if your heart can be
Sleeplessly sincere
To your soul,
Then your life of perfection
Can never, never remain a far cry.

5679.

If you live in the desire-world,
Then God's transcendental Pride
Will never be able to claim you
As its own, very own.

5680.

If the mind can derive satisfaction
From its promising life,
Then the heart can derive
    satisfaction
From its perfecting life.

5681.

O bewildered humanity,
You are longing for a
    satisfaction-life.
You can fulfil your longing
Only by crying for the capacity
To unreservedly listen
To your heart's inner dictates.

5682.

If you want to see
The complete exhaustion and
    extinction
Of your sorrows,
Then control the turbulent
    currents
Of your teeming desires.

5683.

Tranquillity will inundate your
    mind
If your mind gets a new lesson:
The lesson of breathless
    perfection.

5684.

If you are a lover
Of all that breathes in God's
    creation,
Then God the supreme Lover
Will not only crown you
But also place you
On His transcendental Throne.

5685.

Each time an uncomely thought
Invades your mind,
Feel that your mind is totally
    pierced
By a venom-arrow.

5686.

A beginner may be caught
In the tenacious miracle-net.
But a well-advanced seeker must
    escape
The miracle-net
To run always the fastest
In his heart of aspiration
And his life of dedication.

5687.

A seeker does not need
A monastic silence.
He does not need
An ascetic silence.
What he needs
Is a soulful and aesthetic silence
To dive deep within
And reach the deepest depth
Of an all-embracing reality.

5688.

Secretly, cheerfully and
    unconditionally
God has fed your aspiration-life.
Will you not offer Him
One soulful smile
From your life's
    perfection-satisfaction?

5689.

Your long and eager
    expectation-night
Will now be transformed
Into satisfaction-day
Because your heart is flooded
With the fresh tears
Of a new creation.

5690.

If you try to desert your lower self,
You will not succeed.
When the opportunity arises,
Your lower self
Will bite you very hard.
So do not try to desert your lower
    self;
Only try to transform your lower
    self.
Once your lower self is
    transformed,
Light and delight will be
Your life-long friends.

5691.

If your outer steps lead you
To your inner shrine,
God the Beauty will come to you
With a never-dying
And ever-illumining sweetness.

5692.

Since God's Forgiveness-Heart
Has not allowed God to defend
   Himself,
It is the bounden duty of your
   gratitude-heart
To defend God.

5693.

There is always a choice
Between what your desire-life
Wants you to be
And what God's Compassion-Eye
Wants you to be.

5694.

If you do not care for
A purer heart and a better life,
It is as good as returning
To your stone-life.

5695.

God has asked a very simple
   question:
Do you want to be like Him?
He is eagerly waiting
For your open-hearted answer.

5696.

What indefinitely delays
Your God-realisation?
Not your feeble incapacity
But your powerful unwillingness.

5697.

When God smiles,
Even the doubting mind
Totally forgets
That it has the capacity to doubt.

5698.

If you are seeking something
Beyond your present capacity,
Do not listen to the dictates
Of the false voice that says you
   cannot.
Listen only to the dictates
Of the voice that says
You can and you shall.

5699.

The promise-maker
Has a great mind.
The promise-fulfiller
Is a good heart.

5700.

Each prayerful day
Of my heart
Is a blessingful and fruitful Smile
Of my Beloved Supreme.

5701.

The concept of impossibility
My Lord does not accept,
So how can I?
My life will be changed totally.
I just have to be patient.
It is only a question of time.

5702.

A self-controlled life
Will guarantee salvation.
A self-giving life
Will guarantee liberation.

5703.

Happiness follows him
Who follows the footsteps
Of a God-intoxicated lover.

5704.

Your new-made friendship
With your conscience-life
Will save you,
Perfect you
And finally illumine you.

5705.

Watch your sincerity
And pray for your purity.
You will never fall into the abyss
Of temptation-night.

5706.

The modern age of electronics
And the age-old life of inner poise
Deliberately want to be ignorant
Of each other.

5707.

Obey His Commands
If you want your life to be soulful,
Your heart to be fruitful
And, finally, your breath
To be supremely useful
To your Lord Supreme.

5708.

My heart's silence-poise
Is not only my life's confidence
But also my Beloved Supreme's
Satisfaction-Delight.

5709.

A soulful heart,
A self-disciplined mind
And a practical life
God proudly treasures on earth.

5710.

Walk with the Eternal God.
Fleeting time
Will not be able to torture you.
Adamantine will-power
Will descend from Above
And make you a real member
Of God's Heavenly Kingdom on
   earth.

5711.

Make friends
And cherish your friendships,
So you can stop making
Once and for all
Any kind of warship.

5712.

It is Heaven's Compassion-Sky
And not earth's eloquence-flood
That has illumined my heart
And transformed my life.

5713.

If you pray even for five minutes
For the wrong thing,
You may suffer unimaginably
For the rest of your life.

5714.

The faithfulness of my life
And the fruitfulness of God's
   Heart
Are always extremely fond of each
   other.

5715.

During the day
I need only one thing:
God's Vision-Eye
To guide me.
During the night
I need only one thing:
God's Compassion-Heart
To illumine me.

5716.

Success cannot hide
Its futile emptiness,
But progress can hide
Its soulful fruitfulness.

5717.

Be happy, be happy!
Unless you are happy,
Your outer life will not succeed
And your inner life will not
    proceed.

5718.

A life of unhappiness
Is a contagious disease.
The world is already full of misery.
Allow not your unhappiness
To increase the world's misery.

5719.

A heart of magnanimity
Carries at once
The beauty and the power
Of divine electricity.

5720.

Our heart must weep
And our eyes must smile
If we want to totally transform
    ourselves.

5721.

The sound of the sea
Inspires me to become
Something great.
The silence of the sea
Aspires in and through me
To make me good.

5722.

An infallible truth:
A heart of genuine aspiration-cry
Is God's proudest possession.

5723.

Your soul has built
Your life's future-tower today.
Now it is high time
For your heart to stand
Smilingly and soulfully
On its summit-height.

5724.

The difference between
The outer blindness and the inner
   blindness
Is this:
The outer blindness
   unfortunately
Cannot see the light.
The inner blindness deliberately
Does not want to see the light.

5725.

You have everything within.
To find your true self
Just love more
Your heart's soulful cry
And your eyes' powerful smile.

5726.

A new philosophy:
To teach is to learn.
To learn is to reveal constantly
One's inner perfection.

5727.

He is a real discoverer.
He has discovered that
His life's teeming weaknesses
Are all inside the
   Compassion-Heart
Of his Beloved Supreme.

5728.

Pray soulfully.
You will be able to wash away
Your worries.
Meditate silently.
You will be able to create
A totally new life
For yourself.

5729.

Man's perfection-life:
This is what God clearly needs.
God's Satisfaction-Heart:
This is what man sleeplessly
   needs.

5730.

I confess that I have done
Many foolish things in this life.
But why do you have to revive
   them
And torture me infinitely more
Than I actually deserve?

5731.

One soulful cry of the heart
Can not only lighten
The weight of sad depression
But also enlighten
A God-searching mind.

5732.

O Heaven, please remember
That all I have told you
About weak earth
Is in supreme secrecy.
O earth, please remember
That all I have told you
About indifferent Heaven
Is in supreme secrecy.

5733.

O ignorance-night,
So far I have not fought with you
Either sincerely or vehemently.
But once I start fighting,
I will neither expect nor give
An iota of compassion.

5734.

If you are sincere
And your needs are essential,
How can God be unreasonable?
God will tell the whole world
That all your soulful needs
Are only for His
   Satisfaction-Light.

5735.

Two are the thoughts so futile:
I can live
Without the world.
I can find mistakes
In the life of the cosmic gods.

5736.

When you see
Death's tremendous nearness,
Can you not immediately unveil
Your inseparable oneness
With God's Omnipotence?

5737.

Without an instant's hesitation
I shall tell earth
How miserable it looks
Without the blessing-smile of
   Heaven,
And I shall tell Heaven
How unimportant it looks
Without the aspiration-cry of
   earth.

5738.

O my Lord Supreme,
Do grant me Your sovereign Will
To obliterate my earth-bound
   needs
And liberate my impurity-bound
   self-doubts.

5739.

In the morning
The clutch of evil thoughts
Makes me blind, totally blind.
In the evening
The clutch of evil thoughts
Compels my death, unavoidable death.

5740.

I need the courage that is far above
The so-called morality-bound truth,
So that I can serve my Lord Supreme
In His Life's Vision Transcendental.

5741.

My Lord Supreme,
Out of His infinite Bounty,
Tells me that His Weight is at once
As light as my heart's aspiration-cry
And as heavy as my life's ingratitude-frown.

5742.

I refuse to become
A victim to untold miseries
Simply because
I did not think of my Lord Supreme
Centuries ago,
Or even yesterday.
But my heart
Shall be smitten to pieces
If I do not think of my Lord Supreme
From today on,
Forever and forever.

5743.

The stiff mind questions:
Is God-realisation worthwhile?
The flexible heart answers:
It is never worthwhile
To answer a question about God
From the wrong person.

5744.

Our aspiration is accountable
To God's Vision-Light.
Our dedication is accountable
To God's Reality-Delight.

5745.

To be absolutely perfect,
Yesterday I needed a heart of
   beauty,
Today I need a life of purity
And tomorrow I shall need
A smile from Heaven's Divinity.

5746.

Only a perfectly liberated soul
Can meet with the extraordinary
   demands
Of unaspiring human life.

5747.

Once again I wonder
That I still exist.
Once again I wonder
That God still forgives me.

5748.

The measure of your life's
Richest fulfilment
Depends entirely on your heart's
Fullest enlightenment.

5749.

Be careful with your success-life.
Your success-life may hide
Many precious things,
Even your most precious
   progress-delight.

5750.

A moment without a soulful cry
For the ever-transcending Beyond
Is undoubtedly an age-long
Failure-life.

5751.

You are telling me
That your life is committed to the
   future.
How do you then expect
To collect the rich harvest
Of today's reality's silence-peace?

5752.

I sail all night
In my aspiration-boat
Towards Heaven.
I sail all day
In my dedication-boat
Towards earth.

5753.

When my heart's inner flames
Soulfully, quickly and powerfully
Ascend,
God's Compassion-Flood
Lovingly, cheerfully and
  unreservedly
Descends.

5754.

The human mind
Is a self-appointed dictator.
The divine heart
Is a God-appointed lover.

5755.

A moment of self-indulgence
May throw you
To the ferocious and devouring
  tiger,
Death.

5756.

If you are ready today,
I shall announce
God's express arrival.
If you will not be ready until
  tomorrow,
Then I shall announce
God's slow and cautious arrival.

5757.

Spirituality is not like coasting
But exactly like climbing —
Climbing ten thousand
  Himalayas.

5758.

When your mind's determination
  is low,
Go and talk to God immediately.
He is always there inside your
  heart.
No appointment is necessary.

5759.

Reformation means
A new powerful promise.
Regeneration means
A new soulful achievement.

5760.

Heaven has given my mind
The message of transformation.
Earth has given my heart
The message of perfection.
God has given my life
The message of satisfaction.

5761.

A happy heart
Receives the earliest invitation
From God.

5762.

You want to see God's Face
To satisfy yourself.
God wants to embrace your heart
To satisfy Himself.

5763.

As your self-praise
Does not need God,
Even so, God's Vision-Reality
Does not need your great
   contribution.

5764.

Mine is a little cry.
God's is a big Smile.
Yet they live in perfect harmony.

5765.

Sometimes,
When there is no other way
For Him to convince me
Of His Love for me,
God gently strikes me.

5766.

I cry
With my mind's poverty.
I smile
With my heart's plenty.
I dance
With my soul's Infinity.

5767.

My Lord,
May I be reborn every day
With a gratitude-heart,
A surrender-life
And a perfection-soul.

5768.

God does not want to punish us
By blessing the heads
Of our countless desires.

5769.

My mind is fond
Of the visible God.
My heart is fond
Of the invisible God.
My soul is fond
Of the inevitable God.

5770.

Fear and faith—
They do not know each other.
Doubt and love—
They do not know each other.
Aspiration and failure—
They do not know each other.

5771.

Read and read
And see how many things you
    need.
Pray and pray
And see what God has to say
About your needs.

5772.

A visible ally:
God's Compassion-Ocean for me.
An invisible ally:
God's Faith-Sky in me.

5773.

I must know that
God is under no obligation
To listen to my emergency prayers
Since I do not pray daily,
Faithfully, soulfully and
    unreservedly.

5774.

If you have faith in the world,
You will be able to lead the world.
If you doubt the world,
You will be forced to follow the
    world.

5775.

Be careful
When you tell the wrong person
About the right Person: God.

5776.

Singing a soulful song soulfully
Is exactly the same
As enjoying a ride on an express
    train:
Panoramic views on either side.

5777.

God's Transcendental Height
Is not only for special seekers
But also for ordinary human
    beings
Like me.

5778.

Since God is always more than
   ready
To deal with my problems,
Why do I not let Him,
At least for today?
Who knows,
God may fulfil His Promise
And make me really happy.

5779.

God the Question and God the
   Answer
Do not live separately.
They live together
Inside my small, secret
And sacred heart-room.

5780.

Before I meditate,
God places His
   Compassion-Drink before me
And asks me to help myself.
After I have meditated,
God places His Satisfaction-Feast
   before me
And asks me to help myself.

5781.

You have enough real sufferings.
Why are you adding imaginary
   ones
To them, you fool?

5782.

God tells me
That I can touch His Feet
Only if I can dream of seeing the
   truth
Deep inside my heart.

5783.

Human curiosity
Curiously asks.
Divine authority
Authoritatively answers.

5784.

If you have the heart
To help me,
And if you have the soul
To illumine me,
Then you can criticise me,
You can even punish me,
To your heart's content.

5785.

Because your mind
Does not aspire,
You are forced to become
A sleepy onlooker.
Because your heart
Aspires and surrenders,
You have cheerfully become
An expectant uplooker.

5786.

Even jealousy and insecurity
Are curable,
But not ingratitude.

5787.

During his meditation
His stupid mind thinks of
His body's position,
But his wise soul is concerned about
His heart's condition.

5788.

The valid passport
To enter into the inner world
Is not what your mind has
But what your heart is.

5789.

God does not want to delay
His Vision-Plans for you,
But if you desert His
　　Compassion-Heart,
Then naturally He has to delay.

5790.

To succeed triumphantly
Is the miracle of a moment.
To proceed unconditionally
Is the task of a lifetime.

5791.

Soulfully give to God
What you have:
Faithfulness.
Gladly God will give to you
What He is:
Fruitfulness.

5792.

Your mind is full of questions,
But do not worry.
Your heart is full of faith,
Which will answer
All your mind's questions
Most satisfactorily.

5793.

Believe in God soulfully
For a minute,
And you can receive
For a full year
What God offers you
Cheerfully.

5794.

What has happened to me?
I have become a sincere seeker.
What has happened through me?
A satisfying experience for God.

5795.

You may not be proud
Of your achievements,
But your achievements
Are extremely proud of you.
If you do not believe it,
Then give them a chance
To prove it to you.

5796.

Before you allow others
To speak to you,
Give them lovingly
What you have for them:
Your heart's oneness-smile.

5797.

No harm if you misquote
What you have read
In your mind-book
About God.
But if you misquote
What you have read
In your heart-book,
You will be in very serious trouble.

5798.

O my mind,
Stop your mad and helpless rush.
O my heart,
Start your sacred and soulful
   journey.

5799.

Every leaf is a miracle.
That is what my aspiring heart
   feels.
But even if God Himself
Stands right before me,
My doubting mind
Will not consider it a miracle.

5800.

O my gratitude-flames,
Every day you are newly reborn
Inside my heart.
I see it and I know it.
It may not be known to anybody else,
But as long as God, the all-loving
And all-judging Witness, knows it,
You and my heart can remain
In perfect satisfaction-delight.

5801.

Unless I hear
God's beating Heart
Inside my heart of aspiration,
How can I ever see
God's loving and guiding Hands?

5802.

He sees that he was totally wrong.
His Master's compassion-eye
Does love him,
Plus need him.

5803.

If humanity really understood
The importance of a gratitude-heart,
Then humanity would walk much faster,
And much more safely,
Towards its destined goal.

5804.

Whose stupid mind has told you
That your Master, although near you,
Is far away?
Whose insecure heart has told you
That your Master, although he loves everyone,
Does not love you?

5805.

His earnest and determined resolve
Has blotted out
All his previous deplorable mistakes.

5806.

You may withdraw
To your secret cell,
But do not dare to expect
Any happiness whatsoever.

5807.

You have become a problem for
  yourself
Because you do not care to know
The beauty and duty
Of God's Vision-Self in you.

5808.

Unless we consciously and
  lovingly
Feed our hopes daily,
All our promises to Heaven and
  earth
Will remain unfulfilled.

5809.

I declare resolutely
That we gain everything
By accepting God's Vision-Reality
  in us
And lose nothing
By avoiding temptation-nets.

5810.

I never need
The cry of ignorance-sleep,
But I do need
The smile of silver dreams.

5811.

How to use the spiritual energy
You get from meditation?
Do not use it all immediately.
It is like your hard-earned
Earthly wealth.
If you treasure it and keep it safe,
You will be able to bring it
  forward
At God's choice Hour,
To please God in His own Way.

5812.

How many books have been
  written
About the spiritual Masters!
But the most important events in
  their lives
Are not to be found
In these accounts.
For them, the only true biography
Is the inner biography,
Where every hour of every day
Would fill countless pages.

5813.

The West gets satisfaction
From large-scale things.
The nature of Japan
Is diametrically opposite.
It likes to create things
Tinier than the tiniest
And capture the Infinite Supreme
Inside finite man-made forms.
Therein lies Japan's
Message of perfection.

5814.

In America
Things are quite often massive.
In Japan
Things are quite often
    diminutive.
Both embody equally
The Satisfaction of the Supreme.

5815.

The river may be crossed
Either in a vast steamship
Or in a tiny boat.
If we take many individual boats,
We may reach the shore sooner
Than if we wait for all the
    passengers
To fill a huge steamship.
With this approach
Japan has touched her goal.

5816.

Outside: water,
Soothing and soft.
Inside: only
Determination-fire.
Such is
The Japanese nature.

5817.

The Japanese nature
Is a very good combination.
The outer nature
Is like a lion resting.
The inner nature
Is like a lion roaring.
Both are extremely powerful.

5818.

God's choice Hour
Will wait for no one,
Not even for a fraction of a second.
No seeker may claim or preserve
God's choice Hour
At his sweet will.
The seeker must ensure
That he is available
Whenever God's Hour strikes,
At any time of day or night.

5819.

In your outer life
If you can feel
Consciously and soulfully happy
Even while doing
Ordinary, mundane things,
God will consider this
Your real meditation.

5820.

Wherever you are,
Whatever you are doing,
Try to be really happy!
Your psychic happiness
Will help you maintain
A pure and soulful consciousness.

5821.

If you are enjoying yourself
In the excitement-world,
God will not consider it
As part of your meditation.
Soulful happiness,
Integral happiness,
Lies elsewhere.

5822.

The spiritual Master has come
For no other reason
Than to give
His spiritual children joy,
And they in turn have come
To give their Master joy.
It is meditation that serves
As the golden bridge between
   them.

5823.

Obedience is not humiliation.
Obedience is not submissiveness.
Obedience is one's amazingly
   profitable union
With one's own higher self.

5824.

Unless my heart is grateful,
How can my mind be faithful?
Unless my mind is faithful,
How can my life be fruitful?

5825.

You value neither your
   aspiration-heart
Nor your dedication-life.
Perhaps you do not know that
Whether you value them or not,
Whether others value them or not,
Your Beloved Supreme will always
   value
His precious gifts to you
And hope that you will use them
Carefully, devotedly, soulfully
And sleeplessly.

5826.

You cannot expect abiding joy,
You cannot expect any kind of joy,
Unless you have unmistakably
   and soulfully
Accepted the fact that your
   spiritual life
Not only has the joy that you need
But also is joy,
Far, far beyond the need
Of your entire life here on earth.

5827.

Time the destroyer
Cannot touch him
Because he is already devotedly
   seated
At the Protection-Feet
Of his Beloved Supreme.

5828.

My Supreme Lord,
I shall not accept any defeat,
Not because my ego-life
Cannot accept defeat,
But because Your transcendental
   Will
Does not want me ever to accept
   defeat on earth.
It is Your Will that You are
   executing
In and through me,
Your dauntless instrument.

5829.

Many have come
Into the Supreme's Golden Boat;
Many have left.
Many have appeared
And many have disappeared.
Many are outwardly following the
   spiritual life,
But inwardly they are elsewhere,
Millions of miles away.
Again, some seekers are inwardly
   with God,
But outwardly they want to lead
   another life –
A life of lethargy, indulgence,
   disobedience,
Unconscious if not conscious
   self-deception,
Plus self-mockery.

5830.

The spiritual life is arduous.
But the sincere seekers,
Who will ultimately hold
The banners of divine Light
And supreme Delight,
Will forever and forever remain
    faithful
To their inner Captain.

5831.

For the faithful ones
There is no defeat,
There can be no defeat.
For the unfaithful ones
There is no victory,
There can be no victory.

5832.

My Beloved Supreme,
You want me to watch
The unfaithful seekers.
I am watching them.
You want me to wait for them.
I am waiting for them.
Again, it is You who have told me
That there shall come a time
When You will ask me to put an
    end
To my watching and waiting
    games.
Then You will give me a new game
    to play:
The game of justice-light.

5833.

When a spiritual Master
Plays the game of justice-light
At God's express Command,
Very few seekers—
They can be counted on one's
    fingertips—
Will remain in the Boat of the
    Supreme.

5834.

No other weakness
Is as damaging and destructive
As deliberate disobedience.
Those who indulge
In deliberate disobedience
Already have one foot in their
    spiritual grave,
And the other foot
Is fast approaching.

5835.

I shall soulfully do my duty:
I shall illumine my heart.
God will cheerfully do His Duty:
He will perfect my life.

5836.

Each uncomely and undivine
   thought
Wanders restlessly inside my
   mind's
Tiny, unlit cave.
Each pure and flower-like thought
Grows and glows inside my
   heart's
Mightiest kingdom.

5837.

The animal in me thinks
That it does not need
Anything from God.
The human in me thinks
That it needs
Only a few things from God.
The divine in me feels and knows
That it needs
Everything and everything from
   God,
Only from God.

5838.

The new year has commenced
Its momentous journey today.
From today on, during the entire
   year,
I shall not offer my
   volcano-ambition
To the world.
I shall offer the world
Only my moonlit heart's flaming
   aspiration.

5839.

My Lord Supreme,
May the birth of the new year
Herald Your supreme Victory
In and through Your obedient,
   self-giving
And satisfaction-loving children.

5840.

Each new year
The seeker comes to learn
How far away the mind is
From God's Compassion
And how close the heart is
To God's Satisfaction.

5841.

My mind may not know
What others can or will
Do for me.
But my heart knows
What I should and must
Do for others.

5842.

No rhyme, no reason —
O anxiety-cruelty,
You torture me,
My simple mind
And even my pure heart.

5843.

Argument and enlightenment
Purposely and eternally remain
Strangers to each other.

5844.

Two totally dissatisfied friends:
Blindness and uselessness.
Two fully satisfied friends:
Openness and fulness.

5845.

To unburden
The burden of knowledge
Can never be
A simple and easy task.

5846.

Bitterness yields to sweetness
Only when oneness
Is discovered and manifested.

5847.

Nothing can collapse in life
If the faith-foundation
Remains unshakably firm.

5848.

Self-deception
Is the beginning of danger
In the mind
And the beginning of destruction
In the heart.

5849.

A complaint
Quite often
Unconsciously arouses
A sleeping frustration-doom.

5850.

The corruption of the vital
Puzzles the mind.
The corruption of the mind
Starves the heart.

5851.

Desire-life
Withers our flower-heart,
Weakens our searching mind
And imprisons our earth-life.

5852.

When my consciousness descends,
I starve the divine in me,
Resume my old friendship
With the human in me
And am once more tempted
To dance with the animal in me.

5853.

In the ordinary life
Emptiness is nothing short of
   barrenness.
In the spiritual life
Emptiness marks the glorious
   beginning
Of an unprecedented fulness.

5854.

You will not and cannot
Suffer from the blows
Of insufficiency
If you learn how to smile
Soulfully and unreservedly.

5855.

Misfortune dogs your steps
Because you enjoy
The bewildering images
Of life's illusions.

5856.

My surrender-life
Is a secret plan
Of God the Compassion.
My gratitude-heart
Is a sacred place
Of God the Perfection.

5857.

If you really want to be happy,
Then discard once and for all
Your connection with
Your impure vital
And
Your obscure mind.

5858.

The moment his vision-eye
Reached Heaven,
He saw God's Bliss-bestowing
    Hands
All ready.

5859.

I hate my mind
Because it knows
Only how to preach.
I love my heart
Because it knows
Only how to persuade.

5860.

O lovers of the past,
Leave aside
Your ancient mistakes!
Live in the happiness-heart
Of the Eternal Now!

5861.

Only the chosen few
Can escape life's false realities
And live in Eternity's
Golden Day.

5862.

You may use
Your suspicious mind
Before you love the outer world,
But you must use
Your believing heart
Before you love the inner world.

5863.

Today you are afraid
To do the right thing.
Tomorrow God will think
A million times
Before He will grant you
Another chance to do the right
    thing.

5864.

If you want to be happy
In your own way,
God will not mind.
He will just tell you:
"My child,
I shall not criticise you.
But I can't assure you
That I shall be at all happy
In My own Way."

5865.

Today you are facing
A big decision:
Whether you will continue
   surrendering
To the ignorance-night around
   you
Or whether you will start
   surrendering
Right from today
To the wisdom-light within you.

5866.

What do I see
Inside the creation?
Perfect restlessness.
What do I see
Inside that restlessness?
A perfect whisper
From perfect stillness.

5867.

Only Eternity can reveal
What man has.
Only Immortality can manifest
What man is.

5868.

If I see purity
Inside your heart,
How can I misunderstand
The sincerity inside your mind?

5869.

I may not learn anything
From what you are saying,
But I shall definitely learn
Something truly important
By observing what you do.

5870.

You can have perfect peace
Only when you can halt
Your mind's journey
At God's Forgiveness-Feet.

5871.

The entire world
Is expert at playing
The self-satisfaction-game.
But it pretends
That playing this game
Is beneath its dignity.

5872.

"God is all Love."
"I am all for Him."
These are the thoughts
A seeker can cherish.
All other thoughts
He should consider as
Sheer distractions.

5873.

Beauty does not have to explain
Its existence in the outer world.
Purity does not have to explain
Its existence in the inner world.
Divinity does not have to explain
Its existence in God's universe.

5874.

Those who are ready to struggle
While aspiring
Are bound to find
Permanent happiness.

5875.

I may be wrong
When I say he is fooling himself,
But I am absolutely correct
When I feel I am fooling myself.

5876.

Inside the cave of the mind
Man's greatness talks to the world.
Inside the palace of the heart
Man's goodness talks to God.

5877.

The mind does not see darkness
Even when darkness has engulfed
Its entire existence.
The heart feels delight
Even when delight
Is in the heart of someone else.

5878.

My Lord Supreme says to me:
"My child,
I love you, good or bad.
Just do not consciously enjoy
Any more
Your ignorance-sleep."

5879.

You are seeing the sunrise
Inside your aspiration-heart.
Who knows,
In a few days
God may appear before you —
Perhaps today!

5880.

Self-glory
I choose for myself.
Self-discovery
God chooses for me.

5881.

Do you want
To change the world?
If so, then come to me
For some special advice.
Are you trying
To change yourself?
If so, then I am immediately
Coming to you
For some special advice.

5882.

An unawakened mind thinks
That it can do everything.
An awakened heart feels and knows
That only God does everything
In and through it.

5883.

What a strange experience!
You are afraid of the light
That is trying to illumine you,
But you are not afraid of the darkness
That is devouring you.

5884.

Only a false spiritual Teacher
Thinks and feels
That he alone is perfect,
And that the rest
Of the spiritual Teachers
Are all false.

5885.

You lack the courage to say
What you want to say,
Yet you have the audacity
To criticise others,
Even when they say
Absolutely the right thing.

5886.

Imagination has power.
Imagination is power.
Therefore, be sure to have
A good and elevating imagination.

5887.

When I want to change
My outer life,
God uses His Vision-Eye
To smile at me.
When I want to change
My inner life,
God uses His Reality-Heart
To embrace me.

5888.

In a fraction of a second
He saw into my heart
And told me that I shall become
A perfect Truth-seeker
And
A perfect God-lover.

5889.

My present life
Of hopeful promise
Is a song of Eternity.

5890.

To my heart's extreme joy,
My searching mind no longer
Accepts the false as true.

5891.

In public he openly says
That he knows nothing.
In his heart he secretly insists
That he knows everything.

5892.

To rise above ourselves
Means to go far above
Our stupidity-head
And sit at the Compassion-Feet
Of our Beloved Supreme.

5893.

Do not keep inside you
The confusion-mind
If you want to achieve
An illumination-heart.

5894.

An impure mind thinks
That there can be
No pure heart.
A pure heart feels
That everything is pure,
Including the mind.

5895.

You cannot even give
A single soulful smile.
Yet you tell the whole world
Not only what to do
But also how to do it.

5896.

Be not afraid of your emptiness.
Your emptiness is preparing itself
To receive God's Fulness
From God Himself.

5897.

You think you have escaped
From ignorance-slavery.
Can you not ask God
If you are correct?

5898.

Each undivine, unaspiring
And ugly thought of yours
Pinches others for a minute
And then comes back to you
To box your nose for an hour.

5899.

My mind's simplicity
Helps me pray sincerely.
My heart's sincerity
Helps me meditate soulfully.

5900.

My Beloved Supreme lovingly
And compassionately whispers,
"My child, are you Mine,
Are you only Mine,
Or are you for ignorance-night as well?"
The human in me tells my Lord Supreme,
"O Lord, give me some time
To think it over and decide."
The divine in me immediately responds,
"My Beloved Supreme, I am for You,
Only for You.
Throughout Your own Eternity
I shall be for You, for You alone.
Do mould me, shape me and guide me
To fulfil Yourself in and through me
In Your own Way."

5901.

I may not know
What God is doing for me now,
But I do know
That I am desperately trying to please God
In God's own Way.

5902.

I may not know where God is now,
But I do know where I am.
I am now in His Forgiveness-Boat
Sailing towards His
   Satisfaction-Shore.

5903.

I may not love God
   unconditionally,
But I do know what God's
   Compassion
Is doing for my heart sleeplessly
And what God's Forgiveness
Is doing for my life
   unconditionally.

5904.

Only three swimmers are allowed
To swim in the sea of Peace:
A God-lover,
A self-giver
And
An ignorance-destroyer.

5905.

I see no difference
Between your thoughtless
Temptation-flames
And your soulless
Destruction-pyre.

5906.

Because of your suspicion-mind,
Your poor heart-plant is withering
Before it can burst into flower.

5907.

O Truth-seeker, O God-lover,
You do not have to say
Anything about yourself.
Your whole biography is already
   written
In golden letters
On the Tablet of God's own Heart.

5908.

I may have a dry mind,
But I also have a pure heart.
I may have a restless vital,
But I also have a fruitful soul.

5909.

Earth, O earth,
When are you going to stop
Hoisting the banner
Of ridiculous helplessness?
Heaven, O Heaven,
When are you going to stop
Hoisting the banner
Of cruel indifference?

5910.

Do you know
What has conquered for you
Your vital's volcano-pride?
Your aspiration's mountain-cry.

5911.

The dark forest
Of man's desire-life
Can never bathe
In Heaven's golden sunshine.

5912.

Your mind is cherishing regrets.
Your heart is fearing misfortunes.
Such being the case,
What can you expect from your life?

5913.

His dreamless heart
Is now invaded
By impurity's ignorance-sleep.

5914.

A purity-heart
Not only has the necessity
But also is the capacity
To enlarge itself for God's use.

5915.

On earth nothing is more beautiful
Than God's Patience-Light.
In Heaven nothing is more beautiful
Than God's Compassion-Light.
In me nothing is more beautiful
Than God's Forgiveness-Light.

5916.

God can play and will play
His
    Perfection-Manifestation-Game
Only with those choice children of
    His
Who are always apt to deny
    themselves.

5917.

An unoffered life
Will always be doomed
To an unanswered prayer.

5918.

Something divine may be
Beyond your need today,
But it can never remain
Beyond your need forever.
For every day
A new message from Heaven
Is touching the earth-shore.

5919.

Only God's Compassion
Is deeply interested in
And truly concerned with
The perpetual cry of man's heart.

5920.

The doubter thinks
That he alone thinks of himself
Since God has no time to think of
　him.
The believer knows
That God always thinks of him
Even when he thinks of himself.

5921.

Sincerity's sweetness and
Humility's soulfulness
Are of paramount importance
In a seeker's heavenward journey.

5922.

What your mind has
Is a pygmy aim.
What your heart is
Is a brittle hope.
How, then, can you expect God
To smile at you,
Sing for you
And
Dance with you?

5923.

Because you are a born dreamer,
You have a special place
In God's Heart-Garden.

5924.

His sense of perfection thunders
When he enters into
The vital world.
His sense of satisfaction whispers
When he enters into
The psychic world.

5925.

I see no difference
Between your mind's
Frustration-poverty
And your life's
Destruction-reality.

5926.

O man of silence,
My heart needs you desperately.
My heart painfully tells me
That even the best talker
Is the worst possible intruder.

5927.

Present regrets
Are killing his searching mind.
Future fears
Are killing his aspiring heart.
Alas, how can he proceed
In his inner life of aspiration
And how can he succeed
In his outer life of dedication?

5928.

If you can feed
The unconquerable hope-seed,
Then your success-height
And progress-delight
Will not remain a far cry.

5929.

When I look at my mind,
I hear a painful cry.
When I touch my heart,
I hear a breathless sigh.

5930.

Perfection-poise
Is my Lord's Beauty
Inside my heart.
Satisfaction-choice
Is my Lord's Duty
Inside my life.

5931.

Man's ancient roots:
His cries and smiles.
Man's modern fruits:
His laughter and sighs.

5932.

If you are ready
To live outside the reason-fort,
Then God will grant you
His own
    Perfection-Satisfaction-Home.

5933.

His attacks
On self-styled earth-bound
    authorities
Are more than justifiable.
Your attacks
On God-ordained authorities
Are absolutely unpardonable.

5934.

It is your heart's orphan-cries
That will help you reach
The heights of God's Beauty
    Supreme.

5935.

Your oneness-life
Is your forgotten Eternity.
Your fulness-heart
Is your forgotten Infinity.
Your vision-eye
Is your forgotten Immortality.

5936.

At long last
My heart's aspiration-cry
And my mind's inspiration-smile
Are working together
To manifest the Immortal in me.

5937.

Your silence does not have to
Convert anybody.
Your silence will help man
Invent something
Most precious in his own life.

5938.

When dark doubts want to assail
   you,
If your resistance is persistent,
You will without fail
Be able to climb up
The heights of Himalayan
   Satisfaction.

5939.

If you value time,
Then you must try to save time.
If you can save time,
Then you are definitely
Bringing to the fore constantly
The newness-reality of a
   fulness-dream.

5940.

His life is all happiness
Because during the day
He walks along his
   surrender-bridge
And at night
He walks along his
   gratitude-bridge.

5941.

Self-mastery means
The joy of the heart's
Blossoming rose-petals.

5942.

Duty is the purity
Of man's crying heart.
Beauty is the duty
Of man's smiling life.

5943.

Only the
    illumination-combination
Of a perfection-mind
And a satisfaction-heart
Can and will rouse
The sleeping world.

5944.

No greater loss
Than to be ignored by God.
No greater gain
Than to be needed by God.

5945.

Ignorance has disowned him.
Therefore, his life is perfection.
God now owns him.
Therefore, his heart is satisfaction
    within
And satisfaction without.

5946.

To me
The outer life of a seeker
Is not precious
Unless his inner life
Is gracious.

5947.

Man's body usually has two lords:
Lethargy-lord
And
Frustration-lord.

5948.

Do not decline God's
    Hospitality-Invitation.
Who knows,
He may invite others tomorrow.
Who knows,
He may not invite you any more.

5949.

God tells me
That He will teach me
How to sail my own life-boat
Only on two conditions:
My mind must not worry
And
My vital must not hurry.

5950.

My Lord Supreme,
What will You do for me
If I give You my heart's
    blossoming faith?
"My child,
I shall take away
Your mind's brooding doubts."

5951.

The outer beauty
Is an expensive frustration-sigh.
The inner beauty
Is an expansive satisfaction-sky.

5952.

As it is not too late for you to
    realise
That your mind is doing the
    wrong thing
By roaming inside a thick
    thought-forest,
Even so, it is not too late
For God to grant you
His Infinity's ever-transcending
    Delight.

5953.

You are not allowing
Your soul to sing for you
Its silence-songs of the Beyond.
Therefore, your life is compelled
To dance the dance of utter
    futility.

5954.

A man of prayer
Becomes the vision-light of a seer
Even without asking.

5955.

The dearest wish of my new-born
    life
Is to go and sit at the Feet
Of my hopeful Lord Supreme.

5956.

He is completely lost
In between his mind's
Indifference-sea
And his heart's
Forgetfulness-sky.

5957.

You know that you enjoy
    immensely
Deafness-game.
Why then do you find fault with
    God
When He plays His own
Blindness-Game?

5958.

You want your guilty mind to
    hide,
But God wants to bring
Your guilty mind to light
So that some day He can enjoy
Its transformation-perfection-
    height.

5959.

Now that you have surrendered,
Nothing that belongs to you is
   guilty.
No, not even your
   suspicion-enjoying mind.

5960.

My heart has three comrades:
A hopeful prayer,
A soulful meditation
And
A fruitful surrender.

5961.

His is a contradiction-life:
His mind is a restless fly,
But his heart is a quenchless
   God-thirst.

5962.

I poison my own life-breath
When I callously criticise
My Lord's endless
   Compassion-Length.

5963.

This morning I offered a fervent
   prayer
To my Lord Supreme.
I prayed to Him to touch my mind
With His smiling and dancing
   Sincerity-Heart.

5964.

Yesterday he lived
With his life's blazing errors.
Today he is living
With his mind's terrifying terrors.
Tomorrow he will live
With his heart's streaming tears.

5965.

If your mind clings to truth,
Your soul and heart
Will share with your mind
Their sea of perpetual delight.

5966.

Who says that self-giving
Is an expensive pleasure
And not an expansive treasure?

5967.

The Beauty of God's Face
Entirely depends on the purity
Of my heart's rays.

5968.

My life's stormy night
Needs nothing other than
An endless streak of patience-light
To see the smile-worlds
Of the Transcendence-Beyond.

5969.

My union with God
Made my pure heart
Extremely happy.
My reunion with God
Is making my sure heart
Extremely happy.

5970.

What the searching mind needs
Is a silver trance.
What the aspiring heart needs
Is a golden dance.

5971.

His heart feels
That his life is nothing but
A blessingful preparation
For God's arrival.

5972.

He is enjoying a feast
With his heart's ascending sun
And his Lord's descending Grace.

5973.

Today's aspiration-man
And
Tomorrow's Manifestation-God
Are inseparable
And immortal friends.

5974.

Now that his pride is imprisoned,
He has every hope of becoming
A soulful seeker
Of the Absolute Lord Supreme.

5975.

There is only one message of
   Time:
First become the heart of Light
And then see the face of Truth.

5976.

When I think of God,
I think of many things
At the same time.
When God thinks of me,
He thinks only of my heart's
Perfection-cry.

5977.

How can my weak mind please
   God?
Impossible!
How can my pure heart displease
   God?
Impossible!

5978.

God is at once
My heart's unchanging cry
And my life's changing smile.

5979.

He who cries for perfection
At God's outer Door
Will receive illumination
At God's inner Door.

5980.

My Lord Supreme,
Why do You love me
Since You know perfectly well
That I shall never be perfect?
"My child, I love you
Since I know perfectly well
That for Me nothing is more
      worthwhile
Than loving you."

5981.

Indeed, I know many things,
But one thing I do not know.
I do not know how to replace
My life of failure-sighs.

5982.

Inside a self-giving purity-heart
I see always
A thousand smiles shining
      brightly.

5983.

Why does God
Still need me?
Why do I
Still love God?

5984.

He is totally lost
In between his mind's
Lawless confusion-night
And his heart's
Flawless aspiration-light.

5985.

What I need today
Is a liberated life.
What I shall need tomorrow
Is my Lord's manifested Glory.

5986.

Yesterday I was my mind's
Utter stupidity.
Today I am my heart's
Endless insecurity.
Tomorrow I shall be my soul's
Deathless aspiration.

5987.

Mine is the life
That has the slow and steady
　speed
Of an earthly tortoise.
Mine is the heart
That has the amazing and
　lightning speed
Of a Heavenly deer.

5988.

My justice-light
Is my theoretical God-life.
My compassion-light
Is my practical God-life.

5989.

I do not know
How to separate my mind
From confusion-night.
I do not know
How to unite my heart
With perfection-day.

5990.

Each individual soul
Is a harbinger
Of God's reality-manifesting
Vision-Eye.

5991.

Alas, my mind does not have
A nourishing sky.
Alas, my heart does not have
A liberating sun.

5992.

Belief tells us
That we have a soul-bird
Inside us.
Faith tells us
That the soul-bird flies and flies
In the illumination-firmament.
Promise tells us
That we are of God's Divinity
And for God's Immortality.

5993.

An unbinding love
And
An unattached service
Are Eternity's two complementary
   friends.

5994.

Your mind lives
For earth's admiration.
Your heart lives
For God's Love.
Your soul lives
For God's Satisfaction.

5995.

Since you are the impotence
Of your mind's brutal rage,
How can you see the sky
Of God's beautiful and beaming
Satisfaction-Face?

5996.

You are miserable.
Do you know why?
Because your mind refuses
To be with God
And your heart refuses
To be with man.

5997.

Neither you nor God is successful.
You are trying to succeed
In fascinating humanity.
God is trying to succeed
In liberating you from your
   stupidity.

5998.

Because you do not love
The warm heart of the Heavenly
   sun,
You are forced to suffer
From the cold touch of earthly
   years.

5999.

The callousness of the heart
Is completely blind.
The indifference of the mind
Is unthinkably cruel.

6000.

God came to me
Long before I knew
Who He was.
I am going to God
Knowing unmistakably
That He has given me the capacity
To become another God.

6001.

The Road that my Lord Himself
Walked once upon a time
Is now right before me.
Who else is so divinely fortunate?
Who else has this chance
To be supremely perfect?

6002.

I most sincerely deplore
Only one thing:
My eternal Now
Still remains unexplored.

6003.

Many, many times in his life
Silence has proved
Not only to be
The only answer
But also to be
Absolutely the best answer.

6004.

For the betterment of this world,
I am able to offer only three
    things:
My soul's promise,
My heart's hope
And
My life's service.

6005.

Promise!
Eventually you will succeed.
Pray!
Continuously you will proceed.

6006.

Remind me, my Lord,
From time to time,
That You have taught me
How to love the world
    unconditionally.

6007.

Once I was blinded by ignorance,
But now I can see
That I desperately need God,
Especially His Love,
Only His Love.

6008.

Because your mind is slow
To forgive your past,
God is also slow
To grant your mind
The overwhelming delight
Of the future.

6009.

Alas, I believe in everything
Except one thing:
My life's unlimited potential.

6010.

Helplessness is now
Enveloping my life
Because I have allowed hopelessness
To envelop my heart.

6011.

Unfettered freedom-joy
Abides only in
Unconditional love.

6012.

God tells me,
"Take from Me whatever you want.
You do not have to bother the world
For anything."

6013.

You will never see
The Face of God
In this lifetime
At the rate you have been
Oversleeping
In ignorance-night.

6014.

His mind schemes,
His life screams,
His heart dreams,
And he sinks and sinks.

6015.

Imagination tells him
What he can do.
Patience does it for him.

6016.

If you entertain your doubt-life,
How can your faith-life
Enlighten your heart?

6017.

You may magnify
Your troubles,
But nobody is going to minimise
Your stupidity.

6018.

True,
I do not know
Who I am,
But I do know
Whose I am.

6019.

Two secrets, but open ones:
God loves me infinitely more
Than He needs me.
I need God infinitely more
Than I love Him.

6020.

A self-centred man
Thinks and dreams of a happy life.
A God-centred man
Lives and radiates a happy life.

6021.

God made my life
To grow lovingly and slowly.
God made my heart
To glow brightly and steadily.

6022.

You are doomed
To barrenness
Because your mind does not
Want newness
And your heart does not
Need oneness.

6023.

Only a perfected individual
Can dare to dream
Of a perfect humanity.

6024.

My Lord,
I have a sincere need.
"My son,
I have an abundant supply."

6025.

What I call
My self-cultivation,
God calls that very thing
His own Self-Revelation.

6026.

May my life-boat ply between
My self-mastery
And
My God-discovery.

6027.

Slow me down, my Lord;
I am restless.
Show me quickly, my Lord;
I am doubtless.

6028.

When I open my eyes,
I see that I am
My fearful incapacity.
When I open my heart,
I see that I am
My Lord's powerful Capacity.

6029.

If aspiration does not begin
With the individual,
Then it does not begin.
The same is true for realisation,
And also for manifestation.

6030.

An immature man
Dealing with mature problems:
This is precisely what human life is.

6031.

"I do not need God."
This tragedy in human life
Is incomparable.

6032.

The ultimate in human goals
Is to reach the Himalayan heights.
The ultimate in divine goals
Is to become God's choicest instrument.

6033.

What is God's Compassion-Light
If not my own confidence-height
In the world of becoming and
   transcending
And transcending and becoming?

6034.

The Peace, Light and Bliss of
   Heaven
Surround my heart openly.
The fear, doubt and frustration of
   earth
Surround my mind secretly.

6035.

The mind has to forgive the past
Before the heart
Can completely obliterate it.

6036.

My Beloved Lord
Has counteracted my stupidity
And converted my impurity
Into purity.

6037.

Between me and my past blunders
God the Compassion cries
And
God the Forgiveness smiles.

6038.

Yesterday I sang the song
Of renunciation.
Today I am singing the song
Of co-operation.
Tomorrow I shall sing the song
Of perfection.
And the day after I shall sing the
   song
Of God's complete Satisfaction.

6039.

When I soulfully and sleeplessly
Love God,
Everything loves me,
Even my ruthless past.

6040.

You can achieve everything in life
If you can dare to believe
That your soul is having a
   continual adventure
In the heart of God's
Evolving and transcending
   universe.

6041.

I have a heart of love.
Therefore,
I needs must be
A loving man.

6042.

A procrastination-mind is
　responsible
For a frustration-heart.
A frustration-heart is responsible
For a destruction-life.

6043.

The bitterness of failure
And the sweetness of success
Shall find me unswerving
As I climb towards
My summit-goal.

6044.

As my mind has the capacity
To determine my life,
Even so, my heart has the capacity
To determine my mind.

6045.

He is so sad that his mind
Is running away from God.
He is so sad that his life
Is running away from his heart.

6046.

My Lord Supreme,
You gave Realisation to Sri
　Krishna.
Do give it again – this time to me.
My Lord Supreme,
You gave Liberation to the
　Buddha.
Do give it again – this time to me.
My Lord Supreme,
You gave Salvation to the Christ.
Do give it again – this time to me.

6047.

I belong not to the God-preacher
Who says that he has.
I belong to the God-lover
Who knows that he is.

6048.

My life belongs
To humanity's hope.
My heart belongs
To divinity's promise.

6049.

Doubt and impurity are the sunset
Of a seeker's life.
Faith and purity are the sunrise
Of a seeker's heart.

6050.

How can the life
Be empty,
If the heart
Is receptive?

6051.

A wise man knows
What to tell,
How to tell
And
When to tell.
A clever man foolishly tells
More than he knows
Or less than what
He is supposed to tell.

6052.

Because my heart was too slow
In loving God the creation,
God the Creator has withdrawn
His Beauty's Hope and Purity's
    Promise
From my heart.

6053.

If your life is chained
To earthly possessions,
How can you expect your heart
To be a Heavenly satisfaction?

6054.

If you can stab the heart
Of your ignorance-pride,
Then your life will not meet
With any failure.

6055.

Science tells me
What it can do for my life.
Spirituality tells me
What I can do for God's Heart.

6056.

If I am available,
Then the Supreme is ready to send
The lovable cosmic gods
To play with me.

6057.

A heart of beauty
And a heart of purity
Can soulfully fall in love
With God's ever-transcending
    Divinity.

6058.

The lighthouse of a self-giving life
Is a powerhouse of God's
Perfection-Vision and
   Satisfaction-Reality.

6059.

Awareness is ability.
Ability is advancement,
In secrecy supreme,
In the inner world.

6060.

The pendulum that swings
Between man's tears and man's
   smiles
Is always guided
By the Concern-Hand of the
   Beyond.

6061.

His life may belong to
The race of timid cats,
But his heart definitely belongs to
The race of powerful lions.

6062.

If you are a lavish doubter,
You will be compelled to become
A swimmer in life's confusion-sea.

6063.

Only a born dreamer
Has the rightful confidence
To announce the
   transformation-message
Of human life.

6064.

Your dry mind
Does not dare to cry.
Your timid heart
Does not dare to smile.
And you
Do not dare to become
The song of self-offering.

6065.

Love is at once
Aspiration-plant
And
Perfection-tree.

6066.

My heart would like to know
If God is pleased with it.
God would like to know
If my mind is pleased with Him.

6067.

God blows His Victory-Horn
The moment He sees
A climbing cry
And
A spreading smile.

6068.

If you continuously sing
Your self-aggrandisement-songs,
Then the world will force you
To enter your ready-made
Destruction-pyre.

6069.

The mind enjoys
Fantasy's might.
The heart enjoys
Ecstasy's height.

6070.

The perfect evolution
Of possibilities
Is the essence of excellence.

6071.

Just a small suggestion:
Do not allow your hope-joy
To act like a greedy fellow.

6072.

As long as the stupid mind
Enjoys concealment,
The pure heart cannot acquire
Enlightenment.

6073.

The faith of the mind
Starts its journey with
    uncertainty.
The faith of the heart
Speedily runs towards
Its destined goal.

6074.

As I cannot imagine
God's Fondness for me,
Even so, my fondness for God
The world cannot imagine.

6075.

Yesterday
I thought it was better
To have than to be.
Today
I feel it is better
To be than to have.
Tomorrow
I shall keep the same feeling
As today.

6076.

When I want God,
I shall immediately say "No"
To myself.
When God wants me,
I shall immediately say "Yes"
To Him.

6077.

I am God's personal property.
If you really need me,
Then ask God
And see what He says.

6078.

I have received a very special message:
"God not only lives inside
Your heart-room,
But also sleeplessly cares for you."

6079.

I do not need miracles, please.
I do not even want
To see miracles, please.
I need and expect only
A crying heart and a smiling life.

6080.

God has no time for me
Unless He is
The only Way for me.

6081.

My faith is something
That God has created for me
To use inside humanity's heart
Soulfully and carefully,
But never to use
Carelessly and extravagantly.

6082.

I have to put
God's Compassion-Bud
Inside my heart
If I want to see
God's Satisfaction-Flower
Upon my face.

6083.

My poor soul,
Do not worry.
I shall not fail you.
I shall not even disappoint you!

6084.

My concentration is another name
For my fearlessness.
My fearlessness is another name
For my cheerfulness.
My cheerfulness is another name
For my Lord's Closeness,
Fondness and Oneness.

6085.

My soul belongs
To God's descending Promise.
My body belongs
To God's ascending Hope.

6086.

My Lord says to me:
"My child, I wish to play
The give-and-receive game.
Can you not give Me
Your ever-increasing fears
And ever-multiplying doubts
And receive from Me
My all-conquering Power
And all-illumining Light?"

6087.

My mind's colossal loss
Will lead my life
To an amazing and permanent
    gain.

6088.

My prayers and meditations
Are only my necessity-seeds
That will become my
    ecstasy-plants
In the near future.

6089.

God's Blessing-Waves
And my obedience-drops
Always live together
In stupendous
    satisfaction-delight.

6090.

God is sleeplessly planting
The seeds of forgiveness
Inside my heart,
And I am continuously planting
The seeds of hope
Inside His Heart.

6091.

I shall always try to travel
With a soulful heart
And a prayerful life.

6092.

I am inside
My Lord's Compassion-Book.
My Lord is inside
His own Vision-Look.

6093.

Six words have changed
My entire life:
"God loves me.
God wants me."

6094.

Utterly disappointed,
Time took back from him
Its supreme compassion-gift.

6095.

I will take "no" for an answer
From earth.
I will take "no" for an answer
From Heaven.
I will take not only "no"
But also "never" for an answer
From God, only from God.

6096.

I talk to God
About His Generosity.
God talks to me
About my receptivity.

6097.

If you can keep your eyes
Inside your heart,
Then God will unreservedly grant
　　you
His own Beauty's Heart.

6098.

Am I an out-and-out idiot
That I shall send
God-messengers away
Empty-handed?

6099.

Constant aspiration
Is not a thing one can achieve
On the strength of one's own
　　capacity.
It is an unconditional gift from
　　Above.

6100.

Am I doing all I can?
The human in me is telling me
That I am doing infinitely more
Than I can.
The divine in me is telling me
That I am doing as much
As I can.
The Supreme in me is telling me
That I have done nothing
And I can do nothing,
But that He has done
And will continue to do
Everything in and through me.

6101.

Because your heart needs God,
God is calling you.
Because God is calling you,
You can rest assured
That He will make you feel
He loves you infinitely more
Than you love yourself
And His Concern for you
Will stay with you for all Eternity.

6102.

Earth-bound time
Drives the desiring man backward
Fast, very fast.
Heaven-free time
Pilots the aspiring man forward
Faster than the tornado-speed.

6103.

Perfection-race
Is the old race on earth.
Hope-race
Is the older race on earth.
Promise-race
Is the oldest race on earth.

6104.

The human realisation
Sees no armour against fate.
The divine realisation
Sees that fate is nothing
But a man-made toy.

6105.

Your uncertain mind,
Your doubtful mind,
Your suspicious mind
Is only an inch away
From your total
    destruction-dance.

6106.

God openly shows me
What He does for me:
Compassion-cultivation.
God secretly hopes
For something from me:
Satisfaction-harvest.

6107.

Eternity's Beauty-Cry
And
Infinity's Perfection-Smile
Are Immortality's
    Satisfaction-Treasure.

6108.

If your life needs beauty's speed
And your heart needs purity's
    speed,
Then the Goal of the Beyond
Cannot remain a far cry.

6109.

Oblivion is challenging you
Because you are not crying
    sleeplessly
For God's God-Satisfaction
Inside your aspiration-life.

6110.

Unless you become today
God's Satisfaction-Grace,
How will you see tomorrow
God's Perfection-Face?

6111.

What he has
Is a dangerous vital.
No wonder he is craving
Instant enlightenment.

6112.

You can expect God to be
Your constant supporter
Only after you have become
His sleepless lover.

6113.

When my heart's faith is dry,
My mind's doubt proves
That life is a useless
And ceaseless cry.

6114.

O seeker of the Absolute Truth,
You want your life to be
Fruitful of transcendental deeds.
Then why are you delaying
In smashing the shackles
Of your little "I"?

6115.

Perhaps you do not know,
Perhaps you may never know,
That your suspicious mind
Has the capacity and is the
    potentiality
For your universal disaster.

6116.

I saw myself forsaken.
I knew not why.
God came to me and said
Unless I look for the way out
Of the forest of my desire-life,
I shall forever remain forsaken.

6117.

A seeker's life
Lives in between
The evolution of possibilities
And the perfection of necessities.

6118.

In the morning he is drunk
With aspiration-light.
In the afternoon he is drunk
With surrender-light.
In the evening he is drunk
With gratitude-light.

6119.

At long last
He is determined to send
His mind's curiosity
And his heart's insecurity
Into Eternity's exile.

6120.

The aspiration of a soaring seeker
At once renounces
Man's failure-night
And announces
God's Victory-Delight.

6121.

Because of your unlit sound-life
You are denied
God's sunlit Silence-Sky.

6122.

At the eleventh hour
His soul-bird flew down
And snatched away the inner
    victory
From the grasp of his outer
    failure-life.

6123.

Man's first suspicion-night
Tells him
God does not exist.
Man's last suspicion-night
Tells him
God does not care for him.

6124.

Nobody has to stumble
At the feet of Truth.
Everybody can sit and take shelter
At the feet of Truth.

6125.

Each Heaven-descending message
Accepted soulfully
Marks the beginning
Of my self-discovery.

6126.

If you want to make
Real and safe progress,
Then forcefully silence
Your outer noise-world.

6127.

Earth's aspiration-ascent
Is dutiful and beautiful.
Heaven's illumination-descent
Is powerful and fruitful.

6128.

Surrender, surrender!
During the day
You must surrender
Your fear of God's Power.
Surrender, surrender!
During the night
You must surrender
Your fear of God's Peace.

6129.

My mind is completely lost
Between my fruitless
    self-assertion
And
My hopeless desire-choice.

6130.

If you can regain
Your aspiration-flames,
You will eventually rediscover
Your realisation-sun.

6131.

During the day I pray
To the illumination-increasing
   sun.
During the night I pray
To the compassion-flowing moon.

6132.

The beauty of Heaven
Descends speedily
When the purity of earth
Ascends soulfully.

6133.

As there are only two problems,
Birth and death,
Even so, there are only two
   solutions,
Surrender and smile.

6134.

What the demanding vital
Sees as progress
May easily be a regression
In the heart's aspiration-life.

6135.

Because you have
A heart of vision-delight,
God is granting you
A death-challenging dart.

6136.

Because of your
   self-announcement-song,
God has withdrawn today
His yesterday's unconditional
   Grace.

6137.

Your stupidity's existence-reality
Will never be able to discover
God's Compassion-Sun
Inside your heart.

6138.

My Eternity's
Indispensable necessity
Is my Immortality's
Perfect gratitude.

6139.

If yours is a life of prayer
And a heart of meditation,
Then you will not try to cover
Your outer life
And you will not hesitate to offer
Your inner life
To your Inner Pilot.

6140.

Because you have been convicted
By your conscience-light,
You have every chance to look
For a better day,
A brighter sun
And a more nourishing delight.

6141.

If you do not cancel
Your own ignorance-night,
Then God will be unwilling
To inundate your mind
With His own God-Thoughts.

6142.

Humility is exempt
From fear.
Purity is exempt
From division.
Nobility is exempt
From frustration.

6143.

Constant somnolence
Is the source of humanity's
Teeming incurable maladies.

6144.

O my mind,
You are always enjoying
A useless tornado-motion.
Do you not care for a promotion
From your long-lasting
Nothingness-futility?

6145.

In me, science wants to show
Its amazing capacity.
In me, spirituality wants to show
My own ever-transcending
    capacity.

6146.

He no longer gives himself
To noisy boasting.
Therefore, he is now ready
To partake of the concentrated
Wisdom of the ages.

6147.

He is not the Lord
Who demands obedience-flames.
He is the Friend
Who begs for oneness-sun.

6148.

If you renew your heart's beauty
Every morning,
God will come to you
Every evening
With His multiplying Divinity.

6149.

Each century has
Something special to offer.
The special offering
Of the twentieth century
Is that despair shall not mark
Its journey's close.

6150.

Two realities
Are not born for death:
My surrender-life
And
My gratitude-heart.

6151.

Do not foretell a hopeless battle
Even if you have failed time and
      again
In the battlefield of your
      aspiration-life.
You are bound to eventually
      succeed.
What you always need
Is a mind of patience
And a heart of fortitude.

6152.

My heart is pleased with me,
My soul is pleased with me
And
My Lord Supreme is pleased with
      me
Only when I water
My life's gratitude-plant
With my streaming tears
Born and yet to be born.

6153.

Paradise is the place
Where my heart wants to grow.
Paradise is the place
Where my mind wants to know.
Paradise is the place
Where my soul wants to sow—
Sow the seed of perfection.

6154.

When hope guides my steps,
The vision of Eternity's Reality
Comes running towards me.

6155.

If you can intensify
Your mind's commitment to God,
Then God will not only
Purify your mind
But also beautify your thoughts.

6156.

Science tells me
How I can be proud of myself.
Spirituality tells me
How I can make God proud of me.

6157.

If you cannot make friends
With hope-light and
 promise-delight,
Then you will be forced to live
In the kingdom of perpetual
 night.

6158.

The inner revolution
Longs to see
The Arm of God's Power.
The outer resolution
Longs to see
The Eye of God's Beauty.

6159.

I spoke ill of God.
Nevertheless,
God does not hesitate
To obliterate my hostile past.

6160.

Each time I compromise
With ignorance-night
I kill the beauty and purity
Of my climbing heart-plant.

6161.

My heart's heavenward history
And my soul's intimate friendship
With God's Vision-Light
Can never be fables.

6162.

If you are a staunch votary
Of ignorance-night,
Naturally destruction-sleep
Will linger long
Inside your body-bound
    earth-life.

6163.

Yours is a mind of dangerous
    curiosity.
Destroy it sooner than at once!
Otherwise, the brooding forces
Of darkest night
Will envelop the real in you:
Aspiration.

6164.

There are two sleeping secrets
Inside my heart:
God loves me infinitely more
Than I can possibly love myself.
God needs me infinitely more
Than I can ever need myself.

6165.

While others dream,
He asks his mind
To climb far above the
    doubt-clouds,
And he asks his heart
To dine with the vastness
Of perfection-sun.

6166.

What my heart needs
Is a tiny gratitude-flame,
For this flame alone
Will show my entire life
Perfection's core.

6167.

The cry of insufficiency
Was not born with me.
I was born
Not only with my
    sufficiency-smile
But also with God's
    Infinitude-Smile.

6168.

If you can become
Your heart's surrender-light,
Then you can most soulfully play
On God's Self-Amorous Flute.

6169.

My humility-breath
Is every day expanding
God's Vision-Light for me.

6170.

As long as you keep the mind-wall
Of doubt and disbelief
In your aspiration-life,
You will always be carrying with you
A heap of useless ashes.

6171.

Just beyond your thought-dominion
Is your today's impossibility-peak:
God's Perfection-Eye and Satisfaction-Heart.

6172.

O my heart's little hope-birds,
Every day you are inundating my life
With your beauty-making powers.

6173.

The more you enjoy empty moments,
The nearer will you be
To the kingdom of self-doubt
And self-mockery.

6174.

If you want to distinguish yourself
By your mind's giant actions, you can.
But God is not going to grant you
His smiling Face.
If you want to distinguish yourself
By your heart's selfless deeds,
Then God will grant you
Not only His smiling Face
But also His Vision-feeding Nest.

6175.

You never have enough time
For your conscious self-mastery.
But you always have unbounded time
For your unconscious self-mockery.

6176.

I do not need admiration
From Heaven.
I do not need admiration
From earth.
What I need is affection
From my Beloved Supreme.

6177.

What are my credentials?
My credentials are these:
My Lord Supreme sleeplessly cries
In me, through me and for me,
And I cheerfully and confidently
   dance
With His Vision-Light.

6178.

His heart is empty of hope
And his life is a perfect stranger
To perfection,
For his mind's sense
Of perfection and satisfaction
Is founded upon human love.

6179.

Who says that I am alone?
Am I not with the broken wings
Of my hopes
Inside the abyss of darkness?
Who says that tomorrow
I shall be alone again?
No, I shall not!
Tomorrow my entire earthly
   existence
Will swim in the sea of
   God-Delight.
How?
I do not know.
But it is all God-planned
And God-arranged.

6180.

My Lord Supreme,
Do grant me a boon.
"My child, I am giving you the
    boon
To come near Me selflessly."
My Lord Supreme,
Do grant me another boon.
"My child, I am giving you
    another boon:
To see the world
The way I see the world."
My Lord Supreme,
May I have one more boon,
A last boon, from You?
"Certainly, My child.
I shall make you
My perfect emissary on earth,
To become inseparably one
With earth's excruciating pangs
And streaming tears
The way I have been doing
Throughout My entire Eternity."

6181.

When I free myself
From my ego-interference,
I really and truly appreciate
God's Compassion-Magnet.

6182.

God's Feet blessingfully touched
My surrendered head.
Lo, I have now touched the peak
Of my hope-perfection-mountain.

6183.

The rapture of inspiration
Does not believe in
Either the intellectual climate
Or the ultramodern climate.

6184.

Unless we appreciate and admire
The most powerful silence
Of our soul,
Our doubtful mind will always
    create
An explosive noise.

6185.

Do you not realise
That your mind's perpetual
    procrastination
Is shamelessly useless
In your heart's aspiration-life?

6186.

Your heart is timid.
It is always frozen with fear.
It does not look forward,
Upward and inward.
Its blindness-night is the root
Of all your ceaseless problems.

6187.

Because of his mind's doubt-wars,
His heart is denied
His soul's treasure-dream.

6188.

Two warnings from God:
I must not belittle myself.
I must not delay in inviting God
To enter into my heart-room.

6189.

Alas, my strong desire
For world-dominion
Has overpowered not only
My reasoning mind
But also my Heaven-climbing
   heart.

6190.

Existence-Consciousness-Bliss.
Existence I need
To tell the world
How great God is.
Consciousness I need
To tell the world
How good God is.
Bliss I need
To tell the world
That God's Greatness and
   Goodness
Are not only for me
But also for His entire universe.

6191.

What God has and is
All the time
Is Concern for you.
Can you not show God
Even on rare occasions
Your inner courage
And outer adamantine will?

6192.

If you believe in God,
God will grant you His Beauty.
If you believe in God's
   Compassion,
God will grant you His Smile.
If you believe in God's
   Forgiveness,
God will grant you His
   Protection-Feet.

6193.

If you want to go
Beyond the body,
Then try to remember
Only one thing:
Your Beloved Supreme
Is your Eternity's
　Oneness-Companion.

6194.

If I want my Lord's Prosperity,
He will grant me His Prosperity.
But if I want my Lord's Divinity,
He will grant me
Not only His Divinity
But also His Life of Immortality.

6195.

Attention is preparation.
Preparation is the beginning
Of perfection.
Satisfaction is the culmination
Of perfection.

6196.

A sincere self-giving seeker
Feels and knows
That his life is at once
God's Compassion-Light
And
God's Satisfaction-Delight.

6197.

God has given man
The power to hope
In wisdom-light.
Man has given himself
The power to grope
In ignorance-night.

6198.

You can best your enemy
Either by virtue of
Your unprecedented
　determination
Or on the strength of
Your unconditional love.

6199.

War-mongers
Are around us.
Peace-lovers
Are within us.

6200.

I am happy
Not because I have done
Something momentous.
I am happy
Not because I have become
Something precious.
I am happy
Because inside my tiny little heart
God has sowed the seed
Of His Confidence-Light and
   Delight.

6201.

If you plant a seed of purity
Inside your heart,
Then God Himself will water it
   every day
And take care that it grows
Into a tree of divinity.

6202.

Everything is possible.
Fear-tremor can be transformed
Into destruction-terror,
And destruction-terror
Into perfection-love.

6203.

The desire-life vacillates
Between hope and fear.
The aspiration-life oscillates
Between perfection and
   satisfaction.

6204.

His vital is all
Vainglorious demonstration.
His heart is all
Auspicious aspiration.
Unbelievable, but true.

6205.

Self-mastery
Has a free access
To an ultramundane life.

6206.

Flattery now titillates your mind.
Therefore, for you to realise God
Is an impossible task.

6207.

The presence of teeming doubts
In the mind
Is tantamount to the beginning
Of a destruction-life.

6208.

Only a heart
Of soulful silence
Can have a life
Of sacrosanct blessing.

6209.

The pride of personality
Will one day hide
Under the warm blanket
Of satisfaction-unity.

6210.

Cancel your impotence-heart.
God is all ready to grant you
His indomitable
   Strength-Delight.

6211.

Aspire, aspire!
Your heart's aspiration-flames
Will unmistakably show you
The way to come out
Of your thick desire-forest.

6212.

Value the perfection
Of your heart's soft voice
If you want your outer
   confusion-life
To be illumined and perfected.

6213.

I have not seen the Face of God.
I have not felt the heart of man.
Therefore, I am wrapped
Only in my powerfully painful
   thoughts.

6214.

You will see yourself forsaken
If you deny
The indomitable strength of hope.

6215.

Each time you compromise
With ignorance-night,
You tarnish the beauty
Of your soul's perfection-promise
To the world.

6216.

Cheerfully accept your heart's way
And vehemently reject your
    mind's way
If you really want to free yourself
From the fetters of ignorance.

6217.

If your outer name is obedience
And your inner name is surrender,
Then you will never suffer
From periods of spiritual dryness.

6218.

My aspiration means
My heart's non-stop
Fast-rising flames.

6219.

If you just extinguish
The fire of desire,
Then you do not have to
    relinquish
Anything else.

6220.

When even his worst adversary
Does something great and good,
He will extol his foe to the skies.
Indeed, such nobility
Is not foreign to his nature.

6221.

A genuine seeker's life-story
Is nothing other than
God's own Satisfaction-Glory.

6222.

Those who tolerate
    ignorance-night
Cannot expect to reach
The wisdom-sky of vision-light.

6223.

Your do-nothing attitude
Is responsible
Not only for the complete failure
Of your own life
But also for the sad failure
Of your big world-family.

6224.

If you are great,
Then nobody will be able
To understand you.
If you are perfect,
Then nobody will be able
To replace you.

6225.

A mind without inspiration,
A heart without aspiration
And a life without imagination
Will be denied
God's Satisfaction-Smile.

6226.

God's Compassion helps me walk
On the road to perfection.
God's Forgiveness helps me walk
On the road to satisfaction.

6227.

If you do not aspire
Soulfully and sleeplessly,
Then God's Dreams for you
Will turn to useless dust.

6228.

Unless I destroy
My life's ignorance-night,
How can I ever reach
God's God-Height?

6229.

Because my life
Is a visionless ignorance-sky,
I am doomed to become
The king of stupendous failure.

6230.

What is impossibility
If not its own lifeless obscurity
And its own useless futility?

6231.

Not because I insult God,
Not because I find fault with God,
Not because I cannot see
Eye-to-eye with God,
But because I love only myself,
I am compelled to dwell
In my own abysmal
   ignorance-cave.

6232.

You say that you have nothing to do.
Then will you do something for me?
Will you dispatch your frustrated failure
Once and for all,
Just to please me?

6233.

If you invite God
To enter into your heart-room,
Do not forget to ask Him
To push you forward
To see His Eternity's Light
And to pull you upward
To feel His Infinity's Delight.

6234.

Hope-tree protects my life.
Therefore
I see satisfaction,
Feel satisfaction
And become satisfaction,
No matter where I am,
No matter what I am doing.

6235.

As night is the precursor
Of a beautiful and fruitful dawn,
May my mind become the precursor
Of a prayerful and soulful heart.

6236.

In my hermit-heart
I pray to feel only one thing:
God's ocean-deep Victory-Delight.

6237.

At any time I can pierce
Everything that I see
Within and without
Save one thing:
The Compassion-Canopy
Of my Beloved Supreme.

6238.

My Lord,
You have come to me
To revive my climbing heart.
My Lord,
Will You not allow me
To clasp Your descending Feet?

6239.

What my life needs
More than anything else
Is the fire of certainty.
Therefore, I am now sending
My uncertainty-thoughts
Into destruction-exile.

6240.

Because of my soulful morning
   prayer
I am immensely enjoying
Two most special things:
The burial of my deceased mind
And
The fragrance-beauty of my
   Himalayan smile.

6241.

When we live in the body,
The animal in us bites the world.
When we live in the heart,
The human in us inspires the
   world.
When we live in the soul,
The divine in us illumines the
   world.

6242.

Today's self-giving seed
Germinates into tomorrow's
God-becoming plant.

6243.

You can become
Divinity's reverberating
   clarion-call
If you do not allow
Your mind to be affected
By the world's venom-doubts.

6244.

Powerful is his success,
Fruitful is his progress
Because he has become
The naked sword
Of his own conscience-light.

6245.

His mind is
The arrow of concentration.
His heart is
The bow of meditation.
His soul is
The target of contemplation.

6246.

In the morning
My Lord secretly uncovers
   Heaven.
In the evening
My Lord blessingfully shows me
How to discover Heaven.

6247.

In your life's journey
Let God make the choice for you.
Rest assured,
God will let you enjoy the victory
All by yourself.

6248.

If you can think and feel
That God is yours,
You can easily cross to the other shore
Of the uncharted ignorance-sea.

6249.

Insecurity is a disease
That is unconsciously cheerless within
And consciously shameless without.

6250.

Perfection-poise
Is the satisfaction-heart
Of God's God-Beauty
In man.

6251.

A confidence-heart
And an assurance-mind
Are undoubtedly
Two immortal boons from Above
To humanity.

6252.

To intensify my commitment-life,
What I need first
Is an enlightenment-heart.

6253.

When I pray to God for my own sake,
I see His Compassion-cultivation.
When I pray to God for His sake alone,
I enjoy His Satisfaction-harvest.

6254.

The desire-life is good.
It liberates us from unpardonable idleness.
The aspiration-life is better than the best.
It helps us reach God's Palace
And freely and confidently
Dine with God.

6255.

To think of the past
Is indeed a painful task.
To carry the past
Is indeed a fruitless burden.

6256.

Every day try to meditate
On God's Silence-Beauty.
Then you are bound to become
His Heart's Flower-Fragrance.

6257.

A doubting mind and a dividing life
Are the unmistakable sources
Of man's teeming maladies.

6258.

Discard your worthless worries
As dirty, worn-out garments,
If you never want to abandon yourself
To wild despair-disaster.

6259.

If yours is a life of devoted service,
Then yours is also
A mind of inspiration,
A heart of aspiration
And
A soul of God-manifestation.

6260.

Your mind may be enjoying
An encircling gloom.
Your heart may be enjoying
An increasing confusion.
But your soul will always remain
A beckoning light.

6261.

An insincere seeker
Can unimaginably weaken
The life of a sincere seeker.
A sincere seeker
Can unimaginably inspire
The life of an insincere seeker.

6262.

To look at him
Is to be thrilled
With a silver faith in man
And a golden satisfaction in God.

6263.

An impossible task:
For a borrowing mind
Ever to console
A sorrowing heart.

6264.

A foolish mind thinks
That it needs a mountain-cave
For its illumination.
A stupid heart feels
That it needs a forest-grove
For its satisfaction.

6265.

You are wise twice:
Once when you are ready
To live in the world,
And once when you are ready
To look far beyond the world
While remaining in the world.

6266.

When the vital weaves
The rope of desire
It does not know
That it violently strangles
The climbing child in man.

6267.

You can remain
Not only unchanged
But also unchangeable
In this world of cataclysmic
    changes
If you can make your life
Into a soulful flower-offering.

6268.

If you think of God,
God will love you more.
If you love God,
God will need you more.
If you need God,
God will be at once
More proud of you
And more proud of Himself.

6269.

You are a sinner:
You have allowed your mind
To convince you of this.
You are a saint:
When are you going to allow God
To convince your heart of this?

6270.

His life is totally lost
Between his mind's emptiness
And his heart's fulness.

6271.

You do not want to stop living
In the uncertain future,
Yet you do not realise
What you are doing:
You are driving your life-car
From danger to disaster.

6272.

You want to remember
What you were in substance:
A sinner.
God wants you to see
What you are in essence:
A perfect saint.

6273.

The imperfections of your life
God has already forgiven,
But the exploitation of your mind
God is not sure
Whether He will forgive or not.

6274.

To be late to pray
Is common,
But to patiently wait to receive
Is always uncommon.

6275.

You have a humility-life.
What does it mean?
It means that you have
A magnanimity-life.
What else does it mean?
It means that you have embarked
On Eternity's Quest.

6276.

Only two indispensable realities
Can conquer the world:
A humility-mind
And
A purity-heart.

6277.

The cross of Christ
At Calvary
Was astonishingly prayerful.
The meditation of Buddha
At the foot of the Bodhi tree
Was astonishingly beautiful.
The flute of Krishna
At Brindabhan
Was astonishingly soulful.

6278.

If you can give up
The desire to be known,
Your aspiration-heart
Will not be able
To remain unknown.

6279.

What your mind has
Is a storm-tossed boat.
What your heart knows and sees
Is a silence-flooded shore.

6280.

There are two ways
To make constant progress:
The way of the heart
And the way of the life.
The way of the heart
Is to look up
High, higher, highest.
The way of the life
Is to look ahead
Far, farther, farthest.

6281.

Anxiety hounds your steps
Not because you have not
Done the right thing
But because you are unwilling
To accept the right thing
As your own, very own.

6282.

If your heart really loves
The mount of vision,
Then your life can easily,
Soulfully and satisfactorily
Sing the song of perfection.

6283.

Each time my aspiration ascends
I clearly see two things:
The assurance of my inner
 revolution
And the confidence in my outer
 resolution.

6284.

To destroy the shackles
Of my earthly bondage
I must become inseparably one
With my soul's silence-world
And renounce my mind's
 sound-world.

6285.

God feels sad
When he sees that you are caught
In unnecessary struggles
Against the wrong forces
Of your unaspiring friends,
For He knows that you also have
Your own problems and shortcomings
Which you have to conquer
In order to become perfect.

6286.

I weep
Not because I have not tried,
But because I have never asked
My Lord Supreme
What I am supposed to be
In His own Eternity's Vision-Light.

6287.

Don't watch for your weaknesses.
Pray first
And then watch for your weaknesses.
After you have prayed
Your weaknesses will lose their strength
And be ready to accept
The life of illumination.

6288.

The thought-world is a beggar's world.
Nobody can force you
To stay in this beggar's world
Unless you yourself are willing.
You can easily remain
In an emperor's will-power-world
If that is what you ever long for.

6289.

If you do not cooperate
With the desire-world,
Then the aspiration-world
Will wing towards you
To liberate your self-tortured life.

6290.

A humility-life,
A purity-heart
And a spontaneity-mind
Are the three special requisites
Needed for a free access
To God's infinite personal Property.

6291.

Aspiration is the beginning
Of my journey's start.
Surrender is the perfection
Of my gratitude-flooded heart.

6292.

A life of silence
Is the fragrance and beauty
Of God's
　　Self-Transcendence-Song.

6293.

Your teeming doubts
And your strangling suspicions
Will eventually bury you alive
Long before death invites you.

6294.

When you learn the art of
　　self-giving,
You definitely become
A conscious and inseparable part
Of the world-soul.

6295.

Today I have only an iota of
　　soulfulness
Because I am spiritually weak.
Tomorrow I shall become
　　spiritually strong
And become a sun-vast
　　soulfulness
Plus fulness.

6296.

Your life may perish,
But your oneness-smile with
　　Heaven
And your gratitude-heart to earth
Will always survive.

6297.

The wise man
Is he who prays to God
Not to show him
The ugly face of problems
Unless it is absolutely necessary
For his self-perfection.

6298.

You can start
With either sincerity or purity
Or with both.
But you can never stop
With either of them.
You have to continue with them
Forever and forever,
For your realisation
And for God's Manifestation.

6299.

Hope-flames are purifying my
　　heart
So that I can appreciate,
Admire, love and grow into
Heaven's ceaseless sun-vast smiles.

6300.

My Lord,
You have given me what I wanted.
How is it that I am not happy?
"My child,
How can you be happy
Unless you ask Me
For what you actually need?"
What do I need, My Lord?
Please tell me.
"My constant Satisfaction in you."

6301.

You have a multitude of
   questions,
But there is only one answer:
The road is right in front of you,
And the guide is waiting for you.

6302.

As parents disown their children
If they are extremely bad,
You can disown
The children of your mind.
But if a thought
Produced by your mind is good,
Then embrace it with a mother's
   love
And claim it as your own, very
   own.

6303.

No matter how many bad things
You have done over the years,
If you have done even ten good
   things,
Then all is not lost.
When you are depressed or
   assailed by doubt,
Think of these good things,
For they have tremendous power
And can give you the strength
To overcome your inner enemies.

6304.

If you want to drag behind you
A long train with many cars,
You can.
Again, if you want to go
Faster than the fastest
With just an engine,
You can.
To reach your destined goal
You don't need to carry the
   passengers
Doubt, fear, anxiety,
Worry and frustration.

6305.

Even if a mature seeker
Is doubting his own spirituality,
Even if around him
Is nothing but frustration and hell,
He still has a golden chance
To rediscover in himself
The divine qualities
Which he has temporarily lost.
How? Just by sincerely encouraging
The new seekers who have come after him.

6306.

Old seekers and new seekers
Have much to offer one another.
The old ones should encourage the new ones
At every moment.
Indeed, they must make sacrifice after sacrifice
For their younger brothers and sisters.
The freshness and eagerness
Of the new ones
Will give the old ones
Boundless joy and enthusiasm.
It is mutual inspiration
Founded upon true family-oneness.

6307.

Advanced seekers are like tall trees;
Beginning seekers are like small plants.
Overnight a plant cannot become
As tall, powerful and beautiful
As the trees
That have been ascending heavenward
For many years,
With roots firmly in the ground
And branches aiming at the highest height.
The trees can give the plants inspiration
And aspiration.
The trees can give the plants protection
So they will not be blown away
By doubt, suspicion and other negative forces.
But only patience-light
Can turn the aspiration-plants
Into realisation-trees
In God's Forest.

6308.

The day you made
A sincere commitment to God
You started running along
   Eternity's Road
With bullet-speed.
Now you are going
At bullock-cart speed.
True, the race may be
Longer than the longest,
But that does not mean
Your inner speed has to become
Slower than the slowest.

6309.

Take your Master's words
As coming directly from the
   Absolute Supreme.
You will find that his messages
Will satisfy and fulfil you
Beyond your wildest hopes
And brightest dreams.

6310.

If you have the sincere necessity
To do something,
Then God will give you the
   capacity
To do that very thing.
If you have the sincere necessity
To become something,
Then God will give you the
   capacity
To become that very thing.

6311.

God's supreme Message:
"Please Me in My own Way
And do not expect Me to please
   you."
If you expect God to please you
In any way,
Then in the inner world
You have already failed.
Again, there is no difference
Between your failure and God's
   failure.
If a flower does not blossom,
The gardener takes the blame.

6312.

I have only one prayer:
I wish my heart to become
The Flower-Fragrance
Of my Lord's Heart.

6313.

If a seeker
Does even one thing wrong,
Rest assured,
In the inner world
He has gone millions of miles
Away from his Lord Supreme.
If a seeker
Does one thing right,
Even in the thought-world only,
Rest assured,
In the inner world
He has taken a giant step
Closer to his Lord Supreme.

6314.

Do not speak ill of yourself.
The world around you
Will always gladly do that
On your behalf.

6315.

For God to please us
In our desire-world
Is not a difficult task.
But God is eager to please us
Only in our aspiration-world.
He wants to please the few
Who long for Him only.
To others He silently offers
His compassionate Heart of
   Oneness.

6316.

If his mouth has the capacity
To criticise you,
Then your mind definitely has the
   capacity
To ignore him.

6317.

Be careful!
The human in your Master
May tolerate your weaknesses
   indefinitely,
But the Divine in your Master
May one day be compelled
To use His Justice-Light,
Which is only another name
For His Compassion-Height.

6318.

When you accepted
The Path of the Supreme,
You made an inner commitment
To please your Lord Supreme
All the time in His own Way.
Remember this commitment
All your life
As you walk, march, run and fly
Towards the Golden Beyond.

6319.

If you accept the inner life
With the hope that God
Will please and fulfil you
In your desire-life,
You will always remain a failure.
But if you accept the inner life
With the hope that God
Will satisfy your divine hunger
And quench your divine thirst,
You will never be disappointed.
I assure you,
God can and God will
Fulfil your divine hopes
In the near or distant future.

6320.

My Lord Supreme,
I shall not pretend
To be good and perfect any more.
Only make me worthy
Of Your Compassion-Sea,
If so is Your Will.

6321.

When the Master
Outwardly encourages his
　　disciples
In any field,
He is showing his most sincere
Blessingful concern.
For it is absolutely necessary
For them to bring to the fore
Their good qualities
For their own perfection.
These good qualities
Are truly gifts from God,
To be manifested in His own Way
At His choice Hour.

6322.

A true disciple feels
That no journey is too long
If it brings him to the feet
Of his beloved Master.
A false disciple feels
That the shortest distance is too
　　far
For him to go to receive
His Master's highest Peace,
Light and Delight.

6323.

Try to remember
Absolutely the first time
You saw your Master
Or when he accepted you
As his true disciple.
Try to remember
What you felt
Deep inside your heart.
Remember your soul's joy and thrill.
Remember the aspiration, dedication
And surrender
That you offered to the Supreme in him.
Try to remember!

6324.

If you allow your capacities to remain dormant
Inside your heart, mind and body,
Then God may even go to the length
Of arguing with Himself
About whether He did the right thing
In bringing you down
Into the world-arena.

6325.

Because you have tried over the years
And failed,
You must not feel
You are a hopeless case.
Always continue trying
With more intensity and enthusiasm.

6326.

To please the Supreme
In His own Way
Is not possible overnight.
If you are sincerely and consciously trying,
What you need is patience.
Patience is light,
Patience is strength,
Patience is peace.

6327.

If you do not receive
What you are expecting from God,
Feel that it is
The greatest blessing.
Your expectation
Is nothing but stupidity
Which can eventually become
Your own destruction.

6328.

I had a heart-to-heart talk
With my mind.
At long last my clever mind
Wants to become wise.
It does not want to enjoy any more
The self-doubt and world-doubt
   games.

6329.

The human in us
Must not remain hidden.
It has to be unveiled
For its real transformation.
The divine in us
Must not remain concealed.
It has to be revealed
For its full manifestation.

6330.

Your mind is paralysed
With fear.
Your heart is overwhelmed
By despair.
The Hour of God
Is hesitating to approach you.
Alas, you are your own lonely
   world
Of constantly brooding misery.

6331.

Everything can smile,
Even your mind's ugliness.
But you will be satisfied
Only with the smile
Of your heart's soulfulness.

6332.

God and His Vision-Eye
Together live
Inside the heart-garden of
   Heaven.
God and His Mission-Heart
Together live
Inside the body-fort of earth.

6333.

My Lord Supreme,
Do give me a beautiful life
So that I can invite You
To visit my heart.
My Lord Supreme,
Do give me a powerful breath
So that I can embody You
To our mutual satisfaction.

6334.

A single breath of impurity
Has the capacity
To totally empty
An ocean of faith.

6335.

My tiny boat plies
Between my mind's curiosity
And my heart's uncertainty.
Therefore, illusion is my inner
   name
And frustration is my outer name.

6336.

Your heart's forgiveness-light,
Your life's oneness-delight
And your Lord's Self-transcending
   Height
Shall forever remain inseparable.

6337.

Inside my heart-garden
I see the purity
Of humanity's cry
And the beauty
Of Divinity's Smile.
Also I see something else:
The ceaseless and sleepless flow
Of God's Heart-Delight.

6338.

I have accepted man as my friend
Not because his mind is great
And his heart is good
But because the Eye of my Inner
   Pilot
Is all the time dreaming through
   him.

6339.

A moment's ignorance-pleasure
Can easily shatter
The sky-climbing tree
Of a seeker's life.

6340.

My Lord, You ask me to come
And sing with You.
How can I sing with You
When I live all the time
With my mind's impurity-clouds?
"My child, just come.
My magic Touch will clear away
Your mind's clouds."

6341.

One little desire man has:
He wants to become
As powerful as God.
One little desire God has:
He wants to see man
Sincerely happy.

6342.

The difference between humanity
And divinity is this:
Humanity cries for
What it does not have,
Whereas divinity knows that
Anything it does not have
Is not worth having.
It also knows something else:
Its own satisfaction-smile
Is for the transformation
Of humanity's present
　　dissatisfaction-cry.

6343.

When I sail my hope-boat
Towards the Golden Shore,
To my wide surprise
I see my Fate-Maker
Seated inside my boat
Sweetly smiling at me.

6344.

He who has an undisciplined life
And obeys Himalayan falsehood
Will never be able to take shelter
Under the canopy of God's
Transcendental Satisfaction.

6345.

Where do I live?
I live in a land of hope-light.
What do I see there?
The complete end of my
　　yesterday's
Totally barren life.

6346.

When you learn
The language of your divine heart,
God will immediately grant you
The Fragrance of His own
　　Flower-Heart.

6347.

First be absolutely sure
That you know the truth
Before you talk to others
About the truth.

6348.

When I love God the man,
I live inside my perfection-nest.
When I love man the God,
I enjoy my satisfaction-rest.

6349.

My Lord,
If my heart is awakened once
    more,
What will You give me?
"My child,
I shall give you
My own Immortality's Banner
Of Silence-Peace."

6350.

If you become
A self-indulgence-life,
What can you expect from your
    soul
Save and except
A helplessly crying
    reality-existence?

6351.

My past pain was:
I did not want to see
God's Face.
My present pain is:
I do not want to live
Inside God's Heart.
My future pain will be:
I shall not need God
For God's sake.

6352.

When I offer my heart's
    blossoming gratitude
To my Lord Supreme,
He shows me His Infinity's
    smiling Face.
When I offer Him
My Eternity's unconditional
    surrender-oneness,
He grants me His Immortality's
    Crown
While dancing inside
His ever-expanding universe.

6353.

Your body sleeps shamelessly.
Your vital fights shamelessly.
Your mind doubts shamelessly.
Your heart hesitates shamelessly.
Therefore, your soul, the
    God-messenger,
Is sleeplessly pining
For the total transformation
Of your life-family.

6354.

For your perfect perfection
Your mind must silence
The noise of impatience
And your heart must hear
The voice of patience.

6355.

My yesterday's invention:
God does not care for me,
Only I care for Him.
My today's invention:
Not only God the Creator
But also God the creation
Cares for me.
My tomorrow's invention:
Even if I do not care for God,
I shall always be taken care of
By God the Creator and God the creation.

6356.

You have a heart
And it does its duty:
It gives you its tearful cries.
You have a mind,
But it does not do its duty.
Can you not ask your mind
To do its duty
By mixing with your life's
Fruitful faith?

6357.

Do you want to learn?
Then stop arguing.
Do you want to teach?
Then start loving
And firmly establishing
Your oneness-heart.

6358.

If you love knowledge-light
And if you love and need
Wisdom-delight,
Then every day,
Just for a few fleeting seconds,
Dive deep within.
You are bound to see
A rising inner sun
With ever-increasing golden rays.

6359.

You are such a fool!
You want to discover the limits
Of your Heaven-free soul.
Yet you cannot even discover
The limits of your own
Earth-bound body.
Indeed, anything that God creates
Embodies the unlimited
　Vision-Light
Of God's Infinity.

6360.

O champion votary of
　ignorance-night,
Can you not see
That death-night is enveloping
Your outer body,
Your inner hopeful promise
And
Your God's blessingful Concern?

6361.

What else can save me
From the hunger of my
    desire-swoon
If not my Lord's
Daily Compassion-Boon?

6362.

When I rely on my mind,
I unmistakably rely
On my mind's teeming doubts.
When I rely on my heart,
I invariably rely
On my heart's increasing
    insecurities.
When I rely on my soul,
I sleeplessly and eternally rely
On my soul's earth-illumining
And God-satisfying Infinities.

6363.

Humanity's aspiration-core
And Divinity's satisfaction-door
Every day without fail
Dream of each other.

6364.

If you confide in me,
You will not be the loser.
I shall grant you a hope-dawn,
A promise-sun
And my own Satisfaction-Lord
    Supreme.

6365.

God has told me His only Secret:
He has safely kept
His Immortality's Crown for me.
I have told God my own secret:
I do not want to be another God,
I want to be His own
Eternity's perfect slave.

6366.

My mind is my attachment-forest.
My life is my problem-world.
What can my poor heart do?
It has forgotten to offer
Its own self-giving breath to
    humanity.

6367.

When my life grows into a
    deer-speed,
God comes to me and plays
On His Flute of Delight
For me to appreciate, admire,
Adore and finally love.

6368.

My Lord and I exchange
Our mutual smiles.
In my smile my Lord finds
His Vision of the Infinite.
In His Smile I find
My aspiration for Eternity.

6369.

You think that nobody is
   following you,
That only you are following,
Cleverly and deliberately,
Your doubting mind.
Look behind! Can you not see
The wild calamities following
   you,
Secretly but powerfully?

6370.

If you cannot face yourself,
Then how will you have
The inner courage to face others?

6371.

Each prayer
Is an earth-illumining flame
Of the seeker's heart.
Each meditation
Is a Heaven-reaching plant
Of the seeker's soul.

6372.

Who has the power?
He who has not surrendered
To the world-noise.
Who is the power?
He who is always drunk
With Heaven-silence.

6373.

Your sleepless dreams
Are for your achievement-glories.
God's sleepless Dreams
Are for your heart's
Everlasting satisfaction.

6374.

If over the years
You have lost instead of
   intensified
The inspiration, aspiration,
Inner joy and thrill
That you had when you first
   accepted
The spiritual life,
Then you must strive to bring
   back
Your original intensity and
   eagerness.
Only then will you once again feel
The utmost sweetness and
   loveliness
Of your spiritual quest.

6375.

Once upon a time
You felt that many things
Were necessary in your spiritual
    life,
And you worked very hard for
    them.
Now tremendous relaxation
Has assailed your body, vital,
    mind
And perhaps even your heart.
Rid yourself of this destructive
    relaxation!
Walk, march, run and fly
To reach your destined goal!

6376.

There are those who blame their
    Master
For not giving enough importance
To meditation.
But who are the ones who really
    meditate?
Those who really need God
And God alone,
Those who see the Supreme in
    their Master
As their only Guru,
Are the ones who sleeplessly,
Soulfully and breathlessly
    meditate.

6377.

If you are a genuine seeker,
Beware of the constant tug-of-war
Between the sincere and insincere
    members
Of your spiritual family.
Until the boat reaches the Golden
    Shore,
Either side can win.

6378.

Meditation does not only mean
To sit at one place
With closed eyes.
Meditation also means
Loving thought, pure thought,
Self-giving thought,
In our daily life of aspiration.

6379.

If you avail yourself
Of the ample opportunities you
    receive
To meditate with your Master,
Then you can easily
Make the fastest progress
In your inner life
And achieve the greatest success
In your outer life.

6380.

The spiritual life is a marathon,
An inner marathon which never ends.
The Supreme is begging
All His seeker-children
To be excellent runners —
To run speedily, like deer —
In this eternal inner journey.

6381.

One drop of doubt
Is enough to ruin
A faith-cup
Filled to the brim.

6382.

My outer resolution
Silences the world of my outer noise.
My inner revolution
Awakens the world of my inner voice.

6383.

The Master's inner determination
And outer hope
Save his spiritual children
And keep the Master alive on earth.
His determination is
His adamantine will.
His hope is his commitment
To his Beloved Supreme in humanity.

6384.

In one second of cheerful obedience
And willingness
You make Himalayan progress.
In one second of disobedience
And unwillingness
You become your own Himalayan failure.

6385.

He makes friends with empty days,
Empty weeks and empty months,
And then he asks himself
Why he has not pleased God
And why he is not pleased with himself.

6386.

If you are carrying
The frustration of yesterday,
Just say, "The past is dust."
If you can remember this mantra,
You can free yourself from the frustration
That is darkening your life.

6387.

Cherishing frustration in your inner life
Is like carrying a dead elephant
On your shoulders.
Why do you have to carry this elephant?
If you continue, you are a fool,
A rank fool.

6388.

My Lord Supreme,
Make me worthy
Of my spiritual life
And make me worthy
Of pleasing You
In Your own Way
At every moment.

6389.

A bad disciple will try
To please his Master in one way,
Hoping his Master
Will please him in nine ways.
A clever disciple will try
To please his Master in nine ways,
Hoping his Master will forgive him
For not pleasing him in the tenth way.
A good disciple will prepare himself
To please his Master in every way,
And he will succeed!

6390.

What I always need
Is an open life
Inside my Lord's hidden Heart.

6391.

There are two kinds of bondage:
The attachment-bondage
Of an ordinary man
And the compassion-bondage
Of a spiritual man.

6392.

O my mind,
You and I have travelled
For a long time
And covered
A very long distance.
Now we must part.
I must embark on a new journey
With my new friend:
Heart.

6393.

As the year comes to an end,
Your mind and vital may feel tired
And not want to continue
The great spiritual journey.
But the divine in you
Will always feel that each new year
Offers another opportunity –
A new hope, a new aspiration,
A new determination –
To completely obliterate the
   unfortunate past.

6394.

"If ever I lose my Beloved
   Supreme,
How shall I be able
To continue my life?"
If this question echoes and
   re-echoes
Inside your heart,
Your fast-declining spiritual life
Will reverse its course
And you will be saved.

6395.

Bring to the fore as soon as
   possible
All the good qualities of your
   followers.
Otherwise, they can easily play the
   role
Of great traitors.

6396.

Almost everybody feels he knows
What is best for himself.
But fortunately there are some
   truth-seekers
Who have accepted the spiritual
   life
Only because they feel
That God knows better than they
   do.

6397.

There was a time
When you thought that God
Knew what was best for you.
Now you think
That God does not know what is best
Either for you or for others.
Alas, your spiritual life
Has reached its untimely end.

6398.

As long as you can feel
That what God does for you and
    for others
Is absolutely the best thing,
You will be able to remain
In God's Golden Boat.

6399.

My Lord,
Why is it that today
You are not doing the same thing
For me
That You did yesterday?
"My child,
Perhaps I know a little better
Than you do
What is good for your heart and
    soul
Both yesterday and today."

6400.

Inside my sleepless eagerness
Man's doubtless newness
And God's earth-transforming
    Fulness
Shall blossom.
This is the message supreme
Which my heart's blue bird
Has brought to my self-giving life.

6401.

I am praying
To have a white bird
Flooded with purity
To fly in my heart's blue sky.

6402.

Alas, because of my weak body,
Vital, mind and heart,
I have been unable to manifest
My Beloved Supreme
According to the promise I made
    Him
Before I came into the
    world-arena.
Alas, alas!

6403.

The human philosophy runs:
The mind cannot be separated
From doubt-thorns.
The divine philosophy runs:
God will be satisfied
Only when He can show the mind
That it has the capacity to go
   beyond
Its own self-styled discoveries —
Doubt, suspicion and
   frustration —
And sing and dance
With God's perfection-children —
Peace, Light, Delight and Power.

6404.

My child, I have given you
My most precious Wealth:
My Heart's Satisfaction-Smile.
Will you not give Me
Your most precious wealth:
Your heart's oneness-cry?

6405.

My Beloved Supreme
Most sincerely loves me.
Therefore, He does not answer
Quite a few prayers of mine,
Especially prayers of my mind.

6406.

I may fail.
You also may fail.
But somebody will definitely
   succeed
In proving to the world at large
That the Supreme's Message
Is absolutely perfect.

6407.

Since I have no strong liking
For my inner cry,
I do not know how my Lord
   Supreme
Can ever grant me
His Infinity's Perfection-Core.

6408.

Your mind lives
In the house of negligence.
Your heart lives
In the house of impatience.
Therefore, you do not realise
That you have already uprooted
Your life's hope-tree
For good.

6409.

Nobody is safe!
Even excellent instruments
Of the Lord Supreme,
Devoted pilgrims on the spiritual path,
Can become lame and crippled
And be totally devoured
By ignorance-forces.

6410.

The ferocious ignorance-tiger
Is all around us.
This tiger may not be about to leave us
Right now,
But eventually it has to leave us
For good.

6411.

Now that you have discovered
The incense-purity inside your mind,
You will be liberated from the prison-cell
Of your fast-approaching spiritual death.

6412.

Vital tears are born
In the soil of self-deception-night.
Psychic tears are born
In God's God-Eternity's
Self-amorous Delight.

6413.

Yesterday you disobeyed
Your Inner Pilot.
Today you do not believe in
Your own inner capacity.
Tomorrow you will utterly ruin
Your life.

6414.

An outer smile carries
Today's earthly dawn to Heaven.
An inner smile carries
Tomorrow's Heavenly sun to earth.

6415.

At long last my mind
Has gone beyond itself
To grant me the joy
Of the unknown.

6416.

Conquer ignorance here and now!
If you think you can go elsewhere
And escape your enemy,
You are totally mistaken.
For even while you are planning
Your escape,
Your enemy will devour you.

6417.

When ignorance-tiger attacks you,
Just remind yourself who you are:
The supremely chosen instrument
Of your Beloved Supreme
For His divine Manifestation
On earth.

6418.

Why do you hesitate
To talk to God?
He never demands
Silence from you.
On the contrary,
He is expecting you
To say something to Him,
Even if it is not something nice.

6419.

If at every moment
I can convince my mind
That I am of God alone
And I am for God alone,
Then my love for God will grow
And inundate my life
With light and delight.

6420.

My Lord's Heart of
   Compassion-Beauty
Not only saves my life time and
   again
But also assures me
That it is my Eternity's only Way
And my Immortality's only Goal.

6421.

When you forget
Your connection with God,
Ignorance attacks you
Because it sees a yawning gulf
Between your aspiration and
   God's Compassion.
But if you can strengthen
Your oneness with your Beloved
   Supreme,
Ignorance is bound to leave you
   alone.

6422.

What do I see in others?
My own imperfection-spots.
What do I see in God?
My own dissatisfaction-panther.

6423.

If your heart is inspired
To cry like an orphan,
Then God the Father and God the Mother
Will definitely come to you
And teach you how to dance with Them
Their own Immortality-Dance.

6424.

As you run along the Path of Eternity,
Pay all attention to your own inner race.
If you try to carry
Your slower brothers and sisters
While running fast, faster, fastest
To your goal,
Your own frustration will come forward
Again and again
And unmistakably delay
Your spiritual progress.

6425.

Just because another seeker
Has failed in the spiritual life,
Does that mean you also will fail?
No, you have your own name.
When your Beloved Supreme
Calls you,
No other person will come
And appear before Him.

6426.

Every day is your birthday
When you are good.
Every day is your death day
When you are bad.

6427.

Yesterday, for the first time,
I appreciated something in myself
That I had never before appreciated,
And that was my thirsty heart.
Today I am appreciating
Something in myself
That I never thought I would appreciate
In this life,
And that is my Lord's
Uninvited Compassion-Tears.

6428.

You want to know
What God looks like.
I tell you,
He looks exactly like
The beauty of your hope
And
The purity of your promise.

6429.

Yesterday God came to me
With a blue and hungry heart.
Today God has come to me
With a green and nourishing
   hope.
Tomorrow God will come to me
With a golden and fulfilled
   promise.

6430.

If you stay in the Golden Boat,
You will be called.
But if you are no longer in the
   Boat,
Why should the Boatman call
   you?
So stay with your Beloved
   Supreme,
O seeker, stay in His Golden Boat.

6431.

If you have faith in the spiritual
   Teacher
You have chosen,
Then your sincere devotion to him
Will make you feel
That what he has inwardly and
   outwardly
Is more than enough for you.

6432.

The human in us
Wants to know
God's secret Dreams.
The divine in us
Wishes to become one with
God's open Realities.

6433.

If you have an inner will,
Then use it properly!
Use it to control
Your outer life.
If you have an outer will,
Then use it properly!
Use it to feed and please
Your inner life.

6434.

If you withdraw from your inner
   bank
All the good qualities
You have put into your spiritual
   life —
Gratitude, love, devotion,
   surrender,
Concern and affection —
And do not deposit anything
In their place,
Then your account will become
   empty
And your inner life
Will be totally bankrupt.

6435.

If you withdraw one dollar
From your inner bank account,
Then the next day, without fail,
You should be sure to deposit
Five dollars in its place.
This will be all your own wealth.
Nobody else can claim it.

6436.

You can unmistakably know
Your soul's will
By discarding once and for all
The messages of your binding
And blinding mind
And by consciously and sleeplessly
Loving and embracing
The messages of your crying
And dreaming heart.

6437.

The seeker's highest reality
And his lowest reality
Are all the time fighting against
   each other.
For the sincere seeker,
The highest is bound to win
In the near future.
For the insincere seeker also,
The highest is bound to win,
But in the far distant future.

6438.

It is not necessary
For me to know
What God the Perfection
Does for me.
But it is absolutely necessary
For me to know
What I the imperfection
Do for God.

6439.

If your life is your own dream
And not God's Dream,
Then you are bound to live inside
Your own mind's illusion-prison.

6440.

How can you survive
The attacks of ignorance-night
When your mind loves to dance
In darkness
And your heart is too timid and
  weak
To protest against your mind's
  behaviour?

6441.

If you know that God
Is all for you,
Then you are also bound to be
All for God,
No matter how much others
Speak ill of God,
No matter how much others
Speak ill of you.

6442.

To have a true friend
Is to have an added opportunity
To increase your spirituality,
For two friends can easily
Offer to each other
What they inwardly receive.

6443.

Each good thought is a new
  Heaven.
Each new Heaven is a new
  perfection
Of God's Vision
And a new satisfaction
Of God's Reality.

6444.

When I look at God,
I see His Eternity's sleepless Eye.
When I look at myself,
I see my insecurity's helpless "I".

6445.

If your heart-delight
Is walking with God,
That means your
  body-consciousness
Also is walking with God.

6446.

When I live inside my mind,
I offer my Lord Supreme
An unparalleled
　　frustration-prison.
When I live inside my heart,
I grant my Lord Supreme
An unparalleled opportunity
To receive me, shape me,
Mould me and make me
An exact prototype of His own
Heaven-Vision in earth-Reality.

6447.

As long as I live in the hope-world,
My Lord Supreme will appear
Time and again.
But when I no longer live in the
　　hope-world,
Not only will my Lord disappear,
But also my own Heaven-free
　　reality
Will disappear.

6448.

Frustration and satisfaction
Stand before you side by side.
It is up to you to choose.
While you are cherishing
　　frustration,
Satisfaction remains out of reach.
But the moment you cast
　　frustration aside,
Satisfaction is yours.

6449.

Your mind does not aspire.
Therefore, your heart suffers.
Your heart aspires,
But not to the satisfaction of your
　　soul.
Therefore, your soul suffers.

6450.

You are walking
Along the wrong road
Because you are not feeding
Your mind's little thoughts
With your purity-sincerity-flames.

6451.

Promotion:
This is what my mind demands
From the world.
Protection:
This is what my heart needs
From Above.

6452.

In the morning
I am the beggar
Of my Lord's Compassion-Eye.
At noon
I am the beggar
Of my Lord's Oneness-Heart.
In the evening
I am the beggar
Of my Lord's Satisfaction-Breath.

6453.

When you love yourself
And nobody else,
You must know that
Your heart is not,
And perhaps will never be,
As vast as you think.

6454.

His clever vital
Is torturing his uncertain mind.
His intelligent mind
Is torturing his loving heart.

6455.

If you know that a negative force
Is bound to attack you,
Do not delay!
Attack that force
Before it attacks you.

6456.

If you see the ignorance-tiger
Standing in front of you
About to attack,
Do not run away.
Do not wait for the hour
When Peace, Light, Bliss and Power
Will descend into you in infinite measure.
Do not wait until you have more strength
In your mind and heart.
The hour of battle is now!
Just conquer and destroy the tiger
Immediately.

6457.

Nobody is my enemy
Except my mind,
The manufacturer
Of my restlessness-life.

6458.

If your mind enjoys
Living inside the prison cell
Of dark impurity,
How can poor God grant you
His Heart's Love-Nectar-Delight?

6459.

My life's hesitation
Is cleverly beckoned
By my mind's imperfection.

6460.

An imperfect
Institution-mind
Is a perfect
Destitution-life.

6461.

I am so glad that my mind
Is now totally blind.
It can no longer see
The falsehood-mountain.
I am so glad that my life
Is now totally blind.
It can no longer see
The deception-volcano.
I am so glad that my heart
Has regained its perfect vision.
It can not only see God once more
But also feel God's
   Satisfaction-Heart.

6462.

There may be a great difference
Between the peace
That I receive from within
And the peace
That I offer without.

6463.

I love the world
Not because the world
Is trying to be perfect.
I love the world
Because my Lord is evolving
Through the world's constant
   failures
And rare successes.

6464.

I have already found my Lord
Inside my heart-garden,
And now I am looking for Him
In the depths of my mind-forest.

6465.

One divine message is flowing
   down
And touching my earth-home:
My Lord Supreme will make my
   life
His own Illumination-Joy.

6466.

Because I have not disciplined my
   life
I am forced not only to see
The dance of darkness
But also to participate in
The dance of destruction.

6467.

The blue bird of my green heart
Has a special message today:
Before long I shall see
The lotus-red Feet of my Lord
    Supreme
Inside my surrender-life and
    gratitude-heart.

6468.

Man is happy only when
He has his powerful imagination
    with him.
God is happy only when
He has His fruitful Satisfaction
    with Him.

6469.

There are many ways for a seeker
To acquire overwhelming joy
Inside the depths of his heart.
But the easiest and most effective
    way
Is to tell the world:
"I am in you, true!
But I am for God,
I am of God
And I am with God."

6470.

Because of your
    flower-fragrance-humility
God enjoys inside you
The Delight of His own Divinity.

6471.

My only freedom
Is my constant obedience
To my Inner Pilot.

6472.

He has definitely descended
Because his mind
Has stabbed his heart.

6473.

I sincerely do not mind
Who thinks of you,
So long as you are thought of
Affectionately, sleeplessly
And unconditionally.

6474.

My heart's sleepless progress
Is my life's
Shadowless destination.

6475.

When you lose your outer
   strength,
You can gain it back again
Almost at once.
But when you lose your inner
   strength,
Recovery is more difficult.
For that you have to cry and cry to
   God
With all the sincerity
At your command.

6476.

In the outer life
If you do not eat for two days,
Nothing serious will happen to
   you.
But in the inner life
If you do not aspire for even one
   day,
All the world's hostile forces
Can attack you,
And your inner wounds may
   linger
For many days.

6477.

My mind's inspiration
Is divinely beautiful.
My heart's aspiration
Is supremely powerful.
My life's realisation
Is eternally fruitful.

6478.

Each man
Is his yesterday's
Heavenly promise
And his today's
Earthly hope.

6479.

My Lord has saved me
By fulfilling my heart's cry.
My Lord has saved me
By refusing to fulfil
My vital demands.

6480.

The mind thinks
That any change
Is painful.
The heart feels
That any change
Is powerful.

6481.

A crystal-clear glimpse of reality
Has shown him that each heart
Is a green plant of hope
And each life
Is a blue tree of promise.

6482.

It is the hostile forces
In the inner world—
Not those in the outer world—
That try to take you away
From your spiritual life.
These hostile forces take your faith
And give you doubt,
Take your security
And give you insecurity.
But as long as you are vigilantly cultivating
The seeds of faith and security
In the inner world,
You do not have to worry.

6483.

The seeker can stop
His yesterday's inner storms
Only if he knows how to smile
A soulful surrender-smile.

6484.

His heart is completely lost
Between Heaven's chilling indifference
And earth's burning attachments.

6485.

My mind is demanding
A newness-world.
My heart is crying for
A fulness-world.

6486.

Self-giving is not
The climbing of my heavy body
But the coasting of my light life.

6487.

It is not inevitable
That some people become rich
While others remain poor.
No, it entirely depends on
Their eagerness for wealth.
Even so, your spiritual wealth
Depends on your eagerness
To become spiritually rich.

6488.

You may tell the whole world
That your Inner Pilot is not responsible
For your destruction.
You may rightfully blame
Your previous negligence
And present unwillingness.
But do you think that your Inner Pilot
Will be satisfied
Because you are not blaming Him?
On the strength of His Eternity's Oneness
With you,
He feels your failure is unmistakably
His failure too.

6489.

If your heart can bask
In its own open smile,
Then all the deathless dreams
Inside your heart
Will blossom into perfect realities.

6490.

His mind enjoys
The trumpet of prophecy.
His heart enjoys
The flute of soul-illumining
And life-transforming
Oneness-satisfaction.

6491.

With your soul's mustered might
You can easily destroy
Your mind's age-long slumber.

6492.

Gratitude is an inner flower
That can never die
Once it has blossomed
Inside your heart-garden.

6493.

Human friends are good
If they inspire and encourage you
On the journey along Eternity's Road,
But God is your only real divine Friend.

6494.

My life needs only three things:
An emptiness-mind,
A oneness-heart,
A fulness-soul.

6495.

Oppression's volcano-mind
And depression's thunder-vital
Are his inner and outer
  companions.

6496.

If you are ready to suffer
For other's misery,
Then you are fiercely thirsting
To disperse
The ignorance-clouds
Of humanity's cruelty.

6497.

If you can give the hostile forces
A serious warning,
You are bound to see a new light
Inside your heart,
Rising suddenly like the moon.

6498.

If you want to have,
Then talk to others.
But if you want to become,
Then talk to God.

6499.

My mind's faithfulness
Considerably adds to
My heart's soulfulness.

6500.

Your mind is learning
The language of surrender-light.
Therefore, your Lord Supreme has
  granted you
His own Flute of
  Oneness-Delight.

6501.

See the beauty of God's creation
With your sleepless eyes.
See the purity in God's creation
With your breathless joy.
Then your life will be ready
For perfection-splendour.

6502.

A new me I became
The day I learnt the twin arts
Of beautiful surrender
And soulful gratitude.

6503.

God's Compassion cures
My heart.
God's Smile immortalises
My life.

6504.

God keeps all
His transcendental Promises.
My sterling faith
Is the absolutely sincere witness.

6505.

Your heart is aching
Because you do not feed your soul
Even once a week
With a prayerful cry
And a soulful smile.

6506.

Some people proudly judge your
  heart
Only after they have carefully seen
Your life.

6507.

There are two places to hide
Our imperfections:
One place is inside
Our Lord's Compassion-Eye,
And the other place is under
Our Lord's Forgiveness-Feet.

6508.

To try to go to Heaven
Without your heart's soulfulness
Is like trying to open a locked door
Without the key.

6509.

Death cannot say
"Yes"
When my heart says
"No".

6510.

His heart's purity
Enjoys incessant increase.
Therefore, the human in him
Is proud of him
And the divine in him
Is fond of him.

6511.

Trust-flames beckon us,
To illumine our aspiration-heart.
Distrust-fires beckon us,
To baffle us and finally destroy us.

6512.

The outer difference
Between man and God is this:
Man does not know,
Whereas God knows.
The inner difference
Between man and God is this:
Man is not ready to please God,
Whereas God is not ready
To renounce man.

6513.

O Boat of Delight,
I am your new passenger
With a new heart
And a new aspiration
For a God absolutely new.

6514.

Each uncomely thought
Eventually throws the mind
Into a chasm of bleeding despair.

6515.

One man's insufficiency
Can sadly prove
How weak this world is.
One man's sufficiency
Can unmistakably prove
That man is the golden bridge
Between God the Love Divine
And God the Beloved Supreme.

6516.

Between two thieves,
Doubt and insecurity,
I shall make no choice,
For they are equally dangerous
And destructive.

6517.

When I travel Home with God,
I travel very close to Him
So nothing can travel in between us,
Especially not disappointment.

6518.

May my self-giving will
Be infinitely swifter
Than my man-conquering
    thought.

6519.

All doubts are dissolved
When a seeker sincerely
   surrenders
To the Will of his own highest
   Self:
God the Compassion-Heart.

6520.

When your heart's tranquillity
Climbs up,
You are bound to notice
The complete exhaustion
Of your life's sorrow.

6521.

His mind is desperately trying to
   grow
Into a belief-plant,
Whereas his heart has already
   become
A huge faith-tree.

6522.

Before you enter the jaws of death,
Make two requests of Mother
   Earth:
O Mother Earth,
Do forgive me
My life's countless mistakes.
O Mother Earth,
Do forever keep
My heart's gratitude-garland
Which I am placing
At your feet.

6523.

There are three ways
To be special.
One way
Is through possession.
Another way
Is through renunciation.
The third way
Is through acceptance:
Acceptance of God's Will
In God's own Way.

6524.

I shall accept my Master
Unconditionally
Even if he rejects me
Totally
In front of everybody.
This is my oneness
With his heart and soul.

6525.

Accept, accept your Master!
Accept him with the hope
And with the determination
To become his choicest
    instrument.
The moment your surrender
Is complete and permanent,
You will be his best disciple.

6526.

Better days are coming!
Better worlds are emerging!
Better skies are descending!
Better perfection is evolving!

6527.

You have accepted the spiritual
    life.
Do you feel a special love
For what you are doing?
Do you feel a special devotion
To what you are doing?

6528.

My Lord's Satisfaction-Sky
Lies inside my conscious
    acceptance
Of His Vision-in-Reality
And His Reality-in-Vision.
His Vision-in-Reality:
In Heaven I was His Promise.
His Reality-in-Vision:
On earth I am His Manifestation.

6529.

You will find the smile of silence
Inside your heart's sleepless cry.
Cry is the night.
Inside the night is the day.
As the night holds the day,
So the cry holds the smile.

6530.

My Lord,
What do You usually do
During the day
And
During the night?
"My child,
During the day
I watch and wait.
During the night I use either
My Compassion-Height
Or
My Justice-Light."

6531.

Believing is an act
Of earthly will.
Loving is an act
Of Heavenly will.
Surrendering is an act
Of supreme will.

6532.

My music-life invokes
God's Presence
Inside my heart.
My song-life is all prepared
For God's Arrival
Inside my heart.

6533.

I surrender
To the In-Dweller in him,
For my Beloved Supreme
Has manifested much more
Purity and divinity through him
Than through me.

6534.

True freedom is not
In the satisfaction-beauty
Of your face,
But in the perfection-oneness
Of your heart.

6535.

All seekers of the Absolute
  Supreme
Have the sacred responsibility
Of universal fraternity.

6536.

Daily think a few times
Of your future victories in Heaven
Instead of thinking all the time
Of your present defeats on earth.

6537.

Today's pure thoughts
Are resources
For tomorrow's inner
  emergencies.

6538.

If your life does not give joy
To others,
Then how can you expect
Your heart to give any joy
To you?

6539.

The mind depends on
The strength of doubt.
The heart depends on
The strength of oneness.
The soul depends on
The strength of delight.

6540.

You are a stupid fellow
If you are looking for
A perfect man.
You are a wise man
If you are trying to become
A perfect man.

6541.

Failure is a matter of the mind.
If I do not mind,
Then failure is of no consequence.

6542.

My aspiration-heart
Knows no want
Since my illumination-soul
Is its supplier.

6543.

God is everything:
This is a great discovery.
God is in everything:
This is a great revelation.

6544.

My Lord, as a poet
You have made me creative.
Will You not make me creative
Not only when I do something
But also whenever I think
    anything?

6545.

Because my soul
Is a soul of promise,
My life
Is a life of hope
And my heart
Is a heart of peace.

6546.

God the Heart
Loves only one thing:
My heart's breathless inner cry.
God the Eye
Loves only one thing:
My life's measureless outer smile.

6547.

Who cares for the continuous
   increase
Of your mind's reputation
If the soulful capacity of your
   heart
Declines?

6548.

If you use your heart's inner poise
In a constructive way,
Then Blessing-Showers from
   Above
Will be all yours to treasure.

6549.

There is only one cure
For the suspicion-mind,
And that cure is
To deliberately excommunicate
   the mind
From the assembly of the heart
   and soul.

6550.

If you fear God's Power,
Then how will you wake up
And be ready to receive God
When God's God-Hour strikes?

6551.

You may not be great,
But your gratitude-heart
Is exceptionally great
And perfectly good.

6552.

When it comes to prayer,
Wake up, pray,
And do not give up.

6553.

If you are jealous,
If you are insecure,
Think of your Master.
Your jealousy and your insecurity
Will not be able to increase
When you think of your Master.

6554.

My only confidential request
To the children of this world:
"I am totally tired,
But do not breathe a word of it to
   Heaven,
For Heaven does not appreciate
My helpless tiredness."

6555.

Life is a series of adventures,
And he who is ready to enjoy
These adventures
Has a special place
Inside the blessingful Heart of God.

6556.

There are countless approaches to God,
But the easiest and most effective approach
Is to sow the seed of gratitude
And watch it growing every day
Inside the depths
Of your silence-flooded heart.

6557.

You call it imperfection,
But God calls it your preparation.
You call it emptiness,
But God calls it your future fulness.
You call it impossibility,
But God calls it the mask
Of unveiled reality.

6558.

I pray soulfully
So that my mind
Can know the truth
Unmistakably.
I meditate silently
So that my heart
Can grow high enough
To touch God's Heaven-Feet.

6559.

The mind is unhappy
Because it cannot escape
The frequent attacks of merciless pride.
The heart is happy
Because it is incapable
Of any kind of pride.

6560.

When your mind is no longer entangled
In pitch-dark confusion-night,
You will be able to see
The beauty of your inner face
And
The purity of your inner heart.

6561.

Your soulful surrender-heart
Is the holiest of all shrines.
No other shrine can equal it
In this wide universe.

6562.

My Lord Supreme,
Do spare me from name and fame.
My heart consciously, soulfully
And devotedly
Longs to play only with You
In Your Cosmic Game.

6563.

Fear, doubt and anxiety
Together live
In their earthly existence-family.
Hope, promise and dedication
Together live
In their Heavenly
  existence-family.

6564.

If your entire life
Is an insecurity-ant,
How will you ever dare
To drink deep the Nectar-Heart
Of your Beloved Supreme?

6565.

At every moment
If you are not conscious
Of the Height transcendental,
The powerful magnets of the
  lower worlds
Will pull you down
Into the abyss of oblivion.

6566.

The guardian angel
Of my daily life
Is my one
Soulful morning song.

6567.

God became his perfect slave
When he became his heart's
Completely surrendered life.

6568.

Cheerfulness
Is something encouraging.
Calmness
Is something enlightening.
Oneness
Is something fulfilling.

6569.

God has lovingly given my mind
His lightning Speed to enjoy.
God has blessingfully given my
   heart
His immortalising Feast to enjoy.

6570.

His is the heart
That thirsts for God's Nectar-Sea.
His is the life
That dines with God's
   Summit-Satisfaction.

6571.

Your soul was the witness
When God asked your mind
To play with His own
   Sincerity-Smile
And when God asked your heart
To play with His own Purity-Cry.

6572.

How can he succeed in his outer
   life
When earth is so jealous of him?
How can he proceed in his inner
   life
When Heaven is so callous to him?

6573.

God is always able to enjoy
His Victory-Drum
Because He never strikes it hard.
Therefore, He does not produce
   loud sounds
That deafen His Ears.

6574.

Vastness-smile:
This is what the mind
Will ultimately become.
Oneness-dance:
This is what the heart
Will eventually become.

6575.

I shall shorten
My heavenward journey
Just by strangling
My doubting mind.

6576.

Cry within breathlessly,
Smile without sleeplessly.
No nagging dissatisfaction
Will mar your life's
Swift heavenward journey.

6577.

Beauty is tempting and fleeting
In the human mind.
Beauty is self-giving, abiding,
Illumining and God-manifesting
In the divine heart.

6578.

Earth unconsciously welcomes
The messenger of disaster.
Heaven consciously welcomes
The messenger of helplessness.

6579.

Without any preliminary
  preparation
You may see the Face of God,
But without full preparation
You can never become the Heart of
  God.

6580.

Seeing his own helplessness,
He does not want to see
Any blossoming newness on earth
Or any illumining fulness in
  Heaven.

6581.

A human hope
Is a very subtle slavery.
A divine promise
Is a very tangible harbinger
Of self-mastery.

6582.

If you watch closely,
You will see that nobody cares to
  know
Whether you have already realised
  God
Or are going to realise God
In the near or distant future.
Everybody minds his own
  business.
And he ought to!

6583.

If you live in your self-governed
  world,
God will not dislike you,
Never!
But the God-governed world
Will not be at all inspired
To remember you
Either.

6584.

Do not worry
About speaking to the world
About yourself.
Your heart's confidence-light
Is always ready to do that for you.

6585.

Courage is the watchfulness
Of my vision-eye.
Gratitude is the fulness
Of my reality-life.

6586.

Be not afraid
Of the pre-dawn darkness.
The golden morning
With its rainbow-dance
Is blossoming faster
Than you can imagine.

6587.

His self-determination
Powerfully governs his mind.
Therefore, he is now chosen by
   God.
His self-purification
Soulfully feeds his heart.
Therefore, God is inviting him
To be a very important member
Of His inner Family.

6588.

My poor, tiny mind,
I fully sympathise with you.
How can you brave
The ruthless and sleepless
   onslaughts
Of a multitude of uncomely
   thoughts?

6589.

Do not tell God
That you do not know.
God does not like to hear it.
Do not tell man
That you know.
Man does not like to hear it.

6590.

The human life is a difficult
Cross-country run.
The divine life is an easy,
Charming and Heaven-enjoying
Fun-run.

6591.

God the Eye
Threatens the proud.
God the Heart
Transforms the proud.

6592.

Why are you ashamed
Of your imperfections?
God Himself is not ashamed
Of His imperfect creation.

6593.

I do not hate the world,
Not because I do not know
How to hate,
But because God does not want me
To hate.
I love the world,
Not because I know how to love,
But because God,
Out of His boundless Bounty,
Loves the world
In me, through me and for me.

6594.

Two most sacred secrets to keep:
God wants my soul
To be His representative
Here on earth.
God has given me the capacity
To transform the face and fate
Of mankind.

6595.

Only two miracles are worth
   seeing:
The miracle of loving
And
The miracle of forgiving.

6596.

Who are the builders
Of the heavenward road
If not God's Compassion-Eye
And my own aspiration-heart?

6597.

India's secret weapons:
The transcendental Vision-Light
Of the Vedic seers,
The universal
   Consciousness-Delight
From the Vedic code.

6598.

A doubtful mind
Hurts a faithful heart.
A faithless heart
Puzzles a beautiful soul.

6599.

If your heart is all aspiration,
And if your life is all gratitude,
Then you become God's cheerful
And constant responsibility.

6600.

Not because I need a special favour
From my Lord Supreme
Do I obey Him,
But because when I obey Him,
To my utter astonishment,
My own heart swims
In the sea of Light and Delight.

6601.

Take just one positive step.
Every day say:
"My heart is of God
And my life is for God."

6602.

Centuries come and go.
My mind does not know
What it has been doing all along,
But my heart knows
What it has been doing.
It has been crying
For the presence of the Infinite
Inside the tiny body-cave
Of the finite.

6603.

Somehow I have lost my way.
Alas, I now see the road ahead
Constantly lengthening,
Bewildering and frightening me.

6604.

God has invited you to His Party.
Do not forget to carry with you
Your heart's gift:
Absolutely pure gratitude.

6605.

If you are willing
To run the race of oneness-light,
Then only can you enjoy the prize:
The freedom of true
　　independence.

6606.

If you are bathed
In God's Forgiveness-Light,
Then no dust of earth
Will be able to cling to you.

6607.

The beckoning Hands
Of God's hopeful Smile
Will, without fail, one day greet
The fruitful cries
Of man's prayerful heart.

6608.

My steady mind sits and dreams
At the foot of my Lord's
   Perfection-Tree.
My ready heart climbs up and
   devours
My Lord's Satisfaction-Fruits.

6609.

Your mind's confusion-boat will
   sink
Only when you are ready to sail
Your heart's illumination-boat.

6610.

Your friendship with humanity
Is founded upon your curiosity.
Therefore, do not blame God
If you find yourself completely
   lost
Inside a dark nothingness-night.

6611.

Because yesterday your mind
Enjoyed its indifference-night,
Today your orphan-life
Is drowning in the sea of
   helplessness-night.

6612.

How do you dare pressure God
To invite you to His Delight-Feast,
When you are all the time
   treasuring
Your heart's insecurity-hunger?

6613.

The silence-touch of Eternity
Has unconditionally granted me
A lasting and transcending
Oneness-connection with God.

6614.

His mind lives for
   knowledge-light.
His heart lives for
   affection-delight.
His life lives for perfection-might.
His soul lives for
   transcendence-height.

6615.

His mind's new discovery:
God is Forgiveness-Delight.
His heart's new discovery:
God is Justice-Light.

6616.

How can you be always happy
When your life does not go beyond
The domain of your mind's
Superficial investigation?

6617.

A transformed man
Is the perfect manifestation
Of a blossomed God.

6618.

Earth's beauty
Is in its soulfully smiling hope.
Heaven's beauty
Is in its peacefully loving promise.

6619.

Your world's future guide
Is not your promise,
Not your hope,
Not even your surrender,
But your heart's gratitude-plant.

6620.

A mind of simplicity,
A heart of purity
And
A life of duty
Live together
In their perfect oneness-home.

6621.

Trials in the outer world
Awaken you.
Trials in the inner world
Illumine you.

6622.

God's Compassion-Supply
Is more abundant
Than even our extravagant
    requirements.

6623.

His heart's purity
Penetrates the impenetrable.
His life's surrender
Wins the Transcendental.

6624.

Man is nothing but a quenchless
   pride-flame.
Therefore he has no choice.
Helplessly he is humiliated
By a stark ignorance-frown.

6625.

The love of a pure oneness-heart
Has every right to correct
If necessity demands.

6626.

You fool,
You have been dangling
For such a long time!
When will you seize the
   opportunity
Or feel the necessity
To untangle the taut knot
Of your bondage-life?

6627.

What has God's
Unconditional Grace done?
It has made me see
That I the finite
Not only embody
God the Infinite
But will some day reveal
God the Infinite.

6628.

No matter how much you eat
Of your desire-food,
You are bound to be frustrated.
No matter how little you eat
Of your aspiration-food,
You are bound to be eventually
   emancipated.

6629.

Hope illumines my mind.
Promise liberates my heart.
Perfection immortalises my life.

6630.

A singular stroke of light
Has liberated him
From his long-cherished
Fanciful illusions.

6631.

Follow God's Example!
He does not want to plumb
The depth of my life's
   ignorance-sea.
He only wants to measure
The height of my heart's
   surrender-plant.

6632.

Jealousy sees too much.
Insecurity imagines too much.
Pride knows too much.
Doubt destroys more than the most.

6633.

Heavenly words should be weighed
And not counted.
Earthly words should be forgotten
And not treasured.

6634.

An earth-bound life
Is impurity's nothingness.
A Heaven-free life
Is purity's Immortality.

6635.

Each time I think of Him,
I become His Beauty's
Perfection-Bird
And His Duty's
Satisfaction-Wings.

6636.

A pure thought
At a God-chosen Hour
Can and shall
Save this poor and weak world.

6637.

Unlike illusory dreams,
All realities have a special purpose,
A special goal in the Creation-Game
Of the Lord Supreme.

6638.

I need a place to keep my heart
Where nobody will tell me "No!"
I need a place to smile
Where nobody will ask me "Why?"

6639.

God's Compassion-Sea
Has seized his inspiration-mind.
God's Satisfaction-Shore
Has seized his aspiration-heart.

6640.

Indulgent earth did not realise
That it was keeping his life
　imperfect.
Indifferent Heaven did not want
　to feel
That it was keeping his
　aspiration-heart starved.

6641.

Because of his powerful feet,
We see his lofty head
Far above the hurtful clouds
In an ignorance-nourished sky.

6642.

Your mind unconsciously
　treasures
Illusory phantasmagoria.
Therefore, you are consciously
　forced
To remain in a world
Where imperfection reigns
　supreme.

6643.

A man of thought thinks he
　knows
Because he has knowledge-light.
A seeker-heart unmistakably
　knows
Because it is all
　satisfaction-delight.

6644.

As my thought-flags are obedient
To my illumined mind-breeze,
Even so, my surrender is
Unconditionally obedient
To my liberated soul's vision-eye.

6645.

Do not allow earth
To resist your heart's
Perfection-hoping cries.
Do not allow Heaven
To ignore your soul's
Life-illumining smiles.

6646.

Where is the difference
Between a giant mind
And the futility of
　confusion-discovery?

6647.

Each impure thought is a sleeping cancer
Which will soon play its role
Most successfully
In weakening your heart
And taking away your life-breath.

6648.

An ignorance-heart
Is a huge reservoir
Of great disaster
In life's unknown abyss.

6649.

The pinnacle-height of love
Can never be challenged.
The immeasurable depth of silence
Can never be revealed.

6650.

If you are ready to wrestle
With your darkness-mind,
Then God is also ready,
More than ready,
To nurture your soulful heart's
Aspiration-cry.

6651.

My mind says to my heart:
"Will you please praise God for me?"
My heart says to my mind:
"Will you please pray to God
To bless me?"

6652.

Success depends on
Only one thing:
Inspiration.
Progress depends on
Only one thing:
Aspiration.

6653.

The animal anger
Eventually surrenders
To the heart-breaking tears and sobs
Of the loving heart.

6654.

It is bad enough
To have today
As a goalless day,
But to have Eternity
As a goalless reality
Would be an unthinkable
And unfathomable tragedy.

6655.

If your life is afraid
Of reality,
How can God transform
Your human mortality?

6656.

Earth's imperfections
To go unnoticed?
Impossible!
Heaven's compassion
To disown the world?
Impossible!

6657.

If you are caught
By the expectation-chain,
How can you escape
The powerful blows
Of despair-night?

6658.

How can God walk beside you
When you have allowed
Disappointed hopes
To invade you?

6659.

As your mind has the power
To command your
   life-movements,
Even so, your heart
Must develop the power
To control, command and
   transform
Your mind.

6660.

Inwardly he was fearful,
Outwardly he was bashful
And secretly he was sorrowful
Before he met God.

6661.

What stabs my life most
   mercilessly?
The helpless and sorrowful tears
Of my innocence-heart.

6662.

By magnifying the heaviness
Of my life's burdens,
My mind gets tremendous
   pleasure.
By totally ignoring my life's
   burdens,
My heart receives soulful joy
And powerful satisfaction.

6663.

My Lord Supreme can and will
Clasp my hands
Only when I prayerfully and
   soulfully
Love His Heart
Beating inside my own little heart.

6664.

Only a genuine God-dreaming
   seeker
Can eventually become
A peace-manifesting God-lover.

6665.

True, each thought
Is not a striking thing,
But it is a living thing.
True, each man
Is not manifesting the truth,
But he is definitely embodying the
   truth.

6666.

First be the lover
Of consecration.
Then become the ladder
Of perfection.

6667.

Not I, but God in me
Is absolutely responsible
For my nature's total
   transformation.
Not God, but I myself
Have caused intolerable suffering
For both God the Creator
And God the creation.

6668.

My poor mind needs
Only one particular salvation:
Immediate relief from its
   self-declared war.

6669.

O my gold-shining mind,
I sincerely admire you.
O my diamond-distributing heart,
I sleeplessly need you.

6670.

To reach the summit of Heaven
I shall have to get
Either a sleepless cry-push from
   earth
Or a spotless smile-pull from
   Heaven.

6671.

Your head-knowledge
Must be transformed
If you want to be truly happy.
Your heart-wisdom
Must be continuously
    transcended
If you want to be perfectly perfect.

6672.

To meet God without an
    intermediary
May not be impossible,
But it is surely the loftiest
Mountain-climbing task.

6673.

Before God-realisation
No thought can be completely
    perfect.
After God-realisation
The reign of imperfect thought
    collapses.

6674.

Your heart will be shattered by
    sorrow
If you force it to live
In tomorrow's ephemeral
    imagination-world
Instead of in today's eternal
    Reality-Now.

6675.

Unhappy at being unhappy:
This is a deplorable human
    incident.
Happy at being happy:
This is a valuable divine
    experience.

6676.

Do not allow your doubting mind
To lord it over your God-loving
    heart.
Your God-loving heart
Is your unparalleled treasure.

6677.

Discard your worthless worries
As dirty, worn-out garments
If you never want to abandon
    yourself
To wild despair-disaster.

6678.

Time and space contradict each
    other
Because of my conscious
And deliberate unwillingness
To sing with time
And embrace space.

6679.

Two are the sublime contents
Of consciousness-height:
A self-giving existence-light
And a God-becoming
   oneness-delight.

6680.

Perfection must dawn
In your aspiration-cry.
If not, you can never succeed
In your inner journey.

6681.

Who can satisfy God
In God's own Way?
He who yearns to see
God's universal Reality-Delight
Inside His transcendental
   Vision-Light.

6682.

No torture
Is as excruciating
As your long-cherished
Self-doubt.

6683.

My consecrated heart stopped
Not only the cries
Of the descending man
But also his descent.
My liberated soul not only raised
   high,
Very high,
The life of the ascending man,
But also increased enormously
The beauty of his smile.

6684.

What I need
Is a soulfully receptive world
To hear
My heart's blue bird singing.

6685.

Why do you have to worry
Whether others cherish your
   talents,
As long as God cherishes them?
Why do you have to worry
Whether others please your heart,
As long as you please God's Heart?

6686.

At last you have made me truly
   happy
By confessing that your bitterness
Is all due to the fact
That others are enjoying
A life with no suffering.

6687.

Because he thinks and knows
That it is imperative
For us to change ourselves,
A supernal radiance
Has filled his face.

6688.

What is the meaning of life?
Perfection-flower.
What is the meaning of work?
Satisfaction-fragrance.

6689.

He who sincerely aspires
And soulfully serves,
Does not, cannot and will not
   retire.

6690.

How do you bind yourself?
Not with a rope
But by not appreciating
Others' divine qualities.

6691.

Nobody except your own soul
Has the right to tell you
What is right in front of your life,
What is right inside your life
And what is right above your life.

6692.

A seeker touches the abysmal
   abyss
Of foolishness
When he thinks and feels
That God's earth-intense
   Closeness
And His Heaven-free Closeness
Will remain a far cry.

6693.

My soul-bird loves my body-cage
Only when it is kept fit,
Pure and absolutely immaculate.

6694.

If you dare to breathe in
   ignorance-night
With no fear of being strangled,
How is it that you do not
Try to breathe in wisdom-delight
To be completely liberated?

6695.

Sweet was the sound-life
Before we accepted the life
Of self-giving spirituality.
But now extremely bitter is the
   sound-life,
For the silence-life has dawned
And is illumining our heart
   within
And our life without.

6696.

You will realise
That yours is a life of total futility
When your heart is completely
   empty
Of God's Promise-Light
And God's Satisfaction-Height.

6697.

Sincerity you need
Before you need humility.
Simplicity you need
Before you need sincerity.
God's Compassion-Divinity you
   need
Before you need simplicity.

6698.

A theoretical surrender-life
Is better than
A doubtful and unaspiring life.
A practical surrender-life
Is nothing other than
A cheerful
   God-manifestation-life.

6699.

Your earthly sojourn will be
   tortured
By sharp pangs,
If you fail to pray and meditate
With your heart's silence-joy.

6700.

What is the fare
From earth to Heaven?
The fragrance-beauty
Of a gratitude-heart.

6701.

God knows
That He has already accepted
Every problem of yours
Into His Compassion-Care.
But will you believe it?
Will you ever dare?

6702.

Unless you stop searching
For false teachers to deliver you,
You and your deliverance will remain
Like the North Pole and the South Pole,
Eternally at an unbridgeable distance.

6703.

Suicide is a fatal nourishment
And fulfilment
Of a cleverly unknowable temptation.

6704.

Finally my mind
Has made my life happy
By dropping all its disputes
With my life.

6705.

If you want to overcome an enemy,
Secretly think highly of him
And openly remain low.

6706.

In my heart
I never shall deny him.
But in my mind
I deny him vehemently
Because I have no other way
To enjoy my own imagined heights.

6707.

Soulfully pray
To submit yourself.
Lo, the summit has come down
To manifest itself through you.

6708.

Success is to have
Outer friends.
Progress is to discover
Your only Friend, your Inner Pilot.

6709.

What I do may not concern God,
But what I feel does concern God,
Always.

6710.

Faith is the art of seeing
Without looking.
Aspiration is the art of becoming
Without hesitating.

6711.

To have a pure mind
Is to have a newborn life,
And this newborn life
Will help you in countless ways.

6712.

No aspiration, no perfection.
No perfection, no manifested God.
No manifested God, no satisfied God.

6713.

He is great
Because he has read the powerful message
That is written in the sky.
He is good
Because he has become the soulful message
That is inscribed in his heart.

6714.

Consciously and sleeplessly
Steel your heart
Against the blighting hand
Of misfortune.

6715.

O my mind,
You must slow down immediately.
You must not interfere with
My heart's aspiration-cry.
It wants to reach my soul's height quickly.

6716.

When it comes to meditation,
Imagine the radiating sun,
And try to radiate like the sun,
Never ceasing, day or night.

6717.

An ignorant jealousy-mind
And a wise ecstasy-heart
Are two uncompromising
   neighbours.

6718.

You are great
If you think that you are
Of the strong.
You are good
If you feel that you are
For the weak.

6719.

The doubting mind's
   division-frown
Cannot remove
The illumined heart's
   oneness-crown.

6720.

My heart's gratitude-smile
Is the only thing that Heaven
Smilingly allows me to take with
   me
On my way to the higher worlds.

6721.

Adversity
Is a hidden opportunity.
Opportunity
Is my Lord's powerful Smile.
My Lord's Smile
Is the beginning of my
   perfection-life.

6722.

God's Compassion must come
   first,
Long before you can muster
All your faith-strength
   To realise Him.

6723.

My heart's aspiration-cry
Entirely depends on
My Lord's Compassion-Smile.

6724.

When your own sincerity
Satisfies your heart,
God's Compassion-Heart will
Immediately run towards you.

6725.

I shall discover what I have:
World-knowledge.
I shall become what I truly am:
God's Transcendence-Light.

6726.

A heart of pure hope
And a life of spontaneous
   cheerfulness
Can gloriously play together
Like cosmic gods.

6727.

I seek sincerity
Inside my mind's inexhaustible
   source.
I seek purity
Inside my heart's inexhaustible
   source.
I seek divinity
Inside my life's inexhaustible
   Source.

6728.

O my mind,
You are your own unqualified
Self-styled commitment
To truth-discovery
And God-manifestation.

6729.

By virtue of faith
If you want to see God's Face,
God will run after you
With His Heart of Love and
   Compassion
To speedily help you
In your inner journey.

6730.

Today God may whisper in your
   ear
How you can become a good
   seeker.
Tomorrow God will thunder
   before you
So that you will be compelled
To become a good seeker.

6731.

You are cherishing your doubts.
But I am telling you
That doubt is also cherishing you
And punishing you all the time.

6732.

You want to know the truth.
But make sure
You want to know the truth
To perfect yourself
And not to instruct others.

6733.

Your artificial life
Is an unconscious imitation
Of others' lives.
Your natural life
Is the spontaneous revelation
Of God the Life.

6734.

The same God who taught you
How to love Him
Will also teach others
How to love Him.
Therefore, you do not have to worry
About others.

6735.

To see the Face of God,
Do not pray to
God the Power
But meditate on
God the supreme Lover.

6736.

Heaven is always ready
To accept you,
But are you ready
To please Heaven
By running towards it immediately?

6737.

If you can correct
The doubter in you,
The Enjoyer in you
Will teach you and help you
To dance with Him
Immortality's Dance.

6738.

When you pray soulfully
And when you meditate powerfully,
Be careful of one thing:
Do not allow any uncomely thought
To capture your attention.

6739.

You are such a fool.
You think that only you,
And nobody else,
Know how to play successfully
The pretence-game.

6740.

Never forget one thing:
The Ultimate Truth is your friend
And not your enemy.

6741.

How can you fly
In the sky of joy
Unless your heart-bird
Has developed two purity-wings?

6742.

You do not have to be
   discouraged.
Just allow God-Compassion
To encourage you a little more.

6743.

A doubting mind
Is impurity's unlit cave.
A trusting heart
Is purity's sunlit palace.

6744.

If you are a sincere
   hero-worshipper,
Then easily you will be able to win
The Heart of God,
The Hero Supreme.

6745.

If you can crucify your desire-life,
You will be happy.
If you can purify your desire-life,
You will be happy, plus perfect.

6746.

An unaspiring life
Will eventually suffer
From the piercing arrows
Of destruction-night.

6747.

Each God-lover has a special
And beautiful soul-bird.
This bird has a soulful heart-wing
And a prayerful life-wing.

6748.

Because of your faith
In this world,
You were able to take birth
   happily.
Now if you can have faith
In the other world,
When your hour arrives you can
   die happily.

6749.

Your heart's bright faith
Should, can and will save you
From the world's
   fast-approaching
Doubt-volcano explosion.

6750.

God's three Silence-Instructions:
My mind must cry for peace,
My heart for oneness
And my life for perfection.

6751.

The best he has within him
Is his sincerity-river-heart.
The worst he has within him
Is his confusion-mountain-mind.

6752.

Do you ever care to know
That your very birth on earth
Is your perfect divinity
In supreme disguise?

6753.

Your great God-hunger
Is the only valid ticket
For your absolutely new
Satisfaction-life-journey.

6754.

Do not try to barter
Your life of constant
   contradictions
For God's transcendental
Life-transforming Smile.

6755.

If you really want to have
A satisfaction-day,
Then immediately cancel your
   friendship
With lethargy-night.

6756.

Ruthlessly destroy
Your mind's disbelief-net
If you want to receive
Your soul's divinity-message.

6757.

God is more than ready
To applaud your every forward
   step.
But are you truly happy
With your life's progress-light?

6758.

Walk in confidence-hope.
Look, the promise-land
Is eagerly awaiting
Your auspicious arrival.

6759.

You are your own abiding trust
In God.
God is His own abiding
Promise-Manifestation-Dream
In you.

6760.

His surrender-life moved many
To reform and transform their
    own lives.
His gratitude-heart moved God
To shed tears of Light and Delight.

6761.

I shall be more than happy
To agree with you
Since you are so remarkably brave
As to declare that you are without
    sin.

6762.

He has all kinds of trouble
With doubt in his mind,
But he has no trouble
With faith in his heart.

6763.

If you can once more live
A life of innocence,
Then God's constant Intimacy
Cannot hide from you.

6764.

To know him
Is to love him.
To study him
Is to be a very special instrument
Of God-Satisfaction.

6765.

A selfless being
Is by far
The greatest God-revealer.

6766.

A surrender-heart
In a purity-smile
Is divinity's imperishable
Protection-shield.

6767.

O God-lover,
Do stand before me.
O world-thinker,
Do stand behind me.

6768.

In the inner world
There is no such thing
As spiritual greed
Or excessive appetite.

6769.

Do not build your life
Upon the hope-sands
Given to you by others.

6770.

Unless you consciously surrender
To God's Will
Soulfully, smilingly and
   unconditionally,
Your desire-life will, without fail,
Continue to plant impurity-seeds
Inside your heart-garden.

6771.

The length of your
Perfection-achievements
Entirely depends on
Your Lord's unreserved
Compassion-Enlightenment.

6772.

Allow everything else to vanish
Save and except your cherished
   dreams,
For your cherished dreams
Are treasured sleeplessly
By God Himself.

6773.

You are a Vision-Reality of God.
Alas, you are completely unaware
   of it.
What is worse,
You never have any longing
For God's eternal
   Satisfaction-Smile.
Therefore, are you not a miserable
   failure
In God's creation-awakening
   Vision?

6774.

It is your inexhaustible energy
That will grant you the capacity
To consciously cry for
God the Perfection
And consciously smile with
God the Satisfaction.

6775.

Nothing will remain unchanged.
Even your wild, restless vital
Some day and somehow
Will be brought under control
By your soul's indomitable will.
Just wait and see.

6776.

What you have
Is a sleepless sky above you.
What you have
Is a spotless moon within you.
What you have
Is a rising perfection-sun before you.

6777.

What I want to see
Is a happy oneness-marriage
Between earth's ascending aspiration-cry
And Heaven's descending satisfaction-smile.

6778.

Your lack of enthusiasm
In your spiritual life
Will cause your unparalleled destruction.
Enthusiasm is the road
That is eagerly waiting to serve you.
Accept its service immediately, O runner,
And run and run with a gratitude-heart!

6779.

There is only one way
To strengthen the feeble
And that is to consciously place
Your concern-will for them
At the Lotus-Feet of your Beloved Supreme.

6780.

Because you are an art-lover,
God is happily teaching you
How to see Him as the Supreme Artist
And also how to place Him
Before the art-world
Of man's quenchless thirst
For beauty's breath.

6781.

Each soulful song
Sung by humanity
Will touch the Ecstasy-Heart
Of the Inner Pilot.

6782.

You were a fool when you wanted
To discover others inside your
   heart,
Rather than inside God's Heart.
Now you are a pioneer
Because you are discovering
The ever-changing,
   ever-transcending
And ever-illumining vision-dawn
Within your own heart.

6783.

In the battlefield of life
Do you know what saved me?
My life's cheerfully surrendered
Helplessness.

6784.

God does not approve of
My entertaining you.
Therefore, I shall not
Explain my life to you.

6785.

If you have really accepted
The spiritual life,
That means you have already
   decided:
"Not my choice but my Master's,
Not my voice but my Master's."

6786.

My thinking-power
Cannot understand you.
My understanding-power
Cannot love you.
My loving-power
Cannot transform you.
Therefore, how can I be so stupid
As to tell you
That I shall be responsible
For your perfection?

6787.

As long as your mind
Loves inspiration,
As long as your heart
Loves aspiration,
As long as your life
Loves dedication,
You do not have to worry
About anything else.

6788.

Do not kill yourself worrying
About false teachers.
Your sincerity-shield will protect
   you
And also definitely help you
Find a real teacher.

6789.

Why do I invite God
To come and visit me every day?
I invite Him precisely because
He is my life's very old Friend
And my soul's only Friend.

6790.

My heart's belief
Is my life's strength.
And my Compassion-Lord
Always takes care of
My life's strength.

6791.

I have changed my mind.
It now really needs God.
I have changed my heart.
It now really wants God,
And God alone,
In God's own Way.

6792.

Soulfully tell your heart
What you need.
Powerfully tell your mind
What you want.

6793.

When unconsciously you treasure
Your hopeless life,
Consciously your soul suffers
From a helpless reality.

6794.

My self-deception means
My deliberate revolt
Against my Lord's universal
Oneness-Satisfaction.

6795.

God loves me
When I need Him.
Humanity loves me
When it needs me.

6796.

I believe,
Therefore I exist.
I exist,
Therefore my Lord Supreme
Has confidence in His own
  creation.

6797.

I have found another way
To walk along the path of
  aspiration
And another way
To please my Lord Supreme:
The self-giving way.

6798.

Do not be discouraged
And disheartened!
I can clearly see
That you have many
Good and important things to do
Both for God the Creator
And God the creation.

6799.

Alas, my mind is afraid
Of choosing God,
My heart is afraid
Of inviting God
And my life is afraid
Of loving God.

6800.

Do not follow me.
Follow the eternal runner
Who is running along Eternity's
  Road.
And who is that eternal runner?
The eternally awakened God-lover
  in you.

6801.

My Lord,
May I make it
My only satisfaction-ocean
To do immediately
All the things that You command.

6802.

Who wants to prolong a useless
Marathon discussion
With humanity's unwilling
And unaspiring mind?

6803.

Imagination
Is birthless and deathless.
Its power
Is inexhaustible.

6804.

His disproportionately overgrown
Doubt-mind
Has sent a tornado of fear
To his hope-heart.

6805.

How can you have
Even an iota of trust
If you so obstinately adhere
To your giant mistrust?

6806.

Your imagination-dawn does not create
Your golden future.
It is your aspiration-day that creates
Your golden future.

6807.

I do not care to know
What will happen to my stupid mind
If it does not surrender
To my wise heart.

6808.

The dust of my Lord's Feet
Gives me the unparalleled faith
To brush aside
My teeming self-doubts.

6809.

Unravel the tangles of your mind
To travel with your soul
In God's Immortality-Country.

6810.

If you can flatter yourself
With self-love,
Then you can easily lie
To God.

6811.

Your heart is under
No obligation
To fear the monster-doubts
That your mind has created.

6812.

I wish to live always
In the adamantine security
Of God's choicest God-Hour.

6813.

An express train
Of consecutive great ideas
Has brought me to my Himalayan
　goal:
The sleepless service of humanity.

6814.

A shout of success
He wants.
A song of progress
He needs.

6815.

My heart loves
Your sincerity-drops,
But it does not need
Your stupidity-flood.

6816.

I am happy
Because my mind
Is shock-proof.
I am happy
Because my heart
Is despair-proof.

6817.

My mind's
Insecurity-thought-children
Will not leave my heart
In peace.

6818.

Easily you can exhaust
Your heart's gratitude,
But not your mind's ingratitude.

6819.

His stupendous self-devoted love
Does not allow him to receive
The life-transforming Love
From Above.

6820.

Simplicity, sincerity, humility,
Purity and divinity:
A series of man's gradual
God-approaching ascents.

6821.

You are a genius.
So what?
Unless your heart is precious to
　God,
I shall never need you.

6822.

What is my despair-heart
Gazing at?
It is gazing at the unmistakable
Statue of death.

6823.

My mind has at last admitted
That it has not thought of God
  enough.
My heart has always admitted
That it can never think of God
  enough.

6824.

Each daily prayer of mine
Is a sincere God-adorer.
Each daily meditation of mine
Is a pure God-lover.

6825.

God is inside my heart.
I have seen Him there.
Now let me look for Him
Inside my mind,
In case He happens to be there,
  too.

6826.

My humility-light
Is the direct
And immediate result
Of my sincerity-cry.

6827.

O earth's orphan-cries,
You belong to me.
O Heaven's emperor-smiles,
I belong to you.

6828.

Father, my Father Supreme,
Do give me a guileless
Morning prayer.
Father, my Father Supreme,
Do give me a thought-free
Evening meditation.

6829.

God is always fond
Of climbing down
Man's obedience-tree.

6830.

My prayer unmistakably means
My preparation.
My meditation inevitably means
The start of my Eternity's
    conscious journey.

6831.

I was totally mistaken
When I thought I loved God
Unconditionally.
I was completely mistaken
When I thought God did not need
    me
At all.

6832.

God is eagerly waiting
To demolish my fault-tower.
But what can He do,
Since I am not ready to believe
In His Mercy-Power?

6833.

Three things every day I need:
The inspiration of giving,
The aspiration of becoming,
The realisation of loving.

6834.

When we worship
We sincerely feel
That there is no need
For us to have any warship.

6835.

All I need to know
Is if my heart's cry for God
Is completely genuine.

6836.

Dedication
My Lord needs from me.
Perfection
I need from myself.

6837.

O earth, my earth,
I shall pray to God
Soulfully.
Do not worry about me.
O Heaven, my Heaven,
I shall serve the God in man
Devotedly.
Do not worry about me.

6838.

My Lord and I constantly argue
With each other.
My Lord tells me I *can*,
And I tell my Lord I *can't*.

6839.

This time my soul
Has come back to the world
With a more sublime promise
To God.

6840.

What is my surrender-delight?
The compass to guide me
To my Beloved Unknown.

6841.

His mind carefully watches.
His heart soulfully waits.
His soul peacefully smiles.

6842.

My Lord,
Do release me
From the endless round
Of bitter failure-memories.

6843.

Alas, there is a yawning gulf
Between your imagined self
And the Truth of the Beyond.

6844.

Each man
Is an information-expert.
Each angel
Is an illumination-expert.

6845.

Try to maintain
Your heart's beauty
In spite of your mind's
Disheartening uncomeliness.

6846.

Do not quote me
When I say,
"I am not God."
Quote me
When I say,
"No matter what you and I do,
God always loves us
Unconditionally."

6847.

When God gives you His soulful
    Smile
And His powerful Blessing,
Do not feel your role is over.
You must now carefully preserve
What you have received from God,
Or it will all vanish.

6848.

Your aspiration, dedication,
    surrender
And gratitude
Bring you measureless Heavenly
    treasures.
Alas, so often you carelessly lose
Your hard-earned inner wealth.
So often you foolishly squander
God's precious Blessings.

6849.

He was struck
By the sudden realisation
That the worst disaster
Is the heart's loneliness.

6850.

How can I possibly forgive
My mind
When it has dashed
My heart's dreams
To pieces?

6851.

God's Satisfaction in God's own
    Way:
This, indeed, is the only thing
That is always worth treasuring
In your aspiration-heart
And your dedication-life.

6852.

His useless mind
And his helpless heart
Are the fragments
Of his shattered past.

6853.

Your doubting mind is fully
    responsible
For the loss of your heart's lustre
And the loss of your soul's rapture.

6854.

God has forgiven him.
Whether or not he wants
God's Forgiveness
Is altogether a different matter,
A totally unimportant thing.

6855.

His hopes are soaring
And his promises are manifesting
For the first time in years.

6856.

To combat your mind's confusion
Open your heart's door
And gather strength
From its inmate: your soul.

6857.

I am sure my ancestors
Have not suffered as much as I
From the self-destructive disaster:
Doubt.

6858.

Dauntlessly he said good-bye
To his past despair-life.
Soulfully he is saying hello
To his future hope-life.

6859.

I have two constant visitors:
My eternally doubting mind
And
My infinitely forgiving God.

6860.

Because I am not a real
And divine friend to myself,
I cannot get rid of my unwanted
And constant companion:
Fear.

6861.

If you correct yourself,
God will gladly direct Himself
To you.

6862.

Death is at once
The end of the body's
Old journey
And the beginning of the soul's
New journey.

6863.

A life of surrender
May seem like a bitter medicine,
But it is by far
The best oneness-remedy.

6864.

Two things he does not know:
Where his love of sincerity
Has gone
And where God's bright
    Satisfaction
Has gone.

6865.

With my prayer
I have bound God mercilessly.
With my meditation
I am slowly and steadily
Liberating God.

6866.

My duty is
The Voice of God
And the smile of Heaven.

6867.

How to change your world?
Just commit fewer mistakes
And smile heartily.

6868.

When you sing, remember,
You are singing for those
Who appreciate you
And not for those
Who criticise you.

6869.

My prayer is a dark road
For the beggar in me to walk on.
My meditation is a sunlit road
For the prince in me to march
    along.

6870.

A flood of joy
Comes to my mind
Not only when I least expect it
But also when I least deserve it.

6871.

A self-giving heart
Will, without fail,
Win what it so rightly deserves.

6872.

I offered my Lord
My mind full of facts.
My Lord gladly accepted it and
    said:
"I shall treasure your head.
Now I am offering you
My Heart full of Love.
Accept it and treasure it
In the same sincere way
That I shall treasure your mind."

6873.

A dedication-life
Likes to prove
The immortality of oneness-love.

6874.

To have a gratitude-heart
Is a supreme art
That we all must learn.

6875.

The mind needs
A listening ear.
The heart needs
Another receiving heart.

6876.

An ambition-mind
Hates comparison.
An aspiration-heart
Needs no comparison.

6877.

Humility is the conscious
    expansion
Of our vastness.
On the strength of our inner
    oneness
With God's entire creation,
We use our humility-light.

6878.

If the father does not reach down,
His child cannot receive anything
    from him.
It is the father's
    oneness-compassion
That compels him to reach down.

6879.

Humility is not humiliation.
Just as a tree is not humiliated
When it bows down
To offer its fruits,
Even so, by showing humility
We offer the best in ourselves
To humanity.

6880.

If we do not have humility,
It is because inwardly
We have nothing to give.

6881.

As a mother reaches down
To offer a fruit to her child,
Even so, God the Infinite
Reaches down to offer Himself
To the finite.

6882.

When God reaches down
To touch the finite,
We call it Compassion.
When man bows down
In self-offering to humanity,
We call it humility.

6883.

Keep all your meditation-wealth
Safe inside your heart-wallet.
Then when you are attacked by fear,
Doubt, anxieties or worries,
Just bring forward the peace, joy and love
Which you have safeguarded.

6884.

His prayer is thoughtless,
His meditation is soulless.
Therefore, his outer life
Is denied earthly success,
And his inner life
Is denied Heavenly progress.

6885.

O Heaven, my Heaven,
I shall once more renew my promise:
I shall never disobey you.
O earth, my earth,
I shall once more renew my promise:
I shall ever love you.

6886.

The Master's fruitful answers
To his children's soulful questions
Are as meaningful to them
As their highest meditation,
For his answers convince
Their physical mind
Of the messages they receive
From their spiritual heart.

6887.

Two earth-born companions of mine:
Desire-cry and bondage-tear.
Two Heaven-born companions of mine:
Aspiration-smile and freedom-dance.

6888.

Heaven does not want
To correspond with me,
For my heart is wanting
In purity-flames.
Earth does not want
To correspond with me,
For my mind is wanting
In certainty-light.

6889.

His choice of peace
Sleeplessly gives him
A voice of love.

6890.

Today's struggling heart
Is, without fail, going to become
Tomorrow's beckoning hand.

6891.

In the inner world
I can have sunshine every day,
For my inner faith is founded upon
God's infallible Promise-Light.

6892.

From his morning thought
He comes to learn
That life is a love-pretending snare.
From his evening thought
He comes to learn
That love is life illumined.

6893.

Your faith in yourself
Works only after you think.
Your faith in God
Works long before you dream.

6894.

You just think
Of your own aspiration-flame.
God has already started meditating
To grant you a realisation-sun.

6895.

The prayer that soars above
Unlocks the perfection-door for
 you.
The mind that dives within
Shows you the satisfaction-room.

6896.

If you want to live
Beyond the snare of doubt,
Then stay in the freedom-sky
Of your blossoming heart.

6897.

To the unawakened earth
My message is:
"I shall be for you."
To the illumined Heaven
My message is:
"I shall be with you."

6898.

You will see your heart's inner
 bird
Singing and soaring
Beyond your expectation-summit,
If you can allow
Your heart's morning star
To beckon your outer life.

6899.

Congratulations!
Your doubting mind has finally
 exploded.
Today you have made your inner
 world
Really happy, supremely happy.

6900.

Between sunrise and sunset
He has only one silent
Express train of thought:
"I love God the man only,
I serve man the God only."

6901.

My Lord,
Without You I may at most
Try to be good,
But with You
I am perfectly perfect.

6902.

Time's wild flood is rising
Because you have befriended
Your impure mind's dark doubts.

6903.

Today's keen pangs of separation
May turn into tomorrow's
Stupendously illumining
Oneness-satisfaction.

6904.

Each earth-bound
Human breath
Is a never-fading
Desire.

6905.

I love You, my Lord,
Not because of what
You are going to do for me,
But because of what You are
In Your Eternity's Vision-Delight.

6906.

My Lord,
You have made me Your friend.
Can You not make me Your slave instead,
To give me more joy?

6907.

Two unimaginably valuable things
You may never recapture:
Your sincerity's cry
And your humility's smile.

6908.

I am,
Not because I do.
I am,
Because my heart sleeplessly cries
And my life breathlessly smiles.

6909.

My life's chief concern
Is to wait soulfully
For God's choice God-Hour.

6910.

Alas, there are so many
Unbridgeable misunderstandings
Between man's binding desire-life
And his liberating aspiration-life.

6911.

An experience-life
Is beautiful.
A realisation-life
Is fruitful.
A satisfaction-life
Is divinely beautiful,
Supremely fruitful
And absolutely perfect.

6912.

God has taught me
How to work.
I am begging Him to teach me
How to continue.

6913.

Our outer
　intelligence-conversation
Is artificial.
Our inner
　intuition-communication
Is always beautiful.

6914.

My good fortune's greatest smile
Is the blue depth
Of my heart's golden sky.

6915.

The human in me
Helplessly calls it compulsion.
The divine in me
Lovingly calls it liberation.

6916.

On the whole
I do not hate anybody,
But I do have a deep-rooted hatred
For power-hungry human
　authority.

6917.

My Lord Supreme tells me
How I can either receive Him
　soulfully
Or deceive Him successfully.

6918.

If you make greatness your
　companion,
You may suffer.
If you make goodness your
　companion,
You will not only prosper
But you will also have God
As your Companion.

6919.

My Lord Supreme,
Do tell me once again
Why You love my heart
And why You need my life.

6920.

Alas, how is it possible for Heaven
To disown my human breath?
Alas, how is it possible for earth
To disown my divine life?

6921.

Deliberately
My mind doubts.
Helplessly
My heart suffers.

6922.

Heaven is cruel.
Therefore, it delays
My God-realisation.
Earth is ignorant.
Therefore, it delays
My God-manifestation.

6923.

When I was about to fall down
From the wisdom-tree,
My Lord's Compassion-Eye
   caught me
Lovingly and powerfully.

6924.

My mind does not want to
   unlearn.
Therefore, I am suffering
From the worst flood
Of ignorance-torture.

6925.

You call it
A mere hesitation.
I call it
Your armour of suspicion.

6926.

At first the enormity of truth
May bewilder you.
But later the divinity of truth
Will illumine you.

6927.

His all-loving heart
Sincerely dislikes wrestling
With his all-doubting mind.

6928.

You want abiding happiness,
Yet you do not want to surmount
The mountain-barriers
Of your confusion-enjoying mind.

6929.

Do you know why I cannot aspire?
I cannot aspire because of
Heaven's sleepless indifference
And
Earth's shameless interference.

6930.

What is the difference
Between a complicated mind
And contradictory thoughts?
No difference, none!

6931.

To please my Lord Supreme
Every day I shall cry
With earth's heart
And every day I shall smile
With Heaven's soul.

6932.

As the human mind is the master
Of useless swiftness,
Even so, the divine heart is the master
Of useful fulness.

6933.

My mind consciously enjoys
Reckless confidence.
My heart smilingly enjoys
Doubtless confidence.

6934.

His mind is permanently employed
By the owner of doubt-factory:
Ignorance-king.

6935.

O earth, from you
I do not need anything more
Than a few comforting words.
O Heaven, from you
I do not need anything more
Than an illumining message.

6936.

What will you do
With your random flood of words?
Live instead in your silence-heart,
For your Silence-Lover: God.

6937.

What has betrayed me?
No, not my teeming doubts,
Not my Himalayan pride,
But my eyeless unwillingness.

6938.

Alas, I am not ready
With my receptivity,
But God is all ready
With His Infinity.

6939.

Alas, what I have
Is a greedy mind
And what I am
Is a starving heart.

6940.

My Lord granted me
His Compassion-Smile
Long before I even wished
To deserve it.

6941.

If God can be
His own Goodness,
I can at least try to be
My own soulfulness.

6942.

What I need
Is a desert of thought
And a mountain of will-power.

6943.

My Lord,
My heart has only one question
To ask You:
Will it have the capacity
To satisfy You eventually?

6944.

The moment I touch
My Lord's Protection-Feet,
My Lord's Compassion-Eye gives chase
To my roaming thoughts.

6945.

The beauty of human perfection
Is the unparalleled necessity
Of human aspiration.

6946.

Either defy or deny
Your sombre past
If you wish God to certify
Your heart's present smile.

6947.

Every day there is only
One thing to learn:
How to be honestly happy.

6948.

God's Heart has a special love
For him
Because he has unconditionally
    placed
His heart at God's Feet.

6949.

Two things God wants
To do for you cheerfully:
He wants to celebrate
Your mind's self-mastery,
And He wants to celebrate
Your heart's God-discovery.

6950.

My heart's only unfailing desire
Is to remain perpetually a
    God-lover,
A perfect stranger
To the world of fame.

6951.

My mind never dares
To wander
Inside my heart's
Will-power-garden.

6952.

I may not be helpful to you,
But I shall always be hopeful
For your success-life
And progress-heart.

6953.

Although my mind is useless,
Although my heart is worthless,
Although my life is soulless,
I shall not give up,
Never!

6954.

Let me see who can and will
Answer my two questions:
Why do I still love man
When he secretly thinks so poorly
   of me?
Why do I not think of God
When He openly speaks so highly
   of me?

6955.

Your mind's bondage-night
You must defy
If you want to enjoy
Your heart's freedom-sky.

6956.

You may offend my mind's pride,
But my heart shall always
Defend your right to do so.

6957.

I carry only one thing:
My Lord's sleepless Smile.
My Lord carries only one thing:
My shadowless satisfaction.

6958.

My heart's sacred flame
Sings only one song:
Earth's self-transcendence-song.

6959.

When my teeming doubts
And my tormenting fears
Are in collusion,
Frustration becomes my outer
   name
And destruction becomes my
   inner name.

6960.

Your mind-boat is plying
Between criticism-shore
And cynicism-shore.

6961.

I bow to the light
That never dims.
I bow to the delight
That never fades.

6962.

If you wage war against fear,
You are divinely great.
If you wage war against doubt,
You are supremely good.

6963.

You do not have to seek
Your mind's
　imperfection-impurity.
Your mind's
　imperfection-impurity
Will inevitably find you.

6964.

Another opportunity-smile
God has granted me today
To meditate on Him
　unconditionally.

6965.

If your heartbeats cling
To God's Golden Boat,
Then your life will never sink.

6966.

May all my achievements,
Good and bad,
Die of inattention.

6967.

He is his mind's inner poverty.
No wonder his outer life
Is a barren desert.

6968.

I have already gone
To the very end
Of the world's doubt-voyage.
Now I am going back
To the very beginning
Of my faith-voyage.

6969.

Two unnecessary questions:
Does God love me?
Do I need God?

6970.

I am crying inside
My sincerity-heart
To humble the pride
Of my haughty intellect.

6971.

Since your heart
Is not used to deception,
Your life will before long
Be granted perfection.

6972.

Your simplicity-mind-tree
Must not bend.
Your sincerity-heart-tree
Must not break.

6973.

Alas,
His heart's silence-smile
Has been chased away
By his mind's reckless thoughts.

6974.

The thoughts that nestle
Inside his searching mind
Are pure, man-loving
And God-serving.

6975.

Celestial compassion-moon
My aspiration-heart today
Again and again implores.

6976.

His searching mind
May be obscure,
But his aspiring heart
Is revelation itself.

6977.

I think of God
Because I know I need Him.
God thinks of me
Because of my wisdom-filled need.

6978.

A cynic does not walk alone.
He walks with his monstrous eye
And murderous tongue.

6979.

Keep on steering straight ahead.
The Golden Shore will not
Be denied you.

6980.

My mind is destined to become
The morning's deep glow.
My heart is destined to become
The sun's golden lustre.

6981.

To me,
Each heavy thought
Is an unanswerable
Plus unpardonable question.

6982.

Each beautiful thought
Comes from a far-off land,
Cradled by God's compassionate
Vision-Eye.

6983.

My heart is exactly the place
Where yesterday I saw my Lord,
The Satisfaction-Giver.

6984.

If you are brave enough
To sing through darkness,
Then light will sing through you
And for you.

6985.

Each human mind
Is a demanding question.
Each divine heart
Is a loving answer.

6986.

On earth I expected to see
The same God I knew in Heaven,
My soul's God.
But instead what I see here
Is my mind's newly-invented God,
The Science-God.

6987.

How can you expect to see
Your heart's silvery beams
Under your mind's gathering
   shadow?

6988.

My heart is gazing into
Tomorrow's distance-light.
It is empty of even
A speck of fear.

6989.

My mind wants to be satisfied
With astonishment.
My heart wants to be satisfied
With enlightenment.

6990.

Your mind's
Lack of enthusiasm
And your heart's
Lack of determination
Will, before long,
Cripple your spiritual life.

6991.

Is there no greater purpose
For your existence
Than mere thinking and
   brooding?

6992.

The hallucination-foundation
Of his outer life-tower cracked
When he saw that his grandiose achievements
Were nothing short of painful imperfections.

6993.

If your heart is not
With me,
That means your mind
Is against me.

6994.

Each beautiful and soulful morning
Is the haven
Of my thirsty and hungry hopes.

6995.

From Nothingness-Fulness
We came.
To Fulness-Nothingness
We shall retire.

6996.

The desire-bound world
Is not for my aspiring heart.
The aspiration-free world
Is not for my desiring vital.

6997.

The swiftness of his own uncomely thoughts
Not only puzzles his mind
But also weakens his heart.

6998.

My heart does love God
And my mind does need God:
Now is the moment of certainty.

6999.

His aspiration-heart bitterly cries
When his mind is engulfed
By endless thoughts.

7000.

My heart tells me
That I have not offered anything
To my Lord's Heart
Unless and until
I have placed everything
At my Lord's Feet.

7001.

A single God-Touch
From God's Compassion-Height
Can transform man's
   unimaginable
And countless weaknesses
Into God's own infinite,
Immortal and omnipotent Power.

7002.

His mind failed to help him
Be a God-thinker,
But his heart helped him
Become a God-lover.

7003.

Go beyond yourself.
Ecstasy-sky is all ready
To receive you.

7004.

Transcend the mind.
Your life will immediately
Have a new meaning:
Perfect satisfaction.

7005.

Do not fear.
He who fears cannot stay near
God's Compassion-Eye
And God's Forgiveness-Feet.

7006.

My success-light learns from me
About the stillness of the mind.
I learn from my progress-delight
About the universal oneness
Of existence-height.

7007.

My mind likes
Opinion-gongs.
My heart loves
Liberation-songs.

7008.

Your mind is responsible
For your own success-train.
Your heart is responsible
For the world's progress-boat.

7009.

You should say
What you want to say.
You must become
What you want to become.
Just say no
To the ridiculous demands of others.
Just become
A self-giving instrument of God.

7010.

By helping the undeserving,
You cannot make them worthy
Of Heaven's Delight.

7011.

My Lord Supreme does not mind
My total unfitness.
He cares only for
My cheerful willingness.

7012.

Negate what you proudly know.
Propagate what you soulfully are.
You will definitely please God.

7013.

Just to say
That you are going to commence
Is itself a striking commencement
Of your life's very long journey.

7014.

The perfection of an old cry
In my heart
Is the realisation of a new smile
In my life.

7015.

Why should I be embarrassed
To try something new in my life?
Who knows,
My newness may turn out to be
Another name for my universal oneness.

7016.

You are not thinking at all.
Therefore, you are not moving.
He is thinking too much.
Therefore, he is moving
   backward.
I am thinking neither too little
Nor too much.
I am just surrendering myself
To my Inner Pilot.
Therefore, the human in me is
   succeeding
And the divine in me is
   progressing.

7017.

O my mind,
Do anything else you want,
But please do not try
To hide yourself
From my heart's concern.

7018.

There are only two superior ways
To realise God:
My life's surrender-way
And my heart's gratitude-way.

7019.

I shall not cry for my satisfaction.
That is my Lord's Task.
I shall cry for my perfection.
Indeed, that is my task,
My only task.

7020.

My outer frustration
Is desperately looking for
Its lost friend:
My inner satisfaction.

7021.

My closeness-promise
Is my right action.
My oneness-hope
Is my perfect action.

7022.

To feel God's Presence
Inside your heart
Is to forget the long-sought
   fulfilment
Of your desire-life.

7023.

Self-examination has two other names:
Self-perfection
And
God-satisfaction.

7024.

As I can see
What I know,
Even so, I must become
More than I know.

7025.

Self-deception-experience
I did not need.
Even then, I had it.
Self-liberation-realisation
I do need.
And just because I need it
I shall have it.

7026.

God has already started meditating
On your life's fulness.
Look, you have not even started thinking
Of your heart's soulfulness.

7027.

Who has instigated you
To immigrate
To unreality's dream-land?
Not God, but somebody else!

7028.

By seeing what you have seen,
I shall see the Compassion-Eye
Of God.
By becoming what you have become,
I shall become the perfection-instrument
Of God.

7029.

If I can correct
My thought-train,
God will immediately grant me
His own Perfection-Plane
To fly all over
His entire creation.

7030.

Today's problems are torturing you
Mercilessly.
Tomorrow's problems, do not invite!
Who knows, they may bring with them
The message of your unwanted
But inescapable and premature
Death.

7031.

My Lord,
Save my vital and free my mind
From the dangerously contagious disease:
Sadness.

7032.

If you have a beauty-mind
And a purity-heart,
Then you can participate
In the soul's freedom-game.

7033.

In my mind's descent-life,
No news is good news.
In my heart's ascent-life,
No news is sad news.

7034.

Every morning in the inner world
I look for and long for
Only one thing:
Hope-news.

7035.

My definition of man:
Self-congratulation.
My definition of God:
Oneness-Satisfaction.

7036.

In the inner world
I have written many books.
But one book I shall never write
And that is the book called
"Doubt-torture."

7037.

Bury the desire-prince
Of your vital
If you want to be really happy
As a perfect satisfaction-king.

7038.

There is only one thing
We can easily do
Without being taught,
And that is to fly desire-kites.

7039.

Two unavoidable consequences
Of your doubt-life:
You lose your beauty's eyes;
You lose your purity's heart.

7040.

My Lord,
I wish to tell You that I know,
Beyond the slightest doubt,
That I have become a perfect
    victim
To my own exhaustion-mind.

7041.

At last I have written
A long-neglected letter
To my Lord Supreme
Giving Him this special message:
Mine will soon be the life
Of unconditional surrender.

7042.

Infinity's eternal soul-melodies
Are what I wish to have
Deep within me.

7043.

Unless you are first a dreamer,
How can you become a darer?
Impossible!

7044.

Today's teeming demands
Are simply killing you.
Why do you have to think
Of tomorrow's countless
    demands,
You abysmal fool?

7045.

No desire-bound outer hope
Can be forbidden.
No aspiration-free inner hope
Can be smitten.

7046.

My outer world does not know
What I inwardly wanted,
But it does know what I now have:
A weeping defeat.

7047.

My heart
Cannot and will not stay
With defeated dreams.

7048.

Each human being pines
For an immortal life
But, alas, is forced to live
With mortal hopes.

7049.

Fears are great liars.
Do not allow them
To lead your eyes
And guide your life.

7050.

Since you can enjoy
Either ignorance-sleep
Or wisdom-awakening,
Make your life's choice
Here and now!

7051.

Indeed,
I am fond of many things.
But I am extremely fond of
Beauty's song in the morning sun
And purity's dance in the evening
    sky.

7052.

Unless you stop climbing
The ladder of earth's ambition,
You will not be able to climb
The ladder of Heaven's
    illumination.

7053.

God does not want you to die.
He only wants your
    depression-night
To die.

7054.

Satisfaction-lion
Will postpone its visit
Because aspiration-deer
Has not yet started its journey.

7055.

Intruding thoughts, stop!
Interfering mind, stop!
Fearful heart, stop!
Illumining soul, start!

7056.

Transcendental heights
Are always founded upon
God's indispensable
Vision-spreading Depths.

7057.

You do not have to hurry
God's Hour.
God Himself will hurry it.
You just make your aspiration
More intense
And your dedication
More immense.

7058.

Frequent visits
Of depression-night
Are nothing other than
Premature introductions to death.

7059.

The path of the unillumined
Is so narrow
That the illumined cannot
    proceed along it
To spread the light
Of aspiration-flames.

7060.

My Lord,
I have not forgotten You
Even for the first time.
Will You not for all time
Remember me?

7061.

There was a time
When I wanted to enjoy God's
    Fellowship
Only to become
An extremely important member
Of God's cosmic Society.
Now I enjoy God's Fellowship
Only to unlearn
What the ignorant world
Has taught me forcefully
Over the years.
There shall come a time
When I shall enjoy God's
    Fellowship
Only to offer to the world at large
One message in supreme silence:
Just because God knows
What we truly are,
He needs us infinitely more
Than we need Him.

7062.

My Lord Supreme
Has liberated my soul.
My soul is trying
To liberate my heart.
But because of my heart's
Fear of vastness and oneness,
My soul is finding it
An extremely difficult task.

7063.

My heart knows
It is not liberated.
Therefore, it does not try
To liberate my mind.
But my clever mind
Wants to liberate my restless vital,
In spite of knowing
That it is not liberated itself.

7064.

My vital, like my mind,
Is far, far away from liberation.
Yet it shamelessly and falsely feels
That its restless and destructive
  qualities
Are the signs of liberation.
Therefore it wants to liberate my
  body,
Which is also enveloped by
  inconscience.

7065.

Before, I felt the human necessity
Of solving my problems
All by myself.
Now I feel the divine necessity
Of invoking God's Compassion,
Forgiveness and Concern
To solve all my problems for me.
There shall come a time
When I shall feel the supreme
  necessity
Of bringing to the fore
My unreserved surrender-life
And my unconditional
  gratitude-heart
While simultaneously invoking
The Presence of my Beloved
  Supreme
To solve all my life's teeming
  problems.

7066.

To me, earthly power
Is no peace.
To me, Heavenly joy
Is no peace.
To me, my Lord's daily
  Satisfaction-Smile
Is the only peace.

7067.

God's Smile is the victory
Of today's man.
Man's smile is the Victory
Of Eternity's God.

7068.

My vision-eye is the sanctuary
Of the unborn creation
Of my Lord Supreme.
My realisation-reality is the sanctuary
Of the Perfection-Satisfaction-Message

Of my Lord's ever-transcending
Light and Delight of the Beyond.

7069.

Two disasters he has inherited
From his many ignorance-lives:
A doubting mind
And
An unaspiring heart.

7070.

How can you break
Your impurity-enemy's resistance?
Just imagine your heart
Bathing in the soul-light
Of your purity-dawn.

7071.

When I live inside my hurtful mind,
I see all around me
Nothing but bitterness.
When I live inside my prayerful heart,
I see all around me
Nothing but sweetness.
When I live inside my blossoming soul,
I see all around me
Nothing but God's continuous Fondness
For me.
When I live inside my Lord Supreme,
I see and feel all around me
Only one thing:
God's sleepless Oneness with me.

7072.

God creates.
My heart discovers.
My mind distrusts.

7073.

Enthusiasm and success
Are immediate neighbours.
Aspiration and perfection
Are immediate neighbours.

7074.

Each time you fall
It is a human experience.
Each time you rise
It is a divine realisation.

7075.

For your true self
There is no need to hide.
For your false self
There is no place to hide.

7076.

Those who know the truth
And those who distribute the
   truth
Are apostles of earth's perfection
And Heaven's satisfaction.

7077.

First try to know God,
And then try to know your mind.
First try to silence your mind,
And then think of feeling my
   heart.

7078.

If your heart becomes
The beauty's morn,
Then God will become
Your victory's horn.

7079.

Enthusiasm has success
In it.
Enthusiasm is progress
In itself.

7080.

What I need is
A God-climbing heart
And not
A God-manufacturing mind.

7081.

I shall no more roam
In my mind's unlit jungle.
I now clearly see
And soulfully admire
The blossoming of my
   heart-flower.

7082.

Each good and inspiring thought
Easily unlocks
Heaven's will-power-door.

7083.

If your mind continues
To harbour wrong thoughts,
You cannot reclaim
Your life's divinity.

7084.

My prayer unheard
Is a soulful dream.
My prayer heard
Is a powerful reality.

7085.

The sunshine-hope
In man's aspiration-heart
Will last for a very long time,
For the heart of mankind
Is a deep, conscious and
Promise-treasuring core.

7086.

The higher nature commands
The birth of
A very new life.
The lower nature demands
The revival of
A very, very old life.

7087.

When and where
Soulful qualities are unreservedly
    valued,
Heaven immediately descends.

7088.

He who has
At times may be alone.
But he who is
Can never be alone.

7089.

There are only two reality-lovers:
One is God
The immortal Singer,
The other is God
The eternal Listener.

7090.

His mind is helplessly
And completely lost
In the crowd of contradictory
    thoughts.

7091.

O my mind,
What I need from you
Is just a little determination
And nothing more.
O my heart,
What I need from you
Is just a little aspiration
And nothing more.
O my life,
What I need from you
Is just a little dedication
And nothing more.

7092.

The sudden joy
Of the aspiring heart
Is quite often painful and
   destructive
To the doubting mind.

7093.

Mental clouds appear
From time to time
To challenge and strengthen
My psychic sun.

7094.

Preserve the precious moments
In your life
Sacredly
So that God can invite you
Into His Life
Proudly.

7095.

His mind is a stranger
To stillness.
His heart is a stranger
To soulfulness.
His soul is a stranger
To happiness.

7096.

When I encounter an intellectual
   giant,
I really feel sorry for him,
For he has everything
Except the divinity of sweetness
In his heart.

7097.

You are the right person
To ask your mind
If God needs it.
You are the wrong person
To ask God
If He needs your heart.

7098.

Your treasure-house
Is inside your own heart's cry
And not inside the world's frown.

7099.

My Lord,
Please warn me before You come.
Otherwise, You may come
   unrecognised
And go back unloved.

7100.

Alas, how is it I did not know
For such a long time
That my silence-heart is so special
To my Lord Supreme?
Alas, how is it I did not know
That it is inside my silence-heart
That my Lord's Victory-Drum
Will herald the new dawn
Of His perfect creation?

7101.

If you are ready
To risk all,
You are truly worthy
To receive all.

7102.

He is descending
To his spiritual death
Because every day he bathes
In the river of impure pride
And dark ingratitude.

7103.

Each morning
Has a special game to play
With my heart's snow-white hopes
And my soul's blue-gold promises.

7104.

Your number one earthly disease
Is impurity.
Your number one Heavenly
   disease
Is uncertainty.

7105.

My Lord does not care for
My mountain-capacity,
But He does care for
My fountain-availability.

7106.

Attention-light I needed.
Dedication-height I need.
Perfection-delight I shall need.

7107.

God's supreme Secret:
Man will eventually please God
In His own Way.

7108.

The beauty of your heart
Is your life.
The impurity of your life
Is your death.

7109.

Doubt,
You are showing too much!
Do you not see
That I have two big
Perfectly functioning eyes?

7110.

Fear, you are torturing me
Too much!
Do you not feel that my heart's
Inseparable oneness with God
Will destroy you before long?

7111.

Even your stark enemies
Feel sorry for you
Because you are wedded
To endless and useless worries.

7112.

Your ignorance-night
Will no longer endure.
The express arrival of
    wisdom-light
Is absolutely sure.

7113.

His indecision-mind
Is fully responsible
For his life's repeated
Devastating failures.

7114.

God's Compassion-Machine
Is eternally powerful.
My gratitude-machine
Has recently become soulful.

7115.

Jealousy is not
An incurable disease.
But your unwillingness
To surrender your jealousy
Unfortunately is.

7116.

Delight, delight!
I have nothing but delight.
Why?
Because I have done everything
That my Lord wanted me to do.

7117.

Each good thought
Experiences freedom-joy
From all the snares of
   poison-doubt.

7118.

Do guide my eyes, my Lord,
Into the ways of beauty's joy
And purity's peace.

7119.

My Lord,
I need Your Magnet-Feet.
My Lord,
I need Your Protection-Feet more.
My Lord,
I need Your Forgiveness-Feet
   most.

7120.

I know I will not get
The right message from your soul
Because your mind is the
   interpreter
And not your heart.

7121.

Someone is singing,
Perhaps God.
Someone is threatening my
   ignorance.
Who else can it be,
If not my Beloved Lord?

7122.

I do not believe in
My mind,
With its eternally hungry
Abysmal abyss.

7123.

Your devotion has to be deeper
Than an ocean.
Your surrender has to be higher
Than a mountain.
Only then will you feel
What you mean to God.

7124.

My body needs only one thing:
Movement.
My vital needs only one thing:
Discipline.
My mind needs only one thing:
Obedience.
My heart needs only one thing:
Gratitude.
My life needs only one thing:
Transcendence.

7125.

If you need faith,
You are good.
If you have faith,
You are perfect.

7126.

Your utter stupidity makes you feel
That you do not need God.
But never dare to expect
That others are going to follow you.

7127.

I can find myself,
Since my Beloved Supreme
Is searching with me.

7128.

God is already
My personal Friend.
Now I am trying hard
To make Him
My most intimate Friend.

7129.

Only God can grant you
Spiritual security.
No, not even your soul can do that.

7130.

A heart of gratitude
And a life of surrender
Never drink tears.
They drink only nectar-delight.

7131.

Today you are puffed up
With exorbitant pride.
Tomorrow you will be bitten ruthlessly
By doubt-snakes.

7132.

Since my prayer to you is sincere,
Can you not also show me sincerely
What you are truly made of,
O my puzzling mind?

7133.

Perfection slowly comes
And happily stays
In the same room
With patience.

7134.

Our easy-going ways
Are solely responsible
For the failure
Of our life's journey.

7135.

Each unaspiring moment
Will prove to be
A frustration-shore
Of nowhere-land.

7136.

"When will God's Work be done?"
This is the question
That breaks the hearts
Of true God-lovers.

7137.

God is the vision
Of man.
Man is the Satisfaction
Of God.

7138.

Do not undervalue yourself
Unnecessarily,
For that work is done by others
Far better than you can ever do it.

7139.

Victory usually means
Temporary peace.
But peace is
Eternity's victory.

7140.

My mind is totally blind.
It cannot see
The perfection-eye
Of my heart.

7141.

I am anxious to see
Where God is hiding His
   Compassion.
God is anxious to see
Where I am hiding my
   enthusiasm.

7142.

You want to be your own teacher.
Do you not know
That this is God's Task?

7143.

Do not satisfy an undivine person
In his own way
If you really care for
His future perfection.

7144.

If it is a question about God,
Who can answer with more
   authority
Than the heart's blue bird:
The soul?

7145.

The divine love of the heart
Can only be felt.
It cannot be revealed,
It cannot be seen.

7146.

Nothing is wrong with me:
So says my vital.
Something is wrong,
But it can eventually be corrected:
So says my heart.

7147.

Since everything is bound to
   change
Eventually,
My life's total transformation
Will not always remain a far cry.

7148.

Earth means
Birthless and deathless hopes.
Heaven means
Birthless and deathless dreams.
God means
Birthless and deathless Realities.

7149.

God asks me to give Him
The things that I myself
Do not at all care for:
My imperfections.

7150.

I am suffering
From myself
Because I am not desperately
    looking
For myself.

7151.

Each heart knows
How to cry for God.
Each soul knows
How to fly with God.

7152.

In my life's humility-nest
My Lord has chosen to enjoy
His enduring Rest.

7153.

You love your inner life.
That means God has
A very special Concern for you.

7154.

When I am inside my mind,
I look for God the Doctor.
When I am inside my heart,
I look for God the Singer.

7155.

Fear ends only when I realise
That fear is nothing
But punishment unsought.

7156.

Since your confidence has failed
    you,
Try God's Compassion-Light.
It will definitely work!

7157.

I do not depend on others' faith
In me.
I depend only on my faith
In God.

7158.

Sincerity gives my mind
Indomitable strength.
Purity gives my heart
Unfathomable joy.

7159.

My heart's sleepless gratitude
Is the only fitting tribute
To my Lord Supreme.

7160.

The tears of an orphan-heart
Enter straight into
The Compassion-Heart of God.

7161.

The soulful oneness of the
　universe
With a seeker's aspiration-heart
Is the bond inevitable.

7162.

He has unlearnt all the lessons
That he received from his
　ignorance-teacher.
Therefore he has all the marks
Of a great and genuine seeker.

7163.

Before it is too late,
My heart must start growing
And my mind must start glowing.

7164.

The envelope of light
Contains my beautiful
　Immortality.
The envelope of darkness
Contains my immediate death.

7165.

Must I curb my quest?
Yes, if it is an earth-conquering
　quest.
Must I curb my quest?
No, if it is a surrender-blossoming
　quest,
Never!

7166.

How can it be possible
For a small mind with weak
　thoughts
To long for liberation?

7167.

My Lord's Compassion-Touch
Immediately mends my mind
And heals my heart.

7168.

O my sick mind,
Because of you
I am unable to strengthen
My heart's aspiration-life.

7169.

Aspiration and dedication
Are two friends
Who affectionately teach us
How to approach perfection.

7170.

My Lord
Will You not reconsider my case?
I really would like to have
A taste of Nectar-Delight.

7171.

You must command your
    thoughts,
Not vice versa,
If happiness is something
That you are looking for.

7172.

If you want to stand
God-revealed,
Then first stand
Self-concealed.

7173.

Concentration means
Success immediate.
Meditation means
Progress ultimate.
Surrender means
Satisfaction within,
Satisfaction without.

7174.

Do not trust your mind
Unless it is soulfully
Searching for God.

7175.

God loves my entire being.
Can I not at least try to love
Only one part of my being:
My heart?

7176.

I shall always remember
What God once told me:
I am a dream of His
Inside His Eternity's Dream-Boat.

7177.

Humility is the best song
Sung by a God-seeker
In his outer life.
Purity is the best music
Played by a God-seeker
In his inner life.

7178.

At the assembly of hearts and
　souls
Certain greedy minds come to talk
About the perfection-satisfaction
Of democracy.

7179.

So often my heart cannot persuade
My mind, vital and body
To meditate.
They are so obstinate!

7180.

What my heart needs
Is an indefinite vacation
From my unaspiring mind
And my demanding vital.

7181.

Are you a great fighter?
If so, use your fighting capacity
Against your doubting mind.
Are you a great lover?
If so, offer your love to God
Only for Him to use.

7182.

Enlarge your dedication-circle
To make yourself happy.
Enlarge your surrender-circle
To make God happy.

7183.

A doubting mind in itself
Is an affront to our inner divinity,
Our universal oneness.

7184.

My love
Of universal oneness
Is God's
Unparalleled Dream.

7185.

Heaven's Himalayan
   encouragement
And earth's Atlantic
   encouragement
Simultaneously echo and re-echo
In his soft, tender and flower-like
   heart.

7186.

His heart has only
One inner resolve:
To restore everyone's
Freedom-right.

7187.

I soulfully smile
When I want to please myself.
I powerfully cry
When I wish to please God.

7188.

The mind thinks
That it knows God.
The heart feels
That God knows it.

7189.

What is necessary
Man does not know.
What is unnecessary
God does not know.

7190.

You must be careful
Of what you say.
You must be careful
Of what you do.
But you do not have to be careful
Of what you think of God.

7191.

My mind is happy
Because it is intelligent.
My heart is happy
Because God is compassionate.

7192.

I may not know myself,
But I do know my Father:
My Forgiveness-Lord.

7193.

Real spirituality
Can easily be described
In one word:
Delight.

7194.

He holds perfection.
You behold perfection in him.
That means you yourself
Are on the road to perfection.

7195.

May my mind's vastness
And my heart's oneness
Be translated into immediate acts.

7196.

God always wants
The powerful mind to surrender
To the soulful heart.

7197.

"My joy is for me."
This is the division-man
Speaking in me for himself.
"My Joy is for all."
This is the Oneness-God
Speaking in me for everyone.

7198.

Say what
Makes the world happy.
Do what
Makes God happy.

7199.

Your misfortune teaches me
How to be perfect.
Therefore, I wish to share with
 you
My unconditional gratitude.

7200.

The first thing in life
Is soulful self-giving.
The last thing in life
Is unconditional self-giving.

7201.

The more I think of Him
And the more I speak of Him,
The more my heart is transformed
Into a masterpiece of devotion.

7202.

His is the mind
That enjoys sleepless struggles.
His is the life
That enjoys useless unrest.

7203.

My soul taught my heart
How to fly.
My heart taught my mind
How to cry.
But my mind is now teaching my life
How to sigh.

7204.

The Silence-God
Of the ever-transcending Beyond
Has opened my heart's
Aspiration-room
And my life's
Dedication-door.

7205.

A desire-bound life
Is ruthlessly and inevitably seized
By the indomitable strength
Of an unappeasable hunger.

7206.

Your life can succeed
And your heart can proceed,
But you cannot be the judge
Of their success and progress.

7207.

There is no such thing
As insignificant work.
Therefore, we must needs do everything
With our heart's love
And our life's respect.

7208.

Sweet are my heart's silence-tears.
How I wish I could keep them
Safe inside the happiness-palace
Of my soul.

7209.

His mind never proceeds
Further than his long-treasured
Himalayan plans.

7210.

An impurity-mind,
An insecurity-heart
And a futility-life:
These are his
Three imperishable sorrows.

7211.

To preserve my heart's
Burning faith
Is to unveil my soul's
Sacred promise.

7212.

Alas, my mind does not want
To stop following
The aimless contours
Of the confusion-shore.

7213.

Do not encage your earthly
　　minutes
If you want to fly
Like your soul
In the liberty-firmament.

7214.

The imaginations
Of the human mind
Are quite liberal.
The realisations
Of the divine heart
Are quite conservative.

7215.

In a seeker's gratitude-heart
God finds the panorama
Of His own transcendental
　　Sweetness.

7216.

If your mind's faith wavers,
How can your heart breathe in
Adoration for your Lord Supreme?

7217.

My Lord,
I came to You with empty hands,
But You have discovered
My empty heart too.

7218.

Ingratitude is man's
Undeniable name,
All due to his excess
Of ignorance-dream.

7219.

Each time I long for
A new success
And get a new success,
What do I see?
The usual disillusionment.

7220.

Depression exhausts me.
Depression blinds me.
Depression strangles me.

7221.

Let me give a little credit
To my life of outer sincerity.
Let me give a little more credit
To my life of inner purity.
Let me give all credit
To my Lord's Compassion-Heart.

7222.

My strong desire
To bind the heart of humanity
And blind the eye of humanity
Is unfortunately and unmistakably
An unforgivable fantasy.

7223.

My heart of unconditional oneness
With the Will of my Lord Supreme
Is Heaven's ecstasy-nest.

7224.

My desires make my vital ugly,
My mind lonely
And
My life unfriendly.

7225.

My Lord,
Your boundless Bounty
Has granted me breath.
Now I am praying to You
To grant me a willingly
Self-giving breath.

7226.

Yesterday God taught me one secret:
How to transcend my mind.
Today God is teaching me another secret:
How to please Him
In His own Way.

7227.

My heart's real helplessness
Someday, somehow
Will reach God's God-Ecstasy.

7228.

Since he satisfies God
In his dream-world,
He expects God to satisfy him
In the reality-world.

7229.

My Mother India commands me
To learn that there is no such
   thing
As confusion.
Everything in God's creation
Is on the clear road
To illumination.

7230.

My Mother India announces
The synthesis between
Her mountain-high promises
And her ocean-vast hopes.

7231.

There was a time
When my heart cried and cried
To find God.
Now my heart
Is crying and crying
Not to lose God.

7232.

A chosen instrument of God
Will undoubtedly become
An all-around excellent seeker.

7233.

God's Compassion-Eye
And God's Forgiveness-Heart
Work even in the face
Of man's inborn ingratitude.

7234.

The other day I met God
Walking down the street.
To my extreme happiness
He said to me
That His Heart of
   Compassion-Ocean
Would wash away
All my teeming imperfections.

7235.

This world will try to corrupt you.
Before it can do so,
Try to seek God's Companionship.
Do it as soon as possible!

7236.

When great souls come down
They try to make some special
    rules
To better the consciousness
Of this eyeless and stone-deaf
    world.

7237.

The desire-river of our human
    vital
Finally enters into
The destruction-sea
And nowhere else.

7238.

I shall live on earth
To see tomorrow,
Not the way my vital desires
To see tomorrow
But the way my soul envisions
Tomorrow's perfection
And tomorrow's satisfaction.

7239.

Be patient with yourself
In exactly the same way
That God is patient with you.

7240.

A universal man
Does not have to claim anyone.
He is more than satisfied
That he has been claimed by
    everyone
And by everything.

7241.

My mind, in a terrible rush,
Says to my heart,
"O heart, why are you so insecure
All the time?"
My heart quietly, very quietly,
Says to my mind,
"O mind, why are you so impure
All the time?"

7242.

If you want perfection,
Then long for truth.
If you want satisfaction,
Then long for constant
    self-giving.

7243.

His hunger for world-applause
Does not allow him to live
Inside his own heart-poise.

7244.

The very quest for truth
Is not only challenging and
　gratifying
But also illumining and fulfilling.

7245.

Two supreme gifts
From the Absolute Supreme:
A heart of oneness-duty
And a life of fulness-purity.

7246.

The soulful purity of God-lovers
Surprises all human beings,
Especially the intellectual giants.

7247.

Choose your thoughts carefully
At every moment
If you want your life-boat
To sail in the sea
Of light and delight.

7248.

You and I are two human beings
Who are now on our way
To transformation.
One day we shall become perfect.
How is it that we still
Have not forgotten
Our animal life
And find it so hard
To appreciate each other?

7249.

Those who serve the world
　constantly
Do not have time
To criticise others,
While those who do not serve
Others selflessly
Have endless time
To criticise the whole world.

7250.

How can you live
In wisdom-delight
If you think always of the snares
Of ignorance-night?

7251.

Falsehood tells me
That I simply cannot do it.
True truth tells me
That I have already done it.
Something more,
Since I have already done it,
I have not only become
But I am, eternally am.

7252.

God opens up my heart's gates
Every morning
Only to see them in the evening
Automatically plus firmly closed.

7253.

There is no self-offering
Without God-becoming,
No God-becoming
Without universal
   oneness-revealing.

7254.

The eternal and uninterrupted
   message
Of human life:
Today's cry is unknown;
Tomorrow's unknowable.

7255.

Give up your foolish insecurity.
It is destroying your heart's purity,
Your soul's beauty
And
Your inborn liberty.

7256.

My Lord, why have You postponed
Your visit?
Is it because I no longer
Have any special love for You?
Is it because You are tired of loving
The ingratitude-heart in me?

7257.

A truth-seeker and God-lover
Has abundant capacity to awaken
Even the unwilling souls
From the world of lethargy.

7258.

If your mind is consumed
With disproportionate pride,
How can your heart be inundated
With oneness-delight?

7259.

I have already enjoyed
My life's ignorance-sleep.
Now I want to enjoy
Immortality's infinite Deep.

7260.

My soul is the eternal sufferer
Caught between my mind's
 confusion
And my heart's frustration.

7261.

My sweet Lord,
I am giving You back
My soft heart.
Will You not give me back
Your strong Feet?

7262.

On the road of self-giving
The seeker is most generously
 blessed
With God's cherished Friend:
Smile.

7263.

Do not falsely and stupidly think
That God is not granting you
His Heart's Compassion-Sky
Although you are roaming blindly
In the dark alleys of ignorance.

7264.

Silence your endless
Earth-necessity
Secretly.
Fulfil your soulfully pure
Heaven-necessity
Immediately.

7265.

He knows
Who loves.
He is right
Who does.
He is perfect
Who is God-revealing.
He is another God
Who is Truth-manifesting.

7266.

Although he was forced
To kiss the humiliation-dust of
 defeat,
His blind-elephant-revolt
 continued
Against the Wisdom-King.

7267.

A life of self-sufficiency
Will always remain
Beyond my imagination's flight.

7268.

Beauty tempts the weak.
Beauty inspires the strong.
Beauty gladdens the Supreme.

7269.

I think of God
So that I can immediately become
   good.
God thinks of me
So that I can eternally be perfect.

7270.

Each desire-bound life,
In a spiritual sense,
Is not only mischievous
But also treacherous.

7271.

Each pure thought
Is a perfection-builder
In man and for God.

7272.

When I am weak,
I think of others' capacities.
When I am strong,
I think of my own
Yet unnoticed incapacities.

7273.

Ambition cannot challenge him.
Ambition cannot even find him.
Yet ambition wants to befriend
   him.

7274.

My faith is a peerless bridge
Between my heart's soulful hope
And my Lord's fruitful
   Self-Giving.

7275.

Heaven is a place I cannot reach.
Why can't I reach it?
Because my life does not want to.
Why not?
Because I am already deeply
   attached
To the place where I am now:
Hell.

7276.

The lamp of the mind
Thinks it is most powerful.
The lamb of God
Knows that God alone is most
   powerful
And most beautiful.

7277.

The secret of contentment:
Give what you have,
Your mind's poise,
And become aware of what you
   truly are,
A perfect choice and immortal
   voice
Of God.

7278.

Harsh words
Slay everybody
And delay everything.

7279.

In my soul's lustre-surrender
I give to God
What God Himself needs
For His own Self-Transcendence
And His own earth-Manifestation.

7280.

You do not have to be
Completely versed
In any sacred book.
Just make your heart
The fragrance of a purity-flower.
Lo, God the
   Compassion-Satisfaction-Heart
Is fast approaching you.

7281.

Rapture-realisation is not
   founded
Upon torture-experience.
Rapture-realisation is founded
Upon the oneness-manifestation
Of the aspiring heart.

7282.

A born sacrificer,
A God-lover and
A truth-seeker:
These three are inseparably one
In the same body.

7283.

Nobody but God Himself
Encourages and energises me
To walk fast, very fast,
Along my realisation-road.

7284.

A surrender-heart
Is purity's smile
And beauty's dance.

7285.

God and His Satisfaction-Smile
Always accompany man
On his aspiration-journey.

7286.

What can God's
   Compassion-Readiness do
If my body wants to sleep
And my mind wants to daydream?

7287.

When I do not aspire,
I enjoy the world's thunder-noise.
When I aspire,
I love God's self-transcending
Silence-Voice.

7288.

Each soul-prayer of mine
Is my life's heart-fragrance
Which pleases at once
Both Heaven and earth.

7289.

As you have tremendous
   confidence
In your heart,
Even so,
God has tremendous Love and
   Fondness
For you.

7290.

Each unfulfilled hope
Of humanity
Is an unmanifested promise
Of divinity.

7291.

Have you reserved
The most special room for God
In your heart-hotel?
If so, then God is definitely
And gladly going to take it
At your highest rate.

7292.

My heart's ecstasy-palace
Is built upon the foundation of
God's Self-Dedication-Palace.

7293.

The impurity-elephant
Inside mankind
Has completely forgotten
How to sleep.

7294.

Perpetual necessity means
The perfect revelation
Of an inner inevitability.

7295.

Trust your hope-dreams;
They are harmless.
Trust your promise-realities;
They are peerless.

7296.

God does not want to know
Why I cry
But He does want to know
Why I do not smile.

7297.

My words shall live longer
Than my deeds.
Therefore, my words have to be
At once cautious and precious.

7298.

Is my sincerity-mind enough?
Perhaps it is enough.
Is my surrender-life enough?
Definitely it is enough!

7299.

When I started practising
   self-control,
The animal in me frowned,
The human in me
Was totally dismayed
And the divine in me
Came to the fore to crown me.

7300.

Breathlessly I cry
And selflessly I try
Only to see my soul's
Rainbow-sky.

7301.

In our inner life
Everyone and everything will fail us,
Except our meditation.
Meditation is our friend,
Our soul's old friend,
Our Beloved Supreme's eternal friend.
If this friend ever leaves us,
We shall have nobody to take care of us,
Nobody!

7302.

No matter how many mistakes
You make,
No matter how useless
You feel yourself to be,
No matter how many weaknesses
You consciously and unconsciously cherish,
If you can maintain your friendship
With your ever-loving, ever-inspiring
And ever-illumining friend, meditation,
Then you will, without fail,
Discover the true meaning of your life.

7303.

You are a genuine seeker
Of the absolute Truth.
Therefore, the highest planes of consciousness
Will not and cannot forever remain
A far cry.
Continue walking along
The path of Eternity.
You will one day reach
Your soul's glorious heights.

7304.

You are a lover of meditation.
That means you do believe
In an inner world,
For you have been there many, many times.
If you get joy from that world,
Your eagerness to meditate
Will carry you far, farther, farthest
Towards your destined goal.

7305.

Abysmal failure has touched his life
Because he lives
Either inside his impulsive mind
Or inside his destructive vital.

7306.

I admit
I have a weak heart.
But I must also say
I have a very pure heart.

7307.

No matter what I do or say,
I am always disturbed
By the unwanted presence
Of my doubting mind.

7308.

I allow myself
To do everything else
Except introduce myself
To my Lord's Satisfaction-Smile.

7309.

My heart, stop crying.
You have cried enough.
Now start smiling.

7310.

Every day
My Lord approaches me
With His self-giving
 Compassion-Light.
Every day
I approach my Lord
With my self-giving
 gratitude-delight.

7311.

Lethargy is so useless
That it always enjoys performing
The stupid nothingness-dance.

7312.

I may not have the right
To think for you,
But I do have the right
To think of you.

7313.

Your aspiration-flames must
 climb up
To the mountain-high throne of
 light.
Then only can you reach
 tomorrow's
Immortality-Shore.

7314.

Only a life of constant surrender
Can soulfully and smilingly walk
Along the sunlit road.

7315.

To cherish doubt
Is a certain way
To achieve self-destruction.

7316.

I want to stand at the start
Of faith
And not at the start
Of understanding.

7317.

Be careful of your doubt-tiger.
It can easily destroy
Your tiny and tender faith-plant.

7318.

An uncertain and unaspiring mind
Is the cause
Of a shaky spiritual foundation.

7319.

Do not look around
To see if somebody else
Is making faster progress than you.
Just look deep within
And be grateful for whatever progress
You are making.
Just look high above
And be ready and eager
To make still faster progress.

7320.

The great contribution
Of the human life:
Mind over matter.
The supreme contribution
Of the divine life:
Heart over mind.

7321.

Be practical within.
You will immediately become
Earth's perfect cry
And Heaven's perfect smile.

7322.

No life that yields
To ignorance-night
Can hear the songs
Of beauty's light
And duty's delight.

7323.

You rely upon nothing,
Yet you think
You are doing something great
And becoming someone good.

7324.

My heart,
I want you to be proud of me
Not because I am perfect,
But because I am all gratitude
To my Beloved Supreme.

7325.

Carry on the struggle.
You will eventually win.
Strive with vigour.
You will quite certainly win.
Depend entirely on God's Grace.
You will immediately win.

7326.

My unaspiring heart
And my doubting mind
Are deplorable failures:
So feels my ever-loving
And ever-illumining soul.

7327.

What my mind has
Is sheer stupidity.
What my mind is
Is God's hidden Divinity.

7328.

Each moment
Of prayerful surrender
And soulful gratitude
Brings perfection-light
And satisfaction-delight.

7329.

I use my curiosity-power
To see the beauty of the outer
    world.
I use my sincerity-power
To see the purity of the inner
    world.

7330.

If you really value
Your pure heart,
Then love it infinitely more
Than you love anything else.

7331.

The silence-light
Of my gratitude-heart
Is God's thundering
   Victory-Dream.

7332.

Although my mind
Is an experienced wisdom-reality,
It is nowhere near
God's Illumination-Smile.

7333.

Rest assured,
He who strangles you
With fears and doubts
Will not be allowed to be with you
In the highest world.

7334.

His desire-bound life
Is completely lost
Inside his absurd hopes
And grave fears.

7335.

Liberation means
To soulfully claim
God's Cosmic Vision
And consciously disown
Man's tempting illusion.

7336.

Since you know
You cannot guide yourself,
What is wrong in asking
Your ever-ready Inner Pilot
To guide you?

7337.

If you are painfully aware
Of your inner mistakes
But still maintain your eagerness
To do the right thing,
You will make far better progress
Than those who complacently
   fool themselves
By thinking they are already
Absolutely perfect.

7338.

Do not cherish unhealthy ideas.
If you feel that the world
Thinks ill of you,
Who knows,
Perhaps you are unnecessarily
    torturing
Your life's purity-heart.

7339.

Compromise begins
In useless stupidity
And ends in lifeless futility.

7340.

The purification of the mind
Must follow
The enlargement of the heart.

7341.

Severe psychic treatment is
    needed
For serious doubt-sickness.
God the Doctor tells this
To his spiritually sick children.

7342.

Every day God voraciously eats
Your surrender-fruits
And proudly tells the cosmic gods
All about you.

7343.

You are a dauntless,
Death-challenging hero-warrior.
That means you soulfully care for
God's Satisfaction in you.

7344.

Your heart's soulful readiness
And your life's powerful
    fruitfulness
Sing the song
Of satisfaction-smile.

7345.

Jealousy hides
Only to be caught
For its eventual transformation.

7346.

O my sound-life,
You may be insignificant,
But you are also powerful.
You have extinguished
My heart's aspiration-flames.

7347.

Beautiful is my mind's
Newness-dawn.
Soulful is my heart's
Oneness-day.
Powerful is my soul's
Satisfaction-sun.

7348.

One aspiration-flame of my heart
Has illumined the road
That leads to my soul's
Perennial smile.

7349.

Yesterday's unconditional Grace
And today's dauntless
  determination
Are turning me into a pure
  instrument
Who treasures God's
  Protection-Feet.

7350.

An amazing improvement:
My mind's damaging frowns
Have now become
My mind's lamenting sighs.

7351.

God's Compassion has given me
The capacity to pray.
God's Forgiveness has given me
The capacity to aspire.

7352.

If you are always ready to play
The self-giving surrender-game,
Then God-realisation
Is within your easy reach.

7353.

Ignore the pinch of insecurity.
Lo, your mind's brooding doubts
Have all disappeared.

7354.

Utter loneliness awaited him
When he unmindfully stopped
His morning meditations
And
His evening prayers.

7355.

For a God-lover,
The time-honoured throne of Heaven
Is not something to look at and admire
But something to sit upon and enjoy.

7356.

I appreciate your mind's serenity-seeds.
I admire your heart's purity-plants.
I adore your life's divinity-trees.
I love your soul's Immortality-fruits.

7357.

Be faithful to the fruitful:
Your loving soul.
Be powerful to the unfaithful:
Your doubting mind.

7358.

Deception and meditation
Do not go together.
Meditation and satisfaction
Can and do go together.

7359.

Beautiful emptiness
My mind needs.
Soulful fulness
My heart needs.
Blessingful fruitfulness
My life needs.

7360.

Not your winning race
But your soulful face
Has transported me to Heaven.

7361.

One dedication-drop from my life
Has destroyed ignorance
The betrayer
And won God
The Lover.

7362.

My silence-life creates.
My sound-life destroys.
God's Compassion-Heart revives.

7363.

My heart's beauty-sky:
I know not where it is.
My soul's divinity-sun:
I know not if it even exists.

7364.

Your heart's insecurity
Has concealed your soul's
Spontaneous happiness.

7365.

Your doubt-life has destroyed
Your hope-blossoms
And your enthusiasm-boughs.

7366.

Your service-tree
May not be exceptionally tall,
But your service-flower-fragrance
Is extraordinarily beautiful.

7367.

Today every man is a blunderer,
But tomorrow every man will be
The pioneer-founder
Of God's ever-transcending
   Delight.

7368.

Every heart-cry
Awakens the sleeping world.
Every soul-smile
Nourishes the searching world.

7369.

Every heart-cry
Purifies my mind.
Every soul-smile
Enlightens my life.

7370.

Tomorrow's perfection-face:
Is it my mental hallucination?
Is it my wishful thinking?
No, it is my
   promise-announcement.

7371.

God's Compassion-Flames
I do not deserve,
But I do deserve
Earth's sincerity-drops.

7372.

God's eternal Compassion-Flame
Has at last illumined
My mind's age-old
   confusion-game.

7373.

God is never in a hurry.
If I long to be His choice
   instrument,
Then I must not be in a hurry
   either.
Today I imitate God;
Tomorrow I shall be as perfect
As God eternally is.

7374.

Take on a new role:
Play the role of a God-lover.
No more play the role
Of a man-hater.

7375.

I shall not allow my body
To delay me.
I shall not allow my vital
To torture me.
I shall not allow my mind
To deceive me.
I shall not allow my heart
To talk to ignorance.

7376.

With a prayerful heart
Learn only from Him
Who is your own Eternity's
Inner Pilot.

7377.

Did you say hello to God this
   morning?
"I did not remember."
Did you thank God this morning?
"I did not remember."
Did you criticise God this
   morning?
"Yes, I did, I did."

7378.

My teeming troubles
Are all beginning now
Because I no longer feed my heart
With soulful cries.

7379.

I breathed a silent prayer.
Now I see that my Lord
Will not forsake me
And that my world
Will not disappoint Him.

7380.

Do you think
God has nothing better to do
Than to tell you all the time
That He loves you
Infinitely more than you love
   Him?

7381.

Days passed by;
Months, too.
Yet I do not know
Why I did not pray
At my Lord's Feet
And why I did not meditate
On my Lord's Heart.

7382.

Two miracles in one day
I can hardly believe:
This morning
I saw God's Face,
And this evening
I am touching God's Feet.

7383.

Your mind will be infected
With doubt
If you do not frequent
The faith-temple
And sit at the altar
Of aspiration.

7384.

No exaggeration can be too great
When we try to describe
The self-transcending beauty
Of the Universal Soul.

7385.

The rules of Heaven
My mind does not want to learn
But my heart has already learnt:
Smile sleeplessly,
Love unconditionally.

7386.

The blending of old and new we observe
When a doubting mind
And a loving heart
Are lost in each other.

7387.

I am not departing even an inch
From the actual facts
When I say that I love God
More than I love myself
And that God has definitely told me
I shall soon be one of His choice instruments.

7388.

You are doing the right thing:
You should and you must value
Your heart's breathless aspiration-cry.

7389.

An invisible wound I create
Inside my heart
Each time I become unmindful
Of my great promises
To the world.

7390.

A medley of smiles and tears
Can never be the answer
To man's birthless and deathless
Self-enquiry.

7391.

You have broken both your
   promises.
Now you neither want to sit
At God's Feet
Nor want God to live
Inside your mind.

7392.

Your mind-sky is overcast with
   doubts,
But their days are numbered.
Your inner sun will reappear,
For God has not sanctioned
And will never sanction
Doubt's permanent rule.

7393.

When the veil of illusion is torn,
Each man sees that he loves
Only one Person,
God the Creator,
And serves only one Person,
God the creation.

7394.

If you believe in God
And want to enjoy eternal oneness
   with Him,
Then meditate here and now.
Your present meditation will
   determine
Your future realisation.

7395.

Let God be your inner Coach.
If you can correct any defects
That your inner Coach finds,
Then rest assured,
Your inner speed will
   immediately increase
And you will please God
Far beyond your imagination.

7396.

Selfless service means thinking
Not of your little self
But of your largest Self, the
　　Supreme.
Selfless service is undoubtedly
The great, greater and greatest
　　opportunity
To make the fastest progress.

7397.

If God is disgusted with you,
Then the story will end there.
But if God is simply disappointed,
It is not a hopeless case.
He will give you ample
　　opportunity
To transform this disappointment
Into His true Satisfaction.

7398.

For a spiritual seeker
The inner life is not only
More important than the outer
　　life,
But is actually the only life.

7399.

A child is ready and eager
To play all the time
Because it gives him joy.
A spiritual seeker should be ready
　　and eager
To meditate all the time
Because it gives him joy.

7400.

I fold my hands
When I speak to God.
God holds my hands
And caresses my eyes
When He speaks to me.

7401.

My Lord,
What will happen
If I deepen my faith
In You?
"My son,
My rich Heart
Will grow richer and richest
In you."

7402.

Mine is the mind
That longs for
A simplicity-smile.
Mine is the heart
That longs for
A sincerity-cry.
Mine is the life
That longs for
A perfection-run.
Mine is the God
That cares for
My transcendence-flight.

7403.

I concentrate
For success in my life's journey.
I meditate
For progress in my life's journey.
I contemplate
For God-process in my life's
   journey.

7404.

What is success?
My expansion-ability.
What is progress?
My perfection-necessity.

7405.

I have scheduled my time
Carefully and perfectly.
Nothing can dare to interfere
With my appointment
With my Eternity's Beloved
   Supreme.

7406.

Now is the time of rejoicing!
My inner world tells me
That my Lord is all Compassion.
My outer world tells me
That I am all aspiration.

7407.

If you want to maintain
A very close connection with your
   Master,
Here on earth and there in
   Heaven,
Your meditation will always be
Your direct line to him.

7408.

Because you have a purity-mind
And a sacrifice-heart,
Your inner reserves are unlimited.

7409.

What your mind has
Is inexplicable inspiration.
What your heart has
Is unfathomable aspiration.
What God is going to give you
Is insurmountable realisation.

7410.

Do you see something
Deep inside yourself?
It is the epitome of a new gospel:
Your heart's selfless love.

7411.

At the God-appointed Hour
His earthly sorrows appeared
One final time,
Only to disappear forever.

7412.

Each incident in life
Must not be orchestrated
But liberated
From life's ignorance-dream.

7413.

To weather the crisis
Of self-indulgence,
I shall not hide
But openly lead a life
Of loving sacrifice-light.

7414.

Success has made his outer life
Completely godless
And his inner life
Unthinkably useless.

7415.

To become generous
Is not a difficult task.
To begin with,
Be more generous
With your own
    self-appreciation-smile.

7416.

If you want to make progress,
You need only one thing:
Inner eagerness.
Real inner eagerness
Comes only from the heart.
This eagerness the heart receives
From the soul
And the soul receives
Directly from God.

7417.

Your own heart
Can be absolutely perfect.
Just give it a chance,
A mere chance,
If possible, unconditionally.

7418.

If you are a true truth-seeker,
How can you forget
Early in the morning
To invite God, your Friend,
Your real Friend, your only
  Friend,
To walk along with you
During the entire day?

7419.

I have blindfolded myself
By allowing my success
To remain totally ignorant
Of the purity and divinity of
  progress.

7420.

What you have
Is outer authority.
But this outer authority
Can never overrule
The oneness-purity
Of the constant God-lover in me.

7421.

You want to measure God
By your own discouraging
And disheartening standard.
How, then, can you ever hope
To see the Face of God
In this entire life?

7422.

You have missed the
  salvation-boat.
How, then, can you expect
To reach the Golden Shore?

7423.

The very nature of purity
Is to give the mind
A new vision-eye
And
A new manifestation-arm.

7424.

Your heart excuses
The weaknesses of your entire life.
Your mind excuses
Only its own weaknesses.
It cannot and does not want to
  excuse
Anything or anybody else on
  earth.

7425.

If you sincerely want God
To give you the capacity
To pray and meditate
And to become good and divine,
Then rest assured,
The capacity has already been granted.

7426.

Truth misused, misplaced
And misdirected
Always causes severe pain
In the Heart of God
And in the mind of man.

7427.

Yesterday I saw the depth
Of my pride-ocean.
Today I am seeing the length and breadth
Of my pride-ocean.
But now what my Lord is telling me
Is simply unbelievable:
Tomorrow I shall see the depth,
Length and breadth
Of my oneness-compassion-ocean
All at once!

7428.

Out of His infinite Bounty
God has given me many good qualities
Which I am trying to preserve and expand.
Alas, I have given myself one quality
Which I have been trying for so long
To get rid of,
And that quality is
My excess of earthly knowledge-pride.

7429.

My desire-life is not ending.
My aspiration-life is not beginning.
Still I am living the life
Of living death.

7430.

You can possess peace-light
Only after you have planted
The faith-plant
Carefully and devotedly.

7431.

God will be ready to convince you
Only when your own belief in
   Him
Is strong
And not when you are plying
Your life-boat
Between trust and mistrust.

7432.

Do you know how to praise
   yourself?
That means you know
How to abruptly open
At your sweet will
The gates of self-destruction.

7433.

You are always ready to love
   others,
But you are not ready to love
The Divine and Real in yourself.
Therefore, how do you expect
To tear yourself away
From ignorance-night?

7434.

Everybody laughed at him
When he was on earth
Because he knew nothing about
   Heaven.
Everybody laughs at him
Now that he is in Heaven
Because he is totally ignorant of
   earth.

7435.

I know that I am imperfect,
And my imperfections disturb me
More than they disturb others.
But what pains my divine heart
   most
Is my conscious and clever
   unwillingness
To accept my Lord's Will
As my very own.

7436.

I am such a fool!
Every day I am dying
To have a new friend.
Yet easily I can have not one
But countless friends
Just by welcoming divine,
   inspiring
And illumining thoughts.

7437.

Each thought embodies
Either the destruction-frown
Of darkest night
Or the Treasure-Smile
Of my Lord Supreme.

7438.

Hope is my precious treasure
That I keep inside the heart-safe
Of my God-dreaming life
And God-distributing soul.

7439.

Mere acceptance of the spiritual life
Is not enough.
You must avail yourself
Of each golden opportunity,
And throw your heart and soul
Into your progress-life.

7440.

Two things could not wait:
God's Justice-Light could not wait
For my ignorance-night,
And my hope-flames could not wait
For God's choice Hour.

7441.

My aspiration-heart is bursting
With two most important secrets:
At long last I am able to love God
And God alone;
God is pleased with me
Far beyond my imagination's flight.

7442.

Two strange misconceptions
Are torturing my mind:
My mind does not believe
That it can offer its very existence
To my heart,
And my mind does not believe
That God sleeplessly cares for it.

7443.

If I feel the Presence
Of my Beloved Supreme
Inside my crying heart,
Then my life is truly valuable.
If not,
It is as useless and insignificant
As a tiny ant.

7444.

Do not wrestle
With uncomely and undivine
   thoughts.
You are bound to lose.
Just invoke the Wrestler of
   wrestlers —
Your heart's Inner Pilot —
To fight the battle for you.
Lo and behold,
Your victory is already won.

7445.

When a seeker of the highest
   Truth
Is blessed with inner
   encouragement
From his Inner Pilot,
He can summon all his giant
   strength
To establish the supreme Victory
Of his Lord Supreme
Here on earth.

7446.

Unless your life becomes
A life of surrender,
Unless your heart becomes
A heart of gratitude,
You will be doomed to live
Under the ruthless pressure of
   dragon-time,
And your mind will be filled
   constantly
With deathless apprehension.

7447.

Since you always enjoy curiosity,
Try to be curious
About only two things:
When you will be able to see
The Face of God
For the first time,
And how you will become
Absolutely the choicest
   instrument
Of your Beloved Supreme.

7448.

Challenge the pride
Of ignorance-power
Since you soulfully and sleeplessly
   love
God and His God-Hour.

7449.

He listens to two voices:
The voice that inspires his heart
And the voice that feeds
And satisfies his mind.

7450.

Ascent is aspiring.
Descent is strangling.
Surrender is at once
Perfect and illumining.

7451.

You feel you have nothingness
In the depths of your heart,
But that is a misconception.
What you have is the beginning
Of an illumining newness
And a satisfying God-fulness.

7452.

If I fail in my spiritual life,
That does not mean
I shall stop praying and
    meditating.
If I succeed in my spiritual life,
That does not mean
I do not need a deeper hunger
And a more abiding love
For my Lord Supreme.

7453.

Not by hook or by crook,
But by legitimate means,
God wants us to transcend
    ourselves.

7454.

Yesterday
I desired to become a great man.
My Lord said,
"That is not enough."
Today
I desire to become a good man.
My Lord says,
"That is not enough."
I ask my Lord,
"Is there anything
Beyond greatness and goodness?"
My Lord says,
"Yes, I want you to be
Integrally perfect."

7455.

God has been waiting and waiting
To give me His Nectar-Delight.
It is I who am delaying and
    delaying.
Yet my Lord does not give up
    hope.
My Lord does not give up
His Promise to my soul.

7456.

I see what I have.
God sees what I am.
What I have
Is an endless sigh.
What I am, according to God,
Is a birthless and deathless
God-Oneness-Satisfaction.

7457.

This world does not believe
In perfection.
It thinks perfection
Will always remain a far cry.
Such being the case,
God's Satisfaction-Delight
Does not want to arrive here.

7458.

Indeed, there is nothing wrong
  with me.
I just do not want to mix too much
With the misunderstanding
And misunderstood world.
I want to be alone
So that my inspiration-bird
And aspiration-flames
Can claim me as their own,
And my confidence-tree can grow
In silence-light and
  surrender-delight.

7459.

Although he prays regularly,
His searching mind is not in it.
Although he meditates regularly,
His aspiring heart is not in it.
Although he serves regularly,
His sacrificing life is not in it.

7460.

You want to know
Why everything goes wrong for
  you.
Everything goes wrong because
Your mind consciously treasures
A deluge of doubts.

7461.

God killed him
With His Indifference-Eye.
Now God is giving him a new life
With His Compassion-Heart.

7462.

A selfless lover is he
Who has learnt to wait
For his perfection-tower to be
  blessed
By God's Satisfaction-Hour.

7463.

Your life has become
An incurable failure
Precisely because you have allowed
False freedom to govern your mind.

7464.

Your life is the hyphen
Between a gratitude-cry
And a surrender-smile.

7465.

Your beauty's soulfulness
And your purity's sweetness
Have granted you a heart
That is proudly treasured
By God Himself.

7466.

Each time you delay
In praying and meditating,
You go further down the road
That will cleverly and swiftly lead you
Back to your original start:
Desire-market.

7467.

A sincere seeker
Will take every opportunity
To meditate and serve.
An insincere seeker
Will find every possible excuse
To stay at home and sleep.

7468.

Joy can never rule the day
Of the human being
Who plays with doubt
And dances with suspicion.

7469.

Because of his immense faith
In his higher self,
He enjoys a daily feast
In the inner world.

7470.

Do not try to climb too quickly.
If you do, there is every possibility
That you will fall on your way,
Although only temporarily.

7471.

On earth you can have true friends
Only if you continuously bury
Their stark faults.

7472.

There are many things
That can make your human heart
    happy,
But to make your divine heart
    happy,
Obedience-life has no parallel.

7473.

He thinks that humility
Is a strange thing.
He feels that divinity
Is a strange thing.
Such being the case,
He will remain a stranger
To the higher worlds.

7474.

Dynamism begins with discipline.
If you are regular and devoted
In your meditation,
Your dynamism will, without fail,
Come to the fore.

7475.

A singing heart
Is an immediate openness
To God's Oneness.

7476.

God is thinking of you
At this very moment,
But you are not thinking of Him.
Therefore, ignorance is your lord
And Compassion is God's Lord.

7477.

Praising God in secret
Is loving God
In perfect perfection.

7478.

Keep your eyes wide open.
You are bound to see
God the divine Dispenser.
Keep your heart wide open.
You are bound to see
God the supreme Lover.

7479.

Do what your Inner Pilot asks,
For He wants you to be
Cheerfully and unmistakably
His outer Voice.

7480.

His heart has already said
Good-bye to fear.
Now his mind is saying
Good-bye to doubt.

7481.

If you have an aspiring heart,
Then make it famous
By inundating it with faith.
If you have a dynamic vital,
Then make it famous
By inundating it with courage.

7482.

You are now a man of sorrow.
If you want to be a man of joy,
Then surrender your sorrow
To the God who loves your heart
And to the Lord who needs your life.

7483.

God will not overload you.
He is your heart's Eternity's
Father Supreme.
He is your soul's Immortality's
Friend Supreme.

7484.

God is not confused when I tell Him
That my mind does not want Him
But needs Him.
God is not confused when I tell Him
That my heart loves Him
But does not treasure Him.

7485.

Practise loving the world
Before you ever dare to knock
At God's Heart-Door.

7486.

In the morning he says hello
To his heart's ceaseless cries.
In the evening he says good-bye
To the world that loves him
But does not need him.

7487.

In the wisdom-department
No clever man,
No proud man,
No ungrateful man
Will ever be allowed to work.

7488.

Who is the happy man?
Certainly not the one
Who is afraid of fear
But the one who is always
A friend of faith.

7489.

God's Compassion-Eye
Tells me to relax.
God's Forgiveness-Heart
Allows me to renew
My God-oneness-documents.

7490.

We can, we must and we will
Bring down God the Supreme
　Sovereign.
We can, we must and we will
Lift up man the lost soul.

7491.

If you have faith,
Then you are already a real
　member
Of God's
　Perfection-Satisfaction-Family.

7492.

Jealousy will devour your life
Because you do not believe
In your universal
　oneness-freedom-life.

7493.

A happy listener to the inner voice
Is another name
For a God-Satisfaction-lover
In this confusing and confused
　world.

7494.

Who is first in my life?
Not he who rules,
Not he who overrules,
But he who always cheerfully
　studies
In God's School.

7495.

Because he loves God sleeplessly,
God cheerfully agrees to own
His life's teeming mistakes.

7496.

During his marathon talk with
   God,
One special thing he learnt:
God is eagerly looking forward
To seeing teeming Gods like
   Himself.

7497.

If it is God's Will,
You can try to please others
Instead of yourself.
But when it is your time to pray
   and meditate,
You should try to please only one
   Person —
God.

7498.

Seekers of the same calibre
Should always play together
On the same aspiration-team.
Otherwise, the good
   seeker-players will feel
That they are wasting their
   precious time,
While the bad seeker-players will
   feel
That they can never reach
The necessary standard,
And they will give up the game
   altogether.

7499.

If you want inspiration and
   encouragement,
Remain with seekers of your own
   standard.
Even if you make mistakes,
You will know that others also
Are making similar mistakes,
Or are learning from your
   mistakes.
Together you are succeeding,
Together you are proceeding
Towards your destined goal.

7500.

My Lord, I do not want the peace
That tells me I need nothing
   more.
No, I want the peace that creates
   in me
Constant hunger to receive You
In every way
And distribute You
In every widening heart.

7501.

If you ask me
Why I am so happy,
Then I shall unmistakably tell you
That is what happens
When you live for God alone.

7502.

Your mind may resent you
Because nowadays you are paying
Less attention to it.
But do not be a fool.
Do not again become a good
   friend
Of your mind.
Eventually there will come a time
When you will pay no attention at
   all
To your desire-bound,
   doubt-bound mind.
That will be the time
When you and your faith,
Like two little children,
Will play inside the garden
Of your soul.

7503.

I know at least
One thing well:
Unmerited suffering.

7504.

If you really love God,
Then do not tire Him
With your endless complaints.

7505.

In the inner life
Insecurity is a dead-end road.
In the outer life
Doubt is a dead-end road.

7506.

Indecision is
The confusion-frustration-dance
Of division.

7507.

Simplicity is
The beautiful beginning
Of Divinity.
Sincerity is
The powerful beginning
Of Immortality.

7508.

A suspicion-mind
Is by far the best authority
On life-exhaustion.

7509.

Aspiration illumines
The inner confusion.
Determination destroys
The outer confusion.

7510.

My prayer-life is fond of
My Lord's Sound-Body.
My meditation-life is fond of
My Lord's Silence-Eye.

7511.

Impurity
Invades my mind
Only to pervade
My heart.

7512.

My prayer-life tells me
What I can receive from God.
My meditation-life shows me
How I can manifest God.

7513.

Undedicated money-power
Is more dangerous
Than doubt-poison.

7514.

At the halfway mark
Between life and death,
We are forced to watch
The oneness-dance
Of hope and despair.

7515.

A life of deplorable indecision
Walks along the slow road
Of destruction.

7516.

Am I ever going to transcend
　myself?
This is the only question
That is haunting me.

7517.

A great mind
Wants to know more.
A good heart
Wants to love more.
A perfect life
Wants to satisfy God more.

7518.

It is only ignorance-night
That loves me
When I speak to ignorance-king.

7519.

Remember,
God is watching your mind!
Remember,
Your mind is ignoring God's
　Heart!

7520.

As long as God has given me
The capacity to please Him,
I do not have to think
Of pleasing myself.

7521.

When I fail to aspire,
My life becomes
A complicated calculation
And an impassioned frustration.

7522.

As long as I do not
Find fault with God,
How can I be useless?
As long as I love
And need God only,
How can I be useless?

7523.

My mind's perfection
Is my concern.
My heart's satisfaction
Is my Lord's Concern.

7524.

My mind does not know
What to say.
My heart knows
What to say.
My soul knows
All that my heart knows
Plus how and why to say.

7525.

Your mind enjoys
Nerve-racking arguments.
My mind enjoys
Time-consuming arguments.
Alas, both our stupid minds
Are sailing in the same boat.

7526.

My mind powerfully pushed
My heart aside.
My heart lovingly invited my mind
To walk alongside.

7527.

My mind wants to know
If you are thinking of me.
My heart wants to know
If you are thinking of God.

7528.

Your mind cannot have fear
Because your mind
Is astonishingly clear.

7529.

My sincerity-heart
Is confused, puzzled
And even unimaginably surprised
When people say
That I am perfect.

7530.

My self-control
Openly helps me
And secretly helps others.

7531.

Alas, my mind does not think
That it is deliberately unprepared
For God's Compassion-Eye
And God's Satisfaction-Heart.

7532.

If your heart knows how to cry
For oneness
With God the universal One,
Then you cannot have a lonely life.
If your life knows how to smile
At God the transcendental One,
Then you can never have a lonely death.

7533.

This morning my Lord Supreme
Gave me two pieces of tragic news:
My mind consciously loves
Self-deception,
And my heart consciously enjoys
Self-limitation.

7534.

Even winning
Has its most deplorable problems,
For a winner becomes
An immediate victim
To exorbitant pride
And feels that God's Help
Was, after all, not indispensable.

7535.

God-discovery is possible
Only when you have gone
Far beyond the domain
Of self-styled perfection.

7536.

Although I cannot lead my life
To the Beauty of God,
I shall not allow my life to lead me
To the ultimate human despair.

7537.

A limited viewpoint:
Earth-bound nature has no chance
To be illumined,
And thus it will never be able
To satisfy God in God's own Way.
An unlimited viewpoint:
At God's Hour
Impossibility surrenders to
　possibility.

7538.

A self-invented self-portrait
Can please neither Heaven nor
　earth.
It can only please
The stupidity-unreality.

7539.

My mind needs
The inspiration of Infinity
From the Infinite.
My heart needs
The aspiration of Eternity
From the Eternal.
My life needs
The love of Immortality
From the Immortal.

7540.

My soul's only sacred dream:
My body will be totally
　transformed.
My body's only secret dream:
My body will breathlessly listen
To the dictates of my soul.

7541.

If you are always thinking
Downhill thoughts,
How can you see the beauty and
　divinity
Of uphill will-power?

7542.

I have no right to be what I am
   now.
I have only the right to say
That my Lord Supreme loves me
Infinitely more than I can ever
Love myself.

7543.

Silence waves its transcendental
   wings
When I drink deep
The nectar-delight of my
   gratitude-heart.

7544.

Upon the rock of inner
   illumination
His life is dancing.
Therefore, earth is fond of him,
And Heaven is both fond of him
And proud of him.

7545.

His heart's gratitude-song
Is deathless
In its purity-beauty.

7546.

The source of an ascending cry
Is the great heart of humanity.
The source of a descending Smile
Is the good Soul of Divinity.

7547.

Surrender is the newness
That glows.
Gratitude is the fulness
That grows.

7548.

Two major mistakes in my life:
I blame my soul
When I do anything wrong;
I underestimate the Compassion
Of my Source
And the beauty of
My heart's Godward journey.

7549.

Do not be afraid
Of doing great things.
Just regard these things
As quite normal and natural,
And do them spontaneously.
This is the only way
You can bring to the fore
God within you
For His own supreme
   Manifestation.

7550.

To adore God the Dream
And to love God the Dreamer
Is the very beginning
Of the life that lives only for Him.

7551.

I pray to receive.
I meditate to achieve.
I love to become.
I have what God is.

7552.

Nothing helps like self-giving
At every moment.
Nothing destroys like insecurity
In the physical world,
The vital world,
The mental world
Or even in the psychic world.

7553.

Although he is totally undivine,
I must give him another chance
To transform his life
Of complicated insincerity.

7554.

He thinks he is a saint
And therefore his mind does not
    have to
Search for God
And his heart does not have to
Pray to God.
Luckily, the world does not need
A saint like him.

7555.

The destructive happiness of an
    insane man
Is real torture
To the man whose sanity
Is in perfect order.

7556.

If you have a sorrowful experience
In your inner life,
Disappointment must not break
    your heart.
For you have deep within you
The wisdom to transform
This sorrowful and painful
    experience
Into a joyful and fruitful
    realisation.

7557.

When man forgets
His love for God,
His heart loses
Its Olympian joy.

7558.

Since he has successfully escaped
From the futile shallowness of the
   mind,
His heart will be powerfully
   blessed
By the fulness-beauty of his soul.

7559.

Shock the mind into waking.
Shock the heart into rising.
Shock the life into flying.
You will then be running fast
Along the sunlit road
To the perfection-temple.

7560.

The book of your heart's light
Is an excellent book.
Keep it always on your reading
   desk
To serve as your ever-ready
   reference book,
Especially when you enter into
The library of ignorance-night.

7561.

A soulful oneness-experience
Is man's international dream.
A powerful oneness-satisfaction
Is God's universal Reality.

7562.

A breath of self-effacement
Is the immediate birth
Of my life's enlightenment-sky.

7563.

If you want to succeed,
Allow not any disappointment
To set you back.
If you want to proceed,
Accept the invitations of a
   cheerful hope
And a fruitful promise.

7564.

Alas, it was you who chose death
Long before you had any idea
Of the beauty and divinity of life.

7565.

Heaven's Compassion did not
   help me
Because I was too weak
To be helped.
Earth's jealousy did not disturb
   me
Because I was too strong
To be disturbed.

7566.

For a true seeker of the Infinite
It is an impossible task
To long for death
Before God-manifestation.
For an ordinary man
It is an impossible task
To strive to live
With a higher ideal in mind.

7567.

A heart of silence
Teaches me how to swim
In God's Compassion-Sea.
A mind of sound
Tells me that it can teach me
How to empty God's
   Compassion-Sea.

7568.

He who soulfully listens
Can powerfully speak.
He who powerfully speaks
Is a true messenger of God.
A true messenger of God
Ushers in God's final Victory on
   earth.

7569.

The union of my dreams
And God's Reality
Takes place inside my
   perfection-cry
And God's Satisfaction-Smile.

7570.

Believe it or not,
He gets infinitely more pleasure
From the defeats of others
Than from his own teeming
   victories.

7571.

I have yet to learn
The meaning of loneliness,
Since my Lord Supreme
Has not created loneliness for
   those
Who serve Him unconditionally
In this lifetime.

7572.

Man's desire-life
Never expects to surrender
To God's all-illumining
　　Vision-Eye.

7573.

Although God is infinite,
He prefers to live
Inside a tiny
Man-built nest.

7574.

God introduces me
To His immortal Life every day.
I introduce God
To my immediate death every day.

7575.

I am ready to believe in everything
Except one thing,
And that is the radical
　　transformation
Of my desire's hot breath.

7576.

Every day God does
Two most significant things for
　　me:
He loves my innocence-life
And treasures my security-heart.

7577.

A whisper from my totally
　　helpless
Insecurity-life
Can completely ruin
The flower of my morning prayer
And
The fruit of my evening
　　meditation.

7578.

Earth's soulful love,
With sweet care and dear concern,
Asks man to sing
His own self-transcendence-song
Melodiously and perfectly.

7579.

Your soul-power can baffle death
If your heart invokes
The Compassion-Flood of God,
The universal Protection.

7580.

If you do not aspire every day
Soulfully and unreservedly,
You are bound to see
   unquestionably
Your own heart's fading flames.

7581.

When your heart becomes
The flower of beauty,
Your life will produce
The fruit of earth-nourishing
   reality.

7582.

I shall see
What I can do for God
Since I am not doing
Anything worthwhile for man.

7583.

Since I love even man's
   treacherous mind,
I do not think it will be
A difficult task
For me to love God's
   compassionate Heart.

7584.

My sincerity-mind tells me
That I have not done anything
   great.
My humility-life tells me
That I have not done anything
   good.
My purity-heart tells me
That I have not done anything
   perfect.

7585.

Determination within,
Determination without
At every moment!
Lo, unimaginable achievements
Are within your easy reach.

7586.

I do not want to know
What God thinks of me,
But I do want to remind myself
Of what I can do
To deserve God's infinite
   Compassion.

7587.

Yesterday God-realisation
Was a colossal hope.
Today God-realisation
Is a free Heaven-climbing rope.

7588.

Be careful of your
    silence-commitment.
Be careful of your
    sound-commitment.
If you are careful,
Then happiness will be your
    name.

7589.

Be prepared for surprises.
Today God may invite you.
Be prepared to immediately
    accept.
Again, today the hostile forces
May invite you.
Be prepared to make the strongest
    refusal.

7590.

You do not have to imitate
Others' successes.
You do not have to learn
From others' mistakes.
Just follow your intuition.
Your intuition embodies
The beauty of success
And
The purity of progress.

7591.

As you climb the ladder of success,
Do not forget
It is your determination
That is enabling you to succeed.
As you climb the ladder of
    progress,
Do not forget
It is your surrender
That is enabling you to proceed.

7592.

It is a serious mistake
To broadcast your opinions all the
    time.
Keep your wise opinions to
    yourself
So you can escape the ridicule
Of the world
And also save the world
From having to tolerate your
    stupidity.

7593.

First punish your unruly vital,
Then show it an illumining light.
You will see that it is not
A difficult task
To immortalise your life
Of self-dedication.

7594.

An ordinary human life
May at times be sweet,
But the life of a soulful seeker
Is always incomparably sweet.

7595.

Each painful thought
That you are experiencing today
Is due to the pressure
Of your disobedience-life.

7596.

My life of hope is fast perishing.
Will my heart's sky of sorrow
Also perish
Along with my hope-life?

7597.

If ever I look behind,
What do I see?
Purity? No.
Sincerity? No.
Love of God? No.
I see only the constant birth
Of an all-devouring hunger.

7598.

If your vital indulges
In selfishness,
Then your poor heart's thirst
Will remain ruthlessly
    unquenched.

7599.

You unconsciously resent
    perfection.
Therefore, you don't care to see
God's Satisfaction-Smile
Inside His evolving universe.

7600.

My smiling eyes tell me
My Beloved Supreme
Is coming towards me.
My crying heart tells me
My Beloved Supreme
Has come.

7601.

God touches my heart
So that I can fly on the wings
Of His ever-ascending
    Vision-Smile.

7602.

Be brave
Where your heart is concerned.
Be sincere
Where your mind is concerned.
Then you will see how easy it is
To live your life
In a supremely better consciousness.

7603.

My will was made
For God's Satisfaction.
God's Will was made
For my perfection.

7604.

Curb your negative feelings.
Otherwise, before long,
You will have to retreat
From the world's heart-garden.

7605.

I cry because
I am so imperfect.
I smile because
My Lord tells me
That I am not a hopeless case.

7606.

God the Compassion
Is before my eyes.
God the Satisfaction
Is within my heart.
God the Perfection
Is inside my aspiration-cry.

7607.

I must not forget
To tell Heaven
That poor earth
Is always willing to try.

7608.

There is no difference
Between collecting and storing garbage
And identifying with the impure thoughts
Of the human mind.

7609.

Look at yourself soulfully sometimes
So that you do not exaggerate
Your imperfection-cry.

7610.

Since each thought
Is an atomic power,
You can give each thought
A diplomatic death.

7611.

If my heart
Knows you well,
I shall not keep
My mouth shut
When the world does not value
Your aspiration-heart
And dedication-life.

7612.

The unaspiring human mind
Is forced to enjoy
The tug-of-war
Between strangling doubt
And embracing faith.

7613.

No matter what you say,
No matter what you do,
God will not discredit your
   talents,
For His Heart of Satisfaction
He has already placed inside you.

7614.

My aspiring heart is familiar
With sincerity-seekers.
My undivine mind is familiar
With anxiety-mongers.

7615.

My Lord Supreme,
I desperately need You
Early in the morning
To tell me that my heart
Can be as pure
As Your Vision-Eye.
My Lord Supreme,
I desperately need You
Late in the evening
To tell me that my life
Can be as perfect
As Your Compassion-Heart.

7616.

Simplification is nothing other
Than unification.
When I simplify my complex
And complicated mind,
I unify my earth-bound life
With my Lord's eternally free Life.

7617.

There can be no iota of doubt
Inside your illumined mind.
Such being the case,
Your heart is now in a position
To enjoy citizenship in Heaven.

7618.

If you can cheerfully veil
Your spiritual greatness,
God will quickly unveil
Your spiritual goodness,
Plus tell the whole world
That you are His unparalleled
 instrument.

7619.

God is his life's unwritten
 compassion.
God is his mind's mystic
 inspiration.
God is his heart's psychic
 aspiration.
Therefore,
God dreams of His own perfect
 Satisfaction
In and through him.

7620.

What is the difference
Between falsehood and truth?
Falsehood is not afraid
Of earth's ignorance-night,
But it is afraid
Of Heaven's wisdom-light and
 delight.
Truth is not afraid
Of earth's ignorance-night
Or of Heaven's wisdom-light and
 delight.
Therefore the omnipotent
 Supreme,
Omniscient Supreme
And omnipresent Supreme
Loves truth and not falsehood.

7621.

Even during the sunset years
Of his life,
His heart longed for solid security
And his mind longed for bright
 hopes.

7622.

His days die with sombre sleep.
His nights die with giant groans.
What can you expect
From such an ill-fated
And Heaven-denied man?

7623.

We imitate a person
For our self-glorification.
We imitate God
For our life-liberation.

7624.

Just because you have
The opportunity-hour,
You cannot say you are going to use
Your creativity-power.
But if you have creativity-power,
Someday, somehow,
You will discover
Your opportunity-hour.

7625.

If you remain in your child-heart,
No matter how many mistakes you make,
You will try to rectify them
And not repeat them.
If you remain in your adult-mind,
You will not even try to rectify
Your mistakes.
You will only prepare yourself
For your coffin.

7626.

When the hour strikes,
Nobody is going to look for you.
You have to remain wide awake
And respond immediately.

7627.

Silence speaks soulfully and powerfully.
Everybody loves to hear it speak,
And so do I.
Sound speaks loudly and foolishly.
Nobody understands a word it says.
Everybody laughs,
And so do I.

7628.

The satisfaction of life
May not be ours,
But the beauty of hope
Is all ours.

7629.

God is more than willing
To grant me the beauty
Of perfection-blossoms.
But alas, where is my receptivity?
Where is it?

7630.

Where can I announce my Lord's Victory?
Not inside my mind's sound-sea,
But inside my heart's silence-sky.

7631.

No sincere heart-cries
Will give birth
To devastating frustrations
And heart-breaking realisations.

7632.

My Lord,
I pray to You to shelter me
And everything of mine,
Except two things which I have created:
My fearful vital and my doubtful mind.

7633.

Two ancient universal questions:
How can I realise God
Immediately?
Is unconditional surrender
Ever possible?

7634.

You will be able to outlast
The perils of your temptation-life
If your aspiration is intense
And your dedication is immense.

7635.

Because you do not believe
In the mind's search,
Because you do not believe
In the heart's cry,
Your joy is speeding
Towards death.

7636.

O chosen son of God,
Yours is not the life of empty hopes.
Therefore, for you
Every hour is a long stride
Towards God.

7637.

Cherish not, even unconsciously,
The cave of despair.
Only then will you be able
To sing and dance
On the silver mountain
Of satisfaction-delight.

7638.

His heart's light-giving lamp
God lovingly takes
As His own unveiling
Satisfaction-Sun.

7639.

"I love God."
This thought starts from my heart
And runs and runs towards God.
"I do not love God."
This thought starts from my mind
And carries me away from God.

7640.

Since you immensely enjoy
Dry intellectual jargon,
You are blessed with
A mercilessly perplexing
   labyrinth
Of futile human opinions.

7641.

What have I to conceal?
My ignorance-night?
No, I shall not conceal it.
The sooner I reveal it,
The sooner my Lord's
   Compassion-Eye
Will be able to transform it
Into wisdom-delight.

7642.

God laughs and laughs
When He sees that I am not at all
   anxious
To come out of my failure-night,
That on the contrary,
I am quite comfortably sleeping
   there.

7643.

Nothing gives me greater joy
Than to see my exorbitant pride
Weeping bitterly.

7644.

Dedicate your life divinely
And dare to smile soulfully.
Soon you will hear
God knocking at your heart's
   door.
Once He comes in,
He will stay there forever and
   forever.

7645.

Every day you can walk along
The inner road
With your life of prayer
And your heart of meditation.

7646.

Purity is the Heaven-born music,
And this Heaven-born music
Can be heard only by those
Who are spiritually strong.

7647.

Silence was my goal.
But my Lord Supreme tells me
That He will take me far beyond silence
To an infinitely superior goal.

7648.

As an individual
Often dresses in different clothes,
Even so, Krishna, the Buddha, the Christ
And many others
Are the same God
Clothed in different garb.

7649.

If you see a hungry heart
Inside someone,
That means his truth-life
Has already begun.

7650.

He is totally lost
Between his happy dream of Heaven
And his sad existence on earth.

7651.

O my mind's suspicion-night,
Do you not realise
That you are nothing other than
A joy-devouring beast?

7652.

My gratitude-heart
And my surrender-life
Are already stationed
Among the immortals.

7653.

Everything is imperfect.
Everyone is imperfect.
But God has promised me
That He will definitely make
His entire creation perfect,
And it will be done quite soon.

7654.

A seeker of the supreme Truth
Has only one necessity,
And that necessity is
The earth-liberating
And Heaven-manifesting God.

7655.

Do you want to know
How close you are to God?
Then dive deep within,
To the inmost region of your
    inner life.
Only there will you find
The correct answer.

7656.

Your thunder-vital will never be
    able
To conquer the heart of the world.
It is your sweet violin-heart
That will conquer —
In fact, has already conquered —
The heart of the world.

7657.

Because of my surrender-light
Of today,
My Lord Supreme has forgiven
My neglected aspiration of the
    past.

7658.

The stupid mind thinks
That time is sleeping.
The wise heart knows
That time is perishing.
And I know
That time is illumining.

7659.

If you cling desperately
To your desire-life,
You will never be able to deny
The stark frowns of
    dissolution-night.

7660.

Neglect not
Your heart of promise-light.
If you neglect it,
Yours will be, before long,
The destruction-doom.

7661.

You want your mind to wither.
But how can it wither
As long as you allow it
To nourish itself with false
    imaginings?

7662.

Man speaks ill of God.
Man revolts against God.
Yet God does not change His decision
That man will be His chosen instrument
To manifest Him here on earth.

7663.

What can doubt do?
It can easily destroy
The beauty and purity
Of oneness-friendship-joy.

7664.

Remove resentment
From your entire being
If you want enlightenment
Within and without.

7665.

Unless you sever yourself
From the obscurity
Of your suspicion-mind,
How can your heart
Ever be happy?

7666.

Happiness
Will follow you
If your heart remains
Undisturbed by trifles.

7667.

Man's first disobedience-night
And
Heaven's first indifference-torture
Are inseparable.

7668.

As a tree that has countless leaves,
Flowers and fruits
Bows down to offer them
To the world at large,
Even so, a truly great seeker
Humbly bows down
To offer the fruits of his inner life
To mankind.

7669.

Unless we invoke today
The presence of tomorrow's
All-illumining dawn,
Our life may sadly end
In a heart-breaking,
All-important failure.

7670.

Heaven's first-born child:
Promise-sun.
Earth's first-born child:
Hope-sea.

7671.

Your monstrous anger
Heralds the fast-approaching
   hour
Of your life's
Total destruction.

7672.

Alas, the forest of uncomely
   thoughts
In your mind
Is threatening and frightening
Your heart's climbing cry.

7673.

Soulfully try to accept
God's timeless
   Compassion-Height.
Your heart-cries will be
   transformed
Into blossoms of enlightenment.

7674.

To feed a seeker's heart,
Heaven, in its infinite beauty,
Every day smilingly, lovingly
And compassionately descends.

7675.

Your constant craving
For world praise
Has forced your heart's
   aspiration-cry
To cease speedily.

7676.

A defective and contagious
Loneliness-heart
Sleeplessly breeds
Hidden fears.

7677.

Your inner wound is deepening
And will continue to deepen
Unless you stop obeying
Your mind's loud voice
And listen only to God's
Secret and sacred Whispers.

7678.

It is you who have allowed
    yourself
To become a slave
To your stark fate.
How then can you enter
Into the delight-palace
Of silence-kingdom?

7679.

A succession of calamities
Shall without fail
Mark the reign
Of your wild desire-life.

7680.

We think that opportunity leads
    us
To something precious:
God-realisation.
But opportunity not only leads us
To something precious.
Opportunity itself is precious.

7681.

Because your mind is a slave
To teeming doubts,
You cannot enjoy
The beauty and satisfaction
Of a perfect reality.

7682.

My heart's
Shadowless satisfaction-cry
Is the crown of my life's
Soulful efforts.

7683.

Can you believe that your mind
Is not missing God right now?
Can you believe that your heart
Is not loving God any more?

7684.

God needs manifestation.
That is why He is touching our
    feet.
We need realisation.
That is why we are breaking God's
    Head.

7685.

When he was in Heaven,
His heart-flower opened
And he compassionately said:
"Let me go down and help
The suffering earth."
Alas, when he came to earth,
He immediately said:
"Is there anybody in God's
    universe
As stupid as I?
Let me go back to Heaven!"

7686.

A sense of incompleteness even
   God has.
He has divided Himself
Into two realities:
Heaven and earth.
These two realities need each
   other
And fulfil each other.
Only when Heaven and earth are
   united
Will God feel complete.

7687.

Our goal is not fixed;
It is always transcending itself.
When we are about to reach
Our long-awaited goal,
We immediately see a new goal
In front of us.
To reach this new goal
Is not a one-inch journey.
It is also a very long distance away.

7688.

Our first goal in meditation
Is not to have undivine, ordinary
   thoughts.
Our second goal
Is to have divine, progressive
   thoughts.
Our third goal
Is to have no thoughts at all.
Consciously or unconsciously,
We must always strive for a new
   goal.

7689.

God always keeps His Promises to
   man.
If He does not fulfil one of His
   Promises,
We have to know
That He will fulfil a new and
   better Promise.

7690.

You were waiting for
A phone call from God.
But poor God was exhausted
And could not dial
His Heavenly telephone.
Instead, God just grabbed your
   soul
And fed it,
Giving it divine and supreme joy
Far beyond your expectations.

7691.

An immature seeker may believe
That the faster he chants the names
Of the cosmic gods and goddesses,
The faster will be
His inner progress.
A mature seeker knows
That the more soulfully
He prays and meditates,
The more fruitful will be
His inner progress.

7692.

Since during the day
He sings soulful God-songs,
At night God allows him
To have beautiful God-dreams.

7693.

A true spiritual Master must shoulder
The countless responsibilities
Of his spiritual family.
But still he remains
In a childlike consciousness
To fill his seeker-children
With the joy and delight
Of God the eternal Child.

7694.

If you feel you are young,
Then you will see each moment
As an opportunity to grow.
If you feel you are old,
You may not be able to see
Any opportunities at all
In your life.

7695.

Opportunities appear before us
In millions of ways.
Alas,
To lose these opportunities
We have also found
Millions of ways.

7696.

If you are unable to reveal
The light you have received
During your meditation,
Do not worry.
You will not lose it.
It will only remain dormant
Until God's Hour,
When you will have the inner wisdom
To use it in the right way
For the right purpose.

7697.

Every new year
The Supreme gives us a new
 Message.
If we take His Message seriously,
Our progress can be great,
Greater and greatest.

7698.

In the inner world
You can never say
You have received enough.
While God's Love is entering
Into your heart,
It is creating even more hunger
For His Love.
While God's Compassion is
 descending
Into you,
It is creating an even larger vessel
To hold His Compassion.

7699.

Our earthly hunger can be fed
With a limited amount of earthly
 food
And then be satisfied.
Our Heavenly hunger can be fed
With Peace, Light and Delight
In infinite measure
And still cry for more.

7700.

Give me, give me.
This was the prayer
I offered to God yesterday.
Receive me, receive me.
This is the prayer
I am offering to my Lord today.
Transform me, transform me
And make me Your very own.
This is the prayer
I shall offer to my Lord Supreme
 tomorrow.

7701.

He knows the first divine rule:
Love God, only God.
He knows the last supreme rule:
Love God sleeplessly
Plus unconditionally.

7702.

A sincere seeker will not mind
If God does not speak to him.
An insincere seeker will not be
 satisfied
Even if God does speak to him.
He will be furious that God
Did not speak to him sooner.

7703.

All religions are part of one
   God-Tree.
This God-Tree has many branches,
Flowers and fruits.
If you climb up a tree
And rest on a particular branch,
Will the tree be displeased?
Similarly, if you take a flower or
   fruit,
No matter from which branch,
The God-Tree will be pleased,
For each branch is part and parcel
Of the tree itself.

7704.

When you eat too much earthly
   food,
The world tells you that you are
   greedy.
When you eat too much Heavenly
   food,
God tells you
And the whole world tells you
That you are an absolutely
Choice instrument of God.

7705.

If you fail in your aspiration-life,
In the evening of your life
You are bound to see
Your own failure-sigh
Hovering between earth and
   Heaven.

7706.

Before fear invades your heart,
You must invade and conquer
Your own insecurity-life.
Before doubt invades your mind,
You must invade and conquer
Your own impurity-thoughts.

7707.

If I can always have
A childlike confidence,
Then my Lord Supreme
Will, without fail, become
My sleeplessly self-sacrificing
   Friend.

7708.

Misunderstanding is
The order of the day.
Therefore, even my own mind
Misunderstands my own
   infallible heart.

7709.

Since God has killed me
With His Love,
I am going to kill Him
With my gratitude.

7710.

Fear, why do I have to worship
   you?
You are not going to
Make me happy.
You are not going to
Make me immortal.

7711.

I am totally convinced
That a pure heart
Is the only king on earth.

7712.

Why do I have to believe him
Who tells me
That my heart is not of God
And that my life is not for God?

7713.

As each evil thought
Is a problem-maker,
Even so, each divine thought
Is an immediate problem-shooter.

7714.

My falling tears
In no time are captured
By God's descending
Compassion-Concern-Smile.

7715.

I stumbled only to realise
That my stumbling itself
Was a stepping-stone
Towards my speedy
   God-realisation.

7716.

I do not know where
My prayers have disappeared to.
Alas, my life is strewn
With deathless sorrows.

7717.

O my vital,
You are craving for rich comfort.
But alas, do you not see the
   death-dart
Fast approaching you?

7718.

Human life
Will not meet with
   disappointment
If it keeps
Its daily appointment with God.

7719.

O my mind,
Everybody misunderstands you,
But not my loving heart
And my illumining soul.

7720.

One tiny inch
In any wrong direction
May be the cause
Of a stupendous inner loss.

7721.

What do I expect from you?
A soulful love
And a powerful promise.

7722.

The most difficult task
Is to bring to the fore
The best you have within you.
But this most difficult task
Is not impossible,
For God is always ready to help
   you
With His open Heart.

7723.

The soul does not come and go in
   vain.
At the end of each earthly sojourn
The soul strengthens its
   determination
To manifest the Supreme
   infinitely more
In its future incarnations.

7724.

To satisfy my Lord Supreme
I must treasure my heart's
   aspiration-cry
And my life's dedication-smile.

7725.

Faith is beauty's
Climbing cry.
Beauty is life's
Glowing smile.

7726.

Only one thing
God hesitates to take from me,
And that is
My mind's telephone number.

7727.

God's compassionate
   Rainbow-Lustre
Can be safely treasured and
   preserved
Only by the inner purity
Of aspiring hearts.

7728.

Doubt inserts its poisonous knife
Only when faith is afraid
Of challenging doubt's audacity.

7729.

You can deny and ignore
   everything
Except the ultimate fact of life:
Death.

7730.

O my stupid mind,
From now on
I shall not receive from you
But I shall direct to you
All my wise decisions.

7731.

My Lord,
If You care for me,
Then at least run with me
If You do not want
To run for me.

7732.

My Lord,
Why are You so angry with me?
"I am not angry with you.
I am angry with Myself."
Why? Why?
"Because still I have not been able
To perfect you."

7733.

Loving myself alone
Was my past weakness.
Not loving God alone
Is my very strong present
   weakness.

7734.

God's Oneness-Heart
And my newness-life
I once upon a time thought
Were my mental hallucinations.

7735.

At last my heart
Has challenged my mind,
Not to defeat it
But to transform it.

7736.

Nobody hears anything.
Nobody wants to hear anything.
Nobody needs to hear anything.
But who can avoid hearing
The fast-approaching footsteps
Of death?

7737.

Your great penance has gratified
　you alone.
That's all!
But his self-giving heart for
　mankind
Has not only thrilled my heart
But also illumined my life.

7738.

I live on earth
Only to catch a glimpse
Of my Lord's Compassion-Eye
And Forgiveness-Feet.

7739.

Each undetected desire
Has the unthinkable capacity
To strangle our snow-white
　aspiration-life.

7740.

The increase of self-indulgence
Is the immediate decrease
Of beauty's purity and duty's
　divinity.

7741.

A saint knows and feels
That he is inside
The Satisfaction-Eye of God.
A sinner does not know
Or dare to feel
That he is inside
The Compassion-Heart of God.

7742.

A flood from his thought-sea
Has totally destroyed
The life-illumining music
Of his soul.

7743.

When I am in my Master's heart,
I see everything
Save and except one thing:
Death-dart.

7744.

Nothing is more illumining
Than my silver faith.
Nothing is more fulfilling
Than my golden surrender.
Nothing is more satisfying
Than my diamond gratitude.

7745.

My heart's hope
And my soul's promise
Are showing me the way
To God's Omniscience-Light.

7746.

To live on the outskirts of hope
Is not enough.
Cultivate a hope-life
Inside the very breath
Of your moment-to-moment
    existence.

7747.

Eternity shows its shortest road
To him who does not want to wait
For ignorance-prince.

7748.

There is a better name for earth:
Permanent hospital.
There is a better name for man:
Incurable patient.

7749.

Now that I am not playing any
    more
The self-proclamation-game,
My Lord Supreme is so happy
    with me
And so proud of me.

7750.

If you can have a clear awareness
Of what is happening
In your aspiration-life,
It is an easy task
To cultivate a diamond heart.

7751.

Excellence is the sweet
   permanence-life
Of self-transcendence
In God's Beauty and Duty
   unknowable.

7752.

My Mother India commands me
To learn that comparison
Is not a nice game.

7753.

My Mother India commands me
To learn that her ancient beauty
Far transcends the capacity
Of Western curiosity.

7754.

My Mother India tells me
That her body may be meant
For a silence-life,
But her soul is definitely meant
For the direct manifestation
Of God the Sound.

7755.

My Mother India commands me
To unreservedly honour
One of her main virtues:
Patience.

7756.

My Mother India commands me
To learn that life's divinity
Is founded upon oneness-purity.

7757.

My Mother India announces to me
That by virtue of my heart's
Constant cries,
I can go beyond the soaring
   imagination-flight
Of the modern world.

7758.

When your mind returns to God,
He may not even say hello
To your mind.
But when your heart returns to
   God,
The first thing He will do
Is embrace your heart.

7759.

Unless your heart
Is a dance of hope,
How can your life
Be a song of peace?

7760.

My Lord Supreme,
I am ready to lose everything
Save and except two things:
My heart's beautiful hope
And my soul's powerful promise.

7761.

My Lord,
I try, only to fail.
"My child,
Do not give up.
Soon you will try,
Only to succeed."

7762.

My Lord,
I do not want to know
When I will be able
To please You.
I just want to know
If ever I will be able
To please You.

7763.

A complicated mind wants to see
God's Vision-Eye.
A simple heart wishes to feel
God's Compassion-Heart.

7764.

O my mind,
I am for your
Perfection immediate.
But I am not with
And I shall never be with
Your imperfection.

7765.

There will always be
Some people on earth
Who will save humanity
From total insanity.

7766.

His is the mind that enjoys
Sleepless struggles.
His is the life that enjoys
Useless unrest.

7767.

A God-lover knows
That each pure thought
Is a soulful glimpse
Of beauty's height.

7768.

His ceaselessly and unfathomably
Happy heart
Has cancelled all the injunctions
Of his fateful destiny.

7769.

Who practises truth?
Certainly not you,
Not he, not I,
Not earth, perhaps not even
    Heaven.
Only Eternity's hope
Practises truth.

7770.

Lord, since You have opened
My heart's door,
I am now going to give You
My only treasure:
My life's gratitude-smile.

7771.

He does not hide anything,
Not even his shameless
    unwillingness
To surrender to God's Will.

7772.

Life has denied me
My Lord's Face,
But I am sure death
Will never do that.

7773.

Practical fears
Are very rare experiences.
Theoretical fears
Are daily occurrences.

7774.

Alas, the blue bird
Inside my heart
Instead of singing Heaven-free
    songs
Is hearing earth-bound sighs.

7775.

Each time I speak
To my foolish mind,
I enlarge the gulf
Of my incomprehension.

7776.

With my heart's obedience-flames
I have created a hallowed dawn
To welcome God, the Beautiful
   One.

7777.

From my life my Lord wants
One service-tree.
From my heart my Lord wants
Seven gratitude-fruits
And nothing more, nothing more.

7778.

My heart,
You do not often misunderstand
But you are always
   misunderstood.
I feel simply miserable
That I can be of no help to you
In spite of my soulful intention.

7779.

My constant longing for peace
Is bravely captured
By strong despair.

7780.

Unless we daily and faithfully
Purify the mind,
We will be forced to live
Inside the thick jungle
Of ignorance-night.

7781.

Your unlimited patience
Will earn for you
The unlimited Joy of God.

7782.

Unless my heart takes care
Of my conscience,
How can my conscience take care
Of my complicated life?

7783.

My heart's deathless hope
Is that someday
In this lifetime
I shall please my Lord Supreme
In His own Way
At least for a fleeting second.

7784.

The farther away you are
From inner light,
The nearer you are
To your spiritual death.

7785.

O my mind,
Cry to please God.
O my heart,
Dream to please God.
O my life,
Smile to please God.
O my soul,
Do not leave my body.
I have yet to please God.

7786.

He has made his final decision:
No more world-deception;
Only a self-giving life of
   dedication.

7787.

My vital never learns.
It is so stupid!
My mind never unlearns.
It is equally stupid!

7788.

To gain the comradeship
Of God the Transcendental
Is to claim the ownership
Of God the Universal.

7789.

God has given my
   aspiration-flames
The capacity to whisper secret
   truths
Into His sacred Ears.

7790.

There is only one ideal fragrance
That can come to the seeker's
   rescue,
And that is the Fragrance
Of the yet-unknown God-Flower.

7791.

High above there is a voice
That commands him to love
God the Transcendental Beauty.
Deep within there is a voice
That commands him to serve
God the Universal Purity.

7792.

Every day my Lord asks me
Not to hide His Vision-Beauty
But to carry it and spread it
   all-where
Soulfully and sleeplessly.

7793.

The human mind does not know
Where progress-light abides.
The divine heart knows
That there is no place on earth
Where progress-light
Cannot be seen and manifested.

7794.

God tells us
That there are limitless
   opportunities
For us to love Him
And become His perfect
   instruments.
He also tells us
That the cosmic gods are
   descending
To show us the only way
That leads to His supreme
   Vision-Height.

7795.

The outer sun makes him feel
How insignificant he is.
The inner sun makes him see and
   feel
That for aeons he has been
   admiring
And adoring
Its divine vision
And supreme perfection.

7796.

You do not have to know
About tomorrow.
You do not have to know
Even about today.
You only have to know one thing:
God will not disappoint you.

7797.

In the inner world
The best short-cut
Is to soulfully give
And unconditionally become.

7798.

Your heart must become
A sea of love.
Your mind must become
A river of detachment.

7799.

The future holds for you
Only one thing:
Your complete satisfaction
Within and without
In God's own Way.

7800.

My Lord Supreme,
I am not asking You to receive me.
I am praying to You only to give me
The capacity to remember You
And feel You are my Eternity's All
In both the world of earthly hope
And the world of Heavenly promise.

7801.

My Lord Supreme,
Your Beauty's Eyes
Sleeplessly love me.
In return, may I not love
Your Divinity's Heart
Breathlessly?

7802.

Will this poor and feeble world
Ever be liberated?
Will this helpless and hopeless world
Ever awaken
To a single golden dawn?

7803.

You think that by practising
The life of outer relinquishment
You are fast approaching
The life of inner enlightenment.
It is impossible!

7804.

Since your mind
Is overburdened with problems
Created by none other than yourself,
How can your life ever dream
Of rich salvation?

7805.

There is no such thing
As the near future.
Anything but here and now
Is a mental hallucination.
Therefore, do what you can now,
And be what you are supposed to be
At this very moment.

7806.

The life that unreservedly serves
   humanity
Is unsophisticated.
The heart that unconditionally
   loves God
Is uncluttered.

7807.

I needed a listener.
Alas, nobody wanted to be a
   listener.
Now my Lord is telling me
That I will never have a listener
Unless and until
I have become a lover.
I must love earth
With my service-delight.
I must love Heaven
With my aspiration-height.

7808.

He tries to free himself
From curiosity,
For he feels God-realisation
Is not a matter of curiosity
But a matter of wisdom-light.

7809.

Your mind may enjoy
The comfort of fantasy,
But for your poor heart,
Satisfaction remains a far cry.

7810.

If you suspect the world
And its motives,
Your outer life may not suffer
   much,
But your inner life will starve to
   death.

7811.

You are fond of staying
Inside your desire-bound mind.
No wonder you are indefinitely
   detained
Inside your own doubt-fort.

7812.

The smile of justice-light
Can alone grant you
The blessing of peace-delight.

7813.

When my heart permanently has
The excellence of a
   surrender-flower
And a gratitude-fruit,
God-Perfection shall not
Remain a far cry.

7814.

Two unthinkable things you
   think:
That ignorance-night
Can completely envelop others,
But not you,
And that God loves you only.

7815.

My Heavenly capacities cannot
   cry.
My earthly capacities cannot
   smile.
But someday there will come a
   time
When I shall transcend the
   necessities
Of cry and smile.

7816.

To the soul's festival in Heaven,
Earth was not able to come.
But it sent its representative:
A deathless sigh.

7817.

Yesterday you wept silence-tears.
Therefore, today you have become
The blossom of an illumining life.

7818.

Place your own flower-heart
At the blue Feet of the Lord
   Supreme,
In exactly the same way
As morning places its flowers
At the red feet of the planet sun.

7819.

Even his own wild curiosity
Is not interested in carrying
His suspicion-mind towards God.

7820.

You fool!
How can you expect anything
Beautiful and fruitful
From your self-imposed
   blindness-life?

7821.

Your mind is getting ready
For its deathbed devotion.
Your heart is already ready
For its Immortality's perfection.

7822.

You have the capacity
To see your follies.
Indeed this is the beginning
Of your Godward journey.
Soon you will have the capacity
To observe the mistakes of the
    world.
What will you do then?
You will just correct them
One by one.

7823.

Who can appreciate the fierce
    songs
Of his mental life?
Who can admire the maniacal
    dance
Of his vital life?
Who, tell me, who?

7824.

Every day try to hasten the
    completion
Of your God-ordained task:
The transformation of
    earth-bound sorrow
Into Heaven-free joy.

7825.

Do you want to know
Where I am going?
I am going to Heaven.
Do you want to know why?
Just so I can come back again
With more compassion-light
And more forgiveness-delight.

7826.

What is human life, after all,
If not overwhelming anxiety?
What is divine life, after all,
If not ever-increasing security
In the Heart of the Supreme?

7827.

The immensity of his self-offering
Has buried the frustration-life
Of earth-hunger.

7828.

Do not run away from trouble.
Your aspiring heart will before long
Perform a miracle:
It will cause trouble itself
To run away from you,
Utterly frustrated.

7829.

I have received an invitation
From God.
I shall go and sing for Him
My heart's crying songs
And dance for Him
My soul's ecstasy-manifesting dances.

7830.

As long as you are busy
With your own ridiculously
Insignificant affairs,
Your life's inner tumult
Will never subside.

7831.

The greatest difficulty
In human life
Is the bitter frown
Of misunderstanding-night.

7832.

My obedience to my inner voice
Is my unparalleled confidence
In my tomorrow's life.

7833.

Yesterday gave me
What it had for me:
Two curiosity-eyes.
Today is giving me
What it has for me:
One sincerity-cry.
Tomorrow will give me
What it will have for me:
The inseparable oneness
Of my perfection-life
And God's Satisfaction-Heart.

7834.

If we keep our inner appointments
Cheerfully and punctually,
No disappointment-night
Can darken our heart's aspiration-door.

7835.

There are only two inner
    teachings
That each seeker has to learn:
Man is unveiling God
Slowly and steadily,
God has become man
Cheerfully and unconditionally.

7836.

The torture of ignorance-night
    disappears
Only when the seeker sleeplessly
    values
The lustre of his heart's inner
    moon.

7837.

To the known God I say,
"I have come with gratitude."
To the unknown God I say,
"I have come with surrender."
To the unknowable God I say,
"I have come to my Source."

7838.

Unless you offer your imprisoned
    life
Unconditionally
To your Inner Pilot,
How can you ever dream
Of constant aspiration,
Constant dedication
And constant satisfaction?

7839.

When unwillingness to abide by
    God's Will
Becomes a habit,
Man becomes a perfect victim
To perfect destruction.

7840.

Do you want to work for God?
Then love Him more.
Do you want to love God?
Then serve Him more.
Do you want to serve God?
Then become one with Him more.

7841.

You think that you alone
Know how to postpone
Your life of perfection-light.
But do you not think that God, too,
Knows how to indefinitely delay
His choice Hour?

7842.

You do not have to broadcast
Your conviction.
Your commitment to your inner life
Will not only do that for you,
But will do it far better
Than you can ever do it.

7843.

God may not be always available,
But God's Compassion-Sea
And Forgiveness-Sky
Are always available.

7844.

God has always been inside you
With His Vision-Light.
Can you not be inside Him,
Even for a second,
With your heart's perfection-delight?

7845.

Ignorance and God
Are playing their respective roles
Constantly in my life.
Ignorance tries to blind me
To prove its power-night.
God tries to liberate me
To prove His Power-Light.

7846.

You are looking at
Your failure-life.
When are you going to look for
God's Blessing-Delight?

7847.

Yesterday I sowed faith-seed.
Today I am discovering
A beautiful and fruitful peace-tree.

7848.

To love man unreservedly
Is to discover God in one's own heart
Immediately plus unconditionally.

7849.

God has the time to convince
Only the genuine seekers
Who have already started
   believing
That He loves them,
Feeds them and needs them.

7850.

Beauty knows how to shine.
Purity knows how to give.
Divinity knows how to become.
Immortality knows how to
   transcend.

7851.

One haunting doubt
Can unbelievably weaken
A long-abiding belief.

7852.

I have two final questions:
Is God the Dream as beautiful
As God the Reality?
Are God the Creator and God the
   creation
Satisfied with each other?

7853.

His outer life powerfully enjoys
Wild laughter.
His inner life soulfully enjoys
Sweet tears.

7854.

Gently command,
If you have to command,
Your heart.
I assure you,
It will obey you immediately.
Mercilessly command,
When necessity demands,
Your vital.
Then only will it obey you.

7855.

To entertain the angels
What I need is
A heart of beauty's dawn
And a soul of purity's sky.

7856.

You do not have to wait and hope
Indefinitely,
For you know how to love God the
   One
Swiftly, soulfully, selflessly
And unconditionally.

7857.

Earth does not need me.
Heaven has disowned me.
I can nowhere cause commotion.

7858.

The satisfaction-smile
Of his Master's vision
Is his Heaven-sent haven.

7859.

Curiosity awakens
The sleeping man in us
But saddens and disheartens
The aspiring man in us.

7860.

Many may know who God is
And where God is,
But very few can know
Or will ever know
How God always is.

7861.

His mind's addiction to falsehood
Makes him feel that he is great.
His heart's devotion to truth
Makes even the world feel that he
   is good.

7862.

Your mind's secret duty
Is to be pure.
Your heart's sacred duty
Is to be perfect.

7863.

A man of good will
Has the master key
To open all the doors
In God's Compassion-Palace.

7864.

To me, everything depends on
My life's integrity
And not on my mind's ability.

7865.

My Lord accepts me
As I am,
But my mind will accept me
Only if I become another God.

7866.

Two things you do not know:
When the passion-dance
Of your vital will end
And when the illumination-trance
Of your heart will begin.

7867.

To love the world soulfully
Is his life's outer preoccupation.
To love God unconditionally
Is his heart's inner preoccupation.

7868.

What kind of faith is it
If it is strangled every day
By its mischievous enemy:
Doubt?

7869.

The more you want to possess
The world,
The farther and faster you will
    travel
Away from freedom-light.

7870.

If your mind enjoys collecting
Earthly secrets,
Your aspiration-heart will be
    devoured
By giant discouragement.

7871.

An unerring hour
Has the power to remove
A long-lasting mountain of pain.

7872.

God created my faith
Compassionately plus invisibly.
I created my doubt
Deliberately plus visibly.

7873.

I believe in
Forgiving seconds
And not unforgiving hours.

7874.

He has nothing important to do.
Therefore he indulges in
Imagination-memories
Of the finished past.

7875.

What my heart needs
Is a little co-operation
From my mind.
What my mind needs
Is a little aspiration
From my heart.

7876.

As I have no opinion
Of Heaven's Compassion-Light,
Even so, Heaven has no opinion
Of my aspiration-height.

7877.

My Lord Supreme,
Do give me a heart
That can quench Your Thirst
At Your choice Hour.

7878.

He succeeds always
Because his heart's intensity
Is infinitely more powerful
Than the most brilliant noontime sun.

7879.

Because of your mind's conscious addiction
To serious follies,
Your heart-flower cannot grow
To please the Eye of the Lord Supreme.

7880.

Behold, the beauty and purity
Of your heart's dawn
Are helping your mind fly away
From its own ridiculous, fearful life.

7881.

His mind is always
On good terms with God.
Therefore, the Prince of Gloom
Does not dare to be
His mind's companion.

7882.

There was a time when I had
A sleepless fancy
For man's outer achievements.
But now I am developing
A sleepless love
For man's inner hunger.

7883.

My mind wants to be powerful
To converse freely
With the outer world.
My heart longs to be beautiful
To commune soulfully
With the inner world.

7884.

The abiding perfection-life
Of a seeker
Is far beyond the reach
Of his mind's temporary
   triumphs.

7885.

Inside my Lord's
   Compassion-Smile,
And nowhere else,
My aching heart's cure lies.

7886.

At last his long-treasured
Earth-bound mind
Has decided to climb up
Time's Heaven-free steps.

7887.

To be a true athlete of God
You must delete leisure-pleasure
From the schedule of your life.

7888.

Only the discovery of perennial
   truth
And not an amalgam of truth and
   legend
Can transform the face and fate
Of the world.

7889.

O world vital, sleep!
Even your wild emotions
Are dead tired
And are quite anxious to sleep.

7890.

The medicine for a doubting mind
Is either a powerful soul
Or a tearful heart.

7891.

God will entertain
Your aspiration-heart
If you will disdain
Your desire-mind.

7892.

God does not want to give you
What humanity calls love.
God only wants to give you
What divinity calls Delight.

7893.

O super-cautious world,
Do not be afraid of my mind.
My mind hides no thorn
To hurt you.

7894.

I shall lovingly and
　unconditionally
Watch you
Until your sorrowful life
Becomes soulful ecstasy.

7895.

O my unfortunate friend, mind,
I do not know how
I can dare to love you
And your teeming follies.

7896.

The human mind is ready to
　measure
The measureless depths of God's
　Love
But is always reluctant to measure
The depth of its own dire
　infirmities.

7897.

My vital the climber may fall.
My mind the climber may fall.
But my heart the climber never
　falls,
Never!

7898.

No earthly mischief can blight
The powerful beauty
Of his soulful purity-heart.

7899.

My heart's adamantine will
Must transform
My ignorance-enjoying earthly
　days.

7900.

A life of surrender
In silence soars.
A heart of gratitude
In silence triumphs.

7901.

Do first things first.
Do not try to prove to the world
That God exists.
Just try to see your total existence
Inside God's Compassion-Heart.

7902.

If you have inner poise,
You will be able to see
Immediately
How much pretence
Not only the world around you
But also you yourself enjoy.

7903.

If you are ready
To correct your life,
Then you are bound to see
That God is more than ready
To direct His Dream-Boat towards you.

7904.

You want to change the world.
The world wants to change you.
Neither of you succeed
Or will ever succeed
Unless you invoke
A third party, God,
To transform both of you.

7905.

Do not be a fool!
The divine Love of God
Is not going to satisfy you
Since you are already so satisfied
With the temptation-love
Of the human life.

7906.

When you defend the animal in yourself,
Do you not realise that you offend
Not only the divine in you
But also the human in you?

7907.

The ever-mounting flame
Of my heart's aspiration-cry
Is the source of my life's
Ever-increasing joy and delight.

7908.

"I am not responsible
For what I say and do."
This can never be the message
Of the illumined,
Divine reality in me.

7909.

Look at the clever human mind.
Outwardly it sneers at
But inwardly it admires
The beauty and purity
Of the heart.

7910.

Since you have learnt so well
The art of deceiving others,
I am sure you will perfect your art
Until you can deceive yourself as
   well.

7911.

My loving soul is always grateful
Because it is a living portion
Of my Beloved Supreme.
My aspiring heart is always
   grateful
Because it has established
Its inseparable oneness
With my soul.
Alas, my useless mind
Has not established its oneness
With anything.
Therefore, my mind's
   gratitude-life
Has a fleeting breath.

7912.

Even if my mind believes
For a fleeting second
In the existence of my soul,
It may not be willing
To accept the soul's dictates.

7913.

If you pray and meditate
Soulfully,
You will become strong
In the inner world.
If you pray and meditate
Sleeplessly and unreservedly,
You will become stronger
In the inner world.
If you pray and meditate
Unconditionally,
Only to please God in His own
   Way,
You will become stronger than the
   strongest
In the inner world.

7914.

The fastest way to transform the
   vital
Is the way of wisdom:
Think of the vital
As rarely as possible
Or, with tremendous
   determination,
Do not think of the vital at all.

7915.

If you want to conquer the vital,
Feel that you have already
    conquered it
Or will conquer it sooner than at
    once.
Then you will have the inner
    assurance
That the victory-capacity is yours.

7916.

First you think of your vital,
Then you bring it to the fore,
Then you feed it generously.
No wonder your vital is now
Destroying your inner life!

7917.

As long as you remember
That you came
From the Infinite Consciousness,
That you are of the Supreme
And for the Supreme,
You will automatically have
Inner and outer confidence.

7918.

If you have something divine
    within,
It is only a matter of time
Before it will manifest itself
And be received,
Consciously or unconsciously,
By the entire world.

7919.

The very presence of a spiritual
    Master
Is unconsciously received
By the unaspiring world
And consciously received
By the aspiring world.

7920.

There is no such thing
As a sunlit frontier for the mind.
There is only a pitch-dark fortress.

7921.

I would rather embrace a quick
    death
Than gradually befriend
Lethargy-night and impurity-sky.

7922.

O Lord Supreme,
You are the object of my
   meditation.
You are my meditation itself.
You are the result of my
   meditation.

7923.

If your heart's likes
And your mind's dislikes
Keep you constantly angry with
   the world,
How can you see the beauty
Of a satisfaction-dawn
Along the road of your life's
Birthless and deathless journey?

7924.

India is not just a place.
India is not just a people.
India is the celestial music,
And inside that music
Anybody from any corner of the
   globe
Can find the real significance of
   life.

7925.

India is not Hindu, Muslim or
   Buddhist.
India is India.
Its tolerance is more than ready
To freely house all religions.

7926.

India holds and will forever hold
A special charm and a special
   beauty
For all spiritual seekers:
The illumining and fulfilling
   message
Of the soul.

7927.

See India with your aspiring heart.
Then inside even its outer
   weaknesses,
Inside its helplessness and
   hopelessness,
You are bound to feel
Its heart-illumining
And soul-fulfilling uniqueness.

7928.

To feel what India has and is
You must have
What you do not yet have:
A new vision, a perennial vision.

7929.

The body of India
May be discouraging.
The mind of India
May be disheartening.
But the heart of India
Still maintains its pristine beauty
   and purity
Which will forever remain
Untouched by human ignorance.

7930.

We have only to start our inner
   journey.
Even those who start
Out of curiosity
May someday become great
   seekers.

7931.

If you want to receive
Inspiration and aspiration
From God's creation,
Then always try to see
Only its best aspects.

7932.

When God observes His children,
He does not think.
He only cries and cries
Because so many are lost.

7933.

Only one gift of yours
God will forever treasure,
And that gift
Is your inner and outer obedience.

7934.

If "future perfection"
Is your permanent address,
Then your life of complete
   satisfaction
Will always remain at a distance.

7935.

Since you want to reject
Your doubtful mind,
Why not make your rejection
A permanent one?

7936.

If you find it difficult
To offer God your unreserved
And unconditional obedience,
Try to offer Him
Your cheerful obedience.
If that too is impossible,
Then try at least to offer Him
Your unwilling, reluctant obedience.
Today's unwilling, reluctant obedience
Will eventually be transformed
Into tomorrow's unreserved
And unconditional obedience.

7937.

Superficial and artificial
Outer obedience
Will never be able to give you
Natural and spontaneous
Inner obedience.
But inner obedience in its pure form
Is bound to give you
Outer obedience.

7938.

Yesterday's little disobedience
And today's little disobedience
Add up, over the years,
To tomorrow's giant failure.

7939.

On God's team
Every member has to play his role.
If one member does not do his part,
It becomes the bounden duty of others
To do it for him.

7940.

The life of promise
Never disappoints us.
It is the life of hope
That not only disappoints us
But at times destroys us.

7941.

Death came from hell
To shake hands with him
And say:
"Your heart of bounty
I will not be able to house."

7942.

Curiosity took him to see
How bad the Master was.
Lo, many years have passed by
And still he is sitting
At the feet of the Master.
Idle curiosity was the start
Of his inner journey.
Illumining oneness will be the end
Of his inner journey.

7943.

The first message of the material world:
"Have more, have more, have more!"
The last message of the material world:
"Since you have so much,
Why not enjoy more, enjoy more, enjoy more?"
These two messages are nothing short of
The complete ruin of your life.

7944.

As darkness is totally different
From light,
Even so, man's desire-hunger
Is totally different
From man's aspiration-feast.

7945.

Until purity takes full possession
Of the human mind,
The higher worlds
Cannot do anything properly
In and through the human mind
For God-Manifestation on earth.

7946.

Even as the world
Is progressing and transcending,
God's Transcendental Consciousness
Is ever-transcending.

7947.

Who has abundant enthusiasm?
Only those who feel they are
The chosen children of God.
Every day God is trying to act
In and through these children
With His own boundless Enthusiasm.

7948.

My soul exists only for God.
My heart exists for God and myself.
My mind exists for itself alone.

7949.

Earthly days advance
Only to make us feel
The serenity and purity
Of the departing nights.

7950.

He who sees you praying and
 meditating
May not immediately follow you.
But someday when he is full of
 misery,
He will remember that he saw
Something very special in you.

7951.

Soulfully and powerfully invoke
Pristine peace and poise
During your daily meditation.
Once you have their tremendous
Inner strength,
The life of worry and hurry
Will be totally unknown to you.

7952.

I weep a fountain of tears
When I long to see
My Lord's Compassion-Feet.
I smile a fountain of smiles
When I long to see
My Lord's self-transcending
 Dance.

7953.

God is your Eternity's quest.
You are His Immortality's nest.
Only your heart's peace
Can declare and guarantee this.

7954.

If you cannot feel
That you have a child-heart,
Then you are no better
Than a fossilized human being.

7955.

There is not even one person
Who does not know
What he must do
Inwardly and outwardly
To please the Supreme.

7956.

It is not your broken heart
But your golden heart
That can play with the Smile
Of God's ever-transcending
 Beyond.

7957.

His mind is no longer
A slave of fears.
His life is no longer
A slave of tears.
Therefore, he now has
 God-Satisfaction
As his Eternity's unparalleled
 compeer.

7958.

Inner awareness
Brings enthusiasm
And enthusiasm
Brings more inner awareness.

7959.

My Lord Supreme, I know, I know,
You value only those
Who value Your Vision
And Your Mission.

7960.

An easy way to love God,
An easier way to satisfy God
And the easiest way to become
 another God
Is to sing and sing, dance and
 dance
The songs and dances of
 self-offering.

7961.

If you want God to satisfy you,
Then you are not even a
 truth-seeker.
If you want to satisfy God,
Then you are not only a
 truth-seeker
And a God-lover,
But also a God-fulfiller.

7962.

In the spiritual life
Everything you do
Is important,
Every second of your life
Is supremely important.

7963.

Ask yourself every morning
How many things
God has asked you to do
And how many of these things
You have actually done.
Then feel that this day
Is the last day of your life,
And try to please God
At least for this one day.

7964.

When your entire being
Is surcharged with divinity
By virtue of your meditation,
Your very presence will inspire others.

7965.

No matter what he is doing,
He carries within him
Solid and powerful divinity
Which is freely available
To the entire world.

7966.

Those who consciously do the right thing
Will always get
Immediate appreciation from God.
Those who consciously do the wrong thing
Will always get
Immediate retribution.
For their own good
God is very strict
With His spiritual children.

7967.

If you cannot cheerfully receive
God's Punishment-Illumination,
Then your spiritual death
Is fast approaching you.

7968.

Each day you get up early
To pray and meditate,
You are running very, very fast
In your inner race.
Each day you are unwilling
To get up early,
You are walking slower than the slowest.
The inner victory is only for those
Who run with the fastest speed.

7969.

The day you get up early
To pray and meditate,
You will see and feel
The progress you make.
The day you do not get up early
To pray and meditate,
You will feel and become
A sea of misery.

7970.

As the countless drops
Of the boundless ocean
Or the myriad leaves
Of a huge banyan tree
Peacefully remain side by side,
Even so, all human beings
Will someday live side by side
In a perfect oneness-world.

7971.

You create receptivity in others
By becoming spiritually strong
   yourself.
When others see your inner
   strength,
Naturally they want to follow you.

7972.

If you keep a tape measure
Around your heart,
You will immediately see
How much your heart expands
When God receives your
   gratitude.

7973.

When you offer gratitude,
You give your most precious
   possession
To your own highest Self: God.

7974.

The joy that we get
From our body's indulgence
Can never be real.
The joy that we get
From our soul's victory
Is not only real
But also sacred.

7975.

If you do not separate yourself
From your Source,
The world will eventually see
That you are a drop
Of God the Ocean,
Part and parcel of His vast
   Existence.

7976.

When you feel deep inside you
Something very beautiful
Which you have never felt before,
You will know that God has
   received
The sweet and charming fragrance
Of your heart's blossoming
Gratitude-flower.

7977.

Your soulful self-offering
Is your immediate hotline
To the very depths
Of God's Heart.

7978.

Inwardly you can talk to God
As long as you want to.
Therefore, talk, talk, talk!
Give Him all your sadness and
    frustration
As well as your love and joy.
He will keep them all for you
Inside His divine Heart-Safe.

7979.

He who shows sympathy
Towards your aspiration-life
Must needs also be
A true truth-seeker.

7980.

How to help a seeker-friend?
Meditate on your heart-flower.
Then as silently as a divine thief,
Very carefully place that flower
Inside his heart.
There it will blossom
Into beauty, purity and oneness.

7981.

When you offer anything to God,
Your immediate joy
And God's immediate Acceptance
Always go together.

7982.

An aspiring heart
Is a grateful heart,
For an aspiring heart
Knows and feels
What the soul is doing for it.

7983.

The sun may be covered by clouds,
But eventually its full light
Will be revealed.
Similarly, if you become
Bright, brighter, brightest
In the inner world,
Your inner light will not be able
To remain hidden.

7984.

Every moment can be
An opportunity to meditate,
No matter where you are
Or what is going on around you.
It is all a matter
Of where your consciousness is.

7985.

When your good qualities
Go and touch others,
Their good qualities come
   forward
To receive from you.

7986.

Always remember the joy you get
When you do the right thing.
This joy will give you
The inspiration, aspiration
And determination
To continue doing the right thing.

7987.

Yesterday
By virtue of your determination,
You did the right thing
And made yourself happy.
Remember your yesterday's
   happiness
If you don't want lethargy-night
To destroy today's new
   determination.

7988.

If you need intensity
In your aspiration-life,
Just feel that countless flames of
   purity
Are burning inside the very
   depths
Of your heart.

7989.

The earth-bound mind
Cannot and will not forever
   remain
A confusion-jungle.
The aspiration-flames
Of the Heaven-free heart
Will eventually climb high,
   higher, highest
And illumine the lightless
   jungle-mind.

7990.

The psychic tears
Of your soul's joy
Can secretly touch
The inmost recesses of others'
   hearts.
Then only time will tell
What miracles they will work
   there.

7991.

Even when we do not receive
Any outer appreciation,
We may receive an inner award
Which we can value infinitely
   more.

7992.

Creation means self-giving.
From one
God became many
By freely giving Himself.
When you create,
You give yourself
And become your larger Self.

7993.

Unless God can bring His children
Up to His own highest Height,
Where will be the successful
   ending
Of His Manifestation-Story?

7994.

For a genuine truth-seeker
The outer life and the inner life
Are one,
And that one life
Has only one message:
God comes first,
Spirituality comes first.

7995.

The outer life is the body,
The inner life is the heart.
What can one do without the
   other?
Wherever one goes,
The other has to follow.

7996.

We constantly cry to God
To give us this or that.
But the moment we can say,
"Let Thy Will be done",
Our heart becomes
A flood of gratitude.

7997.

We free ourselves
From the temptation-net,
Only to be caught
By the expectation-net.

7998.

He enjoyed the pleasures of this
   world
To his heart's content,
Thinking that in the evening of
   his life
He would be able to discipline
   himself
And make spiritual progress.
He was such a fool!

7999.

Do not delay a moment!
Right from today
Start running along the path of
    aspiration,
No matter where you are now.
How do you know
You will be inspired tomorrow?
How do you know
You will even be alive tomorrow?

8000.

My Lord Supreme,
The Pinnacle-Height
Of Your Transcendental
    Consciousness
Is my only cherished Goal.
To reach that Height
Will be the culminating
    achievement
Of all my past and future lives.

8001.

Yesterday I prayed to God
To let me know who I really am.
Today I am praying to God
To make me feel that my heart
Really loves Him
And that my life
Really needs Him.

8002.

Why do I cry?
I cry because
My clever mind
Has betrayed my soulful heart.

8003.

No matter where you are,
You do have the hidden capacity
To climb higher and dive deeper,
Even if it is just an inch.

8004.

Self-examination means
Self-perfection.
Self-perfection means
God-satisfaction.
God-satisfaction means
Universe-transformation.

8005.

If you are suffering
From world-doubts,
Then learn the art of inner
    deafness.
You will be happy
And your life will be amazingly
    progressive.

8006.

Your mind's blind restlessness
And your vital's dark attachment
Cause your life's ceaseless pangs.

8007.

Walk along the path of purity.
Easily and effectively
The smile of your heart
Will be able to eradicate
Your imperfection-life.

8008.

If you become a prayerful seeker
Of God's Love-World,
God will grant you His
   Vision-Delight
To treasure always.

8009.

In the heart of life
There is only one thing: hope.
In the heart of death
There is only one thing: peace.

8010.

Not your mind's restless
And incessant calling
But your heart's love
Is the quickest fulfiller
Of your dreams.

8011.

The Silence-Blessing
Of my Lord's Vision-Eye
Is my Eternity's Nectar-Food.

8012.

What can force you to improve?
Not the expectations of others.
No, not even your own desires.
Then what can?
Only your constant love of God.

8013.

When my consciousness lives on earth,
I see and become
   frustration-night.
When my consciousness lives in Heaven,
I become Heaven's
   illumination-flight
And satisfaction-delight.

8014.

If your life is swimming
In the river of sorrow,
Then burn the incense of your
　heart
And inundate your entire being
With Eternity's Light and
　Infinity's Delight.

8015.

If you can make your heart
　become
A ceaseless flow of love,
Then the waters of liberation
Will not remain a distant goal.

8016.

When I dive deep within,
I see no imperfection-jungle
Or even difficulty-fern,
But only the smile of perfection
And the dance of
　satisfaction-delight.

8017.

I can conquer my body's pitiful
　poverty
And make my life happy
If I listen to the sweet melody
Of my divinely wealthy heart.

8018.

Who asks you to walk
Through an endless
　darkness-tunnel?
Do you not see that the road of
　light
Can easily be part and parcel
Of your life's treasure-trove?

8019.

If you love your heart's journey,
Then rest assured the nectar-goal
Will not be able to forget you
Or ignore your life.

8020.

If you have a life of dreams
And want your dreams to be
　fulfilled,
Then be as pure as the dew of the
　dawn
And play on your heart-violin
　every day.

8021.

If you truly have
An illumined mind-life,
Then my heart and I are more
　than ready
To be your regular supportive
　listeners.

8022.

You have shattered all earthly
   bondage.
Therefore, the doors of Heaven
Are wide open for you
To see God's Smile of
   Vision-Plenitude.

8023.

Rest assured, I never see
The heavy weight of your
   imperfection-plight.
What I always see is
The crown-glory of your
   self-offering
To the supreme cause of
   life-perfection.

8024.

If God is His
Compassion-Flow,
Then I am my
Aspiration-gratitude-flow.

8025.

If you cry with hope,
Your liberated heart will one day
Be able to experience the
   silence-delight
Of God's Transcendental Heights.

8026.

How long can you continue
With your false hope-dreams?
Do you not realise that your life
Is as useless as dust?
Is it not high time for you
To end your friendship
With self-deception-night?

8027.

My tenebrous mind
Is enveloped in the black shadow
Of my world of sorrow
And desperate self-destruction.

8028.

If you want to throw away
Something from your life,
Then throw away
Your fear-arrow and your
   doubt-spear.

8029.

His right eye embodies
The eternal sun of power.
His left eye embodies
The eternal moon of love.
His outer heart embodies
God-Confidence.
His inner heart embodies
God-Satisfaction.

8030.

Ask your mind to create
   something
That is infinitely faster than
   thought.
Then ask your heart to purify it,
Your soul to liberate it
And God to play with it.

8031.

As long as you love
Your questioning mind,
How can you expect a smile
From your illumining soul
And a dance
From your loving heart?

8032.

My Lord, I see Your Smile-River
Flowing across my eyes.
Can I not show You
Soulfully and unconditionally
My heart's dance of flame-delight?

8033.

My Lord,
When I tell You that I am a
   hopeless case,
What do You think of me?
"My child,
I think of giving you immediately
A new dream:
The dream of God-Satisfaction
In your giant mind."

8034.

What the world needs
Is an all-loving God-Hour,
But what the world is running
   after
Is an all-devouring giant power.

8035.

If you can think of yourself
As a true earth-child,
Then God will definitely think of
   you
All the time
As a satisfied Heaven-Father.

8036.

If you keep your heart-fountain
   flowing,
Your body and vital
Will be able to play sleeplessly
In the fields of Immortality.

8037.

Today your heart is
Your unconscious incapacity.
Tomorrow your life will be
Your fulfilled capacity.

8038.

The beauty of his soul
Has penetrated his outer life.
The confidence of his outer life
Has satisfied his Inner Pilot.

8039.

Since my body
Lives in this world,
Can my heart not be
For this world?

8040.

Failure is at times
A blessing-gift in disguise.
Even then, nobody likes
To accept this gift.

8041.

Those who want to destroy the world
Have already become prey
To their own suicidal commitment.

8042.

If you want to protest,
Then protest against your own
Hidden inner crimes
By virtue of your own
Sterling faith in God.

8043.

Bury all your mental education
If necessity demands,
But never bury the beauty,
Purity and divinity
Of your intuition-flames.

8044.

The prayerful life you now lead
Has the powerful capacity
And the fruitful necessity
To disown your deplorable past.

8045.

His life is all happiness
Because sincerity-inevitability
Always holds his heart
In its adamantine embrace.

8046.

By nature
Each and every earth-bound
   thought
Is inhospitable.
By nature
Each and every divine thought
Is not only cordially hospitable
But also astonishingly adorable.

8047.

Each special prayer to God
Is a green hope
And a blue promise
To emancipate the human in us
From the binding shackles
Of the animal in us.

8048.

A seeker's soulful smile
Is an everlasting flower
In the Heart-Garden
Of his Beloved Supreme.

8049.

If there is any purpose in
   thinking,
It is so the thinking process itself
Can try to transcend
Its own extremely limited
   existence-reality.

8050.

Each preceding sorrow
Tells us that life is a journey
Into the unknowable.
Each succeeding sorrow
Tells us that everything
Has its own preordained
Earth-limited finality.

8051.

Even if you fail time and again,
Never surrender your precious
   hope-heart
To eyeless, life-denying despair.

8052.

With your heart's loving gratitude
You can easily gain
God's Transcendental Beatitude.

8053.

Your breath of cunning
And intoxicating malice
Has lowered the climbing
Heart-beauty of humanity.

8054.

Each stupid man
Thinks he is entertaining a foolish
  hope
When he thinks of the
  transformation
Of his own nature.

8055.

My heart's gratitude-breath
Is constantly blessed
With the beautiful ripples
Of dynamic energy-light.

8056.

Be careful of your mind's
Undivine thoughts.
Not only do they increase and
  multiply,
But also they can force you
To die a million deaths
Before your life's final hour
  strikes.

8057.

You talk so much
About your mind's maladies.
When will you start talking
About your heart's remedies?

8058.

Unless your mind cares
To be useful to your heart,
How can anyone
Make your life fruitful?

8059.

The human life
Is like a frustration-lion
Loving a frustration-tiger.

8060.

If you want to understand a thing
Sooner than the soonest,
Then do not try to interpret it.
Just love it
And become inseparably one with
  it.

8061.

Suspicion
Is the poison-food
Prepared by the weak
For the weak.

8062.

What you have inside you
Is a heart of beauty's dawn
And a soul of divinity's day.

8063.

The human mind does not
   progress
Because it wants to have
An independent life
In the heart of a dependent life.

8064.

If you love the world,
Then why do you hide from it?
If you hate the world,
Then why do you live in it?

8065.

If you want your mind
To understand the world,
If you want your heart
To be loved by the world
And if you want your life
To be treasured by God Himself,
Then do not think!

8066.

A life of silence
Is always an inner challenge.
Its goal:
To hasten the choice Hour of God.

8067.

Fear and doubt
Never want to listen to anybody
Even though they are tortured
Not only by others
But also by themselves.

8068.

What have you done with
The time that God has given you
To love the beauty of His creation
And inspire the world
With the purity of your inner
   vision?

8069.

If you want to know more
About God the Creator,
Then become a song of service
To God the creation.

8070.

I believe,
Therefore I see.
I believe,
Therefore I become.
I believe,
Therefore I eternally am.

8071.

Each uninspired day
Marks the beginning
Of a painful failure
That ends in an inner death.

8072.

Do not accept the spiritual life
Unless it means everything to you
Now and from now on.

8073.

In the morning
His heart's sincerity
Makes him soulful.
During the rest of the day
His life's purity
Keeps him soulful.

8074.

If your aspiration-heart
Spreads the beauty and purity
Of sunshine,
Then your life becomes
An unparalleled blessing
To yourself and to others.

8075.

I have nothing to do
With failure.
I run my life's business always
With success
Just by virtue of my heart's
Inner surrender-light.

8076.

A soul of beauty
Is the perfection-search
For a life of duty.

8077.

A heart of tranquillity
Is the beauty of the Beyond
That nourishes the hunger
Of unawakened humanity.

8078.

Your love for God
Can make your life beautiful,
But it is God's Love for you
That can make your life fruitful.

8079.

Do not try to satiate
The wild vital.
It is undoubtedly
An endless and useless task.

8080.

God usually does not hide from me
Except when I search for Him
Inside my doubtful mind.

8081.

My Lord,
I am grateful to You
Because yesterday You did not listen
To my prayer for desire-fulfilment.
My Lord,
Tomorrow I shall be grateful to You
If You do not listen
To my prayer for life-satisfaction.
My Lord,
I beg You to listen
To only one prayer of mine:
"Let Thy Will be done."

8082.

Your heart's excellence
You do not have to advertise.
That is God's job,
And He does not want you
To take it away from Him.

8083.

Self-control in the outer life
Is another name for
God's Compassion-Patrol
In the inner life.

8084.

His mind's love of God's creation
Is very limited.
His heart's love of God's creation
Is unlimited.
His soul's love of God's creation
Is not only unlimited
But constantly self-transcendent.

8085.

As imagination runs
Before reality,
Even so, aspiration can run
Before imagination.

8086.

You are unwilling to be brave.
Indeed, you are a fool!
You are unwilling to accept the light
From others who are already brave.
That means you are
Worse than a fool!

8087.

There can be only one reality
In my life, not two:
Either my daily God-appointment
Or my daily sad disappointment.

8088.

If you rely on your friends,
You are clever.
If you rely on yourself,
You are wise.
But if you rely on God alone,
You are perfect
Both inwardly and outwardly.

8089.

When I look up to Heaven,
I have only one urgent duty:
My surrender-duty.
When I look at the world,
I have only one urgent duty:
My gratitude-duty.

8090.

You are sailing
Your mind-boat and your
   heart-boat
In two directions at the same time.
What can poor God do?
He wants to be a passenger
In only one boat,
For the Goal cannot be
Here, there and everywhere.

8091.

If you have a pure heart,
Definitely it will add
To others' happiness.
If you have a clever mind,
Definitely it will subtract
From others' happiness.

8092.

God does not want you
To criticise your mind all the time.
He only wants you
To love your heart
More, ever more.

8093.

O dark world-ignorance,
I am not afraid of you.
You will soon see my soul's smiles
Even inside your wildest frowns.

8094.

He was tired of life.
Therefore he was constantly
   looking
For something that would
Lovingly and convincingly lure
   him
Towards dear and sweet death.

8095.

Pleasure-thoughts before long
Will be shrouded
With abysmal
   torture-experiences.

8096.

I shall have to know the difference
Between the sacred happiness
Of the heart
And the secret happiness
Of the mind
So that I can perfect my life
In God's own Way.

8097.

A soulful song
Can easily soothe the tortures
Of any cruel day.

8098.

If you can sing soulfully
And love the world
   unconditionally,
Then you are bound to hear
The soul-illumining music
Of the trance-world.

8099.

Inner beauty has to penetrate
The outer world.
Outer surrender has to penetrate
The inner world.

8100.

I love God,
Not because one day
He will make me perfect
But because He has given me,
Out of His infinite Bounty,
The capacity to be happy
All the time.

8101.

If I accept my Supreme Lord
Supremely and unconditionally,
Then only will I be able to read
What He has inscribed
On the golden tablet of my heart:
That He loves me unconditionally.

8102.

Burn doubts away immediately.
Otherwise, dark death's stretching
   sea
Will soon drown you,
Your entire life.

8103.

When the mind is all darkness,
It brings endless disgrace
To the aspiring heart
And the illumining soul.

8104.

Fat old idleness
Has a shameless eye.
It can never be invited
To the precious awakening
Of human life.

8105.

O my sweet soul,
Stay inside my heart, stay!
I shall no more offer you
My voice of melancholy.
I shall offer you only
My heart's echoing love and peace.

8106.

Keep your belief always
   unstained.
Then you will be able to swim
In the waters of perpetual delight.

8107.

With steps unswerving,
Our heart must approach God.
On the way there should not be
Any blind interchange
Between our heart's faith
And our mind's doubt.

8108.

Pain hangs heavily in his life
And his heart is twisted with grief.
In spite of his powerful
   attachment
To this life,
He is now saying
His inevitable farewell to earth.

8109.

Invisible flames of aspiration
Can not only brighten the soul's
   light
But also create fuel
For life's heavenward journey.

8110.

His doubtful mind
And his fearful heart
Are desperately trying
To thwart each other.
Alas, this is his deplorable fate.

8111.

My mind speaks whisperingly.
My heart speaks soulfully.
My soul speaks delightfully.
Alas, why does my life
Have to speak strangely?

8112.

The blue bird deep inside my
   heart
Tells me that when I reach
The summit of my
   realisation-mountain
I shall see that the beauty of truth
Is in life itself.

8113.

O my mind,
Can you not fly away
From the crowd of thoughts?
O my heart,
Can you not fly away
From your insecurity-cave?
O my life,
Can you not fly away
From the grasp of
   ignorance-night?

8114.

He is at once
Useful and useless.
He is useful when his heart
Sees truth in all things.
He is useless when his mind
Sees no truth in anything.

8115.

One characteristic
That distinguishes a great man
Is this:
Even if he is engulfed
In the fires of adversity,
He will try to remain
A God-believer.

8116.

The perfection of my life
Is my promise to myself.
The satisfaction of God
Is my promise to God.

8117.

You have something.
Therefore, you desire to achieve
Something more.
Can I suggest to you
What you need most?
God-Satisfaction
In God's own Way.

8118.

What kind of independence is this
When you depend so much upon
What you are going to say,
What you are going to do,
What you are going to become?

8119.

God has already allowed my soul
To lean its whole weight
On His Perfection-Arms.
Now He is asking my life
To lean its whole weight
On His Lotus Feet.

8120.

Man has his Eternity's
Infinite questions.
God has His Immortality's
Only answer:
Oneness-embrace.

8121.

Your old mind
Is tired of living.
Your new heart
Is afraid of dying.
Your uncertain life
Is crying one moment
And smiling the next—
Crying for possession
And smiling with renunciation.

8122.

He made two great decisions:
Not to speak ill of humanity
Any more,
To love God infinitely more
From now on.

8123.

Death, you have given me fear.
Take it away immediately!
Heaven, you have given me
    delight.
Allow me to keep it permanently!

8124.

When my mind and my heart
Are at war,
What do I do?
I bring forward my soul
To help my real friend, my heart.

8125.

Each good thought vanishes
Faster than it appears.
Alas, each man is doomed
To have this experience.

8126.

He gets satisfaction,
Soulful and fruitful,
When he struggles and struggles
In the face of the inevitable.

8127.

No earth-bound power
Can be permanently effectual
Unless Heaven-created
   Compassion
Sleeplessly supports it.

8128.

If you deliberately ignore
The Will of God,
Then you are bound to have
An incurable disease:
Unhappiness.

8129.

When your mind and vital start
   enjoying
Various degrees of
   self-complacency,
Then your life's progress comes
To an abrupt and total end.

8130.

Develop soulfully pure tears
Of oneness-love.
Then the universal life of beauty
Will be all yours.

8131.

Can you believe
That my Lord Supreme loves
Everything that I say and do,
Even my unimaginably feeble
Tribute to Him?

8132.

My morning prayers
And my evening meditations
Are sleeplessly devoted
To the manifestation
Of God's Compassion-Light
Here on earth.

8133.

If you do not feed your heart's
   hunger
Daily plus cheerfully,
Then your heart will soon become
A totally ruined paradise.

8134.

O my stupid mind,
When will you stop laughing
At my heart's fathomless despair?

8135.

What we need from life
Is a visible dedication.
Otherwise, an invisible
   frustration
Will chase our life.

8136.

If your mind loves
Your uncomplaining life,
That means your mind is ready
For total illumination.

8137.

My Lord, I do not want
To be chained to time any more,
For I wish to unveil Heaven
In its birthless and deathless
   Delight.

8138.

As self-contempt clings
To your impure vital life,
Even so, self-enlightenment
Will permanently cling
To your pure psychic life.

8139.

If you want to run away
From the wild world,
Then you do not need
Two swift feet.
What you need is sleepless
   devotion
To God's Compassion-Heart.

8140.

His heart's sleepless hunger
Is crying
For God-Satisfaction-dreams.

8141.

The doubting mind must
    surrender
To the aspiring heart.
Otherwise, the stumbling life will
    suffer
In a mournful mist of tenebrous
    fear.

8142.

You are a man of belief.
How is it that you dare not believe
That your earthly grief
Itself is mortal?

8143.

Speaking ill of God
Is like fighting an unseen enemy
Who can be found anywhere
    inside
A limitless void.

8144.

Two things he cannot
    understand:
Why humanity fears him
And why divinity is indifferent to
    him.

8145.

O my hope-world,
I have your tomorrow
Inside my today's hungry heart.

8146.

O fearful heart,
Do believe that God does not
    know
How to punish.
God knows only how to illumine
And thus satisfy His Eternity's
Infinite Vision-Dreams.

8147.

A questioning mind does not give.
A strong heart not only gives
But also becomes.
What does it give and become?
God the eternal Dreamer.

8148.

If your mind is critical
Of everything,
Then your mind is useless.
If your heart is pleased
With nothing,
Then your heart is worse than
   useless.

8149.

Your faith is not worthless.
Your faith is not trivial.
Your faith is its own
Splendid victory.

8150.

If your life is locked in a prison
Of self-indulgence,
Then your self-image will
Without fail
Eclipse your God-image.

8151.

When I live inside my vital,
Superiority damages my life.
When I live inside my mind,
Inferiority damages my life.
When I live inside my heart,
Satisfaction illumines my life.

8152.

Even though he gives all that he
   has
And all that he is
To mankind,
He does not see a flicker of hope
For God-Manifestation
In God's own Way
Here on earth.

8153.

His soul has planned
From the beginning of time
To reduce his mind's desire-life
And diminish his vital's
   frustration-life.

8154.

If you carry God only sometimes
In your heart,
How can you expect God
To be your Friend
All the time?

8155.

This is a crisis-filled world.
Here you meet with
Either dire destruction
Or unforgettable failure.

8156.

If I can express my instant
    readiness,
Then only can I become
A true candidate
For the sunlit path.

8157.

True, his mind has the capacity
To enter into self-delusion,
But his heart has the capacity
To cry for self-perfection.

8158.

If you are an all-devouring ego,
Then how will you know
Where you are supposed to go
And who will go with you
After you reach your
    frustration-goal?

8159.

My Lord's Fulness-Heart
Always answers my heart's
Soulful appeal.

8160.

O my Lord,
Do turn my life into an open book
And place it right before
Your Vision-Eye and
    Compassion-Heart.

8161.

What I need is a mind
Perpetually interesting.
What I need is a heart
Universally inspiring.
What I need is a soul
Transcendentally illumining.

8162.

From earth's most remote corners
I receive only one message:
"Earth and progress do not
    rhyme."

8163.

Remember, an endless future is
    before you,
Not behind you.
Therefore, you can easily make
    friends
With endless happiness-hopes.

8164.

If you have oneness-faith
In God's Vision-Eye,
Then your life will be
Heaven's transcendental choice
And earth's universal voice.

8165.

Heaven itself will cheerfully
Accompany a God-lover
If he turns his life
Into a gratitude-song
For his Beloved Lord to sing.

8166.

If you are afraid
Of silence-light,
That means you are not meant
For God's Nectar-Delight.

8167.

Mine is the heart-song
That invokes the unknowable
With the cheerful help
Of the unknown.

8168.

When we talk of world peace,
We are actually talking secretly
Of our own self-interest.

8169.

If pleasure is a sheer dream,
Then pain is also a dream,
A mere dream.

8170.

God does not look at me,
Not because my mind is impure
But because my heart is unsure.

8171.

You are not happy
And you will never be happy
Because you do not lose yourself
Enough to find yourself—
I mean your true self.

8172.

He lives in empty silence.
Therefore his ignorance-life
Is lengthened
And his knowledge-life
Is shortened.

8173.

Everywhere is a demanding vital.
Everywhere is a doubting mind.
Everywhere is a God-loving heart.

8174.

No doubt you love God soulfully,
But do you ever think
Of loving God's Heart
And serving God's Body
Unconditionally?

8175.

His curiosity-mind wants to know
The weak secrets
Of the past world
And the strong secrets
Of the future world.

8176.

There is only one way for me
To renounce my curiosity-life,
And that is to constantly feel
That I am of man the God
And for God the man.

8177.

I love God, I need God.
This is what I can say
For the time being.
Let time tell the rest for me.

8178.

If God has stopped looking
At your face,
That does not mean
You cannot look
At God's Feet.

8179.

Although I delay
My heavenward journey,
My heart is always for
The perfection-satisfaction
Of Heaven's smile.

8180.

Each soulful heart
Is haunted by Eternity's
   hunger-cry.
I know it
And my heart knows it.

8181.

His outer life is rich,
His inner life is deep,
His higher life is sure
And his love of God is perfect.

8182.

The equal of a gratitude-heart
Will never be available
Either here on earth
Or there in Heaven.

8183.

My Lord, break me,
My mind and my life,
So that I can claim You
As my own, very own,
And love You infinitely more
Than I can right now imagine.

8184.

Who says that you are doing
The wrong thing
By enjoying the crowd
Of your supernal memories?

8185.

Everybody knows
When I talk about God.
But alas,
Does anybody care to know
When God talks about me?

8186.

Since I am happy with what
I am doing for myself,
Why do I then find fault
With both God the Creator
And God the creation?

8187.

Unconsciously I tell the world
That God is great.
Consciously I tell the world
That God is good.
Soulfully I must tell the world
That God is always absolutely
    perfect.

8188.

God has told me many things
During the years
Since I first accepted the spiritual
    life,
But I have told God only one
    thing:
I need more Love from Him.

8189.

I thought God was going to
Perfect my life.
God thought I was going to
Surrender my heart to Him.
Unfortunately we are both the possessors
Of fruitless expectations.

8190.

Each human being wants to know
What he can do for himself.
Alas, does he ever care to know
What God, out of His infinite Bounty,
Has already done for him?

8191.

My heart may not know
How to love God soulfully.
My life may not know
How to serve God cheerfully.
But my mind knows
How to delay God's appearance
Indefinitely.

8192.

Each day begins
With a soulful hope.
Each day ends
With a powerful promise.
This is the human life-story.

8193.

The heart that cries sleeplessly
Knows what God looks like.
The soul that smiles constantly
Knows who God is
Plus where God is.

8194.

The humility of a tree
Pleases my life.
The purity of a flower
Pleases my heart.
The divinity of a fruit
Pleases my soul.

8195.

The heart that loves
The Divinity of God the Creator
And the Beauty of God the creation
Is always a universal favourite.

8196.

If you want to break asunder
The chains of bondage-life,
Ask your heart to play
On the golden harp
Inside your soul's dream-boat.

8197.

I do not remember everything
That I did in Heaven,
But what I do remember clearly
Is the unconditionally cheerful
   sharing
Of the advanced souls.

8198.

Before I came to realise
Who God is,
God told me who I am:
The glowing promise
Of His Vision-Eye.

8199.

In this fast-paced world
You are trying to do something
Quite unusual:
You are trying to have
A relaxed mind and a listening
   heart.

8200.

True, God has not given me
Everything,
But He has given me
Two firm convictions:
He loves me
No matter what I do;
I shall need Him
No matter what I become.

8201.

My Lord,
Do teach me how to create
Waves of enthusiasm inside my
   mind.
My Lord,
Do teach me how to create
A sea of love inside my heart.

8202.

These are his three secret
   misfortunes:
He does not love God.
He does not need God.
He wants his life
To remain unchanged.

8203.

Before we achieve self-mastery,
Life is nothing but
A most painful failure.

8204.

No path can be
Too hard for you
If you have one God-Gift:
Faith in yourself.

8205.

God is anxious to reassure you
That you can be a good
   instrument of His
If yours is a life
Of sleepless surrender.

8206.

Do not waste any more
   opportunities.
All your opportunities
May suddenly and unexpectedly
   end.

8207.

The heart cannot see the Supreme
If the heart is unprepared.
The soul cannot manifest the
   Supreme
If the soul is unprepared.
But God can love man
Even if man is unprepared.

8208.

Do not try to deceive your heart.
If you deceive your heart,
Yours will be a life
Of endless tragedy.

8209.

The heart is always ready
To slow down
So the mind can catch up with it,
But the mind wants to go alone
At its own unimaginably slow
   speed.

8210.

My life's surrender
Is the first chance I have
To satisfy God.
My heart's gratitude
Is the last chance I have
To satisfy God.

8211.

Human life is not
A fleeting picture.
It is an abiding portrait
Done by God's own Hands.

8212.

A doubtful mind
Means an unfulfilled life.
An unfulfilled life
Is the soul's great disadvantage.

8213.

Because you have a believer's
   mind,
Because you have a lover's heart,
Because you have a server's life,
God has chosen you
As His divine instrument.

8214.

Each animal thought
Is a bitter destruction.
Each human thought
Is a sad failure.
Each divine thought
Is a supreme victory.

8215.

Each human being
Is a satisfaction-dreamer
But not a perfection-lover.

8216.

Enthusiasm is a satisfactory
   moment
Longing for an endlessly
Satisfactory hour.

8217.

Each seeker must live
A spotless life of hope.
Then only will he be able to enjoy
His soul's eternal journey.

8218.

He who has no faith inside his
   mind
Will eventually disappear
Into outer darkness.
He who has no promise inside his
   heart
Will eventually disappear
Into inner darkness.

8219.

To satisfy either the heart's hope
Or the soul's promise
Is not a trivial task.
It is an immensely difficult
   endeavour.

8220.

Each seeker's searching mind
Has amazing possibility.
Each seeker's crying heart
Has illumination-inevitability.

8221.

A gratitude-heart keeps a
   catalogue
Of God's complete Life.
An ingratitude-mind keeps a
   catalogue
Of its own empty life.

8222.

No human being is ready to face
The unthinkable treasury
Of his own wild emotions.

8223.

Do not blame Heaven
And do not blame earth
For your loneliness.
You are travelling the ways of
   loneliness
Because your mind has not tried
   to conquer
The darkness of
   frustration-frown.

8224.

Faith-seeds precede
Wisdom-bud.
Wisdom-bud precedes
Peace-flower.
Peace-flower precedes
Satisfaction-fruit.

8225.

I have watched myself
Only to be exasperated.
I have watched my body
Only to be disgusted.
I have watched my mind
Only to be disappointed.
I have watched my heart
Only to be excited.
I have watched my soul
Only to be delighted.
I have watched my Lord Supreme
Only to be fulfilled.

8226.

O my mind,
Take as long as you want
To investigate my heart.
I am keeping it right in front of
   you.
But do not doubt my heart.
If you doubt,
You will lessen the beauty
Of my heart-moon
And destroy the purity
Of my heart-sun.

8227.

What you need
Is a life of innocence.
What you need
Is a heart of purity.
What you need
Is a mind of sincerity.
Do you need anything else
To realise God?
No! This is enough,
More than enough.

8228.

If you think and feel
That you were born
To do something great for
   yourself,
You may be right.
But if you think and feel
That you were born
To do something good
For God and God alone,
Then you are absolutely perfect.

8229.

Pray first, then act.
This is the right thing to do.
Act first, then declare.
This is the right thing to do.

8230.

The music of the trance-world
Can act like a lance
To stab the impurity
Of ignorance-night.

8231.

Dedication is the beginning
Of liberation.
Liberation is the beginning
Of satisfaction.
Satisfaction is the beginning and
   end
Of the inseparable oneness
Of God the Dreamer and God the
   Lover.

8232.

Do not think of your present life
As a wasted opportunity.
Think of your present life
As a needed experience,
And think of your future life
As the beginning of God's new
   creation
Inside you.

8233.

Your mind thinks
Of success and failure.
Your heart feels the necessity
Of aspiration and dedication.
Your soul promises
God-realisation and
   God-manifestation.
All you have to do
Is become a conscious and
   constant instrument
Of your Lord Supreme.

8234.

Do not think
Of your past desire-life.
It will present you
With a net full of painful
   memories.
Think of your today's
Aspiration-life.
Then you will see Light and
   Delight
Fast approaching you.

8235.

What can I make new
Out of yesterday?
Confidence-light.
What can I make new
Out of today?
Promise-height.
What can I make new
Out of tomorrow?
God's transcendental
Satisfaction-Delight.

8236.

He who has
A short-sighted capacity
Cannot have
A long-lived quality.

8237.

The most important question
Of my life once was:
"Does God ever care for me?"
The most important question
Of my life now is:
"Will I ever be able
To unconditionally surrender
To my Lord Supreme?"

8238.

The curse of a troubled mind:
I think God is the product
Of man's mental hallucination.
The gift of an untroubled mind:
I know God is Peace
And Peace is Satisfaction.

8239.

My Lord wants me to give Him
The heavy weight of my past
   failures
And to keep with me
The tall height of my present
   dreams.

8240.

God knows my weaknesses
Better than I do.
I don't think He will
Allow me to fail Him
Constantly and permanently.

8241.

If the human mind neglects
To meditate every day,
Then if ever it gets peace,
This peace will be without fail
Both fleeting and fragile.

8242.

If you are not quick
To forgive the world,
Earth's hatred will be
Too much for you
And Heaven's love will be
Too little for you.

8243.

If you do not know how to speak
The language of love
And want to learn,
Then God will definitely teach
   you.
But if you do not know
And do not want to know,
Then you will never be able to fit
Into God's Cosmic Plans.

8244.

I once chose my desire-life
To be happy.
My needs and demands
Were numberless.
But now that I have chosen God,
I have only one need:
God's Life, and nothing more.

8245.

Every morning my heart's hope
Shows me a new sky.
Every evening my life's promise
Tells me that someday
I shall own a permanent sunrise.

8246.

Today be satisfied
With what you have.
Tomorrow try to be satisfied
Not only with what God has
For you
But also with what God is
For Himself.

8247.

My life is forgiven by God.
Therefore, my heart feels obliged
To forgive the world around me.

8248.

If you are a truth-seeker
And a God-lover,
You will, without fail, inherit
God's Perfection-Throne
And Satisfaction-Palace.

8249.

Do you want to stop dying?
If so, soulfully and
    unconditionally say:
"God comes first, always!"

8250.

If God has Power,
Then you can at least try
To use His Power.
If God has Love,
Then you can at least try
To accept and treasure His Love.

8251.

God wants to walk with me today,
But my mind is doubting Him.
Because my mind is unwilling
To walk with God,
My heart, which is claiming God
In every possible way,
Is miserable.

8252.

If you want to have real rest,
Then there is only one place for
    you,
And that is God's peace-flooded
Satisfaction-Kingdom.

8253.

God has given you
His Power to use.
God has given you
His Love to use.
God has given you
His Perfection to use.
God has given you
His Satisfaction to use.
And what are you giving God
In return?
Can you not give Him
Even a ray of hope
That you will accept Him
As your own, very own,
Unconditionally?

8254.

God's Love is willing
To transform my life,
But my earth-bound life
Does not care
For either God the Doer
Or God the Action.

8255.

Just because I am loved
By God's Heart,
I shall love humanity.
Just because I am forgiven
By God's Compassion,
I shall definitely try to forgive
  myself.

8256.

Your mind knows
What doubt is.
Your heart knows
What faith is.
And you are trying to know
What Eternity's Satisfaction-Life
  is.

8257.

There is no certainty
That you will be happy
Unless you have implicit faith
In God's inner Cosmic Dance
And outer Cosmic Smile.

8258.

You want to possess God
And God wants to possess you.
Have you not realised by this time
That God is infinitely stronger
  than you?
How then do you expect to win?

8259.

My Lord, I have already placed
  You
On the throne of my silence-heart.
Now do give me the capacity to
  keep You
In the thick forest of my mind.

8260.

When I sing in the silence of my
   soul,
I become the creator of a new age
And the destroyer of my wrong
   thoughts
From ages ago.

8261.

Although the darkness
Of your mind-sky
Is threatening you,
You do not realise it
Because the inexhaustible Source
Of divine Love
Is still coming to your rescue.

8262.

If your mind lives
In the wasteland of false beliefs,
How can you claim happiness
As your birthright?

8263.

God paints a new sky every day.
If you pray to God,
Every day He will paint
A new heart for you.
Just pray, and see it all being done.

8264.

When my soul said good-bye to
   Heaven,
Heaven said, "I shall guide you
Right from here."
When my heart said good-bye to
   earth,
Earth said, "You cannot go
   anywhere
Without carrying me."

8265.

Only a God-tuned heart
Can fly in the plane of silence
In Infinity's sky.

8266.

When the Peace of God
Rules my aspiring heart,
I see God smilingly walking
Side by side with me,
Towards His own
   Vision-illumined Home.

8267.

If I want to see the flowers of joy
Blossoming inside my
   heart-garden,
What do I do?
I do not allow myself to be
   intoxicated
By the forces of self-delusion.

8268.

Because you are great,
I think of you.
Because you are good,
I think for you
With the hope
That you can become perfect.

8269.

Two things I desperately need:
A heart of gratitude-depth
And a life of surrender-length.

8270.

When I promise,
I see the sun of my soul.
When I love,
I see the moon of my heart.

8271.

If your meditations
Are blue-gold silences of love,
Then you will, without fail,
Have a silver-rose heart of joy.

8272.

A sad smile
Has made my heart pure.
A happy smile
Is making my life sure.

8273.

Life's fulfilment-poise
Comes from the heart's
Enlightenment-choice.

8274.

What a strangely hungry world!
Every day without fail
It enjoys eating
Hopeless imperfections.

8275.

The whole world in unison
Tells me it does not hate me,
But it hates my
    self-announcement-gong.

8276.

His life is beautiful and soulful
Because his heart is as pure
As his prayer-cry.

8277.

Each promise
Is duty's oneness-course.
Each hope
Is beauty's newness-source.

8278.

My heart-tears are serving
God's Forgiveness-Feet.
My life-smiles are serving
God's Satisfaction-Eye.

8279.

I am satisfied
With my heart's cry.
May this world be satisfied
With my Lord's Smile.

8280.

If you know
The heart-surrender-way to God,
Then you will be given
The world-perfection-key.

8281.

My Lord is my
Perfection-Dreamer.
I am my Lord's
Satisfaction-dreamer.

8282.

I do not know
What I can do for man,
But I do know
What I can do for God.

8283.

Only a God of Satisfaction
Can dare to create
A man of perfection.

8284.

I know my climbing heart
Loves God.
I know my soaring soul
Loves man.

8285.

To have faith
Is to dream of God.
To dream of God
Is to eventually become
A perfect instrument of God.

8286.

He who desperately needs God
Will definitely reach the
  mountain-summit
Of God's infinite Love-Light.

8287.

God does not smile
When the time is not right.
God does not smile
When my aspiration is not genuine.
God does not smile
When I do not share my realisation
With the rest of the world.

8288.

When I think of my mind,
I deal with possibility-seeds.
When I feel God's Heart,
I deal with inevitability-fruits.

8289.

God will definitely help you
If you want to please Him
In His own Way.
But first you have to know
Whether you are sincerely
And absolutely ready.

8290.

Have you decided when you are going
To begin your spiritual journey?
Have you decided how long you will take
To complete your journey?
Have you decided what you will offer
To your Beloved Supreme
At the end of your journey?

8291.

God whispers
That I can afford to have everything
Except a doubting mind.

8292.

Each trouble may not know
That it embodies opportunities,
But each trouble must know
That it will someday, somehow
Give way to new realities.

8293.

God does not love
Your insecure shyness with Him.
God loves only
Your pure oneness with Him.

8294.

God does not laugh at our prayers,
No matter how insincere they are.
But God does laugh when we think and feel
That our prayers will never be answered.

8295.

You are afraid of the future.
Perhaps it is true that the future
Holds only torture for us.
But can you not be wise?
Do not invoke the future.
Just live cheerfully
In the eternal Now.

8296.

You are great
Because you have committed yourself
To God the creation.
You are good
Because you have committed yourself
To God the Creator.
You are perfect
Because you have committed yourself
To God the ever-transcending Supreme.

8297.

God does not want to surprise me
With His Compassion.
God does not want to surprise me
With His Perfection.
God does not want to surprise me
With His Dedication.
But God wants me to surprise Him
With my own aspiration.

8298.

Lord, can You not bless my tomorrows,
Since I am forced to embody
My yesterday's mind-forest
And my today's vital-volcano?

8299.

Your mind may be filled
With your own great achievements,
But do not expect God to surprise
Either you or your heart
With His Compassion-Height.

8300.

My Lord,
You have given me the capacity
To feel the throb of my heart
In the hearts that love You dearly.
Will You not also give me the
   capacity
To become a gratitude-flower
At Your Compassion-Feet daily?

8301.

I know, I know,
My heart's purity-life
Is my safest haven.

8302.

If discouragement defeats your
   heart,
Then God will not be enthusiastic
In accepting you
As His Eternity's partner.

8303.

My Lord Supreme,
I need only one thing from You:
Do give me the capacity
To startle and awaken my body
From its easy slumber-life.

8304.

My mind does not get tired
Of doing everything wrong.
My heart does not get tired
Of doing everything right.
My Lord does not get tired
Of transcending His outer Beauty
And His inner Divinity.

8305.

My mind is dealing with
An unreachable God.
My heart is dealing with
A distant God.
My soul is dealing with
An immediate God.

8306.

My life has misused
God's Freedom-Gift.
Therefore, my Lord does not want
To unveil my heart.

8307.

He is soulfully trying
To be himself.
Therefore, God is inviting him
To bask in the golden rays
Of His transcendental Sun.

8308.

You have the master key
To unlock God's secret
   Heart-Door,
And that master key
Is your sleeplessly unconditional
   surrender.

8309.

Each moment my heart tries
To sacrifice itself on God's Altar.
Each moment God grants my
   heart
The Ecstasy of His Eternity's
   Oneness.

8310.

His mind is willing.
His heart is obedient.
Therefore, God has appeared
   before him
With His Delight-Embrace.

8311.

God wants to hear
All your problems,
But your unlit mind
Does not want you to share
Your problems with God.

8312.

If your life has a moment
Of true consecration,
Then God will have a full day
Of true Satisfaction.

8313.

Because his life-arrow
Has missed its mark,
His is an inner life of turmoil,
Beginningless and endless.

8314.

You think it is necessary to worry.
I tell you, it is absolutely
   unnecessary.
What is worse, when you worry,
God feels sad
That His Vision of Perfection
Is not revealing itself inside you.

8315.

You cannot win God's Love
By surprise,
But God can catch
Your careful unwillingness
By surprise.

8316.

Why are you grumbling against
   God?
Is it because you feel
He does not love you enough?
Is it because you feel
The need for a better God?
Or is it because you are
A total failure?

8317.

My climbing prayer
Cannot persuade God,
But my divine surrender
Can and does persuade God.

8318.

When a world of doubt
Captured his searching mind,
No other reality,
Either from the inner world
Or from the outer world,
Came to his rescue
Save and except God's
   Compassion-Sun.

8319.

The outer voice demands.
The inner voice commands.
But God's Voice neither
   commands
Nor demands.
It only unconditionally awakens
The seeker in me.

8320.

If your mind strives to think
   divinely,
Then you are bound to be
   embraced
By God's transcendental
   Delight-Beauty.

8321.

The sigh that the sound-life
   heaves
Can eventually touch
The Compassion-Feet
Of the Lord Supreme.

8322.

Respect your hopes,
Love your hopes,
For your hopes are destined
To see God's Vision-Eye
And feel God's Salvation-Heart.

8323.

God is ready
With His Saviour-Heart.
Alas, when shall I be ready
With my believer-heart?

8324.

When I pray,
My prayer tries to reach
God the tallest Height.
When I meditate,
My meditation tries to reach
God the vastest Breadth.

8325.

The silence of the heart
Is an unparalleled joy
Unattainable by the doubting
   mind
And the strangling vital.

8326.

The heart is born to pray.
The mind is born to hesitate.
The vital is born to fight.
The body is born to forget.
The soul is born to forgive
And illumine.

8327.

A doubting mind knows how
To plague the heart.
A loving heart knows how
To illumine the mind.

8328.

A realised soul
Is a fortress of Eternity
To protect humanity
From the inconscience-blows of
   death.

8329.

It is not responsibility
That weighs you down.
It is insensibility
That weighs you down
And destroys your heart's
Oneness-happiness.

8330.

His doubt-enemy is in his grasp.
Do you know why?
Because his faith-friend has given
   him
A most powerful gift:
Confidence.

8331.

Do not keep God waiting
Any longer.
He has been waiting for you
For millennia.

8332.

So far your unconscious life
Is unforgettable,
But do not allow it to become
Unforgivable.

8333.

When the purity-channel is open,
Your higher nature gets an
   immediate chance
To reign supreme.

8334.

What foolishness is this?
Your mind will not give you peace,
Never!
It is your aspiration-heart
That will give peace
Not only to you
But to your uninspired mind as
   well.

8335.

Heaven and earth, sooner or later,
Will pass away.
What will forever remain
Is your life's eternal hunger,
And something more:
Your heart's infinite thirst.

8336.

His heart is a river
Of hopelessness.
His mind is an ocean
Of sadness.
His life is a desert
Of helplessness.
Yet he dreams of God's
Constant Closeness.

8337.

His mind was born to satisfy God
In His own Way.
His heart was born to love God
Unconditionally.
His soul was born to grow into
Another God.

8338.

If your mind is driven
By demonic dreams,
How can the lustre
Of your hidden divinity
Shine on your outer life?

8339.

When a human being puts his ego
On display,
His love-life with himself
Needs immediate correction.

8340.

At last my mind and my vital
Have signed a peace treaty.
Therefore, my soul-bird is flying
Happily and proudly
In God's Satisfaction-Firmament.

8341.

Compassion and justice
Need each other.
Compassion needs justice
For newness-light.
Justice needs compassion
For oneness-delight.

8342.

When will you realise
That your self-righteous pride
Is the constant companion
Of your failure-life?

8343.

God has given me the
    responsibility
To love Him and serve Him.
I have given God the
    responsibility
To strike me and perfect me.

8344.

His heart's soulful smile
At once disarms the ugliness
Of his doubting mind
And captures the beauty
Of his loving soul.

8345.

Insecurity-drops
Have paralysed your heart.
Impurity-flood
Has paralysed your mind.
Ignorance-sea
Has paralysed your life.

8346.

When his mind became
A silenced noise,
God gave him His own Heart's
Satisfaction-flooded soundless
    Voice.

8347.

I can escape
Neither my powerful mind-forest
Nor my soulful heart-garden.

8348.

Justice is not enough.
Compassion is not enough.
Oneness is not only enough,
But more than enough.

8349.

The outer world is suffering
From its immoral insanity.
The inner world is suffering
From its indifferent insanity.

8350.

How can you have a glimmer of hope
When your hope does not long for
The august company of your soul?

8351.

Your life is filled with
Love-seeds,
Devotion-plants
And surrender-trees.
No wonder you have a safe path!

8352.

There are only two indispensable things
On each man's life-agenda:
Complete perfection
Of his outer nature
And total satisfaction
Of his Beloved Supreme.

8353.

Your mind has extinguished
Your hope-flames.
Therefore, stark disappointment
Is hammering at your heart's door.

8354.

The human mind
Is dying to see God's Face.
But, at the same time,
It does not want to shun
The company of ignorance-night.

8355.

A determination-eye
Is his life's outer history.
An aspiration-heart
Is his life's inner history.

8356.

Mental love is investment
In the outer world.
Psychic love is enlightenment
Within and without.

8357.

To graduate
From the life-experience-school,
The seeker has to be rescued
From his own ordinary self.

8358.

Because you do not love
God the Creator,
Yours is a life
Of teeming questions
  unanswered.

8359.

You have allowed your mind's
  impurity
To poison your heart.
Therefore, yours is now the
  untimely
Death-grave.

8360.

When the human in me
Unconsciously goes to sleep,
The divine in me
Immediately wakes up
And also dives deep.

8361.

When the mind is ready
For self-examination,
It sees God the Dreamer
Dancing inside it.

8362.

As earth has no monopoly
On God's Compassion,
Even so, Heaven has no monopoly
On God's Pride.

8363.

Do not discard your
  mind-instrument.
It is just out of tune.
Tune it carefully and devotedly.
It is bound to give you
Boundless satisfaction.

8364.

You are stamped as a second-rate
   seeker
Because you are not willing
To be a caretaker
Of this doleful earth.

8365.

A purity-mind,
A gratitude-heart
And a surrender-life
Are born of their own divine
   needs.

8366.

If I desire to conquer the world
By God's Grace-Flood,
Then I am bowing
To a false God.

8367.

His heart is totally indifferent
To its own needs.
Therefore, God Himself is secretly
And proudly
Nourishing his heart
With His own Love-Delight.

8368.

What can poor God do
When the seeker begins
   hero-worshipping
His own deplorable self?

8369.

His powerful heart
Deliberately chose to be weak
So that he could become
   inseparably one
With earth's excruciating pangs.

8370.

No difference between
My heart's aspiration-power
And my life's liberation-hour.

8371.

In the mind
There is only one question:
"How long?"
In the heart
There is only one answer:
"Not too long!"

8372.

Earth knows how to hope.
Heaven knows how to be
  indifferent.
God knows how to smile at earth
And frown at Heaven.

8373.

Alas, the human mind
Not only loves
But also accepts
The unacceptable: doubt.

8374.

Your mind's impurity is secretly
  sapping
Your heart's strength-tree.
How then can you ever hope to see
The Face of your Beloved
  Supreme?

8375.

When his suffering finally ceases,
Man will have a new name:
God's Self-transcendence-Song.

8376.

Sincerity is meant for living.
Purity is meant for loving.
Oneness is meant for fulfilling.
Satisfaction is meant for being.

8377.

If your heart has climbing
  aspiration,
Then you cannot go backward.
You can only go forward.

8378.

He ran down the stairs of memory
Only to be bitten
By a destructive ignorance-wolf.

8379.

Together God and I have seen
My mind's failure-life.
Now together God and I are seeing
My heart's success and
  progress-life.

8380.

Nothing divine
Can be accidental,
But everything divine
Can be ephemeral.

8381.

My Lord Supreme,
You have given me
An innocent heart.
Can You not also give me
A translucent mind?

8382.

Ask nothing!
Lo, you are ascending.
Give everything!
Lo, God is descending.
Finally, you are unmistakably
In the company of God.

8383.

Why do I seek my Beloved
   Supreme?
I seek Him because I need to see
His Vision-Eye in me
For my
   perfection-satisfaction-smile.

8384.

Suppression is not transcendence.
Suppression is future destruction
In perfect disguise.

8385.

Desire, please say good-bye
To my tired mind.
Aspiration, please say hello
To my freshly awakened heart.

8386.

Do not say,
"I am going to try"
Or "I am going to do".
Only say,
"God is doing it in me"
And "God has done it for me".

8387.

There was a time
When I could not live a moment
Without ignorance-night.
Now I cannot live a moment
Without my Lord's
   Compassion-Eye
And Forgiveness-Feet.

8388.

O desire-life,
Now that I know
You have hidden dangers,
I have nothing to do with you
Any more.

8389.

Now I weep, now I laugh
Because of my mind's
　impurity-frown
And my heart's purity-crown.

8390.

The mirror reflects
His diamond-face,
Flooded with the delight
Of his soul's infinite Peace.

8391.

When your heart and mind
Greet each other,
Your soul's promise-beauty
Is bound to increase
In a most astonishing way.

8392.

Since impurity-thoughts are
　darting
Through your mind,
How can your heart dare to sing
Fruitful songs of hope?

8393.

My Lord, my heart is tied
To Your divine Feet.
Therefore, mine is the
　perfection-beauty
That will never fade.

8394.

The sons of morning sang
And reminded me of God the
　Power.
The daughters of evening sang
And reminded me of God the
　Peace.

8395.

May each page of my
　aspiration-life
Contain only two messages:
Gratitude-song and
　surrender-dance.

8396.

God has not asked you
To become a lover of loneliness.
How then can you blame Him
For your life of utter uselessness?

8397.

The day you deliberately started
Making friends with
    ignorance-night,
You saw the farewell-beam
Of your inner sun.

8398.

A life of increasing perfection
Is undoubtedly a peerless solace
To every aspiring heart.

8399.

Each human being is nothing
But a tiny drop in the
    Eternity-Sea.
Yet quite often he enjoys
His superb frown of pride.

8400.

My heart is so grateful
To have only You, my Lord,
And to claim You as the sole
    possession
Of my surrender-life.

8401.

As my heart's adoration-bird
Spreads its wings,
My life swims in the Power-Sea
Of my Lord's Love.

8402.

If you do not manifest
The Supreme,
You will be buried
By your own hidden capacities.

8403.

Hard is it to escape
From doubt,
For it wears
A million disguises.

8404.

Her insecurity has triggered
Her insincerity.
Her insincerity has triggered
Her devastating failure
Within and without.

8405.

You are fond of living
Inside your mind's doubt-fort.
No wonder you are so
   accident-prone
In your inner life.

8406.

Because you always unleash
Your animal anger upon the
   world,
The cosmic deities within you
Are quite often forced to starve.

8407.

Every human being can be
Out of tune
With God's Justice-Light
But not with God's
Compassion-Height.

8408.

As forgiveness can illumine
A human life,
Even so, love can enlarge
A human mind.

8409.

O my mind,
Do not compete with my heart
For supremacy.
If you want to compete
With anything or anyone,
Then compete only for
God's constant
   Compassion-Light.

8410.

If you can make your heart
A ceaseless song of newness,
Then your life of God-fulness
Cannot remain a far cry.

8411.

In case you have not noticed,
There is an inevitable link
Between the human desire-life
And ceaseless frustration-night.

8412.

You do not love God.
You do not pray to God.
You do not meditate on God.
Do you think
That these are only minor
   incidents
In God's Cosmic Drama?

8413.

The human life-river flows.
The divine life-river
Flows and glows.
The Supreme Life-River
Carries everywhere
The Satisfaction-Heart
Of the Absolute Supreme.

8414.

Your lack of faith in God
Is nothing short of
A beginningless and endless dark
   tunnel.

8415.

When God governs your inner life,
Your outer life becomes
God's own sleepless Dream-Boat.

8416.

If you are a secret
Lover of God,
And if you are a sacred
Instrument of God,
Then ignorance has no right
To exist in your life.

8417.

If you are overcome
By the trivia of the ordinary
   world,
Then your past failures
Will always remain alive
Inside your tightly earth-bound
   life.

8418.

Every day you must learn anew
How to maintain silence
In your mind-world.
Every day you must learn anew
How to offer peace
To the world at large
From the world of your
   aspiration-flames.

8419.

To discover the darkness
Of your mind's night,
You do not have to go anywhere.
Just look within
Carefully!

8420.

If you want to become
God's Victory-Drum,
Then ask your heart
To pray to God
To know His outer
And inner Programme.

8421.

The unaspiring human in me
Not only protests but also cries
When it sees that the divine in me
Wants to be awakened
To illumine the world within and
　without.

8422.

If you love spirituality
Sincerely and generously,
God will undoubtedly
Crusade for your victory.

8423.

Your heart's surrender-life
Is not even a single heartbeat away
From God's Satisfaction-Life.

8424.

Your heart of love
And your life of light
Must always appreciate and
　admire
The mountain-high beauty of
　your soul.

8425.

God Himself will keep
A good grip on your life's reality
If you just master the art
Of faith-fidelity.

8426.

If you know how to surrender
Cheerfully, soulfully and
　unconditionally,
Then you are bound to see
The swift opening of Heaven's
Life-illumining and
　soul-fulfilling door.

8427.

I shall not allow
My thronging thoughts
To intrude upon my heart's
Supremely precious
Oneness-life with God.

8428.

My gratitude-heart breathes
Only to see the face
Of my perfection-life.

8429.

You have cast aside
Your disbelief-life.
Therefore, you have become
A specialist in God's Love.

8430.

My dear soul-bird,
If you do not want to teach me
How to fly for you,
Then at least teach me
How to fly with you.

8431.

Peace in my outer life
Is my perfection-smile.
Dynamism in my inner life
Is my satisfaction-dance.

8432.

His inner actions
Have made his heart
Divinely beautiful.
His outer silence
Has made his life
Supremely powerful.

8433.

Cheer up
And give up your failure-life!
Look at your heart's
   gratitude-flames.
This time God will definitely
Be on your side.

8434.

Because he is his heart's
Ceaseless silence,
He is also his life's
Endless joy.

8435.

My secret prayers
Deal with my mind's
Undivine thoughts.
My sacred meditations
Deal with my heart's
Soulful feelings.

8436.

Now that purity
Is your heart's new name,
You can live inside the garden
Of your soul's illumination-sky.

8437.

When I shut my mind's
Disbelief-door,
Peace unfolds its brightest bloom
For me.

8438.

Cheerful self-giving
Is the master key
To the mystic door
Of God-discovery.

8439.

There are so many ways
To please our Beloved Supreme,
But the ways of patience,
   surrender
And gratitude
Are very special.

8440.

My Lord Supreme,
An atom of Your Light
Liberates my bondage-mind;
An atom of Your Delight
Immortalises my aspiration-heart.

8441.

In my outer life
I own nothing but my feeble
   hopes.
In my inner life
I own many things,
Even God's Vision-Eye.

8442.

Yesterday's fear
Has captured me.
Tomorrow's doubt
Is capturing me.
And today's utter helplessness
Is about to capture me.

8443.

My confidence in my heart
Is my only joy.
My soul's confidence in me
Is my only peace.

8444.

O my heart,
You are meant for perfect
    perfection.
God will not grant you
Even a small margin for error.

8445.

The silence of humility
Cheerfully follows
And successfully replaces
The sound of stupidity.

8446.

Mine is a completely new effort
To start smiling
The final smile.

8447.

Inside a tiny moment-drop
I do hope to see the Presence
Of my Lord Supreme.

8448.

I phoned God
And asked Him
To do something about my
    impurity-life.
He told me that He knows all
    about it
And that He is definitely
Going to take care of it.

8449.

Smile!
It will bring you out of the prison
Of wasted thoughts.

8450.

Your life's dedication-light
Is your free passport
To freedom's delight.

8451.

Man loves the winner,
But God loves the lover
Of experience-light.

8452.

I wish to be an eternal slave
To serve my Lord's Lotus Feet.
I wish to be an eternal dreamer
To adore my Lord's Vision-Eye.
I wish to be an eternal lover
To manifest my Lord's
   Oneness-Heart.

8453.

O my mind,
My soul is a very close friend
Of Immortality's diamond
   dreams,
And my heart is a very close friend
Of Infinity's golden dreams.
Can you not be even an ordinary
   friend
Of Eternity's silver dreams?

8454.

His heart of patience
And his life of perseverance
Have at long last granted him
Heaven's ever-increasing
   ecstasy-sky.

8455.

Between my self-inquiry
And my self-discovery
Two divine existence-realities
   abide:
My heart's soulful cry
And my life's powerful smile.

8456.

A mind flooded with doubts
Is at once Eternity's sadness
And
Infinity's madness.

8457.

Unless you carefully watch
Your inner treasures,
Your faith, love and gratitude,
How can you expect God
To sleeplessly watch
Your doubt, hatred and
   ingratitude?

8458.

Where is the difference between
Your heart's adamantine
   will-power
And your life's unparalleled
   God-Hour?

8459.

Purity's love
Is my inner electricity.
Beauty's concern
Is my outer electricity.
Divinity's satisfaction
Is my supreme electricity.

8460.

My heart's junior partner
Is my earth-born mind.
My heart's senior partner
Is my Immortality's soul.

8461.

A whisper of inspiration
Has totally changed his face.
A whisper of aspiration
Has completely changed his life.

8462.

If your life is ready
To challenge the invisible,
Then your heart will definitely
Be embraced by the unknowable.

8463.

You are denied the satisfaction
Of God's Presence
Not because you do not need God,
Not because you speak ill of God,
But because you have become
An absurd and shameless
    self-lover.

8464.

Each negative thought
Is a positive intruder.
Each negative feeling
Is a positive destroyer.
These are the elementary lessons
The seeker receives
When he enters into the spiritual
    life.

8465.

No man-acquired achievements
Can forever last,
But all God-granted achievements
Will forever and forever last.
This is the supreme lesson
That all human beings must learn.

8466.

Inspiration is the nectar-delight
Of my searching mind.
Aspiration is the nectar-delight
Of my crying heart.
Realisation is the nectar-delight
Of my self-giving life.

8467.

This world may not need
A great spiritual Master.
This world may not need
A great saint.
But this world definitely needs
A perfect gentleman.

8468.

The human mind
Does not want to know
Where God is.
The human heart
Does not know
What God looks like.
The human life
Does not understand
Why God delays.

8469.

Do you want to transcend your
   mind?
If so,
Then either sell your mind to
   humanity
For good
At a very high price,
Of offer your mind to God
Unconditionally and
   permanently.

8470.

I came from God
To learn the meaning
Of His "Why?"
I shall go back to God
After I have learnt the meaning
Of His "How?"

8471.

If you are a beginner-seeker,
Then yours can be
God's Compassion-Sea.
If you are an advanced seeker,
Then yours should be
God's Justice-Sky.

8472.

God does not care to know
Whether or not you are satisfied
With Him,
But God does want to know
How you can be satisfied
With your ignorance-self.

8473.

Before you think of God,
Think of yourself
As a sleepless seeker.
This will definitely help you.
Before you meditate on God,
Think of yourself
As an unconditional God-lover.
This will definitely help you.

8474.

In Heaven my soul and I
Received the message
Of God-Manifestation.
On earth my heart and I
Received the message
Of God-Perfection-Satisfaction.

8475.

If you want to argue with
    someone,
Why don't you argue
With your doubting mind?
If you want to hate someone,
Why don't you hate
Your devouring vital?
If you want to awaken someone,
Why don't you awaken
Your sleeping body?

8476.

When I live inside my mind,
I long for quantity's Infinity.
When I live inside my heart,
I long for quality's Immortality.
When I live inside my soul,
I long for neither quality nor
    quantity.
I long only for the supreme
    Satisfaction
Of my Beloved Supreme
In His own transcendental Way.

8477.

Doubt has a free permit
To exercise inner tyranny
In a careless seeker's
    aspiration-life.

8478.

Has there ever been a time
In God's creation
When human beings have not suffered
From the pressure of inner weaknesses?

8479.

A heart of constant
And cheerful self-giving
Will not be dogged
By despair.

8480.

He is not happy
Because he has imposed upon himself
The task of reassessing each day
His own life.

8481.

True, you are not a God-lover.
True, you are not even a truth-seeker.
But you can easily be
A faithful and meticulous observer.

8482.

If you deliberately cherish
A doubt-life,
Sooner or later you will fall
Into life's deepest chasm.

8483.

Each soulful seeker
Has only one necessity.
What is that necessity?
A golden God-necessity-chain.

8484.

If you fall again and again
Into the trap of self-deception,
How can you dance inside your heart
With your soul's sunbeams?

8485.

You do not need
A vast kingdom.
You do not need
A deep solitude.
What you need is
A mind of blossom-poise.

8486.

There is a world far from ours
Where beauty's heart, purity's life
And divinity's soul
Grow and glow
To reveal God the Eternal
   Dreamer
And manifest God the Immortal
   Lover.

8487.

If your human mind
Is overpowered by the sound-life,
How can you expect
To sing soul-stirring songs
In your silence-heart?

8488.

Once upon a time
Inside my heart
Hope was shining bright.
Alas, now my heart is the place
Where hope gropes in the
   darkness
Of frustration-night.

8489.

Because you know how to scatter
The dew of earth-delight,
God has granted you
His own Eternity's immortal
   Height.

8490.

I long to remain
In a sacred corner of my
   heart-room
Where my self-giving life-music
Can please the Satisfaction-Ear
Of my Beloved Supreme.

8491.

The presence of teeming doubts
Not only weakens the seeker's
   heart
But also lengthens the seeker's
   failure-life.

8492.

He made the wrong approach:
He wanted to conquer the world
With words of hate.
He is now making the right
   approach:
He is conquering the world
With acts of love.

8493.

Outwardly he does not want to
   hear
What the world says,
But inwardly he is always eager to
   know
What the world feels.

8494.

He is now ready to achieve
The life of perfection-delight
Because his human life has
    become
A dead leaf on the desire-tree.

8495.

He does not know
Why his faith has left him.
How can he know
Unless he invites his heart's inner
    King
To return to the throne
Inside his earth-bound and
    Heaven-free life?

8496.

There is no difference
Between a desire-breath
And a disgrace-life.

8497.

Each beautiful life
Is indeed a satisfaction-child
Of Divinity's God-Hour.

8498.

An impurity-breath
Is the only place
Where Heaven's God-Flowers
Never want to grow.

8499.

His mind is a shattered hope.
His heart is a battered promise.
Alas, this is the kind of life he has.

8500.

My life's devoted receptivity
Has and is the capacity
To make my heart feel
That it is not only close
To my Lord Supreme,
But closer than the closest.

8501.

No need of miracles!
Ask man and God for nothing.
Let the beauty of silence
Reign supreme in your life.

8502.

Do not try to bind love,
For love alone
Can change the face
Of this ill-fated earth.

8503.

He is not the loser
And he can never be the loser,
For his heart's surrender-flower
And his life's gratitude-fruit
God has proudly accepted.

8504.

Your first question is:
Is God-realisation
Everybody's birthright?
Your second and last question is:
How can the human cry
Be transformed into a divine
 smile?

8505.

If your life has a sacred thirst,
Then God is bound to grant you
His own secret Well to quench it.

8506.

Love your heart ever more.
And do something further:
Reawaken your imprisoned
 heart-flames!

8507.

My desire,
Stay where you are.
I am running towards you.
What for?
To reduce your life's
Loud clatterings.

8508.

Sleepless perfection,
Will you ever be mine?
Sleepless satisfaction,
Can I be yours, only yours?

8509.

I once promised myself
That I would not try to escape
Any appropriate punishment
If I misbehaved in my inner life.
Yet my promise remains
 unfulfilled.

8510.

Beautiful is his heart's loyalty.
Soulful is his mind's enthusiasm.
Fruitful is his life's obedience.

8511.

Unless I cross the mind's barrier,
How can I see beauty's face,
Purity's heart
And divinity's soul?

8512.

What can my little hands do?
They can paint the Face
Of God the Beauty.
What can my heart's soulful will do?
It can liberate man,
The bondage-slave.

8513.

A purity-heart
Has the capacity
And is the capacity
To live inside
The heart of Infinity's Love-Light.

8514.

If I can keep my life safe
From my mind's ignorance-dreams,
Then I do not see why and how
I cannot become a perfect instrument
Of my Beloved Supreme.

8515.

If humility is mighty,
Then purity is almighty.
If surrender is powerful,
Then gratitude is all-powerful.

8516.

No matter how divine and how perfect
A human being is,
He is subject to the scorn
Of multitude-tongues.

8517.

If God's Mind is subtle,
His Heart is simple.
If God's Compassion-Eye is powerful,
His Satisfaction-Life is blessingful.

8518.

Each human desire
Is an arrow
Which is quite often apt
To miss the target.

8519.

As a flower is blessed
With fragrance and beauty,
Even so, each human being is blessed
With inner purity and divinity.

8520.

Because he has divine thoughts
As his unparalleled inheritance,
His life is a constant expression
Of his heart's intense gratitude.

8521.

His firm belief:
Unless his entire being cries
For fulness-splendour in life,
Tears will drain
His aspiration-heart dry.

8522.

When imagination fails you,
Do not feel sad.
Just smile and remain serene.
From Above you will get another chance
To catch the imagination-bird.

8523.

Just refuse to sing with your mind.
Behold!
Your heart is all ready
To teach you its own soulful songs.

8524.

If you can cherish
What you have already received from God,
God will, without fail,
Grant you His Eternity's Treasure-Smile.

8525.

Be sure to know
What hurts you more:
To teach the world
Or to learn from the world.

8526.

No matter what your physical appearance,
There is always a most beautiful person
Inside your heart
Who can make your face truly beautiful.

8527.

As there is no such thing
As a perfect desire,
Even so, there is no such thing
As imperfect
   aspiration-surrender.

8528.

A doubtful mind,
A fearful heart
And a hateful life
Are the unmistakable and
   powerful causes
Of sudden death in the spiritual
   life.

8529.

We need many, many things from
   God
To become His divine
   instruments.
But what we need most of all
Is to keep our heart's door
Sleeplessly open to Him.

8530.

If you do not know how to smile
When you descend,
Then God in His Infinite
   Compassion
May not appear
To help you ascend once again.

8531.

You say you are
A genuine God-lover.
If so, how is it
That your imagination-bird
Is mercilessly locked up
In a tiny cage,
And your aspiration-bird
Is tightly locked up
In a tiny cave?

8532.

You can love the world dauntlessly
Because God is always for you.
You can serve the world
   unconditionally
Because God is always with you.

8533.

As my doubting mind is aware
Of God's Compassion-Eye,
Even so, my unaspiring life is
   aware
Of God's Forgiveness-Heart.

8534.

When I use my heart
As God intended,
Only then can I say
That I live for God's Love alone.

8535.

Do you not see
That God is unfolding Himself
Before your very eyes?
Do you not see
That your heart and God's Heart
Are two open books to each other?

8536.

You say that you pray every day.
But if you really prayed,
Your prayer would definitely sink
   into
Your aspiration-heart and
   gratitude-life.

8537.

His heart is crying
For God's Supreme Love.
His mind is crying
For man's lofty appreciation.
Alas, what is man doing?
Man is dying
To see his fall.
And what is God doing?
God is unveiling Himself
To be claimed powerfully by him.

8538.

The mind tells the heart
That it will never see
The Face of God.
The heart receives Blessing-Light
From the soul,
Which buries the curse of the
   mind
In oblivion-night.

8539.

When my soul invites me,
It is all in perfect silence-light.
When I invite my soul,
It is all in imperfect sound-might.

8540.

When you meditate,
If thoughts are flocking,
Then try to imagine
That God Himself is rocking
Your heart-cradle.

8541.

When the mind reigns over
   matter,
You can conquer the outer
   heights.
When the inner depths conquer
   the mind,
Your aspiration-dedication-life
Becomes unparalleled.

8542.

My Lord is not pleased
When I say I am not worthy of
   Him.
My Lord is pleased
Only when I say
I am definitely going to be
His choice instrument.

8543.

Nothing is worth believing:
This is what the human mind
Tells us.
Doubt is worth nothing:
This is what the divine heart
Tells us.

8544.

The cynical eye distrusts.
What does it distrust?
It distrusts man,
The God-representative on earth.

8545.

His heart called out,
"Doubt, the bandit,
Must be seized and imprisoned!"
Doubt immediately surrendered,
And longed to be transformed
Into the heart's choice
   instrument.

8546.

My dedication to the world
Should be a beautiful gift
And not a demanding
   expectation.

8547.

His mind has unparalleled poise.
Do you know why?
Because his heart is in constant
   touch
With Eternity's Silence-Smile.

8548.

Do you know what has crushed
Your life's pride?
It is your huge,
Fallen self-expectation-tree.

8549.

What the weeping multitudes
   need
Is a divine strength
Beyond human hope.

8550.

Although you are not aspiring
To His Satisfaction,
Just because you are still aspiring,
The unexpected Supreme Guest
Will come to you
With His inexplicable Splendour.

8551.

Sorrow-rain will eventually
Fall heavily on you
If you always remain
Self-enamoured.

8552.

Aspiration is the beginning
Of self-mastery.
Self-mastery is the halfway point
To God-discovery.

8553.

My heart's sleepless cry
Is my Lord's earth-born child.
My soul's matchless smile
Is my Lord's Heaven-born child.

8554.

Determination is my mind's God.
Hope is my heart's God.
Promise is my soul's God.
Surrender is my life's God.

8555.

Why do I choose to hide?
Not because I am a thief,
But because the God-Hour
Has not yet struck
For me to reveal myself.

8556.

My search for satisfaction within
Is yet unfinished.
My search for perfection without
Is yet to begin.

8557.

At your slightest hint
Of surrender-light
God will come to you
With His Infinity's
   Satisfaction-Delight.

8558.

Expand your heart,
Transcend your mind!
Lo, your ego-life
Is all gone.

8559.

Open the door
Of your gratitude-heart.
Anxiety, the treacherous queen,
Will no longer be able
To rule your life.

8560.

To serve mankind
You need only two clean hands.
To serve God
You need only one pure heart.

8561.

A doubtful mind
And a fearful heart
Are indeed
Two monsters of waste.

8562.

Self-contempt will cling to you
Unless you become aware
Of your earthly role:
You are Eternity's pilgrim
On Immortality's road.

8563.

If you allow your mind
To be chained to time,
How can you be God's choice
    instrument
In the heart of mankind
Or even in the Heart of God?

8564.

There is only one God-trodden
    path,
And that path lies
Inside your heart,
Not before your eyes.

8565.

If you keep your heart-eye veiled,
Naturally you will be pierced
By the wild shafts
Of darkness-night.

8566.

His heart of love
And his life of service
Are always guided
By his inner glimpse
Of God's outer Smile.

8567.

When the heart does not listen
To the dictates of the soul,
The heart is bound to become
A ruined paradise.

8568.

How can you proceed today
If you do not laugh
At your yesterday's despair-night?

8569.

Unless I become
A visible aspiration-flame
In the depths of my heart,
An invisible frustration
Will torture my life.

8570.

If you are silent
And uncomplaining,
God will cheerfully allow you
To join Him
In His own eternal Hunger
For self-transcendence.

8571.

Fear, doubt and worry
Will have to leave eventually
With their family of sighs.

8572.

You do not have to run away
From yourself.
God not only will carry your burden
But He will also carry you,
For He knows that He alone
Is the universal Burden-Bearer.

8573.

A questioning mind
Does not want to perceive.
A questioning heart
Does not want to receive.
A questioning life
Does not want to achieve.

8574.

O fearful heart, believe me!
This world is not as undivine
As you think.
This mind is not as important
As you think.
Heaven is not as remote
As you think.

8575.

How can your heart be pleased
With anything here on earth
When your mind is critical
Of everything there in Heaven?

8576.

Your outer service to mankind
Will give your inner faith
A splendid victory.

8577.

Because your life enjoys
Trivial and worthless activities,
Your God-loving heart
Is still locked
In an amazingly cruel prison.

8578.

O unbelieving mind,
I shall show you
Where God is.
O unaspiring heart,
I shall tell you
Who God is.

8579.

His Heaven-life saw
A mountain of promise.
His earth-life is now dying for
A flicker of hope.

8580.

Because your soul has planned
    your life
From the beginning of time,
You are eager to extinguish
Your earth-desire-flames.

8581.

O fearful freedom,
Who wants to have you?
No, not my crying heart.
O soulful freedom,
Who wants to have you?
No, not my doubting mind.

8582.

When I live in the very depths
Of my heart,
I run towards my destined goal.
When I live inside my mind,
My desire-life runs towards me
Fast, very fast.

8583.

My mind is not satisfied
With newness.
Therefore, I am unhappy.
My heart is not satisfied
With fulness.
Therefore, I am unhappy.
My Lord and I are satisfied
With our oneness.
Therefore, we are eternally happy.

8584.

A money-minded seeker
Is on the wrong train.
His train will have no destination.
No, never!

8585.

My Lord,
My dream-sky exists
Only for You.
My reality-clouds exist
Only for You.

8586.

You are a broken-hearted seeker
Just because your heart has
    become
A self-confessed insecurity.

8587.

If your outer liking
And your inner disliking
Of the world
Keep you always upset,
Then invoke the presence
Of peace;
It will grant you
Eternity's oneness-reality.

8588.

Since you are no longer
The slave of fear,
I shall shed a fountain
Of joy-tears.

8589.

If you want to become
Eternity's peace-distributing self,
Then never give in
To the falsehood-power of
    neutrality.

8590.

My Lord,
You do not have to break
The chains of my sinful life.
Just show me how I can chain
  myself
To Your Compassion-Feet.

8591.

Do not allow your hope
To disappoint you.
Let your hope be
The sunlit frontier
Of your God-searching mind.

8592.

If you can become
An unconditionally surrendered
  seeker,
You will see that few
Will take birth on earth
To equal you
And your unparalleled
  achievement.

8593.

Because of your beauty's mind,
Because of your purity's heart,
Because of your divinity's life,
You have become a universal
  favourite.

8594.

Perfection means constant
  rejection
Of your desire-life.
Perfection means constant
  acceptance
Of your aspiration-heart.

8595.

Each time a new wave of faith
Enters into him,
His mind marshals
His life's doubt-clouds.

8596.

Disobedience is
The beginning of death
In the spiritual life.
Ingratitude is
Permanent death
In the spiritual life.

8597.

I pray and meditate
To lengthen the day
Of my heart.
I pray and meditate
Not only to delay but also to cancel
The arrival of ignorance-night.

8598.

A spiritually full man
Is he who fans the flame
Of his aspiration
Each new day
More cheerfully and more
   powerfully.

8599.

God helps the seeker
Create his tomorrow's world
   today
When the seeker's life becomes
A surrender-moon and a
   gratitude-sun.

8600.

My Lord,
You have my tomorrow
Inside Your Heart.
Can I not have Your Today
Inside my heart?

8601.

I shall not allow my aspiration-life
To become my forgotten past.
I shall keep it always
As my chosen present.

8602.

I am enjoying at one and the same
   time
The feast of inner triumphs
And the fast of outer defeats.

8603.

The glory of learning
The desiring mind knows.
The glory of unlearning
The searching mind must learn
Before it can dive deep
Into God's Ecstasy-Sea.

8604.

His doubt-enemy
Can easily be brought under his
   control
If he does the needful
Cheerfully and powerfully
With his faith-friend.

8605.

What is extremely difficult for
   man
But extremely easy for God?
A constant Satisfaction-Smile.
What is extremely easy for man
But extremely difficult for God?
An endless dissatisfaction-cry.

8606.

You feel sad that your defeat-life
Has arrived so quickly.
But I assure you that your future
    success-life
Will arrive not only quickly
But also certainly.

8607.

His heart is enjoying
His today's Heaven-bound flight.
His mind is enjoying
His yesterday's ignorance-failure.

8608.

Your mind's doubt-cloud
Has totally eclipsed
Your heart's hope-moon
And your soul's promise-sun.

8609.

He and his heart
Are permanent residents of
    Heaven,
And do not care for earth at all.
Therefore, he and earth
Cannot be of any real help
To each other.

8610.

If God wants me to succeed
In my life's outer journey,
Then He will give me
His Vision-Eye.
If God wants me to proceed
In my life's inner journey,
Then He will give me
His Satisfaction-Heart.

8611.

In the inner world
His heart's purity-smile
Is his supreme assistant.
In the outer world
His mind's sincerity-cry
Is his supreme assistant.

8612.

Who says the dead are forgiven?
No, they are not!
Only those who again and again
Try to transcend themselves
Will be cheerfully forgiven
In God's Compassion-Heart
By God Himself.

8613.

If a simple mind
Can imagine God,
Then a pure heart
Can easily reveal God.

8614.

You may not know
When I think of God,
But I know
When you think of God.
You think of God when God tells me
That He has two
Supremely chosen instruments.

8615.

My humble prayer is eager to see
What God has for me.
My proud mind is ready to show
What it has for God.

8616.

If you can be consistent
Like the ancient truth-seekers
And God-lovers,
You will soon be schooled
In enlightenment.

8617.

Not because you are clothed
In a frail body,
But because of your obdurate
Unwillingness to change,
Your life is a misery-haunted house.

8618.

Love your soul more and more.
Your soul will teach you
How to break ignorance-chains
And untie bondage-knots.

8619.

Each soul-boat is anchored on earth
For a brief sojourn.
Then it goes back to its
  Heaven-harbour
To renew its
  God-manifestation-promise.

8620.

Do not give up!
He who gives up
Never reaches the
  Satisfaction-Shore.
Who knows?
Each attempt of yours may bring you
Many exceptionally
  heart-enlightening
Heaven-prosperities.

8621.

O my present life,
Can you not forget my past
The way my future life
Will forget your own
　　ignorance-torture?

8622.

If your heart-life is thirsty,
Then quench it immediately
With your soul's all-loving
　　promise
To God
And with His Eternity's
　　Immortality's
Will-power.

8623.

Since the Divinity of my soul
Has not changed,
How can the Eternity of my life
Change?
It is simply impossible
Plus unnecessary.

8624.

You have already seen
Your mind's limitation-room.
Now what you are going to see
Is your soul's vastness-kingdom.
Just soulfully and unconditionally
　　wait.

8625.

Delighted, I say to God:
"Father, let Thy Will be done."
Disgusted, God says to me:
"Son, let your temptation-greed
　　fulfil itself."

8626.

Unless a seeker's life
Is a sleeplessly cheerful
　　commitment
To God-realisation,
His goal will always remain
A far cry.

8627.

Cry deep within
Unreservedly
If you want to collect
The harvest of God's Smile.

8628.

O my mind,
If you can never regain
Your lost simplicity,
How can you ever receive
God's Satisfaction-Delight?

8629.

Just because you want to become
A true truth-seeker
And a perfect God-lover,
Yours cannot be the life
Of criticism and
    complaint-luxury.

8630.

Because his inner life has learnt
To love the unparalleled hardship,
God is sharing with him
His Immortality-ownership.

8631.

I see incessant disputes
Between the impurity of my mind
And the aggression of my vital.
Alas, I am completely helpless!

8632.

There is no such thing
As an uneasy peace.
Peace is always
Divinity's ease.

8633.

To obey at every moment
God's transcendental Decisions
Is to continually manifest
    God-Satisfaction
In God's aspiring creation.

8634.

The revelation of what you have
May not please the world,
But the revelation of what you are
Is definitely going to teach the
    world.

8635.

When uncomely thoughts
Walk into your mind,
You have to know
That your old friend, ignorance,
Is telling you he still wants to
    keep you
Under his firm jurisdiction.

8636.

If you want to solve
All the confusion-problems
Of your mind,
Then resolve to live
Inside the illumination
Of your heart-sky.

8637.

If you do not allow yourself
To be perfected by God's
 Compassion-Light,
Then you will without fail
Belong to the Heaven-rejected
 category.

8638.

Each forward step of his
Is an upward and inward
 dedication
To the all-pervading God.

8639.

Do not expect.
Do not demand.
There are higher things on earth
Than expectation and demand.
Try a heart of gratitude
And a life of surrender.

8640.

Look what your expectation-train
Has done to you:
It has brought you speedily
To the helpless moans
Of your despair-station.

8641.

The morning of God's Hour
Is beauty's smile.
The evening of God's Hour
Is purity's song.
The night of God's Hour
Is divinity's silence-flooded dance.

8642.

If you allow your mind to doubt
And at the same time
Ask your heart not to be
A victim of despair,
Do you not think
That you are trying to succeed
At an impossible task?

8643.

If education is a sophisticated
Mental exercise,
Then I do not need it
And I definitely do not want it.
But if education is self-cultivation
And longing for God-Satisfaction,
Then I badly need it
And I definitely want it.

8644.

To see the gate of Heaven wide open
Is undoubtedly your reward
For having silver faith in yourself
And golden faith in your Lord Supreme.

8645.

When I love God,
God agrees with me more.
When God agrees with me more,
He tells me something secretly:
"My child, your heart has now become
My perfect Home."

8646.

Why do you have to take a detour
On your spiritual journey?
Why?
Is it because
Your heart's sincerity is not enough?
Is it because
Your mind's determination is not enough?
Is it because
Your life's integrity is not enough?

8647.

If I am not afraid to start again,
Then there is no reason
Why my Lord Supreme
Will not be compassionate enough
To help me with my new start.

8648.

If my mind can give God
More time
And if my heart can give God
More trust,
Then my Lord will give me
Not only a better
But a better than the best
Life of satisfaction-peace.

8649.

The world-mind has given you
Countless troubles.
The world-heart will give you
Ever-transcending triumphs.

8650.

I shall help you
Defeat your mind.
I shall help you
Discover more good qualities
In yourself.
I shall help you
See God singing and smiling
Inside your peace-flooded heart.

8651.

If I love God's Love
For myself,
Then I am really great.
If I love God's Love
For humanity,
Then I am really good.
If I love God's Love
For God's Revelation
In God's own Way,
Then I am really perfect.

8652.

Each aspiring heart
Must be the hyphen between
Heaven's forgiveness
And
Earth's happiness.

8653.

What kind of faith is it
That does not produce
Power in your mind,
Love in your heart
And peace in your life?

8654.

If every day you do not clean
Your mind-room,
Then rest assured that every day
You will have to face
Your life's unavoidable doom.

8655.

If you want the capacity
To grant wings to your dreams,
Then you must develop the
    capacity
To see a beautiful soul-bird
In your life-reality.

8656.

You trust God.
Therefore, God will always rescue
    you.
You need God.
Therefore, God has given you
His own heart-satisfying
    Meditation.

8657.

The human mind says
To the human being:
"God is so great.
Why and how should He speak to
    me?"
The divine heart says
To the divine being:
"Just because God is so great,
He is always ready to speak to me."

8658.

Just because I know
I am God's child,
I can be happy.
Just because I know
God loves me,
I should be kind to myself.
Just because I know
God is playing
His Satisfaction-Game
In and through me,
I must make myself
Cheerfully perfect.

8659.

Do you think God will ever allow you
To destroy His transcendental Dream
Of the ultimate perfection
Of your earthly journeys
Which He has been nourishing for millenia?

8660.

A true truth-seeker and God-lover
Is he whose outer and inner life
Are powerfully anchored
Inside his heart's starlit faith.

8661.

True, suffering has reality in it.
Who denies it?
But the transcendence of suffering
Also has reality in it.
Who can disbelieve it?

8662.

To suffer and not to speak
Is the sign of
Either a stupid fellow
Or a genuine seeker.

8663.

A great idea can change failure
Into success.
A good idea can transform human aspiration
Into God's own transcendental Satisfaction.

8664.

When I fail,
I must not think
That God is not for me.
When I fail,
I must think
That God, out of His infinite
    Bounty,
Is giving me a much-needed
    experience
For my earth-bound life
And heavenward journey.

8665.

The closer a seeker is
To God's Compassion-Light,
The clearer it becomes to him
That it was he who loved
Ignorance-night,
Not ignorance-night
That loved him.

8666.

At long last my life has found
Its life-illumining "yes"
In its surrender-heart
To God's blessingful Vision-Eye.

8667.

Have more faith in your own
    heart.
Your heart is your own
    divinity-magnet
Which will pull you up
To God's Transcendental Heights.

8668.

Take each problem in your life
As your self-examination,
And each self-examination
As your Lord's Satisfaction
In your heart's perfection-cry.

8669.

How can I have a sorrowful life
When my Lord Supreme does not
    have one?
How can I have a fearful heart
When my Lord Supreme does not
    have one?
How can I have a doubtful mind
When my Lord Supreme does not
    have one?

8670.

God the Infinite needs
Man the finite.
What else is a miracle?
Man the finite can easily love
God the Infinite.
What else is a miracle?

8671.

The door
That God's Compassion-Height
    opens,
No one can shut.
The door
That God's Justice-Light shuts,
No one can open.

8672.

God is not
In your uselessness,
But God is always
In your selflessness.

8673.

When God did not call him
On the phone,
He did not feel sad.
The very fact
That God had wanted to call him
In the first place
Was enough to flood his whole
    being
With joy.

8674.

Your mind has already failed
In God's Vision-Eye,
But your life will never fail
In God's Compassion-Heart.

8675.

If I think that I am personally
　responsible
For the purification of my mind,
Then I am not mistaken.
If I think that I am personally
　responsible
For the transformation of my life,
Then I am not mistaken.
If I think that I am personally
　responsible
For the satisfaction of my Lord,
Then I am not mistaken.
But if I think that I am personally
　responsible
For the transformation of God's
　creation,
Then I am totally, totally
　mistaken.

8676.

You want to know
If I consulted God
Before advising my mind to be
　pure
And my heart to be sincere.
I must say
That I did not consult God,
But God Himself commanded me
To speak to my mind
About its purity
And to my heart
About its sincerity.

8677.

As soon as you see a
　gratitude-flower
In your heart
And a surrender-fruit
In your life,
Offer them to your Lord Supreme,
Not only cheerfully,
But also unconditionally.

8678.

Nothing has to be taken as
　possession
Either in the inner life
Or in the outer life.
But everything should be taken
As soulful and powerful
　progression
In both the inner life
And the outer life.

8679.

What my mind solely needs
Is God's Justice-Length.
What my heart solely needs
Is God's Compassion-Strength.

8680.

The outer man wants success.
The inner man wants progress.
The supreme man wants
    self-transcendence.
And God wants Satisfaction
In His entire creation.

8681.

God loves us even after
We have failed Him.
We need God even after
We have realised Him.

8682.

The loud music of the
    sound-universe
Tells me what God does
For its perfection.
The sweet music of the
    silence-universe
Tells me what God is
For His own Satisfaction.

8683.

If you continuously prolong your
    life
Inside your mind-desert,
When and how can you expect to
    live
Inside your heart-garden?

8684.

Since you are concerned only
With satiating your wild vital,
The thirst of your pure heart
Will always remain unquenched.

8685.

Frustration-sound
Is the pilot of human fate.
Illumination-silence
Is the pilot of divine fate.

8686.

It is imperative to see
Where your mind is running,
Where your vital is sleeping,
Where your heart is dying.

8687.

The hesitation of the mind
Forces man to take
Unforgettable lessons
From the sorrow-teacher.

8688.

Each man
Can at least try to nourish
His own heart's feeble gratitude
To God.

8689.

Ask your present life
To forget your past life.
Ask your future life
To illumine your past life
And liberate your present life.

8690.

Although his life is pierced
By the poison-shaft of envy,
He is trying with all his heart
To carry envy to the Light of
   Infinity.

8691.

The future ignores
The mighty past
And deplores
The failing present.

8692.

Our lampless outer universe
Will have to weep
Until earth's sorrow
Becomes Heaven's ecstasy.

8693.

His heart of self-offering
Is a stupendous smile
Amidst earth's dark frowns.

8694.

Each undivine thought
Leaves the seeker
With a sad memory.

8695.

Control your animal vital,
Or this vital of yours
Will be the annihilation
Of your heart's aspiration-life.

8696.

Unless a seeker soulfully prays
And selflessly meditates,
His ignorance-bound life
Will return like the revolving
   years.

8697.

Each aspiration-heart
And each dedication-life
Is a hallowed thirst
For the Lord Supreme.

8698.

If you can have a new hope,
God will give you a new heart.
If you can have a new heart,
God will give you a new oneness.
If you can have a new oneness,
God will give you a new
   satisfaction.

8699.

God wants to teach me
Three simple lessons:
A soulful cry,
A beautiful smile
And a fruitful life.

8700.

When divine beauty
Penetrates the world,
Truth reveals
Its all-perfecting wings.

8701.

Every day you can create
A miracle in your life
Just by cherishing one positive
   thought:
"I will be able to conquer
   ignorance
And become a supremely chosen
   instrument
Of my Beloved Supreme."

8702.

A single unwilling, lethargic
And negative seeker
Can slow the progress
Of all those on the same path.

8703.

For the Supreme to please you
In your own way
Is for Him to make friends
With ignorance,
And that friendship is impossible.
But for you to make friends
With the Supreme
And please Him in His own Way
Is not a difficult task at all.

8704.

Each moment on earth
We are pleasing someone or
   something.
Since we are always pleasing
   someone,
Why not let that someone be
The Supreme within us?

8705.

He who does selfless service
    cheerfully
Is in no way inferior
To he who meditates soulfully.
Where one's consciousness dwells
Is the all-important question.

8706.

If outer success comes naturally,
Then welcome it.
But if you have to strive for it,
Then it is only temptation,
Which is the harbinger of
    destruction.

8707.

Your mind wants you to know
Where you were.
But I want you to know
Where your heart-home
Eternally is.

8708.

Man says to God,
"Be kind, be kind, be kind!"
God says to man,
"Be good, be good, be good!"

8709.

Man says to God,
"Be quick, be quick, be quick!"
God says to man,
"Be patient, be patient, be
    patient!"

8710.

Why do you have to suffer
In the stormy winter of the mind?
Just take a permanent vacation
In the sunny tropics of the heart.

8711.

When you serve the Supreme,
Do not allow
Any expansion of your ego.
Otherwise, He will be forced
To give you a zero
As your selfless service-grade.

8712.

You cannot stay
In the Supreme's Golden Boat
With an ego larger than the
    largest.
You can stay in God's Boat
Only by transforming your
    "I-ness"
Into oneness.

8713.

If you have lost
Your enthusiasm,
You will ultimately lose
Your aspiration-race.

8714.

Even the divine pathfinders
Can be deeply disappointed,
For although they may have found
A new path,
Others may not want to follow
    them.

8715.

He did not actually
Come before his time.
The time was right,
But the world was not willing.

8716.

A self-giving man-server
Will automatically become
A silent man-leader.

8717.

Ego can grow
Even in one who has nothing.
The poorest person on earth can
    say,
"I can manage without anything,
Whereas you cannot."

8718.

You will truly appreciate life
Only when you can see
That on a higher reality-plane
Everything is perfect.

8719.

When your Beloved Supreme
Scolds you,
Listen only with your heart.

8720.

Conquering doubt
Is not just a matter of time.
Doubt can be conquered
Only by the cry from within
And the Grace from Above.

8721.

At times God sees
An imminent world disaster,
But what can poor God do?
He will definitely save the world,
But He must wait
For the world's receptivity.

8722.

You can be most receptive
When you echo the inmost cry
Of a true sannyasin:
"I am ready to give up everything
For my Beloved Supreme."

8723.

It was the Supreme alone
Who gave you
The inspiration and
   determination
To do something good.
Will you not, therefore,
Offer Him the result,
And your gratitude as well?

8724.

If you have faith in God,
Then the Supreme Doctor Himself
Can and will cure
Your imperfection-illness.

8725.

In His transcendental aspect,
God is the Lord of nature.
In His universal aspect
God is nature itself.

8726.

True progress
Does not stop to look around
For appreciation.

8727.

Inner obedience and outer
   obedience
Always go together.
If you are not listening
To your Master outwardly,
Then rest assured,
You are not listening to him
Inwardly, either.

8728.

At every second you can please
Either your faithful heart-reality
Or your doubtful mind-reality.
Therefore, use your time wisely.

8729.

There is no such thing
As an unimportant action
In a seeker's life.
Each action has its own meaning
And value
At the proper time.

8730.

If you say no to your wrong
　thoughts
And yes to your inspiration
To become God's perfect
　instrument,
Then boundless receptivity
Will immediately be yours.

8731.

You do not have to look at others
To see where you stand.
You are standing inside the Heart
Of your Beloved Supreme.

8732.

When we feel
That we are of the Supreme
And for the Supreme,
We become His,
And His Wealth becomes ours.

8733.

Each positive thought
Has the atom-bomb-capacity
To destroy the negative in us.
Each negative thought
Has the atom-bomb-capacity
To destroy our whole world.

8734.

When God deals with human
　beings
Who have limited receptivity,
For Him there is no failure.
It is only an experience.

8735.

To walk along the spiritual path
Is not an easy task.
Therefore, be not complacent,
For wrong forces can attack you
At any moment.

8736.

He does not believe in fate.
His goal is only
To transcend his limitations.

8737.

What is fate,
If not a limited reality?
A truth-seeker must always aim
At the unlimited Reality,
The infinite and immortal
   Supreme.

8738.

The soul's will-power
Can easily change the face
Of the body's destiny.

8739.

When I was a tiny bud,
I was ready to give myself to God.
Now that I am a fully-blossomed
   flower,
God has already offered me to
   humanity.

8740.

Your two legs,
Aspiration and dedication,
Must both be functioning
If you want to run the fastest
In the spiritual life.

8741.

Do not hide
In the Himalayan caves.
It is here on earth,
In the very heart of life,
That you have to conquer
   ignorance.

8742.

Always be a climbing flame
If you do not want your life
To be caught in ancient patterns
Of demoralising decay.

8743.

In the morning
I discover the beauty of peace.
In the evening
I discover the peace of beauty.

8744.

For a human being,
To offer gratitude
Is as difficult a task
As asking the mind
To surrender to the heart.

8745.

Even if you sit in meditation
Until an anthill grows on your
   head,
If intensity is lacking,
Your realisation will remain
A far cry.

8746.

He who is well-established
In his inner life
Does not need to possess
Anybody or anything on earth.

8747.

If you have accepted a spiritual
   Master,
Do not delay in trying to please
   him.
If you are not inspired to please
   your Master
During his lifetime,
Why should you be inspired to
   please him
After he leaves this earth?

8748.

While a spiritual Master is on
   earth,
At the foot of the tree,
He is like a child,
Giving out candy to all.
When he climbs back up
To the top of the tree,
He will throw candy only to those
Who really cared for his affection,
Compassion and concern.

8749.

Every wrong thought
Is a leak in your life-boat.
Even if it is tinier than the tiniest,
Fix it immediately
Before it becomes larger than the
   largest
And causes your life-boat to sink.

8750.

He lived an austere life
To discover the spirit of nature,
But God wanted him to discover
The original spirit of Delight
From which Consciousness and
   Existence came.

8751.

If you conquer your weaknesses
Even on one plane,
You have already started walking
On the road to your total
   perfection.

8752.

Unless you climb upward
With your aspiration-cry
Every day, every hour,
Every minute, every second,
Your heart-paradise
Will remain empty
And your Beloved Supreme
Will remain absent.

8753.

The world of negative thoughts
Envelops your mind
Because you are not cautious.

8754.

I pray to God
For the ignorance-challenging
   power,
Not to lord it over others,
But to better manifest my oneness
   with them.

8755.

Peace, Light, Bliss and Power
Are one and the same
On the highest plane of Reality.
Invoke one and, lo,
All the others are yours.

8756.

Not the power to conquer others
But the power to become one with
   others
Is the ultimate power.

8757.

A song sung
Without soulfulness
Can never be
God's Song.

8758.

Unless you consciously try
To better your aspiration-heart
And dedication-life,
Your entire being will be
   inundated
With fruitless and bitter
   memories.

8759.

Give ambition its due value.
In the ordinary human life
A person without ambition
Is worse than a solid wall.

8760.

Do not blame the poor
And innocent world.
It is you and nobody else
Who deliberately allowed yourself
To be surrounded
By self-styled obligations.

8761.

You ask me which I want:
The spiritual life or the earthly
    life.
I want both,
But only if my earthly life
Will add to my spiritual life.

8762.

Lord, lift me up
To the Himalayan heights.
Make me Your excellent
    instrument
To please You in Your own Way.

8763.

To meditate soulfully
For a few minutes
Is infinitely more valuable
Than to sit for hours and hours
With a restless mind.

8764.

A God-realised soul
Is a spiritual pioneer
Who clears a path
For others to follow.

8765.

Your Beloved Lord is offering you
A most delicious inner meal.
He alone knows how difficult it
    was
For Him to prepare it.
You have only to eat
To your heart's content.

8766.

Until your body, vital and mind
Are illumined,
They will never care
For your true happiness.

8767.

If your vital wants to enjoy
The sound of success-hours,
Then your heart will not be able to
   enjoy
The silence of progress-days.

8768.

For ages humanity
Has been trying to get joy
By dividing reality
And analysing the pieces.
When will humanity learn
That joy can be found
Only in oneness?

8769.

If you attempt to work
Beyond your body's limited
   capacity,
Your body will revolt.
Let the body's capacity
Gradually grow and progress
In the soul's effulgent light.

8770.

If you have a divine goal,
Then the heart and soul
Of both Mother Earth
And Father Heaven
Will be divinely pleased with you
And supremely proud of you.

8771.

His wild criticisms
Of his fellow seekers
Proved that he was not, after all,
A genuine truth-seeker.

8772.

Today I may be undivine and
   imperfect.
But one thing I know for sure:
God will someday make me,
Without fail,
His divine and perfect
   instrument.

8773.

True, the temptation of the world
Is powerful.
But even if for lifetimes
The soul does not make progress,
A day will eventually dawn
When once again it will start
Its progress-journey.

8774.

Just because the past
Has not given me everything,
God has created the present.
And even the present has a higher
   purpose:
To make the future better.

8775.

Be totally sincere.
Otherwise you will be helplessly caught
Between your aspiration-cry
And your frustration-frown.

8776.

You think of problems.
That is why problems
Are thinking of you.
Can you not start thinking
Of peace-light?
Lo and behold, to your wide surprise
You will see that peace-light
Has always been thinking of you.

8777.

To study nature's beauty
Is good,
But to realise God the Beauty
Is infinitely better.
God created nature and then said,
"You and I are one."

8778.

The inner wealth you discover
Only when you calm your mind.
A difficult task, true!
But once you achieve it,
The inner world and the outer world
Become your intimate friends.

8779.

The difference between morning
And evening is this:
Morning is preparation,
Evening is realisation.
Preparation is the seed,
Realisation is the fruit.

8780.

Insecurity means separativity.
If you want to be secure,
Establish your true oneness
With God's entire creation.

8781.

Except for a God-realised soul,
No human being on earth
Can unmistakably declare
That he is truly secure.

8782.

Constructive will-power
Can change darkness into light.
Destructive will-power
Can change day into night.

8783.

On the inner plane
There is no such thing as luck.
Whatever good happens in your life
Is the result of conscious or unconscious
Inner preparation.

8784.

A wave of unhappiness
Has entered into you,
Not because you are neglecting
Your prayer and meditation,
But because you are unconscious of
Your roaming vital-elephant.

8785.

Do not be afraid to act.
If you act and succeed,
You will be able to declare:
"I have done it."
If you act and fail,
At least you will be able to say:
"I tried."

8786.

Real oneness with others
Can only be founded upon
Mutual faith.

8787.

He was such a fool!
He wanted to possess someone
For his own security.
Alas, when he fulfilled his desire,
He saw that the one he possessed
Was infinitely more insecure than he.

8788.

Think of the good things
God has done for you
And the good things
You have done for God.
Lo, the negative forces
Which are threatening you
Will all disappear!

8789.

When man wants something,
He cries and begs.
When God wants something,
He wills and creates.

8790.

He is not an animal,
He is not a human,
He is not even a divine being.
In his highest Transcendental
    Consciousness
He is the Supreme Himself.

8791.

God's children are His true
Arms and legs.
If His arms and legs are defective,
Is God not still imperfect?

8792.

The so-called freedom-life of earth
Is nothing other than
A vagabond-life.

8793.

The body is not real.
The vital is not real.
The mind is not real.
Only the soul is real.

8794.

If your mind is willing
To be deluded,
Your heart will soon be
Blank with nothingness.

8795.

True, in my reality-life
I cannot do anything.
But in my dream-life I have
    transformed
This world of monstrous
    wilderness
Into a pure and life-enlightening
    garden.

8796.

Human life need not swim
In ignorance-sea
If it starts loving the
    Compassion-Height
Of God the Creator.

8797.

When your mind becomes
A world of simplicity,
Your life begins to enjoy
The satisfaction of Heaven's
Unbelievable beauty.

8798.

Your doubting mind
And your destructive vital
Will soon be found together
At the same light-forsaken place.

8799.

My heart does not love God.
My mind does not need God.
Is it not ridiculous for me
To expect God to grant my life
Even an iota of His sleepless
   Delight?

8800.

I shall not live in the past.
Even if only one second ago
This world gave me a sad
   experience,
I shall not remember it.
No, I shall not!

8801.

God is giving you a special chance
To please Him.
You have only to sleeplessly feel
That He loves you most.

8802.

He lives with the hope
That someday, somehow,
Someone will realise the Supreme
   in him
So he can fulfil his Lord
Here on earth.

8803.

O truth-seeker, aspire,
Aspire constantly!
Otherwise, you will be fooling
Not your Lord Supreme
But only yourself.

8804.

Alas, it often happens
That the good souls must suffer
Because of the bad ones.
Such is the fate
Of God's creation.

8805.

In his Master's presence
He pretended to be full of light,
But out of his Master's sight,
He became the darkest possible
   night.

8806.

One does not have to be
A God-realised soul
To know what is happening
Inside others' hearts.
Just raise your consciousness high
   enough
And you will be able to know
What others are feeling.

8807.

My mind quite often makes me feel
That it is drinking nectar
Even while it is drinking
Doubt-poison.

8808.

No other power on earth
Will be able to please God
Except your heart-power.
It is heart-power alone
That God will always treasure.

8809.

When God says
That He is not completely satisfied
With any human being,
Each individual thinks
That he is an exception.
When God changes His opinion
And says that He is pleased
With each and every human being,
Each individual thinks
That God is infinitely more pleased with him
Than with the rest of the world.

8810.

Only a gift
That has been offered
With the heart's oneness-power
Is worth receiving.

8811.

Your Beloved Supreme is ready to give you
Something infinitely more significant
Than God-realisation,
And that is His supreme Satisfaction
Unparalleled.

8812.

God is far more satisfied
With a blade of grass
Embodying the message of humility
Than with a highly advanced seeker
Who still embodies the message of pride.

8813.

Alas, most seekers love the
    Supreme,
Manifest the Supreme
And please the Supreme
In their own way
And not in His Way.

8814.

Your soul wants to be proud of
    you
At every moment.
Therefore, sleeplessly your soul
Encourages you,
Inspires you
And energises you
To become a most perfect
    instrument
Of your Beloved Supreme.

8815.

If you want to lead the life
Of a god or goddess on earth,
Love your Beloved Lord
In His own Way.

8816.

When your Lord Supreme blesses
    someone,
If you expand your consciousness,
You can receive the same blessing.

8817.

Widen your vision-eye,
Intensify your aspiration-heart,
Enlarge your dedication-life.
This is all God wants from you,
And it will always remain so.

8818.

Do not wait for tomorrow
To listen to God's blessingful
    Requests,
For that tomorrow may never
    dawn
In your aspiration-life.

8819.

When his Lord Supreme
Finally lost faith in him,
His own soul, out of bitter
    disgust,
Weakened his spiritual capacity
And diminished his inner
    receptivity.

8820.

When a soul enters into a body,
The Lord Supreme dreams the Dream
Of His Manifestation-Light.
When a body becomes the soul-consciousness,
The Lord Supreme smiles the Smile
Of His Satisfaction-Delight.

8821.

If there is something divine
That you are planning to do,
Do it immediately.
If there is something undivine
That you are planning to do,
Think of doing it tomorrow.

8822.

When God the Captain
Blows His divine whistle,
He wants His team to run
And cheerfully do the needful.

8823.

The cosmic gods never sleep.
At every moment they serve the Supreme
Both here on earth and there in Heaven.

8824.

For an unaspiring man,
Work is punishment,
Work is torture.
For an aspiring man,
Work is a blessing,
Work is a joy.

8825.

The spiritual Master is a flower
And his students are the petals.
Without the flower,
There can be no petals.
Again, if the petals have fallen away,
Who will appreciate the flower?

8826.

He endured humanity's physical pain
Because he saw the Absolute
Not only inside the smile of Heaven
But also inside the cry of earth.

8827.

True, he is an unfortunate seeker
Because he wants to reach his goal
By false means.
But, alas, you are no better.
You are so complacent
That your goal does not even
 exist!

8828.

The energising power
Of your own climbing aspiration
Can prevent those who are still
Wallowing in the pleasures of
 ignorance-night
From making deplorable
 mistakes.

8829.

Because of his disobedience,
He was unable to progress.
Because he could not progress,
He fell far behind in the inner
 race.

8830.

As long as your heart compels you
To remain in God's Boat,
God will exercise His divine
 Authority,
Which is nothing other than
His inseparable oneness with you.

8831.

You feel that your Master
Has achieved something
Which you have not yet achieved.
But can you not feel
That just because you are
His spiritual child,
You also have achieved that very
 thing
In and through Him?

8832.

The heart believes that purity
Is the beginning of the spiritual
 life.
The mind believes that sincerity
Is the beginning of the spiritual
 life.
The vital believes that obedience
Is the beginning of the spiritual
 life.
The body believes that
 wakefulness
Is the beginning of the spiritual
 life.
And I must say
That their beliefs are perfect.

8833.

Talent is not unattainable.
If you aspire,
God's Grace will descend
And God's own Talent will develop
In and through you.

8834.

If you have been blessed with talent
In any field,
Take the golden opportunity
Not only to use it
But also to increase it
As quickly as possible.

8835.

A heart that is pure
Is Heaven's perpetual Bliss.
A mind that is impure
Is hell's dragon-frown.

8836.

Tremendous success,
If it is to last,
Must always be followed
By continuous progress
Both inner and outer.

8837.

To meditate longer
Will be of no avail to you.
What you must do
Is meditate more soulfully.

8838.

Your Beloved Supreme may forgive you
If you want to please Him
In your own way,
But your own soul will not be satisfied,
Never!

8839.

At every second you may give God
Earthly poison,
But God will always offer you
Only Heavenly Nectar.

8840.

Sweeter than the sweetest
And purer than the purest
Is our gratitude
To our Beloved Lord Supreme.

8841.

God's Compassion and your
   receptivity
Together make it possible
For God to keep you safely
Inside His Golden Boat.

8842.

Only if you live in your heart
Will your soul be able to offer you
Its divine messages.

8843.

When he told God
That he didn't want to serve
God's divine Mission on earth,
God appreciated his sincerity
But was totally ashamed
Of his lack of dedication.

8844.

At each moment we are
   surrendering,
But it is up to us
Whether we surrender to the
   undivine forces
Or to the Will of our Beloved
   Supreme.

8845.

If you want to take God's side,
At every moment you have to be
Alert, aspiring and self-giving.

8846.

If you make your life
An emblem of sincerity,
God will definitely give you
An invaluable gift in the inner
   world.

8847.

If you see where you are
And where you once stood,
You will realise one undeniable
   truth:
There is no one who more deserves
Your constant gratitude-heart
Than your Beloved Supreme.

8848.

When gratitude is absent,
There is only inner destruction.
When gratitude is present,
There is continuous inner
   progress.

8849.

Because of your obedience,
Both inner and outer,
You are everything to God
And He is everything to you.

8850.

Each wrong thought,
No matter how tiny,
Can easily become as destructive
As an atom bomb.

8851.

Everything in your life
Can and will desert you,
Except your pure oneness-heart
With your Beloved Supreme.

8852.

If God sees His children aspiring,
He gets tremendous joy.
If He sees them not aspiring,
A sharp, pointed arrow
Enters into His Heart.

8853.

There is Someone in Heaven
Who loves you infinitely more
Than you can ever love any
　human being,
Including yourself,
And that Person is none other
　than
Your Beloved Supreme.

8854.

Because he failed to please his
　soul,
There came a time when his soul
Became indifferent to him,
And totally withdrew
From his false
　aspiration-dedication-life.

8855.

Work devotedly.
Lo, you are meditating soulfully.
Meditate soulfully.
Lo, you are serving devotedly.

8856.

On the strength of his oneness
　with God,
He is all security
Within and without.

8857.

No one expects a child to carry
Too heavy a load.
Since you are a child of the
   Supreme,
Do you think He will ask you to do
   something
Without giving you
More than the necessary capacity?

8858.

Gratitude that starts in the mind
Cannot last.
Each time an unhealthy,
Contradictory thought arises,
Sooner than at once
Mental gratitude disappears.

8859.

If you feel that your Beloved
   Supreme
Is disappointed with your inner
   life,
Then bring back your
   determination
And aspiration,
And again do the right thing.
Lo, His blessingful Smile
Will once more be yours.

8860.

O foolish seeker,
You have developed your ego
To such an extent
That you are trying to make God
   feel
As you yourself already feel:
That you are indispensable.

8861.

Why do you worry?
You worry simply because
The physical reality in you
Is hopelessly attached
To the earth-consciousness.

8862.

The earth-magnet pulls
Our body-reality.
The Heaven-magnet pulls
Our soul-reality.

8863.

Always identify with the highest
   reality
In yourself, your soul-bird,
Which flies above and beyond
All the worries of the earth-plane.

8864.

Devotion and gratitude
Are like two spiritual legs.
Both should be equally strong
If we are to run the fastest.

8865.

The desire-world unconsciously
  craves
And seeks satisfaction from
  excitement.
The aspiration-world consciously
  strives for
And finds satisfaction in
  enlightenment.

8866.

How can God be happy
If your lack of oneness with others
Is making them sad?
How can you be happy
If your lack of oneness with others
Is making God sad?

8867.

The human in us says,
"His misconduct is intolerable.
I will punish him
So he will change."
The divine in us says,
"Perhaps I would have done the
  same
In his position.
Therefore, let me cultivate
Compassion and forgiveness
To illumine both him and myself."

8868.

If I cannot have
  compassion-power,
Let me have forgiveness-power.
If I cannot have
  forgiveness-power,
Let me have tolerance-power.
If I cannot have tolerance-power,
Let me at least delay
My judgement-power.

8869.

Because he contained his anger,
The divine forces had the
  opportunity
To act in and through him
And finally to illumine him.

8870.

My Lord Supreme,
One thing I know for sure:
I can be truly happy
Only when You replace my anger
With forgiveness,
Then with compassion
And finally with oneness.

8871.

The vision-light of America's
   creators
Is not being accepted by America
   today,
But a day will dawn when a new
   generation
Will manifest the divine vision
Of America's immortal founders.

8872.

If you do something right,
You will see God's Smile.
If you do something wrong,
You will feel God's Sadness.

8873.

He lived in the world of jealousy,
Insecurity, impurity and
   ingratitude.
But he smiled at his Master
Just to get a smile in return,
So he could fool himself into
   thinking
That everything was all right.

8874.

You say your present-day
   problems
Are killing you.
But do you not remember
That once upon a time
Peace, Light and Bliss
Were absolute realities for you?
Those were not your fantasy-days!
They were as real as today.
If you want to have them back,
Nothing on earth can prevent you.

8875.

To be well-established
In the spiritual life
Is to be happy in the only way
One can really be happy.

8876.

When advanced seekers lead
A pure spiritual life,
Their very presence transforms
Their younger brother-seekers.

8877.

Beauty is the enrichment
Of the aspirant's heart.
Beauty is the enlightenment
Of the heart's cry.

8878.

When the soul comes forward,
The heart very often offers
Its special gratitude to the
   Supreme
Through human tears.
Remember those tears and
   treasure them,
For they are something most
   precious.

8879.

If you want to study yourself,
Remember that your heart
Is your own true mirror.

8880.

His are not the tears
Of disappointed expectation.
His are the tears
Of unexpected inner joy.

8881.

Do you not see
That you are comfortable
But not soulful
When you ask God for His
   Forgiveness-Light?
Such being the case,
God and His Forgiveness-Light
Will never knock at your heart's
   door.

8882.

When God remains
In His highest Heights
And ignores the demands
Of His earth-bound children,
You can be sure
It is always for their own good.

8883.

If your outer sincerity
Is based on inner insincerity,
Then your service to others
Has no real value.

8884.

To see a glimpse of the highest
   Truth
Is an easy task.
But to be absolutely obedient and
   faithful
To that highest Truth
Is a most difficult task.

8885.

Today you may think of God
And feel God,
But tomorrow, without fail,
You must become
Another God.

8886.

If your suffering, frustration
And undivine qualities can reach
   God,
Do you not think that your love,
Devotion and surrender can also
   reach Him?

8887.

Try to live a life
That breathes an everlasting hope
Which can never be subdued
By frustration-dragon.

8888.

You are forcing your heart
To become an exact duplicate
Of your mind.
Even God cannot believe it!

8889.

If you mercilessly weigh
Your faults,
Then God will cheerfully weigh
Your heart's mountain-faith.

8890.

People have many dreams,
But I have only three:
Perfect peace between
The soul and the body,
The total transformation
Of my nature,
And complete satisfaction
In God's entire creation.

8891.

The world can tell you
Where to go unmistakably.
But the world can never tell you
How to go,
Even slowly,
Not to speak of speedily.

8892.

I want my animal life
To become totally extinct,
But my Lord says this is wrong.
What He wants from me
And for me
Is the transformation of my
    animal life
Into an illumined and manifested
    divine life.

8893.

Because he did not want
Satan in him,
He started praying to God.
Because he did not like
The impurity in him,
He started meditating on God.
Therefore, he is grateful
Even to the undivine
For helping him on his spiritual
    journey.

8894.

I was wrong and you were right!
Each human being
In God's creation
Is the World-Creator
In complete disguise.

8895.

Doubt is extremely poisonous.
Don't mix with doubt,
And don't mix your dark doubts
With your bright faith.
Otherwise, your faith, too,
Will become poisoned.

8896.

Direct your vision-eye
In every conceivable direction.
You will be able to illumine
Even the world's division-eye.

8897.

Because his earthly existence
Is in stark bondage-chains,
His heart is compelled to live
In the deserts
Of birthless and deathless
    frustration.

8898.

If you are restlessly
And blindly searching
For the beauty and fragrance
Of nectar-delight,
How can God's Hour
Knock at your heart's peace-door?

8899.

What he wants to see
Is only a God-Throne
And nothing else
Inside the aspiration-cry
Of his surrendering heart.

8900.

You alone and nobody else
Can be an absolutely divine
    soldier,
The world's most remarkable,
Powerful and beautiful
Chosen child of God.

8901.

A series of daring visions:
I shall love the world
The way my Lord Supreme
Loves the world.
I shall become as perfect
As my Lord Supreme
Wants me to be.
I shall never, never miss
My God-appointment-hour.

8902.

The spiritual message of tennis:
Love, serve
And finally surrender
To the Supreme in the winner.
The loser who cheerfully
    surrenders
To the Supreme in the winner
Becomes himself a real winner
In the inner world.

8903.

My heart is meant for crying,
Crying for oneness, constant and
    inseparable,
With my Lord Supreme.
My soul is meant for smiling,
Smiling in oneness, constant and
    inseparable,
With my Lord Supreme.

8904.

When my soul identifies
With my body, vital and mind,
It embraces suffering.
When my soul identifies
With its own highest Reality,
Easily it can remain
Far beyond the realm of sorrow.

8905.

If you can sincerely feel
That your mind is an instrument
   of God,
Then God will definitely turn
   your mind
Into His own Monument of
   Delight.

8906.

Adversity may hide
Possibility-buds,
But adversity can never hide
Inevitability-flowers.

8907.

Although you do not care
To have anything from God,
God wants to give you His
   Kingdom.
Although God does not need
Anything from you,
He wants to give you His Throne.
Be wise and accept them
With a gratitude-heart.

8908.

God is more than eager
To cancel your teeming
   weaknesses
If you are ready to cancel
Your friendship with fleeting faith
And establish your friendship
With abiding and soulfully
   childlike faith.

8909.

Your life will remain
A life of unanswered questions
Because your heart does not keep
   alive
The Message of God's Love.

8910.

Sooner or later
You will be able to escape
Your mind's stupidity-sea,
But your life will never
Be able to escape
God's Compassion-Sun.

8911.

Alas,
This world of ours
Takes enormous pride
In its cynical eye
Of dark distrust.

8912.

Your mind thinks
Nothing is worth believing.
Your heart feels
Nobody is worth loving.
No wonder your life
Is constantly begging for
    happiness
Here, there and everywhere.

8913.

His is a very strange life:
He soulfully keeps his heart
In the company of God,
While he deliberately keeps his
    mind
In the company of man.

8914.

It is good to have friends,
But be careful of those
Who try to lean very heavily on
    you
And sap every drop of your
    spiritual energy.
Are they friends?
No, they are just leading your soul
To a life of bankruptcy.

8915.

Each uttered word
Can be a revealing experience.
Each unuttered word
Can be a rewarding experience.

8916.

My mind is crying pitifully
At the confusion-shore.
My heart is crying sleeplessly
At the frustration-shore.
My soul is smiling blissfully
At the perfection-shore.

8917.

Impurity,
Stop biting my mind!
Ingratitude,
Stop killing my heart!
Because of you two
My Lord is postponing His Visit.
Needless to say, I am miserable.

8918.

Only the chosen few
Will not be subdued
By the ruthless torture
Of inhuman earth-life.

8919.

There is absolutely no difference
Between his pleasure-life
And his unholy mind.

8920.

You are now fully ready
To accept God's Vision for your
   life,
Because you feel you have been
   tortured enough
By the agony of your
   long-lingering
Pleasure-life.

8921.

Do not allow your pure
   flower-heart
To inherit the shameless
   corruption
Of your blind and wild mind.

8922.

His hands are concern-machines.
His eyes are
   compassion-machines.
His heart is an
   illumination-machine.
And he himself is a conscious
God-manifesting machine.

8923.

If I love God,
Then what is wrong in expecting
   God
To help me?
If I love my ignorance,
Then how can I blame my
   ignorance
For embracing me?

8924.

Not your mind's Himalayan
   excellence
But your heart's sleepless
   surrender
Is the key to your inner and outer
   success.

8925.

Your vision-light will have
No reality-delight
Unless your life becomes
The constant flow
Of a self-giving river.

8926.

Attraction unconsciously binds
The human in us.
Aversion consciously strengthens
The inhuman in us.

8927.

Anyone who will listen to his soul
Will see a new future
Blossoming in the heart
Of his tomorrow's happiness.

8928.

Rock the ignorance-child to sleep.
Otherwise,
This child will, without fail,
Destroy your love of God
And your oneness-joy with God.

8929.

The world is completely lost
Between your manifested stupidity
And your unmanifested divinity.

8930.

The secret of success
Is an outer commitment
And an inner enlightenment.

8931.

If you want to be a man of integrity,
Then what you need
Is a heart of morning purity
And a life of evening simplicity.

8932.

Ego-boosting praise
And a self-defeating life
Will eventually be found living together
Inside the futility-night of ignorance.

8933.

I was what I was:
A mind of phantom-moment.
I am what I am:
A heart of aspiration-hour.
I shall be what I shall be:
A life of illumination-day.

8934.

Mine is the silence
That hurts my Lord Supreme.
My Lord's is the Silence
That illumines my life.

8935.

Wrong seeing
Is torturing the world.
Wrong thinking
Is ruling the world.

8936.

When the time arrives for you
To leave this life for another life,
If you wish to go
To a beautiful and soulful world,
Then you will need a valid
    passport,
And that passport is your
    meditation
Here on earth.

8937.

Do not take your Lord Supreme
    for granted.
When you go to the other world,
You may not be able to see Him
At your sweet will
If you have not sincerely tried to
    satisfy Him
During the years and years He
    offered you
Countless opportunities on earth.

8938.

He was an unfortunate Master.
He had poor instruments.
But still he continued to serve his
    Beloved Supreme,
Only waiting for the day
When his fate would change
And he would have new and
    excellent instruments
To manifest the Vision
Of his Beloved Supreme.

8939.

You are sitting at the feet
Of your Master,
But your wandering thoughts
Are taking you away from him
Farther than the farthest!

8940.

How to invite your own spiritual
    death?
Make friends with
Self-satisfied complacency.
How to prove you are a real
    God-seeker?
Climb higher and dive deeper
To transcend your teeming
    weaknesses.

8941.

Many precious chances
Have passed away.
Alas, my heart is still without
A soulful cry
And my life is still without
A fruitful smile.

8942.

Do not expect
Anything from Heaven.
Do not demand
Anything from earth.

8943.

Heaven's brightest morning
Shines only on the minds
That live far away from
The doubt-country.

8944.

Miracles are everywhere to be
   found
When I surrender my infinite
   desires
To my immortal aspirations.

8945.

I was late in almost everything.
I did not mind.
I am late in almost everything.
I do not mind.
I shall be late in almost
   everything.
I shall not mind.
But I was not late,
I am not late
And I shall never be late
In one thing:
My awareness of
My Lord's Compassion infinite
Since He began His
   Vision-Reality-Game
In and through my Heaven-free
   soul
And my earth-bound life.

8946.

Be it known
To the whole world
That I am no longer
Desire's friend.

8947.

Do you know
That you have deliberately
   enchained
Your soulful heart?
Perhaps not!
Do you know
That you have completely
   forgotten
Your fruitful soul?
Perhaps not!

8948.

I do not mind
If you want to become
A missionary,
As long as you first become
A universal light
And a transcendental delight.

8949.

O my mind,
I most sincerely feel sorry
That you have been suffering
So much from yourself.

8950.

The longing for perfection
Is the illumining beginning
Of God's God-Satisfaction in man.

8951.

Ask Truth if you are correct.
Do not ask anybody,
Not even yourself,
If Truth is correct.

8952.

Meditate now,
At this very moment!
Who knows?
Your soul may not get
Another opportunity to inspire
    you
In this lifetime.

8953.

God the Beauty
Loves to live
Inside my heart's cry.
God the Power
Loves to live
Inside my life's smile.

8954.

Opportunity enthusiastically
Asks me to run.
Ability cautiously
Asks me to crawl.

8955.

Every day I make
The same stupid mistake:
I do not care to speak to God
Inwardly or outwardly,
Prayerfully or selflessly.

8956.

A brilliant mind
May know where the truth is,
But a pure heart
Unmistakably and lovingly
Embodies Infinity's eternal Truth.

8957.

O my mind,
Can you not leave a few speeches
Undelivered here on earth?
I would be so happy;
The entire world would be so
    happy;
Perhaps, eventually, you too!

8958.

As there is no substitute
For a gratitude-heart
In my inner life,
Even so, there is no substitute
For a surrender-mind
In my outer life.

8959.

The human mind enjoys
Living in the land
Of perpetual preparation.
The divine heart enjoys
Living in the land
Of soulful action.

8960.

You are swayed
By the winds of emotion.
Therefore, danger will meet you
In the morning,
Disaster
In the afternoon
And destruction
In the evening.

8961.

If you sincerely want to make
    progress,
Try to see divinity in everything.
If you don't want to make
    progress,
You need not see divinity in
    anything,
Not even inside
God's own transcendental
    Perfection.

8962.

I may not be succeeding,
But I am soulfully trying
To bathe all human beings
In my purity's love-river.

8963.

O world, although I am in you,
Since I am not of you,
I am not for you.
Because I am of God,
I am not only with God
But also for God.

8964.

Each divine thought
Is a new window
Which a God-lover can open
Onto a realm of God's
Self-Transcendence-Delight.

8965.

His heart of consolation,
His soul of illumination
And his life of perfection
Have the stamp of Immortality's
Brightest satisfaction-smile.

8966.

You say that you are all alone,
But I see within you and without
   you
God's Compassion-Flood and
   Forgiveness-Sea.
Such being the case,
Are you not your shameless
   ingratitude?

8967.

Alas, we worship the elusive flame
Inside our mind
Instead of the illumination-sun
Inside our heart.

8968.

A mind of wisdom-light
And a heart of vision-delight
Breathlessly enjoy
Each other's company.

8969.

Self-delusion
Is the root cause
Of your continued existence
In the abyss of lifeless
   nothingness.

8970.

God is away, far away
From my sound-prayer.
God is near, very near,
In fact, right inside,
My silence-meditation.

8971.

My heart shall sleeplessly follow
The footsteps of faith
So that it can safely and swiftly
   reach
The Palace of my Lord Supreme.

8972.

His mind does not know who he
   is.
Yet it tries to describe him.
His heart does not know who he
   is.
Yet it tries to reveal him.
His soul knows who he is.
Therefore, his soul and his God
Are taking care of him
All the time.

8973.

Do not pretend
To be good.
God wants you to be sincere.
Your sincerity-drops
And God's Satisfaction
Will, without fail, meet together.

8974.

You are looking for the unknown.
Someday you are bound to meet
   with it.
Will you be happy then?
No, you will not!
You will be happy
Only when you meet with the
   Unknowable,
For that Unknowable Reality
Is your Beloved Supreme.

8975.

A life of surrender is always
   needed
Either to please the soul of Heaven
Or to please the body of earth.

8976.

You will be happy only when
Yours is the heart that longs
For the Transcendental Smile
And yours is the life that longs
For the Universal Cry.

8977.

Promise, promise,
How beautiful you are,
How powerful you are!
Each time my soul comes down,
It brings you
With a higher and deeper inner
   conviction
To manifest my Lord Supreme.

8978.

My mind is a sleeping
Child of God.
My heart is a crying
Child of God.
My soul is a self-giving
Child of God.
And I am a dreaming
Child of God.

8979.

You think you are very wise,
But you are not.
You are just a clever man.
What you have learnt is nothing
But how to shoplift in the
   ignorance-store.

8980.

God does not want you
To relearn yesterday's sorrow.
He just wants you
To learn and live in
Today's joy.

8981.

There are countless questions
About God,
But only one answer:
God is His own Eternity's
Satisfaction-distribution.

8982.

The less the human mind knows
About ignorance-night,
The better.
The more the divine heart knows
About God's Vision-Eye,
The better.

8983.

If you hide your aspiration-cry
From your own heart,
Then who is going to look for it?
Nobody!
No, not even God,
The Compassionate One.

8984.

There is nothing wrong with you.
What you need is only
A little more soulful effort
To satisfy your Eternity's Inner Pilot.

8985.

Why do you ask me to repeat
My frustration-life, O earth?
Do you get malicious pleasure
In my tearful failure-cry,
Or is it all due
To your brutal indifference?

8986.

My heart is suffering
From chronic pain,
Not because my mind
Does not love God,
Not because my mind
Does not need God,
But because my Lord Supreme
Has tried in vain, time and again,
To illumine and immortalise my mind.

8987.

You are abandoning God
In order to make friends
With doubt's insecurity-cry.
Ask your soul if you are doing
The right thing.
Ask your soul if there is any way
It can awaken you.

8988.

Your unconsidered action
Is a well-preserved complacency
That will meet in the end
With the wildest
   destruction-frown.

8989.

I am my mind's sound-fear.
I am my heart's silence-tear.
I am my life's helpless beggar.
Yet I long to be a faithful
   instrument
Of my Lord Supreme.

8990.

My Lord must give His world
Another heart,
So that this new heart can capture
His Aspiration-Vision
And His
   Perfection-Manifestation.

8991.

O God-seeker,
If you sing heedlessly
The glory of the world's
   desire-life,
Then you are painting disaster
And nothing else
In your Heaven-forsaking and
   earth-bound life.

8992.

If a seeker can remain
Inside his aspiration-heart
For one fragile hour,
He can stem the flood
Of all his yesterday's sorrows.

8993.

If you can treasure
Your soul's unmeasured flames,
God will definitely ask you
To become a choice instrument
In His Vision-Reality-
   Manifestation-Game.

8994.

A self-giving seeker
Has a heart flooded with peace,
And this heart can easily outlive
The world's inner war
And outer destruction.

8995.

Do not listen to your mind!
If you listen to your mind,
You will not see the Golden Boat
That plies between your
    soul-shore
And your God-Shore.

8996.

There was a time
When adversity
Was his heart's only rival.
Now prosperity
Is his life's only rival.
In the future he himself
Will be his only rival.
Himself he will transcend
Not in his own way,
But in God's Way.

8997.

When my heart sings
The song of newness,
My life becomes
The dance of fulness.

8998.

There is no difference
Between today's desire
And tomorrow's shame.
There is no difference
Between today's aspiration-cry
And tomorrow's realisation-smile.

8999.

If you allow yourself
To be chained to mortal fame,
How can you play with God
His immortal Game?

9000.

Surrender your common sense:
That you are only a human being.
Surrender your earthly goal:
Name and fame.
Receive immediately what God
    has for you:
His Eternity's
    Immortality-Crown.

9001.

My Lord,
Do give me the capacity
To see the Divinity
In everything You do
And to grow into that Divinity
At every moment.

9002.

True gratitude can never come
From the mind.
It has to flow from the heart
To the mind, vital and body
Until everything that we have and are
Is a sea of gratitude.

9003.

At night
I treasure my golden dreams.
In the morning
I put them immediately to work.

9004.

Do not have the same unaspiring thought
Again and again.
Have a new thought this time,
A God-loving thought.

9005.

Love divine
Is the fragrance-purity
That the Unknown uses
To bring to the fore
The hidden divinity
Of the known.

9006.

O human mind,
Your incalculable mischief-life
Is past correction.
Yet I shall not give up on you,
For I need your perfection-smile.

9007.

Since God is interested in human affairs,
Can you not humbly and gratefully
Turn to God alone
For His supreme Guidance?

9008.

Because I know
That my life is nothing but
A perpetual possibility,
With my heart's lucid stillness
I try to advance progressively forward,
Always forward.

9009.

If you do not train your mind,
There shall come a time
When your life will be forced
To strain itself
And you will be thrown
Into a disaster-sea.

9010.

It is not a hard task
For enthusiasm to grasp
The beauty and purity
Of excellent intention-flowers.

9011.

There was a time when my life lived
In the blue dwelling of divinity.
Alas, now it is forced to endure
The pangs of mortality.

9012.

Do not crave ceaseless glory.
You will be forced to experience once again
The failure-life of your hoary past.

9013.

Smiling is easier than crying.
Therefore, I smile.
Loving is easier than smiling.
Therefore, I love.
Surrendering is easier than loving.
Therefore, I surrender.

9014.

Save yourself inwardly first,
And then try to save others.
Only if you are saved inwardly
Can you become a perfect instrument
Of your Beloved Supreme
And a perfect helper of mankind.

9015.

There is only one way
In God's entire creation
To be happy,
And that way
Is to make God happy.

9016.

When the unbending champion
Bows with humility,
He immeasurably adds to the glory
Of his previous victories.

9017.

To reap the richest harvest
Of my aspiration-heart,
I shall listen
To the silence-flooded Whispers
Of my Inner Pilot.

9018.

What I needed was an orphan-cry.
This was the message
That I received from my Lord
   Supreme
Last year.
What I need is an emperor-smile.
This is the message
That I have received from my Lord
   Supreme
This year.

9019.

Beware of outer sympathy,
For its immediate neighbour
Is attachment-net.

9020.

He wanted to conquer
The ugliness of his mind.
He wanted his heart-garden
To grow Heaven-flowers.
He has not succeeded in fulfilling
Either desire.
Therefore, his hope-life is now
Completely shattered.

9021.

A pure and self-giving heart
Is always the key
To Truth's transcendental Door.

9022.

I come to earth
To offer my silver dreams.
Alas, earth does not
Care for them.
I go to Heaven
To offer my golden dreams.
Alas, Heaven already has
Plenty of them.

9023.

Now that you are depending
Entirely upon God the
   Forgiveness,
God the Compassion
Will turn your evil scars
Into divine stars.

9024.

I have already informed my soul
That I shall from now on
Implicitly listen to its commands.
I have already informed my
   intellectual life
That I shall no longer
Continue my friendship with it.

9025.

True happiness
Is not a mental hallucination.
True happiness
Is not a complacent feeling.
True happiness
Is the spontaneous feeling of joy
That comes from knowing
You are doing the right thing
And leading a divine life.

9026.

A God-lover is a joy-distributor
In the inner world
And an ignorance-hunter
In the outer world.

9027.

Aspiration without dedication
Is like a slow runner
Who knows where the goal is
But is bound to arrive shockingly
   late.

9028.

Every day renew your spiritual
   life.
Every day think and feel
That yours is the life
Of blossoming beauty and
   nourishing purity.

9029.

Every day offer yourself
   consciously
To your ultimate Vision and
   ultimate Reality.
Your ultimate Vision tells you
That you are of the Supreme.
Your ultimate Reality tells you
That you are for the Supreme,
The Supreme alone.

9030.

God will reveal
All His Secrets to you
Only when He sees
That you are not false to yourself.
You are false to yourself
When you think you already are
Another God.
You are false to yourself
When you feel you can never
   become
Another God.

9031.

You are true to yourself
When you constantly think and
   feel
That your heart's cry
Comes from God alone
And your life's smile
Goes to God alone.

9032.

The Supreme is extremely sad
Because two seeds He has planted
    inside you
Are not germinating:
Your life's purity-seed
And your heart's gratitude-seed.

9033.

If you want to make God happy,
Every day pray and meditate
Lovingly,
Soulfully
And selflessly.

9034.

You enjoy playing hide-and-seek
With ignorance-night:
This is your bad quality.
You sometimes compromise
With ignorance-night:
This is your worse quality.
You surrender quite often
To ignorance-night:
This is your worst quality.

9035.

When God gave you
The body, vital, mind and heart,
They were so beautiful!
Alas, you have not properly used
    them.
Therefore, their beauty is now
    deeply hidden.

9036.

There is only one way
To use God's Gifts properly,
And that is the way of obedience,
Inner and outer.

9037.

Your soul listens to the Supreme
Consciously and constantly.
That is why it always maintains
Its unparalleled beauty.

9038.

The mind knows what obedience is,
But it wants to enjoy
The world of doubt
Infinitely more than the world of faith.
The vital knows what obedience is,
But it wants to enjoy
The world of destruction
Infinitely more than the world of dynamism.
The body does not even know
What obedience is.
Therefore, what can you expect of the body?

9039.

The heart at times cherishes
The mistaken belief
That the body, vital and mind,
In spite of their disobedience,
Live in the world of joy.
Alas, the pure oneness-heart
Is tempted to join them,
Only to began its immediate descent.

9040.

Your soul is the only reality
That obeys the Supreme
Sleeplessly, breathlessly and unconditionally.
Therefore, your soul is happy
And will remain eternally happy.

9041.

Happiness,
Not pleasure,
Is another name for beauty.

9042.

Obey your Lord Supreme
Inwardly and outwardly.
In no time you will grow into
His Beauty transcendental
And His Beauty universal.

9043.

My sweet Lord,
Why do I fail again and again
In my spiritual life?
"My child,
You fail again and again
Because deep inside you there is
    something
That cleverly and secretly
    instigates you
To enjoy a failure-life
Infinitely more than a
    success-life."

9044.

You are not meant to fail.
You are meant always to succeed
    and proceed.
When you stop cherishing
Your insecurity, jealousy
And feeling of unworthiness,
You are bound to succeed
As well as proceed.

9045.

Your Beloved Supreme wants you
To succeed,
For He desperately wants His
    Dream
To be fulfilled.

9046.

The courage of the vital
Is dynamism.
The courage of the mind
Is its acceptance
Of only pure thoughts.
The courage of the heart
Is its oneness with the Vast.

9047.

No, no, no!
No to darkness,
No to ignorance,
No to unwillingness!
Yes, yes, yes!
Yes to soulful love,
Yes to sleepless devotion,
Yes to breathless
And unconditional surrender!

9048.

He prayed to God
For an iota of peace.
Alas, when God offered him
A boundless Peace-Flood,
His tiny heart became frightened,
And his psychic courage vanished.

9049.

Along life's pathway
Happiness will ride with you
In your chariot
If you smilingly and lovingly
Feed your heart's aspiration-cry.

9050.

A spiritual Master is a living
   dynamo
Who at every moment
Inwardly and outwardly offers
Inspiration and aspiration in
   abundant measure.
The world has only to accept
   them.

9051.

Music is meditation
If it is sung soulfully by good
   singers
Or even sung badly by singers
With soulful hearts.

9052.

A good leader cares only for
The manifestation of the
   Supreme.
Therefore, he will always try to
   receive
New inspiration and aspiration
From the eagerness of those
Who are following him.

9053.

Secretly observe
Those who are spiritually strong
So that by following their
   example
You can conquer your own
   weaknesses.

9054.

His sincere progress-life
Came to a halt
When complacency powerfully
   entered
His inner and outer life.
Why did complacency enter?
Because he allowed his ego to
   make him feel
That he was perfect, absolutely
   perfect.

9055.

The soul's abundant peace
We have not brought into the heart.
What little peace the heart has
We have not brought into the mind.
And where is peace in the vital or body?
Only when we have established peace
In our entire being
Can there be peace all over the world.

9056.

What separates
The countries of this world?
The human mind.
When the mind develops
The divine love which the heart has,
World-division will be transformed
Into world-oneness.

9057.

He is not meditating
For his own realisation.
That is already done!
He is meditating
For your illumination.

9058.

Repeat God's Name
During your highest meditation
And listen to its echo
Deep inside your heart.

9059.

Imagine a beautiful Golden Boat
Sailing on a river
Towards a Golden Shore.
You are in that Boat, O seeker,
Sailing on that very river,
And eventually, without fail,
You will reach that Golden Shore.

9060.

As long as you can remember
That you have done
And will continue to do
Something great and good for God,
You will be able to maintain
Constant joy and enthusiasm
In your inner life.

9061.

These hands must obey my Lord Supreme.
These eyes must obey my Lord Supreme.
This mind must obey my Lord Supreme.
This heart must obey my Lord Supreme.
Everything that I have
And everything that I am
Must obey my Lord Supreme.

9062.

He remained in the psychic consciousness
Through years of higher education.
You proudly remain in the mind,
Though you are totally uneducated.

9063.

Who is strong?
He who is sincerely happy
In his spiritual life.

9064.

There is Someone from whom we came
And to whom we are going back,
Consciously or unconsciously,
Slowly or speedily.

9065.

If you are awakened,
Just run towards God!
You will not actually leave
Anyone behind,
For soon others will also wake up
And run towards the same Goal.

9066.

Today
I am no longer sleeping,
I am no longer crawling,
I am no longer walking.
Today I am running
Faster than the fastest
Towards my destined Goal.

9067.

Just start your inner race
Without waiting to see
Who else is ready to run with you.
When others see you have reached your goal,
They will also be inspired to run.

9068.

When you have a smiling face
And a loving heart,
You allow your Master to live
In Heaven itself.
When your face is sad
And your heart is miserable,
You force him to live in a place
Worse than hell.

9069.

If you want to be happy,
See yourself always
As a four-year-old child
Playing inside the Heart-Garden
Of your Beloved Supreme.

9070.

Because God Himself
Is an Eternal Child,
He has infinite hope.
God's Hope and God's Promise
Both live inside
His chosen children.

9071.

God cannot do anything
For those who think
That they are too old to begin.
But He can and will do everything
For those who feel
That they are eternally young.

9072.

If you feel you are a child,
You will not have to run after
    purity.
Purity will run after you.

9073.

Spiritual energy is like the Ganges
Flowing from the Himalayas.
It must be channelled
If it is not to be wasted.

9074.

I am more than ready
To be called a fanatic
So long as I can remain
In the Supreme's Boat.
For it is only the Supreme's Boat
That can safely carry me
To my Satisfaction-Goal.

9075.

You do not need
Any other human being
To tell you that you are crazy.
Your own mind
Quite often tells your heart
That it is crazy to compel you
To get up so early to meditate.

9076.

He did not follow you
On your spiritual journey,
But because he was your friend,
His love and concern compelled him
To help you in every way.

9077.

Your soulful service requires
Both your inner life's
Aspiration-heart
And your outer life's
Dedication-hands.

9078.

Each moment is an opportunity
To think of God
And to feel God's Presence.
In everything that you do,
Feel that you are touching
The very Breath
Of your Beloved Supreme.

9079.

Because he knew that his Beloved Supreme
Was suffering from earth's excruciating pangs,
He felt it was his bounden duty
To shoulder some of his Beloved's responsibility
And suffer some of the same pain.

9080.

True, your Lord Supreme is asking you
To think first of your own self-discovery,
But that is no excuse to allow
Meanness towards others
To enter into your life in any way.

9081.

If you do something wrong,
I shall not feel miserable.
I shall only pray to the Supreme
To illumine you
So that you will not make
The same mistake again.

9082.

If you are always thinking
Of those who are not aspiring,
Neither you nor they
Will ever approach perfection.
Strive always to remain in the
    room
That is illumined.
A time will come when those
Who are in darkness
Will come to join you there.

9083.

The Supreme is taking care
Of each of His children
In a very special way.
Surrender your dear ones to the
    Supreme
In the same way you have
    surrendered
Your own life to Him.

9084.

After he jumped out of
The Boat of the Supreme,
He cast the temptation-net
To try to take others with him,
So that they, too, would not reach
The Golden Shore.

9085.

He who has inwardly asked you
To serve Him
Is acting in and through you
With His own divine Capacity.
If today you accept and use
His Capacity,
Then tomorrow you will be able to
    receive
Even more capacity
To become His more perfect
    instrument.

9086.

Always be grateful to your soul,
For it is your soul that has
    inspired you
And led you
To walk along the sunlit road of
    aspiration.

9087.

First discover your own
    illumination-room
And dwell in it all the time.
Only then will you be able
To welcome inside it
Others who seek your help.

9088.

Yesterday he saw his Master
As a friend.
Today he is feeling his Master
As his best friend.
Tomorrow he will realise his Master
As his only friend.

9089.

Who is your true family?
Your spiritual brothers and sisters
Who are following the same road,
Eternity's Road,
To the same supreme Goal.

9090.

Look! The Hand of the Supreme
Is beckoning us:
"Come, My children, come!
The Hour has struck for you."

9091.

He left those who were still sleeping
To grow in Eternity's lap
And found his true joy and satisfaction
In serving those
Who wanted to run like deer
Towards the destined Goal.

9092.

If you can always remember
The Compassion, Concern and Love
That God has given you,
Then no hostile force can ever stand
Between you and your Beloved Supreme.

9093.

Continue to perform soulfully
The work which God has given you.
To serve God is the greatest honour,
Even if the world does not recognise it.
Then, one day, even the world will admit
That you, and nobody else,
Served God faithfully
In His own Way.

9094.

My foolish human nature
Thinks that nothing I get in life
Is meaningful,
While everything that others get
Is supremely meaningful.

9095.

Winter does not last forever.
When spring arrives,
Winter fades away.
Even so, attacks by the negative forces
Cannot last forever.
They are eventually succeeded
By a new life-awakening.

9096.

Remain always in the sunshine
Of your heart
Until you see that its illumining rays
Have also flooded your mind.

9097.

You say you are discouraged
Because you are still far away
From the Golden Shore.
I say it does not matter
Whether you are near your Goal,
But only whether you are for God
And will always be for God.

9098.

He entered into the Himalayan caves
For solitude and peace
Only to discover that his undivine mind
With its impure thoughts
Had accompanied him even there.

9099.

I do not worry about others.
If I can reach my perfection-goal,
At least there will be
One less imperfect being
On this earth.

9100.

From now on
I shall have only love
In my heart,
And this love will be only
For my Beloved Supreme.

9101.

My Lord,
I wish to be a burning flame
Climbing high, higher, highest
Inside the Temple of Your Heart.

9102.

I have counted
My soulful tears
And I have counted
God's powerful Smiles.
The outer loser has won
The inner Winner.

9103.

I pray, and my prayers are
　fulfilled.
Since my prayers are fulfilled,
I should offer the transcendental
　prayer
For God-Satisfaction
In God's own Way.

9104.

If I can sincerely feel
That my heart is all emptiness and
　readiness,
Then my Lord Supreme will,
　without fail,
Make my life feel
The beauty and divinity of His
　Fulness.

9105.

When I live for God's Love alone,
I am divinely great and supremely
　good.
When I live for God alone,
I am absolutely perfect.

9106.

There is no risk
In accepting the spiritual life
If you have a sincerity-mind,
A purity-heart
And an integrity-life.

9107.

Who is so stupid
As to waste time here on earth,
Knowing perfectly well
That his earth-hours are
Extremely limited?

9108.

You want to advise God
About how to change the world.
Do you think you can give Him
A few more years
And see if He is making
This world of His better?
In the meantime,
Can you not change your own life
For the better,
So that God can start
His World-Perfection-Life
In and through you?

9109.

You think that God
Cannot change this world
Because He has lost
Complete control of it.
But do you ever care to know
And do you ever care to feel
That God the Aspiration
Lived at the Vision-beginning
And God the Manifestation
Will live eternally
At the Reality-end?

9110.

Your doubting mind does not feel
At ease with God,
But your loving heart does.
Therefore, God has given your heart
The unparalleled capacity
To scale His own Transcendental Heights
With Him.

9111.

In the inner and outer race
I will not say,
"God wants me to win",
But
"Let God's Will be done".

9112.

Unless my Lord Supreme
Forcefully opens my heart-door,
I do not think my frustration-life
Will ever grow into
My satisfaction-heart.

9113.

He is a fool.
He surrenders to God out of fear
That God or others will speak ill
   of him
If he does the wrong thing.
She is an opportunist.
She surrenders to God with the
   hope
That by pleasing Him today
She will be able to receive a special
   favour
From Him tomorrow.

9114.

How can the world find peace
In its machine-mind?
How can the world find perfection
In its dissatisfaction-vital?
How can the world find
   satisfaction
In its oblivion-life?

9115.

My Lord,
I have already taught myself
How to bend others
To my will.
Now will You kindly teach me
How to bend myself
To Your Will alone?

9116.

Selfless service
Is immediate progress.
Instead of working for our little
   self,
We serve our large Self,
The Supreme.
Selfless service helps us come out
   of
Our limited body-dimension
And our limited mind-boundary.

9117.

Although he has touched rock
   bottom
In his aspiration-life,
Because of his adamantine
   determination
He will soon be making progress
   once again.

9118.

Why make friends with
   fault-finders?
You are having enough trouble
Trying to conquer your own
   weaknesses
Without being constantly
   reminded
Of the weaknesses of others.

9119.

America means speed:
Speed to run the fastest.
America means victory:
Victory over ignorance.

9120.

If you want to run the fastest
In the inner world,
You have to do everything
    regularly,
Punctually and perfectly.

9121.

Each time you enter a new year,
Be determined not to bring
Your old self with you.

9122.

Why not take today
As your golden opportunity
To cast aside the undivine
    problems
Which you have been dragging,
Like dead elephants,
For so many years?

9123.

How can there be any such thing
As a new year for you
If you are still leading
Your old unbearable life?

9124.

Examine your compassion
And see if it is true divine
    compassion
Or just your own attachment
In disguise.

9125.

A true truth-seeker knows
That his Beloved Lord rebukes
    him
Only on the strength
Of His absolute Oneness.

9126.

Your Master's aspiration
And your Master's songs
Are inseparable.
When you sing his songs soulfully,
You become the pristine purity
Of his aspiration
And the supernal beauty
Of his songs.

9127.

To sing even one song
Soulfully
Is to have a profound meditation
Unmistakably.

9128.

Because he consciously or
    unconsciously
Enjoys wrong forces,
There is every possibility
That he will be strangled
In the inner world.

9129.

Be extremely sincere
And extremely brave!
You will undoubtedly make
The fastest progress.

9130.

Let me renew each day
My prayer and my promise
To be a perfect instrument
Of my Beloved Supreme.

9131.

My Lord Supreme,
Since I do not have
A pure enough heart
To conquer Your Heart,
Do give me the capacity to sit
Soulfully and unconditionally
At Your Feet.

9132.

How to feel always secure?
Each one has an answer,
But the only answer
That will satisfy man's heart
Is the perfect oneness-answer.

9133.

You will be routed
At the very beginning
Of your spiritual journey
If you do not have a simple life
And a loving heart.

9134.

Your dreams cannot be
As beautiful and powerful
As the purity and divinity
Of your self-giving heart.

9135.

What is humility
If not a well-protected harbour
In your expanding life-sea?

9136.

God's Compassion-Height
Is automatic.
Can we not have a gratitude-heart
That is equally automatic?

9137.

All your hopes are shattered
Because your vital is afraid
To challenge ignorance-night
And your mind is afraid
To challenge ignorance-frown.

9138.

Two most ancient desires:
To enjoy ignorance-night
Without the inevitable
   repercussions
And to dine with wisdom-day
Without the necessary
   qualifications.

9139.

Between desire and faith
There is only one
Sweet and life-illumining breath.
When the mind desires
Something from God,
The heart feels
More faith in God.

9140.

The only prayer that God
   appreciates
Is the prayer of self-offering
Founded upon God's
Life-illumining Vision-Light.

9141.

I cannot reject anything,
Not even my suspicion-mind,
For my existence-cry and my
   existence-smile
Are an integral reality.

9142.

Don't try to please God the
   creation.
It is an almost impossible task.
Do try to please God the Creator.
You will succeed,
For you yourself are a secret player
In God's Vision-Game.

9143.

If you want perfection,
Then do one thing:
Stretch your self-giving arms
Towards the perfection-harbour
   alone.

9144.

My life is soulful and fruitful
When I see that my Lord
Smilingly drinks in my
   gratitude-drops
Every moment of my life.

9145.

There can be no trouble-free
   performance.
There can be no anxiety-free
   performance.
There can be no rivalry-free
   performance.
But there can be
An unconditionally self-giving
   performance
By a seeker whose life
Is all surrender-satisfaction.

9146.

If you are really spiritual,
Then no part of your being
Will be unnecessarily theatrical,
For a spiritual life
Is nothing other than a natural
   life.

9147.

Quantity-advice
Foolishly and wilfully
My mind gives to my heart.
Quality-advice
Lovingly and unconditionally
My heart gives to my mind.

9148.

Doubt is a useless weakness,
Yet it has the capacity
To cleverly and convincingly
Don the robe of wise judgement.

9149.

When we strike
The truth-bell,
Man quite often
Does not want to hear it,
For he thinks it is hurtful
Instead of blissful.

9150.

If you do not run every day
In the outer world,
The human in you may forgive
   you.
But if you do not run every day
In the inner world,
The divine in you will not forgive
   you,
For the destined goal
Will always remain a far cry.

9151.

Just keep your heart's door open.
At every moment
You are bound to receive
Something special
From your Beloved Supreme.

9152.

He simply had no idea
What would happen to him
When he took the side of
   ignorance.
She simply had no idea
What would happen to her
When she took the side of God.

9153.

Only if you throw your heart and
   soul
Into your
   aspiration-dedication-life
Can you claim to be
A true truth-seeker.

9154.

Do you really care for God?
Then you must be ready to please
   Him
In His own divine Way.

9155.

Alas, because he did not have
   implicit faith
In his Master
And did not love him soulfully,
The longer he stayed in his
   Master's presence,
The greater became his insecurity
And jealousy.

9156.

Those who have faith in God
And love for God
Will discover the unimaginable
   things
God's Power can do
In and through them.

9157.

O truth-seekers,
Since you are consciously awake,
You must accept more of the blame
For the problems of the world
Than those who are not yet awakened.

9158.

Even he who does not pray and meditate
Knows that your prayer and meditation
Indirectly give him peace.
In the heart of his heart
He knows that you really love him
And he loves you.

9159.

You do not need to participate
In every divine task,
But you do need to have the broad heart
To appreciate those
Who have the enthusiasm and inspiration
To do the needful.

9160.

You are finding it difficult
To *achieve* something for God.
But God wants you to go
Even one step further.
He wants you
To *be* something for Him.

9161.

Work soulfully.
Lo, you will not be able
To find any difference
Between Heaven and earth.

9162.

His soulful music expressed
His aspiration,
His realisation
And his oneness
With the Universal Consciousness.

9163.

If you sail in your Master's boat
To the Supreme,
Then you and your Master will sing together
Eternity's Oneness-Song.

9164.

Always think of your life
As only one day,
Today,
And just for this one day
Be truly spiritual.

9165.

Wherever your Lord Supreme
Asks you to work,
That particular place
Should be Heaven to you.

9166.

True progress
Belongs to those who,
With their aspiration and
    dedication,
Soulfully manifest the Supreme.

9167.

Maintain your inner freshness.
You will be able to sail always
In the Boat of the Supreme,
And He will always have
Boundless confidence
In your heart and soul.

9168.

My Lord,
Why have I not achieved
All the things I wanted to achieve?
"My child,
Just purify your mind.
Lo, all your problems are solved."

9169.

Never allow your pure heart
To become insecure,
Not even for a second!

9170.

Because I am
What my Father has and is,
I can never be insecure.

9171.

If your whole heart
Cries for God,
Then God's whole Heart
Will come to you.

9172.

Do not ask your Master to come down
From his Himalayan heights
Just to give you an outer smile.
You may be satisfied with only a smile,
But your Master will be miserable
That he has not been able to give you
His inner height.

9173.

If we doubt God
Today or tomorrow,
God will forgive us.
But if we doubt ourselves,
Then there is nothing God can do
To save us.

9174.

You say,
"I am an ordinary human being;
I can never realise God."
God says,
"Your self-doubt is your own creation.
Now you take care of your creation."

9175.

If you are truly spiritual,
God's Compassion, Love
And Blessings
Will act directly in and through you.

9176.

Spirituality is inside everyone.
But while some are trying consciously
To bring it to the fore,
Others are still fast asleep.

9177.

Because he was not receptive,
God tried to work through him
In an indirect way.
Therefore, he was God's
Unconscious representative.

9178.

Because God loves you,
First He will try with Love
To make you do the right thing.
If that fails,
Then He will use Force,
Which is just another form
Of His Love.

9179.

Ignorance-forces may try to extinguish
Your flame of aspiration,
But they will never succeed.
Your aspiration-flame will continue to burn
Bright, brighter, brightest.

9180.

Every day I tell my Beloved Supreme
That I can be absolutely perfect.
Every day my Beloved Supreme tells me
That I am His chosen child.

9181.

If you feel
You have reached the abysmal abyss,
You can use your determination
To again climb up.
If you feel
You are making satisfactory progress,
You can use your aspiration
To do better.

9182.

Remember,
Every day,
During each meditation,
You can transcend your past heights.

9183.

You say you have
Neither the time nor the inclination
To do selfless service,
But one day you will realise
The supreme necessity of serving
Humanity and divinity
Sleeplessly and unconditionally.

9184.

Although I try and fail,
Again and again I strive
To become a good runner
In my inner life.

9185.

Be always aware of your aspiration,
Your dedication and your goal.
Do not throw away
Your great, greater, greatest opportunities
To make the fastest progress.

9186.

All your fellow seeker-servers
Are sailing in the same boat
Towards the same goal.
Individually there may be
   differences,
But collectively you are all bound
   to reach
The Golden Shore.

9187.

When you serve your Beloved
   Supreme,
Outwardly you may not become
Richer than the richest,
But inwardly you become
A true millionaire
From His soulful and bountiful
   Blessings.

9188.

Because he did not avail himself
Of his God-given opportunities,
God no longer wanted him
As His choice instrument.

9189.

What prevents you
From manifesting the Supreme?
Not your helpless inability,
But your conscious unwillingness.

9190.

God has already given you
More than the necessary capacity
To do everything He has asked
   you to do.
Just dive deep within.
An inexhaustible source
Of energy and capacity
Is waiting there for you
Not only to receive
But also to become.

9191.

Whatever is destined
Will one day be accomplished
In the manifestation of the
   Supreme.
If today's chosen instruments fail,
New instruments will come to the
   stage
To play the necessary roles.

9192.

A narrow escape from death
Made him wiser.
He discovered compassion
Inside his newly-increased
   gratitude-power.

9193.

During his devoted prayer
His folded hands
Increased his soulful intensity
And, like a magnet,
Drew the Blessings of the
  Supreme.

9194.

Avail yourself of every
  opportunity
That the new day brings,
For every day may not have
Equal possibilities.

9195.

He is now devotedly walking
In the footsteps
Of his glorious predecessors
Who have worked very hard
For the Vision and Mission of the
  Supreme.

9196.

When the Supreme brings down
Celestial Light from Above,
Your receptivity gives Him
Immense Joy.

9197.

It is not the spiritual Master,
But the Supreme inside him,
Who deserves and receives
The seeker's devotion.

9198.

He gave credit to his own
  aspiration
For his outer success and inner
  progress,
But he did not want to give poor
  God
Credit for anything.

9199.

He embodies divinity
Not only when he is in
Deep meditation-trance,
But also when he is in
The midst of his life-dance.

9200.

In your pure heart
The Supreme is alive
At every moment.
Through your pure heart
The Supreme is working
At every moment.

9201.

My sweet Lord,
Something inside me is making me feel
That You are my journey's start
And You are my journey's only Goal.

9202.

The future-tree is nothing but
The Eternal-Now-Tree,
Which is eternally blossoming
Right in front of you.
You have only to climb up
To satisfy your immortal hunger.

9203.

The Supreme has a special message
For you:
"Be happy and remain happy!"

9204.

True happiness comes
From your discipline-life
And not from your pleasure-life.

9205.

Of all the gifts
You have offered to God,
Your happiness-gift
He treasures most.

9206.

Do you want to fight heroically
Against the ignorance-giant?
Then be happy!

9207.

Work, pray and meditate soulfully.
You are bound to remain happy
And make most satisfactory progress.

9208.

From the discipline-life-bud
The happiness-flower blossoms
Into immediate progress.

9209.

No one else has to tell you
When you have fallen
In your spiritual life.
Your own conscience
Is the best judge.

9210.

He could not even fool himself.
When his sincerity pinched him,
He saw what he was
Once upon a time
And what he had now become.

9211.

To try to cross the ignorance-sea
Without a divine boat
Is an almost impossible task.
Therefore, if you have a boat
And a boatman,
Just stay in the boat
Until you reach the Golden Shore.

9212.

Every day feel that you are
A most beautiful, fresh flower
And offer yourself to your Beloved
   Supreme.
Otherwise, as the years advance,
You will feel you are becoming
A dry, withered flower
That cannot even be placed on the
   shrine.

9213.

To keep your inner newness
And freshness,
You need only one quality:
Cheerfulness.

9214.

When they see your
   cheerfulness-shield,
Frustration, depression, doubt,
Anxiety and worry
Will not dare to attack you.

9215.

Obedience is salvation.
Salvation is satisfaction.
Satisfaction is nothing other than
God Himself.

9216.

To be a good student of life
You must feel the necessity of
   going
Not only to the outer school
But also to the inner school.

9217.

Right now the spiritual life
Is illumining and fulfilling
Only on the psychic plane.
But I assure you,
Eventually the physical, vital
And mental planes
Will also be illumined and
   fulfilled.

9218.

Everybody has to realise God
Eventually,
But God Himself expedites
That golden Hour
For His chosen children.

9219.

O seekers of the ultimate Truth,
You are God's chosen children.
He is giving you the greatest
　opportunity
In every possible way
To walk, march and run
Along the spiritual road
To realise the Highest Absolute.

9220.

If you become
A lover of all that lives
In God's entire creation,
Then God the Supreme Chooser
Will, without fail, grant you
His Vision's earth-transforming
　Voice.

9221.

If you make a mistake
In spite of your best intentions,
Remember this mantra:
"The past is dust".

9222.

If your Himalayan blunders
Are torturing you,
Tell yourself,
"I am walking along Eternity's
　Road.
Tomorrow I will have another
　chance
To do the right thing."

9223.

I was supposed to be granted
God-Victory's transcendental
　Glory.
Alas, what have I done?
I have allowed myself to be
　pierced
By the poison-arrow of self-doubt.

9224.

Courageously surmount each
　obstacle
On your spiritual journey,
And continue to walk, march and
　run
Along the sunlit path.

9225.

Although you make deplorable
 mistakes
Time and again,
You are not a hopeless case.
You will be given
Opportunity after opportunity
To transcend and illumine your
 mistakes.

9226.

Your undivine life
Is a thing of the past.
You are no longer
The same spiritual infant
Who once enjoyed that childish
 life.
In you wisdom-light
Has finally dawned.

9227.

Start doing the right thing!
Lo, you have made considerable
 progress
In your human life,
Not to speak of your divine life.

9228.

O my soul,
If you want to come down,
Then come down with your
Eternal moon of love.
O my body,
If you want to go up,
Then go up with your
Eternal sun of strength.

9229.

Work cheerfully, soulfully
And devotedly
With a spirit of oneness.
That is true spiritual service.

9230.

When each day dawns,
Meditate on what is most difficult
For you to achieve in your
 spiritual life,
For each day brings
A new opportunity
For you to achieve that very thing.

9231.

Choose the right medicine:
Doubt-disease
Needs faith-medicine;
Impurity-disease
Needs purity-medicine.

9232.

Alas, my two age-old enemies,
Doubt and impurity,
Are destroying my hope
Of ever achieving conscious oneness
With my Beloved Supreme.

9233.

If doubt enters your inner life,
See yourself as a little child
Who is all faith.
If impurity enters your inner life,
See yourself as a beautiful flower
Which is all purity.

9234.

In the Universal Consciousness
Of the Supreme,
Everybody has always existed,
Everybody always exists
And everybody will always exist.
Therefore, you need not wait for others
To accept the spiritual life.
Just run the fastest
Towards your destined goal.

9235.

Because he has a heart
Larger than the largest,
The Supreme has given him
His own God-Wisdom to use.

9236.

If you want to love God,
First you have to get that love
From God.
If you want to give joy to God,
First you have to get that joy
From God.

9237.

On your inner journey
Wait only for those
Who are just one step behind you.

9238.

Your Master is the sacred bridge
To help you cross the turbulent life-river
And reach your destined goal.

9239.

Never feel
That you have received everything
From your inner life.
Never allow
Relaxation to be
Your inner or outer name.

9240.

Practise spirituality soulfully:
It is your immeasurable inner gain.
Practise spirituality mechanically:
It is your inconceivable inner loss.

9241.

Do not look backwards
Or even sideways!
You will stumble
And slow your aspiration-pace.
Run forward
With one-pointed concentration
Towards your destined goal.

9242.

Spirituality is the life
Of your choice.
God-realisation will be the fruit
Of your hard work.

9243.

Make your choice!
Choose conscious union with God
Or be forced to face
Cold oblivion-night.

9244.

I am a tiny drop.
At last I am ready
To throw myself into the ocean.
But let me not look around!
Let me be absolutely blind
Or I shall immediately see
That other drops are also
Ready to jump.
O my stupid insecurity!

9245.

Do not remember
Your ancient scars.
Otherwise you will continue to meet
With ever-new disasters.

9246.

Offer your heart's gratitude
To the soul of your country.
Not by chance were you born there,
But to fulfil God's special Purpose.

9247.

Every morning I pray to God
To forgive my doubtful mind.
Every evening I pray to God
To forgive my ungrateful life.

9248.

Once your inner sun
Comes to the fore,
Your spiritual life
Will be all sunshine.

9249.

In the sky you see only one sun,
But inside your being there are
 many suns.
The light from even one of these
 inner suns
Can easily illumine
The darkness of your lower self.

9250.

My Lord Supreme,
What do You do with those
Who do not please You?
"My son,
As long as they do not
Deliberately displease Me,
I just keep silent."

9251.

Loneliness is not
A sign of greatness.
Loneliness is not
A sign of goodness.
Loneliness is your ignorance-life's
Self-styled reality.

9252.

True, you are a good seeker,
But that does not mean
You should not sincerely and
 soulfully
Try to become better.

9253.

Make a desperate effort
To go beyond
What you have already
Received and achieved!

9254.

The path of unconditional
 surrender
Always remains
Unfrequented.

9255.

Although he was an advanced
 seeker
With much inner wealth,
He regularly withdrew from his
 heart-bank
Until ultimately he became
Spiritually poverty-stricken.
Although she was a new seeker
With no inner wealth,
She regularly deposited
Into her heart-bank
Until eventually she became
Spiritually wealthy.

9256.

However great your inner capacity
 may be,
Continue increasing it.
The Supreme will be
Much more pleased with you
Than with those who have
Even greater capacity
But are not using it.

9257.

Visible man
With Eternity's hunger.
Invisible God
With Infinity's Feast.

9258.

O concentration-weakening
 thoughts,
I shall conquer you and your pride
With my Lord's all-conquering
Compassion-Waves.

9259.

If the Supreme is confident
That you will not go back
To your life of doubt, insecurity
And impurity,
Then He will choose you
To come back into the world
To hold aloft His Victory-Banner.

9260.

Those who do not please the
 Supreme
Will come again and again
Into the world,
Not to manifest Him,
But only to free themselves
From the fetters of ignorance.

9261.

My Lord Supreme,
My life has no joy
Because I am listening
To my earth-bound mind
And not to my Heaven-free heart.
"My child,
Since your heart is so pure
And your mind is so impure,
Why do you care for your mind
More than you care for your
   heart?"

9262.

To train your eye
So that it can see
The birth of Truth,
What you need first
Is God's Compassion-Eye
Inside His Forgiveness-Heart.

9263.

God's Compassion-Magnet
Is always ready to draw
Both our good qualities
And our bad qualities.

9264.

On the strength of our surrender
We become happy.
When we are happy,
We become perfect.
This is our self-discovery
And our God-satisfaction.

9265.

Ego is like a balloon.
How easy to burst a balloon!
Just grab it and break it.
Ego is like a firecracker.
It makes a dazzling display,
But how long does it last,
And why do we need it?

9266.

God is waiting for us.
Either we have to open ourselves
So that He can come in,
Or we have to empty ourselves
So that He can fill us.

9267.

A spiritual Master is not God,
But he is trying to be
God's devoted and obedient dog.

9268.

He who cheerfully and devotedly
Serves the Supreme
Instead of meditating
Can receive more inwardly
Than he who outwardly meditates
   for hours
While inwardly remaining fast
   asleep
In ignorance-night.

9269.

God-realisation and
   God-manifestation
Are destined, true.
But how often the tempting
   earth-ignorance
Unnecessarily delays them!

9270.

Everyone has a good soul,
But some souls, like unfortunate
   parents,
Have mind-children and
   vital-children
That will not listen to them.

9271.

Do you know when I get
The most special Love from God?
Not when I have a fearful heart,
Not when I have tearful eyes,
But when I have a self-giving heart
And two smiling eyes.

9272.

Life is a divine game.
Truth-seekers are the
   aspiration-team.
Their Captain, none other than
The Supreme Himself.

9273.

Which kind of freedom is
   desirable?
The freedom that can declare:
"I am God's
Supremely chosen child.
I am eternally His.
Sleeplessly I shall be
For Him alone."
No other freedom is real
Save and except this one.

9274.

Who can dream?
Who is dreaming?
Who will always dream?
Only the God-lover
In the seeker's aspiration-heart.

9275.

If your mind doubts
God's Compassion-Heart,
Then satisfaction
Will never take birth
Inside your life.

9276.

Because you are consciously
   spiritual,
On each of your birthdays
Your soul comes to you to energise
   you,
Inspire you and give you
   additional strength
To go forward in your
   aspiration-life.

9277.

Indifference is the best weapon
Against cynicism,
For no matter how much
Kindness and forgiveness
You offer to a cynic,
You will not be able to change
   him.

9278.

The braver you are
In telling the world
What you are and what you stand
   for,
The greater will be the world's
Appreciation for you.

9279.

No matter where you go,
No matter what you do,
You can always carry with you
The inspiration and light you
   receive
From your inner life.

9280.

The very nature of kindness
Is to spread.
If you are kind to others,
Today they will be kind to you,
And tomorrow to somebody else.

9281.

Two questions have stung me:
Why have I not told God
The entire truth?
Is there anything
That I have learnt
Which it would not be better
If I unlearnt?

9282.

A single blessingful Smile
From his Beloved Supreme
Can make a sincere truth-seeker
   feel
That he has finally reached
   Heaven.

9283.

There is not a single seeker
Who cannot inspire others.
There is not a single seeker
Who cannot be inspired by others.

9284.

Your Beloved Supreme
Is all gratitude to you
Because you have the courage
To show your inner faith
To the outer world.

9285.

His aggression-vital came to the
   fore
To challenge the world.
But, alas, when the world
Accepted his challenge,
His coward-vital was frightened
   to death.

9286.

It is not such a difficult task
To be the torch-bearer
Of a new creation.
Start right from this very moment
By intensifying your
   aspiration-life.

9287.

Not in vain
Did you enter the Boat
Of the Supreme.
Not in vain
Have you stayed in His Boat
For so many years.
Not in vain
Are you going to stay in His Boat
For all Eternity.

9288.

If you really want to continue
Walking along Eternity's Road,
Who can prevent you?
If you really want to make
The fastest progress,
Who can prevent you?

9289.

He is always successful
Because beauty-blooms and
　purity-blooms
Have soulfully and powerfully
　starred
His aspiration-dedication-path.

9290.

Increase, always increase
Your aspiration-cry.
If you allow your aspiration
To decrease,
It will be your real disgrace.

9291.

An unavoidable necessity
Can quite often be
An unexpected opportunity.

9292.

If you do not value
Your spiritual life,
How can you expect
To get much benefit from it?

9293.

The longer he followed
The spiritual life,
The weaker became his aspiration
And the stronger became the
　disappointment
Of his Beloved Supreme.

9294.

You feel you are always pleasing
　God
No matter what you do or say,
But this is all deception –
Not God-deception but
　self-deception.

9295.

The heart and the soul
Are friendly neighbours.
Whenever the heart wants
To become one with God's Light,
It just knocks at the soul's door
And enters.

9296.

The prayer of a conditional seeker:
"My Lord Supreme,
I have pleased You
For quite a few years.
Is it not time
For You to please me?"
The prayer of an unconditional
    seeker:
"My Lord Supreme,
Through Your boundless Grace
I have been able to please You
For so many years.
If such is Your Will,
I will continue pleasing You
    forever."

9297.

When he ascended, he did not feel
Immediate satisfaction
According to his expectation.
Therefore, deliberately and
    vehemently
He chose to descend.

9298.

His Inner Pilot repeatedly asked
    him
To pray more intensely,
To meditate more soulfully
And to serve more
    unconditionally.
Finally he listened
And became the perfect
    instrument
Of his Pilot's choice.

9299.

He started his inner journey
With no love,
No devotion,
No surrender —
Only sheer curiosity.
But now, years later,
He is running fast
Along his inner road
Of love, devotion and surrender.

9300.

God alone knows
When the Kingdom of Heaven
Will finally descend on earth.
In the meantime,
God is begging His aspiring
    children
To try to create
At least a tiny island
Which He can call Heaven on
    earth.

9301.

Your Beloved Supreme is inviting you
To walk with Him
And learn from Him the Song
That He eternally enjoys most:
His Eternity's Oneness-Song
With your heart,
In your life
And for your breath.

9302.

Since I wish to become
An excellent God-seeker,
I must get used to saying no
To the debris of the past,
And I must get used to saying yes
To the edifice of the future.

9303.

Purity without sincerity
Is an unusual achievement.
Purity with sincerity
Is an invaluable achievement.

9304.

Since you are for God
And for God only,
My Eternity's aspiration-heart
Is all yours
And my Infinity's dedication-life
Is all yours.

9305.

An obedient disciple
Is a permanent student
At his Master's heart-university.

9306.

Only an obedient disciple
Has a free access
To his Master's heart
Of infinite Peace
And his Master's soul
Of infinite Bliss.

9307.

I do not know who God is,
But I do know what God's Compassion is:
The eternal beginning
And immortal continuation
Of my soul's Godward journey.

9308.

My ego talks,
My humility acts.

9309.

God, I cannot please You
Because I am not always pure.
"Man, I cannot please you
Because you and your pride
Are always cocksure."

9310.

Yesterday I did not know
What I was supposed to tell God.
Today also I do not know
What I am supposed to tell God.
Tomorrow I sincerely hope
That God will tell me
What I am supposed to tell Him.

9311.

Greatness and glory
Live together.
Goodness and satisfaction
Live together.

9312.

My Lord,
Since I am not always conscious
Of what I do,
Right now I may not know
What I am doing.
But I do know
What You are doing right now.
You are thinking of me
And forgiving me.

9313.

My sweet Lord,
When I entered the spiritual life,
I thought I would realise You
Sooner than at once.
I have been praying
And meditating for years.
How is it that the Goal
Still remains a far cry?

9314.

God can give you His Consolation,
But consolation cannot give you
    illumination.
If you do not get illumination,
Then you will not get
    realisation-satisfaction.

9315.

Every day ask yourself three
    questions:
Do you think of God only?
Do you need God only?
Do you love God only?
If the answers are all in the
    affirmative,
Then prove your answers
In your aspiration and in your
    dedication.

9316.

If God can see the perfect manifestation
Of your aspiration
In your everyday existence,
Then He will give you
The realisation of His highest Height
And His deepest Depth.

9317.

Dive deep within for the answers
To your life's questions.
Once you have the answers,
Then manifest them in and through
Your heart's ceaseless cries
And your soul's ceaseless smiles.

9318.

Where is God?
He is inside my doubtful mind.
What is He doing there?
He is desperately trying
To transform my doubtful mind
Into His own faithful Heart.

9319.

If you are truly pleased with God,
With what He is doing
With you, in you and for you,
Then you will not have any interest
In your desire-life, comfort-life,
Pleasure-life and achievement-life.

9320.

In the outer world
Fear may prevent you
From revolting against God.
But in the inner world is there any day
That your mind does not argue with God,
Your vital does not rebel against God
And your physical does not find fault with God?

9321.

God has not been able
To please him,
And God will never be able
To please him,
For his way is not God's Way.

9322.

If your Lord Supreme pleases you
In your own way,
Immediately you will embrace
 destruction.
But if you please your Lord
 Supreme
In His own Way,
Yours will be a life
Of continuous delight.

9323.

The day you close your door
To myriad interests
And have God as your only
 interest,
You and God will be able to
 celebrate
Both your victory and His Victory.

9324.

A blind disciple is he
Who thinks he can do everything
All by himself,
Although he has a spiritual
 Master.
A blind disciple is he
Who thinks his Master
Will do everything for him,
Even if he does not pray or
 meditate
Or do anything to please his
 Master.

9325.

A seeker can do nothing,
Absolutely nothing,
Without God's help.
Again, God can do little,
Next to nothing,
Without the seeker's conscious
 awareness
And conscious co-operation.

9326.

Even though your aspiration is
 tremendous,
Do not ignore purity.
I tell you a supreme secret:
Purity is an added advantage,
Ever unimaginable.
Even though your dedication is
 continuous,
Do not ignore humility.
I tell you a supreme secret:
Humility is an added advantage,
Ever unimaginable.

9327.

Each outer gift soulfully offered to God
Increases the seeker's sweet and strong
Oneness-capacity with God
And gives God a unique opportunity
To express His blessingful
And powerful Gratitude
To the seeker.

9328.

God has only two Demands:
The perfection of oneness
In your inner life
And the satisfaction of perfection
In your outer life.
You can fulfil His Demands easily
If you can all the time have
One sleeplessly crying heart
And two sleeplessly smiling eyes.

9329.

Do not give up!
There is every possibility
That you may surprisingly succeed
In the battlefield of your self-giving
And God-becoming life.

9330.

O Lord Supreme,
We, Your children,
May unimaginably delay You,
But we shall not ultimately fail You
In Your God-Manifestation-Promise.

9331.

God wants you to know
What you can eventually become
And what you eternally are.
You can eventually become
His choicest instrument.
You eternally are
His Oneness-Heart.

9332.

Money-power will not last.
Personality-tower will crumble.
Popularity-flower will fade away.
Only my heart's God-Hour
With my Beloved Supreme
Will forever and forever last.

9333.

O truth-seeker,
Why have you lost your inner joy?
You have lost your inner joy
Because you did not value it.
You mistakenly cherished the idea
That you could have inner joy for
    the asking.
Therefore, you began
Secretly drinking pleasure-soup
With your body, vital and mind.

9334.

Your cleverness and meanness
Have turned you into
An unthinkable opportunist.
You want joy, appreciation, love,
    concern
And even gratitude from God.
But you do not want God Himself
For His own sake.

9335.

God uses His Justice-Light
When it is the only way
To awaken you
And make you see and feel
The importance of the inner life.

9336.

Once you lose your inner wealth,
You have to start over
Right from the very beginning,
Where sincerity, humility, purity
And self-offering are waiting
To run with you, in you
And through you once more.
Do not disappoint them,
Or yours will again be the life
Of immediate failure.

9337.

For years and years God will lavish
His invaluable
    Blessing-Opportunities upon
    you.
But if He is seriously displeased
    with you,
He not only can but also does
Withdraw these
    Blessing-Opportunities.

9338.

In my life of aspiration and
    dedication,
Either I must avail myself
Of God's inner and outer Gifts,
Or I shall be forced to accept
A life of unimaginable failure
And a heart of total
    disappointment.

9339.

Each time a birthday comes,
Mortal death knocks at our body's
    door.
But the immortal soul inside the
    body-room
Calls out,
"You are knocking at the wrong
    door.
Go away, go away!"

9340.

When I am the body,
Which is limitation in every sense,
I see death at every moment
Here, there and everywhere.
When I am the soul,
Which is unlimited freedom in
    every sense,
There is no death,
But only endless Immortality.

9341.

If your ignorance
Does not torture you,
I do not mind.
But if your ignorance
Pleases and satisfies you,
Then I accuse you of committing
The greatest inner crime.

9342.

O body, my body,
Think of the soul.
For with the help of the soul
You will grow into
Eternity's Poise, Peace, Light and
    Bliss.
O soul, my soul,
Think of the body.
For it is in and through the body
That you will have to manifest
    your divinity.

9343.

The body and fleeting time
Are synonymous.
Each fleeting second
Is a fleeting life-breath.
Therefore, do everything as soon
    as possible
In and through the body.

9344.

My Lord Supreme is not asking
    me
To see if others are accompanying
    me
On my upward path.
He is only asking me
To sleeplessly march
On my upward path.

9345.

If you deliberately hide something
From your Lord Supreme,
He will give your mind a new
    name:
Destruction;
Your heart a new name:
Frustration;
Your vital a new name:
Futility;
Your soul a new name:
Failure;
And Himself a new name:
Indifference.

9346.

I am under no obligation
To explain myself to others,
But it is my bounden duty
To see their God
In them,
As I see my own God
In myself.

9347.

I exceed in order to become.
I exceed my usual reality
In order to become my real vision,
Which is the perfection of man
For the Satisfaction of God.

9348.

Each act is a work of art.
The Supreme Artist, my Beloved
    Supreme,
Has already completed
The Supreme Work of Art.
But alas, I have not yet started
My own artwork,
And I do not know
When I shall start.

9349.

How can it be possible?
You love God,
But you do not love
The chosen children of God.
How can it be possible?

9350.

If you say there are no
Infallible God-seekers
And God-lovers on earth,
Then why don't you try yourself
To prove to the world
That it is possible?

9351.

O truth-seeker,
Do not care for those
Who scoff at your devoted
    meditation
And doubt your fruitful sincerity.

9352.

My Lord Supreme,
Do You think I can bind You?
"My child,
You will not be able to bind Me,
Never!"
My Lord Supreme,
Do You think You can bind me?
"My child, I can bind you,
But I shall not.
Mine is not the Way
To bind My creation.
Mine is the Way
To grant freedom to My creation."

9353.

In the morning
God appears before you
As divine Opportunity.
At noon
God appears before you
As supreme Capacity.
In the evening
God appears before you
As immortal Reality.

9354.

Try to grow in freedom-light
Inside your Lord's Oneness-Heart,
Where Nectar-Delight is there for
   you
To drink to your heart's content.

9355.

The unparalleled height
Of man's rare gratitude-heart
Still remains unmatched.

9356.

A moment's vast inner strength
Can easily nullify
A year's stupendous outer
   ignorance-life.

9357.

I know, I know,
There will be at least a few
Supremely chosen instruments
Of our Beloved Supreme
Who will remain absolutely
   faithful
To the Boatman
And who will remain soulfully
   seated
In the Boat
Until the Golden Shore
Is unquestionably reached.

9358.

An obedient seeker-disciple
Is his Master's invaluable
    possession
In the outer world
And his Master's incomparable
    promise
In the inner world.

9359.

A heart of gratitude
And God's lightning Smile
Are always found together.

9360.

Each soulful seeker must
    surrender
Money-power to heart-power
To illumine his mind
And save his life.

9361.

I can hear the Heartbeat of the
    Supreme
Only when I feel the
    Compassion-Power
Of His Lotus Feet.

9362.

Sweetness purifies our heart.
Brilliance strengthens our mind.
When sweetness enters into
    brilliance,
The victory of brilliance is soulful.
When brilliance enters into
    sweetness,
The victory of sweetness is
    powerful.

9363.

Here on earth when I surrender
To God's Will unconditionally,
There in Heaven God plays
My victory-drum breathlessly.

9364.

God feels sorry that you have no
    time
To watch the victory-flag
That He has unfurled on the
    wings
Of your gratitude-soul.

9365.

There are only two ways
To achieve and declare
The supreme Victory in life.
One way is to feel
That you are nothing, absolutely nothing,
On the strength of your sincere humility.
The other way is to feel
That you are everything, absolutely everything,
On the strength of your perfect oneness
With God's Love, Peace and Power.

9366.

God uses His destructive Power
For the transformation of human ignorance
And the illumination of human life.

9367.

When one is flooded
With divine consciousness,
One becomes a perfect representative
Of God on earth.

9368.

Sometimes in the inner world
What you have
Is an imaginary disobedience
And what you are
Is an imaginary arrogance.
Detect them and dismiss them,
For God loves you as His own, very own.

9369.

When negative thoughts
Assail your mind
And assault your life
Of aspiration and dedication,
You have to convince yourself
That they can never be permanent,
Never!
When positive thoughts
Inspire and encourage you,
You have to convince yourself
That they not only can but also will be
Unquestionably permanent.

9370.

The two worst negative thoughts:
I am not of God;
God does not care for me.
The two best positive thoughts:
I am eternally of God;
I am unconditionally for God
And God alone.

9371.

Give up, give up, give up
What you usually are.
Accept, accept, accept
What you really are.
What you usually are
Is a friend of ignorance-night.
What you really are
Is an inseparable friend of
　wisdom-delight.
Ignorance-night is nothing but
Slow, steady and unerring death.
Wisdom-delight is nothing but
God's God-Satisfaction
In man's perfect Perfection.

9372.

To a friend,
The best thing you can give
Is your heart's sweetness.
To an enemy,
The best thing you can give
Is your soul's forgiveness.

9373.

He may not have high inner
　experiences,
But he does obey God inwardly
　and outwardly.
You do have high experiences,
But you do not listen to God.
Therefore, he is far dearer to God
　than you.

9374.

Although the soul-bird has
　allowed itself
To be caught inside the tiny
　body-cage,
It still carries the message
Of the boundless
　Reality-Freedom-Sky.

9375.

Finally his body is getting up,
His vital wants to manifest God
And his mind has stopped its
　doubt-train.
Therefore, his soul is now coming
　forward
Very powerfully.

9376.

The Message of the Supreme
For aspiring humanity:
"If you have,
Then be happy;
If you don't have,
Then be equally happy."

9377.

On his birthday
He was both happy and unhappy.
He was happy because
His friends were congratulating him.
He was unhappy because
He had accomplished so little
During so many years on earth.

9378.

Human music
Feeds the vital of mankind.
Divine music
Serves the heart of mankind.

9379.

Enamoured of the beauty
Of the world-tree,
He appreciated not only
The root and boughs,
But each and every one
Of its countless leaves.

9380.

How to expedite your progress,
Inner and outer?
Be cheerful, be dynamic
And always do the needful,
Inwardly and outwardly.

9381.

If you do not take
Your spiritual life seriously,
No outer calamity may take place,
But you will definitely incur
Serious inner damage.

9382.

Meditate, serve
And wait patiently for God's choice Hour.
Your journey to God
Is bound to be successful and fruitful.

9383.

Dive deep within and you will discover
That inside your body is your heart,
Inside your heart is your soul,
And inside your soul is God.

9384.

It is very easy to surrender
What we have:
Ignorance.
But it is very difficult to remember
Who we are:
God's chosen children.

9385.

An intelligence-mind I needed,
And I achieved it.
A wisdom-heart I need,
And I amply have it.
A perfection-life I badly need,
And God's Compassion-Smile
Is descending with it.

9386.

Peace does not mean
Seclusion.
Peace means the perfection
Of oneness-life.

9387.

His mind is flooded
With teeming queries.
His heart is flooded
With beaming reveries.

9388.

You want to climb up to Heaven,
Yet your mind enjoys living
In the abysmal abyss
Of darkness-night.

9389.

What my mind needs
Is a new inspiration
To please God's Eye.
What my heart needs
Is a new aspiration
To please God's Heart.

9390.

With astonishing swiftness
I must reawaken my heart
For the clear and complete
    manifestation
Of my Beloved Supreme.

9391.

Because of his angelic speed,
His heart enjoys
The beauty and purity
Of the higher worlds.

9392.

Two lives I must sincerely love:
My heart's crying life
And
My soul's dreaming life.

9393.

If the world wants to give you
In small measure,
Don't be a fool.
Just take it.
If you want to give to the world
Without measure,
Don't be a fool.
Just do it.

9394.

If you always borrow
From others' thoughts,
Then naturally someday,
Sooner or later,
Sorrow will sleeplessly
Follow your steps.

9395.

Your heart-bird cannot use
Its blue-gold wings
Unless your diamond faith has
    attained
Total sufficiency.

9396.

Aspiration discovers doubts.
Dedication challenges doubts.
Revelation cheerfully, powerfully
And unmistakably disperses
    doubts.

9397.

His mind is not satisfied
With newness.
His heart is not satisfied
With fulness.
His life is not satisfied
With richness.
But he is satisfied with his Lord's
Constant Fondness.

9398.

When others pray to God
    soulfully,
It looks so simple,
It sounds so simple.
Yet how is it that I cannot sail
In the same devotion-boat
With the same
    aspiration-boatman?

9399.

To please God
All you have to do
Is offer your soul's smile.
To please man
All you have to do
Is offer your heart's cry.

9400.

There was a time
When God wrote the work-story
And I took the success-glory.
But now we work together
And write our success-story
   together.
There shall come a time
When together we will compose
A progress-song
And we will continue singing it
Forever and forever.

9401.

A surrender-prayer is the only
   prayer
That God immediately answers.
Therefore, from today on
My life shall grow into
A surrender-prayer.

9402.

Out of His infinite Compassion,
My Beloved Supreme told me
A supreme truth:
If I bend my head constantly,
My heart can expand
   immeasurably.

9403.

Sow the seed of divine longing
Inside your heart-garden.
Then your life will never be forced
To live in the unlit cave of
   nothingness.

9404.

Inside each life-breath
God has His supreme Necessity,
Unknown to the human heart,
Unknowable to the human mind.

9405.

Do not try to bind God
With the human in you,
For you will fail.
Bring to the fore the divine in you
And discover your oneness-reality
   with Him.
Then you will see and feel
A blossoming satisfaction-light
That will fulfil not only the divine
And human in you
But also, to your wide surprise,
The animal and
   stone-consciousness in you.

9406.

Inside each heartbeat
There is always God the Quality.
Inside each life
There is always God the Quantity.

9407.

I am divinely happy
That my heart is now
　　experiencing
Eternity's hunger.
I am supremely happy
That my soul is always ready
With Immortality's meal.

9408.

His mind is made
Of flaming faith.
His heart is made
Of illumining love.
His life is made
Of sacrificing breath.
Therefore, God's
　　Satisfaction-Hour
Is fast approaching him.

9409.

The day his mind lost
Its suspicion-eye
And his heart lost
Its apprehension-breath,
He began to shine
With the unparalleled light
Of supreme liberation.

9410.

Your mind is empty of pride.
Your heart is empty of despair.
Both Heaven and earth marvel at
Your Himalayan achievements.

9411.

It is absolutely unnecessary
To allow your mind
To be plagued by repentance.
Just ask your mind
To take shelter at the foot
Of your heart's illumination-tree.

9412.

O suspicion-mind,
Do you ever want to know
Who you truly are?
You are your own hidden
　　brutality.

9413.

If you have the power
To prescribe newness
For your heart,
You can also have the power
To proscribe oldness
Inside your mind.

9414.

Who needs a disobedient mind?
No one, especially not I!
Who needs a disheartened heart?
No one, especially not I!
Who needs a disturbing and
    disturbed life?
No one, especially not I!

9415.

As long as each human being
Remains a self-employed
    indulgence-prince,
The effulgence of self-perfection
Will always remain a far cry.

9416.

In my one secret letter to God
I have written:
"My Lord, if You really exist,
You are forgiving me,
And if I really exist,
I am somehow getting ready
To please You in Your own Way."

9417.

I admire your abstinence,
But I love your surrender-flames,
Which you have dedicated
To our Beloved Supreme-Sun.

9418.

I may not love God,
But I shall never say
That I do not need Him.
God does not need me,
But He never says
That He does not love me.

9419.

The most important secret is
What God has told me today:
It is my bounden duty
To see Him soulfully
And serve Him carefully
In His creation vast.

9420.

No human being is forced to live
In the whirlwind of dark
    worldliness.
We are all invited to participate
In the newness and fulness
Of life-satisfying delight.

9421.

God was astonishment-struck
When He saw on earth
An endless mass of ignorance,
But He is definitely going
To do something about it,
I am sure.

9422.

When God interviews man,
Man's helplessness breaks His
   Heart.
When man interviews God,
God's Fulness overwhelms his
   mind.

9423.

A good thought is indeed
A guest from paradise.
Welcome it, so your life will
   become
A wave of ecstasy.

9424.

If you are satisfied
With a superficial experience
Of God's Compassion-Light,
Then the divine satisfaction
Of realisation in infinite measure
Will always remain a far cry.

9425.

My Lord Supreme is
His golden Will-Sun
And I am
My silver obedience-flames.

9426.

When the soul compromises
With earth,
It ruins its inner vision-light
And its Heaven-free delight.

9427.

My incapacity saddens my mind.
My capacity gladdens my heart.
My transcendence enlightens
Not only me
But also the aspiration-loving
   world.

9428.

O my heart's insecurity,
When are you going to learn
The art of confidence-life?
O my mind's impurity,
When are you going to learn
The art of purity-manifestation?

9429.

Human insecurity wants security.
Human security wants nothing else
But God's special Attention-Smile.

9430.

My greedy mind wants to be the manager
Of the universal market.
My loving heart longs to be the caretaker
Of the transcendental garden.

9431.

A falsehood-loving man
Is helplessly attached
To his unfulfilled desires.
A truth-loving man
Is sleeplessly devoted
To his unmanifested dreams.

9432.

The outer life of man
Is the strangling love of ignorance.
The inner life of man
Is the blossoming delight of love.

9433.

When I tell my mind
That my Lord's Face
Is extremely beautiful,
My heart immediately tells me
That my Lord's Feet
Are infinitely more beautiful.

9434.

When I can joke
With my mind's tension-world,
God will give me
The needed competence
To become His choice instrument.

9435.

Sincerity is your loyalty
To yourself.
Sympathy is your loyalty
To others.
Surrender is your loyalty
To your Beloved Supreme.

9436.

His life is a temple
In God's Compassion-Field.
His heart is a shrine
In God's Illumination-Home.

9437.

His intellectual mind
Was so badly defeated and
   humiliated
In the inner world
That now he is looking for asylum
Where the utterly helpless
Human souls reside.

9438.

You are an expert
In sleeping long hours
In the night of forgetfulness.
Can you not become an expert
In singing and dancing constantly
In the bright dawn of
   wakefulness?

9439.

The mind wants to invent
A new God.
The heart wants to discover
The ancient and eternal God.

9440.

The first and foremost thing I did
To receive God's Blessing-Light
Was to tell God
That I love humanity, His
   creation,
Sincerely, soulfully and
   unreservedly.

9441.

Each soulful thought
Is a powerful prayer.
Each powerful prayer
Is a fruitful vision of man
That is trying to grow into
The very image of God.

9442.

Your mind is looking
For a short-cut.
Your mind is looking
For an easy way to realisation.
Alas, alas, your mind is not at all
   ready
For God-realisation.

9443.

O my heart, go deeper
If you want to last longer.
O my life, look farther
If you want to last longer.
O my heart and life,
Do you not know that
The soul is supremely immortal
Precisely because it sees the
   Infinite
And is one with the Infinite?

9444.

Unless you have the flame
Of fire-pure aspiration,
How can you transform your
    nature?
How can you love the Divine in
    you
And fulfil the Real in you?

9445.

My Lord Supreme,
I wish to place my heart-flower
At Your Compassion-Feet
So that I can become
My soul's tears of delight.

9446.

What is life
If not a jungle of teeming desires?
What is death
If not a song of the unknown?

9447.

My Lord,
I am sure that my life
Has been at Your Feet
For centuries.
My Lord,
I am sure that my heart
Has been inside Your Eye
For centuries.
My Lord,
I am sure that my soul
Has been carrying Your supreme
    Message
All over the world
For centuries.
Alas, how and why is it
That ruthless oblivion
Is still torturing me?

9448.

Since you are your
    suspicion-mind,
How can the current of ecstasy
Flow through you,
And how can God the eternal
    Satisfaction
Sing and dance before you?

9449.

God is not interested in hearing
Your victory's trumpet-voice.
God is only interested in seeing
Your thunder-will's
    determination-volcano.

9450.

Why are you forgetful
Of your soul's inner promise?
Why are you forgetful
Of your heart's inner peace?
Why are you forgetful
Of your life's inner love?

9451.

If your life loves God
Only unconsciously,
How will you ever see
The sun-flooded room of your
   soul?

9452.

You have no idea
How much pressure
Still remains inside my mind.
You have no idea
How much pleasure
Still remains inside my life.

9453.

We do not appreciate God:
This is our first crime.
We do not trust God:
This is our second crime.
Finally, we betray God:
This is our third, last and
Unforgivable crime.

9454.

Your inner will cannot succeed
Because your outer mind
Has no receptivity
Or sense of responsibility
And has not yet welcomed
Your gratitude-heart.

9455.

If you are negligent in your duty,
God is not going to knock
At your heart's door
Nor grant you the capacity
To see His Beauty's all-illumining
   Sun.

9456.

A God-loving man has two hearts.
One heart suffers
With humanity;
The other enjoys Nectar-Delight
With Divinity.

9457.

We cannot appreciate
An incessant talker,
But we do appreciate, admire and
   love
An incessant self-giver.

9458.

When each day dawns,
The opportunity is again granted
For you to be a perfect instrument
Of your Beloved Supreme.

9459.

How to cure falsehood?
Ask your mind to learn
The formula of
Oneness-love-truth.

9460.

Because I am God's chosen child,
I have every right to disown
The unreal in me, ignorance,
And the unreal around me,
    darkness.

9461.

No sermon can convince his mind.
No logic can convince his heart.
Only a heart of love
Can convince his mind, his heart
And his entire life.

9462.

The mind of my sound-life
I have all along seen.
Now it is time for me to see,
Appreciate and admire
The heart of my silence-soul.

9463.

At long last he has escaped
From the foolish way of life
That shamelessly and ceaselessly
Has tried to exhibit itself
In and through him.

9464.

O my mind,
You are telling me
That you have no work to do.
Can you not cheerfully be
The distributor of God's Goodwill
To each and every human life?

9465.

I shall show my love for God
By doing two things:
I shall build a temple
In each human heart,
And I shall become the sacrificial
    fire
On the altar of each human life.

9466.

There is no such thing
As the mind's worthy desire.
There is no such thing
As the heart's unworthy
   aspiration.
There is no such thing
As the soul's useless realisation.

9467.

Yesterday I buried
My dark disappointments.
Today I am burying
My proud unwillingness.
Tomorrow I shall bury
My earth-suspicion-ugliness.

9468.

My silver dreams
Are extremely powerful and
   beautiful,
For they are creating
My fruitful realities.

9469.

Your failure-life
Will never be punished.
It is your unwillingness
To accept light in God's own Way
That will be severely punished.

9470.

In my sweet dream-life
I walk with God
The Compassion-Sea.
In my harsh reality-life
I follow God
The Justice-Sun.

9471.

It may be a difficult task,
But not an impossible one,
For a seeker's aspiration-light
To grow into an unconditional
Obedience-lamp.

9472.

No cloud passes
Between my aspiring heart
And my illumining soul.
No sunlight passes
Between my doubting mind
And my strangling vital.

9473.

My Lord Supreme,
Can we not share our
   responsibilities?
I shall deal with
The flood of quantity,
And You will take care of
The sea of quality.

9474.

I am so happy
That I have altogether forgotten
My doubtful mind
And have accepted my inner light
Cheerfully, totally and
    unconditionally.

9475.

If you have faith
In your love-power,
Then you can easily expedite
God's choice Hour.

9476.

If you want to accomplish
    anything
Divine and supreme
In your inner life,
Then destroy your train of fear.
If you want to accomplish
    anything
Divine and supreme
In your outer life,
Then destroy your chain of doubt.

9477.

My mind is evolving
By virtue of its self-conquest.
My heart is evolving
By virtue of its self-offering.

9478.

I love my heart's tiny
    humility-nest
Infinitely more than
My mind's huge arrogance-palace.

9479.

Each hope-flame on earth
Awakens the seeker in man
And directs him towards
God-Light in Heaven.

9480.

True, God the Justice-Light
And God the Compassion-Height
Are inseparably one,
But we all long for
Only God the
    Compassion-Height.

9481.

Only a heart of surrender
And a life of gratitude
Are proudly treasured
By our Beloved Supreme.

9482.

You are sad
That you are employed by
   someone
And are not your own master.
But do you not realise
That even God is employed
By His Compassion-Eye
And Forgiveness-Heart?

9483.

My aspiration-cries
And God's Ecstasy-Skies
God created to determine
His own finite and infinite
   Capacities.

9484.

Your vital-life has caused
Tremendous curiosity
In the world.
Your mind-life has caused
Tremendous confusion
In the world.
Your heart-life has spread
Tremendous luminosity
All around the world.

9485.

You will be happy
If you turn your heart
Into a desireless God-seeker.
You will be perfect
If you turn your life
Into a sleepless God-lover.

9486.

Even a mind
Darker than a starless night
Will one day become as bright
As the sunlit day.
God has already decreed it.

9487.

My mind's tension-world
Is crying and dying
To see the face
Of my soul's earth-transforming
   light.

9488.

Sincerity is not dead.
It is the mind
That longs for sincerity
Which is long dead.
Purity is not dead.
It is the heart
That longs for purity
Which is long dead.
God is not dead.
It is the life
That longs for God
Which is long dead.

9489.

God believes in progress.
Therefore, there is always
   self-transcendence
Both in His Universal Life
And in His Transcendental Life.
Can we not imitate God?
Can we not make constant
   progress
And constantly transcend
   ourselves
The way God eternally does?

9490.

In vain my heart is looking
For a smile to borrow
In this ill-fated world.

9491.

God the Justice
Prompts a powerful question.
God the Compassion
Provides a beautiful answer.

9492.

Misunderstanding is
The destroyer of love.
We can destroy the destroyer
By transcending the barriers
Of our own self-love.

9493.

My Lord,
If I am supposed to catch
The ignorance of the world,
Then do give me Your Heart's
Compassion-Net.
If I am supposed to love
The beauty of the world,
Then do give me Your Heart's
Oneness-Embrace.

9494.

My mind wants
Only to acquire.
My heart wants
Only to become.
My soul wants
Only to please the Supreme
In His own Way.

9495.

The human life is a bridge
Between man's mortal hope
And God's immortal Promise.

9496.

Remember,
You are not only the body,
You are not only the vital,
You are not only the mind,
You are not only the heart,
But you are also the soul,
Especially the soul.

9497.

Once you enter into
Your Master's ocean of
   oneness-love,
You will feel miserable for those
Who have not yet entered.

9498.

Even if you are truly pleasing God,
He still has only one message for
   you:
"My child,
Your capacities have no limit.
You can aspire and achieve
   infinitely more."

9499.

God came and knocked at your
   door
To tell you that you are
His supremely chosen
   instrument.
Alas, you left His knock
unanswered.

9500.

My Lord,
You have granted me
A flood of enlightenment.
May I give You my payment
In endless gratitude?

9501.

In the morning
When I soulfully pray,
I clearly see
Compassion-Beams from God's
   Eye
Shining all around me
Like the morning sun.

9502.

My heart is dependent
On God alone.
That means my life
Is independent of others.

9503.

Today's flaming aspiration
Can easily consume
Yesterday's cruel frustration.

9504.

Affection I need
From God's Heart.
Compassion I need
From God's Eye.
Liberation I need
From God's Feet.

9505.

Pay attention
Only to what you do not know
But need to know,
And not to what you already know
But do not need to know.

9506.

In his God-adventure,
Nothing can fracture the
   illumination-mind
Or torture the realisation-heart
Of a master seeker.

9507.

Perfection
Comes from self-command.
Satisfaction
Comes from self-surrender.

9508.

Do not try to make a
   happiness-fountain.
Just try to break your
   unhappiness-tower
And then see where you are:
You are playing in and with
Happiness-power.

9509.

Fulfilment means
The enlightenment of the human
   in us
And the manifestation of the
   divine
Through us.

9510.

O my heart's fountain-love,
When will you liberate me
From the chains of
   division-blindness?

9511.

Ego is a cruel thief;
So is my earthly anxiety.
Purity is a self-giving saint;
So is my Heavenly humility.

9512.

My vital always insists
On taking a short-cut.
Alas, will it ever realise
That the only short-cut
Is unconditional self-offering?

9513.

The sermon of ignorance-night:
I do not need God;
I do not need anything
Except one thing—
Earth-destruction-dance
Within and without.

9514.

I shall reach the pinnacle-height
Only when my life grows into
The fragrance of a self-giving
    flower.

9515.

Daring enthusiasm and abiding
    cheerfulness
Can accomplish everything on
    earth
Without fail.

9516.

Beauty born of God's
    Compassion-Light
Feeds the lost human beings
And encourages the awakened
    human beings.

9517.

The sacred heart of the moon
Is from the secret Smile of God.
The sacred breath of the sun
Is from the open Dance of God.

9518.

I carry my patience wherever I go,
Hoping to see God the Dutiful
Inside God the Beautiful.

9519.

Alas, my mind
With its strangling doubts
Is challenging my heart's
Fountain-love.

9520.

Each child has a pure heart.
Each child loves
God's sleepless Breath.
To each child God tells one special
   secret:
That he is the beginning of
A new dawn.

9521.

Those who are serving the
   Supreme
Unconditionally
Are receiving His most powerful
   Gratitude.
Those who are serving the
   Supreme
Even conditionally,
Will still receive His Gratitude,
For eventually they too may serve
   Him
Unconditionally.

9522.

Leave behind the vain questioning
   mind.
God will grant you the ancient
   wisdom
Of the sages and seers
Of the hoary past.

9523.

I enjoy the voice of unseen
   loveliness
Inside my mind.
I enjoy the choice of
   oneness-perfection
Inside my heart.

9524.

Do you remember when you took
The spiritual life very seriously?
What purity, sweetness and
   gratitude
You felt inside your own heart and
   life!
What Blessings, Concern and Love
You felt inside your Lord
   Supreme!

9525.

Only if you lead
A pure and disciplined life of
   self-giving
Will your heart make you feel
What your Master stands for on
   earth.

9526.

The ultimate and deplorable fate
Of an unaspiring human being
Is infinitely more painful
Than I ever dreamt.

9527.

My future will not need
Any deathbed sincerity
If my present has
A volcano-determination.

9528.

Whom do I need?
Only God!
Whose help do I require?
Only my Master's!

9529.

Do not try to convince others
That you are good.
God will do that for you.
Just try to love God
A little more.

9530.

O my doubting mind,
I have a very special message
For you today:
My heart's rekindled faith
Is guaranteeing your immediate
    collapse
And permanent death.

9531.

Because of your mind,
Today you are weak.
Because of your heart,
Tomorrow you will become
Strong and perfect.

9532.

Immortality is the soulfulness
Of climbing earth
And the fruitfulness
Of descending Heaven.

9533.

Face your anxiety!
It will fade away.
Face your fear!
It will die away.
Face your doubt!
It will fly away.

9534.

My ascending heart
And my descending soul
Meet inside God's Vision-Eye
To become His Reality's choice
    instruments.

9535.

Earth loves him
Who loves.
Heaven loves him
Who is love within
And love without.

9536.

He who knows
Is great in his own eyes.
He who is
Is perfect in God's Eye.

9537.

The mind thinks that God
Is all complication.
The heart feels that God
Is all Compassion.
The soul knows that God
Is all Illumination.
God knows that He is
His own Eternity's Dedication.

9538.

How can I see God in my future
When I do not care for
His past Compassion
And His present Forgiveness?

9539.

God came to me unannounced.
Alas, He is returning
　　unappreciated.
Now what shall I do?
Shall I not build a oneness-bridge
Between my Lord and my crying
　　heart?

9540.

How can the Hand of God
Remain far away
If I dive deep within
And allow my tiny heart-island
To be surrounded
By God's Compassion-Heart
And Dedication-Life?

9541.

Sleepless aspiration
Needs no outer recognition.
It is its own self-transcending joy
Unparalleled.

9542.

There was a time
When I had God the Delight
In boundless measure.
Alas, all I have now
Are my Eternity's birthless
And deathless sighs.

9543.

I feel so sorry
That the confusion of the
    philosophy-world
Has tainted your mind,
Eclipsed your heart
And flooded your life.

9544.

Do not fail your Master repeatedly
In this world,
For in the other world
He will be only for those
Who have pleased him
Or have tried to please him
In his own divine way.

9545.

I am supremely fortunate
Because my heart loves me
No matter what I do.
I am supremely happy
Because my soul loves me
No matter how I live
Here on earth.

9546.

Where is hope
If there is no faith?
Where is faith
If there is no love?
Where is love
If there is no self-giving?

9547.

An intelligent mind
Is only a certificate of competence.
It can never be
A guarantee of success.

9548.

If I know that my Source is the
    Supreme,
The Infinite,
Then how can my heart
Be insecure?

9549.

Since you love God
And God loves you,
It is His bounden Duty
To command you,
And it is your bounden duty
To obey Him.

9550.

O sweet death,
I have only one question:
How do you keep your silence-life
So secret and so powerful?

9551.

In our aspiration-life,
Each uninspiring thought
Is nothing but a dreadful dream
In a phantom hour.

9552.

I am sorry to tell you
That it is not God's Will
That I should be your teacher.
But I am happy to tell you
That it is God's Will
That I should be
Your eternal well-wisher.

9553.

If you are
A half-hearted seeker,
That means your God is
A half-fulfilled Vision.

9554.

God's permanent Injunction:
Serve Me in man
Sleeplessly;
Love man in Me
Unconditionally.

9555.

My heart's aspiration
Is extremely precious.
God's Compassion
Is eternally and unconditionally
    gracious.

9556.

Your life-plant is growing
Inside a dark earth-bound cave.
Therefore, your prayers never take
    root
In God's Compassion-Heart.

9557.

His mind was searching
For light.
His vital was surcharged
With dynamism.
But, alas, his body was still
    sleeping.

9558.

Your mind is all doubt-filled.
Can you not illumine your mind?
Your vital is all destructive.
Can you not transform your vital?

9559.

Since I cannot exchange money
In Heaven,
On earth I shall use it all
To serve God's earth-transforming
   Hour.

9560.

My Lord Supreme,
I have used Your Compassion-Eye
To see how great You are.
I have used Your
   Forgiveness-Heart
To see how good You are.
I have used Your Oneness-Life
To see how perfect You are.

9561.

Because you doubt your very
   breath,
You cannot see yourself
With God's Vision-Eye.

9562.

O my alarmist mind, stop!
For God's sake and for my sake,
   too,
End your self-styled role
Of fear-supplier.

9563.

God has won me back from
   ignorance,
Not because I have done
   something new,
But because He has done
   something new:
He has used His Love-Sky,
Compassion-Moon
And Forgiveness-Sun
All at once.

9564.

I may enjoy other luxuries,
But not the luxuries of doubt
And suspicion.

9565.

The Power-Light of God's
Compassion-Heart
Has forever silenced
The loud noise of thought
Inside his mind.

9566.

Wake up, my mind!
Already it is too late.
Jump up, my heart!
Already it is too late.
Speak up, my soul!
Already it is too late.

9567.

The Divine may rest,
But the divine Fingers do not rest.
God may rest,
But God's Heart never rests.

9568.

He does not want to return
To Heaven
Because earth's life needs him.
He does not want to return
To earth
Because Heaven's Vision-Eye
   needs him.

9569.

Before death surprises you
With its unexpected arrival,
Try to give some credit
To this ever-compassionate world.

9570.

To walk in a saint's footsteps
Is to discover a new life
Of stupendous delight.

9571.

My mind may be occupied
By earthly thoughts,
But my heart is occupied
Only by God and His Love.

9572.

Do you want to know
How God has won me?
Not with a sudden burst of force,
But with His unconditional
   Oneness-Love.

9573.

Nothing to lose but the ignorance
In your life.
Nothing to lose but the fear
In your heart.
Nothing to lose but the doubt
In your mind.
Nothing to lose but the
   imperfection
In your world.

9574.

Where your heart lives
I know,
But where your mind lives
Nobody knows,
And nobody wants to know.

9575.

To see the Face
Of God the Beauty
And to see the Hands
Of God the Duty
Are impossible delights,
Especially in my case.

9576.

Do not give up, do not give up!
Who knows?
Before long
Your full manifestation of God
May take place.

9577.

O my mind,
Why should I be satisfied with you
When I know that my heart
Is infinitely more beautiful
And that my soul
Is infinitely more powerful
Than you?

9578.

Aspiration without dedication
Is like a flying airplane
Without a passenger.

9579.

I am conscious.
That means I know
How to deal satisfactorily
With earthly sorrows.

9580.

Do not insist on changing
What cannot be changed.
Do not insist on correcting
What cannot be corrected.
If you do,
Even the little poise that you have
Will disappear from your life.

9581.

Animal love
Knows how to destroy.
Human love
Knows how to misunderstand.
Divine love
Knows how to radiate.

9582.

If you are a cheerful loser,
Then in God's Eye
Nobody else but you
And you alone
Is the unparalleled winner.

9583.

The soulful music of the inner life
Builds the hope-temple
And destroys the
   disappointment-tree.

9584.

To be good to all
Is to hear God constantly playing
His own Music of Life
Inside your heart.

9585.

If you have a big heart,
Then use it at once
To quench man's eternal thirst
And satisfy God's immortal
   Hunger.

9586.

In the life of a God-seeker
Gratitude is not a mere word,
But a life-illumining
And God-fulfilling book.

9587.

My surrender to God's Will
Is my unparalleled possession,
Which no human being on earth
Will ever be able to take away
   from me,
Even for a fleeting second.

9588.

If your heart shows me
How deeply you love God the
   creation,
Then I shall easily be able to tell
   you
How close God the Creator is to
   you.

9589.

When I feel weak,
Others exploit me.
When I feel insufficient,
I exploit others.
When I feel strong,
I exploit myself.

9590.

Instead of exploiting yourself,
Instead of exploiting others
And instead of allowing others to exploit you,
From today on play a new exploitation-game:
Exploit God's Compassion-Sea
And God's Forgiveness-Sun.
When you become tired of exploiting
God's eternally infinite Compassion-Sea
And Forgiveness-Sun,
Illumination will immediately take place
In the form of
Your body's awareness,
Your vital's enthusiasm,
Your mind's clarity
And your heart's purity.

9591.

My inner voice
Sees the presence of suffering.
My higher choice
Knows the permanence of delight.

9592.

My inner voice
Carries a very heavy past
On its inner journey.
My higher choice
Carries a very light present
On its higher journey.

9593.

My inner voice mercilessly hates
Artificial spirituality.
My higher choice constantly ignores
Artificial spirituality.

9594.

My inner voice knows
That a false teacher is the beginning
Of his own confusion-darkness.
My higher choice knows
That a false teacher is the beginning
Of his own destruction-night.

9595.

My inner voice begins
The transcendental art of self-union.
My higher choice ends
The universal art of self-division.

9596.

Mind, mind, O my doubting mind,
You are too stupid to learn
Anything divine.
Heart, heart, O my aching heart,
You are too stupid to unlearn
Anything undivine.

9597.

Fear, fear, O my fear,
You think that I am always
    obliged
To listen to you.
I tell you,
I owe you nothing, absolutely
    nothing!
Therefore, I am not at all obliged
To listen to you.
From now on I shall never, never
Listen to you, O fear!

9598.

Jealousy, jealousy, O my jealousy,
You think and you insist
That you have full control over my
    life.
I tell you,
It is an absolute lie,
And I shall prove it!

9599.

Sincerity is in the heart.
Honesty is in the mind.
Eagerness is in the vital.
Purity is in the life.

9600.

Humility is man's perfect glory.
Love is man's sleepless
    oneness-life.
Aspiration is man's unknown
    journey
Towards the Unknowable.

9601.

O my heart's Pole-Star,
I meditate on You,
Cherishing the lofty hope
That someday my life shall
    blossom
In excellence supreme.

9602.

Today if you are
All gratitude and surrender,
Your heart will remember
Yesterday's happy songs
And grow into
Tomorrow's happy dances.

9603.

Destroy your self-importance.
God will immediately grant you
His own Omniscience-Light
And His own
    Omnipotence-Delight.

9604.

You do not need any skill
To enjoy the flights
Of God's Vision-Transcending
    Smile.
Just surrender your will
Devotedly and soulfully
To His Will alone.

9605.

Hate-night is personal.
Love-day is never impersonal
But is ever universal.

9606.

The oriental gods came to me
With the message
That silence is satisfaction,
Silence is all.
The occidental gods came to me
With the message
That sound is more than
    satisfaction,
Sound is more than all.

9607.

He who needs
Is ultimately called.
He who is called
Is ultimately perfect.

9608.

When I go to visit my soul
Inside my heart's silence-beauty,
I see an Eye that invites me to visit
My own transcendental palace.

9609.

Those who have denied
    themselves
Will be able to carry a
    world-message
That will awaken
Slumbering humanity's life.

9610.

If you live only in the heart
And nowhere else,
Then you will never have to
    experience
The brutal torture
Of earth's frightening bondage.

9611.

Try to be conscious
Of your imagination-power,
For this power is nothing short of
God's Promise-Hour
In you and for you.

9612.

Since you unconsciously enjoy
A pleasure-life,
Can you not consciously try to
   make your life
A climbing and glowing
   prayer-tree?

9613.

I need only one assurance from my
   Lord,
And that assurance is that He will
   give me
The capacity to please Him
In His own Way.

9614.

My Lord Supreme has repeatedly
   told me
That no blunder of mine
Will ever dishearten Him.
Each blunder will only
Indefinitely delay my
   God-realisation.

9615.

My curiosity-teacher has taught
   me
For a long time.
What I now need inside me
Is a necessity-student
And a sincerity-teacher.

9616.

When he ceased his forward
   journey
Along Eternity's Road,
It was nothing other than
His soul's defeat.

9617.

Here on earth
God plays in and through His
   representatives,
The human champions.
There in Heaven
Nobody need represent God,
For God Himself is the Champion
In everything.

9618.

Love is the birth
Of newness,
And newness is the birth
Of fulness.

9619.

The supreme message
Of the spiritual heart:
Man's utter helplessness
Will be transformed
Into perfect fulness.

9620.

The freedom-right of the vital
Is the slavery-night of the man
Who has developed a true hunger
For illumination-light.

9621.

Written words may not be
   immortal,
But a giving life
Shall always remain immortal
Inside humanity's
   gratitude-heart.

9622.

If you surrender
To your future temptations,
The chaos of the seven lower
   worlds
Will immediately start
   frightening your heart
And threatening your life.

9623.

To obliterate my painful and
   baneful past,
What my life needs now
Is a tornado-speed
To look forward,
Run forward
And become one, inseparably one,
With my ultimate destination.

9624.

It is I who embrace my silent death
By pretending to know
What I should never know
And by pretending to become
What I must never become.

9625.

To plumb the depth of delight,
Never entertain a wait-and-see
   attitude.
At every moment
You have to sing, play and dance
In the core of silence-light.

9626.

Do not fear dark misfortunes,
Do not cherish wild regrets,
If you really care for
An auspicious heart
And a spacious life.

9627.

God is waiting at your heart's door
To support your hope's beauty
And your life's
   perfection-promise.

9628.

Each time I soulfully pray,
A new world unfolds itself,
A new dimension fills me with
   astonishment
And I discover startling truths.

9629.

Two are the questions
That remain always unanswered:
Does God actually need me?
What will happen
If I become another God?

9630.

All his life he has been feeding
   hope:
The beauty of hope,
The purity of hope
And the divinity of hope.
Hope is his all.

9631.

If you do not believe
In the power-splendour
Of your heart's beauty,
The cries of the finite
Shall always follow you.

9632.

God will inform you
Of His imminent arrival
Only when He sees
That you are ready
With your heart's soulful
And innocent smile.

9633.

To cure falsehood,
Earth needs him.
But, alas, earth has nothing
To pay him.
To distribute truth,
Heaven needs him.
But, alas, Heaven is not giving
   him
Enough gratitude-power-light.

9634.

Destruction's feet are challenging
   you
Because your desire-life fears
And is not ready to receive
A delight-flooded life.

9635.

If you are a perfect devotee
Of the pleasure-life,
You will not be allowed
To see God's Eye,
Although it invisibly lives
Inside your very breath.

9636.

In the morning
Earth is my suffering-sister.
At noon
Earth is my hope-builder.
In the evening
Earth is my surrender-splendour.

9637.

O my heart,
If you excuse my mind
Time and again,
Then you will, without fail,
Be blamed by your superior,
My soul.

9638.

My heart's ancient realisation:
Death is not death
But a new life
With a new purpose –
To please God.

9639.

To you, O earth,
A mere suggestion:
Be constantly conscious
Of what you are not receiving
  soulfully.
To you, O Heaven,
A mere suggestion:
Be constantly conscious
Of what you are not giving
  cheerfully.

9640.

If you do not brave
The life of failure-sighs,
Then you can never expect
The infinite and immortal
  Satisfaction-Sky
Of God's Heart.

9641.

My Eternity's hungry heart
Is God's unhorizoned Choice.
At last I swim
In the sea of wisdom-delight.

9642.

God does not mind at all
If I use His Eye
To see each and every human
   being.
On the contrary,
He deeply appreciates
My wisdom-light.

9643.

This world may damage
   everything
That belongs to him,
But it can never damage
His God-given self-esteem.

9644.

O hostile forces,
Your cannons are roaring,
Your bayonets are flashing
And your drums are rolling,
But I shall not surrender.
At God's choice Hour
I shall conquer you all
With no exception,
Without fail.

9645.

When I swallow my
   tempest-pride,
God immediately grants me
His own Tongue to use freely.

9646.

Each time my mind wants to
   escape
From the reality-life,
My heart sees nothing
But the cruel torture of death.

9647.

You must never think
That your life is made of
Hopeless hopes.
No! Your life is made of
The ever-illumining sun
And the ever-fulfilling sky.

9648.

What I need from my present life
Is a smile from God.
What I need from my future life
Is a dance from God.

9649.

To make myself really happy,
I shall empty myself of
   ignorance-night.
To make my Lord astonishingly
   happy,
I shall empty myself of myself.

9650.

You are consciously on the way
To your goal.
That means at long last
Your soul is going to be
Triumphant.

9651.

Everybody is longing for
   happiness,
Even God.
Although He is all Happiness,
He wants to be even happier
By transcending Himself.

9652.

You are nothing but an
   insignificant creature
When you do not please God
In His own Way.
You are dearer than the dearest
In God's Heart
When you please God
In His own Way.

9653.

You can achieve something
   worthwhile
Either for God or for yourself
Only by virtue of
Your adamantine determination.
Without determination,
Your life is worse than useless.

9654.

He had no idea how sad God was
At his lack of determination.
His life's failure gave God
A most deplorable experience.

9655.

There is always room for
   improvement.
Improvement is the mind's
   enlightenment
And the heart's fulfilment.

9656.

If you have to make any mistake,
Then do it in the higher world,
Not in the lower world.
If you make a mistake in the lower
   world,
You will be destroyed.
If you make a mistake in the
   higher world,
You will be given a chance
To rectify it.

9657.

Through meditation, dedication
And a prayerful inner life,
Let us see how far, how deep
And how high we can go.

9658.

He was chosen by the Supreme
   Himself
To manifest the heights
Of spirituality and divinity.
But unconsciously, if not
   consciously,
He was unwilling to fulfil
His God-ordained tasks.

9659.

When he hesitated to fulfil
The Mission of his Lord Supreme,
The Supreme chose a new
   instrument
To awaken the slumbering world.

9660.

O sincere seeker,
Listen to your heart
When it tells you
That you are pleasing God,
For then you will be able
To please Him more.

9661.

He may not be a tall man,
But his ambition-mountain
Is unimaginably high.
He may not be a promising soul,
But his hope-sea
Is very deep.

9662.

A child's question
Can be answered in one sentence.
The same question
Asked by an adult
Requires a thesis as an answer.

9663.

When dire necessity commands me
To immediately change
The face and fate of mankind,
I vehemently stand against
My own old friends:
Concern, compassion, closeness and oneness.

9664.

My Lord Supreme
Has given me chance after chance
To please Him,
Yet I have not been able
To build a heart-temple
Inside my life-house.

9665.

You do not belong to Heaven.
If you belong to Heaven,
Then where is your heart of delight?
You do not belong to earth.
If you belong to earth,
Then where is your face of beauty?

9666.

If man wants to worship
The perennial Truth,
He can.
But usually he prefers to worship
The eclipse of Truth.

9667.

When I choose
To forgive the world,
My divinity-sun immediately increases
Its unhorizoned power.
When I choose
To live the life of oneness-love,
My humility-moon immediately increases
Its beauty's light and purity's height.

9668.

Darkness knows how to thicken.
Light knows how to brighten.
Earth knows how to bind
The divine in man.
Heaven knows how to liberate
The human from the animal.

9669.

If your mind wants to challenge something,
Then let it challenge peace.
If your heart wants to challenge something,
Then let it challenge love.
If you want to challenge something,
Then challenge perfection.

9670.

When God allows you to fail,
He does not want you to feel humiliated.
Since you are His chosen child,
God wants you to know
The experience of humility
And not the experience of humiliation.

9671.

Both your lethargic body
And your aggressive vital
Must be transformed, without fail,
Into a dynamic life.

9672.

Your mind thinks
That God is unreachable.
Your life believes
That God is quite distant.
And what does your heart feel?
Does it feel God is distant?
Does it feel God is unreachable?
Or does it feel God is where it is itself?

9673.

The aspiration-flames of our inner life
Can win the life-and-death battle
With the desire-night of our outer life
If we need our Supreme Pilot only,
Every day, every hour,
Every minute, every second.

9674.

If I put my Beloved Supreme
Always first in my life,
When I pray to Him
To fulfil my undivine desires,
First He delays
And then He forgets to fulfil
  them.
When I pray to Him
To fulfil my divine aspirations,
He not only fulfils them
Infinitely sooner than my
  expectation
Or even my imagination,
But He also fulfils my innocent
  desires
With utmost Joy.

9675.

What are weaknesses,
If not unlit rooms?
You will be happy
Only when all the rooms
In your life-home
Are fully illumined.

9676.

My heart's latest discovery:
God's Heart is for
My own hidden larger self,
Humanity.

9677.

Before the soul completes
Its final journey,
It manifests its divinity
On earth,
And this divinity is nothing else
But God's Compassion-Light
And Satisfaction-Height.

9678.

My Lord,
Why are You staying inside
My frustration-vital
And not inside
My satisfaction-heart?
"My child,
Your heart-room has pleased me.
Now I want to live in your
  vital-room.
I shall illumine your vital-room
The way I have illumined your
  heart-room."

9679.

You must watch your words.
Each word can reverberate
Inside your heart's purity-temple
Or inside your vital's
  impurity-cavern.

9680.

Allow not your mind to enjoy
The complicated affairs of life
If you want your heart's beauty
To grow deeper and deeper
And your life's duty
To go higher and higher.

9681.

God is my known Friend:
This is the rich feeling
Of my heart.
God is my unknown Friend:
This is the vague opinion
Of my mind.
God is my unknowable Friend:
This is the totally helpless
    conviction
Of my life.

9682.

The strength of passion-torture
And pleasure-torture
Are inseparable.
The love of
    illumination-perfection
And satisfaction-perfection
Is indispensable.

9683.

Always mix with a true God-lover.
It is he alone who can help you
Have a God-adoring heart.

9684.

You say you do not believe
In God and His
    Compassion-Game.
Do you expect me to believe
That you are your own
Self-created vision-flames?

9685.

Smaller than a mustard seed
Is man's sacrifice-drop,
But it has the power
To bring to man eventually
The ecstasies of both
The inner world and the outer
    world.

9686.

His vital and mind together
    sobbed
When he lost the outer race.
His heart and soul together
    sobbed
When he lost the inner race.

9687.

The inner world was indifferent
    to him.
The outer world challenged him.
Helpless, he surrendered
To the dictates of
    ignorance-night.

9688.

You do not know yourself,
So why not trust him?
He will tell you
How you can see God
And how you can touch God's
    Feet.

9689.

I prefer the heart
That creates purity
To the mind
That creates obscurity.

9690.

The doom of the doubt-life
Is not only inevitable
But also visible.

9691.

An instant touch
From the inner world
Can easily cure
Your fractured trust.

9692.

My mind cannot afford
To enjoy the luxury
Of baneful doubts.

9693.

A God-realised soul
Not only feeds his own inner
    hunger
But also sleeplessly tries to feed
The inner hunger of God's entire
    creation.

9694.

Inner stillness
Has a volcano-power.
It destroys the smouldering
    anguish
Of the human heart.

9695.

To make my dry mind happy
What I need is newness.
To discipline my vital
What I need is either strictness or
   soulfulness.

9696.

Time is sacrificing itself every day
So that the aspiration-life
Can be bettered at every moment.

9697.

The world's deep
   midnight-silence
Has seen him not only meditating
But also playing hide-and-seek
With his Lord's Vision-Eye.

9698.

God's Silence preceded God's
   Sound
Amazingly.
God's Sound is preceding God's
   Manifestation
Slowly, steadily plus convincingly.

9699.

You can never reach complete
   satisfaction
In your heavenward journey
Without your heart's
   aspiration-cry.

9700.

Only an inch separates
My gratitude-heart
From God's Satisfaction-Heart,
And I shall bridge that final inch
With my heart's purity-surrender.

9701.

I am great,
Not because I sincerely pray to
   God,
But because God, out of His
   boundless Bounty,
Has given me the unparalleled
   opportunity
To live in His Vision-Eye.
I am good,
Not because I soulfully meditate
   on God,
But because God, out of His
   boundless Bounty,
Has given me the unparalleled
   opportunity
To live in His Compassion-Heart.

9702.

If you are leading a human life,
Ordinary and unaspiring,
Then expectation is your morning
    illusion
And evening frustration.
If you are leading a divine life,
Simple, sincere and pure,
Then aspiration is your morning
    joy
And evening peace.

9703.

O Lord Supreme,
A beautiful day has dawned for us.
Please tell us what we should do
During the entire day.
"My sweet children,
You are now praying to Me
And meditating on Me
Devotedly and soulfully.
The entire day try to think and feel
That you are eternally of Me alone
And eternally for Me alone."

9704.

My Lord,
How can my mind think of You
When it is suffering so much?
"My child,
Tell your mind
That it does not have to think of
    Me.
It only has to think of My Peace."

9705.

My Lord,
How can my heart feel You
When it is suffering so much?
"My child,
Tell your heart
That it does not have to feel Me.
It only has to feel My Bliss."

9706.

My Lord,
How can my vital know You
When it is suffering so much?
"My child,
Tell your vital
That it does not have to know Me.
It only has to know My Oneness."

9707.

My Lord,
How can my body have faith in
    You
When it is suffering so much?
"My child,
Tell your body
That it does not have to have faith
    in Me.
It only has to have faith in My
    Compassion."

9708.

I do not want to know
How I have failed
And why I have failed.
I only want to know
How I can succeed,
For I know that I shall definitely
    succeed.
When?
Soon, very soon!

9709.

Since your heart is
Exceedingly beautiful,
It will not take much time
For you to make your life
Supremely fruitful.

9710.

My Lord Supreme,
I have given You
My aspiration, dedication and
    surrender.
What else do You want from me
So that I can be a perfect
    instrument
Of Yours?
"My child,
Be constantly pure in your
    aspiration.
Be constantly humble in your
    dedication.
Be constantly sincere in your
    surrender.
Then I shall claim you
Not only as a perfect instrument
    of Mine
But also as My own, very own."

9711.

My Lord Supreme, I know, I know,
My insincerity, my impurity
And my doubt hurt You.
Is there anything else that hurts
    You?
"Yes, My child, there is something
    else.
Your unwillingness to change
    your nature
Hurts Me infinitely, infinitely
    more
Than your insincerity, impurity
    and doubt."

9712.

"Children, My dear children,
I shall every day give you
What I have:
My Infinity's Love.
I shall every day give you
What I am:
My Eternity's Compassion."
Father, dear Father,
We shall every day sleeplessly give
    You
What we have:
Our insecurity-lives.
We shall every day soulfully give
    You
What we are:
Our gratitude-flames.

9713.

My sincerity tells me
God is.
My purity tells me
God does.
My receptivity tells me
God is for me,
For me always.

9714.

My Lord Supreme,
Do tell me the easiest way
To please You.
"My child, from today on
Think of yourself infinitely more
Than you think of others,
Until the time comes
When I ask you
To think of Me infinitely more
Than you think of yourself.
This is the absolutely easiest way
To please Me."

9715.

To become a perfect instrument
Of your Beloved Supreme
You need only two things from
    Him daily.
During the day
You need His Compassion
So that in the battlefield of life
Your searching mind can succeed
And your crying heart can
    proceed.
During the night
You need His Forgiveness
Because unconsciously, if not
    consciously,
You make friends with
    ignorance-sleep.

9716.

Soulfully give what you have.
You will realise
That you have given nothing.
Consciously become what you are.
You will realise
That you have become everything:
A perfect instrument
Of your Beloved Supreme.

9717.

Not only every day but at every
    moment
Your Lord Supreme does
    something
Very special for you.
When you are lethargic,
He stands behind you
And pushes you forward.
When you are energetic,
He stands before you
And pulls you forward.

9718.

Since I have taken my duties
Seriously and soulfully
And I have fulfilled my
    obligations,
Inner and outer,
Nobody will be able to delay
My Heaven-bound journey.

9719.

It is unmistakably obvious
That nothing great, nothing good
And nothing abiding
Can ever breathe outside the
    love-citadel
Of one's own inner being.

9720.

His heart he spends in discovering
The beauty, purity and divinity
Of love.
His life he spends in manifesting
The promises of his Heaven-free
Soul-reality.

9721.

Nobody can stop me!
In the inner life
My heart is my own revolution.
In the outer life
My mind is my own
    determination.

9722.

Keep your heart's door closed.
You will see that your own success
Is no success at all.
Keep your heart's door open.
You will see that the success of
    others
Is also your success.

9723.

If you cannot expand your heart
And establish your oneness
With your highest Self,
Then in God's Eye
You will be totally lost.

9724.

He was dearest to God
Because he offered to help others
Without being requested.
He was dearest to God
Because when others requested
 his help
He felt they were carrying
Nothing other than God's
 Message.

9725.

The determination in your heroic
 effort
Will permeate your mind and
 heart
Even after your success or failure
Is long forgotten.

9726.

To please God in His own Way
You know what you are supposed
 to do:
Just live in the heart
And not in the mind.

9727.

Whenever you do something
Great and good,
Your Master feels he has done it.
Whenever your Master does
 something
Great and good,
Try to feel you have done it.
Then the mutual joy in your
 hearts
Will last eternally.

9728.

The dark ignorance-tunnel
May seem endless to you,
But he who has already passed
 through it
Knows it is only a matter of time
Before you will also emerge
Into the effulgence of God's
 infinite Light.

9729.

Although you are experiencing
Repeated defeats and failures,
Do not give up!
Always remember
The Golden Shore is waiting
For nobody else but you.

9730.

The nature of divine friendship:
If one friend loses,
The other's oneness-heart will
    break.
If one friend wins,
The other's oneness-heart will
    make him feel
It is he who has won.

9731.

Although God is prepared to fail
Every day, every hour and every
    minute
When he deals with our human
    nature,
He knows that His is the ultimate
    Victory.

9732.

Human fear is absolutely useless!
Why be afraid of anybody or
    anything?
Cherish only the divine fear
That you may do something
Which will bring suffering
To your Beloved Supreme.

9733.

If you can identify
With your friend's achievements,
You will share his happiness.
If you cannot identify
With your friend's achievements,
You will act like his worst enemy
In the inner world.

9734.

If you cannot conquer
Your outer greed,
You will never be blessed
With an abiding inner hunger.

9735.

Determination is the first rung
On the evolution-ladder,
Not only for unaspiring people
But also for those
Who have wholeheartedly
    accepted
The spiritual life.

9736.

Because he was failing badly
In his life-examination,
He was a disgrace not only to his
    soul
But also to his heart,
Which was sincerely aspiring
To make him a good truth-seeker.

9737.

Although I see failure
All around me,
I shall always strive to maintain
My inner oneness with God.

9738.

If you have the capacity
To please God for one day,
Then, without fail,
You have the capacity
To please Him always.

9739.

Your empty heart
Is the beginning
Of your
   silence-delight-experience.

9740.

I have only one prayer,
And that prayer is simple and
   constant.
What do I pray for?
Purity's oneness-light
Within and without
At each human breath.

9741.

If you want to realise who you are,
Then start acting like
A representative of God
And not a representative of
   ignorance.

9742.

The real in you
And the unknowable in you
Are always the same.
Do not separate them
If you want to live
In the oneness of self-perfection
And God-satisfaction.

9743.

Curiosity cannot create
Positive energy.
Sincerity can not only create
Positive energy,
But can also offer it to others.

9744.

If you do not renounce
Your negative thinking habits,
Then the darkness-forces will
   announce
Their destruction-victory inside
   you.

9745.

What can you expect
From poor God
If you wilfully resist
His unconditional
   Compassion-Arrival?

9746.

Struggle!
Struggle vehemently against
   darkness!
Your soul, the blue bird inside
   your heart,
Desperately wants from you
The transformation of your
   earth-life.

9747.

Be careful!
Your shameless mind's
Heartless resentment
Can indefinitely delay
Your soulful heart's
Supreme enlightenment.

9748.

Since your vital is not ready
To give up the idea of hiding,
How can you expect the world
To give up the idea of exposing
   you?

9749.

Your unwilling mind knows
What resentment is.
Your loving heart knows
What oneness is.

9750.

God granted him
His own
   Self-Transcendence-Smile
Because he was unreservedly for
   those
Whose needs came to his notice.

9751.

Since yours is a calm and serene
   mind,
Your hope of promoting world
   peace
Shall not remain an unfulfilled
   dream.

9752.

I hate your complex mind
Beyond my imagination.
I love your simple heart
Beyond your imagination.

9753.

If God's strictness
Is not to your taste,
Remember that your life's
    barrenness
Is not to God's taste.

9754.

If you really want to accomplish
Something great in life,
Then be quick to battle against
    ignorance
And, if needed, exercise your
    divine authority.

9755.

He who is an unconditional
    God-lover
Is a spark of God's special Light
And the centre of God's special
    Love.

9756.

He has satisfaction.
He is perfection.
Therefore, he has fulfilled
His two Himalayan
    commitments.

9757.

The entire length
Of your life's God-manifestation
Is founded upon the strength
Of your heart's God-vision.

9758.

When I pray,
I start with a beggar's
    nothingness.
When I meditate,
I start with a true God-lover's
    stillness.

9759.

There can be no real agreement
Between what my vital wants
And what my heart needs.

9760.

Do you know
That your faith has enough
    strength
To carry even your impurity to
    God?

9761.

Your aspiration-light
Must always stand above
Your previous desire-night
In its determination-strength.

9762.

My human nothingness
Does not change me.
My divine willingness
Can and does change me.

9763.

My crying heart
Is an inexperienced child.
My doubting mind
Is an experienced fool.

9764.

O my body,
Everybody knows that you are
The great sleeper.
Can you not prove to the world
That you are something else as well:
A sacred temple of the evolving God?

9765.

When God's Breath touches my sleep,
Two things I immediately see:
God's Compassion-Tree
And
My own gratitude-plant.

9766.

You have danced in the desire-world
For many, many years.
Do you not believe in
The ecstasy-breath of newness?
Can you not see
That you have a free access
To the aspiration-world as well,
And that this aspiration-world
Is your only reality-world?

9767.

Dive deep within.
You will see a lion
In its own lion-poise.
The day is fast approaching
When this lion will roar and roar,
Announcing the Victory
Of your Lord Supreme.

9768.

Anxiety and worry,
You are total strangers
To my aspiring life.
I can be of no help to you!
Therefore, why do you not leave me?

9769.

When you speak ill of others,
You have already exposed
Your own inner weakness
To the outer world.

9770.

Unless I become a sleepless dreamer
Of God-Dreams,
My heart shall remain a fount
Of orphan-tears.

9771.

The mind says to the heart,
"I am not ready
And I may never be ready
To pray to God,
But I have a strong curiosity
To see God.
Therefore, will you not take me
In your boat
And pilot me to the Golden Shore?"

9772.

When I disappoint my soul,
I not only weaken my life
But also sadden
My Lord's Compassion-Heart.

9773.

If you are not sincerely aspiring,
Then remember,
The unkindness of the world
Is no match for your own unkindness
To your all-loving soul.

9774.

Tell me, my friend,
What you think of yourself,
Not what you know about yourself,
For that is what
Will definitely inspire me.

9775.

If I do not prevent
Discouraging thoughts from attacking me,
That means I am allowing
Someone to threaten me
With a taut and strangling rope.

9776.

Since truth has repeatedly told
   you
That you are its great friend,
Why do you need falsehood
To befriend you?

9777.

Everybody knows
What the universal disease is:
Doubt.
But does anybody care
For the real medicine,
Or for any medicine at all?

9778.

The enlightenment of a seeker's
   life
Is nothing other than
A very pleasant entertainment
In God's Heart-Garden.

9779.

To love the purity of
   silence-delight
Is to divinely enjoy
A God-manifesting leisure
   activity.

9780.

I always belong
At my Lord's Forgiveness-Feet:
This is my absolutely
Unmistakable conviction.

9781.

I appreciate your mind
Because it sincerely pursues.
I admire your heart
Because it richly achieves.

9782.

My vital does not want
To hear the truth from you,
For it feels that truth is
   punishment.
My heart wants to hear
Only the truth from you,
For it feels that truth is not
   punishment
But illumination.

9783.

God is not an outsider.
God is an insider,
Closer than the closest,
The only one who protects
And illumines you.
Why, then, are you afraid of Him?
Why are you so unkind to Him?
Why do you not love Him?
Why do you feel
That you do not need Him?

9784.

Who told you
That God is an intruder?
He is not!
He is only the greatest
    Perfection-Lover
And Satisfaction-Promoter.

9785.

The ultimate meaning of human
    life
Lies in the sleepless thrill of
    self-giving
To the world of aspiration-heart.

9786.

I had a long talk with God.
He told me two most important
    things
About the mountain-smile
Of my aspiration-heart:
It has conquered the
    division-mind
Of the world,
And it has welcomed God the Doer
Secretly
And God the Lover
Openly.

9787.

What you have is a blundering
    mind.
What you are is a forgotten hope.
What you want to be
Is the question of questions,
Which God alone can answer.

9788.

If your mind loves
Indisputable sincerity,
Then your heart will quickly
    become
The master of your life.

9789.

O my mind,
My heart is so well-liked
By my Lord Supreme!
Therefore, do you not see that it is
An unforgivable insult
When you criticise
My pure and self-giving heart?

9790.

I wanted to admire
The beauty of Infinity.
Alas, my mind's incapacity
And my mind's impurity
Have forced me to surrender
To strangling Eternity.

9791.

Since you are quite comfortable
With your mind's frequent
    inconsistencies,
How can anybody teach your life
Success-progress-stories?

9792.

Unless I become a positive voice
To myself,
My heart shall remain
An utterly disappointed hope.

9793.

Where is God's
    Compassion-Light?
It is inside the sound
Of my prayer-dream.
Where is God's
    Satisfaction-Delight?
It is inside the silence
Of my meditation-mountain.

9794.

His spiritual life was stung
By a piercing criticism-arrow.
Therefore, he deliberately
    shrouded his life
In top secrecy.

9795.

You want to know today
Where my teeming doubts are.
Well, I have found a suitable place
For them to stay.
They are in the cemetery of
    yesterday.

9796.

A vast inspiration flashes across
    my mind:
I shall weep until my heart-bird
Receives from Above
Two ecstasy-wings.

9797.

Now that he has achieved perfection
In his own obedience-life,
His heart is swimming
In the sea of delight.

9798.

Man's love for the unnatural life
And for the finite realities
Has created death
And its good friend, ignorance.

9799.

The outer beauty prays to God
For more beauty.
The inner beauty prays to God
For more responsibility.

9800.

Hope lights the candle of delight
Inside the temple of my silence-heart today.
Once more I am able to claim my Lord Supreme
As my own, very own.
From today on I shall be
The sunshine that crosses my path.

9801.

Discover a new kind of winning,
This time not for yourself
But for the entire world.
Consciously become what you eternally are:
Another God.

9802.

I water my life-garden every day
With my heart's tears
So that I can soulfully sing
And powerfully dance
With my Lord Supreme
In His Vision-Transcendence-Light.

9803.

To permanently change his old habits,
Man needs an absolutely sincere wish
For self-dedication-light.

9804.

I see a new solution
To my new problem.
My new problem is:
I do not know anything correctly.
My new solution is:
As long as I can love my Lord
   Supreme
Soulfully and devotedly,
I do not need anything more.

9805.

My heart's unwavering faith
Has given my mind's meditation
The capacity to become
A silence-expander and
   delight-distributor.

9806.

Book-knowledge-minds
Know how to wrangle and
   strangle.
God-wisdom-hearts
Know how to grow and glow.

9807.

Although he is tremendously
   confused
About who he is,
He enjoys the intoxication
Of self-styled commitments
To all those who are around him.

9808.

Unless you launch your
   Heaven-free heart
On the tide of self-giving love,
Your earth-bound mind
Can never become faultlessly
   pure.

9809.

Loneliness violently attacks the
   world
Every day,
Yet the world survives.
How?
Because God's secret Love-Touch
Is everywhere.

9810.

Your mind is in the dust,
But your heart is not of the dust
And your life is not for the dust.

9811.

My doubtful past cannot touch
My soulful present
And my fruitful future.

9812.

If your mind wants to enjoy
Being a one-man show,
Then be careful.
You may eventually find yourself
In a barren wasteland.

9813.

The message of a curse:
I cannot and I will not.
The message of a blessing:
I have and I already am.

9814.

Each movement need not be
A successful progress,
But each progress
Is a successful movement
Forward, upward and inward.

9815.

His advantages have made him
Slowly and secretly lethargic.
His possessions have made him
Quickly and openly useless.

9816.

As intense outer hunger
Does not find fault
With the food-preparation,
Even so, sincere inner hunger
Does not find fault
With God's Vision-Manifestation.

9817.

The turbulence of an intellectual
   mind
And the silence of a soulful heart
Do not care for each other,
Even in their resting hours.

9818.

The animal in me has changed.
The human in me is changing.
The divine in me has transcended.
The Supreme in me is
   ever-transcending,
Ever-illumining
And ever-perfecting.

9819.

I may at most begin the journey;
God's boundless Bounty
Will have to complete
My heavenward progress-life.

9820.

Sleep instead of sighing
If you are clever.
Sing instead of sighing
If you are wise.
Ascend and transcend instead of sighing
If you are perfect.

9821.

I have only one inner teacher:
A gratitude-flame.
I have only one outer teacher:
A surrender-drop.

9822.

I can have security
Only when I have implicit faith
In my Lord's blessingful Message to me:
"My child,
I shall replace your insecurity-life
With confidence-light
If at least ten times daily
You can claim Me as your own,
Very own."

9823.

When I want to increase
My own heart's purity,
I repeat my Lord's Name
As powerfully as possible.
When I want to increase
Purity in my dear ones,
I repeat my Lord's Name
As slowly as possible
And as quietly as possible.

9824.

Because of his unconditional surrender
To God's Will,
He is the only one
Whom God has entrusted
With the opportunity and capacity
To celebrate His Perfection-Smile
In Heaven
And His Satisfaction-Cry
On earth.

9825.

Stupidity is stronger than logic:
A sincere mind may know it.
Impurity is stronger than aspiration:
No sincere heart will accept it.

9826.

I am half afraid to say
That even my loving
And illumining soul
Is totally disgusted
With my doubting mind.

9827.

Your mind has a monopoly
On wisdom-light.
Your heart has a monopoly
On satisfaction-delight.

9828.

If you are out of practice,
Then start praying to God
Most sincerely.
If you have been praying regularly,
Then start meditating on God
Unconditionally.

9829.

Love likes to remain in a group,
Accessible and available.
Power likes to live apart,
Inaccessible and unavailable.

9830.

You want to know
How you can become perfect?
Ask earth's aspiration-heart
And Heaven's illumination-eye
To answer this question.

9831.

What I need from my Lord
    Supreme
I have told Him.
What He needs from me
He has told me.
We both have decided
That we shall keep our needs
A top secret from the world.

9832.

Can you not see
That God is waiting for you
At His Table?
When will you eat His Food?
When will you drink His
    Nectar-Drink?
How long does poor God have to
    wait
Unnecessarily for you?

9833.

He criticises my mind,
But he loves my heart.
How can I be displeased with him,
Since he immediately
   compensates?

9834.

I speak in defense of earth:
It desperately tries to cry
To Heaven.
I speak in defense of Heaven:
It definitely wants to smile
At earth.

9835.

When the soul cannot properly
Manifest the Supreme,
It sings the song of sorrow.
When the soul is able
To manifest the Supreme,
This song of sorrow is
   transformed
Into an immortal song of joy.

9836.

My morning awareness
Asks the question of questions:
Who is God?
My evening awareness
Asks the question of questions:
Who is not God?

9837.

His life stands crucified
Between his crying desire
And his smiling aspiration.

9838.

Change your mind
If you do not want anybody
To bind your life.

9839.

Each negative thought
Produced by my mind
Is running like a river
That enters into the sea of
   destruction
And adds to its destructive power.
Each immortal expression of will
Produced by my heart
Is running like a river
That enters into
God's ever-increasing
   Silence-Peace
For the ever-increasing
   satisfaction
Of earth's heart.

9840.

God the man was fascinated
When he saw man the God's
Birthless and deathless Golden
   Bridge.
The Absolute Supreme,
Who is both God the man and
   man the God,
Is eagerly waiting for earth's
   receptivity
To claim that Golden Bridge
As its own, very own.

9841.

When the human mind loses,
Even to God,
It immediately starts weeping.
When the divine heart loses,
Not only to God
But also to any divine being,
It immediately starts smiling.

9842.

You are happy
Now that you are not carrying
The burden of scholarship.
You will be perfect
The day you emerge dauntlessly
From your mind's battleship.

9843.

My morning prayer
Challenges the imperfection of
   my life.
My midday prayer
Challenges the uncertainty of my
   mind.
My evening prayer
Challenges the insecurity of my
   heart.
My nighttime prayer
Challenges the power of my own
   insufficiency.

9844.

All your
   battleground-experiences
Must eventually be transformed
Into oneness-fount-experiences.

9845.

The life of austerity
Is an old way.
This old way
Will not work any more.

9846.

He who is clever
Is useless in the spiritual life.
He who is earthly wise and
    divinely unwise
Is equally useless.
But he who is supremely wise
Is constantly perfect.
Who is supremely wise?
He who does not expect anything
From the ignorance-world,
His lower self,
But who expects everything from
    God,
His higher Self.

9847.

Universal oneness
Is the divine necessity
Of the human life.
Transcendental fulness
Is the supreme necessity
Of the divine life.

9848.

One world can bind us:
Fear.
One world can free us:
Love.
One world can place us on God's
    Throne:
Surrender.

9849.

Since God is His own
Self-giving Compassion,
I shall try to become my own
    heart's
Climbing preparation.

9850.

My heart,
You have revealed to me
Many things.
Only one thing more do reveal:
The mountain-smile
Of your aspiration-cry.

9851.

I may not know many things,
But I do know one thing well:
My Eternity's only indispensable
    necessity
Is my Lord's Compassion-flooded
    Heart.

9852.

Because your life lives
In forgotten promises,
Your heart is forced to live
In forgotten hopes.

9853.

If you compete with yourself,
God will give you the capacity
To transcend yourself.
If you compete with others,
Yours will be a blundering mind
And a suffering heart.

9854.

Cast aside half-truths
If you hope to climb up
The peace-crowned heights
Of God's Immortality-fulfilled
God-Hour.

9855.

If your heart gives birth
To sacred God-loving thoughts,
Then only will your life
No longer remain a part
Of the universal aimlessness.

9856.

In tomorrow's world
Many things will illumine
  humanity.
But the thing that will illumine
Humanity's inner and outer life
  most
Is the transcendental temple
Of universal silence.

9857.

You do not have to approach
Your own doom.
Just let your aspiration-flower
Fully blossom
Petal by petal.

9858.

Each time I see newness
In my thought-world,
I see my Lord's Fulness-Smile
Nourishing not only my
  Heaven-free soul
But also my earth-bound body.

9859.

My unlit mind derives satisfaction
From ingratitude-thorns.
My illumined mind derives
  satisfaction
From a gratitude-flower.
I become ingratitude-thorns
When I want to defeat the world.
I become a gratitude-flower
When I walk with the world
And for the world
In my Lord Supreme.

9860.

God's Vision-Eye
Loves God's Newness.
God's Reality-Heart
Loves God's Oneness.
God's Immortality-Life
Loves God's Fulness
In His earth-bound Cry,
Heaven-free Smile
And self-transcending Song.

9861.

The fount of inexhaustible
　willingness
Is discovered only inside
The seeker's heart of sleepless
　selflessness.
Selflessness in the inner world
Is God the Dreamer.
Selflessness in the outer world
Is God the Performer.

9862.

My heart's sincerity-cry
May not be appreciated
By earth's ignorance-life,
But it is fondly treasured
By Heaven's wisdom-flooded soul.

9863.

When my mind is pure,
My Lord Supreme smilingly tells
　me
That I am great.
When my heart is pure,
My Lord Supreme fondly tells me
That I am great.
When my life is pure,
My Lord Supreme smilingly,
　fondly
And proudly tells me
That I am not only great
But also perfect.

9864.

O my mind,
It is high time for me to pierce
The fog of your confusion
With my soul's supernatural
　capacity:
Its inseparable oneness
With my Lord Supreme.

9865.

The Compassion-Eye and
　Forgiveness-Heart
Of my Beloved Lord Supreme
Are identical and
　indistinguishable.

9866.

He and his heart every day run
To reach the ultimate Goal:
The complete satisfaction of God
In His own Way.
While running, they never allow
Earthly emotions to join them.

9867.

My Lord, I have glimpsed many
    times
The immensity of Your Heart's
    Concern.
Now I am eager to hear
Just a few earth-illumining
And life-fulfilling words.

9868.

The vision-eye of a saint
Plays with the beauty
Of the visible world
And with the divinity
Of the invisible world.

9869.

Try to trust the world
At every moment.
If you even secretly mistrust the
    world,
There shall come a time
When your heart may have to
    weep
A rain of sorrows.

9870.

A little of your heart's sweetness
Can easily and unmistakably kill
The bitterness of your
    frustration-vital.

9871.

I am still inside the prison cell
Of the past.
I am totally blind
In my self-styled life.
My life is nothing but
A contrary experience
To my Lord's Vision-Will.

9872.

You may not know everything,
But you do know something
Unusual and rare:
How to cheerfully commune
With your mind's melancholy
    thoughts.

9873.

His is the mind
That is now completely engulfed
By impurity-flood.
His is the heart
That is now utterly shattered
By frustration-night.
Yet he does not want
His life to be sheltered
Under the Compassion-Canopy
Of the Absolute Supreme.

9874.

If you start serving your
    newness-heart
And stop serving your
    foolishness-mind,
Then God's Oneness-Heart
Will be within your easy reach.

9875.

His heart of gratitude
For God's Compassion
And his life of surrender
To God's Will
Became the evening sunshine of
    his life.

9876.

To give pleasure to my Lord
    Supreme,
My soul and my heart
Must exert heavy pressure
On my mind of hesitation
And frustration.

9877.

True love of God
Grows in the soul,
Then glows in the heart
And finally flows through the
    body.

9878.

A man is
What he says to himself.
A man is
What he does for humanity.
A man is
What God thinks of him.

9879.

Your heart's soulful dream
And your life's powerful promise
Can bring God nearer to you
In an unprecedented way.

9880.

Alas, there is a yawning gulf
Between his soul's will
And his life's most tragic fate.

9881.

If your mind enjoys
The breathless silence
Of the Unknowable,
That means God has already kindled
The fire of deathless happiness
Inside you.

9882.

True, my Lord, I need You.
But I need Your Silence-Power more.
Why?
Because I want to silence
Envy's loud invasion of my thoughts.

9883.

My soul,
Since you and I have worked very hard,
Let us go and rest for a while.
My body,
Since you are always reluctant to work
And I cannot force you to work,
You can rest until God's Justice-Light
Descends upon you.

9884.

O my sacred and Himalayan hopes,
I am missing you more and more
Now that I have irretrievably lost
My aspiration-heart
And my dedication-life.

9885.

O my body,
Add not anything more
To your ignorance-sleep.
God's choice Hour has already struck.
If you do not respond now,
Yours will be
A shattering experience.

9886.

Let the whole world go its way.
You just go your own way.
Your way is to feel the divinity
In humanity's heart
And to see the Immortality
In Divinity's soul.

9887.

Yesterday I discovered something new:
My love-thoughts.
These love-thoughts I shall broadcast
And my outer world I shall heal
With my soul-smiles.

9888.

Where is my existence?
It is standing between
My heart's weeping tears
And my soul's enlightening smiles.

9889.

O my soul,
Let us once more try to perfectly manifest
Our Beloved Supreme here on earth.
Are we not His chosen instruments,
Him to manifest,
Triumphantly and unprecedentedly,
In His own cosmic Way?

9890.

Hope is not a momentary flicker.
Hope is Eternity's slow, steady,
Illumining and fulfilling height.

9891.

The vision of power
Is very limited
In the outer world.
The power of vision
Is always unlimited
In the inner world.

9892.

Every day
Early in the morning
And late in the evening
I sing through my heart-tears.
This is indeed the illumining result
Of my Lord's and my joint efforts.

9893.

My hope is
Heaven's cheerful descent.
My promise is
Earth's powerful ascent.

9894.

I never dare to think!
If ever I think,
I immediately drink deep
The joy of an empty hope.

9895.

Because your mind is free
From impurity-charges,
Your heart can now radiate joy
To all seekers
And even to non-seekers.

9896.

If you are powerful,
Then ask your mind to be happy.
If you are soulful,
Then ask your life to be perfect.
If you are self-giving,
Then tell God that everything you claim
To be your own
You have surrendered to His choice Hour.

9897.

If you become sidetracked
In your meditation,
You and your life will be without
The blossoming God.

9898.

Your body obeys
The law of inertia.
Your mind obeys
The law of doubt.
But your heart obeys
Only one pilot:
Your adamantine faith.

9899.

My Lord,
You know that I am praying to
   You.
"My child,
I shall not deny your prayer,
But you must develop a
   purity-mind.
This is what is delaying
My blessingful Boon."

9900.

My Lord,
I want to run with You
Sleeplessly and unconditionally,
But I cannot keep pace with You.
What can I do?
"My child,
Your very eagerness to run with
   Me
Is more than I need.
Sleeplessly think of running with
   Me;
Unconditionally meditate on
   running with Me.
Lo, sooner than at once
You and I will be easily running
Together."

9901.

My Lord Supreme,
No one but You
Will hear my heart's
   gratitude-song.
No one but You
Will watch my soul's
   surrender-dance.
No one but You
Will transform my dream-life
Into Your own Reality-Heart.

9902.

My Lord,
Give me a large heart
So that I can treasure
Your rich Smiles.
My Lord,
Give me a pure life
So that I can discover
The fountain of Your infinite
   Delight.

9903.

From tomorrow on
My morning meditation will be
The offering of my
　aspiration-plants,
My midday meditation will be
The offering of my
　dedication-fruits
And my evening meditation will
　be
The offering of my
　gratitude-heart
To You, my Beloved Supreme.

9904.

He who dreams of God
Does not have to live
In the hope-world.
His dream is the harbinger
Of fast-approaching God-Reality.

9905.

Forgive me, my Lord Supreme,
Forgive me!
I have drunk doubt-poison
Profusely and happily.
Now I want to change my drink.
I want to drink faith-nectar
Immeasurably and spontaneously.
Will You not give me another
　chance, my Lord,
Will You not?

9906.

Forgive me, my Lord Supreme,
Forgive me!
I have made friends
With tenebrous ignorance-night
Consciously and deliberately.
Now I want to change my friend.
I want to accept wisdom-light
As my new friend
Immediately and permanently.
Will You not give me another
　chance, my Lord,
Will You not?

9907.

Forgive me, my Lord Supreme,
Forgive me!
I have not loved You
Sleeplessly and unconditionally.
Will You not give me another
　chance, my Lord,
Will You not?

9908.

Forgive me, my Lord Supreme,
Forgive me!
I have not served You
Soulfully and unreservedly
Inside the hearts of the
　pilgrim-seekers
Walking along Eternity's Road.
Will You not give me another
　chance, my Lord,
Will You not?

9909.

Forgive me, my Lord Supreme,
Forgive me!
I have not spoken to the world
   about You
Confidently and convincingly.
Will You not give me another
   chance, my Lord,
Will You not?

9910.

Forgive me, my Lord Supreme,
Forgive me!
I have not manifested You here on
   earth
Concretely and satisfactorily.
Will You not give me another
   chance, my Lord,
Will You not?

9911.

Forgive me, my Lord Supreme,
Forgive me!
I have not become
What You wanted me to become
Cheerfully and gratefully.
Will You not give me another
   chance, my Lord,
Will You not?

9912.

His life's first prayer
Was to grasp the life of plenitude.
His life's last prayer
Was to become the breath of
   gratitude.

9913.

Since your heart
Has passed Eternity's
   examination,
Your life is now entitled
To receive Infinity's perfection.

9914.

God has given us the mind
To enjoy imagination-feast.
God has given us the heart
To enjoy aspiration-feast.
God has given us life
To enjoy realisation-feast.
God has given us His very
   Existence
To become His universal
   Satisfaction-Song.

9915.

Do not be afraid of your
   desire-life.
Just ask your aspiration-fire
To melt all your desires.
Your aspiration-fire embodies
God the infinite Power.

9916.

My vast thought-world
Is for my Lord Supreme to read.
My tiny aspiration-room
Is for my Lord Supreme to live in.

9917.

What thrills my mind?
Sincerity's song.
What thrills my heart?
Purity's dance.
What thrills my life?
Divinity's embrace.

9918.

In my heart's world
Of light and delight,
My hesitation-frustration-mind
Is an utterly helpless
And useless stranger.

9919.

My body unconsciously protested
When I asked it to be wakeful.
My vital vehemently protested
When I asked it to be peaceful.
My mind cleverly protested
When I asked it to be soulful.
My heart cheerfully agreed
When I asked it to be helpful
To friends and foes alike.

9920.

I challenged yesterday's problems
With my determination-power.
I am challenging today's problems
With my aspiration-cry.
I shall challenge tomorrow's
   problems
With my surrender-smile
To my Lord Supreme.

9921.

Every mind has its greatness.
Every heart has its goodness.
Every life has its fruitfulness.
Yet every human being is dying
Of a beggar's hunger.

9922.

As God is ready to wait
For His Satisfaction,
Even so, you can wait
For your perfection.

9923.

You say you do not have faith
In anything.
Do you not see
That you have tremendous faith
In your own doubt?

9924.

A heart of gratitude
Is the next-to-last step
Before we reach Heaven.
A life of surrender
Is the very last step
Before we reach Heaven.

9925.

How can you succeed in your
    outer life
When you do not have
The power of concentration?
How can you proceed in your
    inner life
When you do not have
The peace of meditation?

9926.

Nothing is as imperfect and cheap
As my mind's outer smile.
Nothing is as perfect and precious
As my heart's inner cry.

9927.

I believe in a big and real God:
My Beloved Supreme.
I do not believe in a small and
    false god:
My doubting mind.

9928.

"God, give me!"
This is a wrong prayer.
"God, take me!"
This is a right prayer.

9929.

My Lord,
My heart knows
That You have been waiting for
    me
For Eternity.
Do give me a new heart, my Lord,
So that I, too, can wait for You
Eternally.

9930.

The past controls the present:
This is a human experience.
The past surrenders to the present:
This is a divine experience.
The past is transformed
And made into a perfect instrument
For the Supreme to use in His own Way:
This is a supreme experience.

9931.

Humanity's three earth-bound houses:
Passion, possession and frustration.
Divinity's three Heaven-free homes:
Illumination, perfection and satisfaction.

9932.

Each time I cry,
I purify my heart.
Each time I smile,
I simplify my life.

9933.

An invisible ascent:
My heart of ecstatic silence.
A visible descent:
My life of bombastic sound.

9934.

There was a time when I fed my mind
With unbelievable fantasies,
But now I feed my heart
With immeasurable ecstasies.

9935.

I am sad that my mind is incapable
Of silence-light.
I am glad that my heart is incapable
Of indifference-night.

9936.

My life may not know
What God's Compassion is,
But my heart does know
What God's Forgiveness is.

9937.

My soul came down
From the Himalayan heights
To see the Protection-Feet
Of my Lord Supreme.
My life shall climb up
To the Himalayan heights
To see the Compassion-Eye
Of my Beloved Supreme.

9938.

My mind is brave.
Therefore, it dares to imagine
The Beauty of God's Infinity.
My heart is pure.
Therefore, it hopes to embody
The Love of God's Immortality.

9939.

My destiny laughs at me
When I tell the world
That I can become.
My destiny touches my feet
When I tell my Lord Supreme
That I am.

9940.

My heart uses its aspiration-cry
To see the Face of God.
My mind uses its
   inspiration-smile
To feel the heart of man.

9941.

A nobility-mind is ready
To wait for the world.
A magnanimity-heart is ready
To die for the world.

9942.

A divine hero-warrior
Does not accept any defeat,
Not because he is proud
But because his Inner Pilot
Has time and again told him
That he is His choice instrument
And that His Vision-Eye will
   succeed
In him
And His Satisfaction-Heart will
   proceed
Along with him.

9943.

My mind calls it
An accident.
My heart calls it
An experience.
My soul calls it
A life-transforming Touch of God.
My Beloved Supreme calls it
His inner Involution
And His outer Revelation.

9944.

Your heart-tears
Have transformed your life.
Your heart-tears
Have satisfied God.
Your heart-tears
Have illumined mankind.
Your heart-tears
Can answer all the past, present
And future questions of the world.

9945.

At last
He is healed of his self-doubt.
Now what is happening?
He is awakening
To his soul's ecstasy-sun.

9946.

Each aspiration-cry
Is a rising flame.
Each desire-smile
Is a sinking boat.

9947.

Determination-fire:
This is what my mind
Precisely needs.
Illumination-sun:
This is what my heart
Soulfully needs.
Satisfaction-God:
This is what my life
Sleeplessly needs.

9948.

To acquire innocence-joy,
What I need most in my outer life
Is a God-searching mind,
And what I need most in my inner life
Is a life-surrendering heart.

9949.

Two frightening shadows
Are chasing me:
One says
My heart does not love God;
The other says
God does not need my life.

9950.

How little do I know
Of my repeated failures
In the inner life.
But I do know
Of my major failure
In the outer life:
I have completely surrendered
To temptation-spear.

9951.

Hearken only to Time Eternal!
Your questioning mind is the dance
Of a very weak and flickering flame-light.

9952.

O my mind,
I do not want you to enjoy
Either the flight
Of fleeting thoughts
Or the train
Of unending doubts.

9953.

In my outer life
I have already wasted
And I may continue to waste
Many precious things,
But in my inner life
I shall never waste
The most precious thing:
My life-surrendering heart-tears.

9954.

My soul was born to teach.
My heart was born to learn.
My mind was born to unlearn.
My life was born to smile inwardly
And cry outwardly.

9955.

One foot is on earth
And one foot is in Heaven.
Therefore, he is equally
Heaven's powerful eye
And
Earth's tearful heart.

9956.

O my heart, look upward!
God and His Satisfaction-Eye
Are waiting for you.
O my mind, dive inward!
God and His Forgiveness-Feet
Are waiting for you.

9957.

My heart's unspoken
And breathless sorrows
Are my life's hallowed
And endless joys.

9958.

God the Lover sleeplessly cries
With earth's cries.
God the Beloved unconditionally
   smiles
With Heaven's smiles.

9959.

I have a deep desire
To teach my restless mind
How to rest.
I have also a deep desire
To be taught by my aspiring heart
How to cry.

9960.

I have seen many things:
God's Compassion-Eye,
God's Forgiveness-Heart,
God's Protection-Feet.
I have been many things:
A life that enjoys ignorance,
A heart that enjoys ingratitude,
A mind that enjoys suspicion.

9961.

My mind admires God
Because He is powerful.
My heart loves God
Because He is beautiful.
My life needs God
Because He is merciful.
My soul reveals God
Because He is fruitful.

9962.

O my clever mind,
You want me to succeed
With my stubborn opinion.
O my wise heart,
You want me to proceed
With my surrendered dedication.

9963.

If you want to hold the banners
Of both the East and the West,
First give to the East
Your heart of aspiration-love,
And then give to the West
Your life of dedication-smile.

9964.

When I look into the mist
Of my past years,
My life of failure sees nothing but
A silver flow of orphan-tears.

9965.

His aspiration-heart is as real
As a supreme Dream of the
    Absolute.
His desire-life is as false
As a failure-experience of the soul,
God's representative on earth.

9966.

There was a time
When you walked with God,
But now you cannot even see Him
    walking.
Why?
Because your watching eyes
Deliberately wanted
To swim in the forgetfulness-sea.

9967.

Am I God's adopted child,
That I have to worry?
Am I not entitled to
God's spontaneous Affection,
Sleepless Love
And unconditional Fondness?

9968.

My life's soulfulness-beauty
Sees God.
My heart's openness-purity
Receives God.

9969.

The agreement between the
    natural
And the supernatural is this:
The natural will always remain
The root of the reality-tree,
And the supernatural will be
Its topmost branch.

9970.

Prepare yourself for self-mastery,
Since God has already prepared
    you
For self-discovery.

9971.

In the morning
My heart cries through my eyes.
In the evening
My life smiles through my soul.

9972.

My ever-increasing
    gratitude-heart
And ever-transcending
    surrender-life
Are invited to dine in the banquet
    hall
Of God's Eternity.

9973.

My inner voice
Is my beauty's flower.
My higher choice
Is my duty's fruit.
My inner voice likes to sing
My Lord's Perfection-Song.
My higher choice likes to dance
My Lord's Satisfaction-Dance.

9974.

I am my mind's
Depression-weight.
My Lord is His Heart's
Compassion-Scale.

9975.

Your life has become a doubt-wave
In a confusion-sea,
Yet you always think
That you are definitely worthy
Of God's arrival.

9976.

The mind tries to imitate
The purity-heart
In a distorted way.
The heart tries to imitate
The divinity-soul
In a self-giving way.

9977.

My Inner Pilot asks me
From this very moment
Not to look even once more
At the ugliness of my doubting
    mind.

9978.

My heart suffers more
From my mind
Than I suffer
From my vital.

9979.

As it is impossible
For me to please God
Without my ever-mounting
    faith-flames,
Even so, it is impossible
For God to please me
Without His ever-increasing
    Compassion-Flood.

9980.

Your heart's oneness-delight
Can alone try to perfect
The world's
    division-dissatisfaction-life.

9981.

His heart's aspiration-mountain
And his life's
   determination-volcano
Have formed a new haven
For earth's ceaseless cries
And endless failures.

9982.

I thank myself
Because I love God.
God thanks Himself
Because in me He has found
His long-lost Victory-Trumpet.

9983.

The landscape listens
To your heart's soulful dictates.
Do you know why?
Because you have already
   appreciated
Its beauty's life
In God's Vision-Light
And its purity's heart
In God's Reality-Delight.

9984.

Every day ride the purity-bicycle
Inside your heart.
If you do not do so daily,
You will not be able to proceed.
Not only that,
You will fall down, I must say,
Very badly.

9985.

Even God's Heart of Compassion
Immediately changed when I told
   Him
That I do not need
   aspiration-hunger
To appreciate His
   Perfection-Satisfaction-Meal.

9986.

Your mind may have
A scarcity of ideas.
Your life may have
A scarcity of ideals.
But your heart can never have
A scarcity of self-transcending
   goals.

9987.

I do not imitate others
To become their friend.
I just love their Source,
God's Oneness-Love.

9988.

Yesterday
My life passed safely.
Today
My heart is crying soulfully.
Tomorrow
My mind shall behave perfectly.

9989.

Your life-boat
Shall not remain unlaunched
Any longer,
For God's Breath
Has finally been able
To touch your sleeping heart.

9990.

Your oneness-heart is happy
Because it lives inseparably
With the entire world.
Your division-mind wants to be
   happy
Without enjoying the
   peace-beauty
Of the inner world.

9991.

My Lord Supreme,
I am tired of constantly colliding
With my lower self.
Do become my only
   Protector-Transformer.

9992.

I do not have to see
Any miracle,
For I myself have become
A living miracle.
Do you know how?
Just by taming
My explosive energy.

9993.

O my mind,
There is no such thing
As instructive doubt.
O my heart,
There is no such thing
As constructive fear.

9994.

Never fear your own
   confusion-mind.
Just challenge it vehemently!
It is high time for you
To become fully acquainted
With your own true self:
Tomorrow's God.

9995.

Since you do not invite faith
Into your heart-room,
How can you expect to chase
The doubt-wolf from your life?

9996.

You think that God has to use
His infinite Power
To silence your mind.
But I tell you,
To silence your mind,
He needs to use only
His sweet Heart-Smile.

9997.

Because he did not want
His insecurity-heart any more,
He started praying
To God the Infinite Power.
Because he did not want
His impurity-mind any more,
He started meditating
On God the Immortal Love.

9998.

What enables us to see God?
Definitely not our
    capacity-strength,
But our heart's gratitude-length.

9999.

When my mind believes in
God's Closeness,
My heart immediately feels
God's Fondness
And my life sleeplessly feels
God's Oneness.
God's Closeness surprises
The human in me,
God's Fondness immortalises
The divine in me
And God's Oneness fulfils at once
The divine lover
And
The Supreme Beloved in me.
The divine lover in me
Is he who knows;
The Supreme Beloved in me
Is He who is.

10000.

O my sound-life!
I love you
Because you are
Powerful.
O my silence-life!
I need you
Because you are
Beautiful.
O my Beloved Supreme!
I at once love You
And need You
Because
Your Eye is my
Dream-Boat,
Your Life is my
Silver Journey
And Your Heart is my
Golden Shore.
O my Beloved Supreme Absolute!
In me is Your Eternity's
   Transcendental Cry,
For me is Your Infinity's Immortal
   Smile.

PART II

207 FLOWER-FLAMES

Author's preface to 207 Flower-Flames

I have selected 207 poems out of 10,000 from my series, *Ten thousand Flower-Flames,* which was originally published in 100 volumes. Here the poet in me is soulfully satisfied, the reader in me is smilingly satisfied and the critic in me is surprisingly satisfied.

My Beloved Supreme, what more can I tell You, and what more do You expect from me?

"Be quiet, My poet-reader-critic-son. The Hour, My Hour, is about to strike."

— Sri Chinmoy

1.

My Lord,
I came to You with empty hands,
But You have discovered
My empty heart, too.

2.

I came from God
The Eternal Dreamer.
I am heading towards God
The Immortal Lover.

3.

Of all the gifts
I have offered to God,
My happiness-gift
He treasures most.

4.

The mind wants to invent
A new God.
The heart wants to discover
The ancient and eternal God.

5.

My Lord,
Please warn me before You come.
Otherwise, You may come
   unrecognised
And go back unloved.

6.

My mind says to my heart:
"Will you please praise God for
 me?"
My heart says to my mind:
"Will you please pray to God
To bless me?"

7.

What is the fare
From earth to Heaven?
The fragrance-beauty
Of a gratitude-heart.

8.

Every time I run away from You
And come back,
I see Your Eyes
More illumining than before,
And I feel Your Heart
More forgiving than before.

9.

My Lord, I am happy
Because You are the Lord of my
 life.
Can You not make me perfect
By becoming the Lord of my
 thoughts?

10.

The miracle of my sound-life:
It can chase God.
The miracle of my silence-life:
It can embrace God.

11.

Two
Are my secret wishes:
I shall show God
Man's transformation-head.
I shall show man
God's Compassion-Feet.

12.

Not beyond man's possibility
Is God-realisation.
Not beyond earth's possibility
Is earth-transformation.
Not beyond my possibility
Is self-transcendence.

13.

I do not interfere in God's Affairs.
Every day I let Him
Create a new world.
God does not interfere in my
 affairs
Either.
Every day He lets me
Destroy an old world.

14.

Your old prayer may not change
   God.
But God can grant you
A new prayer,
And this new prayer
Will make you really happy.
What is your new prayer?
God-Satisfaction
In God's own Way.

15.

To frighten the animal in me
My God is all Justice.
To enlighten the human in me
My God is all Compassion.

16.

Yesterday
I desired to be
God's Lion-Power.
Today
I desire to be
God's Deer-Speed.
Tomorrow I shall desire to be
God's Lamb-Fondness.

17.

God wanted you
To go to Him untouched.
But what you did,
You know!
You went to God unchanged!

18.

Are You, O Lord,
Tired of being good?
It seems You are.
Are You, O Lord,
Tired of being divine?
It seems You are.
Are You, O Lord,
Tired of being perfect?
It seems You are.
O my Lord Supreme,
Then do bless me
With Your Goodness-Heart,
Divinity-Life and Perfection-Role.

19.

God watched me from the sky
With His unchanging
   Compassion.
I watched God from the ground
With my increasing hesitation.

20.

Scold me, my Lord, untiringly.
Insult me, my Lord, unreservedly.
But, my Lord, do not forget Your
　　Boon.
You told me millions of years ago
That You would grant me the
　　capacity
To love You sleeplessly.
Something more,
　　unconditionally.

21.

An unfinished Dream of God
Brought me down.
The God-Hour then struck.
An unending Reality of God
Will take me up.
The God-Hour will once again
　　strike.

22.

Even my shadow avoids me.
Even my body dislikes me.
Even my life disappoints me.
Even my God forgets me.

23.

A heart of gratitude
Is the next-to-last step
Before we reach Heaven.
A life of surrender
Is the very last step
Before we reach Heaven.

24.

Mistaking earth for Heaven,
He sighed.
Mistaking Heaven for earth,
He died.

25.

Can this be true?
No desire binds me,
No temptation haunts me,
No imperfection blights me.
Can this be true?

26.

Don't take a late start.
You may lose the race altogether.
Keep your
　　love-devotion-surrender
Always on the alert.
Then you cannot have a late start.

27.

O descending Blue,
I love you.
O ascending Green,
I love you.
O spreading Gold,
I love you.

28.

Aspiration tells me
That my God is
Compassion-Mother.
Realisation tells me
That my God is
Liberation-Father.
Manifestation tells me
That my God is
Perfection-Friend.

29.

God alone knows
When the Kingdom of Heaven
Will finally descend on earth.
In the meantime,
God is begging His aspiring
  children
To try to create
At least a tiny island
Which He can call Heaven on
  earth.

30.

What has God given me?
A beautiful heart.
What shall I give Him?
A soulful face.

31.

The twentieth century
Is flooded
With self-styled Master-rogues.
The twentieth century
Is flooded
With monster disciple-fools.

32.

A thinking mind
Is a sinking life.
A sinking life
Is a dying promise.
A dying promise
Is a weeping God.

33.

An interesting question:
Where is God?
An inspiring question:
What is God doing?
An illumining question:
Who is God?
A fulfilling question:
Who else's love do I need,
If not God's alone?

34.

My Lord Supreme,
Whether You like it or not,
I shall come to You daily.
Whether You like it or not,
I shall tease You smilingly.
Whether You like it or not,
I shall place You on my shoulders
    surprisingly.

35.

A good place to begin:
My soul's soulful nest.
A good place to continue:
My heart's psychic core.
A good place to transform:
My mind's mental factory.

36.

Indeed,
Science is man's
Breath-taking advance.
Indeed,
Spirituality is God's
Breath-immortalising romance.

37.

Music is entertainment.
Music is enlightenment.
Music is the animal bark
Of man.
Music is the God-Song
And God-Dance for man.

38.

Doubt-elevator never works.
Fear-elevator seldom works.
Confidence-elevator occasionally
    works.
Aspiration-elevator sleeplessly
    works.

39.

My Lord Supreme,
You rang my alarm clock.
How could this be true?
You prayed for my salvation.
How could this be true?
You concentrated on my
    illumination.
How could this be true?
You meditated for my realisation.
How could this be true?
You contemplated on my
    perfection.
How could this be true?
You lived for my satisfaction.
How could this be true?

40.

Heaven, pray for me, please!
I need the dream
Of oneness-perfection.
Earth, pray for me, please!
I need the reality
Of fulness-satisfaction.

41.

My Lord told me a supreme secret:
"My child, I shall never scold you
   any more."
I told my Lord a supreme secret:
"My Father-Friend, I shall never
Disappoint You any more."

42.

God is my outer Coach.
Therefore, I smile and smile
After I succeed.
God is my inner Coach.
Therefore, I dance and dance
Before I proceed.

43.

I have two serious faults:
I underestimate
God's Compassion-Beauty.
I overestimate
Man's ingratitude-reality.

44.

I entertain God
With my promise-power.
God entertains me
With His Compassion-shower.

45.

I chose not to understand God.
I chose not to understand even
   man.
But alas,
I chose to understand my clever
   mind.

46.

Yesterday's God
Belonged to my confidence.
Today's God
Belongs to my promise.
Tomorrow's God
Shall belong to my hope.

47.

God gave me
By way of joke
A little mind.
I am giving God
In dead earnest
A big problem:
My useless life.

48.

My sweet Supreme Lord,
You have helped me
By speaking to me.
Let me help You
By listening to You.

49.

Yesterday
I quickly chose God's Power
To fulfil me.
Today
I am quietly choosing God's Light
To illumine me.

50.

My prayer-wings
Carry me up to Heaven
To see God's Beauty.
My meditation-wings
Carry God down to earth
To see my heart's purity.

51.

God's Forgiveness finds me
No matter where I am.
God's Compassion takes me
Where I ought to go.

52.

I think of God
Because
I need God's Power.
God thinks of me
Because
He needs my love.

53.

I appeared before God
With what I have:
An iota of gratitude.
God appeared before me
With what He is:
Infinity's Satisfaction-Smile.

54.

Precisely because
God loves me infinitely more
Than I love myself,
God cannot afford to be
As careless with my life
As I am.

55.

When I pray
To the false God,
My praying is not enough.
I have to run towards him.
When I pray
To the real God,
He immediately runs towards me.

56.

The old God
Taught me how to fight
Against ignorance-night.
The new God
Is teaching me how to surrender
To His Vision-Light.

57.

God's Greatness and Goodness
Puzzle me.
My weakness and meanness
Puzzle God.

58.

I am not needed
To say the right thing.
I am only required
To be the right thing.

59.

Each heart is the beauty
Of a God-dreamer.
Each life is the delight
Of a God-lover.

60.

Each listening heart
Is not a bud of infancy.
Each listening heart
Is a flower of God-Ecstasy.

61.

Do not waste time.
Time is precious.
Do not exploit God.
God is gracious.
Do not mix with ignorance.
Ignorance is ferocious.
Do not play with doubt.
Doubt is injurious.
Do not cherish insecurity.
Insecurity is infectious.
Do not harbour impurity.
Impurity is dangerous.

62.

If I can see God's Face
Even once,
I am sure He will make
Some room for me
To stay in His Heart
As long as I want to.

63.

Self-imprisonment begins
The day we start playing
With expectation-snare,
And not before.

64.

My heart represents
God the Duty
On earth.
My soul represents
God the Beauty
In Heaven.

65.

Peace needs no interpretation.
Love needs no explanation.
Oneness needs no expression.

66.

Three ultimate absurdities:
I shall fail my Lord.
I am not meant for
   God-realisation.
My Lord is not pleased with me.

67.

God's troubles are these:
The animal in man
Has forgotten Him totally.
The divine in man
Is not manifesting Him
   satisfactorily.

68.

You are mistaken.
God does think of you constantly.
I am mistaken.
God does love us both equally.

69.

Unless I become a sleepless
   dreamer
Of God-dreams,
My heart shall remain a fount
Of orphan-tears.

70.

True,
I do not know
Who I am,
But I do know
Whose I am.

71.

Only two miracles are worth
  seeing:
The miracle of loving
And
The miracle of forgiving.

72.

Darkness knows how to thicken.
Light knows how to brighten.
Earth knows how to bind
The divine in man.
Heaven knows how to liberate
The human from the animal.

73.

Centuries have rolled away,
And still the outer man does not
  know
Where the inner man
Unmistakably is,
And the inner man does not know
What the outer man
Actually wants.

74.

The difference
Between a God-dreamer
And a God-lover
Is this:
A God-dreamer wants to live
In God's birthless and deathless
  Infinity;
A God-lover longs to live
In God's Heart-Cave.

75.

No way
To persuade God.
No way
To deceive God.
But many ways
Not only to realise God
But also to become God.

76.

When I pray,
I pray for the right thing:
Peace.
When I meditate,
I meditate on the right Person:
God.

77.

My heart's constant guest:
God the Many.
My life's constant host:
God the One.

78.

Yesterday
I measured my success
By competing with others.
Today
I measure my success
By competing with myself.
Tomorrow
I shall measure my success
By expanding my heart
To encompass others.

79.

The soulful meditation-line to
　　Heaven
Is never busy
Because
Very few seekers have the capacity
To use that line.
The wild frustration-line to
　　Heaven
Is always busy
Because
Everybody has the capacity
To use that line.

80.

Hope has no real intention
Of deceiving us.
Alas, it has no adequate capacity
To please us.

81.

You are accepted
By Truth.
That means you are liberated
By God.

82.

Two things I must never forget:
My meditation-appointment with
　　God
In the small hours of the morning,
And God's
　　Satisfaction-appointment with
　　me
In the late hours of the night.

83.

Do not blame yourself.
This world will do it for you,
Far beyond your imagination.
Do not admire yourself.
The higher worlds will do it for
　　you,
Far beyond your expectation.

84.

His life's early morning
Saw God's Forgiveness-Feet.
His life's late evening
Shall see God's Compassion-Eye.

85.

You are bound to know
God's Will
If you allow God
To become real to you.

86.

Three Himalayan prayers:
Lord, do give me the capacity
To love Your Forgiveness-Feet
Unreservedly.
Lord, do give me the capacity
To love Your Compassion-Heart
Untiringly.
Lord, do give me the capacity
To love Your Justice-Eye
Unconditionally.

87.

Only a fool
Thinks that he is independent.
Only a fool
Feels that he is indispensable.

88.

Sweet is my Lord
Because He is knowable.
Sweeter is my Lord
Because He is known.
Sweetest is my Lord
Because He invites me
To play hide-and-seek with Him
Every day.

89.

Be aware!
God definitely exists.
Be awake!
God will come and knock
At your door.

90.

If it is true
That Jesus is coming again,
Then it is also true
That you and I should go to meet
  Him
And welcome Him
At the halfway point.

91.

Because I fear God,
I do not have to fear any man.
Because I love God,
I have to love all human beings.

92.

God loves me.
I mean,
My sincere cry.
God wants me.
I mean,
My simple life.
God needs me.
I mean,
My pure heart.

93.

O my Supreme Lord,
I have only one desire:
Do give me the thing
That pleases me for a fleeting day.
O my Supreme Lord,
I have only one aspiration:
Do give me the thing
That pleases You forever and
   forever.

94.

Because of his shallow mind
He is an unfinished man.
Because of his vast heart
He is in unextinguished pain.

95.

I have lost You, My Lord,
Not because my intimate friend
Is tenebrous ignorance-night,
But because I have never dared to
   claim You
As my own, very own.

96.

Attention—
My body needs attention.
Encouragement—
My vital needs encouragement.
Inspiration—
My mind needs inspiration.
Aspiration—
My heart needs aspiration.
Guidance—
My life needs guidance.

97.

You do not have to prove
God's Love for you.
Just feel that you live
Only for God's Love.

98.

God compassionately asks me,
"Will you be available?"
He never asks me,
"Will you be able?"

99.

I have only one inner teacher:
A gratitude-flame.
I have only one outer teacher:
A surrender drop.

100.

Everybody can begin,
But only the chosen
Can divinely continue
And supremely succeed.

101.

If you do not have
A sense of humour,
Then God will not choose you
To be in His close company.

102.

What my mind wants
Is a strong armour of proof.
What my heart needs
Is a sweet ripple of belief.

103.

Greatness is a matter
Of a moment.
Goodness is the work
Of a lifetime.
Oneness is the return-journey
Of birth and death.

104.

As a dreamer,
You are loved by God
Constantly.
As a Lover,
God is loved by you
Unconditionally.

105.

I have only one idol,
And that idol is my crying heart.
I have only one hero,
And that hero is my smiling soul.

106.

Something new happened
This morning:
I came to realise
That God still loves me.
Something new happened
This evening:
God gave me His Heart
And took away my mind
In exchange.

107.

Philosophy embodies
God-information.
Religion embodies
God-aspiration.
Spirituality embodies
God-Satisfaction.

108.

In the morning
My mind tells me:
"Young man,
You are supremely useful."
In the evening
My mind tells me:
"Old man,
You are absolutely useless."

109.

My Lord,
Do take my mind
Out of the tempest.
"My child,
Let Me first take the tempest
Out of your mind."

110.

Do not descend from Heaven
After me.
My heart will feel miserable.
Do not descend from Heaven
Before me.
Your soul will not appreciate it.
God has two supreme Realities:
Togetherness-life
And
Oneness-heart.

111.

In the morning
My search for realisation ends
Inside my Lord's
   Compassion-Heart.
At noon
My search for perfection ends
Inside my Lord's Vision-Eye.
In the evening
My search for satisfaction ends
At my Lord's Beauty-Feet.

112.

Yesterday I was clever.
That is why
I wanted to change the world.
Today I am wise.
That is why
I am changing myself.

113.

Self-observation is the beginning
Of self-perfection.
Self-perfection is the beginning
Of God-Satisfaction.
God-Satisfaction is the beginning
Of God's new Dream.

114.

One thing you must know:
A "no" from your heart
Is infinitely stronger
Than all the hostile forces in the world.

115.

God gave me something special:
Awareness.
I gave God something special:
Willingness.
Now God wants to give me
His Satisfaction
And I want to give God
My gratitude.

116.

My Lord, do You love me
Even when I kill time?
"Yes, My child, I love you."
My Lord, is there any time
When You do not love me?
"Yes, My child, there is a time
When I do not love you."
When, my Lord, when?
"When you think that you are not
A budding God."

117.

Self-mastery and God-discovery
Are the only two things
That each human being on earth
Must take seriously.
Everything else can be taken lightly.

118.

My body,
I have been helping you
For such a long time.
Nevertheless, you are an idler.
My vital,
I have been helping you
For such a long time.
Nevertheless, you are an aggressor.
My mind,
I have been helping you
For such a long time.
Nevertheless, you are a doubter.
My heart,
I have been helping you
Since this morning.
I clearly see that you are a born lover.
My soul,
I have just started serving you.
To my extreme joy I find
That you are the supreme fulfiller.

119.

Every day, before your mind tells you
That it has something special
To give to the world,
Let your heart tell you
That it has something special
To receive from Heaven.

120.

Remember, O my mind,
You have three alternatives:
You can either go
From darkness to light
Or from light to darkness,
Or you can remain where you are:
In your self-created unawareness.

121.

God has the sincerity
To tell me
That He loves me.
Alas, I do not have the sincerity
To tell Him
That I badly need His Love.

122.

My Lord Supreme,
Do grant me a boon:
Before I reach You,
Do allow my gratitude-heart
To precede me.

123.

I affirm what God affirms.
What does God affirm?
He affirms that God-realisation
Is my birthright.
I negate what God negates.
What does God negate?
He negates that I am a member
Of ignorance-society.

124.

Silence
Your endless earth-necessity
Secretly.
Fulfil
Your breathless Heaven-necessity
Immediately.

125.

The difference between
Man and God is this:
Man unknowingly
Crawls towards God;
God compassionately
Runs towards man.
Man thinks that he has God;
God knows that man is God.

126.

I sleeplessly bow to the Light
That never dims.
I breathlessly bow to the Delight
That never fades.

127.

My Beloved Supreme is searching
For my willingness
And not for my capacity.
My Beloved Supreme is searching
For my readiness
And not for my perfection.

128.

Remember what you said to God:
"My Lord, I shall always
Fulfil You unconditionally."
Remember what you said to man:
"My friend, I shall always
Help you unreservedly."

129.

You want to know why you are lonely?
You are lonely because
You never want to hear
Your heart's oneness-song.

130.

The Scriptures teach me
How to love the Saviour.
The Saviour teaches me
How to love the Real in me,
The future God.

131.

I love
Both God the young
And God the old.
From God the young I learn
How to run, jump, fly and dive.
From God the old I learn
How to cry and smile
And how to smile and cry.

132.

When you pray,
You come to realise
That you have a room high above.
When you meditate,
You come to realise
That you have a home deep inside.

133.

In the beginning
An unconditional life
Is a battlefield.
But eventually
An unconditional life
Becomes a playground.

134.

If you have a true and sleepless
Love of God,
Then nobody will be able to
    snatch you away
From the Embrace of God.

135.

A God-seeker thinks
That he can be free.
A God-server feels
That he will be free.
A God-lover knows
That he is free.

136.

I shall forgive and I shall forget.
I shall forgive my past
    unwillingness
To meditate on God.
I shall totally forget
My very, very old friend:
Ignorance.

137.

Do you not remember
That only the other day
You loved God unconditionally?
Do you not remember
That only the other day
You claimed God as your own,
    very own?

138.

Every day my mind turns
Towards the miracle-working
    God.
Every day my heart turns
Towards the life-illumining God.

139.

My Lord,
I shall obey You unconditionally
Provided You tell me
That I am Your best student.
"My child,
I shall tell the world
You are My best student
Provided I am your only Teacher
And you completely give up your
    other teacher:
Ignorance."

140.

I went up
To see God's beautiful Feet.
God came down
To give me His bountiful Heart.

141.

Do You love me, my Lord,
No matter what I say
And no matter what I do against
    You?
"Tell Me first, My son,
Do you need Me
No matter how strict I am with
    you?"

142.

When I use what I have:
A commitment-lamp,
God gives me what He has:
His Contentment-Sun.

143.

The difference
Between my mind and my heart
Is this:
My mind wants to play with God.
My heart longs to work for God.

144.

This is my day;
I love it.
This is my morning God-Hour;
I need it.
This is my supreme moment;
I am it.

145.

Two persons love me:
Satan and God.
Satan loves me
So that he can use me
As his faithful slave.
God loves me
So that He can have me
As His cheerful friend.

146.

My ancient heart tells me
That God is beautiful plus
　powerful.
My modern mind tells me
That God is either unmindful or
　doubtful.

147.

To be closer to God,
Be a better cry
And
Have a better smile.

148.

There is neither a visible
Nor an invisible partition
Between self-giving
And God-becoming.

149.

Be not afraid!
Take the first step.
Go and see God personally.
His Omnipotence will prove to
　you
That it is also His universal Love.

150.

You love God
Because He is supreme.
God loves you
Because you are His powerful
　Dream.
You need God
Because He is eternally perfect.
God needs you
Because you are His choice Project.

151.

Before I call,
God's Compassion-Eye answers.
Before I start,
God's Compassion-Heart
Finishes the race for me.

152.

True, I do not have the capacity
To touch God's Compassion-Feet,
But I do have the capacity
To feel God's Forgiveness-Heart.

153.

Do not say anything
To a self-worshipper,
For God knows how and why
He is stabbing his own heart.

154.

O my heart,
Do not die unsung.
O my mind,
Do not die unsettled.
O my vital,
Do not die unchallenged.
O my body,
Do not die untransformed.

155.

When he realised God for himself,
God said to him,
"My son, I may use you
In the distant future."
When he realised God for others,
God said to him,
"My son, I shall use you
In the near future."
When he realised God for God,
God said to him,
"My son, I am using you
And I shall use you
Sleeplessly and eternally."

156.

A soulful smile
Can kindle the universe.
A breathless cry
Can feed the universe.

157.

Do not ask for too little.
When you do that,
God's Heart of Magnanimity
Is tearfully embarrassed.

158.

God has asked a very simple
    question:
Do you want to be like Him?
He is eagerly waiting
For your open-hearted answer.

159.

My Lord Supreme,
Out of His infinite Bounty,
Tells me that His Weight is at once
As light as my heart's
    aspiration-cry
And as heavy as my life's
    ingratitude-frown.

160.

You want to see God's Face
To satisfy yourself.
God wants to embrace your heart
To satisfy Himself.

161.

Each time I compromise
With ignorance-night,
I kill the beauty and purity
Of my climbing heart-plant.

162.

God has openly fed you
With His Compassion-Sea.
Will you not even secretly feed
    Him
With your heart's
    gratitude-drops?

163.

Man's ancient roots:
His cries and smiles.
Man's modern fruits:
His laughter and sighs.

164.

You have a multitude of
    questions,
But there is only one answer:
The road is right in front of you,
And the guide is waiting for you.

165.

Do not speak ill of yourself.
The world around you
Will always gladly do that
On your behalf.

166.

An outer smile carries
Today's earthly dawn to Heaven.
An inner smile carries
Tomorrow's Heavenly sun to earth.

167.

Never forget one thing:
The Ultimate Truth is your friend
And not your enemy.

168.

I was totally mistaken
When I thought I loved God
Unconditionally.
I was completely mistaken
When I thought God did not need me
At all.

169.

Every day there is only
One thing to learn:
How to be honestly happy.

170.

Two unnecessary questions:
Does God love me?
Do I need God?

171.

God does not want to know
Why I cry,
But He does want to know
Why I do not smile.

172.

What is success?
My expansion-hunger.
What is progress?
My perfection-feast.

173.

The great contribution
Of the human life:
Mind over matter.
The supreme contribution
Of the divine life:
Heart over mind.

174.

There are only two superior ways
To realise God:
My life's surrender-way
And my heart's gratitude-way.

175.

Satisfaction-lion
Will have to postpone its
  momentous visit
Because aspiration-deer
Has not yet started its journey.

176.

I shall see
What I can do for God
Since I am not doing
Anything worthwhile for man.

177.

Since each thought
Is an atomic power,
You can give each thought
A diplomatic death.

178.

Two ancient universal questions:
How can I realise God
Immediately?
Is unconditional surrender
Ever possible?

179.

At last my heart
Has challenged my mind,
Not to defeat it
But to transform it.

180.

God may not be always available,
But God's Compassion-Sea
And Forgiveness-Sky
Are always available.

181.

Two disasters he has inherited
From his many ignorance-lives:
A doubting mind
And
An unaspiring heart.

182.

What I need is
A God-climbing heart
And not
A God-manufacturing mind.

183.

There are only two reality-lovers:
One is God
The Immortal Singer;
The other is God
The Eternal Listener.

184.

Although God is infinite,
He prefers to live
Inside man's tiny heart-nest.

185.

God asks me to give Him
The things that I myself
Do not at all care for:
My imperfections.

186.

Man has his Eternity's
Infinite questions.
God has His Immortality's
Only answer:
Oneness-embrace.

187.

True, God has not given me
Everything,
But He has given me
Two firm convictions:
He loves me
No matter what I do;
I shall need Him
No matter what I become.

188.

Sincerity
Changed my past
Slowly and steadily.
Determination
Is changing my present
Powerfully and convincingly.
Faith
Will change my future
Amazingly and permanently.

189.

God does not laugh at our prayers,
No matter how insincere they are.
But God does laugh when we
   think and feel
That our prayers will never be
   answered.

190.

My dubious prayer-life
May not satisfy God,
But my glowing surrender-heart
Will always satisfy God.

191.

The sons of morning sang
And reminded me of God the
    Power.
The daughters of evening sang
And reminded me of God the
    Peace.

192.

God loves us
Even after we have failed Him.
We need God
Even after we have realised Him.

193.

I came from God
To learn the meaning
Of His "Why?"
I shall go back to God
After I have learnt the meaning
Of His "How?"

194.

Mine are not the tears
Of disappointed expectation.
Mine are the tears
Of unexpected inner joy.

195.

The world is completely lost
Between your manifested
    stupidity
And your unmanifested divinity.

196.

There are countless questions
About God,
But only one answer:
God is His own Eternity's
Satisfaction-distribution.

197.

Aspiration without dedication
Is like a slow runner
Who knows where the goal is
But is bound to arrive shockingly
    late.

198.

The sacred heart of the moon
Comes from the secret Smile of God.
The sacred breath of the sun
Comes from the open Dance of God.

199.

Two are the questions
That I do not know how to answer:
Does God actually need me?
What will happen
If I become another God?

200.

Someday God will forgive me.
It may be soon.
Someday I shall satisfy God.
It may take a little time.

201.

I need three things desperately:
An ancient heart,
A modern arm
And an ultra modern-eye.

202.

A willing breath
Sees the Face of God.
A surrendering life
Becomes the heart of God.

203.

Because I am a truth-seeker
My future flows towards me.
Because I am a God-lover
I live in my Eternal Now.

204.

Take your choice!
Either allow God
To sit inside your head
Or go and sit
At God's Forgiveness-Feet.

205.

Two incredible facts:
God was chasing away my desire-tiger.
My doubting mind was untiringly
Following God.

206.

"God, give me!"
This is a wrong and improper
    prayer.
"God, take me!"
This is a right and proper prayer.

207.

We pray to God the Power,
But God the Lover
Answers our prayers.

207 FLOWER-FLAMES

Note: Two printings of 207 Flower-Flames are extant, both published by Agni Press on February 1985. One has Sri Chinmoy's painting of a rose on the cover, the other has a Jharna Kala painting dated "September 1975". The printing with Jharna Kala painting is slightly different, as set out below.

3.

Of all the gifts
You have offered to God,
Your happiness-gift
He treasures most.

104.

As a dreamer,
He is loved by God
Constantly.
As a Lover,
God is loved by him
Unconditionally.

133.

In the beginning
An unconditional life
Is a battleground.
But eventually
An unconditional life
Becomes a playground.

146.

His ancient heart tells him
That God is beautiful plus
    powerful.
His modern mind tells him
That God is either unmindful or
    doubtful.

188.

Sincerity
Changed his past
Slowly and steadily.
Determination
Is changing his present
Powerfully and convincingly.
Faith
Will change his future
Amazingly and permanently.

194.

His are not the tears
Of disappointed expectation.
His are the tears
Of unexpected inner joy.

202.

One willing breath
Saw the Face of God.
One surrendering life
Became the Heart of God.

203.

Because I am a truth-seeker
The future flows towards me.
Because I am a God-lover
I live in the Eternal Now.

APPENDIX

POEM TITLES AS SELECTED BY
EDITORS FOR FIRST EDITION

POEM TITLES AS SELECTED BY EDITORS FOR THE FIRST EDITION

1. A new marathon
2. Are you not ashamed?
3. Days pass by
4. Afraid
5. The tears of Mother Earth
6. Self-defeat
7. Prayer-cry
8. Inside my silence-life
9. God is not discouraged
10. A small trouble
11. A tamed mind
12. Pride
13. What you need
14. My journey's companion
15. Mine is the life
16. In the field of frustration
17. Two miracles
18. The fever of my life
19. Your aspiration-life
20. My aching urgency
21. An infant God
22. First gift, last gift
23. My progress
24. Try not to rob my heart
25. Competition-separation
26. O my beloved
27. Ambition-noon, affection-moon
28. You have lost
29. You are destined
30. A solemn promise
31. He is God's
32. Beauty born of life
33. Surrender-fulness
34. Prayers are made of tears
35. Two things I immensely enjoy
36. Succeed and proceed
37. A sly deception
38. The telescope of time
39. Your real need
40. Too poor
41. What delays our meeting?
42. Each night, each day
43. Although God loves him
44. Poor little heart
45. Because he loves
46. God does not love me
47. God does not care for me
48. Slowly and steadily
49. The best, the worst
50. All due to jealousy
51. The call of America
52. The stories told
53. Two inseparable friends
54. Finally
55. Clutching the last hope-ray
56. He took up death's challenge
57. Human and Divine Business
58. The supreme Reality
59. Human life, divine life
60. My mind is tired
61. Yesterday, today and tomorrow
62. The blossom of your Heaven-fame
63. The sure Hour of God
64. The same day
65. A sad mistake
66. I do not deserve
67. A God-Knower Master
68. In human nature
69. To teach humanity how to love
70. Desperate needs
71. Why not take a chance!
72. Spread your cheerfulness
73. The message I have heard
74. A simple truth
75. A full harvest of peace
76. The road from heart to heart
77. I live for you alone
78. A secret way
79. Who lives above me?
80. Three are the false excuses
81. True sacrifice glows
82. To speak with authority
83. Heaven descends, earth ascends
84. Two secret wishes
85. Only three strides ahead
86. A dreamless night
87. A wild sound-call
88. My secret rehearsal
89. The lesson supreme
90. Freedom-Immortality
91. The symphony of mental clouds
92. My God-Realisation
93. Not beyond possibility
94. My life is burning out
95. My God-hunger
96. I do not interfere
97. An idle thought
98. Therefore I love
99. Nothing is equal
100. Just for a second
101. What has punctured your joy?
102. My rising horizon
103. A wild depression
104. The Heart of my Lord Supreme
105. Hell's orchestra
106. Persistence
107. Helpless earth
108. My mind's inaccessible corner
109. My hope's resurrection
110. Incredible news
111. Hope comes first
112. Dangerous diseases
113. Push and pull
114. I am hanging
115. If you are ignorant
116. Something cries
117. Aspire to lead and feed
118. The chains of desire-night
119. When I cry for victory
120. Hope alone remains
121. A difficult task
122. Nothing can defeat you
123. A lesson I always enjoy
124. My heart
125. The game
126. Alas, all have forgotten
127. The power of a dream
128. A new prayer
129. The heart of progress-oneness
130. The vision of freedom-might
131. When I am on God's side
132. All I want
133. God's Love-Call
134. A deathless future
135. A new discovery
136. How little I know
137. America's special strength
138. Oneness-land
139. The longest road
140. Three kinds of givers
141. Someday, somehow, somewhere
142. A God-Heart
143. One heart in two bodies
144. An overnight success
145. If you suffer
146. A great teacher
147. Each opportunity
148. God is always watching us
149. Humour and rumour
150. To frighten and enlighten
151. Conquerors
152. God's Lion-Power
153. Declaration of a non-believer
154. Life's fond illusion
155. The mother of my pure thoughts
156. You are not
157. Eternity's sunrise
158. A chainless mind
159. Nowhere
160. My surrendering surrender
161. A perfect gentleman
162. Eternal hunger
163. Almost an impossible reality
164. God the Compassion
165. My summer-tree
166. A free passage
167. God's Football
168. An atom of soulful effort
169. Tempt me no more
170. A colossal hole
171. O incense-breathing morning
172. When I was the victor
173. Your starlit heart
174. You come not alone
175. His true nature
176. Drownings
177. The grown-up God
178. A flower-future
179. Satisfaction is in God-Becoming
180. I smiled in my mind
181. Each journey
182. Just carry one thing with you
183. The thunder-victory
184. The art of surrender
185. A common ability
186. My smiling God
187. A desire-life
188. He who feeds my heart
189. Non-stop magic
190. How to succeed?
191. The arrival of another day
192. Your silence-loving heart
193. Should parents play God?
194. Nothing more, nothing less
195. Who will guard my possessions?
196. I must take nothing for granted
197. Your purity-prayers will help you
198. The common award
199. A short-sighted idea
200. My body does not belong to me
201. The God-Hour strikes
202. What you did
203. The stairway of your dreams
204. Two unchanged obsessions
205. Where, O where, is God?
206. Our creations will crumble
207. God just gives and gives
208. Our faith-life only
209. Yet I shall go on
210. The boon
211. A devoted member of God's Society
212. Two observers
213. The most ancient story
214. Two hopes
215. Let hope once more refresh you
216. Inside there should be
217. Our different ways
218. An aspiration-life means
219. A determination-stride
220. All your dangers
221. Are You tired, O Lord?
222. How far can you go?
223. Her determined speed
224. Three Heaven-bound passengers
225. A mystic gulf
226. I know you will wait for me
227. Although he barks and barks
228. What can I expect?
229. Soulful happiness is my escort
230. Fulfilling faith will rule
231. O my failure-fountain
232. I hear no more
233. To perfect me in his own image
234. An honest unbeliever
235. No longer necessary
236. Ego feeds on attention
237. O my raindrops of hope
238. My need
239. Kindness is not blindness
240. Love mankind here
241. What is silence?
242. A tower of fortitude
243. An impossible task
244. Soon they will be over
245. Pride does not confess
246. God's timeless Dream
247. Beauty without vanity
248. My conscience
249. I see a smile
250. I study alternatives
251. Since nobody wants to play
252. O silver flames
253. No parallel
254. Disturb not the world
255. A fatal experience
256. Even my shadow avoids me
257. Obedience
258. Ecstasy's unplumbed skies
259. This defective life
260. You are not a man
261. Beyond the reach
262. The shortness of the day
263. He has planted his footsteps
264. Sweet thoughts
265. Together they have returned
266. A little more time
267. A very, very long time
268. Perpetual benedictions
269. Who betrays whom?
270. Whips of God
271. Two monumental mockeries
272. They show me
273. Like the sleeping flowers
274. Guardian of my heart
275. Human life is really something
276. What a downfall!
277. O beautiful meditation
278. A sweet silence-thought
279. Make the right choice!
280. A willing God
281. You are all right
282. A sweet disorder
283. Devouring time
284. Do not give up
285. The same old God
286. The midnight dream
287. Idle hopes
288. Beauty
289. Duty
290. How to kill desire
291. Confidence of reason
292. Do dissolve me
293. The smile that conquers
294. When God first created man
295. Let it all end
296. In the ancient Heaven
297. A white Heaven-born thought
298. Mistaking earth for Heaven
299. When the outer world deserts him
300. A serious matter
301. Love before you serve
302. Therefore I discover
303. More than ready
304. Yours is the victory supreme
305. My choice
306. What is the matter with you?
307. A marathon run
308. I go to God twice a day
309. Destination
310. Give your heart a chance
311. A free pass to Heaven
312. The grip of attachment
313. Even God is a disciple
314. A great secret
315. To steal a look at God
316. I am fulfilled twice
317. Why am I so tired?
318. Don't take a late start
319. To see his Compassion-Feet
320. Inside I live
321. A mistake-proof life
322. No real reason
323. A life of indecision
324. Great strangers
325. The power of your sound-life
326. My needs
327. Human mind, human heart
328. The Tent of my Beloved Supreme
329. The real reality
330. Time for Heaven to descend
331. A doubting mind
332. Only one sad thing
333. Each body dies
334. Nothing to equal
335. O descending Blue
336. Nothing compels you
337. Different names
338. Earth is the teacher
339. My sweet Lord's Satisfaction-Delight

340. What can your Master do?
341. Do you need a pure heart?
342. Bitterness unspeakable
343. Lost heritage
344. Loss and gain
345. I am watching
346. I see a garden
347. Playmates of the soul
348. I thought of doing something
349. Just sing a soulful song
350. A caged success
351. God's favourites
352. Oneness-peace
353. Your home
354. Peace
355. What you have
356. I love three dreams of mine
357. Do give me another chance
358. O my foolish body
359. The only way to go
360. Your God-ordained task
361. Aspiration tells me
362. The same sad story
363. His vision-eye
364. A moment of inspiration
365. I am crying
366. One thing haunts me
367. Perfection
368. Friend and foe
369. What is new?
370. Don't blame God
371. Bitterly crying
372. Love is
373. Light enlightens
374. They will cure you
375. A secret source
376. Reveal your insecurity-life
377. Start doing this immediately
378. Every time you love unconditionally
379. God has stopped his game
380. Face your lower nature
381. Not you
382. Known by another name
383. No more
384. Your soul-victory's crown
385. Your old desire-cry
386. We know
387. Yours is great resolution
388. Nothing else God wants from you
389. Yours is a deplorable failure
390. Not ready to learn from God
391. Every aspiration-day
392. What you are within
393. Past, present, future
394. A life of exalted purity
395. Look who treasures you
396. Before you start thinking
397. I am sick of my aspiration
398. I shall not fail
399. To God I have surrendered
400. A very busy day
401. While others are fond of sleeping
402. To consecrate soulfully
403. O sweet touch of silence-peace
404. Satisfy and serve
405. How strong is prayer?
406. O my hope
407. All the evil forces
408. The changer of world history
409. A God-man
410. They will know it
411. Because of venom-doubt
412. Fallen from surrender-tree
413. Summoning the sleepers
414. Three insults
415. O my Lord Supreme
416. To make yourself happy
417. You don't need them
418. Who is happy?
419. The twentieth century
420. Because of You, Lord
421. An interesting question
422. Clever and tricky
423. Unlit and unfit
424. Gratitude
425. Your ignorance-choice
426. My priority-list
427. Just a quick reminder
428. The longest stride
429. Man and machine
430. Blame

431. Never
432. Three tearful prayers
433. Stop shouting!
434. The secret of divine education
435. Ambition is hard work
436. Life is an experience
437. A life of mistakes
438. Learn and unlearn
439. You will be happy
440. Whether you like it or not
441. Two favours from my Lord
442. What does Heaven need?
443. Because of his good heart
444. A good place
445. They never stop
446. Forgive and forget
447. Hope discovered America
448. No preparation, no attempt
449. Sincere desires
450. You will appreciate
451. Science and technology
452. Permanent happiness you wanted
453. Man first came to know of God
454. Another God
455. Science is
456. Keep doing the right thing
457. Do give me the capacity
458. Now what is happening?
459. A baby balloon
460. Philosophy is blind
461. Innocence untouched
462. What you need
463. Why are you in tears?
464. Courage is a kind of beauty
465. My heart-home
466. Your holy steps
467. The bright eye of the sun
468. What you always have
469. The perfect choice
470. If I am great
471. A very far cry
472. I love You
473. I am happy
474. If not grateful
475. Prayer-power
476. Only one favour
477. Exorbitant pride
478. Eye-witness
479. Although you hate God
480. Builders are transformers
481. No peace for you
482. No other choice
483. Science, my friend
484. Spirituality, my friend
485. Who practises what he preaches?
486. Not enough
487. Music is
488. Volcano-sounds
489. Music knows no frontiers
490. Keep up your God-promise
491. Your Himalayan victory
492. You are tired
493. Offering worship to You
494. Ancient rivals
495. My friendship with you
496. Caught in the snare
497. Do not be unreasonable
498. Your supremely ridiculous discovery
499. Illumining is my prostration
500. I don't need salvation
501. This body
502. Not available
503. O my desire-life
504. I remember
505. Nourish your searching mind
506. Scoffers and defamers
507. O my mind-song
508. Another God
509. My dream, my reality
510. My sound-life, my silence-life
511. I know not why
512. No extravagant hopes
513. To brave the sound-life
514. The mouth of my wild desires
515. My life-flute
516. Beyond the sunrise-sky
517. They cannot wait for me
518. A new friend
519. Three things I love
520. A new name
521. Where my journey begins

522. Loving You
523. They know not
524. Can this be true?
525. Life is nothing but this
526. A weeping God
527. Four elevators
528. One thing
529. God will be yours
530. Destitute
531. Only one thing
532. A fleeting smile
533. My Lord invited me
534. My passport
535. Who else is utterly helpless?
536. Two supreme secrets
537. I have already answered
538. How could this be true?
539. Do you know the way?
540. It will help
541. My thoughts
542. Audience with my Inner Pilot
543. Attachment: what is it?
544. They tell me
545. A human life
546. In your presence
547. Do you know what you have?
548. Earth weeps, Heaven weeps
549. I am not alone
550. Far beyond, deep within
551. Deep and ancient
552. Yours is the heart
553. I shall return
554. Pray for me, please!
555. My needs
556. Wrestle with restlessness
557. Heaven's promise, earth's promise
558. Heaven's soul, earth's heart
559. God and I admire
560. A strong love-bond
561. Promise and guarantee
562. In the light
563. When I disagree
564. My growing familiarity
565. Steer clear
566. What I need
567. Secret and sacred truths
568. God thinks of me
569. Something else, something more
570. Thanks to Heaven, thanks to earth
571. Fierce wars
572. Oh now is the time
573. Let me live on earth a little more
574. A traveller between life and death
575. In the chosen ones
576. My earth-born diamond-tears
577. God's Love blessingfully shelters him
578. Oh when my sadness is sweet
579. The dauntless challenge
580. An adventure of incomparable newness
581. O knife of cynicism
582. O belated worshipper
583. My immortal tear-drops
584. My soul-fire
585. Mine is the heart
586. God is my Coach
587. Three short-cuts to God-realisation
588. Aspiration is a cry
589. Our thoughts, our deeds
590. Every moment
591. Temptation is powerful
592. The train of resolution
593. Nothing to sacrifice
594. Nothing to love
595. Nothing to remember
596. Secrets
597. To invite God
598. Good thoughts
599. One code of life
600. What to do
601. My peace of mind
602. No introduction needed
603. Compassion-heart, justice-eye
604. My soulful heart
605. What my restless mind has
606. Why is it hard?
607. A supreme secret
608. An appreciating consolation
609. My dreams have not come true
610. A very long time
611. A fulfilling conversation

612. What has God given me?
613. What my desire-life wants
614. God's Satisfaction-Founder
615. Because you save me
616. God is smiling powerfully
617. Two things for nothing
618. Two eternal friends
619. Do you really want me to be happy?
620. When I ignore my mind quietly
621. Because of the Beauty
622. My mind's game
623. His astounding manifestation-life
624. When you are in hesitation
625. Fault-finding
626. Mine is the heart
627. Two complete failures
628. I have two serious faults
629. Faith nullifies
630. Keep your division-mind
631. You can never get lost
632. Weak are my ears
633. A God-nourishing fruit
634. When I give a soulful cry
635. The secret of realisation
636. A clear conscience
637. Since you are afraid of sins
638. God has given me
639. My earth-bound mind has taught me
640. My dear Lord blesses
641. When I think of the world
642. Your God-necessity-cry
643. If to forgive is divine
644. I fight my ignorance-night
645. Where is your partner?
646. You are surprisingly great
647. Only when you climb it
648. A small mind
649. The prosperity-raptures
650. God came to visit
651. My life-motor clicks
652. My mind is happy
653. A sad, sad experience
654. Important in God's Heart
655. My body needs God's Compassion
656. What lies behind me
657. The seeker's realisation-heart
658. They always return
659. The perfection-train
660. Your meditation-light never works
661. By way of joke
662. Something to do
663. No rival
664. I am so proud of my mind
665. I entertain God
666. What shall I see tomorrow?
667. And it is
668. Slowly, my aspiration-heart is travelling
669. An abiding partnership
670. I can easily enjoy
671. Without a second
672. God has and you are
673. This is the day
674. God gave you
675. What God wants
676. Fear
677. A gift from Above
678. An iota of gratitude
679. You never needed it
680. I love you, I need you
681. Two realisations
682. Let me help you
683. Today's clear world
684. I am the happiest
685. Mine is the life
686. O my soldier
687. O prayer-beauty
688. Aspiration is
689. Because of your beauty
690. I believe
691. The way to proceed
692. My peace lives
693. What do I do with my inspiration-wings?
694. Inseparable friends
695. All are crying
696. What we need
697. You call it self-knowledge
698. Your Compassion-Searchlight
699. I am the owner
700. The ascending saviour

701. Perfection-beauty
702. A halfway Christian
703. O Bible
704. They fear
705. The Christ lives
706. The Christ gave
707. We shall not see Jesus
708. The Christ has come
709. I love God
710. I pray to God
711. At least one person
712. I am happy because
713. God is not surprised
714. I am not willing
715. I am happy
716. I am choosing God's Light
717. Advance knowledge
718. Conversation
719. The dividing line
720. Hope is born to sigh
721. Yesterday's God
722. I am tormented
723. Three things I shall conquer
724. Hope-buds are wide awake
725. What am I?
726. An illumining thought
727. Yesterday I desired to live
728. Hide your cleverness
729. I can and I shall
730. My prayer-wings carry me
731. More than a luxury
732. A seeker's secret adventure
733. When I correspond with the cosmic gods
734. I came from God
735. Nobody is idle
736. Give what you have
737. I chose
738. A crucial difference
739. Something infinitely better to do
740. Conceal and reveal
741. Practical and spiritual
742. Each time
743. Because I am a representative of God
744. I appeared before God
745. I chose God
746. Two things have led me
747. How do I spend my time?
748. Your actual life
749. What you need from the world
750. The only medicine
751. The answer
752. Aspiration-silence is leading you
753. God is waiting for you
754. O my heart
755. Because of God's Justice-Light
756. Because God is all Love to me
757. God is my only Lamp
758. My mind treasures
759. Fear not
760. If you truly love your friend
761. I pray to my pure heart
762. I depend on faith
763. Two medicines
764. The game is complete
765. Happiness
766. Is it possible?
767. Alas, alas!
768. A gigantic hoax
769. The celestial inspiration
770. The inner problem
771. You have not asked yourself
772. His resistance to truth
773. No problem
774. I shall not fumble in vain
775. When my heart's purity radiates
776. A rising sun
777. A shining smile
778. A fleeting separation
779. My heart longs
780. Gratitude is glory
781. How can I believe?
782. His foundation-haven
783. A perfection-man
784. My human life hangs heavy
785. A divine life
786. Heart is the child
787. The cave of sound
788. Each dangerous thought
789. Choice is opportunity
790. Because you are chained

791. I love You still
792. Your soft-speaking eyes
793. An important failure
794. His life's cloudy weather
795. Satisfaction-sun
796. The great conqueror
797. A whole Eternity
798. Mine is the heart
799. Do not imitate
800. A true Master
801. A map of silence
802. While walking
803. You cannot possess two things
804. Even his enemies have forgiven him
805. Only one reason
806. One positive seed-thought
807. Only when I allow
808. O inspiration-sky
809. The beauty born of oneness-love
810. Now I love
811. Anxiety
812. Are you really sure?
813. Lose the map
814. God's morning Compassion
815. Who wants my help?
816. Accept the truth
817. Everything is possible
818. Never fear to watch
819. God's Marathon-Compassion
820. The detachment of the stars
821. My remembrance-light
822. The day I saved
823. This world has nothing for me
824. Spend your thought-power
825. I am determined
826. Excusing myself
827. I have replaced
828. An inner medicine
829. Truth has charmed me
830. Now is the opportunity
831. A sublime truth
832. Two things absolutely unparalleled
833. God will promote you
834. Who will condemn you?
835. When I study
836. Reveal your nervousness
837. What others think of you
838. Nothing else is perfect
839. I love and I serve
840. I need only one thing
841. A false seeker
842. A false student
843. Heaven laughs
844. My mind has enslaved
845. I amuse God
846. Infallible inspiration
847. A supreme truth
848. No advantage
849. God's Forgiveness finds me
850. Let your heart criticise
851. I have nothing to fear
852. No matter how many mistakes
853. You have every opportunity-right
854. The cure
855. Three invaluable Heaven-gifts
856. Why have you surrendered?
857. Happiness is my name
858. Seeing is becoming
859. The happiest man in God's creation
860. So thinks the human mind
861. Sincerity tells me
862. The real wisdom-light
863. The real life of happiness
864. If you want to run the fastest
865. Purity's way
866. The new world
867. The price
868. The Master's compassion-height
869. Your only problem
870. I really love you
871. No difference
872. Truth and falsehood
873. The fight
874. Inspiration descends
875. The human life
876. Truth will not tolerate
877. The relaxation of the mind
878. I cry and cry
879. So easy to forget
880. I smile and smile
881. I want Him

882. A soulful heart questions
883. Another way to live
884. Because I know
885. Suffering is a painful joke
886. So beautiful
887. I think of God
888. Each day
889. I am watching your eyes
890. Faith is the transcendence-glory
891. The happy God tells me
892. The vision I want
893. A heart flooded with poise
894. Preparations
895. Light and life mingle
896. Without the Grace-Power
897. The inner faith
898. Even death cannot escape
899. Harvest of the heart
900. A stronger heart
901. The real in me
902. The heart-land
903. Your right of self-encouragement
904. The defeat of my life
905. Since you do not play
906. Something exists above
907. What I shall have
908. My aspiration-heart tells me
909. My soul has already become
910. A God-Smile
911. The happy result
912. My supreme realisation
913. Helpless and senseless
914. God sees me differently
915. Because God loves me more
916. If we can raise ourselves
917. Man loves his confusion-fog
918. Your foolish mind
919. Pains follow us
920. You must listen
921. Wisdom-light dawned on me
922. The answer
923. Self-glory
924. If you have the courage
925. When you are liberated
926. Mine are the eyes
927. Let me follow my heart
928. When I pray to the false god
929. If you long for peace
930. Beyond the inner barriers
931. If God and Truth communicate
932. Counterfeit victory
933. Remain unseen
934. Two enemies have left me
935. I am not needed
936. You will hurt yourself
937. Divinity fails to hide
938. Truth is paralysing
939. Old God, new God
940. Those who are always late
941. Each heart is the beauty
942. Three tear-drops
943. Special attention
944. An excellent Boss
945. Mine is the vision-eye
946. The habit of trusting yourself
947. Real confidence
948. A great encouragement
949. I shall depend
950. I shall relax
951. I shall not hide from Truth
952. Prison of misunderstanding
953. Your Goal
954. When I understand you and him
955. An inner task
956. Today and tomorrow
957. Whom shall my soul believe?
958. The flower of a reality
959. The science of poison-doubt
960. A zone of indifference
961. No recommendation
962. My human life knows
963. Time bridges
964. The key
965. Where is the strength?
966. The root of prosperity
967. The gift of gifts
968. Time silences the animal in me
969. A master key
970. Time awakens
971. Never for sale
972. If your heart does not know
973. Two neighbours

974. I shall outlast
975. A reality of love
976. The mystery of mysteries
977. To increase faith
978. The roots of your doubts
979. The unbelievable
980. You are a rogue
981. Choice, not chance
982. He who compromises
983. The forced duty
984. My victory, my defeat
985. Nobody can defeat you
986. Each difficulty
987. You are lost
988. My doubts have died
989. A direct gift
990. My enthusiasm
991. The thick forest of solitude
992. Visitor
993. The inevitability
994. What I have become
995. A train of sadness
996. A fountain of God-thought
997. I am helpless as ever
998. The great authority
999. The days of my slavery
1000. My heart's challenging life
1001. No difference
1002. The flame of oneness-life
1003. Confusion-night boasts
1004. My freedom-bird flies
1005. Stupendous victory
1006. Arrows of Light
1007. The Love Divine
1008. A broken wing
1009. Submit to the power-heart
1010. The swimmer
1011. The golden disc of the Beyond
1012. Puzzles
1013. Our supreme secrets
1014. A short vacation
1015. I really wish to know
1016. To please You most
1017. Inside God's Compassion-Heart
1018. An appreciating eye and an admiring heart
1019. Cry and smile
1020. God's problem
1021. The unusual oneness-delight
1022. Each knowledge-day
1023. God-memories from my past
1024. A one-way street
1025. Where is happiness?
1026. Yes, I shall forgive
1027. Each devoted moment
1028. Each listening heart
1029. Because he is not sanctified
1030. Soulful sorrows
1031. Two extraordinary things
1032. O my inexperienced heart
1033. What each knows
1034. Two ultimate absurdities
1035. Two things he has become
1036. Willing souls
1037. Your heart's aspiration-flames
1038. I feel sorry for you
1039. When my prayer is an action
1040. Three diamond thoughts
1041. My indispensable partner
1042. Each impure thought
1043. Bitter disappointments
1044. A stormy thought-world
1045. The city of "God and yes"
1046. Who says?
1047. What is behind me?
1048. Don't act like a fool
1049. O vastness-sky
1050. I purify myself
1051. Keep aloof
1052. The mind of man
1053. How far can ignorance carry you?
1054. The best fighters
1055. A fruitless thought
1056. Two miracles
1057. You are chosen
1058. The pain of death
1059. Your selfless dedication-life
1060. So often you sail
1061. My shadowless awakening-duty
1062. Discovery
1063. A seeker of perfection-silence
1064. Two requests

1065. My mind laughs
1066. Meditation's only food
1067. In the silent Memory
1068. A new role
1069. How do you expect?
1070. Never carry doubt-poison
1071. You will never be able to learn
1072. During the day
1073. Yet I am determined
1074. Your flaw-seeking eyes
1075. This extravagant desire
1076. Cheerful news
1077. Always in my prayers
1078. If you can be aware
1079. Your life-flower is fully blossomed
1080. The beauty of purity
1081. Only one duty
1082. A gift of God
1083. To triumph
1084. Integrity
1085. We long for peace
1086. I thank you
1087. Offering
1088. The right answers
1089. Each human soul
1090. Each thought
1091. My earthly day
1092. To make friends
1093. An attempt
1094. Do not waste time
1095. My supremely soulful joy
1096. His life's departing splendour
1097. The boat of despair
1098. My heart represents
1099. If your mind is too poor
1100. My silver dream-heart
1101. When I go beyond
1102. Self-reliance
1103. I am right
1104. Your suffering-world
1105. The powerfully wise man
1106. Towards my new perfection-life
1107. Any negative thought
1108. Remain cheerful!
1109. Willingness to learn
1110. God will come to you
1111. God has given you
1112. I still care for God
1113. My real nature
1114. Your humility-life
1115. The right thing
1116. Each thought
1117. What is confidence?
1118. Study and give
1119. Keep your inner life sacred
1120. The art of self-encouragement
1121. Since I stopped meditating
1122. You are bound to suffer
1123. The heart of luminosity
1124. My God-oneness tells me
1125. My life-tree crumbled
1126. Cherish the American way
1127. When I invite
1128. An unfinished creation
1129. No real power
1130. A soulful wish
1131. A new kind of prayer
1132. God-awareness transforms
1133. Aspiration-efforts
1134. Wisdom-light
1135. An orderly life
1136. When the heart-plant is changed
1137. Think only of those
1138. When I see the Face of God
1139. To see God in a God-lover
1140. My heart sees the Infinite
1141. God cries
1142. My heart needs God
1143. What shall I learn ultimately?
1144. If you do not know
1145. Your heart's desire
1146. I shall not try
1147. Anything that is right
1148. Where is happiness?
1149. Do not trust your mind
1150. God loves me
1151. Do not distort
1152. A supreme discovery
1153. A lot of doubt
1154. A human being is deceived
1155. How do you expect to sail?
1156. When I pretend

1157. How can you own self-perfection?
1158. Why am I always frustrated?
1159. The supreme glory
1160. You can be aware of two things
1161. Your division-illness
1162. Stupidity's ultimate height
1163. I pray to my Lord
1164. What I need
1165. I can find fault
1166. A tiny negative thought
1167. Your purity-life
1168. Soulful sincerity
1169. Aspiration-heart, dedication-life
1170. What is this earth?
1171. Ask your own heart
1172. Because you are soulfully submissive
1173. My realisation-life
1174. God's God-Gladness
1175. Be not discouraged
1176. Opportunity-delight leads man
1177. A God-satisfying heart
1178. The faultless choice
1179. Self-imprisonment begins
1180. Do you need protection?
1181. The fantasy-prison
1182. Revelation, revelation!
1183. Liberate yourself immediately
1184. Do you want to be perfectly happy?
1185. What you are
1186. Do you want to return home?
1187. The divine always wins
1188. God blesses me
1189. Artificiality and sincerity
1190. To rise above ourselves
1191. My final goal
1192. The supreme discovery
1193. I have sincerely prayed
1194. I do not know
1195. My willingness to love God
1196. My self-giving way
1197. Grasp the golden vision
1198. We love our doubtful minds
1199. To change the world
1200. Mine is the way
1201. When you change your name
1202. If you have the sincerity-courage
1203. Unlearn and learn
1204. If your mind is divinely practical
1205. The deeper you descend
1206. Two things unthinkable
1207. God's Way
1208. If you can brave the shock
1209. We realise the highest Truth
1210. Your destructive impurity
1211. A new intensity
1212. I need God
1213. Conceal your self-interest-cry
1214. Your heart's name
1215. Why do you need another enemy?
1216. Ask your mind to protect itself
1217. Do you know why?
1218. The book of self-knowledge
1219. The only wall
1220. One day you will see
1221. Your volley of questions
1222. Your heart will get satisfaction
1223. A peace-flooded home
1224. God's creative ability
1225. God's Assembly-skies
1226. How can you expect?
1227. God will find you the way
1228. If you come to me now
1229. What can you expect?
1230. A boat that knows no shore
1231. The contradiction-sky
1232. You need an explanation-life
1233. Each senseless thought
1234. Even so
1235. If I can see God's Face
1236. When I am sincerity incarnate
1237. Do not trust
1238. Just relax!
1239. Something really valuable
1240. He is a real danger to himself
1241. The present way
1242. The key to liberty
1243. You do not know
1244. I shall not choose
1245. A perfectly celestial smile
1246. Do not be disappointed!

1247. Two incredible facts
1248. Yours is the mind
1249. Go alone!
1250. A relief to discover
1251. Companions
1252. Do not complain
1253. Your life is not your own
1254. Sacrifice what you have
1255. Peace needs no interpretation
1256. A stranger to deception
1257. Do you really want to be happy?
1258. Let me realise You today
1259. God's Compassion-Eye
1260. How can you be happy?
1261. Soaring wings
1262. My heart's aspiration-light
1263. Your love of soul-freedom
1264. Self-control
1265. Each dream
1266. Aspire or retire
1267. My common enemies
1268. Appreciation is a miracle-power
1269. Life-mastery never stops
1270. Worthy causes
1271. Try to befriend the perfection-will
1272. Each service-heart
1273. Fight against complacency
1274. His life's ignorance-chain
1275. If you have perfect faith
1276. Life-satisfying energy-blossoms
1277. No aspiration is hopeless
1278. His heart thrives on adversity
1279. Every step of progress-smile
1280. A child of yesterday
1281. My self-examination
1282. Secrets of a peaceful life
1283. Do not ignore me
1284. You will reap disaster
1285. A land of orphans
1286. The golden key
1287. A dedicated God-believer
1288. Fools
1289. Two royal paths
1290. A dangerous trap
1291. Someday my Lord will give me
1292. He stood against
1293. Fame is a flickering flame
1294. A Himalayan promise
1295. Human love, human life
1296. My birthright
1297. A friend of sleepless night
1298. The heart has many roads
1299. My mind was born to follow
1300. Silence clings
1301. The beginning finds the end
1302. O mocking eyes of the world
1303. Three ultimate absurdities
1304. Confidants
1305. The only answer
1306. A complete betrayal
1307. Three imaginary convictions
1308. Hope
1309. Each prayer is hard work
1310. Justice-light
1311. The limits of love
1312. A fleeting mortal sorrow
1313. A more reliable disciple
1314. Share
1315. An incurable opportunist
1316. Who has the freedom?
1317. God is all ready
1318. God's troubles
1319. Break your bad habits
1320. The junkyard
1321. Poverty-ideas, prosperity-ideals
1322. A true satisfaction
1323. O my soul, smile!
1324. My ignorance is no excuse
1325. Your wise willingness-heart
1326. What do I do?
1327. Take your choice!
1328. We are mistaken
1329. An unexpected blow
1330. If you are an earthly guest
1331. God's partner
1332. I shall have no more problems
1333. Who says?
1334. At the end of all the roads
1335. Do not think of human grief!
1336. God-life is waiting for me
1337. Each day dies eventless
1338. The usual end of day

1339. What is new?
1340. The snare of imperfection
1341. My heart's inner secret
1342. My diamond thoughts
1343. Twice I was lost
1344. Because I am a truth-seeker
1345. A fleeting experience
1346. A sweet dream
1347. A universal passport
1348. Opportunity and ability
1349. The length of his patience
1350. The depths of his convictions
1351. I am the same
1352. God's Heart of Silence-Delight
1353. Alas, no escape!
1354. God still loves me
1355. This game of progress
1356. Free of aspiration
1357. A prosperous gift
1358. Faithful to every promise
1359. He raised a wall of nothingness
1360. Like an angel
1361. His aspiration-hunger
1362. Progress and transcendence
1363. Great light clasped his mind
1364. Troops of cheerful hopes
1365. I shall not mix with you
1366. A free access
1367. Slow to expect, quick to act
1368. Desire is a game
1369. Let satisfaction be yours
1370. A new-born hero
1371. Your smile of sorrow
1372. Love does everything for God
1373. O my obstinate doubt
1374. A prince of frustration
1375. There are many kinds of wings
1376. The life of possession-madness
1377. A good heart
1378. A breath of my kindness
1379. Your extraordinary credentials
1380. He governs the unwilling
1381. In the abyss of the five senses
1382. A genius
1383. Yet I live and love
1384. My heart will not fade away
1385. Abandoned
1386. Everything else will disappear
1387. Can you not stop trying?
1388. I have lost
1389. By mistake
1390. Love itself is wisdom
1391. A rank fool
1392. In wisdom-light
1393. An ugly thought
1394. God still has faith
1395. His denial of temptation-night
1396. Divinely happy, supremely proud
1397. Only one way
1398. My higher life
1399. The heart's oneness-spreading
1400. The life of man is love
1401. My dream-boat
1402. Your inner hunger
1403. My beloved Comrade
1404. My deeper dream
1405. My sinking eye
1406. You are secretly chosen
1407. The secrets of your heart
1408. When I laugh
1409. I went to visit my Lord
1410. Meditation loves ecstasy
1411. In my silence-memory of God
1412. Dwelling places
1413. The season of self-giving
1414. The moment you become
1415. Your joy, your love
1416. Puppets and soldiers
1417. Our needs answered
1418. Oneness is the only need
1419. Your heartbeats in my heart
1420. In nothingness-nectar
1421. I enjoy conversing
1422. The right thing
1423. I need a breathless second
1424. An aspiration-life
1425. My old and new question
1426. My dream-life invokes
1427. O worshipper of ignorance-night
1428. My beautiful life
1429. God is still waiting for me

1430. An expression of deepening disgust
1431. Only God's Opinion
1432. I do not mind
1433. The greatest disaster
1434. Mankind's common expectations
1435. Time's tallest figure
1436. Centuries have rolled away
1437. A permanent friendship
1438. Imaginative I was
1439. One willing breath
1440. Before the final ruin came
1441. I have found no answers
1442. Another established God
1443. You can be truly happy
1444. The purity of your eyes
1445. My golden hopes
1446. Regular, like the night
1447. The wrong instrument
1448. Defeated completely
1449. Merciless as ambition
1450. Who is advancing towards me?
1451. Ambition obeys no law
1452. Everything else will fade
1453. An enormous effort
1454. The breath of pure ecstasy
1455. My ego needs no nourishment
1456. In his thriving days
1457. Lip service to the Inner Pilot
1458. His constant God-necessity
1459. Immortal as the stars
1460. My heart stands for liberty
1461. Discoveries
1462. Today's plan for progress
1463. Freely I want to live
1464. Open doors
1465. Present your secret ideas
1466. Mystical and musical
1467. Because your eyes
1468. What has meditation given me?
1469. Because you are hospitable
1470. A very pleasing companion
1471. You are magnetic
1472. Pray for a glimpse
1473. Harmonious is my inner nature
1474. A dynamo of creative ideas
1475. God has given you
1476. Because you are faithful
1477. When I love God
1478. To see your Goal
1479. You can be complete in yourself
1480. Your short-fused temper
1481. Success-stars attend you
1482. Art out of beauty
1483. I sincerely like you
1484. Gracious is your God
1485. I wish to be perfected
1486. When God thinks of me
1487. My three teachers
1488. If you love God
1489. Tomorrow I shall give God
1490. I shall tolerate the world
1491. You are doomed
1492. This world is privileged
1493. The conscious steps of purity
1494. I always win
1495. Six things I do
1496. Why do you follow?
1497. If you can dare to face
1498. Your powerful concentration-flames
1499. God has come to you running
1500. Your life is integrity
1501. To change my inner conditions
1502. The presence of faith
1503. To have faith in oneself
1504. Two errors of Eternity
1505. In the morning when I pray
1506. My Lord's Satisfaction-Lion
1507. A God-dreamer and a God-lover
1508. My nights are fractured
1509. My days and nights
1510. Man's soul is a smile
1511. Now I am grateful
1512. Only if you change
1513. The only real danger
1514. The competition
1515. Only one favour
1516. The idea-flames
1517. Many ways
1518. To tie me to God
1519. God's Promises
1520. Divorce
1521. His confused heart
1522. Slowly and quickly
1523. God's Satisfaction-Eye
1524. No preparation is required
1525. Immediate help from God
1526. Suddenly and perfectly
1527. When faith ends
1528. When I proceed
1529. Adversity and prosperity
1530. Tiredness and readiness
1531. When quality-satisfaction begins
1532. Sickness and medicine
1533. Experience and realisation
1534. The wealth of experience
1535. Three processes
1536. For all others
1537. Two hearts
1538. I need, I have, I am
1539. A tempted heart
1540. A chained heart
1541. A praying heart
1542. A faithful heart
1543. No difference
1544. A smiling and dancing world-heart
1545. My clever prayer
1546. My devoted prayer
1547. My needs
1548. When I pray
1549. My five-cent prayer
1550. O my aspiration-life
1551. A series of astonishments
1552. Rest comes not
1553. My expectation-load
1554. When God first told me
1555. Nourish learning
1556. Scoffers and defamers
1557. Three songs
1558. Happiness-givers
1559. Tears unshed
1560. Nurse no extravagant hope
1561. To brave silence
1562. The art of unthinking silence
1563. A hopelessly drowsy death
1564. On good terms
1565. The eyes of my aspiration-heart
1566. My heart's constant guest
1567. Each thought, each life
1568. Death desires me
1569. Beyond the sun-smile
1570. My heart-bridge
1571. The possession of another mind
1572. Marvellous rumour
1573. The longest journey
1574. Translunar music
1575. Your tear-floods are subsiding
1576. The glory that shines
1577. To disarm death
1578. You need eternal rest
1579. The wish of my soul
1580. Two aimless eyes
1581. Silence and sound
1582. Thus runs my dream
1583. A high opinion
1584. I wish to be led
1585. One minute a day
1586. He has departed
1587. The best thing
1588. Seasons
1589. If you can multiply
1590. Morning is the time
1591. I think of God first
1592. Greatness gives me
1593. Relax your body
1594. What is joy?
1595. I shall flood myself
1596. Each time I pray
1597. At least for one day
1598. I measured my success
1599. You are inseparable
1600. Two things I must never forget
1601. The first surprisingly soulful day
1602. The God-Hour
1603. What soulful purity has done
1604. In Heaven the souls are placed
1605. God's choice child
1606. Awake, arise!
1607. Far from your reach
1608. A sorrowful heart
1609. One depression-moment
1610. Because your heart is selfless
1611. Why explain?
1612. A rewarding and illumining experience
1613. They will do it for you
1614. Why disbelieve in God?
1615. Immediate confession
1616. It makes no difference
1617. Transformation
1618. Who says that you have failed?
1619. There must be soulful hearts
1620. The last key
1621. The magic touch
1622. The birth of my importance
1623. Go beyond your life
1624. If you cling
1625. Remembrance
1626. You call it self-command
1627. My Lord's Compassion-Lamp
1628. If you seek a perfection-life
1629. Unreservedly change yourself
1630. The mind that enables you
1631. A peace that lives for me
1632. The real in me
1633. When you do not know
1634. Expectations
1635. A more fruitful thing to do
1636. How I wish to live
1637. The only way
1638. An excellent spiritual Teacher
1639. The Compassion-Eye of my Supreme
1640. All secrets of the world
1641. A totally new life
1642. Neither accuse nor excuse
1643. By virtue of my patience-light
1644. His life is charmed
1645. If you are firm
1646. A cheerful obedience
1647. Give God a chance
1648. You can transform
1649. Your choice
1650. Always take one more step
1651. A natural and divine strength
1652. Each dedication-day
1653. My confidence
1654. My needs
1655. Inseparably one
1656. If you can conquer
1657. Your own terms
1658. Self-betrayal
1659. Conquer and revive
1660. Obscurity and futility
1661. Two lines to Heaven
1662. Capacities
1663. The whispering voice within
1664. I shall obey You
1665. Forgetfulness-slumber
1666. If you are a seeker
1667. A totally lost warrior
1668. A most beautiful toy
1669. Three old things
1670. My tasks divine
1671. Because your heart believes
1672. Two God-fulfilling friends
1673. Satisfaction wants immortality
1674. Crimes
1675. Heart-sermons
1676. A new idol
1677. Time's secret gift
1678. The beginning
1679. An unconscious suicide
1680. A fault ignominious
1681. I am surprised to see
1682. I imitate
1683. Ruin
1684. See and reveal
1685. Opportunity is a dream
1686. If you have
1687. Everybody wants to know
1688. Expect and deserve
1689. If you live a surrender-life
1690. Invited and welcomed
1691. Inspiration is the capacity
1692. An unforgotten dream
1693. Our respective roles
1694. You are on your own
1695. Your daily life
1696. I must know everything
1697. Only one thing
1698. Do not criticise yourself
1699. Intention and capacity
1700. You are great because
1701. Because you are perfect
1702. Think and feel
1703. He wants to help you
1704. Because he is God's representative
1705. On earth, in Heaven
1706. Human life, divine life
1707. He who argues
1708. If you have the soulful capacity
1709. See and know
1710. An aspiration-life
1711. To know the mind of Truth
1712. The brave decision
1713. To employ a doubtful mind
1714. I am happy
1715. Replacement
1716. Be not afraid
1717. Accepted by Truth
1718. First love God
1719. The practical in me knows
1720. I shall only try
1721. You will definitely succeed in life
1722. God's Vision-Reality
1723. True and abiding satisfaction
1724. The real in you
1725. An invisible power
1726. Squander your insecurity-life
1727. Your life's only aim
1728. Your natural confidence
1729. Pairs
1730. Each senseless thought
1731. What to do with God
1732. Because you are great
1733. He secretly buys dream-seeds
1734. Walk along a single path
1735. Your vision-eye knows
1736. Try to be absolutely spiritual
1737. Compensation
1738. Love God
1739. The concert of manifestation-light
1740. When my Lord Supreme forgives me
1741. If you allow your mind
1742. The world soon forgets
1743. If you want to see your friends
1744. Left alone
1745. Your surrender-light
1746. A supremely supernatural exchange
1747. The sun of Grace
1748. Never substitute
1749. Be careful of what you do!
1750. Appearances
1751. Confession is no substitute
1752. The solution of the mind
1753. Encounters with problems
1754. Look within, look above
1755. No God-touch
1756. He jumped to conclusions
1757. Complicated my life
1758. Out of simplicity
1759. No room left
1760. Be pleased with yourself
1761. The prerogative of the heart
1762. To keep awake
1763. In his peaceful hours
1764. The proof
1765. Satisfaction-building
1766. Something infinitely worse
1767. He lives with little
1768. To live in a simplicity-cave
1769. The clever mind
1770. Out of practice
1771. A premature arrival
1772. Painful and fruitful
1773. Right place, wrong time
1774. The compassion-feet of death
1775. Make everybody soulfully happy
1776. Everybody laughs at my incapacities
1777. If you know me
1778. Not free, not free
1779. Patience
1780. Don't eat too much
1781. Confession is the beginning
1782. The only miracle worth performing
1783. You do not have to offer
1784. The next best thing
1785. Three incomparable things
1786. I shall serve my superiors
1787. Two medicines
1788. Only three winners
1789. I shall xerox only three things
1790. If you want only attraction

1791. Feed your heart
1792. Be careful of the frustration-seed
1793. If you cannot proceed further
1794. Peace is an inspiring faith
1795. Sources
1796. To make comparisons
1797. A prayerful life
1798. I need three things desperately
1799. Perfection blossoms in obedience
1800. He is truly happy
1801. How to suffer less
1802. Seven aspiration-flames
1803. Purity-heart and beauty-face
1804. Great and good
1805. In vain
1806. Experience and reality
1807. The greatest masterpiece
1808. Free yourself from tension
1809. How can I be constantly happy?
1810. We must wrestle
1811. Immortality will conquer
1812. If we think of God
1813. A tremendous success
1814. My prayers
1815. I love God
1816. I shall become tomorrow
1817. This world can be truly happy
1818. What I do not have
1819. What I have been preserving for You
1820. Surmount your faults
1821. Reveal an unknown world of beauty
1822. Man's mind
1823. Today's machine-man
1824. Today's man of thought
1825. A creative newness-satisfaction
1826. I must be receptive
1827. God will not deny me
1828. What we are today
1829. Infinity's Abode
1830. Gratitude
1831. Commitments and involvements
1832. An absurdity
1833. The inner hunger
1834. To love the ungrasped
1835. God the Tree
1836. Love and service
1837. Under the Banner of God
1838. Why do you bind me?
1839. Inspiration-flood
1840. My soulful aspiration
1841. Arrangement and rearrangement
1842. God is asking
1843. One step at a time
1844. My heart must succeed
1845. If you know
1846. An indispensable life
1847. Be faithful
1848. Human nature
1849. Change your attitude!
1850. No deception
1851. When you become the Infinite
1852. Happiness
1853. Reject not!
1854. Each thought
1855. I need a new start
1856. The protection-cross
1857. God-discovery
1858. Imitation is not art
1859. You have made me happy
1860. I experience life
1861. Fulness and emptiness
1862. Nobody else
1863. Satisfaction dawns
1864. Let your heart
1865. How can you expect?
1866. The true truth
1867. Be aware of everything
1868. Wake up!
1869. A good intention
1870. Absence demonstrates
1871. An inspiration-sky
1872. Time's error
1873. Signs of God
1874. Aspiration lives
1875. A God-dreamer
1876. He who has no faith
1877. My dream, my vision
1878. What more do I need?
1879. An unconditional marriage
1880. Look beyond appearances
1881. A single blessing-smile
1882. Do not allow tension
1883. Infinite choices
1884. Be not afraid
1885. What my Lord calls protection
1886. Nothing to fear
1887. My soulful prayers
1888. An unnecessary companion
1889. No answer
1890. Allow God to become real
1891. His life's early morning
1892. Soulless competition
1893. Heaven's gratitude-heart
1894. Two Himalayan blunders
1895. Is there any difference?
1896. Pray in the morning
1897. A fertile mind
1898. Oneness-satisfaction
1899. The unrewarded service
1900. Three Himalayan prayers
1901. My life is silent
1902. A great exception
1903. When will it end?
1904. Never allow it to disappear
1905. I think of God
1906. Cancellations
1907. Truth lives
1908. Love the world
1909. The perfect work
1910. We shall be caught red-handed
1911. A purity-heart
1912. A lost mortal
1913. A God-seeker
1914. Faith without surrender
1915. No destruction-fear
1916. The supreme message
1917. Two perfection-crowns
1918. In all my prayers
1919. Immediate needs
1920. God the Truth
1921. Ask and learn
1922. Remembrance
1923. God's religion
1924. Two unparalleled aims
1925. Silence
1926. Man's transformation-hour
1927. My sincerity
1928. I am eagerly waiting
1929. Two blessingful gifts
1930. A touch of sadness
1931. Your flaw-seeking eyes
1932. A perfect stranger
1933. O blossoming moment
1934. The heritage of my soul
1935. His Sun's golden Eye
1936. The art of awakening
1937. The most vehement weapon
1938. Become the heart-beauty
1939. Inspiration, instruction, perfection
1940. I shall need God the Love
1941. Everything becomes illumining
1942. Follow your heart
1943. You are absolutely right
1944. Choose freedom
1945. Only a fool
1946. A man of wisdom
1947. Each prayer
1948. Sweet is my Lord
1949. Every argument
1950. Arguments
1951. Yesterday I was on earth
1952. Almost nobody
1953. The echo
1954. He is taking you
1955. If you want to deceive truth
1956. Love and serve
1957. Strange neighbours
1958. Confusion-cave
1959. The worst danger
1960. The role of a doer
1961. Simplicity is needed
1962. Change yourself slowly
1963. Self-discovery
1964. Explore!
1965. Longing for the undesirable
1966. Be aware!
1967. Even if you stop
1968. Something better
1969. Three self-discoveries
1970. Don't be a fool
1971. Fixed ideas
1972. Do love my self-giving life
1973. Oneness-satisfaction
1974. Your own responsibilities
1975. Your heart-flower
1976. My freedom lives
1977. Read his face
1978. The best definition
1979. Your doubting mind
1980. Long for anything divine
1981. Who can be trusted?
1982. Deepen your faith
1983. Remind yourself
1984. The only satisfaction
1985. Art
1986. Loved and needed
1987. Because we embrace
1988. Lord, will you forgive me?
1989. Lord, do you love me?
1990. My first discovery
1991. My meditation
1992. Around the clock
1993. Because you love God
1994. Because I sincerely love you
1995. My inner journey
1996. I shall not carry
1997. My only satisfaction
1998. The delight in meditation
1999. To be poor and weak
2000. It is never too late
2001. What I need most
2002. A disciplined life
2003. What is an accident?
2004. Ask your heart
2005. Anything worth having
2006. Each experience is an improvement
2007. Realisation-sun
2008. I implore God
2009. What you need
2010. God receives my poor life
2011. If criticism frightens your heart
2012. Too good, too bad
2013. You can be always happy
2014. Why do you forget?
2015. If it is true
2016. God's Compassion, God's Forgiveness
2017. Because I love God
2018. My prayer and my meditation
2019. Useful talks
2020. An emptiness-fount
2021. God tells us to love him
2022. I shall never try to comprehend you
2023. You must choose!
2024. Demotion or promotion
2025. Nothingness-futility
2026. Duet
2027. A God-lover
2028. No future in your heart
2029. You have to do your part
2030. God cherishes me
2031. Obedience is blessing-light
2032. My last day on earth
2033. Now is the time
2034. God will stand starving
2035. God's favourites
2036. Your aspiration-life
2037. Live only for God's Love
2038. Where are you standing?
2039. Why do you climb?
2040. Hope-flower, hope-fruit
2041. The code of your life
2042. Everything is good
2043. Destructive forces in disguise
2044. God's only interest
2045. God compassionately asks
2046. God's position
2047. Never start a day
2048. Improve your self-esteem!
2049. I am not lost
2050. The way
2051. The unusual capacity
2052. What I want
2053. Independence and dependence
2054. God is in full control
2055. Relax
2056. Since I can begin again
2057. Make up your mind
2058. Only the chosen
2059. I am at your door
2060. Simplicity you have lost
2061. Don't forget one thing
2062. If you want me to think of you
2063. Together let us go back
2064. The doorkeeper
2065. Learning is not enough
2066. Purity is wanting
2067. Scholarship and God-worship
2068. I shall never escape
2069. An unbowed head
2070. Desire-pain
2071. When I renounce
2072. An incompetent fool
2073. The one who knows
2074. A oneness-heart
2075. You are great
2076. I shall reclaim
2077. Self-awareness
2078. O my stupid mind
2079. A seeker knows
2080. Self-awakening
2081. Since limitless is the Source
2082. My mind's intensity
2083. Truth will recognise you
2084. You will excel
2085. What I can become
2086. Existence
2087. How can we succeed?
2088. If love is reborn
2089. Forgiveness is happiness
2090. A soulful heart
2091. Each innocent thought
2092. God needs me
2093. One and the same
2094. No difference
2095. Loneliness and unawareness
2096. Unless you are brave
2097. A divinity-ocean
2098. O purity of my surrender-life
2099. A liberated smile
2100. One desire and one aspiration
2101. You have the first place
2102. A moment of self-assessment
2103. Baffled by life?
2104. His mind's astonishment
2105. Two beautiful gifts
2106. The God-like wish
2107. A radiant and spotless heart
2108. Except one thing
2109. My last resort
2110. Sweet is his heart-flower
2111. A silence-breathing God
2112. My heart's liberty
2113. The wings of his mind
2114. O self-applauding stupidity
2115. The pressure of my grief
2116. He knew
2117. A sweetness-prayer
2118. O my hope-life
2119. Only a faithful life
2120. Immediate neighbours
2121. When God was my neighbour
2122. A new heart-dance
2123. Am I meant for You?
2124. The only solution
2125. At another time and place
2126. I take them
2127. Beautiful is the hour
2128. Not the journey's close
2129. Your heart-bank
2130. The positive side of life
2131. My mind spends its strength
2132. A chosen soul
2133. The human mind wants to see
2134. Only a prayer-length away
2135. A visit to nothingness
2136. The only path
2137. To be a friend of humanity
2138. Not to be found
2139. Not easily spotted
2140. An unfinished man
2141. A learning heart
2142. Cyclone-dreams
2143. Faithfulness includes
2144. Death cannot see you
2145. My days know
2146. God will extol you
2147. Hopes Himalayan
2148. A goalless rain
2149. Your Love
2150. Merciless old life!
2151. To invite God
2152. O come back
2153. Journeying towards oblivion

2154. Two things I enjoy
2155. The shadow of deceased desire
2156. Time will crumble
2157. I am a silence-pilgrim
2158. I shall surprise my soul
2159. My eyes silently sleep
2160. Hell-depth
2161. Infinity's sadness-song
2162. The unparalleled joy
2163. To soar from earth-torture
2164. Truth goes alone
2165. I saw earth ascending
2166. Immediate defeat
2167. These earth-bound eyes see nothing
2168. My latest discovery
2169. My watchful Master
2170. My home of endless tears
2171. Two things do not end
2172. His life is torn
2173. The difference
2174. O compromise-flames
2175. Never too late
2176. Truth's worst enemy
2177. They will easily shatter
2178. His emptied mind
2179. Faith was born in him
2180. Sweetness and bitterness
2181. How long have you to stay?
2182. My Heavenward rise
2183. A blind fear
2184. I have learnt more
2185. Brief moments
2186. Faith-nectar energises you
2187. What I need is a heart
2188. A delicate touch
2189. Victory's unparalleled trophies
2190. To reveal the secrets of Eternity
2191. When I lost my Beloved Supreme
2192. Inside the core of the sun
2193. With or without hope
2194. Learn and earn
2195. His life's sound-lion
2196. I have tried but failed
2197. My willing heart
2198. I have lost You
2199. Two things are in my mind
2200. God's perfect messenger-son
2201. I need three things
2202. My promise I keep
2203. My life needs guidance
2204. To pray
2205. Because you are great
2206. Ambassador of concern
2207. Every right
2208. God I can become
2209. To be in God's company
2210. My mind has surrendered
2211. I am divinely proud
2212. When I think too much
2213. My sleeplessly open heart
2214. You have touched God's Feet
2215. You will win me!
2216. You have constant faith
2217. Common sense
2218. One medicine
2219. My heart yearns to please You
2220. My desire-night is long
2221. May my gratitude-plant grow
2222. May my surrender-flower blossom
2223. I daily apply
2224. Two humble God-seekers
2225. A seeker's service
2226. Do not postpone!
2227. How long can the mind carry?
2228. Patience means
2229. Love your Master
2230. The doleful garland
2231. If your heart loves
2232. When I pray
2233. My imprisoned life
2234. What saves me
2235. An ancient story
2236. In spite of my feeble faith
2237. At long last
2238. My desire
2239. When I think of God
2240. A wise forgetfulness
2241. Give me a heart that pounds
2242. God does not chasten us
2243. I am waiting
2244. You are divinely great

2245. Your foes
2246. His Master's silence-tears
2247. Her Master's silence-tears
2248. Meditation and manifestation
2249. A God-realised soul
2250. Advantage-flower
2251. A seeker's fruitful thought
2252. No match
2253. If you are climbing
2254. The real in you
2255. The Master's Justice-Light
2256. The Master's Wisdom-Light
2257. The Master's withdrawal
2258. The power of Eternity
2259. Money-power
2260. The Master's heart
2261. Somebody has placed a flower
2262. Why I am happy
2263. Self-command
2264. So that I will become perfect
2265. You are your goal
2266. A Vision-Reality
2267. When God thinks of you
2268. My mind will not understand
2269. Self-transformation
2270. Yours is the mind
2271. An unawakening sleep
2272. Let us all thank the Supreme
2273. I have saved my heart
2274. The firmness of a Master
2275. Your mind embodies
2276. To love more
2277. The beauty of God's Life
2278. Two things I love
2279. Every day
2280. Lose and gain
2281. A oneness-heart
2282. Surrender your mind
2283. Love-power can be measured
2284. Two mirrors
2285. Is he your friend?
2286. Is he your true friend?
2287. Sweet and secret quarrels
2288. Do not try to understand
2289. Smile once only
2290. Love the souls of your enemies
2291. I like my mind and my heart
2292. Remember only three things
2293. If you live in the heart
2294. God-messengers
2295. Because you are always just
2296. Satisfaction takes birth unseen
2297. Love and lose
2298. The satisfaction-distance
2299. An unforgivable liar
2300. I know
2301. My simplicity and my sincerity
2302. My purity and my oneness
2303. My realisation and my God-satisfaction
2304. You can realise Me today
2305. God's Time
2306. First become a follower
2307. A relationship
2308. Faith means
2309. Supreme truths
2310. Discipline yourself!
2311. Do not surrender to struggles
2312. The light is waiting
2313. You have not failed!
2314. Two Gods
2315. No excuse
2316. Two soulful prayers
2317. Peace above all else
2318. Expectation and frustration
2319. Your own unparalleled reward
2320. My life's oneness
2321. The return-journey
2322. You win God's Crown
2323. A true God-seeker
2324. Conscious self-examination
2325. When the vital challenges
2326. The Supreme likes
2327. Cheerfulness is progress
2328. Disobedience is destructive
2329. To please my Lord Supreme
2330. Beauty from Heaven
2331. I have nothing to tell
2332. My beautiful eyes cannot see
2333. My beautiful heart cannot feel
2334. My beautiful life does not know
2335. Three enemies to conquer

2336. Each prayer
2337. O earth, O Heaven
2338. My three teachers
2339. Three rare achievements
2340. Do you want to be happy?
2341. Start struggling with your body
2342. Start tormenting your vital
2343. Start doubting your mind
2344. Start crying and loving
2345. Start smiling and flying
2346. My heart's peace
2347. One second of hope
2348. If your mind is thought-bound
2349. A kind of strength
2350. My first aspiration
2351. His Master's unwritten message
2352. The same boat
2353. A new affair
2354. An unfamiliar hope
2355. Your peculiar realisation
2356. God gave me instead
2357. The balloons of your pretence
2358. Your volcano-aspiration
2359. Your Himalayan self-command
2360. No failure is final
2361. His mind is now really happy
2362. His heart is now really happy
2363. Success is action
2364. His life's unexplained mysteries
2365. He knows when to fight back
2366. A symphony of prosperity
2367. The company of silence
2368. Sincerity rises
2369. The dependence is mutual
2370. A perfect leader
2371. Dreamers and lovers
2372. A tomorrow that never comes
2373. He will never suffer from defects
2374. Simplicity has solved my problems
2375. The vision-light of Heaven
2376. My Self-Transcendence-Height
2377. Two sure homes
2378. Worries of the mind
2379. They never fail
2380. The hour of patience
2381. Question your mind dauntlessly
2382. God's Compassion-Heights
2383. Saviour of the mind
2384. My heart's sacred thoughts
2385. Three special freedoms
2386. Titan eyes
2387. A smile on his blue-gold face
2388. An armour of proof
2389. The grand palace of will-power
2390. When I look at him
2391. More changeful than the tide
2392. The gates of laughter wild
2393. A flower in his life
2394. When I unconditionally meditate
2395. If your heart is empty
2396. A poor beggar-singer
2397. If your mind surrenders
2398. The perfection-dawn
2399. Silence succeeds
2400. One idol, one hero
2401. The inner game
2402. My adamantine determination
2403. Each new start
2404. A life of fulfilment-tree
2405. The fire of wild separativity
2406. How can he be alive?
2407. Fruitfulness triumphs
2408. His Child-Heart-Smile
2409. To span the yawning gulf
2410. Live with a union-heart
2411. God gave me his Mind
2412. Something new happened
2413. His future friend
2414. Hope is brightness-dawn
2415. His life as he sees it
2416. Only two things I do
2417. An Olympic seeker
2418. My golden future
2419. They are all wrong
2420. My soul and I
2421. You make your own choice!
2422. Do not weep for me
2423. My communion with God
2424. Minus is good
2425. What do I mean?
2426. Someday
2427. God will always come first

2428. Yes or no
2429. In the new hour ahead
2430. In the new year ahead
2431. I learn from man
2432. Prisoners in my world
2433. God's transcendental Paradise
2434. Immortality's Oneness-Love
2435. Too late to change
2436. To make yourself really happy
2437. No orphan
2438. Don't make it too easy!
2439. Unless you unburden yourself
2440. Self-confidence
2441. My life-transcending cry
2442. Each step of purity
2443. Barren thoughts
2444. Tired of thinking
2445. In love with a sweet dream
2446. I shall arrest my thoughts
2447. A trouble-free life
2448. His vital froze to stone
2449. Frequent meetings
2450. Drop a tear
2451. Cosmic energy
2452. Revolving memories
2453. Breathe a prayer
2454. Wrongs and shames
2455. What my sleeping eyes need
2456. I kneel for forgiveness
2457. Do not love despair
2458. A short-lived passion-smile
2459. How can I be happy?
2460. For transient fame
2461. When I cry
2462. Man's descending dove
2463. A oneness-song only
2464. Owing to outer pressures
2465. A fading name
2466. An act of God's Will
2467. No other credential
2468. The sprinter of success
2469. Be not afraid of death
2470. An aspiration-tree
2471. A pure thought
2472. The breath of morning
2473. Unburden yourself
2474. My Lord's blue-vast Eyes
2475. Human friendship
2476. Pray soulfully, meditate calmly
2477. No work to do
2478. The harvest of leisure-life
2479. A spiritual surprise
2480. The sea of Illumination-Delight
2481. If you have peace
2482. The giant progress
2483. Doubt me not
2484. If you fear not
2485. Every day set sail
2486. Becoming is liberating
2487. The inner sunshine
2488. An illumining experience
2489. Unmatched delights
2490. Yet I love you
2491. An ego-thrill
2492. A face can reveal
2493. Each positive thought
2494. If you hesitate to see
2495. Meditation longs to give
2496. I know that I can receive
2497. Your real strength
2498. O my mind-guide
2499. I can be smart
2500. My life's beauty-hunger
2501. Explore new heights
2502. A different promise
2503. You have lost to Truth
2504. Your willingness to receive
2505. He who sleeps
2506. God's higher worlds
2507. My absolutely normal life
2508. If you want to be happy
2509. If your life is awake
2510. A life-illumining sea
2511. The part that loves God
2512. Near the border of your mind
2513. Your realisations shall transcend
2514. This is called self-knowledge
2515. Do you know?
2516. Self-newness is beautiful
2517. A new nourishment
2518. For a progress-life
2519. Let us realise

2520. Freedom-satisfaction
2521. A pure life
2522. Two questions
2523. A self-unfoldment
2524. Only one thing is perfect
2525. Entitled to criticise
2526. Obscurity is not profundity
2527. How many can transform?
2528. The source
2529. Self-perfection we are
2530. Self-glory
2531. Do the most difficult thing first
2532. You can simplify truth
2533. Philosophy embodies
2534. Peace is a twelve-letter word
2535. Great mind, good heart
2536. The fire-pure change
2537. Your only credential
2538. The question of death
2539. An honest thought
2540. In constant repair
2541. Independent of fate
2542. Only an invincible cry
2543. Most powerfully pleased
2544. A breathtaking surprise
2545. We double our joy
2546. I trust my soul
2547. God is all for you
2548. Your mind-tree bears no fruits
2549. Only three questions
2550. When you think of me
2551. Explore the secrets
2552. I know that you care for me
2553. My ambitious plans are exploded
2554. The absence of my outer happiness
2555. Introductions
2556. Two powerful enemies
2557. Mutual prayer
2558. One long prayer
2559. I do not want to include
2560. A suspicious mind
2561. Can you not care?
2562. Go beyond yourself
2563. Cultivate self-insight
2564. No difference
2565. Only one thing to do
2566. Divine capacities
2567. My mind tells me
2568. I can win everything
2569. Guidance has just arrived
2570. Conviction is an awakening
2571. God's magic Wand
2572. Nothing changes
2573. The touch of sincerity
2574. Satisfaction abides in him
2575. An awakened soul
2576. Choose self-discovery
2577. Try to save yourself
2578. You were an angel
2579. Self-deception's body
2580. An abiding sincerity
2581. A false path
2582. Self-deception and self-perfection
2583. Only one thing is not ready
2584. You are ready to be crowned
2585. The dissatisfaction-tiger
2586. Contradiction-power
2587. A first-class opportunist
2588. Falsehood needs everything
2589. The observer doubts
2590. A subtle fear of the world
2591. We all pretend
2592. Twice you are absolutely right
2593. Conscience
2594. Know one thing well
2595. The carelessness-hearts of others
2596. God wants to see you
2597. Just by claiming
2598. Without praying for an escape
2599. Oneness-understanding-power
2600. All gratitude to You
2601. Nothing to become
2602. Take the tempest out
2603. What is precious?
2604. I need your heart
2605. Who says that God forgets?
2606. I was unprepared
2607. I shall not interrupt you
2608. One thing wrong
2609. I do not know
2610. A free access
2611. Duty comes first

2612. Your arms are for extension
2613. My Lord loves me
2614. When we share our struggles
2615. My meditation tells me
2616. Think of others
2617. No and yes
2618. Aspiration is an achievement
2619. Two needed friends
2620. The warmth of your realisation-sun
2621. No more advice
2622. Originality
2623. I love the pristine beauty
2624. He is already occupied
2625. Renounce, renounce!
2626. He has divorced three things
2627. Earth cannot answer
2628. If you want to please a false God
2629. Your imperfection-repetition
2630. Few in number
2631. Be conscious of your strength
2632. You have sailed a long way
2633. How can I stop destroying myself?
2634. Your lack of outer wealth
2635. Turning on the switch
2636. My mind's trial period
2637. The lives of arguments end
2638. My great days
2639. Make your choice
2640. A soulful smile
2641. Wisdom-sun
2642. Who will lead you?
2643. The fountain of forgiveness
2644. Another name for man
2645. The lamp of faith
2646. He knows the secrets of Heaven
2647. An atom-weight of goodness
2648. God will wait for you
2649. If you do not know the truth
2650. Two supreme Realities
2651. The splendour of the firmament
2652. The road of a defeated life
2653. False discoveries
2654. Every day I water Heaven
2655. His Eternity's Sunrise
2656. If truth comes first
2657. Unless you reform yourself
2658. God does not forget!
2659. A new hunger-dawn
2660. Unconditional Forgiveness
2661. You can conquer fate
2662. Make the right choice
2663. He has renewed himself
2664. Supreme discoveries
2665. Inside a sweet dream
2666. What follows a man of silence?
2667. One unforgivable mistake
2668. Fill the heart
2669. Each blazing warrior-soul
2670. Sleep and dream
2671. God's moonlit Thought
2672. God's dinner
2673. The only pain-killer
2674. The daring concentration-spear
2675. The tears of my heart
2676. Rich and poor
2677. Truth never descends
2678. Man's honesty-boat
2679. A flowing dream
2680. O my aspiration-child
2681. The world loves to examine
2682. Ego-life
2683. Drown your glory
2684. Revive not old desires!
2685. Three everlasting penalties
2686. God-hearers
2687. You have accomplished something
2688. O my beautiful hope-soul
2689. Gratitude is something in our heart
2690. What I call enthusiasm
2691. My self-transcendence-life
2692. I choose freedom
2693. God and I shall call it
2694. I claim
2695. Your prayers are important
2696. God cares for you
2697. One thing more
2698. Have faith
2699. My Lord strengthened
2700. My search ends
2701. Today I am wise

2702. Concealing and revealing
2703. The miracle-reward
2704. Two close friends
2705. You do not want to change
2706. The fruit of satisfaction
2707. An insincere mind
2708. Divinely perfect realisation
2709. The inner problem
2710. Give Him what you have
2711. Many are the ways
2712. The human mind
2713. The examination of self-improvement
2714. The only time
2715. No advantage
2716. To see God's Face
2717. How and why
2718. You examine first
2719. Save me from both!
2720. Never possible
2721. Ideas that are not true
2722. Your own feeble faith
2723. Almost impossible to stop
2724. I am happy twice
2725. To see perfection in the mind
2726. Nobody can see
2727. Choose both
2728. The son of time
2729. O forgiveness-light from Above
2730. A radiant ray
2731. The tree of eternal freedom
2732. Each soulful hope
2733. What my heart is
2734. The dreaming eyes of time
2735. My vision-realities
2736. When the silence-night surrounds me
2737. How can you be happy?
2738. The hyphen
2739. Beyond the reach of delight
2740. The light that never fails
2741. Not on speaking terms
2742. The firsthand experience of God
2743. Our soulful tears
2744. Impossibility
2745. The greatest victor
2746. Unnecessary thoughts
2747. Perfect nonsense
2748. The miracle of miracles
2749. The express falsehood-train
2750. To save myself
2751. Change your inner attitude
2752. Implore and explore
2753. God will do it for you
2754. Self-centredness or self-awareness
2755. When you do not wake up
2756. The beginning
2757. The length of your trouble-world
2758. I tell you secretly
2759. If your heart lives
2760. The compromise-world
2761. One of two things
2762. In the same boat
2763. Do you want to increase?
2764. Every atom
2765. The zoo that you are living in
2766. The unique capacity
2767. The fear of a jungle-mind
2768. The real teacher
2769. One thing
2770. Inside the power of love
2771. The world of realisation
2772. The satisfaction-sun
2773. Your own satisfaction
2774. Defeat of my ego-power
2775. Truth-tellers
2776. My deplorable weaknesses
2777. One defeat I shall never accept
2778. The peace of silence-sky
2779. His special Favour
2780. God's amazing intimacy
2781. The thorn-crown of depression
2782. A silence-dawn invites me
2783. The tasteless loaf of idleness
2784. An ingratitude-heart
2785. A special world of God's
2786. A new thought
2787. Do not hope to escape
2788. Taste and renounce
2789. Each pure thought
2790. Each divine thought
2791. I thought I was perfect

2792. The smile of life ever-lasting
2793. The keys of wisdom-delight
2794. What I need from you
2795. The transcendental cure
2796. If you pray to lose yourself
2797. My definition of joy
2798. When we share
2799. When hope is gone
2800. The path of the soul
2801. A feast in the inner world
2802. Not looking for the reality
2803. An opportunist society
2804. If you want guidance
2805. Insecurity, I am a clever man
2806. The heart-grove
2807. Two discoveries
2808. The seed of self-observation
2809. What have you lost?
2810. Unparalleled quality
2811. Sail in the right boat
2812. Two questions
2813. Our real nature
2814. Unless and until
2815. A God-revealing faith
2816. Your sleepless faith
2817. Fly with your soul-bird
2818. An unkind mind
2819. Permanent sunshine
2820. You have shortened the distance
2821. What we give
2822. The fragrance of oneness-light
2823. Only two safe places
2824. The flower and fruit
2825. Make the correct choice
2826. What is your own
2827. A big favour
2828. Today's nectar-meal
2829. A lamb-slave of man
2830. We have to make ourselves ready
2831. Because my game was a pleasure-life
2832. I have learnt many things
2833. A power without equal
2834. Relief
2835. Nobody can dominate you
2836. Give up and accept
2837. Yes and no
2838. Say "No" to your doubt-life
2839. Surrender to your higher life
2840. The higher power
2841. A "No" from your heart
2842. Your friends
2843. A time-wasting idler
2844. Your heart knows best
2845. Do you want to be happy?
2846. To be a good walker
2847. Adhere always to your firm decision
2848. Do not surrender to exhaustion
2849. Demands
2850. Endless talking
2851. My mind is fascinated
2852. Only one competition
2853. He is faultlessly right
2854. The cave of false protection
2855. My life of progress
2856. You have almost realised
2857. The capacity to deceive
2858. In one spacious room
2859. Make haste
2860. When you are ready
2861. Something special
2862. Feast and hunger
2863. To make my Lord happy
2864. You have not forgiven me
2865. No sincere seeker
2866. Thousands of strong reasons
2867. To end your unhappiness
2868. Confidence tells you
2869. The face of your future regrets
2870. You call it misunderstanding
2871. One thing will never frighten you
2872. God the Conqueror
2873. Something new you should know
2874. Not what you appear to be
2875. God's Inspiration-Victory
2876. Only one way
2877. The heart of oneness
2878. Capacity and necessity
2879. Courage means
2880. A divine family
2881. Let your heart-bud bleed

2882. The life-meter clicks
2883. Radios
2884. Only one satisfaction
2885. The uncomely things
2886. Escaping the confusion
2887. The mistakes in your life
2888. We pretend to know
2889. Clever evasions
2890. Discouragement
2891. The more you try to convince yourself
2892. Challenge your frustration-vital
2893. Your false imagination
2894. God's Nectar-Smile
2895. You have come to learn
2896. God's Promise to you
2897. If he is your true friend
2898. A satisfaction-light
2899. Once you start believing your soul
2900. God will do the needful
2901. A good thought
2902. The most expensive thing
2903. The spiritual Master
2904. My image of life-perfection
2905. The destruction-game
2906. Three uncompromising worlds
2907. A better citizen of the world
2908. You are terribly alone
2909. The courage to tell the world
2910. My compassionate Lord
2911. Excruciating pangs
2912. A constantly peaceful mind
2913. The results of my impurity
2914. Will You not come to me?
2915. My tiny world and God's big World
2916. I am happy only twice
2917. I have not been dreaming
2918. What will happen?
2919. What pains You most?
2920. Your complete Manifestation
2921. A time when You do not love me
2922. The real difference
2923. We must soulfully combine
2924. The capacity to become
2925. Open my eyes
2926. My only needs
2927. God has transcended Himself
2928. Self-mastery and God-discovery
2929. I followed you closely
2930. Purify and intensify
2931. A new boon
2932. If you want God to crown you
2933. You are a fool
2934. Only one way
2935. Look for perfection
2936. Courage produces a great man
2937. Two divine gifts
2938. Because He is my only Friend
2939. God will pay you every day
2940. A man of wisdom-delight
2941. Three teachers
2942. Courage means readiness
2943. A poor man wants something
2944. My life wants
2945. Do not whisper
2946. If you believe in God
2947. Think of God
2948. My Immortality's Reality-Shore
2949. God's Capacity and Quality
2950. My life can be satisfied
2951. Inside God
2952. The supreme fulfiller
2953. Three kinds of love
2954. My Beloved Krishna
2955. If you have no courage
2956. Your best friend
2957. Two inseparables
2958. An insincere aspiration
2959. Only one thing
2960. Question yourself
2961. I want to go beyond myself
2962. My present life
2963. Jump off the boat
2964. Develop the capacity
2965. God is exceptionally pleased
2966. God is turning towards you
2967. A new game
2968. God wants to be saved
2969. Sincerity has the capacity
2970. He will take care of everything
2971. To make progress

2972. God's own Treasure
2973. Before your mind tells you
2974. Change your course
2975. He who is divinely practical
2976. God wants you to do that
2977. Who will save me?
2978. What you want
2979. My unmistakable assurance
2980. You want only to rise
2981. Do you want to be happy?
2982. God has something to tell me
2983. My successful day begins
2984. My experience
2985. I can never stop
2986. My life's dedication-smile
2987. Simplicity is the preparation-seed
2988. What can be more heartbreaking?
2989. The Kingdom of Heaven
2990. If you pray to God
2991. Quite often I see a stranger
2992. A false life
2993. Your extraordinary love-power
2994. I shall never forget
2995. Peace you get
2996. Now that you are not praying
2997. What you have lost
2998. Gratitude
2999. Why do we fail?
3000. Just do one thing selflessly
3001. Unless you lose yourself
3002. The main problem with my mind
3003. Your God-attempt
3004. If you want to be perfect
3005. The fond child of God
3006. The art of commanding yourself
3007. I am suffering
3008. Why are you being tortured?
3009. Your soul will please you
3010. My Lord's Quality and Quantity
3011. To solve your problems
3012. Truth helps us in our quest
3013. Time for a new boss
3014. If you have a wrong thought
3015. Always try to remain untouched
3016. They are not ready
3017. Each wants to dominate
3018. You can be happy
3019. You think, I think
3020. Can your life not be satisfied?
3021. Tomorrow's silence-beauty
3022. Run against all odds
3023. On the eve of his venture
3024. Two powerful rivals
3025. A special prayer
3026. If your mind can imagine
3027. I did not listen
3028. Push and pull
3029. A nagging sense of emptiness
3030. Only two significant messages
3031. The life of mendicant-hope
3032. A fruitful peace-life
3033. My grateful eyes and heart
3034. The symphony of a hopeful day
3035. Two inexplicable things
3036. An ardent submissiveness
3037. Under the brightest morning
3038. Why do you pretend?
3039. Oneness is generous
3040. We are given chance after chance
3041. If you know about truth
3042. If you are truly spiritual
3043. You do not have to be a loser
3044. Someone advised you
3045. You have the capacity
3046. If you are faithful
3047. You are with God
3048. Why don't you smile and dance?
3049. If you depend on the positive
3050. My actions lined with religion
3051. A fount of admonition
3052. Three unthinkable suggestions
3053. A mistrusting mind
3054. Another name for absurdity
3055. A fine sense of contrast
3056. His sincerity-life is totally lost
3057. A desire-life is ultimately caught
3058. Three immovable convictions
3059. Stupidity has a free access
3060. Three glorious qualifications
3061. The train of your self-discovery
3062. Each temptation
3063. A profitable partnership

3064. A fearless expectation of success
3065. The world is not listening to you
3066. If you can become a better listener
3067. If your mind develops
3068. Three inevitable companions
3069. Two peerless boons
3070. Question their right
3071. Stand firm
3072. Challenge and regain
3073. Do not be afraid
3074. Three alternatives
3075. Follow your soul
3076. Sail on your aspiration-voyage
3077. God's Freedom-Height
3078. Love enlightenment more
3079. See if I am correct
3080. They choose you
3081. If you persist
3082. Our mutual satisfaction-delight
3083. To believe in human promises
3084. Only God has power
3085. Your loneliness-fire
3086. The real story
3087. You owe your success-life
3088. Truth wants you
3089. My Lord's great Satisfaction
3090. Your last gift
3091. My heart is crying
3092. Empty deception-praise
3093. I am completely lost
3094. I shall need You only
3095. God has the sincerity
3096. Oneness-joy
3097. I shall never be lost
3098. Ask your heart
3099. Every day I am deceived
3100. God has the time
3101. God's God-Beauty
3102. Purity in the heart
3103. A mind of silence
3104. Three peerless gifts
3105. Oneness
3106. God's unconditional Compassion
3107. The ultimate step
3108. The delight of sincerity
3109. Give me a pure heart
3110. Before I reach You
3111. The eyes of purity
3112. The name of this house
3113. My sleepless purity-breath
3114. Obedience in a seeker's life
3115. Obedience is the seed
3116. Humility is the capacity
3117. Humility achieves everything
3118. My conscious self-glory
3119. Appreciation for my prayer
3120. The inner garden of beauty
3121. Oneness with the sound-world
3122. A sea of ecstasy
3123. A self-revealing reality
3124. Two perfect strangers
3125. Since his soul is hungry
3126. A new dawn will appear
3127. Your heart's ingratitude-rope
3128. Roles
3129. Gratitude is the food of faith
3130. If you want to cry
3131. You are weak
3132. I fear God
3133. Trust Russia
3134. My supreme secret
3135. God sees what we see
3136. Two intruders
3137. The situation-cloud
3138. God has made you great
3139. Only two necessities
3140. When insecurity comes
3141. Please only your heart
3142. Your faith-power is stronger
3143. The reward of faith and humility
3144. God needs your life
3145. Do not talk, act!
3146. No whisper
3147. How to achieve more
3148. If you want God
3149. Inseparable friends
3150. Your deplorable involvements
3151. Your real personality
3152. Each helpful experience
3153. We do not know what to become
3154. The company of anxiety
3155. In spite of everything

3156. If you have the right aim
3157. When Truth invites you
3158. Silence teaches me
3159. Your heart's reality-cry
3160. If you are sincerely ashamed
3161. The greatest fool
3162. The path of disproportionate pride
3163. The burden of power
3164. There comes a time
3165. My unsung song
3166. Beautiful is my mind
3167. A lightning-laughter
3168. Into the chasm of despair
3169. I go to You
3170. With a wailing cry
3171. The difference between our songs
3172. The delight of oneness-satisfaction
3173. Your unconditional surrender
3174. A mind of newness-hope
3175. My mind cries
3176. A lengthening stretch
3177. Your aspiring patience-heart
3178. Do not forget one thing
3179. Do not glorify your stupidity
3180. Unless you give up
3181. I am determined
3182. What you actually value
3183. Your willingness
3184. There is only one miracle
3185. Self-reliance
3186. When your mind is fearful
3187. If you make a perfect choice
3188. The only remedy
3189. My peculiar way
3190. A stupid thought
3191. You have every right
3192. If you want to like yourself
3193. Its prediction is perfect
3194. Three life-crowning thoughts
3195. I am smiling
3196. A tragically dying passenger
3197. Each problem is an opportunity
3198. The self-improvement-boat
3199. Can you not play your role?
3200. If you are not pure
3201. The shrine of my heart
3202. O superiority-tree
3203. A questioning mind
3204. It was God's Plan
3205. O blissful independence
3206. My heart has succeeded
3207. In my Lord's Heart
3208. Newness satisfies
3209. Not a difficult task
3210. When I became a candidate
3211. Your capacity for self-delusion
3212. Your Forgiveness-Sun
3213. The smile of my eyes
3214. My dream-eyes exist
3215. When I was a purity-heart
3216. Rather a quick death
3217. I am ready to weep
3218. God Himself is suffocating
3219. The supernal mysteries
3220. If my doubt is mighty
3221. My soul's sacred smile
3222. On the inimitable way
3223. I am realising you
3224. Born to do something great
3225. I have buried my past
3226. My heart and God's Heart
3227. God's Grace-Kingdom
3228. A Source unknowable
3229. Sanctioned and guaranteed
3230. The weight of my ignorance-night
3231. How can fear torture me?
3232. A breathless whisper from afar
3233. O divine Grace
3234. My inevitable choice
3235. My Lord will give His Eternity
3236. To develop beauty
3237. Imperturbable cheerfulness
3238. An increasing brightness
3239. A winning boat
3240. A well-constructed bridge
3241. A noisy and hollow boast
3242. You are mercifully blind
3243. You enjoy perennial bliss
3244. Sorrow I share
3245. I love everything
3246. Nothing less than the highest
3247. Perfect revelations

3248. My witnesses
3249. I affirm what God affirms
3250. Two smiles
3251. An exception
3252. Everything is equally important
3253. The seeker can escape
3254. To proceed confidently
3255. Aspiration-power assures
3256. Man is an imperfect instrument
3257. Discipline is God-interest
3258. Sleep not
3259. Journey's end, journey's beginning
3260. A God-seeker's aspiration-cry
3261. You can earn your place
3262. The flight of your gratitude-heart
3263. Dining with frailties
3264. Sing the self-offering song
3265. Just transcend your mind
3266. The roots of delight-tree
3267. God's choice Hour
3268. Your soul-bird's plumage
3269. Explore the Beauty of God
3270. When I do something wrong
3271. My heart knows how to receive
3272. One kind thought
3273. The height of my victory
3274. In God's Hands
3275. My earthly and Heavenly quest
3276. Aspiration means self-development
3277. The songs of the eternal Now
3278. When I pray to God
3279. Purity can be a daily experience
3280. A safe investment
3281. If the world is challenging me
3282. Its own horrifying curse
3283. The life that will rise
3284. The hunger of possessiveness
3285. What was that nothing?
3286. Every good thought
3287. A fruitful pilgrim
3288. What my mind needs
3289. Inexhaustible enthusiasm
3290. Fabulous fame
3291. My body needs calm confidence
3292. If you make others happy
3293. Pull down the confidence-sky
3294. New hopes and old regrets
3295. Confidence founded upon Grace
3296. If you want to learn
3297. An inch beyond
3298. The pressure of small needs
3299. Because of your great capacity
3300. What can life do to me?
3301. Real joy
3302. Prosperity-palace, purity-cave
3303. A powerful comforter
3304. Any eager and intense attempt
3305. If your heart can dream of purity
3306. A sound and happy co-operation
3307. Human nature's daily food
3308. I need intense concentration
3309. I shall liberate my mind
3310. God's perfection-experience
3311. My inexorable fate
3312. My earth-pilgrimage
3313. My Heaven-pilgrimage
3314. Master, where is light?
3315. Master, where is delight?
3316. The divine in us enters
3317. My heart is God's Choice
3318. Because your heart is detached
3319. You will be happy
3320. You must learn
3321. Man has yet to build
3322. Where construction ends
3323. My morning and evening questions
3324. A supreme secret
3325. You do your own duty
3326. Love has tremendous power
3327. Their shameless ignorance-smile
3328. A fruitful solution
3329. God gives you a new heart
3330. You want to change the world
3331. You are taking God's job
3332. Nothing that God will not do
3333. God's Satisfaction-Sun
3334. Your vital and mind
3335. Your own life's dedication-promise
3336. Learn what you need to know
3337. The fountain of immortal life

3338. You have transformed your life
3339. I owe God everything
3340. Your life's inner emptiness
3341. At times you need outer emptiness
3342. The fulness of your inner life
3343. He alone lives
3344. Changes in our aspiration-life
3345. A self-fulfilled man
3346. Because I strive
3347. As the years advance upon me
3348. The worst possible traitor
3349. The past is the foundation
3350. A liberated man
3351. Conquest of the mind
3352. Newness precedes soulfulness
3353. My heart's contribution
3354. I came from the unknowable
3355. To ascend and transcend
3356. Selfishness-cat
3357. A strange but peaceful smile
3358. Yours are the blessingful Hands
3359. One question worth asking
3360. God's Forgiveness-Eye
3361. The world's good opinion
3362. Desperation ends
3363. You try to exploit God
3364. Unless your heart has wisdom
3365. They are deeply interested
3366. Your God-given sincerity
3367. Who is on your side?
3368. Do not be a fool!
3369. You have to rebel
3370. Eternally fruitful
3371. What you actually want
3372. Your useless mind
3373. An absurd expectation
3374. Two things are always real
3375. Is there anything you cannot accomplish?
3376. The meaning of sacrifice
3377. Never use the word gratitude
3378. The song of innocence
3379. By far the best
3380. God-dreamers and God-lovers
3381. The divinity of the unknowable
3382. God is everything
3383. God will protect you
3384. My life needs intensity
3385. To change your life
3386. Perfect strangers
3387. Inseparable friends
3388. I know what God has for me
3389. The outer and inner teachers
3390. Conquer yourself
3391. If you want God's Goodness
3392. Only the unaspiring qualities
3393. Man crawls towards God
3394. Man thinks that he has God
3395. Your heart will be all right
3396. Our aspiration-cry can do that
3397. The fruit of a transformation-life
3398. Man is perfect
3399. What your heart is
3400. Ignore the pains of your body
3401. If I can love myself
3402. If I can treat myself carefully
3403. If I can examine myself
3404. If I can give myself
3405. If I can think of myself
3406. If I can see myself
3407. If I can purify myself
3408. O locked door of my mind
3409. I keep my eyes open
3410. My Lord comes to me
3411. Wisdom-light
3412. Perfect my imperfections
3413. The thought-world
3414. O my indecisive mind
3415. His heart was his foe
3416. Infinity's Light radiates
3417. Nothing is more beautiful
3418. Oneness fulfils
3419. Because of his self-doubt
3420. You hide because you are afraid
3421. The beauty of the morning
3422. I am very happy
3423. If you see your mistakes
3424. Become a perfect man
3425. A Spiritual Master is strict
3426. O my broken heart
3427. Do not pretend!
3428. You just have to tolerate yourself

3429. Sincerity purifies our eyes
3430. A simple heart has the beauty
3431. Prayerfully cry every day
3432. No longer a counterfeit
3433. Keep determination
3434. Enthusiasm and imperfection
3435. Nothing can be lost for good
3436. Love yourself more
3437. If I unreservedly devote myself
3438. Love yourself more every day
3439. Self-doubt disappears
3440. One day we will all become perfect
3441. God can teach you
3442. The self-giving heart
3443. The Supreme in us loves
3444. How can I forgive myself?
3445. All are fascinated
3446. A direct connection
3447. Glowing remedies
3448. I am eager to learn
3449. In God's Care
3450. Quality-suggestions
3451. My teachers
3452. Proud statements
3453. Cheerfulness-treasure
3454. Malady and remedy
3455. Remembrance of God's Name
3456. Give up everything else
3457. Your heart is all you need
3458. A beacon-light
3459. Surrender is a clarion call
3460. If you have a thought
3461. Only one thing beautiful
3462. My Beloved Supreme is searching
3463. Who says you are cruel?
3464. If you listen to your vital
3465. Your heart can protect
3466. Another name
3467. Your cheerful heart
3468. My perfect desire
3469. The vastness-beauty of the sky
3470. Keep crying
3471. Wisdom is power
3472. Beyond the reach
3473. Purity, purity, purity!
3474. Like being reborn
3475. As the clouds cannot hide
3476. A man of failure
3477. Without the beauty of surrender
3478. A useful seeker
3479. Impossible for a liberated man
3480. I think of you, my Lord
3481. When you live in yourself
3482. Go beyond your mind
3483. Perfect your earthbound mind
3484. Study the art of humility
3485. A fool
3486. What compels me to leave?
3487. Fountain-hearts of aspiration
3488. He who consoles your heart
3489. What do you want from God?
3490. I shall no more desire
3491. The ultimate Truth
3492. Infinitely more difficult
3493. You need both
3494. Your bounden duty
3495. My mental world
3496. An absurd expectation
3497. A right ideal-palace
3498. You want to manifest God
3499. When I see my Lord's Omnipotence
3500. O Truth-seeker, O God-lover
3501. Three are the easy steps
3502. Do you want to enjoy your self?
3503. He shows interest in you
3504. Don't blame your confusion-mind
3505. You can never spare a moment
3506. Dependence-division-hour
3507. What confession actually needs
3508. God's perfect faith in you
3509. A real difference
3510. You are obliged
3511. To know more
3512. Do not be afraid of shadows
3513. The human in you deceives him
3514. A perfectly adaptable instrument
3515. Become the song of oneness
3516. Illumination is imperative
3517. If you are a true seeker
3518. Think only of accepting

3519. I can easily protect myself
3520. If you have a searching mind
3521. God tells me what to do
3522. Outer and inner conquest
3523. Yesterday my mind frightened me
3524. God likes your powerful mind
3525. Two pieces of advice
3526. What do you want?
3527. Before you think of realising God
3528. I love my inner life
3529. I brave the powerful blows
3530. A fruitful life
3531. God does not mind
3532. Someone is waiting
3533. To sit at the Feet of God
3534. I am a fool
3535. My God-strength
3536. My Lord is happy
3537. Golden is Eternity's Road
3538. My mind is afraid
3539. Only one thing satisfies me
3540. Your wee life-boat
3541. You do not deserve
3542. End the inner war
3543. What a strange attitude!
3544. Why do you forget?
3545. You can surmount all obstacles
3546. If you want to learn more
3547. Start to think of a new life
3548. When my dream-tower collapses
3549. For sweet progress
3550. If you dare to know who you are
3551. Why do you have to feel helpless?
3552. If you think you are practical
3553. Confusion-night cannot last
3554. Three false realisations
3555. Believe in the higher visions
3556. Your Himalayan self-transformation
3557. A sure surety-life
3558. Death ennobles
3559. He will succeed
3560. I do not know them
3561. At the mercy of time
3562. Be careful of uninspiring books
3563. God's Benediction-Sky
3564. The right thing
3565. Assist and resist
3566. The blossoms of hope
3567. A right question
3568. Your outer smile
3569. Confess to the right person!
3570. Your constant remembrance
3571. Unless I act from God's Heart
3572. Always an oasis
3573. An unforgettable truth
3574. The right thing to do
3575. You can increase
3576. The eyeless and earless seekers
3577. Ignore your protests
3578. Aspiration without dedication
3579. How can you succeed?
3580. Depending on oneself alone
3581. My Lord Supreme smiles twice
3582. Give up your hiding game
3583. Do you know?
3584. The last thing a saint wants to hear
3585. You fail again and again
3586. God's Independence-Delight
3587. How can you smile?
3588. A volley of borrowed opinions
3589. What my life needs
3590. Sleepless goodness
3591. The strength-tower of sincerity
3592. If you think confusion is necessary
3593. His heart is against him
3594. What you need
3595. The richest life
3596. The mountain of peace
3597. The purification man
3598. Your greatness is fascinating
3599. Do try to be as beautiful
3600. Happiness
3601. Obedience is the fruitful goal
3602. My obedience
3603. The divine capacity and inclination
3604. God-manifesting Light
3605. I have no time
3606. If you do not glow
3607. Your body annoys you
3608. Immediate neighbours

3609. The inner conquest
3610. We have undivine thoughts
3611. Why cry?
3612. Your task, God's Task
3613. If you are an unaspiring man
3614. If you know how to think properly
3615. The trouble-shooter knows
3616. Remember what you said
3617. You can easily feel the truth
3618. Divinity does not know
3619. The divine heart proceeds
3620. My mind's confusion
3621. Delight is an unlimited capacity
3622. To say something deeper
3623. The highest progress
3624. Try to belong to your heart
3625. Do you want to win?
3626. Resist the power of darkness
3627. One more way
3628. One way to win
3629. You will no longer tolerate
3630. No match for you
3631. To know more
3632. What the world has for you
3633. What the mind needs
3634. When unaspiring seekers meet
3635. Preparing for a new game
3636. Imagination tells me
3637. We do not know
3638. You can conquer
3639. No difference whatsoever
3640. The way to conquer
3641. You can expect nothing
3642. Doubt fools the doubter in us
3643. Live up to your Himalayan heights
3644. Stand against your lower self
3645. A sea of silence-night
3646. Uncover and discover
3647. The world does not trust you
3648. Absolutely mistaken
3649. God will definitely blame you
3650. You enjoy doubts
3651. Although I fail
3652. Make no haughty demands
3653. The stillness of the mind
3654. If it is too late
3655. It can never be too late
3656. My hope tells me
3657. The human mind
3658. When I live in the heart
3659. What is active devotion?
3660. Weighing your faults
3661. Unless you believe
3662. Saying good-bye
3663. Self-investigation
3664. Willingness and readiness
3665. Something equally distributed
3666. Your obedience will teach you
3667. I appreciate your heart
3668. Totally lost
3669. The pretence-wings of the mind
3670. Do you want to be happy?
3671. Your heart's oneness-role
3672. If you can see the beauty
3673. Your worried morning
3674. I do not deny
3675. Doubt is powerful and destructive
3676. Two things almost unconquerable
3677. Three things I desperately need
3678. An exceptional privilege
3679. A new form
3680. The seeker who lives a hidden life
3681. You are lonely because
3682. Refuse to surrender
3683. The secret of satisfaction
3684. He who aspires
3685. I shall not avoid you
3686. Why do you listen?
3687. Two perfect strangers
3688. The brightest dawn resides
3689. An earthly gift
3690. Do not ignore your doubting mind
3691. Not like you
3692. A child's sweet hopefulness
3693. A golden shower from Above
3694. Our inner stillness
3695. What can poor God do?
3696. The question of questions
3697. As I prefer knowledge-light
3698. An isolated and deserted life
3699. The rising of my soul-rainbow
3700. Your heart's gratitude-plant
3701. Just stay with me
3702. A thinker shows the world
3703. If I feel love
3704. His transcendental Freedom
3705. God's best Child
3706. As soon as I succeed
3707. I shall prove myself
3708. My Lord, until we meet again
3709. Because I believe in you
3710. I pray to God
3711. I know what to feel
3712. Before I pray to God
3713. I shall sleeplessly love God
3714. My heart loves God
3715. One question is torturing me
3716. There is only one kind of suffering
3717. If you have stopped
3718. The vision of possibilities
3719. A soulful and God-loving heart
3720. A dislike for praise
3721. A rare strength of mind
3722. Eternity's fruitful Bliss
3723. My deliberate errors
3724. Who can determine the distance?
3725. Try to live only one season
3726. The memorial of forgotten faith
3727. One thing can adorn my life
3728. My Heaven-free heart
3729. A uselessly painful affair
3730. Unconquerable indifference-noon
3731. A soft tone of humility
3732. God the Lover
3733. God's unlimited Forgiveness
3734. My mind's sincerity-river
3735. Who wants to know?
3736. What am I waiting for?
3737. I shall keep for myself
3738. The Saviour teaches me
3739. I hope this discovery is true
3740. For you
3741. When I tell God
3742. You enjoy peculiarity
3743. When we cheerfully perform
3744. He who loves life
3745. Unless you believe in God's Help
3746. An idle man
3747. The problem with fault-finding
3748. Unless I believe in the unknown
3749. No matter how bad your mind is
3750. If you have a pure heart
3751. I really feel sorry
3752. A doubtful mind and a fearful heart
3753. Yesterday I was satisfied
3754. God the young and God the old
3755. He likes to play with God
3756. Feel that I am not displeased
3757. The clouds do not last forever
3758. Do not underestimate
3759. If it is true
3760. I am pleased with my mind
3761. A seeker without discipline
3762. Aspiration minus dedication
3763. Because God tells me
3764. I can't believe
3765. God has given up everything
3766. I shall tell you where God is
3767. Twice I shed tears of gratitude
3768. Two ways to conquer ignorance
3769. Two beautiful twins
3770. An unconditional life
3771. Once God sees you
3772. God wants to see
3773. My eyes do not know
3774. Life is sadness
3775. Man's destruction-frown
3776. Who is worthy?
3777. The best way
3778. God's sadness
3779. There is Somebody else
3780. Tell the world
3781. My Lord denied me
3782. Keep counting the flowers
3783. A great difference
3784. Two purposes
3785. You come to realise
3786. Don't pray for useless things!
3787. A second birth
3788. The divinity of hope
3789. My consciousness tells me
3790. The temptation-tree
3791. Soulfully you give
3792. If you have faith in yourself
3793. Have a positive idea
3794. My perfect disciple
3795. Love yourself cheerfully
3796. Give to man
3797. The Power of God's Feet
3798. Since God has not rejected you
3799. I am already up!
3800. My Lord's Oneness
3801. True freedom will come
3802. The secret of your inner progress
3803. God is within me
3804. Give cheerfully
3805. You will really be happy
3806. You are an ideal-sea
3807. God will deny you
3808. The immortality of peace
3809. A great barrier
3810. A soulfully surrendered heart
3811. Anything useless
3812. Self-deception must give way
3813. Inner neighbours
3814. When I think and think
3815. Faith will change his future
3816. You entirely belong to God
3817. You do your duty
3818. An awakened soul
3819. Renunciation-light helps you
3820. You are fully ready
3821. The absolute Fulness of God
3822. A spiritual person liberates me
3823. To run to the unknown
3824. What is right for my heart
3825. Discard this false notion!
3826. You have done my job
3827. Tired of forgiving
3828. A fruitful God-Satisfaction
3829. His bountiful and gracious Heart
3830. God gets the opportunity
3831. The perennial Truth
3832. When I say I belong to God
3833. God's Ecstasy-Heart
3834. The Light of the Beyond
3835. My surrender-life tells me
3836. Intuition knows
3837. Just feel that I am yours
3838. If you are doing something wrong
3839. A big nectar-feast
3840. The pride of ignorance
3841. A self-transcending beginning
3842. Develop a new heart
3843. I need God badly
3844. What you are
3845. An eternal Breath
3846. To see the Face of God
3847. Be aware of your thought-life!
3848. To know more
3849. In the beginning
3850. The answer
3851. The source of all strength
3852. A grateful seeker
3853. Three most significant things
3854. How can God care for you?
3855. An unusual compromise
3856. I shall not give up
3857. Your utter ruin
3858. The way to change your mind
3859. The transformation of man's nature
3860. Why are you so hesitant?
3861. Love alone will rule
3862. God will open his Heart
3863. The key of love
3864. Do you not see?
3865. Your life cannot be rootless
3866. Conquer your idle thoughts
3867. A perfect treasure
3868. Your life will be blighted
3869. He who does not love life
3870. Humility
3871. I am pleased only with my soul
3872. A true and sleepless love of God
3873. God the Justice
3874. A God-lover knows
3875. Patience was the beginning
3876. I must go beyond thought
3877. Obey the small whispers of peace
3878. Ignorance binds us
3879. God Himself has chosen
3880. Your vital ease
3881. If your heart-flower is withered
3882. Two unanswered questions
3883. What does Heaven like?
3884. The things I feel
3885. I thank You for two reasons
3886. A small measure
3887. Your happiness will be multiplied
3888. After you have revealed
3889. If you have a prayerful heart
3890. His heart knows
3891. The wall of cheerfulness
3892. You are most precious to God
3893. Faith is fruitful
3894. A new and perfect boss
3895. Years from now
3896. Truth really loves us
3897. Silence speaks for you
3898. An added delay
3899. A true sense of satisfaction
3900. My mind needed greatness
3901. My heart's only choice
3902. You call it self-command
3903. Our mental power
3904. One of the true immortals
3905. The world's useless gifts
3906. A bright place
3907. The heart's own illumination
3908. A spiritual Teacher knows
3909. I have the heart to thank you
3910. A special way for me
3911. I am sailing
3912. Free and perfect
3913. It seems that you are interested
3914. You do not have to worry
3915. You are haunted
3916. Your self-mastery
3917. If you think you have problems
3918. God the Compassion-Monarch
3919. I try
3920. God exists for me
3921. When you find
3922. To see your bountiful face
3923. Wake up!
3924. When I run with God
3925. Your eyes have the beauty
3926. Two misfortunes in life
3927. Your patience-tree
3928. Oneness-satisfaction
3929. When my Lord pulls me
3930. My life likes to know
3931. If you care to make me happy
3932. My mind wants only attention
3933. A perfect answer
3934. I try to please God
3935. Who is really wise?
3936. Do you want to change yourself?
3937. You want to love them
3938. If you want God the Quantity
3939. God wants one thing in your life
3940. Surrender yourself
3941. If you run fast
3942. He still has a chance
3943. Two compeers
3944. O my heart of beauty
3945. I shall follow you unreservedly
3946. To live in the Eternal Now
3947. Before you can repair your mind
3948. To be one's own teacher
3949. There can be no strength
3950. Surrender to the sky-silence
3951. If I do not dare to fight
3952. Nothing is beyond repair
3953. For my Lord's Compassion-Heart
3954. When I come to you confidently
3955. What you need to have
3956. I gave you what I had
3957. The power of a radiant sunrise
3958. Two miracles
3959. Because you are extremely weak
3960. Your heart's satisfaction-house
3961. Your very old associate
3962. A blessingful gift
3963. The journey's fulfilling initiation
3964. This is your task
3965. I am thanking you
3966. I shall forgive and forget
3967. My God-reliance manifests
3968. Be not a rank fool!
3969. Tell your mind
3970. What a mind you have!
3971. How can you be happy?
3972. Do you know yourself?

3973. His heart wishes
3974. The more you love the divinity
3975. To go beyond yourself
3976. He is not a poor man
3977. Wrongs and rights
3978. If you want to free yourself
3979. The strength of fulness
3980. Each good thought
3981. Unless you lead your own life
3982. You are working for others
3983. Your life's salvation-smile
3984. A clear mind
3985. Awaken the human life
3986. Who is standing in your way?
3987. The end of your mind's confusion
3988. Your own brother
3989. If you can think correctly
3990. Once you stop being frightened
3991. Observe your actions
3992. How can you not succeed?
3993. If you want to expand your mind
3994. To transform your life
3995. If your life is real
3996. If you choose
3997. Do not be discouraged
3998. Awareness is strength
3999. Confidence is calmness
4000. Do you want to be fruitful?
4001. Every time I run away from You
4002. An amazing miracle
4003. You can save yourself
4004. Fear ends in self-defence
4005. To escape the mind-jungle
4006. Ask your body to wake up
4007. I have time to think
4008. God's Compassion-Waves
4009. The choice
4010. Your mind gets an ego-thrill
4011. Cry for another reason
4012. Respect the world
4013. Do you not remember?
4014. Why do you blame God?
4015. Soulfully you love God
4016. Teach what you are being taught
4017. A pure thought liberates you
4018. Your mind can expose you
4019. If you want to change your life
4020. The only way to arrive
4021. Go to the garden of love-light
4022. Give up your lethargy
4023. Deep inside my jungle-life
4024. Without the beauty of a dream-boat
4025. When you are insecure
4026. Take a new look at yourself
4027. Four most fulfilling neighbours
4028. To please the seeker-heart in you
4029. Everything ultimately helps
4030. The brave doer
4031. Do not give up!
4032. Every day my heart turns
4033. A hope-building motto
4034. Each experience of love
4035. If you give lovingly
4036. I call it opportunity
4037. Each experience
4038. When I do something great
4039. I am looking for a miracle
4040. What we have given
4041. The answer I like most
4042. Your heart can change
4043. You aspire and strive
4044. Self-glory and God-discovery
4045. The undivine in me
4046. Wisdom-light is eagerly waiting
4047. More to follow
4048. The clever invitation
4049. I am totally obliged
4050. Your prayerful sincerity
4051. How Do You Dare?
4052. I Shall Obey You Unconditionally
4053. I Am So Pleased
4054. You Have The Capacity
4055. To Conquer Self-Deception
4056. What Can You Expect?
4057. The Job You Alone Can Do
4058. Just Try To Regain
4059. Most Intimate Friends
4060. I Am All Admiration For You
4061. Alas, I Am Not Ready
4062. A Self-Giving, Dauntless Soul
4063. Lovingly Try To Give God
4064. If You Want To Sing
4065. To Pierce The Veil Of Ignorance
4066. If You Wish To Succeed In Life
4067. If You Have Nothing To Do
4068. No Appreciable Difference
4069. He Who Loves Your Heart
4070. Doomed To Carry
4071. His Soulful Prayer To God
4072. Hide-And-Seek
4073. A Wise Man Loves Himself
4074. His Heart Is Praying To God
4075. Automatically They Will Gain
4076. God The Teacher
4077. If You Have A Good Desire
4078. My Sufferings
4079. He Commands
4080. I Shall Respect My Lord
4081. If You Can Love God
4082. The Inner World Needs Him
4083. Do Empty My Mind Completely
4084. Do Not Be Afraid
4085. When I Am In The Psychic Plane
4086. God's Forgiveness-Height
4087. An Unsoiled And Sacred Heart
4088. Each Morning Meditation
4089. Your Mind Does Not Want To Know
4090. Give And Receive
4091. Your Soulful Patience
4092. Patience Is The Purity Of Hope
4093. Patience Lives At The Root
4094. As Rich And Happy
4095. Patience Is The Soul-Power
4096. The Fragrance Of His Life-Flower
4097. My Mind Is Heavy
4098. God Denied Me
4099. Do Give Me The Courage
4100. How Far Can It Take Me?
4101. Today is my day
4102. Every day is the right day
4103. Do not dislike your responsibilities
4104. A whisper of fear
4105. What is despair?
4106. God's secret Means
4107. My God is not as distant
4108. My life
4109. Just peacefully wait
4110. God came down
4111. The surest way to love God
4112. Without a prayerful heart
4113. The invisible forces
4114. Your heart's perfect preparation
4115. Do you love me, my Lord?
4116. I have complete hope
4117. An abiding friendship
4118. My inheritance
4119. Supreme discoveries
4120. An energising vital
4121. You win both
4122. You are useful to God
4123. An excellent beginning
4124. Right decisions
4125. Your soul can erase
4126. My inner life needs liberation
4127. A doubting mind
4128. The world will be in your hands
4129. Destination: nowhere
4130. The perfect beginning
4131. Let me do my duty
4132. God will announce
4133. No real happiness
4134. When your hope is God
4135. God will announce his Victory
4136. Make your choice!
4137. When pride surpasses beauty
4138. Give to God's Eye
4139. Don't act like a fool
4140. Discipline, my discipline
4141. If you start with a purity-heart
4142. God's Whisper
4143. Go to God as you are
4144. Self-transformation begins
4145. To feel secure
4146. The only solution
4147. When stark falsehood disappears
4148. Your soul's pleasure-garden
4149. A cure for imperfection
4150. Please yourself divinely
4151. Your soulful insight whispers
4152. The art of self-giving
4153. I am always saved and fulfilled
4154. Predecessors
4155. Your soul knows how to play
4156. I am not alone
4157. Companions
4158. God's ever-prosperous Smile
4159. Allow your heart to swim
4160. God's revealed Silence-Power
4161. Contradiction disappears
4162. Misery knocks at your heart's door
4163. I tell the earth-bound life-train
4164. A silence-diploma
4165. Now that your mind is ready
4166. Your outer name
4167. I feel sorry for you
4168. A major miracle
4169. Nothing is difficult
4170. A top secret
4171. What you do not want to give
4172. A mountain-high aspiration
4173. A child's heart of innocence
4174. Fearless and indomitable you are
4175. The life-stirring dance
4176. The right place
4177. Your life's amazing victory
4178. God's Consciousness-Coin
4179. Faith and life-energy
4180. Controversy
4181. Allow your mind
4182. Your thought feels and knows
4183. I am offering
4184. Your new inner self
4185. My desire and God's desire
4186. Do not blame your false teacher
4187. When God comes to visit me
4188. When I go to visit God
4189. From tomorrow on
4190. The outer forces
4191. Your madness-pride
4192. To see God's Transcendental Smile
4193. How can you be happy?
4194. A measureless treasure
4195. The connecting link
4196. Ready with only one thing
4197. Choose the right candidate
4198. If your heart has soulfulness
4199. The perfection-seed will germinate
4200. Surrender, my surrender
4201. God shares His Greatness-Height
4202. Proud of depending on each other
4203. My mind trusts you
4204. Unless you depend
4205. My mind is free
4206. My Lord's daily Forgiveness-Heart
4207. A true millionaire
4208. Like a perfect disciple
4209. Both God and I are satisfied
4210. Why do you have to keep it?
4211. I am truly fortunate
4212. The hostile forces tremble
4213. My morning meditation
4214. Stop at this point
4215. A sea of peace rules my heart
4216. Because of your absolute Greatness
4217. The role of a self-excuser
4218. Your life's insincerity-career
4219. You know one important thing
4220. When doubt knocks
4221. Only one sensible action
4222. When my love of God comes in
4223. Your Heavenly responsibilities
4224. Stupidity incarnate is he
4225. My unsung songs
4226. God-love encompasses
4227. Can you not be very good?
4228. God will speak highly of you
4229. Surrender-tree you need
4230. Be a genuine ambassador
4231. Sincerity is not hollow
4232. If your mind is a stranger
4233. God the Boatman will appear
4234. The most unfortunate person
4235. Success comes from
4236. Never surrender to failure
4237. Why waste your precious time?
4238. God's Compassion-Eye
4239. Fruitful echoes
4240. How can God mould your life?
4241. Hitchhiking is forbidden
4242. You will be happy
4243. Say nothing, but be something
4244. To own God's Affection-Delight
4245. You can easily be free
4246. The perfect readiness
4247. Sincerity without determination
4248. My doubtful life
4249. God's Example
4250. The national anthem of Heaven
4251. To have a oneness-realisation
4252. A suffering heart gets better
4253. An important rung
4254. Who says you have to go down?
4255. God has taken my inspiration
4256. How can you be hopeless?
4257. You talk and talk
4258. Gratitude is a puzzling bird
4259. What divine happiness is
4260. More than my usual time
4261. Next door to each other
4262. To walk with God the Justice
4263. If you are a bad seeker
4264. Each mechanical thought
4265. A doubtless mind
4266. Your fearful life
4267. Use your open mind
4268. To make you a humble instrument
4269. God's Promise to me today
4270. A mind that equals Mine
4271. Many seekers secretly think
4272. Meditations without a word
4273. I simply cannot agree
4274. Save your life from your mind
4275. A very rare soul
4276. A cheerfully self-giving heart
4277. Try the surrender-key
4278. A powerful Master
4279. Only our heart-power
4280. You must not allow your vital
4281. If you please your Master
4282. The stamp of Immortality
4283. Your mind does not care for God
4284. Your purity-heart is always perfect
4285. Your future cry
4286. Your illumining heart-sun
4287. His is the jovial heart
4288. An excellent God-lover
4289. Everything amazingly increases
4290. In the inner world run secretly
4291. What I personally treasure
4292. When I give of myself
4293. God is working through you
4294. Anything precious
4295. Nothing is everything
4296. How can you expect?
4297. A gossip-monger deserves
4298. My body likes to be satisfied
4299. A life of tremendous victory
4300. The golden bridge
4301. My Lord will carry the world
4302. Every divine duty unfulfilled
4303. Give me only one century more
4304. A new and profitable way
4305. If you keep your mouth shut
4306. Two great discoveries
4307. You have newness
4308. Never meet for the last time
4309. My aspiring vital
4310. The first Person to applaud
4311. The impossibility-land
4312. The way of cheerfulness
4313. Invoke God's Compassion-Eye
4314. Your soul's freedom-discovery
4315. When I use what I have
4316. Your confidence-heart
4317. Weakness corrupts the divine
4318. If you want to be a good man
4319. Four sorrowful words
4320. The greatest thing in Heaven
4321. Many million steps
4322. Why do I blame my mind?
4323. Live your own life cheerfully
4324. The goal of inner progress
4325. The role of my life
4326. I attract divinity to me
4327. The only crime
4328. Each thought is a force
4329. Your proud self-respect
4330. Try to go with others
4331. Better a flower inside your heart
4332. Don't change your heart
4333. Your job

4334. Best to invoke God's Light
4335. God makes opportunities
4336. A sad failure-life
4337. Life is a beautiful gift
4338. The increase of charm
4339. God likes oneness
4340. There is nothing but opportunity
4341. Nobody has made you impure
4342. The power of your heart's cry
4343. To conquer power itself
4344. Start offering your gratitude-heart
4345. Praise the force of the Source
4346. I shall not forget
4347. The conscious beginning
4348. My sky-vast dream
4349. The silence of love-sky
4350. Because you have the vision-eye
4351. I wish you every favour
4352. An illumining immediacy
4353. Hope is an unparalleled power
4354. Your best possession
4355. An ingratitude-heart
4356. Large is my inner temple
4357. What self-doubt has done
4358. A mountain-high contradiction
4359. Renounce and then taste
4360. Your inner faith shall teach you
4361. What can your poor life do?
4362. Worthy to be His true child
4363. Discover and uncover
4364. Fearful messages
4365. God-Satisfaction blossoms
4366. Competition
4367. Your inner weaknesses
4368. Never fear defeats
4369. Present God, future God
4370. The heights of satisfaction
4371. The path of the self-giving heart
4372. Toil is an outer mask
4373. Do not embellish Truth
4374. Simplicity is power
4375. My Lord of Love comes to me
4376. No more pleasure-songs
4377. Heaven's oneness-fulness-orchestra
4378. His eyes embody prophecy
4379. Beauty-soul and divinity-goal
4380. I am torn between
4381. More than sufficient
4382. I have nothing to do
4383. Your heart will prosper
4384. Your one wee heart
4385. If your mind thinks of liberty
4386. At last my life is ready
4387. Don't allow
4388. Those who deliberately disobey
4389. Inseparables
4390. If you worship God
4391. Patience-sun is the lesson
4392. Don't sleep
4393. You are blessed
4394. Your soul knows how to fulfil
4395. Increase what you are
4396. Your heart will be nourished
4397. Every second counts
4398. Your yesterday's promise
4399. My Heart's Immortality-Sun
4400. My eternally open Heart
4401. My supreme moment
4402. I am able to begin again
4403. Two new ways of thinking
4404. Only one aim
4405. Only one divine interest
4406. No more gloom of doubt
4407. The ecstasy of aspiration-flames
4408. The right to choose
4409. Against my heart's climbing cry
4410. The poor cry of my heart
4411. Your heart is playing with God
4412. If you are truly faithful
4413. One way to do the right thing
4414. First be sure
4415. Your own imperfection-nights
4416. O fault-finder
4417. Only two questions to answer
4418. For your permanent safety
4419. Seconds count
4420. If you want to alter your life
4421. I admire your life
4422. Free access
4423. Two persons love me
4424. A false start

4425. Thank God for everything
4426. A response to God's Call
4427. My heart longs to work for God
4428. Everything that is
4429. The inner world gives me ecstasies
4430. My heart practises forgiveness
4431. Determination unleashed
4432. Two ways to while away your time
4433. Completely safe
4434. Your mind's tempest-doubts
4435. His heart's gratitude-speed
4436. A faithless seeker betrays
4437. Empty to the core
4438. The vision-free intuition
4439. My mind's silence-sea
4440. Do not ignore me
4441. Only one way to be free
4442. Oneness-Home
4443. Believe and obey
4444. Keep your heart always open
4445. Who is right?
4446. A gracious invitation
4447. I must not delay!
4448. Examine your love
4449. Can you not do the same?
4450. Quality, not quantity!
4451. My Supreme's most perfect holiday
4452. Two kinds of persons
4453. With my glowing aspiration
4454. I wish to be that inner cry
4455. Unless I disown my bondage-life
4456. A new start
4457. The inner courage comes to stay
4458. Two most powerful realities
4459. A secure heart
4460. You must not declare
4461. Two questions torment me
4462. A fault-redeemer
4463. Give God the first choice
4464. Two special homes
4465. Where is my perfect perfection?
4466. Why do you think you are alone?
4467. I am on my way back home
4468. Do not just sit there
4469. Your heart will help you
4470. My aspiration is not for self-denial
4471. You are not advanced enough
4472. To live in Eternity's failure-cry
4473. Freedom from imperfection-cave
4474. Ready to forget my past
4475. At God's choice Hour
4476. No time to be sick
4477. Teeming clouds appear
4478. A tremendous loss
4479. A hopeful prince-seeker
4480. The pretence-sword
4481. The God-discovery test
4482. Pray like a truth-seeker
4483. My Lord's Forgiveness-Light
4484. To sing and dance in silence
4485. Somebody to carry your load
4486. Two morning messages
4487. The noisy self-assertion of my vital
4488. My silence-life knows
4489. Pray to God
4490. Not how busy, but why
4491. Were you there this morning?
4492. I am so happy and fortunate
4493. An eternal Now
4494. Make up your mind!
4495. Where is the difference?
4496. How you are old
4497. The creation of Light
4498. Our precious gifts
4499. In the psychic world
4500. God will complete it for you
4501. My life's only opportunity
4502. I am offering
4503. My heart's soulfulness
4504. Do find me a place
4505. As soon as I see my life not aspiring
4506. If you can surrender
4507. Never afraid
4508. Do not waste
4509. Try to be pleased with yourself
4510. God sizes my heart
4511. To become divinely great
4512. If you do not look for the results

4513. Two most special achievements
4514. Everybody wants to crush
4515. The frown of impossibility
4516. The quintessence of spirituality
4517. Never lose your precious treasure
4518. What can oneness do?
4519. Before you can see Infinity's Beauty
4520. What kind of faith is it?
4521. Only one friend
4522. The world of Silence-Peace
4523. I am starting over
4524. A purity-flooded saint
4525. If you can soulfully smile
4526. Your mind's unchanging newness
4527. Do you know where your mind is?
4528. Let us not waste time
4529. Your determination-arrow
4530. To conquer others' minds
4531. God-Realisation at a discount
4532. God knows I am His son
4533. My Lord uses His Silence
4534. An increase of suffering
4535. If your life is blessed
4536. Chasten your impure life
4537. Check each thought
4538. Go beyond yourself
4539. Until you have achieved perfection
4540. A saga of selfless service
4541. An encircling gloom
4542. Do you remember?
4543. No alternative
4544. Rich in hope
4545. Your heart of aspiration
4546. Self-styled sense of responsibility
4547. Pain-giving ailments
4548. Pain-killing drugs
4549. Prosperities of the unknown world
4550. His silent words
4551. A hidden life
4552. I surrender only to necessity
4553. The heart of humanity
4554. To realise my Lord Supreme
4555. His desire-life has dropped
4556. You are divinely brave
4557. The mantra of self-transformation
4558. My dauntless determination
4559. Determination-smiles
4560. My Supreme is not finished
4561. A supremely chosen instrument
4562. I have started blossoming
4563. If you can free yourself
4564. Prayer is the cry
4565. Man-illumination
4566. God is always just
4567. I shall discover truth and beauty
4568. Unless you shun the noise
4569. A cheerful heart
4570. Your appreciation-power
4571. Whenever a special day dawns
4572. My Lord is ready
4573. A revolutionary pioneer
4574. Eagerness in your search for God
4575. A perpetual paradise-tree
4576. Love is not pleasure
4577. Create a new world
4578. Leave behind your gratitude-heart
4579. The dance of desires
4580. If you have inspiration
4581. Sufficient in yourself
4582. The golden city of your heart
4583. If you fear no change
4584. Treasure a flash of hope
4585. Constant expectation
4586. I am poor
4587. My wise heart is following
4588. If you are impressed by impressions
4589. A seeker's aching heart
4590. Two things you do not know
4591. You want something from God
4592. Unless you have walked with God
4593. Go forward to see God's Face
4594. To make God happy
4595. Three ways to happiness
4596. The only answer
4597. A true God-seeker
4598. Who can dominate your mind?
4599. What you actually need is shelter
4600. My Lord's transcendental Height
4601. The lost God-Hour
4602. If your heart has confidence

4603. Two rarities
4604. Two kinds of responsibility
4605. God will keep you from swaying
4606. If you fear God
4607. Compromise-stupidity
4608. Your own most irresponsible slave
4609. A heart of love
4610. If you are awakened
4611. The only offering
4612. Faith does not govern
4613. When will you free me?
4614. God's Eye is upon you
4615. A new world of today
4616. Only one reality
4617. Yield to God's Will
4618. To shun the noise of folly
4619. The manifesting reality
4620. Nothing is so unkind
4621. If your heart is rich in hope
4622. The song of beauty
4623. You are a fool
4624. Your enthusiasm needs devotion
4625. Deathless deserts of Eternity
4626. Cleverly you surrender
4627. The eve of your mind
4628. If your life has the quantity
4629. A pessimistic mind does not know
4630. Fiercer than arguments
4631. Impurity binds you
4632. Tomorrow's ecstasy-hours
4633. A perpetual paradise-garden
4634. God's Satisfaction claims you
4635. God's effulgent interpreter
4636. If you sincerely feel the weight
4637. God the Compassion is watching
4638. God's unparalleled trumpet
4639. His ancient heart tells him
4640. Inspiration, aspiration, dedication
4641. The master of your destiny
4642. God's Satisfaction-Heart
4643. A new day of light
4644. Your negative self-image
4645. God's Protection-Light
4646. Two wisdom-prayers
4647. I shall grow into miracle-delight
4648. A life-perfecting incident
4649. What God needs from me
4650. The freedom of the unifying heart
4651. When the heart functions properly
4652. Truth that needs explanation
4653. Before the heart can discover
4654. Two fulfilling compeers
4655. A stark fool
4656. Experience says
4657. The ancient delight
4658. The hunger of my soul
4659. A speedy deliverance
4660. A most deplorable disappointment
4661. Then you will be protected
4662. Do not overfeed your mind
4663. Empty the mind every day
4664. I shall only look for vision-light
4665. My final choice
4666. Your challenging will
4667. My mind's desire-life thrives
4668. All your requests are granted
4669. The secret of my victories
4670. If God compassionately needs you
4671. The dreaming mind
4672. My surrendering will
4673. The unparalleled winner
4674. Become a breathless dreamer
4675. Eternally mutual admirers
4676. It is time to be ashamed
4677. To be closer to God
4678. God's Heart wants to know
4679. My heart is an aspiration-garden
4680. My loving service
4681. No partition
4682. He discovered God
4683. My Lord's eternally loving task
4684. Something precious for the future
4685. An opportunity for God
4686. The winner of God
4687. What my heart needs
4688. The most fruitful treasures
4689. Let us welcome the inevitable
4690. Your heart-safe
4691. No joy in your mind-cave
4692. Your aspiring heart will lead you
4693. Three obstinate questions

4694. My Lord's illumining Blessings
4695. Even if I change
4696. His heart has experienced
4697. Your mind's constant resistance
4698. My life-boat plies
4699. God's Freedom-Light
4700. Your heart is always infallible
4701. Go and see God personally
4702. Your life-story
4703. An aspiring man
4704. I can afford to lose everything
4705. God's Compassion-Story
4706. A new faith in God
4707. Stand firmly against your mind
4708. The Supreme in me
4709. If your mind purifies
4710. A secret communication
4711. Each soulful dream
4712. Discouragement never glorifies
4713. A God-intoxicated man
4714. No hidden snare
4715. How can you catch a glimpse?
4716. If your heart pines to discover
4717. Accomplices of death
4718. The inner wisdom of self-perfection
4719. The goal of humanity
4720. How can you expect?
4721. The soul knows what purity is
4722. Do not join the giant intellects
4723. The rare opportunity
4724. The good heart of earth
4725. A self-giving life
4726. God's Tower of infinite Delight
4727. Your heart's climbing prayers
4728. The silence that moves my heart
4729. Hope helps my unbelief
4730. A divinely new belief
4731. Do chasten my mind
4732. Your solitude-life
4733. A seeker's first necessity
4734. God-tuned souls
4735. Between your soul and God's Heart
4736. What you are is important
4737. Twice I become a victim to sadness
4738. Take anything you want
4739. Aspiration and dedication
4740. When my mind dictates
4741. The distance
4742. My heart's resources
4743. When I smile and meditate
4744. The only place to hide
4745. A well-devoted life
4746. How can you show your love?
4747. Your heart's fruitful peace
4748. What your soul likes most
4749. Quarreling with happiness
4750. Death's breath is powerful
4751. Your life is mercilessly caught
4752. A complete picture
4753. Each opportunity
4754. Each trial can unveil
4755. The Blessings of God
4756. If you have implicit faith in God
4757. Appreciate your aspiration-heart
4758. Appreciate your dedication-life
4759. If you are so afraid of death
4760. A sincere and soulful thought
4761. It is not true!
4762. Ask the awakened soul
4763. Ecstasy's breath
4764. Your sense of self-importance
4765. Two fond friends
4766. Another chance
4767. My choice must be followed
4768. God's Compassion-Flood
4769. Why do you allow?
4770. The peace-lovers
4771. The throne of self-transcendence
4772. Stop your blind suspicion
4773. The quagmire of my insecurity
4774. You are allowed to speak for God
4775. A faultless man
4776. The crown of life
4777. Heaven's indifferent eye
4778. Two special homes
4779. An answer
4780. Try to have an iota of gratitude
4781. A veil over past differences
4782. On my silver dream's wings
4783. If you are longing for perfection

4784. A paper tiger
4785. Heaven's Eye
4786. Your eyes' omnipresence-calmness
4787. Two indispensable virtues
4788. Crying breathlessly
4789. God's precious Heart
4790. Only a heart of soulful gratitude
4791. Sorrowful evening news
4792. Each cry of aspiration-hunger
4793. Your chastening Eye
4794. To live in a soulful consciousness
4795. Live inside your heart
4796. Your insecurity sees too little
4797. He is both useless and godless
4798. He has conquered
4799. Your tricky mind has taught you
4800. My becoming shall never end
4801. Yearn for the sea of purity
4802. Three Heaven-born messages
4803. His eyes cry in silence-light
4804. The cheapest
4805. Yet everybody expects
4806. Man admires truth
4807. Enthusiasm begins the journey
4808. Failures in the singing-world
4809. Give freedom to your heart
4810. Perfect quietness of heart
4811. Loving cures everything
4812. My victory is Yours
4813. Purity is the music
4814. A precious truth-diamond
4815. Rise like a pure candle-flame
4816. Your life will be cradled by God
4817. The golden chain
4818. Unless you unfold your faith
4819. The mightiest sound
4820. What does failure do?
4821. Each soulful effort
4822. Doomed to suffer
4823. To transform my unlit life
4824. To conquer its sleeping life
4825. To conquer its fighting life
4826. To conquer its doubting life
4827. To love the Supreme more
4828. To manifest the Supreme more
4829. The Supreme meditates
4830. God's Self-Transcendence Message
4831. My purity
4832. You are a tree
4833. For the world beyond
4834. My soul, my heart
4835. The voice of gladness
4836. A lifelong voyage
4837. Only you are authorised
4838. God's measureless Hours
4839. Your Heart's Golden Age
4840. You will be supremely happy
4841. What human life reveals
4842. Forget the bitter past
4843. A reconciliation with God
4844. Learn and love
4845. You must not allow
4846. Conceal and reveal
4847. One step
4848. The weapons of deception
4849. Two favours
4850. I talk to God
4851. A well-read scholar
4852. A cheerful mind and a soulful heart
4853. I cry for my perfection
4854. Concealing your weaknesses
4855. Spontaneous divinity
4856. Heart-perfection
4857. Your perfect sincerity
4858. Dangerous nonsense
4859. The serpent-mind
4860. God's Compassion
4861. Unless you can summon
4862. Galaxies of Light and Delight
4863. A God-spreading life
4864. Nothing is beautiful
4865. You cannot speak ill
4866. What have I been doing?
4867. How I can go back
4868. I have simply no idea
4869. I know your sweet secrets
4870. Tomorrow's world
4871. Another existence-reality-robe
4872. Unless your life is the hyphen
4873. I wonder if it is the same person

4874. If you are a man of courage
4875. He is eternally perfect
4876. Sadness reigns supreme
4877. The apparently easy road
4878. The God-realisation fun-run
4879. His is a heart that defies
4880. An illumining helper
4881. Your heart's supreme glory
4882. To be closer to God
4883. He has to surrender
4884. Some will precede
4885. Man's soul invents
4886. The inner rose
4887. Only one cave
4888. God's Satisfaction-plane
4889. A powerless life
4890. You are loved
4891. How long will they last?
4892. Show sympathy
4893. Natural and supernatural
4894. Your mind insisted
4895. You may not be wrong
4896. Your answer must be perfect
4897. God's Compassion-Eye
4898. If you do not aspire
4899. Go to God
4900. If you love God
4901. I do have the capacity
4902. The weight of ingratitude
4903. A parting benediction
4904. Two important lessons
4905. God's morning Breath
4906. Do not give up
4907. Perhaps I need not know
4908. My golden reality-heart
4909. His is the vision-eye
4910. Oneness-music
4911. God will guide your steps
4912. My heart serves
4913. Each new determination
4914. Its own eternal witness
4915. Suffering chastens my vital
4916. Each mind creates
4917. Contamination
4918. An Amusement-Enlightenment Park
4919. The fellowship of angels
4920. A loser does not really fail
4921. The harvest of silence-delight
4922. A powerful realisation
4923. To succeed in any great enterprise
4924. A pure heart
4925. My heart's only wish today
4926. Richly rewarding experiences
4927. I sat at the Feet of my Lord
4928. One thing eternally fruitful
4929. Enjoy first the harvest
4930. Use your sacred faith
4931. The diamond secret
4932. Prove you are God's instrument
4933. God will be your Announcer
4934. God's sun-vast Satisfaction
4935. The world knows you
4936. A good God-seeker
4937. You are completely wrong
4938. An amazingly powerful capacity
4939. Poise is the hyphen
4940. Heaven is pleased with him
4941. One thing in favour
4942. Let them live separately
4943. Difficult for a contemplative man
4944. Looking for the easiest way
4945. Patience-seeds and forgiveness-seeds
4946. If you think you are self-made
4947. Sympathy
4948. Speak ill of yourself
4949. Surrender is the only way
4950. Our respective tasks
4951. The seekers must colonise
4952. Each experience
4953. The splendour of silence-delight
4954. Stupidity or humility?
4955. The greatest fool
4956. No credentials but yourself
4957. His is the love
4958. Only one Lord
4959. Your own puny God
4960. You wear the crown of miseries
4961. We do not need anything else
4962. What can stand?
4963. The only reality-passport

4964. No God-realised soul
4965. An unfortunate God-seeker
4966. Two divine realities
4967. Perhaps you made a promise
4968. If you have the determination-fire
4969. God will like you more
4970. May my life have the capacity
4971. Certain and precious thoughts
4972. My perfection is the heir
4973. My life is not a transient dream
4974. Your amazing victory-song
4975. You are wise, you are perfect
4976. Disown your mind
4977. What really counts
4978. Love-power sets the pace
4979. Only I can damage
4980. Is there any man?
4981. My satisfaction
4982. Your burning determination
4983. They do not want to remember
4984. To become a satisfaction-emperor
4985. I shall feel sad
4986. God's own Beauty-Plants
4987. Where can I find a man?
4988. A self-worshipper
4989. There is always hope
4990. My songs' prayerful journey
4991. To be perfectly satisfied
4992. No experience is free
4993. Courage I use
4994. Two supremely good partners
4995. God will give Himself to you
4996. The moon's silver feet
4997. Renewed friendship
4998. Heaven does not want him
4999. Do not broadcast my imperfections
5000. When I want to surrender
5001. I have one request
5002. Before I call
5003. My only necessity
5004. You are not happy
5005. Serve the crying earth
5006. A faithless heart
5007. You are bound to win
5008. A reality out of date
5009. Allow him to enjoy
5010. There is always tomorrow
5011. Your right choice
5012. Your only protection
5013. Your self-satisfied grandeur
5014. The power of burning sighs
5015. Your heart's inner purity
5016. Two things you can do
5017. Your choice of autocracy
5018. The heart gives spontaneously
5019. A challenger of stark oblivion
5020. Do not hide yourself
5021. The beauty of Heavenly hours
5022. How can he sleep?
5023. A world-loser
5024. The Lord of my thoughts
5025. Doubt cramps your mind
5026. The game of descent
5027. My heart does double duty
5028. His love of praise
5029. Your defeats will soon be ending
5030. What is my confidence?
5031. My God and I know
5032. My deepest wisdom
5033. God will befriend you
5034. You will be liberated
5035. God does mind
5036. If you believe in God
5037. The paramount questions
5038. A submissive heart
5039. Eternal strangers
5040. You think of God
5041. A starless walker
5042. Stop your self-indulgence
5043. God does not mind
5044. Love-weapons
5045. Do not worry!
5046. To say God has created confusion
5047. Your Master does not hide
5048. If you are a stranger to me
5049. God's Satisfaction-Delight
5050. God has not tempted you
5051. Look what you have done!
5052. The man of aspiration
5053. Because you long for perfection
5054. Since you indulge

5055. God loves you no matter what
5056. Only your suspicious mind
5057. The university of ignorance-night
5058. Faith awakens soulful tears
5059. Punctual in being late
5060. The purity-heart of human life
5061. A sympathetic heart
5062. Heaven will be Heaven to me
5063. Each sad tear
5064. A silver dream-boat
5065. A soulful smile from Above
5066. In just a twinkling
5067. The sunlit path
5068. My heart's sacred dreams
5069. A soulful heart is always available
5070. The best haven
5071. A "must" for every seeker
5072. His rest has deteriorated
5073. Only one teacher
5074. Renunciation-feast
5075. The direct representative
5076. Self-knowledge
5077. Uninvited guests
5078. To see beyond myself
5079. Infinitely more powerful
5080. If you sincerely repent
5081. I close my eyes to pray
5082. The real man in a genuine seeker
5083. Your heart was born to sing
5084. The drop always wins
5085. A weak man
5086. Your creation of truth
5087. Selflessness within
5088. It is all done
5089. Life's shallow amusements
5090. How can there be peace?
5091. God is just
5092. I am all for God
5093. I am not going back to Heaven
5094. A judge suffers
5095. Your self-gratification
5096. So can you realise God
5097. Always ready to die
5098. Two supreme commitments
5099. A risk worth taking
5100. Two opportunities
5101. Choose something different today
5102. Do not expect anything
5103. Yesterday your mind was nebulous
5104. My morning's inner teacher
5105. Two sermons of ignorance-night
5106. Your burning temper
5107. I shall always faithfully follow
5108. The fate of mere mortals
5109. A soulful oneness always wins
5110. If you cannot treasure
5111. Each humility-life
5112. His illumination-mind
5113. My fame is not lasting
5114. My heart's gratitude-world
5115. I shall follow your footsteps
5116. Do not let any chance pass by
5117. My only God-realisation-hope
5118. What God will accept from you
5119. God will transform my mind
5120. More powerful possessions
5121. The river of aspiration-light
5122. Miracles are unnecessary
5123. God has openly fed you
5124. Ignorance and stupidity
5125. Unless you desert your stupid self
5126. My tears
5127. Two souls I have
5128. Two essential truths
5129. Wait for God's choice Hour
5130. In his dying hours
5131. My life's white-green mission
5132. The first and last message
5133. We belong to the Unknowable
5134. Until we can love the Unknowable
5135. Wait for another hour
5136. The higher way
5137. Far from the Will of God
5138. You can easily remember
5139. Think of your highest Reality
5140. Only think of happiness
5141. Be consciously aware
5142. If you want to feel newness
5143. We got everything from the Source
5144. Make your vessel larger
5145. You are more than ready
5146. A subtraction-sadness
5147. If you wage war
5148. Your hands are full
5149. Your life's prayer
5150. Faith
5151. When nobody dares to challenge
5152. Hope is a future reality
5153. Two kinds of faith
5154. Hope says
5155. The outer man
5156. I do not have to remind God
5157. God's sacred Possession
5158. God stands up for you
5159. God has tried
5160. Lingering effects
5161. Your life's integrity-flower
5162. Your tempting tiredness
5163. A matter of self-giving
5164. Unless the seeker asks
5165. A real problem to yourself
5166. God will teach you tomorrow
5167. Simplicity and universality
5168. Neither resist nor resent
5169. The quagmire of contradictions
5170. The glowing desire to be cheerful
5171. Freedom from self-mortification
5172. A maze of misinformation
5173. Buffeted by unreality-strokes
5174. My heart is capable of servitude
5175. A faithless friend
5176. O my God-manifesting heart
5177. A constantly blundering doubt
5178. Fear no wrong
5179. God will help you enrol
5180. The ladder of will-power
5181. You will be able to operate
5182. Do not allow anybody
5183. A most frightening challenger
5184. Each pure thought immortalises
5185. You are afraid to befriend
5186. His universe collapsed
5187. At the Protection-Feet of his Lord
5188. Every uncomely occurrence
5189. Alas, where am I now?
5190. Your mind is shattered
5191. God has freed you
5192. Heaven-free attempts
5193. If you want to be happy
5194. All eyes will be on you
5195. An obedience-thought
5196. Tomorrow's sky
5197. O silence of Eternity
5198. Pale with guilty fears
5199. I live inside the Compassion-Eye
5200. May my heart's purity radiate
5201. Just outside your heart's door
5202. Slavery to ignorance
5203. My first decision
5204. Weakness must aspire
5205. To make your life real
5206. Live in naturalness
5207. What you really need
5208. The power of inspiration
5209. A liberated life knows
5210. An all-existent divinity
5211. A cluster of memorised ideas
5212. The tortures of noisy ambitions
5213. The fragrance of God's Breathing
5214. He who does not suffer
5215. Intuition travels alone
5216. Two perfectly useless concepts
5217. My heart needs the Christ
5218. When the mind does not pray
5219. The inner beauty grows and glows
5220. The most powerful competition
5221. He accuses his soul
5222. The mind can and will find rest
5223. I can realise God
5224. He is supremely beautiful
5225. Do not die unsung
5226. To climb the sky's long stairs
5227. You can never be homeless
5228. The first danger sign
5229. An imperial thunderbolt
5230. The crown of success-light
5231. The first surprise
5232. His strength has failed
5233. True freedom
5234. Unless you live sleeplessly
5235. Love is something to give
5236. The conscious presence of God
5237. An evil thought
5238. The Infinite has embraced the finite
5239. God's Compassion-Sea saves
5240. We really live
5241. A prayerful heart
5242. A sleepless love for the world
5243. A most tragic end
5244. His aspiration wings
5245. The illusion of possibility
5246. History obeys the will
5247. If you want to proceed
5248. The agony of wild impatience
5249. In the same dark room
5250. The last flicker of life
5251. If you choose God
5252. A fresh disappointment
5253. An uncritical friendship
5254. Each dream of my heart
5255. All the ugly faces
5256. A loving chain
5257. I need no nest
5258. Get the correct answer
5259. Perdition is looking for you
5260. A loser's heart of sorrow
5261. Selflessness means
5262. To fulfil a happy promise
5263. A sweet whisper
5264. Chains of expectation
5265. A soulful sacrifice
5266. I am very busy
5267. God yields
5268. An atmosphere of silence-delight
5269. God commands the strength I have
5270. The loneliness of your mind
5271. Success without self-admiration
5272. To have an iota of Bliss
5273. God's Forgiveness-Heart
5274. Before you hurt others
5275. If you acquire wisdom
5276. What your mind needs
5277. An extremely easy task
5278. Before I studied God's Face
5279. What God cares for
5280. Become a flower of purity
5281. The fruitfulness of my fulness-soul
5282. My soul has invited me
5283. I shall fear God
5284. Each faithful heart
5285. An unprecedented joy
5286. My heart pines
5287. Do tell me something new today
5288. A moon of hope
5289. My heart does it
5290. I shall fill my divinity-ocean
5291. What I want to tell the world
5292. I do know where God lives
5293. I am grateful to God
5294. What God desperately needs
5295. Three insoluble puzzles
5296. He will be loyal to God
5297. God is building a prison
5298. The only exception
5299. He saw into my heart
5300. The song of God's manifestation
5301. With equal cheerfulness
5302. Time's telescope
5303. This same life
5304. What you actually need
5305. Wait for God
5306. The heart is beautiful
5307. A very difficult subject
5308. Our faultless choice
5309. An unconditional seeker
5310. Alarming danger
5311. Surrender is peace-expansion
5312. Our conscience-light
5313. Inside God's Heart of Pride
5314. Before you pray and meditate
5315. To love in the aspiration-world
5316. Can you dare to believe?
5317. My illumination-friend
5318. As long as you are willing
5319. A special love
5320. Man's service-hands
5321. A life of daring promise
5322. Choose to live like an emperor
5323. If I lose faith
5324. If each moment of your life
5325. If you want to serve God
5326. Before your mind dares
5327. Perfection-love
5328. What we need now
5329. The divine hunger
5330. God invites us all
5331. Longing for self-effulgence
5332. A negligible distance
5333. I take the Heaven-bound train
5334. My sincerity is the hyphen
5335. Powerful practicality
5336. I shall not mind
5337. My heart's cry
5338. I have tried to please the world
5339. Three old friends of mine
5340. Your powerful nervousness
5341. He has implicit faith in himself
5342. My soul powerfully celebrates
5343. My heart's blue-gold hours
5344. My heart's sleepless complaint
5345. His heart is a cry
5346. God does not mind
5347. God will give him another chance
5348. Humanity's victory depends
5349. My life's first moment of freedom
5350. God's quality of fulness
5351. When danger threatens you
5352. Your pride's ceaseless errors
5353. A pilgrim of inner beauty
5354. Doomed to constant failure
5355. My reality-cries
5356. If your heart has the strength
5357. When he realised God
5358. God loves my life
5359. I serve the Vision-Eye
5360. God's Way is the only way
5361. Do grant me a heart of plenty
5362. Happiness will follow you
5363. The market-noise of my mind
5364. Man's unparalleled gift
5365. A purity-heart is always hungry
5366. A seeker's heart is blessed
5367. Everybody has a life of obedience
5368. A man of purity
5369. The peace of my Beloved Supreme
5370. I need the freedom to adore
5371. My humility-life
5372. I shall surrender
5373. The beauty of self-giving
5374. A gratitude-heart
5375. My life's only task
5376. Spontaneous joy
5377. The endless breath
5378. An experience and a realisation
5379. I need only one courage
5380. Easy to feel security
5381. Your Vision-Satisfaction-Smile
5382. When I establish conscious oneness
5383. My oneness-heart
5384. The four great challenges
5385. Truth is always self-giving
5386. When we look at a flower
5387. My heart knows the truth
5388. I have failed because
5389. Faith in myself
5390. God smiles at everything
5391. God's inner Family
5392. With my purity-soul
5393. The purity-key
5394. Your heart's determination-speed
5395. God's Vision in Reality
5396. A security-heart
5397. A life of discipline
5398. Since You have given me
5399. The Fragrance of his Faith-flower
5400. Miracles
5401. God's life-transforming Hour
5402. Live inside the Freedom-Palace
5403. A labyrinth of contradictions
5404. God's first Hymn
5405. Something refuses to reveal itself
5406. Your devotion to anger
5407. A soaring citadel
5408. The oneness of love and duty
5409. Heaven said hello to him
5410. If confidence is misplaced
5411. Uncouple the soul-divinity
5412. Bravely my mind shall contest
5413. In the middle of Eternity
5414. The paradise of self-compliments
5415. His heart's beauty is starving
5416. Two old questions
5417. The dreamlessness of dust
5418. O wisdom-sun

5419. My sound-life loves
5420. His life's scattering smiles
5421. Time's first sunrise
5422. Where has God gone?
5423. A strange new disease
5424. Unmistakably and completely lost
5425. Mine is a smiling God
5426. God examines every thought
5427. I can't stand my mind
5428. O physical world, stop sleeping
5429. My companions
5430. A never-ending celebration
5431. Heaven's smiles of farewell
5432. The art of pure perfection
5433. Generously erase yourself
5434. Every mind is a new question
5435. When love starts ruling my mind
5436. A secret and sacred passage
5437. An all-consuming ego-night
5438. Heaven and I wept together
5439. Nothing can threaten
5440. The permanence of your body
5441. In secrecy's silence-breath
5442. Simplicity has deserted him
5443. God does not need me
5444. Victory never comes too late
5445. What can I expect from myself?
5446. A spreading wave of anxiety
5447. The enlightenment-bird shall come
5448. A never-slumbering plant
5449. Only the right to announce
5450. God will always be found
5451. When I enjoy labour
5452. I am trying to save my friend
5453. The chill winds of ingratitude
5454. To be amazingly perfect
5455. God always chooses
5456. Each auspicious splendour
5457. Two invaluable gifts
5458. The rapture of inspiration
5459. The rarest opportunity
5460. Three triumphant conclusions
5461. A momentous test
5462. The army of ignorance-night
5463. A thoughtless evil-doer
5464. Why do friendships fail?
5465. My conscience-drops
5466. My faith looks forward
5467. His heart's devotion-stream
5468. Self-doubt refuses to rest
5469. Ego-protection blocks perfection
5470. To solve every problem
5471. Lord, do give me the capacity
5472. Sail beyond the sorrow-river
5473. Awareness is a spiritual power
5474. Life's worst disaster
5475. If I give God only one thing
5476. Chained to an unhappy past
5477. Opportunity does not appear
5478. The most often-asked questions
5479. A soulful smile
5480. What has experience taught me?
5481. This sadness will not last
5482. A precious evolution
5483. Inside my flaming love
5484. In perfect silence-hush
5485. You are more than perfect
5486. Love the battlefield of life
5487. When death invades you
5488. The flood of his remembrance
5489. Consecrate your voyage
5490. A hopeless journey
5491. Suspect your choice
5492. Its nearest neighbours
5493. My hesitation
5494. They will die together
5495. Never-ending changes
5496. The world of Heavenly becoming
5497. Opportunity knocks
5498. If your heart can love
5499. An obedience-smile
5500. Switch your loyalty to God
5501. No more tomorrows
5502. Your silence-mind
5503. Today's mental world
5504. A sincere and dear love
5505. The product of powerful visions
5506. The goalless fighters
5507. Each time I aspire
5508. Victory and defeat
5509. God Himself will be proud of you
5510. Today's proud ambition
5511. An unblossomed bud
5512. Only your heart's aspiration-cry
5513. Fight and fight
5514. Try to outweep
5515. His heart's inner sun
5516. Two ancient playmates
5517. When his life refused to accept
5518. Because your words cast darkness
5519. God's Justice-Light
5520. More important things to do
5521. If you mix with insane thoughts
5522. A haven of silence
5523. Two absurd absurdities
5524. When his heart communes with him
5525. Unconsciously willing victims
5526. A fruitful Eternity
5527. My heart's bounden duty
5528. God does not sanction
5529. My heart is happy
5530. The harvest of happiness
5531. The joy of his song
5532. May oblivion hide
5533. How can you expect to see?
5534. A palace of despair
5535. One with the inner faith
5536. The height of your hypocrisy
5537. His heart's celestial beauty
5538. If you refuse to accept
5539. Hope begins
5540. The voice of beauty
5541. Love ceaselessly struggles
5542. My life's beauty has given me
5543. Eternity's progress-road
5544. The water of self-contempt
5545. There are two prophetic songs
5546. A soulful person
5547. The power of hope
5548. O power of oblivion
5549. Kill the doubt-snake
5550. Do not resist your soul
5551. If you obey God's Will
5552. The uncontrollable vital
5553. Master your resentments
5554. Peace may not follow him
5555. The inner hunger rules
5556. If you have a detached mind
5557. Use your purity-breath
5558. Who can measure?
5559. Wanting in self-control
5560. Be careful in choosing!
5561. The wings of fleeting time
5562. Breathlessly I love You
5563. Reduce the earth-bound mind
5564. A note of the world's deficiencies
5565. His silence-tree
5566. The soul's sorrowful eyes
5567. Two paramount questions
5568. My universe of tears
5569. A victim to earthly fame
5570. His mind is a secret
5571. An ineffectual hope
5572. The whispers of the prophets
5573. Two precious dreams
5574. Inside the circle of anger
5575. Yours is the opportunity
5576. No end to joy
5577. Self-discovery is not an accident
5578. His sadness sadly crawled
5579. The life of aspiration
5580. A citadel against the mind
5581. The world within you
5582. What does my aspiration-cry do?
5583. His will be the role
5584. He expects the fruits
5585. A Dream of God
5586. If Heaven gets tired
5587. A mountain peak of fulfilment
5588. An imperishable message
5589. The arrows of your silence-life
5590. Can you not please me?
5591. One highway to Heaven
5592. The footsteps of envy
5593. Society's cheap joy
5594. Since you resigned
5595. God's supremely chosen instruments
5596. Death's journey begins and ends
5597. Life's journey begins and ends
5598. You cannot escape
5599. The blue bird inside your heart
5600. Make friends with your soul
5601. The year of meditation
5602. The golden opportunity
5603. Meditate, meditate, meditate!
5604. If you do not meditate
5605. Purity and security
5606. Your Master's inner guidance
5607. Be regular, punctual and sincere
5608. My self-transcending horizon
5609. If you resist God's Compassion-Light
5610. When God chooses
5611. Two common sense experiences
5612. In disguise
5613. Absolutely negligible
5614. Suffering is an inner thief
5615. Immortality likes to grow
5616. If man offers
5617. A completely new vision
5618. Divinely inspired God-affirmations
5619. An indefinite delay
5620. An ever-fresh luminosity
5621. Unthinkable stupidity
5622. When the hour of death approaches
5623. The duty of a seeker's heart
5624. A perfection-life
5625. The glorious beginning
5626. The transformation of ambition
5627. Not beyond the range
5628. A self-giving heart
5629. My obedience means
5630. What is belief?
5631. How can you hope to succeed?
5632. One step forward
5633. Gifts I need from Above
5634. A miracle-achievement
5635. Faith helps my heart-flower
5636. The soul-birds come down
5637. Yesterday Eternity came to me
5638. A Heavenly silence-heart
5639. A stepping-stone
5640. Even a great mind
5641. Immediately choose to serve
5642. Your gratitude-companion
5643. Round my silver dreams
5644. The high road to Heaven
5645. A heart-winning man
5646. He is weighed down
5647. Souvenirs from my trip to Heaven
5648. The free play of God's Heart
5649. Miscellaneous thoughts
5650. My foolish prayers
5651. My soul sings
5652. The Lord of my dreams
5653. A faithful companion of God
5654. God will love me infinitely more
5655. Do not ask for too little
5656. Your light-forsaken life
5657. Exulting in Ecstasy
5658. You are heartlessly indifferent
5659. God's Forgiveness-Depth
5660. You will remain unnoticed
5661. My inner world
5662. My heart's peerless friend
5663. A confessed failure
5664. No necessity
5665. The best prayer
5666. New discoveries
5667. My heart's inner revolution
5668. From now on
5669. Humanity's dream
5670. Disobedient people will always fail
5671. Is the Master such a fool?
5672. The easiest thing
5673. Four forbidden words
5674. A good disciple
5675. Three goals in life
5676. Our journey's course
5677. An adamantine determination
5678. Your life of perfection
5679. God's transcendental Pride
5680. The heart's perfecting life
5681. Longing for a satisfaction-life
5682. The currents of your desires
5683. The lesson of perfection
5684. A lover of all that breathes
5685. Your mind is pierced
5686. The miracle-net
5687. A soulful and aesthetic silence
5688. God has fed your aspiration-life
5689. The tears of a new creation
5690. Transform your lower self
5691. God the Beauty will come to you
5692. The duty of your gratitude-heart
5693. There is always a choice
5694. Returning to your stone-life
5695. A very simple question
5696. Your powerful unwillingness
5697. When God smiles
5698. The voice that says you can
5699. The promise-maker
5700. Each prayerful day
5701. The concept of impossibility
5702. A self-controlled life
5703. Happiness follows
5704. Your new-made friendship
5705. Watch your sincerity
5706. The modern age of electronics
5707. Obey His Commands
5708. My heart's silence-poise
5709. God proudly treasures
5710. Walk with the Eternal God
5711. Cherish your friendships
5712. Heaven's Compassion-Sky
5713. If you pray for the wrong thing
5714. The faithfulness of my life
5715. I need only one thing
5716. Success cannot hide
5717. Be happy, be happy!
5718. A life of unhappiness
5719. A heart of magnanimity
5720. Our heart must weep
5721. The silence of the sea
5722. An infallible truth
5723. Your life's future-tower
5724. Outer and inner blindness
5725. You have everything within
5726. A new philosophy
5727. He is a real discoverer
5728. Pray soulfully
5729. What God clearly needs
5730. I confess
5731. One soulful cry
5732. In supreme secrecy
5733. Once I start fighting
5734. All your soulful needs
5735. Two thoughts so futile
5736. Death's tremendous nearness
5737. Without an instant's hesitation
5738. Grant me Your sovereign Will
5739. The clutch of evil thoughts
5740. Far above morality-bound truth
5741. His Weight is as light
5742. My heart shall be smitten
5743. The stiff mind questions
5744. Our aspiration is accountable
5745. To be absolutely perfect
5746. Only a perfectly liberated soul
5747. Once again I wonder
5748. Your life's richest fulfilment
5749. Be careful with your success-life
5750. A moment without a soulful cry
5751. The harvest of silence-peace
5752. I sail all day
5753. When my inner flames ascend
5754. A self-appointed dictator
5755. A moment of self-indulgence
5756. God's express arrival
5757. Spirituality is like climbing
5758. Go and talk to God
5759. Reformation means
5760. The message of satisfaction
5761. The earliest invitation
5762. You want to see God's Face
5763. Your self-praise
5764. In perfect harmony
5765. When there is no other way
5766. I dance with my soul's Infinity
5767. May I be reborn every day
5768. God does not want to punish us
5769. The inevitable God
5770. They do not know each other
5771. Pray and pray
5772. A visible ally
5773. God is under no obligation
5774. If you have faith
5775. Be careful
5776. Panoramic views
5777. Not only for special seekers
5778. God may fulfil His Promise
5779. God the Question
5780. God asks me to help myself

5781. Enough real sufferings
5782. Only if I can dream
5783. Human curiosity asks
5784. You can criticise me
5785. A sleepy onlooker
5786. But not ingratitude
5787. Stupid mind, wise soul
5788. The valid passport
5789. God does not want to delay
5790. The task of a lifetime
5791. Gladly God will give to you
5792. Your heart is full of faith
5793. Believe in God for a minute
5794. What has happened to me?
5795. Your achievements are proud
5796. Your heart's oneness-smile
5797. No harm if you misquote
5798. Start your sacred journey
5799. A miracle
5800. O my gratitude-flames
5801. God's beating Heart
5802. He was totally wrong
5803. A gratitude-heart
5804. Whose stupid mind has told you?
5805. His earnest and determined resolve
5806. You may withdraw
5807. A problem for yourself
5808. Unless we feed our hopes
5809. We gain everything
5810. The smile of silver dreams
5811. Treasure your spiritual energy
5812. The inner biography
5813. Japan's message of perfection
5814. The Satisfaction of the Supreme
5815. The river may be crossed
5816. The Japanese nature
5817. A very good combination
5818. God's Hour will wait for no one
5819. Your real meditation
5820. Try to be really happy!
5821. Happiness lies elsewhere
5822. The golden bridge
5823. Obedience
5824. Unless my heart is grateful
5825. Precious gifts
5826. Your spiritual life is joy
5827. Time cannot touch him
5828. I shall not accept defeat
5829. Many have come, many have left
5830. The spiritual life is arduous
5831. For the faithful ones
5832. A new game to play
5833. Your few will remain
5834. Deliberate disobedience
5835. I shall soulfully do my duty
5836. Each pure and flower-like thought
5837. Everything from God
5838. New year's resolution
5839. The birth of the new year
5840. Each new year
5841. My heart knows
5842. O anxiety-cruelty
5843. Eternal strangers
5844. Friends
5845. The burden of knowledge
5846. Bitterness yields to sweetness
5847. Nothing can collapse in life
5848. The beginning of danger
5849. A sleeping frustration-doom
5850. The corruption of the mind
5851. Desire-life
5852. When my consciousness descends
5853. Emptiness
5854. The blows of insufficiency
5855. Bewildering images
5856. My surrender-life
5857. If you really want to be happy
5858. God's bliss-bestowing hands
5859. I love my heart
5860. O lovers of the past
5861. Only the chosen few
5862. Before you love the inner world
5863. Today you are afraid
5864. In your own way
5865. A big decision
5866. A whisper from stillness
5867. Only Eternity can reveal
5868. How can I misunderstand?
5869. I shall definitely learn
5870. You can have perfect peace
5871. The self-satisfaction-game

5872. Thoughts a seeker can cherish
5873. Beauty does not have to explain
5874. Those who are ready to struggle
5875. I am absolutely correct
5876. Man's goodness talks to God
5877. The mind does not see darkness
5878. My Lord Supreme says to me
5879. You are seeing the sunrise
5880. Self-glory
5881. Some special advice
5882. An awakened heart
5883. A strange experience
5884. A false spiritual Teacher
5885. You have the audacity
5886. Imagination has power
5887. When I want to change
5888. He saw into my heart
5889. A song of Eternity
5890. My searching mind
5891. In his heart he secretly insists
5892. To rise above ourselves
5893. To achieve an illumination-heart
5894. A pure heart feels
5895. Not a single soulful smile
5896. Your emptiness
5897. You think you have escaped
5898. Each undivine thought
5899. My mind's simplicity
5900. Are you only Mine?
5901. I am desperately trying
5902. I am in God's Forgiveness-Boat
5903. God's Compassion
5904. Only three swimmers
5905. I see no difference
5906. Your heart-plant is withering
5907. Your biography is already written
5908. But I also have
5909. When are you going to stop?
5910. Your aspiration's mountain-cry
5911. Heaven's golden sunshine
5912. What can you expect?
5913. Invasion
5914. A purity-heart
5915. Nothing is more beautiful
5916. Those choice children
5917. An unoffered life
5918. A new message from Heaven
5919. Only God's Compassion
5920. The believer knows
5921. Sincerity's sweetness
5922. What your mind has
5923. A born dreamer
5924. His sense of perfection
5925. No difference
5926. O man of silence
5927. Present regrets, future fears
5928. The unconquerable hope-seed
5929. When I touch my heart
5930. My Lord's Beauty
5931. Man's modern fruits
5932. God's Perfection-Satisfaction-Home
5933. Unabashed attacks
5934. Your heart's orphan-cries
5935. Your forgotten Eternity
5936. At long last
5937. Your silence
5938. Himalayan satisfaction
5939. If you value time
5940. His life is all happiness
5941. Self-mastery means
5942. Beauty is the duty
5943. The illumination-combination
5944. No greater loss
5945. God now owns him
5946. Unless his inner life is gracious
5947. Two lords
5948. God's Hospitality-Invitation
5949. God will teach me to sail
5950. What will you do for me?
5951. The inner beauty
5952. It is not too late
5953. Silence-songs of the Beyond
5954. A man of prayer
5955. The wish of my life
5956. Completely lost
5957. Blindness-speed
5958. Your guilty mind
5959. Now that you have surrendered
5960. My heart has three comrades
5961. His is a contradiction-life
5962. I poison my own life-breath

5963. A fervent prayer
5964. With his heart's streaming tears
5965. If your mind clings to truth
5966. Who says?
5967. The Beauty of God's Face
5968. An endless streak of patience-light
5969. My reunion with God
5970. What the searching mind needs
5971. A blessingful preparation
5972. He is enjoying a feast
5973. Immortal friends
5974. He has every hope
5975. One message of time
5976. When God thinks of me
5977. Impossible!
5978. Unchanging and changing
5979. God's two doors
5980. Nothing is more worthwhile
5981. My life of failure-sighs
5982. Inside a self-giving purity-heart
5983. Why?
5984. Totally lost
5985. What I need today
5986. My soul's deathless aspiration
5987. The amazing and lightning speed
5988. My practical God-life
5989. I do not know
5990. Each individual soul
5991. My mind does not have
5992. Belief tells us
5993. Two complementary friends
5994. God's Satisfaction
5995. How can you see the sky?
5996. You are miserable
5997. Two failures
5998. You are forced to suffer
5999. The callousness of the heart
6000. I am going to God
6001. The same road
6002. One deplorable thing
6003. The best answer
6004. I am able to offer
6005. Promise and pray
6006. Remind me, my Lord
6007. I need God's Love
6008. Because your mind is slow
6009. I believe in everything except
6010. Helplessness is enveloping me
6011. Unfettered freedom-joy
6012. Take everything from God
6013. Oversleeping in ignorance-night
6014. He sinks and sinks
6015. Patience does it
6016. Entertaining doubt-life
6017. Magnify and minimise
6018. I know whose I am
6019. Two open secrets
6020. A God-centred man
6021. God made my life
6022. Doomed to barrenness
6023. A perfected individual
6024. A sincere need
6025. My self-cultivation
6026. May my life-boat ply
6027. Slow me down
6028. When I open my eyes
6029. The individual
6030. Human life
6031. Incomparable tragedy
6032. Ultimate goals
6033. My confidence-height
6034. My surroundings
6035. Forgive the past
6036. Counteraction and conversion
6037. Between me and my past blunders
6038. My songs
6039. When I love God
6040. If you dare to believe
6041. A loving man
6042. Responsible
6043. Unswerving as I climb
6044. The capacity to determine
6045. He is so sad
6046. Do give it again
6047. I belong to the God-Lover
6048. My life belongs
6049. Sunset and sunrise
6050. If the heart is receptive
6051. A wise man knows
6052. My heart was too slow
6053. If your life is chained
6054. Stab your ignorance-pride

6055. Science tells me
6056. If I am available
6057. A heart of beauty and purity
6058. The lighthouse
6059. Awareness is ability
6060. The Concern-Hand of the Beyond
6061. The race of lions
6062. A lavish doubter
6063. Only a born dreamer
6064. You do not dare
6065. Love is at once
6066. They would like to know
6067. God blows His Victory-Horn
6068. Your self-aggrandisement-songs
6069. The mind enjoys
6070. The essence of excellence
6071. A small suggestion
6072. As long as the stupid mind
6073. The faith of the mind
6074. My fondness for God
6075. To have or to be
6076. No and yes
6077. God's personal property
6078. A very special message
6079. No miracles, please
6080. Unless
6081. No misuse of faith
6082. Compassion-Bud and Satisfaction-Flower
6083. Do not worry
6084. Another name
6085. God's Promise and God's Hope
6086. The give-and-receive game
6087. Loss and gain
6088. My necessity-seeds and ecstasy-plants
6089. Blessing and obedience
6090. Forgiveness-seeds and hope-seeds
6091. I shall always try to travel
6092. Where are we?
6093. Six words
6094. Time took back
6095. No and never
6096. I talk to God
6097. Keep your eyes inside your heart
6098. God-messengers
6099. An unconditional gift
6100. He will do everything
6101. Because your heart needs God
6102. Heaven-free time
6103. The oldest race
6104. The divine realisation
6105. Only an inch away
6106. God secretly hopes
6107. Immortality's Satisfaction-Treasure
6108. If your life needs beauty's speed
6109. Oblivion is challenging you
6110. Unless you become today
6111. A dangerous vital
6112. Your constant supporter
6113. When faith is dry
6114. Why are you delaying?
6115. Your suspicious mind
6116. I saw myself forsaken
6117. Between evolution and perfection
6118. He is drunk with light
6119. Eternity's exile
6120. Renounce and announce
6121. Your unlit sound-life
6122. At the eleventh hour
6123. Man's suspicion-night
6124. At the feet of truth
6125. Each Heaven-descending message
6126. Real and safe progress
6127. Earth's aspiration-ascent
6128. Surrender, surrender!
6129. My mind is completely lost
6130. Regain and rediscover
6131. During the day I pray
6132. Descent and ascent
6133. Two solutions
6134. Regression
6135. A heart of vision-delight
6136. Self-announcement-song
6137. Your stupidity's existence-reality
6138. My perfect gratitude
6139. If yours is a life of prayer
6140. Convicted by conscience-light
6141. God-Thoughts
6142. Exempt
6143. Constant somnolence

6144. A useless tornado-motion
6145. Spirituality wants to show
6146. He is now ready
6147. Not Lord but friend
6148. Renew your heart's beauty
6149. This century's offering
6150. Not born for death
6151. Do not foretell a hopeless battle
6152. My heart is pleased with me
6153. Paradise is the place
6154. When hope guides my steps
6155. Your mind's commitment
6156. Science tells me
6157. If you cannot make friends
6158. They long to see
6159. I spoke ill of God
6160. Each time I compromise
6161. No fables
6162. A votary of ignorance
6163. A mind of curiosity
6164. Two sleeping secrets
6165. While others dream
6166. A tiny gratitude-flame
6167. The cry of insufficiency
6168. God's Self-Amorous Flute
6169. My humility-breath
6170. The mind-wall
6171. Today's impossibility-peak
6172. My heart's hope-birds
6173. The kingdom of self-doubt
6174. Your heart's selfless deeds
6175. Never enough time
6176. I need affection
6177. My credentials
6178. Empty of hope
6179. It is God-planned
6180. Three boons
6181. When I free myself
6182. God's Feet touched
6183. The rapture of inspiration
6184. The silence of our soul
6185. Your mind's procrastination
6186. Your heart's blindness-night
6187. His mind's doubt-wars
6188. Two warnings from God
6189. My desire for world-dominion
6190. Existence-Consciousness-Bliss
6191. Can you not show God?
6192. God will grant you
6193. To go beyond the body
6194. My Lord's Divinity
6195. Attention is preparation
6196. A self-giving seeker
6197. The power to hope
6198. You can best your enemy
6199. Around and within
6200. I am happy
6201. If you plant a seed of purity
6202. Everything is possible
6203. Between perfection and satisfaction
6204. Unbelievable, but true
6205. A free access
6206. An impossible task
6207. Doubts in the mind
6208. A heart of soulful silence
6209. The pride of personality
6210. Cancel your impotence-heart
6211. Aspire, aspire!
6212. Your heart's soft voice
6213. I have not seen the Face of God
6214. The strength of hope
6215. Each time you compromise
6216. Accept your heart's way
6217. You will never suffer
6218. My aspiration means
6219. Extinguish the fire
6220. He will extol his foe
6221. A seeker's life-story
6222. The wisdom-sky of vision-light
6223. If you are perfect
6224. Denied God's Satisfaction-Smile
6226. God's Compassion helps me walk
6227. God's Dreams
6228. God's God-Height
6229. The king of stupendous failure
6230. What is impossibility?
6231. Not because I insult God
6232. Will you do something for me?
6233. Do not forget to ask God
6234. Hope-tree protects my life

6235. May my mind become the precursor
6236. I pray to feel only one thing
6237. God's Compassion-Canopy
6238. You have come to me
6239. What my life needs
6240. My soulful morning prayer
6241. When we live in the soul
6242. Today's self-giving seed
6243. Divinity's clarion-call
6244. The sword of conscience-light
6245. The arrow of concentration
6246. In the morning
6247. Let God make the choice for you
6248. You can cross the ignorance-sea
6249. Insecurity is a disease
6250. Perfection-poise
6251. Two immortal boons
6252. To intensify my commitment-life
6253. For my own sake
6254. The aspiration-life is better
6255. To think of the past
6256. His Heart's Flower-Fragrance
6257. The unmistakable sources
6258. Discard your worthless worries
6259. A life of devoted service
6260. A beckoning light
6261. A sincere seeker
6262. A golden satisfaction in God
6263. An impossible task
6264. A foolish mind
6265. You are wise twice
6266. When the vital weaves
6267. You can remain unchangeable
6268. If you need God
6269. Sinner and saint
6270. His life is totally lost
6271. The uncertain future
6272. God wants you to see
6273. The exploitation of your mind
6274. To be late to pray
6275. On Eternity's Quest
6276. Two indispensable realities
6277. The cross of Christ
6278. The desire to be known
6279. What your heart knows and sees
6280. To make constant progress
6281. Anxiety hounds your steps
6282. The song of perfection
6283. Each time my aspiration ascends
6284. The shackles of bondage
6285. God feels sad
6286. Because I have never asked
6287. Pray first
6288. A beggar's world
6289. If you do not cooperate
6290. The three special requisites
6291. Aspiration is the beginning
6292. A life of silence
6293. Before death invites you
6294. The art of self-giving
6295. An iota of soulfulness
6296. Your oneness-smile with Heaven
6297. The wise man
6298. For your realisation
6299. Hope-flames
6300. How is it that I am not happy?
6301. Only one answer
6302. The children of your mind
6303. All is not lost
6304. A train without cars
6305. He still has a golden chance
6306. Mutual inspiration
6307. God's Forest
6308. Eternity's root
6309. Your Master's messages
6310. God will give you the capacity
6311. God's supreme Message
6312. Only one prayer
6313. Even one thing wrong
6314. Do not speak ill of yourself
6315. God wants to please the few
6316. The capacity to ignore
6317. The Divine in your Master
6318. Remember your commitments
6319. God will satisfy you
6320. I shall not pretend
6321. Gifts from God
6322. A true disciple feels
6323. Try to remember
6324. Dormant capacities
6325. Always continue trying

6326. Patience is light
6327. The greatest blessing
6328. A heart-to-heart talk
6329. Unveil and reveal
6330. Your world of misery
6331. Everything can smile
6332. God and His Vision-Eye
6333. Do give me
6334. A breath of impurity
6335. Inner name, outer name
6336. Forever inseparable
6337. Inside my heart-garden
6338. The Eye of my Inner Pilot
6339. A moment's ignorance-pleasure
6340. God's magic Touch
6341. One little desire
6342. Divinity knows
6343. I see my Fate-Maker
6344. No shelter
6345. A land of hope-light
6346. The language of your divine heart
6347. Be absolutely sure
6348. When I love
6349. Immortality's Banner
6350. A self-indulgence-life
6351. My pain
6352. When I offer
6353. Your soul is pining
6354. For your perfect perfection
6355. My inventions
6356. Your mind's duty
6357. Do you want to learn?
6358. A rising inner sun
6359. The unlimited Vision-Light
6360. Votary of ignorance-night
6361. My Lord's Compassion-Boon
6362. When I rely on my soul
6363. Two dreamers
6364. If you confide in me
6365. God's Secret and mine
6366. What can my poor heart do?
6367. A deer-speed
6368. Exchange of smiles
6369. Wild calamities
6370. If you cannot face yourself
6371. Each prayer
6372. The power
6373. Sleepless dreams
6374. Strive to bring back
6375. Relaxation has assailed you
6376. Who really meditates?
6377. Either side can win
6378. Meditation means loving thought
6379. If you avail yourself
6380. An inner marathon
6381. One drop of doubt
6382. My inner revolution
6383. Determination and hope
6384. Obedience and disobedience
6385. He makes friends
6386. The frustration of yesterday
6387. A rank fool
6388. Make me worthy
6389. A good disciple
6390. An open life
6391. Two kinds of bondage
6392. I must embark
6393. Another opportunity
6394. If this question echoes
6395. The role of traitors
6396. God knows better
6397. An untimely end
6398. God's Golden Boat
6399. Yesterday and today
6400. Inside my sleepless eagerness
6401. A white bird
6402. I have been unable to manifest
6403. The divine philosophy
6404. Most precious wealth
6405. Prayers of my mind
6406. Somebody will succeed
6407. No strong liking
6408. Uprooted hope-tree
6409. Nobody is safe!
6410. The ferocious ignorance-tiger
6411. You will be liberated
6412. Tears are born
6413. You will ruin your life
6414. A smile carries
6415. The joy of the unknown
6416. No escape
6417. Just remind yourself

6418. To talk to God
6419. My love for God will grow
6420. My Eternity's only Way
6421. When you forget
6422. My own imperfection-spots
6423. If your heart is inspired
6424. Pay attention to your own race
6425. You have your own name
6426. Every day is your birthday
6427. Today I am appreciating
6428. What God looks like
6429. God came to me
6430. You will be called
6431. He has more than enough
6432. The human in us
6433. An inner will
6434. Your inner life will be bankrupt
6435. Withdraw and deposit
6436. Your soul's will
6437. The highest will win
6438. Absolutely necessary
6439. Your own dream
6440. How can you survive?
6441. All for God
6442. An added opportunity
6443. Each good thought
6444. When I look at God
6445. Walking with God
6446. An unparalleled opportunity
6447. The hope-world
6448. Frustration and satisfaction
6449. Your soul suffers
6450. The wrong road
6451. Promotion and protection
6452. The beggar
6453. When you love yourself
6454. Two torturers
6455. Attack the negative forces
6456. The hour of battle is now!
6457. The manufacturer
6458. The prison of impurity
6459. My life's hesitation
6460. An institution-mind
6461. I am so glad
6462. A great difference
6463. I love the world
6464. Now I am looking
6465. One divine message
6466. The dance of darkness
6467. A special message
6468. Man is happy when
6469. To acquire joy
6470. Because of your humility
6471. My only freedom
6472. He has definitely descended
6473. I do not mind
6474. My heart's sleepless progress
6475. You have to cry
6476. Inner wounds
6477. My mind's inspiration
6478. Each man
6479. My Lord has saved me
6480. Any change
6481. A glimpse of reality
6482. The seeds of faith and security
6483. A soulful surrender-smile
6484. His heart is lost
6485. My mind is demanding
6486. The coasting of my life
6487. Eagerness for wealth
6488. Your Inner Pilot is not responsible
6489. If your heart can bask
6490. The flute of satisfaction
6491. You can easily destroy
6492. Gratitude is an inner flower
6493. God is your real Friend
6494. My life needs
6495. His companions
6496. If you are ready to suffer
6497. A new light
6498. Talk to God
6499. My mind's faithfulness
6500. Your mind is learning
6501. Ready for perfection-splendour
6502. Twin arts
6503. God's Compassion cures
6504. The absolutely sincere witness
6505. Your heart is aching
6506. People judge your heart
6507. Two places to hide imperfections
6508. To try to go to Heaven
6509. Death cannot say "Yes"

6510. His heart's purity
6511. Trust-flames beckon us
6512. The difference between man and God
6513. A God absolutely new
6514. Each uncomely thought
6515. One man's sufficiency
6516. I shall make no choice
6517. When I travel home with God
6518. My self-giving will
6519. All doubts are dissolved
6520. When tranquillity climbs up
6521. His mind is trying to grow
6522. Make two requests
6523. Three ways to be special
6524. I shall accept my Master
6525. His best disciple
6526. Better days are coming!
6527. You have accepted the spiritual life
6528. My Lord's Satisfaction-Sky
6529. The smile of silence
6530. What do you usually do?
6531. Acts of will
6532. My music-life invokes
6533. The In-Dweller in him
6534. True freedom
6535. The sacred responsibility
6536. Think of your future victories
6537. Today's pure thoughts
6538. If your life does not give joy
6539. The soul depends on delight
6540. A perfect man
6541. Failure is a matter of the mind
6542. My heart knows no want
6543. A great revelation
6544. Will you make me creative?
6545. A soul of promise
6546. God loves only one thing
6547. Your mind's reputation
6548. Blessing-Showers from Above
6549. Only one cure
6550. How will you be ready?
6551. Your gratitude-heart
6552. When it comes to prayer
6553. Think of your Master
6554. My only confidential request
6555. Life is a series of adventures
6556. To sow the seed of gratitude
6557. You call it imperfection
6558. I pray soulfully
6559. Incapable of pride
6560. No longer entangled
6561. The holiest of all shrines
6562. Do spare me from name and fame
6563. In their existence-family
6564. How will you ever dare?
6565. The Height transcendental
6566. Guardian angel of my life
6567. God became his perfect slave
6568. Something encouraging
6569. God has lovingly given my mind
6570. The heart that thirsts
6571. Your soul was the witness
6572. How can he succeed?
6573. God is always able to enjoy
6574. Vastness-smile, oneness-dance
6575. My heavenward journey
6576. Cry within breathlessly
6577. Beauty in the divine heart
6578. Earth unconsciously welcomes
6579. Without preliminary preparation
6580. Seeing his helplessness
6581. A divine promise
6582. Everybody minds his own business
6583. Your self-governed world
6584. Your heart's confidence-light
6585. Courage is the watchfulness
6586. The golden morning is blossoming
6587. God is inviting him
6588. I fully sympathise with you
6589. Do not tell God
6590. A Heaven-enjoying fun-run
6591. God the Heart transforms
6592. God is not ashamed
6593. I do not hate the world
6594. Two most sacred secrets
6595. Miracles worth seeing
6596. The heavenward road
6597. India's secret weapons
6598. A faithless heart
6599. God's cheerful responsibility
6600. When I obey my Lord Supreme
6601. Just One Positive Step
6602. My Heart Has Been Crying
6603. Somehow I Have Lost My Way
6604. God Has Invited You To His Party
6605. The Freedom Of True Independence
6606. God's Forgiveness-Light
6607. The Beckoning Hands Of God's Smile
6608. My Steady Mind
6609. Your Confusion-Boat Will Sink
6610. Your Friendship With Humanity
6611. Your Orphan-Life
6612. How Do You Dare Pressure God?
6613. A Lasting Connection
6614. His Soul Lives For
6615. His Mind's New Discovery
6616. How Can You Be Always Happy?
6617. A Transformed Man
6618. Earth's Beauty, Heaven's Beauty
6619. Your World's Future Guide
6620. Their Perfect Oneness-Home
6621. Trials
6622. God's Compassion-Supply
6623. His Life's Surrender Wins
6624. Man Has No Choice
6625. The Love Of A Pure Oneness-Heart
6626. The Taut Knot Of Bondage
6627. God's Unconditional Grace
6628. No Matter How Much You Eat
6629. Hope Illumines My Mind
6630. A Singular Stroke Of Light
6631. Follow God's Example!
6632. Jealousy Sees Too Much
6633. Heavenly And Earthly Words
6634. An Earth-Bound Life
6635. Each Time I Think Of Him
6636. A Pure Thought
6637. The Creation-Game
6638. I Need A Place To Smile
6639. God's Compassion-Sea
6640. Indulgent Earth
6641. We See His Lofty Head
6642. Illusory Phantasmagoria
6643. A Seeker-Heart Knows
6644. My Thought-Flags Are Obedient
6645. Do Not Allow Earth
6646. Where Is The Difference?
6647. A Sleeping Cancer
6648. An Ignorance-Heart
6649. The Pinnacle-Height Of Love
6650. If You Are Ready To Wrestle
6651. My Heart Says To My Mind
6652. Success Depends On
6653. Anger Eventually Surrenders
6654. An Unthinkable Tragedy
6655. If Your Life Is Afraid
6656. Earth's Imperfections
6657. If You Are Caught
6658. How Can God Walk Beside You?
6659. As Your Mind Has The Power
6660. Before He Met God
6661. The Tears Of My Innocence-Heart
6662. By Ignoring Burdens
6663. My Lord Will Clasp My Hands
6664. A Peace-Manifesting God-Lover
6665. Each Thought
6666. First Be The Lover
6667. Not I, But God In Me
6668. One Particular Salvation
6669. O My Gold-Shining Mind
6670. To Reach The Summit
6671. Your Heart-Wisdom
6672. The Loftiest Task
6673. Before God-Realisation
6674. Your Heart Will Be Shattered
6675. Happy At Being Happy
6676. Your Unparalleled Treasure
6677. Discard Your Worthless Worries
6678. Time And Space Contradict
6679. The Contents Of Consciousness
6680. Perfection Must Dawn
6681. Who Can Satisfy God?
6682. No Torture As Excruciating
6683. My Soul Raised High
6684. A Soulfully Receptive World
6685. Why Do You Have To Worry?
6686. You Have Made Me Truly Happy
6687. A Supernal Radiance
6688. What Is The Meaning Of Life?
6689. He Who Sincerely Aspires
6690. How Do You Bind Yourself?
6691. Nobody Except Your Own Soul
6692. The Abysmal Abyss Of Foolishness
6693. My Body-Cage
6694. Try To Breathe In Wisdom-Delight
6695. Bitter Is The Sound-Life
6696. A Life Of Total Futility
6697. Sincerity You Need
6698. A Theoretical Surrender-Life
6699. If You Fail To Pray And Meditate
6700. The Fare
6701. Will You Believe It?
6702. You And Your Deliverance
6703. Suicide
6704. Dropped Disputes
6705. To Overcome An Enemy
6706. I Deny Him Vehemently
6707. Pray To Submit Yourself
6708. Discover Your Only Friend
6709. What I Feel Concerns God
6710. Faith Is The Art Of Seeing
6711. A Newborn Life
6712. No Aspiration, No Perfection
6713. He Has Become The Message
6714. Steel Your Heart
6715. You Must Slow Down
6716. When It Comes To Meditation
6717. Two Uncompromising Neighbours
6718. You Are Great, You Are Good
6719. The Heart's Oneness-Crown
6720. My Heart's Gratitude-Smile
6721. My Lord's Powerful Smile
6722. God's Compassion Must Come First
6723. My Heart's Aspiration-Cry
6724. When Sincerity Satisfies Your Heart
6725. I Shall Discover
6726. A Heart Of Pure Hope
6727. I Seek Sincerity
6728. Your Own Self-Styled Commitment
6729. God Will Run After You
6730. Today God May Whisper
6731. Doubt Cherishes You
6732. You Want To Know The Truth
6733. Your Natural Life
6734. God Will Teach Them
6735. To See The Face Of God
6736. Heaven Is Always Ready
6737. Correct The Doubter In You
6738. Be Careful Of One Thing
6739. The Pretence-Game
6740. Never Forget One Thing
6741. Fly In The Sky Of Joy
6742. Do Not Be Discouraged
6743. Purity's Sunlit Palace
6744. The Hero Supreme
6745. You Will Be Happy, Plus Perfect
6746. An Unaspiring Life
6747. A Special Soul-Bird
6748. Because Of Your Faith
6749. Your Heart's Bright Faith
6750. Three Silence-Instructions
6751. The Best He Has Within Him
6752. Your Divinity In Disguise
6753. The Only Valid Ticket
6754. Do Not Try To Barter
6755. Cancel Your Friendship
6756. Your Soul's Divinity-Message
6757. God Is More Than Ready
6758. Walk In Confidence-Hope
6759. Your Trust In God
6760. His Gratitude-Heart Moved God
6761. You Are Remarkably Brave
6762. He Has All Kinds Of Trouble
6763. A Life Of Innocence
6764. A Very Special Instrument
6765. A Selfless Being
6766. Divinity's Protection-Shield
6767. Do Stand Before Me
6768. No Such Thing
6769. Hope-Sands Of Others
6770. Unless You Consciously Surrender
6771. Your Perfection-Achievements
6772. Your Cherished Dreams
6773. A Miserable Failure
6774. Your Inexhaustible Energy
6775. Nothing Will Remain Unchanged
6776. What You Have
6777. What I Want To See
6778. Enthusiasm Is The Road
6779. To Strengthen The Feeble
6780. Because You Are An Art-Lover
6781. Each Soulful Song
6782. You Were A Fool
6783. What Saved Me
6784. God Does Not Approve
6785. You Have Already Decided
6786. How Can I Be So Stupid?
6787. You Do Not Have To Worry
6788. Your Sincerity-Shield
6789. My Soul's Only Friend
6790. My Life's Strength
6791. I Have Changed
6792. Soulfully Tell Your Heart
6793. When Unconsciously You Treasure
6794. My Self-Deception Means
6795. God Loves Me When
6796. I Believe
6797. The Self-Giving Way
6798. Many Things To Do
6799. My Mind Is Afraid
6800. Follow The Eternal Runner
6801. My Only Satisfaction-Ocean
6802. A Useless Marathon Discussion
6803. Imagination
6804. His Overgrown Doubt-Mind
6805. Your Giant Mistrust
6806. Your Golden Future
6807. I Do Not Care To Know
6808. The Unparalleled Faith
6809. God's Immortality-Country
6810. You Can Easily Lie
6811. No Obligation
6812. God's Choicest God-Hour
6813. Express Train Of Ideas
6814. A Song Of Progress
6815. Your Sincerity-Drops
6816. I Am Happy
6817. Insecurity-Thought-Children
6818. Inexhaustible
6819. Self-Devoted Love
6820. God-Approaching Ascents
6821. Unless Your Heart Is Precious
6822. Statue Of Death
6823. My Mind Has Admitted
6824. Each Daily Prayer
6825. Let Me Look For God
6826. The Direct Result
6827. O Earth's Orphan-Cries
6828. Do Give Me
6829. God Is Always Fond
6830. My Prayer Means
6831. Totally Mistaken
6832. What Can God Do?
6833. Three Things I Need
6834. When We Worship
6835. All I Need To Know
6836. Perfection I Need
6837. Do Not Worry About Me
6838. I Can, I Can't
6839. A More Sublime Promise
6840. The Compass To Guide Me
6841. His Mind Carefully Watches
6842. Do Release Me
6843. A Yawning Gulf
6844. Experts
6845. Maintain Your Heart's Beauty
6846. Quote Me
6847. Be Careful To Preserve
6848. Squandered Treasures
6849. The Worst Disaster
6850. How Can I Forgive?
6851. The Only Thing Worth Treasuring
6852. Fragments Of His Shattered Past
6853. Fully Responsible
6854. An Unimportant Thing
6855. His Hopes Are Soaring
6856. Open Your Heart's Door
6857. The Self-Destructive Disaster
6858. Dauntlessly And Soulfully
6859. Two Constant Visitors
6860. My Unwanted Companion
6861. If You Correct Yourself
6862. The End And The Beginning
6863. The Best Oneness-Remedy
6864. He Does Not Know

6865. I Am Liberating God
6866. My Duty
6867. To Change Your World
6868. When You Sing
6869. Two Roads
6870. A Flood Of Joy
6871. A Self-Giving Heart
6872. Exchange Of Gifts
6873. A Dedication-Life
6874. A Supreme Art
6875. The Mind Needs
6876. An Ambition-Mind
6877. The Expansion Of Our Vastness
6878. The Father's Oneness-Compassion
6879. Humility Is Not Humiliation
6880. Nothing To Give
6881. God Reaches Down
6882. We Call It
6883. Your Heart-Wallet
6884. His Prayer Is Thoughtless
6885. I Shall Renew My Promise
6886. The Master's Fruitful Answers
6887. Companions Of Mine
6888. My Heart Is Wanting
6889. His Choice Of Peace
6890. Today's Struggling Heart
6891. God's Promise-Light
6892. He Comes To Learn
6893. Your Faith In Yourself
6894. God Has Started Meditating
6895. The Prayer That Soars
6896. Stay In The Freedom-Sky
6897. Two Divine Messages
6898. Your Heart's Inner Bird
6899. Your Mind Has Exploded
6900. One Silent Train Of Thought
6901. With My Lord
6902. Time's Wild Flood
6903. Today's Pangs Of Separation
6904. A Never-Fading Desire
6905. I Love You, My Lord
6906. Make Me Your Slave
6907. You May Never Recapture
6908. I Am
6909. My Life's Chief Concern
6910. Unbridgeable Misunderstandings
6911. A Satisfaction-Life
6912. God Has Taught Me
6913. Our Inner Communication
6914. My Good Fortune's Greatest Smile
6915. Compulsion Or Liberation
6916. A Deep-Rooted Hatred
6917. My Lord Supreme Tells Me
6918. Make Goodness Your Companion
6919. Do Tell Me Once Again
6920. How Is It Possible?
6921. Deliberately And Helplessly
6922. Heaven Is Cruel
6923. When I Was About To Fall
6924. My Mind Does Not Want
6925. Your Armour Of Suspicion
6926. The Enormity Of Truth
6927. His All-Loving Heart
6928. You Want Abiding Happiness
6929. I Cannot Aspire
6930. No Difference
6931. To Please My Lord Supreme
6932. The Master Of Fulness
6933. Doubtless Confidence
6934. Permanently Employed
6935. I Do Not Need Anything More
6936. Live In Your Silence-Heart
6937. What Has Betrayed Me?
6938. God Is All Ready
6939. A Starving Heart
6940. Long Before I Wished
6941. I Can At Least Try
6942. What I Need
6943. Only One Question
6944. The Moment I Touch
6945. The Beauty Of Human Perfection
6946. Defy Or Deny
6947. One Thing To Learn
6948. A Special Love
6949. God Wants To Celebrate
6950. My Heart's Only Unfailing Desire
6951. My Mind Never Dares
6952. Always Hopeful
6953. I Shall Not Give Up
6954. My Two Questions
6955. Defy And Enjoy

6956. My Heart Shall Defend
6957. I Carry Only One Thing
6958. My Heart's Sacred Flame
6959. In Collusion
6960. Between Two Shores
6961. I Bow
6962. If You Wage War
6963. Your Mind's Imperfection-Impurity
6964. Another Opportunity-Smile
6965. If Your Heartbeats Cling
6966. All My Achievements
6967. His Mind's Inner Poverty
6968. Now I Am Going Back
6969. Two Unnecessary Questions
6970. I Am Crying Inside
6971. Not Used To Deception
6972. Your Simplicity-Mind-Tree
6973. His Heart's Silence-Smile
6974. Inside His Searching Mind
6975. Celestial Compassion-Moon
6976. Revelation Itself
6977. My Wisdom-Filled Need
6978. A Cynic
6979. Straight Ahead
6980. Destined To Become
6981. Each Heavy Thought
6982. Each Beautiful Thought
6983. My Heart Is The Place
6984. If You Are Brave Enough
6985. A Loving Answer
6986. Newly-Invented God
6987. Your Heart's Silvery Beams
6988. Tomorrow's Distance-Light
6989. Astonishment And Enlightenment
6990. Crippling Diseases
6991. No Greater Purpose
6992. The Hallucination-Foundation
6993. With Me, Against Me
6994. Haven Of My Hopes
6995. From Nothingness-Fulness
6996. Not For Them
6997. The Swiftness Of His Thoughts
6998. The Moment Of Certainty
6999. His Aspiration-Heart Cries
7000. My Heart Tells Me
7001. A Single God-Touch
7002. His Heart Helped Him
7003. Ecstasy-Sky Is Ready
7004. Transcend The Mind
7005. He Who Fears
7006. My Success-Light Learns Liberation-Songs
7007. Opinion-Gongs And
7008. Your Heart Is Responsible
7009. Just Say No
7010. By Helping The Undeserving
7011. My Lord Does Not Mind
7012. Negate And Propagate
7013. A Striking Commencement
7014. The Perfection Of An Old Cry
7015. Why Should I Be Embarrassed?
7016. I Am Surrendering Myself
7017. Do Not Try To Hide
7018. Only Two Superior Ways
7019. I Shall Cry For Perfection
7020. My Frustration's Friend
7021. My Perfect Action
7022. To Feel God's Presence
7023. Two Other Names
7024. I Must Become More
7025. Because I Need It
7026. God Has Already Started
7027. Unreality's Dream-Land
7028. By Seeing, By Becoming
7029. God's Perfection-Plane
7030. Tomorrow's Problems
7031. Dangerously Contagious Disease
7032. The Soul's Freedom-Game
7033. In My Mind's Descent-Life
7034. Hope-News
7035. My Definitions
7036. One Book I Shall Never Write
7037. Bury The Desire-Prince
7038. Desire-Kites
7039. Two Unavoidable Consequences
7040. A Perfect Victim
7041. A Long-Neglected Letter
7042. Infinity's Eternal Soul-Melodies
7043. Unless You Are A Dreamer
7044. Today's Teeming Demands

7045. No Desire-Bound Outer Hope
7046. A Weeping Defeat
7047. Defeated Dreams
7048. With Mortal Hopes
7049. Great Liars
7050. Make Your Life's Choice
7051. Beauty's Song In The Morning Sun
7052. The Ladder Of Illumination
7053. God Only Wants
7054. Satisfaction-Lion And Aspiration-Deer
7055. Stop And Start
7056. Transcendental Heights
7057. God Will Hurry It
7058. Premature Introductions
7059. The Path Of The Unillumined
7060. I Have Not Forgotten You
7061. Enjoying God's Fellowship
7062. A Difficult Task
7063. My Heart Knows
7064. My Vital Wants To Liberate
7065. Necessity
7066. The Only Peace
7067. The Victory
7068. The Sanctuary
7069. Two Inherited Disasters
7070. Your Purity-Dawn
7071. I See All Around Me
7072. God Creates
7073. Immediate Neighbours
7074. Each Time You Fall
7075. No Need To Hide
7076. Apostles Of Perfection
7077. First Try To Know God
7078. If Your Heart Becomes
7079. Enthusiasm
7080. A God-Climbing Heart
7081. I Shall No More Roam
7082. Heaven's Will-Power-Door
7083. Wrong Thoughts
7084. My Prayer Unheard
7085. The Heart Of Mankind
7086. The Higher Nature Commands
7087. Heaven Immediately Descends
7088. He Who Is
7089. Only Two Reality-Lovers
7090. His Mind Is Lost
7091. What I Need From You
7092. Painful And Destructive
7093. Mental Clouds Appear
7094. Preserve The Precious Moments
7095. Three Strangers
7096. I Really Feel Sorry For Him
7097. Right Person, Wrong Person
7098. Your Treasure-House
7099. Please Warn Me
7100. My Silence-Heart
7101. Ready And Worthy
7102. He Is Descending
7103. A Special Game
7104. Your Number One Disease
7105. My Lord Cares For
7106. My Needs
7107. God's Supreme Secret
7108. The Beauty Of Your Heart
7109. Two Big Eyes
7110. Do You Not Feel?
7111. Wedded To Worries
7112. The Arrival Of Wisdom-Light
7113. His Indecision-Mind
7114. God's Compassion-Machine
7115. An Incurable Disease
7116. I Have Nothing But Delight
7117. Each Good Thought
7118. Do Guide My Eyes
7119. My Lord's Forgiveness-Feet
7120. The Wrong Interpreter
7121. Who Else Can It Be?
7122. I Do Not Believe
7123. What You Mean To God
7124. Only One Thing
7125. If You Need Faith
7126. Your Utter Stupidity
7127. I Can Find Myself
7128. My Personal Friend
7129. Only God Can Grant You
7130. They Drink Nectar-Delight
7131. Puffed Up With Pride
7132. O My Puzzling Mind
7133. Perfection And Patience
7134. Our Easy-Going Ways

7135. Each Unaspiring Moment
7136. A Heartbreaking Question
7137. The Vision Of Man
7138. Do Not Undervalue Yourself
7139. Eternity's Victory
7140. My Mind Is Blind
7141. Anxious To See
7142. This Is God's Task
7143. Do Not Satisfy
7144. Who Can Answer?
7145. The Divine Love Of The Heart
7146. So Says My Heart
7147. My Life's Total Transformation
7148. Birthless And Deathless
7149. God Asks Me To Give Him
7150. Suffering From Myself
7151. Each Soul Knows
7152. In My Life's Humility-Nest
7153. You Love Your Inner Life
7154. I Look For God The Singer
7155. Fear Ends
7156. Try God's Compassion-Light
7157. I Depend On My Faith
7158. Sincerity Gives My Mind
7159. The Only Fitting Tribute
7160. The Tears Of An Orphan-Heart
7161. The Bond Inevitable
7162. A Great And Genuine Seeker
7163. Before It Is Too Late
7164. The Envelope Of Light
7165. Must I Curb My Quest?
7166. A Small Mind
7167. My Lord's Compassion-Touch
7168. Because Of You
7169. Two Friends
7170. Will You Not Reconsider?
7171. You Must Command Your Thoughts
7172. To Stand God-Revealed
7173. Concentration Means
7174. Unless Your Mind Is Searching
7175. God Loves My Entire Being
7176. What God Once Told Me
7177. Humility Is The Best Song
7178. The Assembly Of Hearts And Souls
7179. So Obstinate!
7180. An Indefinite Vacation
7181. Are You A Great Fighter?
7182. Enlarge Your Dedication-Circle
7183. An Affront To Our Divinity
7184. God's Unparalleled Dream
7185. Encouragement
7186. One Inner Resolve
7187. When I Wish To Please
7188. The Mind Thinks
7189. What Is Necessary
7190. You Must Be Careful
7191. My Heart Is Happy
7192. My Forgiveness-Lord
7193. Real Spirituality
7194. He Holds Perfection
7195. Immediate Acts
7196. God Always Wants
7197. My Joy Is For All
7198. Say And Do
7199. My Unconditional Gratitude
7200. The First Thing In Life
7201. A Masterpiece Of Devotion
7202. His Is The Mind
7203. Teachers
7204. The Silence-God Of The Beyond
7205. An Unappeasable Hunger
7206. You Cannot Judge
7207. No Insignificant Work
7208. My Heart's Silence-Tears
7209. His Mind Never Proceeds
7210. Three Imperishable Sorrows
7211. To Preserve Is To Unveil
7212. The Aimless Centaurs
7213. Fly Like Your Soul
7214. Liberal Imaginations
7215. The Panorama Of God's Sweetness
7216. If Your Faith Wavers
7217. You Have Discovered
7218. Man's Undeniable Name
7219. A New Success
7220. Depression
7221. Let Me Give Credit
7222. An Unforgivable Fantasy
7223. Heaven's Ecstasy-Nest
7224. My Desires

7225. A Self-Giving Breath
7226. God's Secrets
7227. My Heart's Real Helplessness
7228. He Expects God To Satisfy Him
7229. Mother India Commands
7230. Mother India Announces
7231. Now My Heart Is Crying
7232. A Chosen Instrument Of God
7233. Man's Ingratitude
7234. I Met God
7235. Seek God's Companionship
7236. Some Special Rules
7237. The Desire-River
7238. To See Tomorrow
7239. Be Patient With Yourself
7240. A Universal Man
7241. My Mind Says To My Heart
7242. If You Want Perfection
7243. Hunger For World-Applause
7244. The Quest For Truth
7245. Two Supreme Gifts
7246. God-Lovers Surprise Us
7247. Choose Your Thoughts Carefully
7248. We Still Have Not Forgotten
7249. No Time To Criticise
7250. If You Think Of Ignorance
7251. True Truth Tells Me
7252. My Heart's Gates
7253. No God-Becoming
7254. The Message Of Human Life
7255. Your Foolish Insecurity
7256. Why Have You Postponed?
7257. Even The Unwilling Souls
7258. Consumed With Pride
7259. I Have Already Enjoyed
7260. The Eternal Sufferer
7261. I Am Giving You Back
7262. God's Cherished Friend
7263. Although You Are Roaming Blindly
7264. Silence And Fulfil
7265. He Knows Who Loves
7266. His Revolt Continued
7267. A Life Of Self-Sufficiency
7268. Beauty
7269. I Think Of God
7270. Each Desire-Bound Life
7271. Each Pure Thought
7272. When I Am Weak
7273. Ambition Wants To Befriend Him
7274. A Peerless Bridge
7275. Already Deeply Attached
7276. The Lamp Of The Mind
7277. The Secret Of Contentment
7278. Harsh Words
7279. My Soul's Lustre-Surrender
7280. The Fragrance Of A Purity-Flower
7281. Rapture-Realisation
7282. Three That Are One
7283. Nobody But God Himself
7284. A Surrender-Heart
7285. Man's Companions
7286. God's Compassion-Readiness
7287. When I Do Not Aspire
7288. Each Soul-Prayer Of Mine
7289. Tremendous Confidence
7290. Each Unfulfilled Hope
7291. Your Heart-Hotel
7292. My Heart's Ecstasy-Palace
7293. Forgotten How To Sleep
7294. Perpetual Necessity
7295. Trust Your Hope-Dreams
7296. God Wants To Know
7297. My Words Shall Live Longer
7298. It Is Enough!
7299. Practising Self-Control
7300. My Soul's Rainbow-Sky
7301. Our Eternal Friend
7302. Your Friendship With Meditation
7303. Your Soul's Heights
7304. A Lover Of Meditation
7305. Failure Has Touched His Life
7306. But I Must Also Say
7307. I Am Always Disturbed
7308. I Allow Myself
7309. My Heart, Stop Crying
7310. Every Day
7311. Lethargy Is So Useless
7312. I Have The Right
7313. Your Aspiration-Flames
7314. A Life Of Constant Surrender
7315. To Cherish Doubt
7316. I Want To Stand
7317. It Can Easily Destroy
7318. A Shaky Foundation
7319. Look Deep Within
7320. The Supreme Contribution
7321. Be Practical Within
7322. The Songs Of Beauty's Light
7323. You Rely Upon Nothing
7324. I Want You To Be Proud
7325. Carry On The Struggle
7326. Two Deplorable Failures
7327. What My Mind Has
7328. Each Moment
7329. I Use My Curiosity-Power
7330. Love Your Heart More
7331. God's Thundering Victory-Dream
7332. An Experienced Wisdom-Reality
7333. He Who Strangles You
7334. His Desire-Bound Life
7335. Liberation Means
7336. What Is Wrong In Asking?
7337. If You Are Painfully Aware
7338. Do Not Cherish Unhealthy Ideas
7339. Compromise
7340. The Purification Of The Mind
7341. Severe Psychic Treatment
7342. God Voraciously Eats
7343. A Death-Challenging Warrior
7344. The Song Of Satisfaction-Smile
7345. Jealousy Hides
7346. My Sound-Life
7347. My Mind's Newness-Dawn
7348. One Aspiration-Flame
7349. A Pure Instrument
7350. An Amazing Improvement
7351. The Capacity To Pray
7352. If You Are Ready To Play
7353. The Pinch Of Insecurity
7354. Utter Loneliness Awaited Him
7355. The Throne Of Heaven
7356. Your Mind's Serenity-Seeds
7357. Be Faithful, Be Powerful
7358. Meditation And Satisfaction
7359. My Needs
7360. Your Soulful Face
7361. One Dedication-Drop
7362. My Silence-Life Creates
7363. My Heart's Beauty-Sky
7364. Your Heart's Insecurity
7365. Your Doubt-Life
7366. Your Service-Flower-Fragrance
7367. Every Man Is A Blunderer
7368. Every Heart-Cry
7369. Every Soul-Smile
7370. Tomorrow's Perfection-Face
7371. God's Compassion-Flames
7372. God's Eternal Compassion-Flame
7373. God Is Never In A Hurry
7374. A New Role
7375. I Shall Not Allow
7376. Learn Only From Him
7377. Did You Say Hello To God?
7378. My Troubles Are Beginning
7379. I Breathed A Silent Prayer
7380. Nothing Better To Do
7381. I Do Not Know
7382. Two Miracles In One Day
7383. The Altar Of Aspiration
7384. No Exaggeration Can Be Too Great
7385. The Rules Of Heaven
7386. The Blending Of Old And New
7387. Two Indisputable Facts
7388. The Right Thing
7389. An Invisible Wound
7390. A Medley Of Smiles And Tears
7391. Two Broken Promises
7392. Your Inner Sun Will Reappear
7393. When The Veil Of Illusion Is Torn
7394. Meditate Here And Now
7395. Let God Be Your Coach
7396. Selfless Service
7397. If God Is Disgusted
7398. The Only Life
7399. Because It Gives Him Joy
7400. When I Speak To God
7401. If I Deepen My Faith
7402. Mine Is The Mind
7403. My Life's Journey
7404. Ability and Necessity
7405. I Have Scheduled My Time
7406. The Time Of Rejoicing
7407. A Very Close Connection
7408. Your Inner Reserves Are Unlimited
7409. What Your Mind Has
7410. A New Gospel
7411. At The God-Appointed Hour
7412. Each Incident In Life
7413. To Weather The Crisis
7414. Success
7415. To Become Generous
7416. Inner Eagerness
7417. Give Your Heart A Chance
7418. A True Truth-Seeker
7419. I Have Blindfolded Myself
7420. Outer Authority
7421. You Want To Measure God
7422. The Salvation-Boat
7423. The Very Nature Of Purity
7424. Your Heart Excuses
7425. Already Granted
7426. Truth Misused
7427. My Pride-Ocean
7428. My Earthly Knowledge-Pride
7429. The Life Of Living Death
7430. You Can Possess Peace-Light
7431. When Your Belief Is Strong
7432. The Gates Of Self-Destruction
7433. Not Ready To Love
7434. Everybody Laughs At Him
7435. What Pains My Heart Most
7436. Countless New Friends
7437. Each Thought Embodies
7438. Hope Is My Precious Treasure
7439. Each Golden Opportunity
7440. Two Things Could Not Wait
7441. Two Most Important Secrets
7442. Two Strange Misconceptions
7443. My Life Is Truly Valuable
7444. The Wrestler Of Wrestlers
7445. Inner Encouragement
7446. The Pressure Of Dragon-Time
7447. Curious About Only Two Things
7448. Challenge Ignorance
7449. He Listens To Two Voices
7450. Ascent Is Aspiring
7451. You Feel You Have Nothingness
7452. If I Fail
7453. By Legitimate Means
7454. Integrally Perfect
7455. My Lord Does Not Give Up
7456. God-Oneness-Satisfaction
7457. God's Satisfaction-Delight
7458. I Want To Be Alone
7459. Not In It
7460. A Deluge Of Doubts
7461. A New Life
7462. A Selfless Lover
7463. An Incurable Failure
7464. The Hyphen
7465. A Heart Treasured By God
7466. Each Time You Delay
7467. A Sincere Seeker
7468. Joy Can Never Rule
7469. A Daily Feast
7470. Do Not Try To Climb Too Quickly
7471. True Friends
7472. Obedience-Life Has No Parallel
7473. A Stranger To The Higher Worlds
7474. Dynamism Begins With Discipline
7475. A Singing Heart
7476. Two Lords
7477. Praising God In Secret
7478. Keep Your Eyes Wide Open
7479. Do What Your Inner Pilot Asks
7480. Good-Bye To Fear
7481. Make It Famous
7482. A Man Of Sorrow
7483. God Will Not Overload You
7484. God Is Not Confused
7485. Practise Loving The World
7486. In The Morning He Says Hello
7487. The Wisdom-Department
7488. The Happy Man
7489. My God-Oneness-Documents
7490. Can, Must And Will
7491. A Member Of God's Family
7492. Jealousy Will Devour Your Life
7493. A Happy Listener
7494. He Who Cheerfully Studies
7495. Because He Loves God Sleeplessly
7496. God Is Eagerly Looking Forward
7497. Please Only God
7498. On The Same Aspiration-Team
7499. Together You Are Succeeding
7500. The Peace That Creates Hunger
7501. Why Am I So Happy?
7502. You And Your Faith
7503. Unmerited Suffering
7504. Do Not Tire God
7505. A Dead-End Road
7506. The Dance Of Division
7507. The Beautiful Beginning
7508. The Best Authority
7509. Aspiration Illumines
7510. My Lord's Silence-Eye
7511. Impurity's Invasion
7512. My Prayer-Life Tells Me
7513. Undedicated Money-Power
7514. At The Halfway Mark
7515. A Life Of Deplorable Indecision
7516. The Only Question Haunting Me
7517. A Perfect Life
7518. When I Speak To Ignorance-King
7519. Remember!
7520. The Capacity To Please God
7521. When I Fail To Aspire
7522. How Can I Be Useless?
7523. My Lord's Concern
7524. My Soul Knows
7525. Sailing In The Same Boat
7526. To Walk Alongside
7527. My Heart Wants To Know
7528. Your Mind Cannot Have Fear
7529. My Sincerity-Heart Is Confused
7530. My Self-Control
7531. Deliberately Unprepared
7532. If Your Heart Knows How To Cry
7533. Tragic News
7534. Even Winning Has Its Problems
7535. Self-Styled Perfection
7536. Although I Cannot Lead My Life
7537. Two Viewpoints
7538. A Self-Invented Self-Portrait
7539. Love Of Immortality
7540. My Soul's Only Sacred Dream
7541. Uphill Will-Power
7542. No Right To Be
7543. Silence Waves Its Wings
7544. His Life Is Dancing
7545. His Heart's Gratitude-Song
7546. The Source
7547. The Newness That Glows
7548. Two Major Mistakes
7549. Do Not Be Afraid
7550. To Adore God The Dream
7551. I Pray To Receive
7552. Nothing Helps Like Self-Giving
7553. I Must Give Him Another Chance
7554. He Thinks He Is A Saint
7555. Destructive Happiness
7556. A Sorrowful Experience
7557. Lost Olympian Joy
7558. His Heart Will Be Blessed
7559. Shock The Mind Into Waking
7560. The Book Of Your Heart's Light
7561. Man's International Dream
7562. A Breath Of Self-Effacement
7563. If You Want To Succeed
7564. It Was You Who Chose Death
7565. Heaven's Compassion
7566. An Impossible Task
7567. A Heart Of Silence
7568. He Who Soulfully Listens
7569. The Union Of Dreams And Reality
7570. More Pleasure In Defeat
7571. The Meaning Of Loneliness
7572. Man's Desire-Life
7573. Although God Is Infinite
7574. God Introduces Me
7575. I Am Ready To Believe
7576. Two Significant Things
7577. A Whisper From My Insecurity-Life
7578. Earth's Soulful Love
7579. Your Soul-Power Can Baffle Death
7580. Your Heart's Fading Flames
7581. The Flower Of Beauty
7582. What I Can Do For God
7583. Since I Love Man's Mind
7584. My Sincerity-Mind Tells Me
7585. Determination

7586. I Want To Remind Myself
7587. A Colossal Hope
7588. Be Careful Of Your Commitments
7589. Be Prepared For Surprises
7590. Follow Your Intuition
7591. Do Not Forget
7592. A Serious Mistake
7593. Not A Difficult Task
7594. Incomparably Sweet
7595. Each Painful Thought
7596. My Life Of Hope
7597. If Ever I Look Behind
7598. Your Poor Heart's Thirst
7599. You Resent Perfection
7600. My Smiling Eyes Tell Me
7601. God Touches My Heart
7602. Be Brave, Be Sincere
7603. For God's Satisfaction
7604. Curb Your Negative Feelings
7605. I Cry Because
7606. God The Compassion
7607. Always Willing To Try
7608. There Is No Difference
7609. Look At Yourself Soulfully
7610. A Diplomatic Death
7611. If My Heart Knows You Well
7612. The Tug-Of-War
7613. No Matter What You Say
7614. My Aspiring Heart Is Familiar
7615. I Desperately Need You
7616. Simplification Is Unification
7617. Citizenship In Heaven
7618. Veil And Unveil
7619. God Dreams Of His Satisfaction
7620. Truth And Falsehood
7621. During His Sunset Years
7622. His Days Die With Sombre Sleep
7623. We Imitate
7624. Creativity-Power
7625. Remain In Your Child-Heart
7626. When The Hour Strikes
7627. Silence Speaks
7628. The Beauty Of Hope
7629. Where Is My Receptivity?
7630. My Heart's Silence-Sky
7631. No Sincere Heart-Cries
7632. Shelter Me And Mine
7633. Two Ancient Universal Questions
7634. The Perils Of Your Temptation-Life
7635. Because You Do Not Believe
7636. A Long Stride Towards God
7637. The Silver Mountain
7638. His Heart's Light-Giving Lamp
7639. Two Thoughts
7640. Futile Human Opinions
7641. What Have I To Conceal?
7642. God Laughs And Laughs
7643. To See My Pride Weep
7644. Soon You Will Hear God Knocking
7645. Walk Along The Inner Road
7646. The Heaven-Born Music
7647. An Infinitely Superior Goal
7648. The Same God
7649. His Truth-Life Has Begun
7650. Lost Between Heaven And Earth
7651. O My Mind's Suspicion-Night
7652. Among The Immortals
7653. God Has Promised Me
7654. Only One Necessity
7655. The Correct Answer
7656. Your Sweet Violin-Heart
7657. Because Of My Surrender-Light
7658. Time Is Illumining
7659. The Frowns Of Dissolution-Night
7660. Your Heart Of Promise-Light
7661. You Want Your Mind To Wither
7662. God's Unchanging Decision
7663. Doubt Can Easily Destroy
7664. If You Want Enlightenment
7665. How Can Your Heart Be Happy?
7666. Happiness
7667. Man's First Disobedience-Night
7668. A Truly Great Seeker
7669. Unless We Invoke
7670. First-Born Child
7671. Your Monstrous Anger
7672. The Forest Of Uncomely Thoughts
7673. Blossoms Of Enlightenment
7674. To Feed A Seeker's Heart
7675. Your Craving For World Praise
7676. A Loneliness-Heart
7677. God's Whispers
7678. A Slave To Your Fate
7679. A Succession Of Calamities
7680. Opportunity Is Precious
7681. You Cannot Enjoy
7682. The Crown Of My Efforts
7683. Can You Believe?
7684. That Is Why
7685. When He Was In Heaven
7686. When Heaven And Earth Are United
7687. Our Goal Is Not Fixed
7688. Three Goals
7689. A New Promise
7690. God Grabbed Your Soul
7691. A Mature Seeker
7692. Beautiful God-Dreams
7693. His Childlike Consciousness
7694. If You Feel Young
7695. Millions Of Ways
7696. Light Is Never Lost
7697. A New Message
7698. Never Enough
7699. Our Heavenly Hunger
7700. Three Prayers
7701. The First Divine Rule
7702. An Insincere Seeker
7703. The God-Tree
7704. Too Much Heavenly Food
7705. Your Hovering Failure-Sigh
7706. Invade And Conquer
7707. My Self-Sacrificing Friend
7708. Even My Own Mind Misunderstands
7709. Since God Has Killed Me
7710. Why Worship Fear?
7711. The Only King On Earth
7712. Why Do I Have To Believe?
7713. Each Divine Thought
7714. My Falling Tears
7715. A Stepping-stone
7716. My Prayers
7717. Craving For Rich Comfort
7718. Its Daily Appointment With God
7719. Everybody Misunderstands You
7720. A Stupendous Inner Loss
7721. What Do I Expect From You?
7722. The Most Difficult Task
7723. Not In Vain
7724. To Satisfy My Lord Supreme
7725. Faith And Beauty
7726. My Mind's Telephone Number
7727. God's Compassionate Rainbow-Lustre
7728. Only When Faith Is Afraid
7729. The Ultimate Fact Of Life
7730. All My Wise Decisions
7731. My Lord, Run With Me
7732. Why Are You So Angry?
7733. Past Weakness, Present Weakness
7734. My Mental Hallucinations
7735. At Last My Heart Has Challenged
7736. Nobody Hears Anything
7737. His Self-Giving Heart
7738. Only To Catch A Glimpse
7739. Each Undetected Desire
7740. The Incense Of Self-Indulgence
7741. A Saint Knows And Feels
7742. A Flood From His Thought-Sea
7743. When I Am In My Master's Heart
7744. Nothing Is More Illumining
7745. Showing Me The Way
7746. The Outskirts Of Hope
7747. Eternity's Shortest Road
7748. A Better Name
7749. The Self-Proclamation-Game
7750. To Cultivate A Diamond Heart
7751. Excellence
7752. Comparison
7753. Her Ancient Beauty
7754. Her Body And Soul
7755. Honour Patience
7756. Life's Divinity
7757. Beyond The Soaring Imagination-Flight
7758. When Your Heart Returns To God
7759. A Dance Of Hope
7760. Ready To Lose Everything
7761. I Try, Only To Fail
7762. I Just Want To Know
7763. A Complicated Mind
7764. Your Perfection Immediate
7765. Those Who Will Save Humanity
7766. The Mind That Enjoys
7767. A Soulful Glimpse
7768. Destiny's Cancelled Injunctions
7769. Who Practises Truth?
7770. My Only Treasure
7771. He Does Not Hide Anything
7772. Life Has Denied Me
7773. Practical Fears
7774. The Blue Bird Inside My Heart
7775. The Gulf Of My Incomprehension
7776. A Hallowed Dawn
7777. My Lord Wants
7778. Always Misunderstood
7779. My Constant Longing For Peace
7780. Unless We Purify The Mind
7781. Your Unlimited Patience
7782. Unless My Heart Takes Care
7783. My Heart's Deathless Hope
7784. Farther And Nearer
7785. To Please God
7786. His Final Decision
7787. My Vital Never Learns
7788. To Gain The Comradeship
7789. The Capacity To Whisper
7790. Only One Ideal Fragrance
7791. High Above There Is A Voice
7792. Every Day My Lord Asks Me
7793. Progress-Light
7794. God Tells Us
7795. The Inner Sun
7796. God Will Not Disappoint You
7797. The Best Short-cut
7798. A Sea Of Love
7799. The Future Holds For You
7800. The Capacity To Remember You
7801. My Lord's Beauty's Eyes
7802. This Poor And Feeble World
7803. The Life Of Outer Relinquishment
7804. Overburdened With Problems
7805. Do What You Can Now
7806. Unsophisticated And Uncluttered
7807. I Needed A Listener
7808. Not A Matter Of Curiosity
7809. The Comfort Of Fantasy
7810. If You Suspect The World
7811. Indefinitely Detained
7812. The Smile Of Justice-Light
7813. Surrender-Flower, Gratitude-Fruit
7814. Two Unthinkable Things
7815. My Heavenly Capacities Cannot Cry
7816. The Soul's Festival In Heaven
7817. The Blossom Of An Illumining Life
7818. Place Your Own Flower-Heart
7819. Not Interested
7820. Your Self-Imposed Blindness-Life
7821. Your Heart Is Already Ready
7822. You Have The Capacity
7823. Who Can Appreciate?
7824. Your God-Ordained Task
7825. I Am Going To Heaven
7826. What Is Divine Life?
7827. The Immensity Of His Self-Offering
7828. Your Heart Will Perform A Miracle
7829. An Invitation From God
7830. As Long As You Are Busy
7831. The Greatest Difficulty
7832. My Obedience To My Inner Voice
7833. Tomorrow Will Give Me
7834. If We Keep Our Inner Appointments
7835. Only Two Inner Teachings
7836. His Heart's Inner Moon
7837. I Have Come To My Source
7838. Your Imprisoned Life
7839. A Perfect Victim
7840. Do You Want To Work For God?
7841. God Knows How To Delay
7842. Your Commitment
7843. Always Available
7844. God Has Always Been Inside You
7845. Ignorance And God
7846. When Are You Going To Look?
7847. I Sowed Faith-Seed
7848. To Love Man Unreservedly
7849. God Has The Time
7850. Beauty Knows How To Shine
7851. One Haunting Doubt
7852. Two Final Questions
7853. His Life Enjoys
7854. Gently Command
7855. To Entertain The Angels
7856. You Know How To Love
7857. I Can Nowhere Cause Commotion
7858. His Heaven-Sent Haven
7859. Curiosity Awakens
7860. How God Always Is
7861. His Mind's Addiction To Falsehood
7862. Your Mind's Secret Duty
7863. A Man Of Good Will
7864. My Life's Integrity
7865. My Lord Accepts Me
7866. Two Things You Do Not Know
7867. His Preoccupation
7868. What Kind Of Faith Is It?
7869. The More You Want To Possess
7870. If Your Mind Enjoys Collecting
7871. An Unerring Hour
7872. God Created My Faith
7873. Forgiving Seconds
7874. Imagination-Memories Of The Past
7875. What My Heart Needs
7876. No Opinion
7877. A Heart To Quench God's Thirst
7878. He Succeeds Always
7879. Your Heart-Flower Cannot Grow
7880. Your Heart's Dawn
7881. On Good Terms With God
7882. A Sleepless Love
7883. My Mind Wants To Be Powerful
7884. The Abiding Perfection-Life
7885. Inside My Lord's Compassion-Smile
7886. Time's Heaven-Free Steps
7887. A True Athlete Of God
7888. The Discovery Of Perennial Truth
7889. O World Vital, Sleep!
7890. The Medicine
7891. God Will Entertain
7892. God Wants To Give You
7893. My Mind Hides No Thorn
7894. I Shall Watch You
7895. My Unfortunate Friend
7896. Ready To Measure
7897. My Heart The Climber
7898. The Beauty Of His Purity-Heart
7899. My Heart's Adamantine Will
7900. In Silence
7901. Do First Things First
7902. If You Have Inner Poise
7903. God Is More Than Ready
7904. You Want To Change The World
7905. Temptation-Love
7906. When You Defend
7907. The Source Of My Joy
7908. This Can Never Be The Message
7909. The Clever Human Mind
7910. The Art Of Deceiving Others
7911. My Soul Is Always Grateful
7912. Even If My Mind Believes
7913. You Will Become Strong
7914. To Transform The Vital
7915. The Inner Assurance
7916. No Wonder
7917. As Long As You Remember
7918. Something Divine Within
7919. The Presence Of A Spiritual Master
7920. No Sunlit Frontier
7921. I Would Rather Embrace
7922. The Result Of My Meditation
7923. The Beauty Of A Satisfaction-Dawn
7924. India Is The Celestial Music
7925. India's Tolerance
7926. A Special Charm And Beauty
7927. See India With Your Aspiring Heart
7928. A Perennial Vision
7929. The Heart Of India
7930. We Have Only To Start
7931. If You Want To Receive
7932. When God Observes His Children
7933. A Treasured Gift
7934. Your Permanent Address

7935. A Permanent Rejection
7936. Today's Unwilling Obedience
7937. Outer And Inner Obedience
7938. Tomorrow's Giant Failure
7939. On God's Team
7940. The Life Of Promise
7941. Death Came From Hell
7942. The End Of His Inner Journey
7943. Messages Of The Material World
7944. Totally Different
7945. Until Purity Takes Possession
7946. God's Transcendental Consciousness
7947. Who Has Abundant Enthusiasm?
7948. My Soul Exists Only For God
7949. Earthly Days Advance
7950. He Who Sees You Praying
7951. Pristine Peace And Poise
7952. When I Long To See
7953. Your Eternity's Quest
7954. A Child-Heart
7955. To Please The Supreme
7956. Your Golden Heart
7957. His Eternity's Compeer
7958. Inner Awareness
7959. You Value Only Those
7960. Songs And Dances Of Self-Offering
7961. If You Want To Satisfy God
7962. Everything Is Important
7963. Try To Please God For One Day
7964. Surcharged With Divinity
7965. He Carries Divinity Within
7966. God Is Very Strict
7967. God's Punishment-Illumination
7968. The Inner Victory
7969. The Day You Get Up Early
7970. A Perfect Oneness-World
7971. You Create Receptivity In Others
7972. A Tape Measure Around Your Heart
7973. When You Offer Gratitude
7974. The Joy That We Get
7975. Do Not Separate Yourself
7976. The Fragrance Of Your Gratitude
7977. Your Soulful Self-Offering
7978. Inwardly You Can Talk To God
7979. He Who Shows Sympathy
7980. To Help A Seeker-Friend
7981. When You Offer Anything To God
7982. An Aspiring Heart
7983. Your Inner Light Will Be Revealed
7984. An Opportunity To Meditate
7985. Touch And Receive
7986. When You Do The Right Thing
7987. Remember Your Yesterday's Happiness
7988. Flames Of Purity
7989. To Illumine The Jungle-Mind
7990. The Tears Of Your Soul's Joy
7991. An Inner Award
7992. Creation Means Self-Giving
7993. The Successful Ending
7994. One Life, One Message
7995. The Outer Life Is The Body
7996. We Constantly Cry To God
7997. We Free Ourselves
7998. He Was Such A Fool!
7999. Do Not Delay A Moment!
8000. My Only Cherished Goal
8001. Yesterday I Prayed To God
8002. Why Do I Cry?
8003. You Have The Hidden Capacity
8004. Self-Examination Means
8005. The Art Of Inner Deafness
8006. Your Life's Ceaseless Pangs
8007. The Smile Of Your Heart
8008. If You Become A Prayerful Seeker
8009. In The Heart Of Life
8010. Love Is The Quickest
8011. My Eternity's Nectar-Food
8012. What Can Force You To Improve?
8013. Satisfaction-Delight
8014. Burn The Incense Of Your Heart
8015. A Ceaseless Flow Of Love
8016. When I Dive Deep With
8017. If I Listen To The Sweet Melody
8018. The Road Of Light
8019. If You Love Your Heart's Journey
8020. A Life Of Dreams
8021. Your Supportive Listeners
8022. God's Smile Of Vision-Plenitude
8023. The Supreme Cause Of Life-Perfection
8024. God Is His Compassion-Flow
8025. If You Cry With Hope
8026. End Your Friendship
8027. My Tenebrous Mind
8028. If You Want To Throw Away
8029. He Embodies The Eternal
8030. Ask Your Mind To Create Something
8031. As Long As You Love
8032. I See Your Smile-River
8033. A New Dream
8034. What The World Needs
8035. A Satisfied Heaven-Father
8036. Your Heart-Fountain
8037. Your Unconscious Incapacity
8038. The Beauty Of His Soul
8039. This World
8040. A Blessing-Gift In Disguise
8041. Those Who Want To Destroy
8042. If You Want To Protest
8043. Bury Your Mental Education
8044. Your Prayerful Life
8045. His Life Is All Happiness
8046. Every Divine Thought
8047. Each Special Prayer To God
8048. A Seeker's Soulful Smile
8049. Any Purpose In Thinking
8050. Each Sorrow Tells Us
8051. Never Surrender Your Hope-Heart
8052. With Your Heart's Loving Gratitude
8053. The Heart-Beauty Of Humanity
8054. A Foolish Hope
8055. Ripples Of Energy-Light
8056. Be Careful Of Undivine Thoughts
8057. Your Mind's Maladies
8058. Unless Your Mind Cares
8059. A Frustration-Lion
8060. Do Not Try To Interpret
8061. Poison-Food
8062. What You Have Inside You
8063. The Human Mind Does Not Progress
8064. If You Love The World
8065. Do Not Think!
8066. A Life Of Silence
8067. They Never Want To Listen
8068. The Time That God Has Given You
8069. A Song Of Service
8070. I Believe
8071. Each Uninspired Day
8072. Unless It Means Everything To You
8073. His Heart's Sincerity
8074. An Unparalleled Blessing
8075. Nothing To Do With Failure
8076. A Soul Of Beauty
8077. A Heart Of Tranquillity
8078. Your Love For God
8079. An Endless And Useless Task
8080. God Usually Does Not Hide
8081. Listen To Only One Prayer
8082. You Do Not Have To Advertise
8083. God's Compassion-Patrol
8084. Constantly Self-Transcendent
8085. As Imagination Runs
8086. Unwilling To Be Brave
8087. Only One Reality
8088. If You Rely On God Alone
8089. Only One Urgent Duty
8090. Sailing In Two Directions
8091. If You Have A Pure Heart
8092. God Wants You To Love
8093. O Dark World-Ignorance
8094. Dear And Sweet Death
8095. Pleasure-Thoughts
8096. To Know The Difference
8097. A Soulful Song
8098. If You Can Sing Soulfully
8099. Inner Beauty Has To Penetrate
8100. The Capacity To Be Happy
8101. If I Accept My Supreme Lord
8102. Burn Doubts Away Immediately
8103. When The Mind Is All Darkness
8104. Fat Old Idleness
8105. Stay Inside My Heart!
8106. The Waters Of Perpetual Delight
8107. Our Heart Must Approach God
8108. His Inevitable Farewell To Earth
8109. Invisible Flames Of Aspiration
8110. His Deplorable Fate
8111. My Mind Speaks Whisperingly
8112. The Blue Bird Inside My Heart
8113. Can You Not Fly Away?
8114. Useful And Useless
8115. A Great Man
8116. Two Promises
8117. You Have Something
8118. What Kind Of Independence Is This?
8119. My Soul Is Leaning
8120. Eternity's Infinite Questions
8121. Your Uncertain Life
8122. He Made Two Great Decisions
8123. You Have Given Me Fear
8124. I Bring Forward My Soul
8125. Each Good Thought Vanishes
8126. When He Struggles
8127. Heaven-Created Compassion
8128. An Incurable Disease
8129. Degrees Of Self-Complacency
8130. Tears Of Oneness-Love
8131. My Lord Supreme Loves Everything
8132. Sleeplessly Devoted
8133. A Ruined Paradise
8134. My Heart's Fathomless Despair
8135. A Visible Dedication
8136. Your Uncomplaining Life
8137. I Wish To Unveil Heaven
8138. Self-Enlightenment Will Cling
8139. You Need Sleepless Devotion
8140. His Heart's Sleepless Hunger
8141. The Doubting Mind Must Surrender
8142. Mortal Grief
8143. Speaking Ill Of God
8144. Two Things He Cannot Understand
8145. My Today's Hungry Heart
8146. God Does Not Know How To Punish
8147. A Strong Heart Gives And Becomes
8148. Your Mind Is Useless
8149. Your Faith Is Its Own Victory
8150. A Prison Of Self-Indulgence
8151. Satisfaction Illumines My Life
8152. Not A Flicker Of Hope
8153. His Soul Has Planned
8154. If You Carry God Only Sometimes
8155. A Crisis-Filled World
8156. A True Candidate
8157. His Mind Has The Capacity
8158. An All-Devouring Ego
8159. My Lord's Fulness-Heart
8160. Turn My Life Into An Open Book
8161. What I Need
8162. I Receive Only One Message
8163. An Endless Future Is Before You
8164. If You Have Oneness-Faith
8165. Heaven Will Accompany
8166. If You Are Afraid Of Silence-Light
8167. Mine Is The Heart-Song
8168. When We Talk Of World Peace
8169. A Sheer Dream
8170. God Does Not Look At Me
8171. You Are Not Happy
8172. He Lives In Empty Silence
8173. Everywhere
8174. Do You Ever Think?
8175. His Curiosity-Mind Wants To Know
8176. To Renounce My Curiosity-Life
8177. Let Time Tell The Rest
8178. If God Has Stopped Looking
8179. Although I Delay
8180. Haunted By Eternity's Hunger-Cry
8181. His Love Of God Is Perfect
8182. The Equal Of A Gratitude-Heart
8183. My Lord, Break Me
8184. The Crowd Of Supernal Memories
8185. When I Talk About God
8186. Why Do I Find Fault?
8187. God Is Always Perfect
8188. God Has Told Me Many Things
8189. Possessors Of Fruitless Expectations
8190. Each Human Being Wants To Know
8191. My Mind Knows
8192. The Human Life-Story
8193. The Heart That Cries Sleeplessly
8194. The Humility Of A Tree
8195. A Universal Favourite
8196. The Golden Harp
8197. What I Remember Most
8198. The Glowing Promise
8199. Something Quite Unusual
8200. Two Firm Convictions
8201. Do Teach Me How To Create
8202. His Three Secret Misfortunes
8203. Before We Achieve Self-Mastery
8204. If You Have One God-Gift
8205. God Is Anxious To Reassure You
8206. Do Not Waste Opportunities
8207. If The Heart Is Unprepared
8208. Do Not Deceive Your Heart
8209. The Mind Wants To Go Alone
8210. First Chance And Last Chance
8211. An Abiding Portrait
8212. A Doubtful Mind
8213. Because You Have A Believer's Mind
8214. Each Animal Thought
8215. A Satisfaction-Dreamer
8216. A Satisfactory Moment
8217. A Spotless Life Of Hope
8218. He Who Has No Faith
8219. An Immensely Difficult Endeavour
8220. Each Seeker's Searching Mind
8221. Catalogues
8222. The Unthinkable Treasury Of Emotions
8223. The Ways Of Loneliness
8224. Faith-Seeds Precede
8225. I Have Watched
8226. Do Not Doubt My Heart
8227. What You Need
8228. Born To Do Something Good
8229. The Right Thing To Do
8230. The Music Of The Trance-World
8231. The Beginning
8232. Your Future Life
8233. All You Have To Do
8234. Think Of Your Aspiration-Life
8235. What Can I Make New?
8236. A Short-Sighted Capacity
8237. The Most Important Question
8238. The Curse Of A Troubled Mind
8239. My Lord Wants Me To Give Him
8240. God Knows My Weaknesses
8241. If The Mind Ever Gets Peace
8242. If You Are Not Quick To Forgive
8243. The Language Of Love
8244. Now That I Have Chosen God
8245. My Heart's Hope Shows Me
8246. Tomorrow Try To Be Satisfied
8247. My Life Is Forgiven By God
8248. You Will Inherit
8249. Do You Want To Stop Dying?
8250. If God Has Power
8251. God Wants To Walk With Me Today
8252. Only One Place For You
8253. God Has Given You
8254. God's Love Is Willing
8255. Just Because I Am Loved
8256. You Are Trying To Know
8257. No Certainty
8258. How Do You Expect To Win?
8259. The Throne Of My Silence-Heart
8260. In The Silence Of My Soul
8261. The Darkness Of Your Mind-Sky
8262. How Can You Claim Happiness?
8263. God Will Paint A New Heart
8264. When My Soul Said Good-Bye
8265. A God-Tuned Heart
8266. I See God Smilingly Walking
8267. To See The Flowers Of Joy
8268. Because You Are Good
8269. Two Things I Desperately Need
8270. When I Promise
8271. Silences Of Love
8272. A Sad Smile
8273. Life's Fulfilment-Poise

8274. What A Strangely Hungry World!
8275. The Whole World Tells Me
8276. His Life Is Beautiful
8277. Each Promise
8278. My Heart-Tears Are Serving
8279. May This World Be Satisfied
8280. The World-Perfection-Key
8281. Two Dreamers
8282. What I Can Do For God
8283. Only A God Of Satisfaction
8284. I Know
8285. To Have Faith
8286. He Who Desperately Needs God
8287. God Does Not Smile
8288. When I Think Of My Mind
8289. God Will Definitely Help You
8290. Have You Decided?
8291. God Whispers
8292. Each Trouble
8293. God Does Not Love
8294. God Does Not Laugh
8295. Live In The Eternal Now
8296. You Have Committed Yourself
8297. God Does Not Want To Surprise Me
8298. Can You Not Bless My Tomorrows?
8299. Do Not Expect God
8300. Will You Not Give Me The Capacity?
8301. My Safest Haven
8302. God Will Not Be Enthusiastic
8303. I Need Only One Thing
8304. My Mind Does Not Get Tired
8305. An Immediate God
8306. God's Freedom-Gift
8307. He Is Trying To Be Himself
8308. The Master Key
8309. Each Moment My Heart Tries
8310. God's Delight-Embrace
8311. God Wants To Hear
8312. A Full Day Of Satisfaction
8313. An Inner Life Of Turmoil
8314. When You Worry, God Feels Sad
8315. By Surprise
8316. Why Are You Grumbling?
8317. My Climbing Prayer
8318. No Other Reality
8319. God's Voice Awakens
8320. If Your Mind Strives
8321. The Sigh That The Sound-Life Heaves
8322. Respect Your Hopes
8323. God Is Ready
8324. My Prayer Tries To Reach
8325. An Unparalleled Joy
8326. The Heart Is Born To Pray
8327. A Loving Heart Knows How
8328. A Fortress Of Eternity
8329. Insensibility Weighs You Down
8330. A Most Powerful Gift
8331. Do Not Keep God Waiting
8332. Your Unconscious Life
8333. The Purity-Channel
8334. Your Mind Will Not Give You Peace
8335. Heaven And Earth Will Pass Away
8336. God's Constant Closeness
8337. Born To Satisfy God
8338. The Lustre Of Your Hidden Divinity
8339. His Love-Life With Himself
8340. A Peace Treaty
8341. Compassion And Justice
8342. Your Self-Righteous Pride
8343. The Responsibility
8344. His Heart's Soulful Smile
8345. Paralysis
8346. God's Satisfaction-Flooded Voice
8347. No Escape
8348. Justice Is Not Enough
8349. Suffering From Insanity
8350. How Can You Have Hope?
8351. A Safe Path
8352. On Each Man's Life-Agenda
8353. Disappointment Is At Your Door
8354. The Company Of Ignorance-Night
8355. His Life's Outer History
8356. Investment And Enlightenment
8357. The Life-Experience-School
8358. A Life Of Questions Unanswered
8359. The Untimely Death-Grave
8360. The Divine In Me Dives Deep
8361. When The Mind Is Ready
8362. No Monopoly
8363. Tune Your Mind-Instrument
8364. Stamped As A Second-Rate Seeker
8365. Born Of Their Own Divine Needs
8366. A False God
8367. God Is Nourishing His Heart
8368. What Can God Do?
8369. His Heart Chose To Be Weak
8370. No Difference
8371. One Question, One Answer
8372. Earth Knows How To Hope
8373. The Mind Accepts The Unacceptable
8374. Sapping Your Heart's Strength-Tree
8375. Man Will Have A New Name
8376. Sincerity Is Meant For Living
8377. You Can Only Go Forward
8378. Down The Stairs Of Memory
8379. God And I Are Seeing
8380. Everything Divine
8381. A Translucent Mind
8382. In The Company Of God
8383. I Seek My Beloved Supreme
8384. Destruction In Disguise
8385. Please Say Good-Bye
8386. Only Say
8387. I Cannot Live Without
8388. Hidden Dangers
8389. Now I Weep, Now I Laugh
8390. The Mirror Reflects
8391. Your Soul's Promise-Beauty
8392. How Can Your Heart Dare To Sing?
8393. Unfading Perfection-Beauty
8394. The Sons Of Morning Sang
8395. Each Page Of My Aspiration-Life
8396. How Can You Blame God?
8397. The Farewell-Beam
8398. A Peerless Solace
8399. His Superb Frown Of Pride
8400. The Sole Possession
8401. My Heart's Adoration-Bird
8402. If You Do Not Manifest The Supreme
8403. Hard To Escape
8404. Her Insecurity
8405. Your Mind's Doubt-Fort
8406. The Cosmic Deities Within You
8407. Out Of Tune
8408. Love Can Enlarge
8409. Compete Only For Compassion-Light
8410. A Ceaseless Song Of Newness
8411. In Case You Have Not Noticed
8412. Minor Incidents
8413. The Life-River
8414. Your Lack Of Faith In God
8415. God's Sleepless Dream-Boat
8416. If You Are A Secret Lover Of God
8417. The Trivia Of The World
8418. Every Day You Must Learn Anew
8419. Just Look Within!
8420. God's Victory-Drum
8421. The Unaspiring Human In Me
8422. If You Love Spirituality
8423. Your Heart's Surrender-Life
8424. Mountain-High Beauty
8425. The Art Of Faith-Fidelity
8426. The Swift Opening Of Heaven's Door
8427. I Shall Not Allow
8428. To See The Face
8429. A Specialist In God's Love
8430. Teach Me How To Fly
8431. Peace In My Outer Life
8432. His Inner Actions
8433. God Will Be On Your Side
8434. His Heart's Ceaseless Silence
8435. My Secret Prayers
8436. Your Heart's New Name
8437. My Mind's Disbelief-Door
8438. Cheerful Self-Giving
8439. Very Special Ways
8440. An Atom Of Your Light
8441. I Own Many Things
8442. Yesterday's Fear
8443. My Confidence In My Heart
8444. No Margin For Error
8445. The Silence Of Humility
8446. The Final Smile
8447. Inside A Tiny Moment-Drop
8448. I Phoned God
8449. The Prison Of Wasted Thoughts
8450. Your Life's Dedication-Light
8451. God Loves The Lover
8452. I Wish To Be An Eternal Slave
8453. A Very Close Friend
8454. Heaven's Ecstasy-Sky
8455. Two Divine Existence-Realities
8456. A Mind Flooded With Doubts
8457. Unless You Carefully Watch
8458. Where Is The Difference?
8459. My Inner Electricity
8460. My Heart's Senior Partner
8461. A Whisper Of Inspiration
8462. To Challenge The Invisible
8463. A Shameless Self-Lover
8464. The Elementary Lessons
8465. The Supreme Lesson
8466. The Nectar-Delight
8467. This World Definitely Needs
8468. The Human Mind
8469. Offer Your Mind To God
8470. God's "Why?" And "How?"
8471. If You Are A Beginner-Seeker
8472. God Does Not Care To Know
8473. Before You Think Of God
8474. Two Messages
8475. If You Want To Argue
8476. When I Live Inside My Mind
8477. A Free Permit
8478. The Pressure Of Inner Weaknesses
8479. A Heart Of Constant Self-Giving
8480. His Self-Imposed Task
8481. A Faithful And Meticulous Observer
8482. If You Cherish A Doubt-Life
8483. A Golden God-Necessity-Chain
8484. The Trap Of Self-Deception
8485. A Mind Of Blossom-Poise
8486. A World Far From Ours
8487. How Can You Expect To Sing?
8488. Hope Gropes In The Darkness
8489. The Dew Of Earth-Delight
8490. A Sacred Corner Of My Heart-Room
8491. The Presence Of Teeming Doubts
8492. The Right Approach
8493. He Does Not Want To Hear
8494. A Dead Leaf
8495. Unless He Invites His Inner King
8496. There Is No Difference
8497. Each Beautiful Life
8498. The Only Place
8499. His Mind Is A Shattered Hope
8500. My Life's Devoted Receptivity
8501. No Need Of Miracles!
8502. Do Not Try To Bind Love
8503. He Is Not The Loser
8504. Two Questions
8505. A Sacred Thirst
8506. Love Your Heart Ever More
8507. Stay Where You Are
8508. Sleepless Perfection
8509. I Once Promised Myself
8510. Beautiful Is His Heart's Loyalty
8511. The Mind's Barrier
8512. What Can My Little Hands Do?
8513. A Purity-Heart Has The Capacity
8514. My Mind's Ignorance-Dreams
8515. Gratitude Is All-Powerful
8516. The Scorn Of Multitude-Tongues
8517. If God's Mind Is Subtle
8518. Each Human Desire
8519. Each Human Being Is Blessed
8520. His Unparalleled Inheritance
8521. His Firm Belief
8522. When Imagination Fails You
8523. Refuse To Sing With Your Mind
8524. God Will Treasure You
8525. What Hurts You More
8526. Inside Your Heart
8527. There Is No Perfect Desire
8528. The Causes Of Sudden Death
8529. We Need Many Things From God
8530. If You Do Not Know How To Smile
8531. Your Imagination-Bird Is Locked Up
8532. God Is Always For You
8533. My Unaspiring Life Is Aware
8534. As God Intended
8535. Do You Not See?
8536. You Say That You Pray
8537. His Heart Is Crying
8538. The Curse Of The Mind
8539. When My Soul Invites Me
8540. If Thoughts Are Flocking
8541. When The Mind Reigns Over Matter
8542. My Lord Is Pleased
8543. Nothing Is Worth Believing
8544. The Cynical Eye Distrusts
8545. Doubt Immediately Surrendered
8546. My Dedication To The World
8547. His Mind Has Unparalleled Poise
8548. Your Fallen Self-Expectation-Tree
8549. What The Weeping Multitudes Need
8550. The Supreme Guest Will Come
8551. Sorrow-Rain Will Fall
8552. Aspiration Is The Beginning
8553. My Lord's Earth-Born Child
8554. Hope Is My Heart's God
8555. Why Do I Choose To Hide?
8556. My Search
8557. Hint Of Surrender-Light
8558. Expand Your Heart
8559. The Treacherous Queen
8560. Only One Pure Heart
8561. Two Monsters Of Waste
8562. Your Earthly Role
8563. God's Choice Instrument
8564. Only One God-Trodden Path
8565. If You Keep Your Heart-Eye Veiled
8566. His Inner Glimpse Of God's Smile
8567. A Ruined Paradise
8568. Laugh At Yesterday's Despair-Night
8569. A Visible Aspiration-Flame
8570. God Will Cheerfully Allow You
8571. Family Of Sighs
8572. The Universal Burden-Bearer
8573. A Questioning Mind
8574. O Fearful Heart
8575. How Can Your Heart Be Pleased?
8576. A Splendid Victory
8577. Because Your Life Enjoys
8578. Who God Is
8579. His Heaven-Life Saw
8580. Your God Has Planned Your Life
8581. Who Wants To Have You?
8582. When I Live In My Heart
8583. My Mind Is Not Satisfied
8584. On The Wrong Train
8585. Only For You
8586. Self-Confessed Insecurity
8587. The Presence Of Peace
8588. A Fountain Of Joy-Tears
8589. Eternity's Peace-Distributing Self
8590. The Chains Of My Sinful Life
8591. The Sunlit Frontier
8592. Few Will Equal You
8593. A Universal Favourite
8594. Perfection Means
8595. His Life's Doubt-Clouds
8596. The Beginning Of Death
8597. The Day Of My Heart
8598. A Spiritually Full Man
8599. God Helps The Seeker
8600. You Have My Tomorrow
8601. My Chosen Present
8602. Feast And Fast
8603. The Glory Of Unlearning
8604. Enemy And Friend
8605. Difficult And Easy
8606. Your Future Success Life
8607. His Heart Is Enjoying
8608. Your Mind's Doubt-Cloud
8609. Permanent Residents Of Heaven
8610. If God Wants Me To Proceed
8611. His Supreme Assistant
8612. The Dead Are Not Forgiven
8613. Imagine And Reveal
8614. You Think Of God
8615. Ready To Show
8616. Schooled In Enlightenment
8617. Unwillingness To Change
8618. Love Your Soul More

8619. Each Soul-Boat
8620. Do Not Give Up!
8621. Can You Not Forget My Past?
8622. If Your Heart-Life Is Thirsty
8623. Impossible Plus Unnecessary
8624. Soulfully Wait
8625. Delighted And Disgusted
8626. A Sleeplessly Cheerful Commitment
8627. The Harvest Of God's Smile
8628. If You Can Never Regain
8629. Because You Want To Become
8630. The Unparalleled Hardship
8631. Incessant Disputes
8632. Divinity's Ease
8633. To Obey At Every Moment
8634. The Revelation Of What You Have
8635. Your Old Friend, Ignorance
8636. Confusion-Problems
8637. The Heaven-Rejected Category
8638. Each Forward Step Of His
8639. There Are Higher Things On Earth
8640. Your Despair-Station
8641. The Morning Of God's Hour
8642. An Impossible Task
8643. If Education Is Self-Cultivation
8644. Your Reward
8645. God's Perfect Home
8646. A Detour
8647. My New Start
8648. More Time, More Trust
8649. The World-Heart Will Give You
8650. I Shall Help You
8651. If I Love God's Love
8652. Each Aspiring Heart
8653. What Kind Of Faith Is It?
8654. Every Day You Will Have To Face
8655. Develop The Capacity
8656. You Trust God
8657. Because God Is So Great
8658. Just Because I Know
8659. God's Transcendental Dream
8660. His Heart's Starlit Faith
8661. The Transcendence Of Suffering
8662. To Suffer And Not To Speak
8663. A Great Idea
8664. A Much-Needed Experience
8665. It Was He Who Loved Ignorance
8666. Its Life-Illumining "Yes"
8667. Have More Faith In Your Heart
8668. Your Self-Examination
8669. How Can I Have A Sorrowful Life?
8670. What Else Is A Miracle?
8671. The Door
8672. Your Selflessness
8673. He Did Not Feel Sad
8674. Your Life Will Never Fail
8675. I Am Personally Responsible
8676. God Himself Commanded Me
8677. As Soon As You See
8678. Not Possession But Progression
8679. What My Mind Solely Needs
8680. The Outer Man Wants Success
8681. God Loves Us
8682. Music Of The Sound-Universe
8683. If I Prolong Your Life
8684. The Thirst Of Your Pure Heart
8685. The Pilot Of Human Fate
8686. It Is Imperative To See
8687. The Hesitation Of The Mind
8688. His Heart's Feeble Gratitude
8689. Ask Your Life
8690. The Poison-Shaft Of Envy
8691. Ignore And Deplore
8692. Our Lampless Outer Universe
8693. His Heart Of Self-Offering
8694. A Sad Memory
8695. Control Your Animal Vital
8696. Unless A Seeker Prays
8697. A Hallowed Thirst
8698. A New Satisfaction
8699. Three Simple Lessons
8700. Truth's All-Perfecting Wings
8701. An Everyday Miracle
8702. A Single Negative Seeker
8703. That Friendship Is Impossible
8704. Let Us Please The Supreme
8705. The All-Important Question
8706. Outer Success
8707. Where Your Heart-Home Is
8708. Be Kind, Be Good!
8709. Be Quick, Be Patient!
8710. Why Do You Have To Suffer?
8711. When You Serve The Supreme
8712. You Can Stay In God's Boat
8713. If You Have Lost
8714. The Divine Pathfinders
8715. The World Was Not Willing
8716. A Silent Man-Leader
8717. Ego Can Grow
8718. You Will Truly Appreciate Life
8719. Listen Only With Your Heart
8720. Conquering Doubt
8721. The World's Receptivity
8722. The Cry Of A Sannyasin
8723. Offer Him The Result
8724. The Supreme Doctor
8725. Two Aspects Of God
8726. True Progress
8727. Inner Obedience And Outer Obedience
8728. Use Your Time Wisely
8729. An Unimportant Action
8730. Say No To Your Wrong Thoughts
8731. Where Do You Stand?
8732. We Become His
8733. Each Positive Thought
8734. Only An Experience
8735. Be Not Complacent
8736. His Goal
8737. Aim At The Unlimited
8738. The Soul's Will-power
8739. When I Was A Tiny Bud
8740. Your Two Spiritual Legs
8741. Do Not Hide
8742. Ancient Patterns Of Decay
8743. Discoveries
8744. To Offer Gratitude
8745. It Intensity Is Lacking
8746. He Who Is Well-Established
8747. Try To Please Your Master
8748. While A Spiritual Master Is On Earth
8749. Every Wrong Thought
8750. God Wanted Him To Discover
8751. If You Conquer Your Weaknesses
8752. Unless You Climb
8753. Because You Are Not Cautious
8754. The Ignorance-Challenging Power
8755. One And The Same
8756. The Ultimate Power
8757. God's Song
8758. Better Your Aspiration-Heart
8759. Give Ambition Its Due Value
8760. Self-Styled Obligations
8761. I Want Both
8762. Lord, Lift Me Up
8763. Infinitely More Valuable
8764. A Spiritual Pioneer
8765. A Most Delicious Inner Meal
8766. Until They Are Illumined
8767. If Your Vital Wants To Enjoy
8768. When Will Humanity Learn?
8769. If You Attempt To Work
8770. If You Have A Divine Goal
8771. His Wild Criticisms
8772. The Thing I Know For Sure
8773. The Temptation Of The World
8774. A Higher Purpose
8775. Be Totally Sincere
8776. Think Of Peace-Light
8777. To Study Nature's Beauty
8778. A Difficult Task
8779. Morning And Evening
8780. Insecurity Means Separativity
8781. Except For A God-Realised Soul
8782. Constructive Will-power
8783. No Such Thing As Luck
8784. A Wave Of Unhappiness
8785. Do Not Be Afraid To Act
8786. Real Oneness With Others
8787. He Was Such A Fool!
8788. Think Of The Good Things
8789. When Man Wants Something
8790. He Is The Supreme Himself
8791. Is God Not Still Imperfect?
8792. A Vagabond-Life
8793. Only The Soul Is Real
8794. Blank With Nothingness
8795. In My Dream-Life
8796. Loving The Compassion-Height
8797. A World Of Simplicity
8798. The Same Light-Forsaken Place
8799. My Heart Does Not Love God
8800. I Shall Not Live In The Past
8801. A Special Chance
8802. He Lives With The Hope
8803. Aspire Constantly!
8804. The Fate Of God's creation
8805. He Pretended To Be Full Of Light
8806. To Know What Is Happening
8807. My Mind Makes Me Feel
8808. Only Heart-Power Pleases God
8809. An Exception
8810. A Gift Worth Receiving
8811. God's Supreme Satisfaction
8812. The Message Of Pride
8813. Not In The Supreme's Way
8814. Your Soul Wants To Be Proud
8815. To Lead The Life Of A God
8816. The Same Blessing
8817. All God Wants From You
8818. Do Not Wait For Tomorrow
8819. His Lord Finally Lost Faith In Him
8820. When A Soul Enters Into A Body
8821. Think Of Doing It Tomorrow
8822. When God Blows His Whistle
8823. The Cosmic Gods Never Sleep
8824. Work Is A Joy
8825. Flower And Petals
8826. He Endured Humanity's Physical Pain
8827. Your Goal Does Not Exist
8828. The Energising Power
8829. Because Of His Disobedience
8830. God Will Exercise His Authority
8831. You Have Achieved That Very Thing
8832. Their Beliefs Are Perfect
8833. God's Own Talent
8834. Use And Increase Your Talent
8835. A Heart That Is Pure
8836. Tremendous Success
8837. Meditate More Soulfully
8838. Your Soul Will Not Be Satisfied
8839. Earthly Poison, Heavenly Nectar
8840. Sweet And Pure
8841. Compassion And Receptivity
8842. If You Live In Your Heart
8843. God Was Ashamed
8844. We Are Surrendering
8845. If You Want To Take God's Side
8846. An Emblem Of Sincerity
8847. One Undeniable Truth
8848. When Gratitude Is Absent
8849. Because Of Your Obedience
8850. No Matter How Tiny
8851. Your Pure Oneness-Heart
8852. If God Sees His Children Aspiring
8853. There Is Someone In Heaven
8854. Because He Failed To Please His Soul
8855. Work Devotedly
8856. On The Strength Of His Oneness
8857. You Are A Child Of The Supreme Mind
8858. Gratitude That Starts In The
8859. His Blessingful Smile
8860. You Are Trying To Make God Feel
8861. Why Do You Worry?
8862. The Earth-Magnet Pulls
8863. Identify With The Highest Reality
8864. Two Spiritual Legs
8865. The Desire-World Craves
8866. How Can God Be Happy?
8867. The Divine In Us Says
8868. If I Cannot Have Compassion-Power
8869. Because He Contained His Anger
8870. One Thing I Know For Sure
8871. The Vision-Light
8872. If You Do Something Right
8873. He Lived In The World Of Jealousy
8874. Those Were Not Fantasy-Days
8875. The Only Way To Be Happy
8876. Their Presence Transforms
8877. Beauty Is Enrichment
8878. When The Soul Comes Forward
8879. Your Own True Mirror
8880. His Are The Tears
8881. Comfortable But Not Soulful
8882. Always For Their Own Good
8883. Your Service To Others
8884. A Most Difficult Task
8885. Today You May Think Of God
8886. If Your Suffering Can Reach God
8887. Try To Live A Life
8888. Even God Cannot Believe It!
8889. If You Weigh Your Faults
8890. Three Dreams I Have
8891. The World Can Tell You
8892. What My Lord Wants
8893. He Is Grateful
8894. Each Human Being
8895. Doubt Is Extremely Poisonous
8896. Direct Your Vision-Eye
8897. His Existence Is In Chains
8898. If You Are Searching
8899. Only A God-Throne
8900. An Absolutely Divine Soldier
8901. A Series Of Daring Visions
8902. The Spiritual Message Of Tennis
8903. My Heart Is Meant For Crying
8904. When My Soul Identifies
8905. God's Monument Of Delight
8906. Adversity May Hide
8907. Be Wise And Accept
8908. Establish Your Friendship
8909. A Life Of Unanswered Questions
8910. You Will Be Able To Escape
8911. Its Cynical Eye Of Distrust
8912. Your Life Is Begging For Happiness
8913. A Very Strange Life
8914. False Friends
8915. Each Uttered Word
8916. My Soul Is Smiling Blissfully
8917. My Lord Is Postponing His Visit
8918. Only The Chosen Few
8919. Absolutely No Difference
8920. You Are Now Fully Ready
8921. The Corruption Of Your Mind
8922. A Conscious God-Manifesting Machine
8923. If I Love God
8924. The Key To Your Success
8925. A Self-Giving River
8926. Attraction And Aversion
8927. A New Future
8928. The Ignorance-Child
8929. Completely Lost
8930. The Secret Of Success
8931. A Man Of Integrity
8932. The Futility-Night Of Ignorance
8933. A Life Of Illumination-Day
8934. The Silence That Illumines
8935. Wrong Seeing
8936. Your Meditation-Passport
8937. You May Not Be Able To See Him
8938. An Unfortunate Master
8939. Your Wandering Thoughts
8940. To Invite Your Spiritual Death
8941. Precious Chances
8942. Do Not Expect
8943. Heaven's Brightest Morning
8944. Miracles Are Everywhere
8945. Late In Almost Everything
8946. Be It Known
8947. Do You Know?
8948. Become A Universal Light
8949. I Sincerely Feel Sorry
8950. The Illumining Beginning
8951. Ask Truth
8952. Meditate Now!
8953. God Loves To Live
8954. Opportunity Asks
8955. The Same Mistake
8956. Infinity's Eternal Truth
8957. A Few Speeches Undelivered
8958. No Substitute
8959. The Land Of Soulful Action
8960. Danger Will Meet You
8961. See Divinity In Everything
8962. My Purity's Love-River
8963. O World
8964. Each Divine Thought
8965. Immortality's Satisfaction-Smile
8966. Your Shameless Ingratitude
8967. We Worship The Elusive Flame

8968. Each Other's Company
8969. The Abyss Of Lifeless Nothingness
8970. God Is Right Inside
8971. The Footsteps Of Faith
8972. His Soul Knows Who He Is
8973. God Wants You To Be Sincere
8974. Looking For The Unknown
8975. A Life Of Surrender
8976. Yours Is The Heart That Longs
8977. Promise, Promise
8978. A Child Of God
8979. Shoplifting In The Ignorance-Store
8980. Live In Today's Joy
8981. Only One Answer
8982. The Less The Human Mind Knows
8983. If You Hide Your Aspiration-Cry
8984. There Is Nothing Wrong With You
8985. My Tearful Failure-Cry
8986. My Heart Is Suffering
8987. You Are Abandoning God
8988. Your Unconsidered Action
8989. I Am My Mind's Sound-Fear
8990. Another Heart
8991. If You Sing Heedlessly
8992. One Fragile Hour
8993. Your Soul's Unmeasured Flames
8994. A Heart Flooded With Peace
8995. Do Not Listen To Your Mind!
8996. His Only Rival
8997. The Song Of Newness
8998. There Is No Difference
8999. Chained To Mortal Fame
9000. Surrender Your Common Sense
9001. Do Give Me The Capacity
9002. Gratitude Flows From The Heart
9003. My Golden Dreams
9004. A God-Loving Thought
9005. Love Divine
9006. I Shall Not Give Up
9007. Turn To God Alone
9008. A Perpetual Possibility
9009. If You Do Not Train Your Mind
9010. Excellent Intention-Flowers
9011. The Pangs Of Mortality
9012. Do Not Crave Ceaseless Glory
9013. Smiling Is Easier Than Crying
9014. Save Yourself First
9015. Make God Happy
9016. The Unbending Champion
9017. To Reap The Richest Harvest
9018. Two Messages
9019. Beware Of Outer Sympathy
9020. His Hope-Life Is Shattered
9021. A Pure And Self-Giving Heart
9022. My Dreams
9023. Depending Entirely Upon God
9024. I Have Already Informed My Soul
9025. Your Ultimate Vision And Reality
9026. A Joy-Distributor
9027. Aspiration Without Dedication
9028. Renew Your Spiritual Life
9029. Your Ultimate Vision And Reality
9030. You Are False To Yourself
9031. You Are True To Yourself
9032. Two Seeds Are Not Germinating
9033. If You Want To Make God Happy
9034. Your Worst Quality
9035. Their Beauty Is Now Deeply Hidden
9036. To Use God's Gifts Properly
9037. Your Soul Listens To The Supreme
9038. What Obedience Is
9039. The Heart's Immediate Descent
9040. Your Soul Is Happy
9041. Another Name For Beauty
9042. Obey Your Lord Supreme
9043. You Fail Again And Again
9044. You Are Not Meant To Fail
9045. He Wants His Dream Fulfilled
9046. The Courage Of The Vital
9047. No And Yes
9048. His Psychic Courage Vanished
9049. Happiness Will Ride With You
9050. A Living Dynamo
9051. Music Is Meditation
9052. A Good Leader

9053. Secretly Observe
9054. His Sincere Progress-Life
9055. When We Have Established Peace
9056. World-Division Will Be Transformed
9057. For Your Illumination
9058. Listen To Its Echo
9059. A Beautiful Golden Boat
9060. As Long As You Can Remember
9061. These Hands Must Obey
9062. You Remain In The Mind
9063. Who Is Strong?
9064. Someone From Whom We Came
9065. Just Run Towards God!
9066. Today I Am Running
9067. Start Your Inner Race
9068. When You Have A Smiling Face
9069. If You Want To Be Happy
9070. God's Hope And God's Promise
9071. God Cannot Do Anything
9072. If You Feel You Are A Child
9073. Spiritual Energy Must Be Channelled
9074. A Fanatic
9075. A Crazy Heart
9076. He Did Not Follow You
9077. Your Soulful Service
9078. Each Moment Is An Opportunity
9079. Suffering The Same Pain
9080. No Excuse
9081. If You Do Something Wrong
9082. They Will Come To Join You
9083. Surrender Your Dear Ones
9084. He Cast The Temptation-Net
9085. Accept And Use His Capacity
9086. Be Grateful To Your Soul
9087. Your Own Illumination-Room
9088. His Only Friend
9089. Who Is Your True Family?
9090. The Hand Of The Supreme
9091. He Found His True Joy
9092. If You Can Always Remember
9093. Continue To Perform Soulfully
9094. My Foolish Human Nature
9095. A New Life-Awakening
9096. The Sunshine Of Your Heart
9097. Are You For God?
9098. His Undivine Mind Followed Him
9099. One Less Imperfect Being
9100. Only Love In My Heart
9101. I Wish To Be A Burning Flame
9102. I Have Counted
9103. Since My Prayers Are Fulfilled
9104. Emptiness And Readiness
9105. When I Live For God Alone
9106. There Is No Risk
9107. Who Is So Stupid?
9108. You Want To Advise God
9109. Do You Ever Care To Know?
9110. God Has Given Your Heart
9111. In The Inner And Outer Race
9112. Unless My Lord Supreme Opens
9113. A Fool And An Opportunist
9114. How Can The World Find Peace?
9115. Will You Kindly Teach Me?
9116. Selfless Service
9117. His Adamantine Determination
9118. Fault-Finders
9119. America Means Speed
9120. If You Want To Run The Fastest
9121. Each Time You Enter A New Year
9122. Your Golden Opportunity
9123. No New Year For You
9124. Examine Your Compassion
9125. A True Truth-Seeker Knows
9126. Your Master's Songs
9127. To Sing One Song Soulfully
9128. Because He Enjoys Wrong Forces
9129. Be Extremely Sincere!
9130. My Prayer And My Promise
9131. To Conquer Your Heart
9132. How To Feel Always Secure?
9133. You Will Be Routed
9134. Your Self-Giving Heart
9135. A Well-Protected Harbour
9136. Automatic
9137. Your Hopes Are Shattered
9138. Two Ancient Desires
9139. Only One Breath
9140. The Prayer Of Self-Offering
9141. I Cannot Reject Anything

9142. A Secret Player
9143. If You Want Perfection
9144. My Life Is Soulful And Fruitful
9145. A Self-Giving Performance
9146. Natural, Not Theatrical
9147. Quantity-Advice And Quality-Advice
9148. A Useless Weakness
9149. When We Strike The Truth-Bell
9150. If You Do Not Run Every Day
9151. Just Keep Your Heart's Door Open
9152. They Simply Had No Idea
9153. A True Truth-Seeker
9154. You Must Be Ready To Please God
9155. Because He Did Not Have Faith
9156. Those Who Have Faith In God
9157. You Must Accept More Of The Blame
9158. Your Prayer Indirectly Helps
9159. You Need The Broad Heart
9160. Be Something For God
9161. Work Soulfully
9162. His Soulful Music
9163. If You Sail In Your Master's Boat
9164. Just For This One Day
9165. Your Heaven
9166. True Progress
9167. Maintain Your Inner Freshness
9168. Just Purify Your Mind
9169. Never Allow Your Pure Heart
9170. I Can Never Be Insecure
9171. If Your Whole Heart Cries
9172. Your Master Will Be Miserable
9173. If We Doubt Ourselves
9174. Self-Doubt Is Your Own Creation
9175. If You Are Truly Spiritual
9176. Some Are Trying Consciously
9177. God's Unconscious Representative
9178. Because God Loves You
9179. Your Flame Of Aspiration
9180. Every Day I Tell My Beloved Supreme
9181. If You Feel
9182. You Can Transcend
9183. The Supreme Necessity Of Serving
9184. Again And Again I Strive
9185. Be Always Aware
9186. All Are Bound To Reach
9187. When You Serve
9188. God No Longer Wanted Him
9189. Your Conscious Unwillingness
9190. More Than The Necessary Capacity
9191. If Today's Chosen Instruments Fail
9192. He Discovered Compassion
9193. His Folded Hands
9194. Every Opportunity
9195. He Is Now Devoutly Walking
9196. Celestial Light From Above
9197. The Supreme Inside Him
9198. No Credit To God
9199. He Embodies Divinity
9200. Your Pure Heart
9201. Something Inside Me
9202. The Future-Tree
9203. A Special Message
9204. True Happiness
9205. Your Happiness-Gift
9206. To Fight Heroically
9207. Work, Pray And Meditate Soulfully
9208. The Happiness-Flower Blossoms
9209. The Best Judge
9210. When His Sincerity Pinched Him
9211. Just Stay In The Boat
9212. A Beautiful, Fresh Flower
9213. To Keep Your Inner Newness
9214. Your Cheerfulness-Shield
9215. Obedience Is Salvation
9216. A Good Student Of Life
9217. All Will Be Fulfilled
9218. God Expedites That Hour
9219. To Realise The Highest Absolute
9220. A Lover Of All That Lives
9221. If You Make A Mistake
9222. You Will Have Another Chance
9223. What Have I Done?
9224. Surmount Each Obstacle
9225. You Are Not A Hopeless Case

9226. No Longer A Spiritual Infant
9227. Start Doing The Right Thing!
9228. Your Eternal Moon Of Love
9229. True Spiritual Service
9230. A New Opportunity
9231. Choose The Right Medicine
9232. My Two Age-Old Enemies
9233. See Yourself
9234. You Need Not Wait
9235. A Heart Larger Than The Largest
9236. If You Want To Love God
9237. Wait Only For Those
9238. The Sacred Bridge
9239. Never Feel, Never Allow
9240. Practise Spirituality Soulfully
9241. Do Not Look Backwards
9242. The Life Of Your Choice
9243. Make Your Choice!
9244. Let Me Be Absolutely Blind
9245. Your Ancient Scars
9246. To Fulfil God's Special Purpose
9247. I Pray To God
9248. Your Inner Sun
9249. Many Suns Inside You
9250. I Just Keep Silent
9251. Loneliness
9252. Try To Become Better
9253. Make A Desperate Effort!
9254. An Unfrequented Path
9255. Deposits And Withdrawals
9256. Continue Increasing Your Capacity
9257. Visible Man, Invisible God
9258. All-Conquering Compassion-Waves
9259. If The Supreme Is Confident
9260. Only To Free Themselves
9261. My Life Has No Joy
9262. To See The Birth Of Truth
9263. God's Compassion-Magnet
9264. On The Strength Of Our Surrender
9265. Ego Is Like A Balloon
9266. God Is Waiting For Us
9267. God's Devoted And Obedient Dog
9268. He Who Serves The Supreme
9269. Destined But Delayed
9270. Everyone Has A Good Soul
9271. The Most Special Love
9272. Life Is A Divine Game
9273. The Only Real Freedom
9274. Who Can Dream?
9275. If Your Mind Doubts
9276. Your Aspiration-Life
9277. The Best Weapon
9278. The Braver You Are
9279. Carry The Inspiration And Light
9280. The Very Nature Of Kindness
9281. Two Questions Have Stung Me
9282. A Single Blessingful Smile
9283. Inspire And Be Inspired
9284. The Supreme Is All Gratitude
9285. His Aggression-Vital
9286. Torch-Bearer Of A New Creation
9287. Not In Vain
9288. Who Can Prevent You?
9289. He Is Always Successful
9290. Your Real Disgrace
9291. An Unavoidable Necessity
9292. If You Do Not Value
9293. The Longer He Followed
9294. This Is All Deception
9295. Friendly Neighbours
9296. I Will Continue Pleasing You
9297. He Chose To Descend
9298. His Inner Pilot Repeatedly Asked Him
9299. Now He Is Running Fast
9300. A Tiny Island
9301. The Song He Enjoys Most
9302. Get Used To Saying No
9303. An Invaluable Achievement
9304. Since You Are For God
9305. His Master's Heart-University
9306. A Free Access
9307. What God's Compassion Is
9308. My Ego Talks
9309. I Cannot Please You
9310. What I Am Supposed To Tell God
9311. Greatness And Glory
9312. What You Are Doing Right Now

9313. When I Entered The Spiritual Life
9314. God Can Give You His Consolation
9315. Ask Yourself Three Questions
9316. If God Can See
9317. Dive Deep Within For The Answers
9318. God Is Inside My Doubtful Mind
9319. If You Are Truly Pleased With God
9320. Revolting Against God
9321. His Way Is Not God's Way
9322. If Your Lord Supreme Pleases You
9323. God As Your Only Interest
9324. A Blind Disciple
9325. Without God's Help
9326. An Added Advantage
9327. Each Gift Offered To God
9328. God Has Only Two Demands
9329. You May Surprisingly Succeed
9330. We Shall Not Ultimately Fail You
9331. God Wants You To Know
9332. My Heart's God-Hour
9333. Why Have You Lost Your Inner Joy?
9334. An Unthinkable Opportunist
9335. God Uses His Justice-Light
9336. Once You Lose Your Inner Wealth
9337. God's Blessing-Opportunities
9338. I Must Avail Myself
9339. Mortal Death Knocks
9340. When I Am The Body
9341. The Greatest Inner Crime
9342. Think Of The Soul
9343. The Body And Fleeting Time
9344. On My Upward Path
9345. A New Name
9346. My Bounden Duty
9347. My Real Vision
9348. Each Act Is A Work Of Art
9349. How Can It Be Possible?
9350. If You Say
9351. Do Not Care For Those
9352. Mine Is The Way
9353. God Appears Before You
9354. Try To Grow In Freedom-Light
9355. Man's Rare Gratitude-Heart
9356. A Moment's Inner Strength
9357. There Will Be At Least A Few
9358. An Obedient Seeker-Disciple
9359. Always Found Together
9360. Each Soulful Seeker Must Surrender
9361. The Heartbeat Of The Supreme
9362. Sweetness And Brilliance
9363. God Plays My Victory-Drum
9364. God Feels Sorry
9365. The Supreme Victory In Life
9366. God Uses His Destructive Power
9367. Flooded With Divine Consciousness
9368. An Imaginary Disobedience
9369. Negative And Positive Thoughts
9370. The Two Worst Negative Thoughts
9371. Give Up And Accept
9372. The Best Thing You Can Give
9373. He Is Dearer To God
9374. Reality-Freedom-Sky
9375. His Soul Is Now Coming Forward
9376. The Message Of The Supreme
9377. Happy And Unhappy
9378. Human Music, Divine Music
9379. The World-Tree
9380. To Expedite Your Progress
9381. Serious Inner Damage
9382. Wait Patiently For God's Hour
9383. Dive Deep Within
9384. Difficult To Remember
9385. A Perfection-Life I Badly Need
9386. Peace Means Perfection
9387. His Mind Is Flooded
9388. You Want To Climb Up
9389. What My Mind Needs
9390. I Must Reawaken My Heart
9391. Because Of His Angelic Speed
9392. Two Lives I Must Love
9393. If You Want To Give
9394. If You Always Borrow
9395. Its Blue-Gold Wings
9396. Aspiration Discovers Doubts
9397. His Mind Is Not Satisfied
9398. It Looks So Simple
9399. To Please God
9400. Work-Story And Success-Glory
9401. A Surrender-Prayer
9402. A Supreme Truth
9403. Sow The Seed Of Divine Longing
9404. Inside Each Life-Breath
9405. Do Not Try To Bind God
9406. Inside Each Heartbeat
9407. I Am Divinely Happy
9408. God's Satisfaction-Hour
9409. The Unparalleled Light Of Liberation
9410. Your Himalayan Achievements
9411. It Is Absolutely Unnecessary
9412. Your Own Hidden Brutality
9413. Prescribe And Proscribe
9414. Who Needs A Disobedient Mind?
9415. A Self-Employed Indulgence-Prince
9416. My One Secret Letter To God
9417. I Love Your Surrender-Flames
9418. I May Not Love God
9419. The Most Important Secret
9420. The Whirlwind Of Worldliness
9421. God Was Astonishment-Struck
9422. When God Interviews Man
9423. A Guest From Paradise
9424. If You Are Satisfied
9425. My Silver Obedience-Flames
9426. When The Soul Compromises
9427. My Transcendence Enlightens
9428. When Are You Going To Learn?
9429. God's Attention-Smile
9430. Manager Of The Universal Market
9431. A Falsehood-Loving Man
9432. The Blossoming Delight Of Love
9433. My Lord's Feet
9434. When I Can Joke
9435. Your Loyalty
9436. His Life Is A Temple
9437. Looking For Asylum
9438. An Expert In Sleeping
9439. The Mind Wants To Invent
9440. The First Thing I Did
9441. Each Soulful Thought
9442. Your Mind Is Not At All Ready
9443. O My Heart, Go Deeper
9444. The Flame Of Fire-Pure Aspiration
9445. My Soul's Tears Of Delight
9446. A Song Of The Unknown
9447. For Centuries
9448. You Are Your Suspicion-Mind
9449. Your Victory's Trumpet-Voice
9450. Why Are You Forgetful?
9451. The Sun-Flooded Room
9452. You Have No Idea
9453. Our Unforgivable Crime
9454. Your Inner Will Cannot Succeed
9455. If You Are Negligent
9456. Two Hearts
9457. An Incessant Self-Giver
9458. When Each Day Dawns
9459. How To Cure Falsehood?
9460. I Have Every Right
9461. The Mind Of My Sound-Life
9462. Only A Heart Of Love
9463. The Foolish Way Of Life
9464. The Distributor Of Goodwill
9465. I Shall Build And Become
9466. No Such Thing
9467. Burials
9468. My Silver Dreams
9469. Your Unwillingness To Accept Light
9470. In My Sweet Dream-Life
9471. Not An Impossible Task
9472. No Cloud Passes
9473. Can We Not Share?
9474. I Am So Happy
9475. If You Have Faith
9476. To Accomplish Anything
9477. My Mind Is Evolving
9478. My Heart's Humility-Nest
9479. Each Hope-Flame On Earth
9480. God The Compassion-Height
9481. Only A Heart Of Surrender
9482. Even God Is Employed
9483. To Determine God's Capacities
9484. Your Vital-Life Has Caused
9485. You Will Be Perfect
9486. God Has Already Decreed It
9487. My Mind's Tension-World
9488. Sincerity Is Not Dead
9489. God Believes In Progress
9490. In Vain My Heart Is Looking
9491. A Beautiful Answer
9492. We Can Destroy The Destroyer
9493. Your Heart's Compassion-Net
9494. My Mind Wants
9495. The Human Life Is A Bridge
9496. You Are Also The Soul
9497. Your Master's Ocean
9498. Only One Message
9499. God Knocked At Your Door
9500. My Payment
9501. Compassion-Beams From God's Eye
9502. Dependent And Independent
9503. Today's Flaming Aspiration
9504. I Need
9505. Pay Attention
9506. In His God-Adventure
9507. Perfection And Satisfaction
9508. Happiness-Power
9509. Fulfilment Means
9510. My Heart's Fountain-Love
9511. A Self-Giving Saint
9512. The Only Short-cut
9513. The Sermon Of Ignorance-Night
9514. I Shall Reach The Pinnacle-Height
9515. Daring Enthusiasm
9516. Beauty Born Of Compassion-Light
9517. The Sacred Heart Of The Moon
9518. I Carry My Patience
9519. Challenging My Heart
9520. God's Special Secret
9521. Those Who Are Serving The Supreme
9522. Leave The Vain Questioning Mind
9523. The Voice Of Unseen Loveliness
9524. Do You Remember?
9525. A Life Of Self-Giving
9526. An Unaspiring Human Being
9527. A Volcano-Determination
9528. Whom Do I Need?
9529. Love God A Little More
9530. My Heart's Rekindled Faith
9531. Because Of Your Heart
9532. Soulfulness And Fruitfulness
9533. Face Your Anxiety!
9534. My Ascending Heart
9535. Earth Loves, Heaven Loves
9536. He Who Is
9537. God Knows That He Is
9538. How Can I See God In My Future?
9539. God Came To Me Unannounced
9540. The Hand Of God
9541. Aspiration Needs No Recognition
9542. All I Have Now
9543. The Philosophy-World
9544. Do Not Fail Your Master Repeatedly
9545. I Am Supremely Fortunate
9546. Where Is Hope?
9547. An Intelligent Mind
9548. My Source Is The Supreme
9549. God's Bounden Duty
9550. Only One Question
9551. A Dreadful Dream
9552. I Am Sorry To Tell You
9553. A Half-Hearted Seeker
9554. God's Permanent Injunction
9555. Precious And Gracious
9556. Your Prayers Never Take Root
9557. His Body Was Still Sleeping
9558. Your Mind Is All Doubt-Filled
9559. God's Earth-Transforming Hour
9560. I Have Used Your Compassion-Eye
9561. You Doubt Your Very Breath
9562. O My Alarmist Mind
9563. God Has Won Me Back
9564. I May Enjoy Other Luxuries
9565. The Power-Light
9566. Already It Is Too Late
9567. God's Heart Never Rests
9568. He Does Not Want To Return
9569. Before Death Surprises You
9570. To Walk In A Saint's Footsteps
9571. My Heart Is Occupied
9572. How God Has Won Me
9573. Nothing To Lose
9574. Where Your Mind Lives
9575. Impossible Delights
9576. Do Not Give Up!
9577. Why Should I Be Satisfied?
9578. Aspiration Without Dedication
9579. I Am Conscious
9580. Do Not Insist On Changing
9581. Love Knows How
9582. If You Are A Cheerful Loser
9583. The Soulful Music Of The Inner Life
9584. God's Music Of Life
9585. If You Have A Big Heart
9586. Gratitude Is Not A Mere Word
9587. My Unparalleled Possession
9588. If Your Heart Shows Me
9589. Exploitation
9590. A New Exploitation-Game
9591. The Permanence Of Delight
9592. Past And Present
9593. Artificial Spirituality
9594. A False Teacher
9595. The Art Of Self-Union
9596. Too Stupid To Learn Or Unlearn
9597. I Am Not At All Obliged
9598. An Absolute Lie
9599. Sincerity Is In The Heart
9600. Man's Perfect Glory
9601. O My Heart's Pole-Star
9602. Your Heart Will Remember
9603. Destroy Your Self-Importance
9604. God's Vision-Transcending Smile
9605. Love-Day
9606. Messages From The Gods
9607. He Who Is Called
9608. When I Go To Visit My Soul
9609. Those Who Have Denied Themselves
9610. If You Live Only In The Heart
9611. Your Imagination-Power
9612. A Pleasure-Life
9613. I Need Only One Assurance
9614. My Lord Has Told Me
9615. My Curiosity-Teacher
9616. When He Ceased His Forward Journey
9617. The Human Champions
9618. The Birth Of Newness
9619. The Supreme Message
9620. The Freedom-Right Of The Vital
9621. A Giving Life
9622. If You Surrender
9623. What My Life Needs Now
9624. I Embrace My Silent Death
9625. To Plumb The Depth Of Delight
9626. Do Not Fear Dark Misfortunes
9627. God Is Waiting
9628. Each Time I Soulfully Pray
9629. Two Unanswered Questions
9630. Hope Is His All
9631. The Cries Of The Finite
9632. God Will Inform You
9633. Earth Needs Him
9634. Destruction's Feet
9635. A Devotee Of The Pleasure-Life
9636. Earth Is My Surrender-Splendour
9637. You Will Be Blamed
9638. My Heart's Ancient Realisation
9639. A Mere Suggestion
9640. The Life Of Failure-Sighs
9641. God's Unhorizoned Choice
9642. God Does Not Mind
9643. His God-Given Self-Esteem
9644. I Shall Conquer You All
9645. When I Swallow My Pride
9646. Each Time My Mind Wants To Escape
9647. What Your Life Is Made Of
9648. A Smile From God
9649. To Make Myself Really Happy
9650. Consciously On The Way
9651. Everybody Is Longing For Happiness
9652. When You Do Not Please God
9653. Your Adamantine Determination
9654. How Sad God Was
9655. Always Room For Improvement
9656. If You Have To Make Any Mistake

9657. Let Us See
9658. Chosen By The Supreme Himself
9659. A New Instrument
9660. Listen To Your Heart
9661. His Hope-Sea Is Deep
9662. A Child's Question
9663. When Dire Necessity Commands Me
9664. A Heart-Temple
9665. You Do Not Belong To Heaven
9666. The Eclipse Of Truth
9667. When I Choose
9668. Heaven Knows How To Liberate
9669. If You Want To Challenge
9670. The Experience Of Humility
9671. Both Must Be Transformed
9672. What Does Your Heart Feel?
9673. The Life-And-Death Battle
9674. If I Put My Beloved Supreme First
9675. Unlit Rooms
9676. My Heart's Latest Discovery
9677. The Soul's Divinity
9678. Your Vital-Room
9679. You Must Watch Your Words
9680. Allow Not Your Mind To Enjoy
9681. God Is My Known Friend
9682. Inseparable And Indispensable
9683. A God-Adoring Heart
9684. Do You Expect Me To Believe?
9685. Man's Sacrifice-Drop
9686. His Heart And Soul Sobbed
9687. Helpless, He Surrendered
9688. Why Not Trust Him?
9689. I Prefer The Heart
9690. The Doom Of The Doubt-Life
9691. An Instant Touch
9692. The Luxury Of Baneful Doubts
9693. A God-Realised Soul
9694. Stillness Has A Volcano-Power
9695. Strictness Or Soulfulness
9696. Time Is Sacrificing Itself
9697. The World's Midnight-Silence
9698. God's Silence Preceded God's Sound
9699. You Can Never Reach Satisfaction
9700. I Shall Bridge That Inch
9701. I Am Great, I Am Good
9702. If You Are Leading A Human Life
9703. A Beautiful Day Has Dawned
9704. How Can My Mind Think Of You?
9705. How Can My Heart Feel You?
9706. How Can My Vital Know You?
9707. How Can My Body Have Faith In You?
9708. I Only Want To Know
9709. It Will Not Take Much Time
9710. Then I Shall Claim You
9711. Your Unwillingness To Change
9712. I Shall Every Day Give You
9713. My Sincerity Tells Me
9714. The Easiest Way To Please You
9715. To Become A Perfect Instrument
9716. Give And Become
9717. Something Special
9718. My Heaven-Bound Journey
9719. It Is Unmistakably Obvious
9720. His Heart He Spends
9721. Nobody Can Stop Me!
9722. Your Heart's Door
9723. If You Cannot Expand Your Heart
9724. He Was Dearest To God
9725. Your Heroic Effort
9726. To Please God In His Own Way
9727. The Joy In Your Hearts
9728. The Dark Ignorance-Tunnel
9729. The Golden Shore Is Waiting
9730. The Nature Of Divine Friendship
9731. The Ultimate Victory
9732. Cherish Only The Divine Fear
9733. If You Can Identify
9734. You Will Never Be Blessed
9735. The First Rung
9736. A Disgrace To His Heart And Soul
9737. I See Failure All Around
9738. If You Have The Capacity
9739. Your Empty Heart
9740. Purity's Oneness-Light
9741. A Representative Of God
9742. Do Not Separate Them
9743. Positive Energy
9744. If You Do Not Renounce
9745. What Can You Expect?
9746. Struggle Against Darkness!
9747. Your Mind's Resentment
9748. Since Your Vital Is Not Ready
9749. Your Unwilling Mind Knows
9750. He Was For Those
9751. Your Hope Of Peace
9752. Beyond Imagination
9753. Not To God's Taste
9754. To Accomplish Something Great
9755. An Unconditional God-Lover
9756. He Has Satisfaction
9757. Your Heart's God-Vision
9758. A True God-Lover's Stillness
9759. No Real Agreement
9760. Your Faith Has Strength
9761. Your Aspiration-Light
9762. My Divine Willingness
9763. My Crying Heart
9764. The Great Sleeper
9765. Two Things I See
9766. Your Only Reality-World
9767. The Lion Deep Within
9768. Total Strangers
9769. When You Speak Ill Of Others
9770. A Dreamer Of God-Dreams
9771. A Strong Curiosity
9772. When I Disappoint My Soul
9773. No Match
9774. What You Think Of Yourself
9775. If I Do Not Prevent
9776. Truth's Great Friend
9777. The Universal Disease
9778. A Very Pleasant Entertainment
9779. A Leisure Activity
9780. My Unmistakable Conviction
9781. I Appreciate Your Mind
9782. Truth Is Illumination
9783. God Is An Insider
9784. God Is No Intruder
9785. The Meaning Of Human Life
9786. A Long Talk With God
9787. What You Want To Be
9788. If Your Mind Loves Sincerity
9789. An Unforgivable Insult
9790. I Wanted To Admire
9791. Success-Progress-Stories
9792. Unless I Become A Positive Voice
9793. God's Satisfaction-Delight
9794. He Shrouded His Life
9795. The Cemetery Of Yesterday
9796. Two Ecstasy-Wings
9797. His Own Obedience-Life
9798. Death And Its Friend
9799. Beauty Prays
9800. The Sunshine That Crosses My Path
9801. A New Kind Of Winning
9802. I Water My Life-Garden Every Day
9803. Self-Dedication-Light
9804. A New Solution
9805. My Heart's Unwavering Faith
9806. God-Wisdom-Hearts
9807. Self-Styled Commitments
9808. The Tide Of Self-Giving Love
9809. God's Secret Love-Touch
9810. In The Dust
9811. My Doubtful Past
9812. A One-Man Show
9813. The Message Of A Blessing
9814. A Successful Movement
9815. Advantages And Possessions
9816. Hunger Does Not Find Fault
9817. Turbulence And Silence
9818. Changing And Transcending
9819. I May Begin The Journey
9820. Ascend And Transcend
9821. Only One Inner Teacher
9822. I Can Have Security
9823. When I Want To Increase Purity
9824. The Only One
9825. Stronger Than Logic
9826. Even My Soul Is Disgusted
9827. Your Mind Has A Monopoly
9828. If You Are Out Of Practice
9829. Power Likes To Live Apart
9830. Ask Earth's Aspiration-Heart
9831. A Top Secret
9832. God Is Waiting For You
9833. How Can I Be Displeased?
9834. In Defense Of Earth
9835. An Immortal Song Of Joy
9836. The Question Of Questions
9837. His Life Stands Crucified
9838. Change Your Mind
9839. Running Like A River
9840. The Golden Bridge
9841. When The Divine Heart Loses
9842. You Will Be Perfect
9843. My Prayer Challenges
9844. Your Battleground-Experiences
9845. The Life Of Austerity
9846. He Who Is Wise
9847. Universal Oneness
9848. One World Can Bind Us
9849. My Heart's Climbing Preparation
9850. You Have Revealed To Me
9851. I May Not Know Many Things
9852. Because Your Life Lives
9853. If You Compete With Yourself
9854. Cast Aside Half-Truths
9855. Sacred God-Loving Thoughts
9856. The Temple Of Universal Silence
9857. Your Own Doom
9858. My Lord's Fulness-Smile
9859. My Mind Derives Satisfaction
9860. Newness, Oneness And Fulness
9861. Inexhaustible Willingness
9862. My Heart's Sincerity-Cry
9863. When My Mind Is Pure
9864. My Soul's Supernatural Capacity
9865. Identical And Indistinguishable
9866. He And His Heart Every Day Run
9867. I Am Eager To Hear
9868. The Vision-Eye Of A Saint
9869. Try To Trust The World
9870. A Little Of Your Heart's Sweetness
9871. A Contrary Experience
9872. Something Unusual And Rare
9873. Under The Compassion-Canopy
9874. Within Your Easy Reach
9875. The Evening Sunshine Of His Life
9876. To Give Pleasure
9877. True Love Of God
9878. A Man Is
9879. To Bring God Nearer
9880. A Yawning Gulf
9881. The Fire Of Deathless Happiness
9882. Envy's Loud Invasion
9883. Let Us Go And Rest
9884. O My Himalayan Hopes
9885. A Shattering Experience
9886. Just Go Your Own Way
9887. My Love-Thoughts
9888. Where Is My Existence?
9889. Let Us Try To Manifest
9890. My Hope
9891. The Vision Of Power
9892. The Illumining Results
9893. My Hope, My Promise
9894. I Never Dare To Think!
9895. Your Heart Can Radiate Joy
9896. If You Are Powerful
9897. If You Become Sidetracked
9898. Your Body Obeys
9899. My Blessingful Boon
9900. I Want To Run With You
9901. No One But You
9902. Give Me A Large Heart
9903. Offerings
9904. He Who Dreams Of God
9905. A Different Drink
9906. A Different Friend
9907. I Have Not Loved You
9908. I Have Not Served You
9909. I Have Not Spoken To The World
9910. I Have Not Manifested You
9911. I Have Not Become
9912. His Life's First Prayer
9913. Your Life Is Now Entitled
9914. God Has Given Us The Mind
9915. Your Aspiration-Fire
9916. My Vast Thought-World
9917. What Thrills My Mind?
9918. A Useless Stranger
9919. My Body Unconsciously Protested
9920. I Challenged Yesterday's Problems
9921. A Beggar's Hunger
9922. You Can Wait For Perfection
9923. Faith In Doubt
9924. The Very Last Step
9925. How Can You Succeed?
9926. Nothing Is As Perfect
9927. A Big And Real God
9928. Wrong And Right Prayers
9929. Do Give Me A New Heart
9930. The Past And The Present
9931. Divinity's Three Heaven-Free Homes
9932. I Cry, I Smile
9933. Ascent And Descent
9934. Immeasurable Ecstasies
9935. They Are Incapable
9936. My Heart Does Know
9937. My Soul Came Down
9938. The Beauty Of God's Infinity
9939. My Destiny
9940. Aspiration-Cry
9941. Ready To Wait
9942. A Divine Hero-Warrior
9943. An Accident
9944. Your Heart-Tears
9945. At Last He Is Healed
9946. A Rising Flame
9947. Determination-Fire
9948. To Acquire Innocence-Joy
9949. Two Frightening Shadows
9950. How Little Do I Know
9951. Hearken Only To Time Eternal!
9952. I Do Not Want You To Enjoy
9953. My Life-Surrendering Heart-Tears
9954. My Soul Was Born To Teach
9955. One Foot Is On Earth
9956. Waiting For You
9957. My Heart's Sorrows
9958. God The Lover
9959. A Deep Desire
9960. I Have Seen Many Things
9961. My Mind Admires God
9962. Opinion And Dedication
9963. The Banners Of The East And West
9964. The Mist Of My Past Years
9965. Real And False
9966. When You Walked With God
9967. Am I God's Adopted Child?
9968. My Life's Soulfulness-Beauty
9969. The Natural And The Supernatural
9970. Prepare Yourself For Self-Mastery
9971. My Life Smiles
9972. The Banquet Hall Of Eternity
9973. My Inner Voice
9974. My Lord's Compassion-Scale
9975. A Doubt-Wave
9976. The Mind Tries To Imitate
9977. My Inner Pilot Asks Me
9978. My Heart Suffers More
9979. It Is Impossible
9980. Your Heart's Oneness-Delight
9981. A New Haven
9982. God's Victory-Trumpet
9983. The Landscape Listens
9984. Ride The Purity-Bicycle
9985. I Do Not Need Aspiration-Hunger
9986. Scarcities
9987. I Do Not Imitate Others
9988. My Life Passed Safely
9989. Your Life-Boat
9990. Your Oneness-Heart Is Happy
9991. My Protector-Transformer
9992. A Living Miracle
9993. There Is No Such Thing
9994. Time To Become Acquainted
9995. Since You Do Not Invite Faith
9996. His Sweet Heart-Smile
9997. Because He Did Not Want
9998. Our Heart's Gratitude-Length
9999. Closeness, Fondness And Oneness
10000. Ten Thousand Flower-Flames

207 FLOWER-FLAMES
EARLIEST NUMBERING

It seems likely the poems specially selected by Sri Chinmoy were originally numbered as follows. First number indicates FFP, second number FF.

1: 7217	40: 554	79: 1661	118: 2952
2: 734	41: 536	80: 1699	119: 2973
3: 9205	42: 586	81: 1717	120: 3074
4: 9439	43: 628	82: 1600	121: 3095
5: 7099	44: 665	83: 1613	122: 3110
6: 6651	45: 737	84: 1891	123: 3249
7: 6700	46: 721	85: 1890	124: 7264
8: 4001	47: 661	86: 1900	125: 3393 & 3394
9: 5024	48: 682	87: 1945	
10: 17	49: 716	88: 1948	126: 6961
11: 84	50: 730	89: 1966	127: 3462
12: 93	51: 849	90: 2015	128: 3616
13: 96	52: 887	91: 2017	129: 3681
14: 128	53: 744	92: 2092	130: 3738
15: 150	54: 915	93: 2100	131: 3754
16: 152	55: 928	94: 2140	132: 3785
17: 202	56: 939	95: 2198	133: 3770
18: 221	57: 1012	96: 2203	134: 3872
19: 212	58: 935	97: 2037	135: 3874
20: 210	59: 941	98: 2045	136: 3966
21: 201	60: 1028	99: 9821	137: 4013
22: 256	61: 1094	100: 2058	138: 4032
23: 9924	62: 1235	101: 2209	139: 4052
24: 298	63: 1179	102: 2388	140: 4110
25: 524	64: 1098	103: 2321	141: 4115
26: 318	65: 1255	104: 2371	142: 4315
27: 335	66: 1303	105: 2400	143: 4427
28: 361	67: 1318	106: 2411	144: 4401
29: 9300	68: 1328	107: 2533	145: 4423
30: 612	69: 9770	108: 2567	146: 4639
31: 419	70: 6018	109: 2602	147: 4677
32: 526	71: 6595	110: 2650	148: 4681
33: 421	72: 9668	111: 2700	149: 4701
34: 440	73: 1436	112: 2701	150: 4875
35: 444	74: 1507	113: 2756	151: 5002
36: 455	75: 1517	114: 2841	152: 4901
37: 487	76: 1548	115: 2861	153: 4988
38: 527	77: 1566	116: 2921	154: 5225
39: 538	78: 1598	117: 2928	155: 5357

156: 5479	170: 6969	184: 7573	198: 9517
157: 5655	171: 7296	185: 7149	199: 9629
158: 5695	172: 7404	186: 8120	200: 2426
159: 5741	173: 7320	187: 8200	201: 1798
160: 5762	174: 7018	188: 3815	202: 1439
161: 6160	175: 7054	189: 8294	203: 1344
162: 5123	176: 7582	190: (NEW)	204: 1327
163: 5931	177: 7610	191: 8394	205: 1247
164: 6301	178: 7633	192: 8681	206: 9928
165: 6314	179: 7735	193: 8470	207: 3732
166: 6414	180: 7843	194: 8880	
167: 6740	181: 7069	195: 8929	
168: 6831	182: 7080	196: 8981	
169: 6947	183: 7089	197: 9027	

Poem FFP 190 cannot be traced from the original *Ten thousand Flower-Flames* set of books. Poems FF 3393 and FF 3394 were consolidated by Sri Chinmoy into poem FFP 125.

BIBLIOGRAPHY

TEN THOUSAND FLOWER-FLAMES (100 VOLUMES)

SRI CHINMOY:

—*Ten thousand Flower-Flames, part 1*, New York, Agni Press, 1979.
—*Ten thousand Flower-Flames, part 2*, New York, Agni Press, 1979.
—*Ten thousand Flower-Flames, part 3*, New York, Agni Press, 1979.
—*Ten thousand Flower-Flames, part 4*, New York, Agni Press, 1979.
—*Ten thousand Flower-Flames, part 5*, New York, Agni Press, 1979.
—*Ten thousand Flower-Flames, part 6*, New York, Agni Press, 1980.
—*Ten thousand Flower-Flames, part 7*, New York, Agni Press, 1980.
—*Ten thousand Flower-Flames, part 8*, New York, Agni Press, 1981.
—*Ten thousand Flower-Flames, part 9*, New York, Agni Press, 1981.
—*Ten thousand Flower-Flames, part 10*, New York, Agni Press, 1981.
—*Ten thousand Flower-Flames, part 11*, New York, Agni Press, 1981.
—*Ten thousand Flower-Flames, part 12*, New York, Agni Press, 1981.
—*Ten thousand Flower-Flames, part 13*, New York, Agni Press, 1981.
—*Ten thousand Flower-Flames, part 14*, New York, Agni Press, 1981.
—*Ten thousand Flower-Flames, part 15*, New York, Agni Press, 1981.
—*Ten thousand Flower-Flames, part 16*, New York, Agni Press, 1981.
—*Ten thousand Flower-Flames, part 17*, New York, Agni Press, 1981.
—*Ten thousand Flower-Flames, part 18*, New York, Agni Press, 1981.
—*Ten thousand Flower-Flames, part 19*, New York, Agni Press, 1981.
—*Ten thousand Flower-Flames, part 20*, New York, Agni Press, 1981.
—*Ten thousand Flower-Flames, part 21*, New York, Agni Press, 1981.
—*Ten thousand Flower-Flames, part 22*, New York, Agni Press, 1981.
—*Ten thousand Flower-Flames, part 23*, New York, Agni Press, 1982.
—*Ten thousand Flower-Flames, part 24*, New York, Agni Press, 1982.
—*Ten thousand Flower-Flames, part 25*, New York, Agni Press, 1982.
—*Ten thousand Flower-Flames, part 26*, New York, Agni Press, 1982.
—*Ten thousand Flower-Flames, part 27*, New York, Agni Press, 1982.
—*Ten thousand Flower-Flames, part 28*, New York, Agni Press, 1982.
—*Ten thousand Flower-Flames, part 29*, New York, Agni Press, 1982.
—*Ten thousand Flower-Flames, part 30*, New York, Agni Press, 1982.
—*Ten thousand Flower-Flames, part 31*, New York, Agni Press, 1982.
—*Ten thousand Flower-Flames, part 32*, New York, Agni Press, 1982.
—*Ten thousand Flower-Flames, part 33*, New York, Agni Press, 1982.
—*Ten thousand Flower-Flames, part 34*, New York, Agni Press, 1982.

—*Ten thousand Flower-Flames, part 35,* New York, Agni Press, 1982.
—*Ten thousand Flower-Flames, part 36,* New York, Agni Press, 1982.
—*Ten thousand Flower-Flames, part 37,* New York, Agni Press, 1982.
—*Ten thousand Flower-Flames, part 38,* New York, Agni Press, 1982.
—*Ten thousand Flower-Flames, part 39,* New York, Agni Press, 1982.
—*Ten thousand Flower-Flames, part 40,* New York, Agni Press, 1982.
—*Ten thousand Flower-Flames, part 41,* New York, Agni Press, 1982.
—*Ten thousand Flower-Flames, part 42,* New York, Agni Press, 1982.
—*Ten thousand Flower-Flames, part 43,* New York, Agni Press, 1982.
—*Ten thousand Flower-Flames, part 44,* New York, Agni Press, 1982.
—*Ten thousand Flower-Flames, part 45,* New York, Agni Press, 1982.
—*Ten thousand Flower-Flames, part 46,* New York, Agni Press, 1982.
—*Ten thousand Flower-Flames, part 47,* New York, Agni Press, 1982.
—*Ten thousand Flower-Flames, part 48,* New York, Agni Press, 1982.
—*Ten thousand Flower-Flames, part 49,* New York, Agni Press, 1982.
—*Ten thousand Flower-Flames, part 50,* New York, Agni Press, 1982.
—*Ten thousand Flower-Flames, part 51,* New York, Agni Press, 1982.
—*Ten thousand Flower-Flames, part 52,* New York, Agni Press, 1983.
—*Ten thousand Flower-Flames, part 53,* New York, Agni Press, 1983.
—*Ten thousand Flower-Flames, part 54,* New York, Agni Press, 1983.
—*Ten thousand Flower-Flames, part 55,* New York, Agni Press, 1983.
—*Ten thousand Flower-Flames, part 56,* New York, Agni Press, 1983.
—*Ten thousand Flower-Flames, part 57,* New York, Agni Press, 1983.
—*Ten thousand Flower-Flames, part 58,* New York, Agni Press, 1983.
—*Ten thousand Flower-Flames, part 59,* New York, Agni Press, 1983.
—*Ten thousand Flower-Flames, part 60,* New York, Agni Press, 1983.
—*Ten thousand Flower-Flames, part 61,* New York, Agni Press, 1983.
—*Ten thousand Flower-Flames, part 62,* New York, Agni Press, 1983.
—*Ten thousand Flower-Flames, part 63,* New York, Agni Press, 1983.
—*Ten thousand Flower-Flames, part 64,* New York, Agni Press, 1983.
—*Ten thousand Flower-Flames, part 65,* New York, Agni Press, 1983.
—*Ten thousand Flower-Flames, part 66,* New York, Agni Press, 1983.
—*Ten thousand Flower-Flames, part 67,* New York, Agni Press, 1983.
—*Ten thousand Flower-Flames, part 68,* New York, Agni Press, 1983.
—*Ten thousand Flower-Flames, part 69,* New York, Agni Press, 1983.
—*Ten thousand Flower-Flames, part 70,* New York, Agni Press, 1983.

– *Ten thousand Flower-Flames, part 71*, New York, Agni Press, 1983.
– *Ten thousand Flower-Flames, part 72*, New York, Agni Press, 1983.
– *Ten thousand Flower-Flames, part 73*, New York, Agni Press, 1983.
– *Ten thousand Flower-Flames, part 74*, New York, Agni Press, 1983.
– *Ten thousand Flower-Flames, part 75*, New York, Agni Press, 1983.
– *Ten thousand Flower-Flames, part 76*, New York, Agni Press, 1983.
– *Ten thousand Flower-Flames, part 77*, New York, Agni Press, 1983.
– *Ten thousand Flower-Flames, part 78*, New York, Agni Press, 1983.
– *Ten thousand Flower-Flames, part 79*, New York, Agni Press, 1983.
– *Ten thousand Flower-Flames, part 80*, New York, Agni Press, 1983.
– *Ten thousand Flower-Flames, part 81*, New York, Agni Press, 1983.
– *Ten thousand Flower-Flames, part 82*, New York, Agni Press, 1983.
– *Ten thousand Flower-Flames, part 83*, New York, Agni Press, 1983.
– *Ten thousand Flower-Flames, part 84*, New York, Agni Press, 1983.
– *Ten thousand Flower-Flames, part 85*, New York, Agni Press, 1983.
– *Ten thousand Flower-Flames, part 86*, New York, Agni Press, 1983.
– *Ten thousand Flower-Flames, part 87*, New York, Agni Press, 1983.
– *Ten thousand Flower-Flames, part 88*, New York, Agni Press, 1983.
– *Ten thousand Flower-Flames, part 89*, New York, Agni Press, 1983.
– *Ten thousand Flower-Flames, part 90*, New York, Agni Press, 1983.
– *Ten thousand Flower-Flames, part 91*, New York, Agni Press, 1983.
– *Ten thousand Flower-Flames, part 92*, New York, Agni Press, 1983.
– *Ten thousand Flower-Flames, part 93*, New York, Agni Press, 1983.
– *Ten thousand Flower-Flames, part 94*, New York, Agni Press, 1983.
– *Ten thousand Flower-Flames, part 95*, New York, Agni Press, 1983.
– *Ten thousand Flower-Flames, part 96*, New York, Agni Press, 1983.
– *Ten thousand Flower-Flames, part 97*, New York, Agni Press, 1983.
– *Ten thousand Flower-Flames, part 98*, New York, Agni Press, 1983.
– *Ten thousand Flower-Flames, part 99*, New York, Agni Press, 1983.
– *Ten thousand Flower-Flames, part 100*, New York, Agni Press, 1983.

Suggested citation key: FF.

207 FLOWER-FLAMES

SRI CHINMOY:

—*207 Flower-Flames,* New York, Agni Press, 1985.

Suggested citation key: FFP.

POSTFACE

Publishing principles

This edition of *The works of Sri Chinmoy* aims to obey the Author's wish: scrupulous fidelity to his original words, use of typographical style by him selected, specific spelling choices, end placement of any editorial content (i.e. not written by Sri Chinmoy himself), particular treatment of some personal nouns in special cases, etc.

Textual accuracy

The text of this edition has been checked to ensure faithful accuracy to the originals. Although much effort has been put in proofreading and comparing different versions of the text, this print may still present a few lingering errors.

The Publisher would be grateful to be apprised of any mistypes via postal mail or facsimile, possibly with scan of the original page where the text is different. Please use original books only, specifying the year of publication. Online versions may be not as accurate and should not be considered authoritative.

Acknowledgements

The Publisher is very grateful to the late Professor Lambert and his équipe for his invaluable advice. For many decades Prof. Lambert conducted a small publishing house specialising in hand-made prints of philological edition of the classics. The standard of this edition would not have been the same without his scholarly advice.

The Publisher is also grateful to the international team of collaborators that spent countless hours proofreading and checking the current text against the originals.

Our deepest gratitude to Sri Chinmoy. His living presence can be felt breathing throughout his writings. It is such a privilege to be involved with his works, in any form.

Citation keys

Citation keys are used throughout *The works of Sri Chinmoy* to allow accurate cross-reference of texts across titles and editions. Examples: EA 13, ST 50000, UPA 7.

Sri Chinmoy Canon

We could not use better words than Professor Lambert's, who kindly offered the name *Sri Chinmoy Canon*:

> «By defining Sri Chinmoy's first editions as *editio princeps* we chose to follow classical scholarship criteria, not because we consider Sri Chinmoy's work antique, but because we believe it is among the few post ‹classical antiquity› works to rightly deserve to be considered a *classicus*, designating by that term *superiority*, *authority* and *perfection*.
>
> «The monumental work Sri Chinmoy is offering to mankind is awe-inspiring and supremely pre-eminent in proportions and quality. It is manifest that Sri Chinmoy's work — which we feel right to call *The Sri Chinmoy Canon* — will be of profound help and source of enlightenment to anyone seeking a higher wisdom, truth and reality supreme.»

[Translated from French by M. G.S.]

TABLE OF CONTENTS

TEN THOUSAND FLOWER-FLAMES	735
207 FLOWER-FLAMES	1417
APPENDIX	1449
POEM TITLES AS SELECTED BY EDITORS FOR FIRST EDITION	1451
207 FLOWER-FLAMES EARLIEST NUMBERING	1481
BIBLIOGRAPHY	1485
POSTFACE	1491
TABLE OF CONTENTS	1495

*Composition typographique par imprimerie
Ab Academia Aoidon, Paris & Lyon.*

*Un grand merci à Prof Knuth pour
l'utilisation avancée de TEX.*

A LYON, LE 13 JUILLET LXXXVI Æ.G.

www.ingramcontent.com/pod-product-compliance
Lightning Source LLC
Chambersburg PA
CBHW030109240426
43661CB00031B/1352/J